Carson McCullers

Carson McCullers

A Life

MARY V. DEARBORN

ALFRED A. KNOPF
New York
2024

THIS IS A BORZOI BOOK
PUBLISHED BY ALFRED A. KNOPF

aaknopf.com

Knopf, Borzoi Books, and the colophon are registered
trademarks of Penguin Random House LLC.

Library of Congress Cataloging-in-Publication Data
Names: Dearborn, Mary V., author.
Title: Carson McCullers : a life / Mary Dearborn.
Description: New York : Alfred A. Knopf, 2024. |
Includes bibliographical references and index.
Identifiers: LCCN 2023007221 (print) | LCCN 2023007222 (ebook) |
ISBN 9780525521013 (hardcover) | ISBN 9780525521020 (ebook)
Subjects: LCSH: McCullers, Carson, 1917–1967. |
Women novelists, American—Biography.
Classification: LCC PS3525.A1772 Z595 2024 (print) |
LCC PS3525.A1772 (ebook) | DDC 813/.52—dc23/eng/20230531
LC record available at https://lccn.loc.gov/2023007221
LC ebook record available at https://lccn.loc.gov/2023007222

Jacket photograph of Carson McCullers,
1940 by Louise Dahl-Wolfe © 2023 Center for Creative Photography,
Arizona Board of Regents / Artists Rights Society (ARS), New York;
Print: Courtesy of The Columbus Museum, Georgia;
The Edward Swift Shorter Bequest Fund

Jacket design by Gabriele Wilson

Manufactured in the United States of America
Published February 27, 2024
Second Printing, February 2024

To the memory of my father

Contents

Prologue   3

1. Wunderkind   9

2. That Rainbow Youth of Mine   30

3. Charming the Skin Off a Snake   50

4. A Young Knight   69

5. Flowering Jazz Passion   88

6. A Bit of a Holy Terror   112

7. I Feel That Book with Something Like My Whole Body   134

8. Practically Paradise   153

9. Our Love for Each Other Is Like a Sort of Natural Law   176

10. Like a Broken Doll   197

11. The Jigger Got Bigger and Bigger   215

12. I Am an Invalid   234

13. Harder Than Marble   249

14. Grappa Rather Than Gin   265

15. A Colossal Power of Destruction   283

16. Endings Are Knives   300

17. I Seen the Little Lamp   318

18. i trust you   334

19. That Green and Glowing Spring   349

20. Insatiability for Living   363

21. The Sad, Happy Life of Carson McCullers   384

Epilogue   411

Acknowledgments   423

Notes   427

Bibliography   461

Index   467

Carson McCullers

Prologue

June 4, 1940. Publication day of *The Heart Is a Lonely Hunter.* Carson McCullers, twenty-three years old, was alone in a cheap boardinghouse on New York's West Side. Her husband of almost three years was elsewhere, on a sailboat with a friend; a new note seemed to be sounding in her marriage since her book was, after more than two years of writing, finally seeing the light of day. She knew almost no one in New York except the kindly older woman acquaintance who had found her the room. She was nearly penniless, but she had to scrape together enough money to buy something to wear to a meeting with her editor the next week. June 4 was a pause. On one side were Carson's years growing up in provincial Columbus, Georgia, and the succession of Southern towns to which her husband's job had called them. On the other side, she assumed, would be the exciting life of an author, living glamorously in New York City, meeting the writers, artists, and musicians who had peopled her fantasies.

Her first novel, *The Heart Is a Lonely Hunter,* had enjoyed significant pre-publication notice. The response to the advance copies that her publisher, Houghton Mifflin, had sent out was very promising, and its sales staff were enthusiastic about selling it. The firm had been eager for her to arrive in the city to promote her book. People inside and outside the publisher's offices reminded each other that Carson's editor, Robert Linscott, almost invariably picked winners.

But the novel itself was an outlier. It did not fit any of the accepted and expected categories of mainstream fiction. It was neither a love story nor a bildungsroman, it did not have characters whom readers could recognize as like themselves, it did not have a happy ending, and it did not have a single strong narrative line. Instead, it followed a striking group of oddballs and misfits, the inhabitants of a small Southern city who individually take their hopes and fears to another oddball and misfit. Ironically named Singer, the listener is a deaf-mute who is in love with another man, also a deaf-mute, and his strange silence provides a kind of moral center, or anticenter, for this outlier community. Besides homosexuality, alcoholism, cross-dressing, and mental illness, the improbable range of difficult if not taboo subjects that Carson took on in this singular novel included Communism, poverty, racism, suicide, and adolescent sex.

What struck almost everyone was the writer's youth. Readers were flabbergasted to learn that this tour de force was the work of someone so young and, despite her gender-ambiguous name, a woman. It was hard to believe she knew so much about the "lonely hearts" of others, said one critic. She seemed sui generis, unique, and as it turned out, as odd as some of her characters. But to find an explanation for something new, critics turned to comparison, and Carson was quickly likened to Hemingway and Faulkner, Sherwood Anderson, Dostoyevsky, and Gertrude Stein. While some of the comparisons were valid, they didn't capture what was unique about her book—and about Carson herself.

On the alert for anything new on the horizon, or what Clifton Fadiman in *The New Yorker* called the "unique accent in first novels that critics have been searching for," reviewers enthusiastically welcomed *The Heart Is a Lonely Hunter*. It was not a novelty by a precocious child-woman, however, but a mature achievement: "One cannot help remarking," said Ray Redman in *The Saturday Review of Literature,* "that this is an extraordinary novel to have been written by a young woman of twenty-two; but the more important fact is that it is an extraordinary novel in its own right." Some readers fretted. The *New York Times* reviewer said she dreaded McCullers's second novel: "So high is the standard she has set, it doesn't seem possible that she can reach it again." The poet May Sarton lamented that it would be "another year or two" before there would be another book by "this extraordinary young woman." But Fadiman said he'd "place a small bet on her future."

She looked like a teenage boy. Tall and gangly, with what Ray Bradbury called "ploppy ways," she cut an unconventional figure in fashion-conscious literary Manhattan. All coltish legs, she sometimes wore abbreviated tennis shorts and sweatshirts, heedless of city customs. (Her husband used to tell her she could be a champion sprinter.) Otherwise, once she could afford them, she favored crisp white men's dress shirts with trousers or a suit, and she almost always wore oxfords, sometimes men's brogans, and favored knee socks, often white. Her brown hair hung straight to her shoulders, cut in short bangs across her forehead, strictly wash-and-wear. Her cropped hair and childish pout (when she wasn't convulsed with laughter) gave her the look of a child swimming in adult clothes. But the clothes themselves were carefully chosen and expensive; she loved fashion and never overlooked anyone's clothing. She did like to add a personal touch, sometimes unfortunately—the white knee socks were but one example—but as soon as she arrived in New York, she sought out distinctive, stylish clothes.

The first time Truman Capote met Carson, he noted that "she was a tall, slender wand of a girl, slightly stooped and with a fascinating face that was simultaneously merry and melancholy." She had large, liquid, deep brown eyes and spoke in the accents of the Deep South. Capote noted that her eyes glowed warmly and that "her voice had the same quality, the same gentle heat, like a blissful summer afternoon that is slow but not sleepy." Yet it was wise to listen closely, for she had a lively, mordant wit and spared no one. Some years later she looked back: "I became an established literary figure overnight and I was much too young to understand what happened to me or the responsibility it entailed. I was a bit of a holy terror."

Carson's early marriage was not in her press packet, so to speak. She had married at nineteen, to a good-looking Alabama-born charmer who had most recently been a credit investigator in a string of small Southern cities. Like Carson, Reeves McCullers—she vastly preferred his last name to her own family name, Smith—was determined to get out of the South, for he was also smart and ambitious. Both seemed to know that New York was a good place for anyone who was in some way different, who did not quite fit in: that there they could find, if not a home, then similarly inclined souls with whom they might feel less alone.

But their marriage was strained by the time *The Heart Is a Lonely Hunter* made its dramatic appearance. The reasons reached beyond Carson's imminent success. Within a month of her arrival, she fell madly in love with a beautiful and talented Swiss writer who was visiting friends in New York. "She had a face," Carson said, "that I knew would haunt me to the end of my life." Annemarie Schwarzenbach soon returned to her travels, dying tragically two years later after a bicycle accident in the Alps. She reciprocated Carson's passion only briefly. But Carson's love for Annemarie established a pattern that would continue almost to the end of her life: falling in love with older, more worldly women who sometimes returned her affection but who, despite her feverish pursuit, seldom wanted the passionate physical relationship she sought.

Reeves within a year began an affair with another man, a composer who had initially fallen in love with both him *and* Carson; the resulting triangle brought pain to all three. Reeves's love for Carson was never in question. It was a central fact of her young life, and for Reeves, she was quite literally the reason he was alive. But he came slowly to understand that his love for other men would not go away; it was only one of what he saw as his many problems, which included alcoholism and a desperate search for a vocation.

Carson, by contrast, was entirely comfortable as a bisexual—although largely lesbian—woman, as comfortable and open about her desires as the still very repressed America of the 1940s and '50s permitted her to be. Gender fluidity is a thread through her major works and is fundamental to the strangeness, the difference that marked the remarkable cast of characters who people her novels and stories. Besides Singer, *The Heart Is a Lonely Hunter* gives us Biff, the popular owner of the café that is the meeting place for the other principal characters, who is also a cross-dresser; and Mick Kelly, the adolescent girl who has sex with a boy for the first time and wants to be a composer. In *The Member of the Wedding,* twelve-year-old Frankie—another sexually ambiguous name—wants to be part of something else, her brother's wedding: what she calls "the we of me." Captain Penderton in *Reflections in a Golden Eye* is a married man tortured by his repressed homosexuality, who becomes obsessed with a young soldier doing work around his house, fueled by a vision of the private riding on a horse, naked. Miss Amelia, the heroine of *The Ballad of the Sad Café,* is an independent, self-sufficient giantess married to a criminal, who falls in love with Lymon, a hunchback who claims to be her distant cousin. A lot of Carson went into Miss Amelia, but she understood Cousin Lymon very well, too.

With the exception of the captain, however, none of these characters, not even those to whom it brings the most grief, are tortured by their sexuality; they simply are who they are. Something was changing in 1940s America, however repressed; gay artists and writers were finding each other, cracking the code that would allow them to create work they could successfully offer to mainstream America. Out of this complex of circumstances came writers like Carson, Tennessee Williams, Truman Capote, Patricia Highsmith, Allen Ginsberg, and some of the other Beats. While still very young, Carson had found this nurturing community on a small scale in her family's living room in Columbus, where her mother had convened a salon of young people of whatever sexual stripe who were passionate about art and their creative futures. Soon after *The Heart Is a Lonely Hunter* came out, Carson moved into a Brooklyn brownstone filled with an "assortment of geniuses," a transatlantic cross-section of sexual nonconformists including W. H. Auden, Jane and Paul Bowles, Benjamin Britten and Peter Pears, and Gypsy Rose Lee. For the rest of her life, most of Carson's closest friends, supporters, and occasionally protectors would be gay men.

The geniuses, oddballs, and occasional psychopaths in Carson's fiction fit well into the literary category that the Virginia novelist Ellen Glasgow was already calling "Southern Gothic," which included Erskine Caldwell and William Faulkner. But her characters' complex sexuality was always up front; they also reflected, much more than do other practitioners of the genre, Carson's attempts to understand the cruel racial politics of the time. And they were drawn from life, many specifically from *her* life. In all her major works can be found a version of herself: from *The Heart Is a Lonely Hunter*'s Mick Kelly, the unhappy musical adolescent, to Jester Clane in *Clock Without Hands,* a white man muddling through his competing desires for the light-skinned, openly gay Sherman Pew and his passion for his dead father's cause, racial justice. But even in rough outline, her autobiographical characters do not represent or explain the often delightful but steadily more troubled Carson McCullers. At times the figure she cut could have been straight out of a play by her friend Tennessee Williams: a sensitive Southern woman, emotionally naked, alive to beauty, ill equipped to bear the harshness of the modern world, but capable of toughness and drive when she needed to be.

Illness made cruel inroads. Two major strokes by the age of thirty left Carson just twenty more, increasingly painful years. On top of that, she drank to excess, which made life a struggle and creative life nearly impossible as she grew more dependent on a crew of enablers and a husband who was himself slipping into alcoholic self-destruction. Beneath illness and alcoholism, however, was a remarkably resilient and uncannily talented artist who proceeded as if she were on a mission to make sense of her existence and express it in her work. In the process, she created what may be American literature's most detailed, carefully observed picture of what it means to be an outsider. It is perhaps not constructive to imagine the characters and fictions—What magnificent heroines! What imaginatively constructed novels, plays, and stories!—that Carson might have created had she lived the usual span of years. All we know is she would have drawn from the same rich wells of inspiration that produced *The Heart Is a Lonely Hunter* at twenty-three, and *Clock Without Hands,* a coming to terms with race and racism, scant years before her death. What she left to us is her art and the example of what she called "her sad, happy life."

1

Wunderkind

Carson McCullers titled one of her first, most directly autobiographical stories "Wunderkind." She was just such a child—which
was, as with so many talented children, both a blessing and a curse.

Her mother, Vera Marguerite Smith (known to all as Bébé), thought
she could discern auguries of greatness while her first child was still
an embryo. In a fit of willfulness that came naturally to her and that
would characterize the lives of all her children—but especially her
firstborn—she vowed to name the child Enrico Caruso. Instead, her
daughter was given two family names, Lula Carson, but was known
to her family as "Sister." With the first breath she drew, the child was
the focus of her mother's life. Bébé let her daughter know that she
was loved, which gave Carson a fundamental security, confidence, and
sense of self-worth, which left her feeling she could succeed at almost
anything she tried.

Bébé was a charming, charismatic, intelligent woman who, her
younger daughter estimated, wrote a letter to "Sister" almost every day
they were apart. The Southern novelist Lillian Smith said that Bébé,
"one of the most engaging" women she'd ever known, was "clearheaded
in [her] collective ambition for 'Sister.'" Bébé was "Sister's slave, as was
the rest of the family." Out of what complex of circumstances was born
this immediately recognized genius, this wunderkind?

On both sides of her family, Carson's ancestry reads like a vest-

Lula Carson Smith, c. 1918

pocket history of the regional fortunes of the Deep South. Her family embraced a full complement of pioneers, planters, enslavers, Civil War veterans, small business people, and the wives and daughters who kept the families knitted together. They were Protestant, although some were more active in their faith than others, and alcoholism was a common condition among the men and a few of the women.

Over the course of the nineteenth century, the Deep South grew into a major cotton-raising region built on the labor of enslaved people, went to war with the Union, and rebuilt itself into a highly stratified commodity economy of planters, sharecroppers, foresters, and textile manufacturers, all in less than one hundred years. Lula Carson Smith's family had prospered in the pre–Civil War years. Afterward, much like the family of another prominent Southern writer, William Faulkner, they had brushed against poverty while struggling to assert themselves as part of the new middle class that was beginning to take root in the cities of the New South. Children like Carson grew up with an immense treasury of family stories, legends, resentments, and fierce loyalties that belied the rather mundane circumstances of their daily lives. Middle-class families like the Smiths of Columbus, Georgia, were like middle-class families in other parts of the country—except that they weren't, entirely, with all the baggage they were carrying.

Bébé, born Vera Marguerite Waters in 1890 in Dublin, Georgia, could trace her ancestry back to Thomas Carson, who emigrated from Ireland—from Newry, County Down, in Protestant Ulster—with his wife and seven children in 1773. Thomas Carson fought in the Revolutionary War in Colonel Elijah Clarke's small company, which battled the British from Georgia up into the Carolinas. After the war, Thomas Carson was rewarded with a land grant in Georgia, probably one of many such grants, of thousands of acres, that Colonel Clarke had obtained, possibly in shady circumstances, and may have given to his soldiers as a kind of reward. (His wife, as a widow of a Revolutionary soldier, also drew land in the land lottery of 1827.) Born in 1802, his son, Joseph Jefferson Carson, married the fourteen-year-old Martha Goodwin Raines in Macon County, eventually moving to Knoxville in Crawford County, where they owned and ran a stagecoach inn. They were a prosperous family that enslaved twenty-six workers by 1850. In that year, these Carsons bought a plantation called Wilburville in the town of Reynolds in Taylor County, fifty-two miles east of Columbus. As a delegate to Georgia's secession convention at Milledgeville in 1861, Joseph Jefferson Carson voted for the ordinance declaring Georgia's departure from the Union.

Joseph Jefferson and Martha had ten children. Four were boys, and two died in the Civil War fighting for the Confederacy. (Another son died young, and Joseph Perryman Carson fought in the war and survived.) The eldest, John Thomas, Carson McCullers's great-grandfather, born in 1825, married Susan Sophronia Howe, whose grandfather had fought in the Revolutionary War as well. At their plantation in Macon County, he and Sophronia enslaved eighteen people in 1860. When the rebellion broke out, John Thomas joined the army as first lieutenant, later captain, and finally major, in Company C, Twelfth Georgia Infantry (known as the Davis Rifles). The company was part of Stonewall Jackson's Shenandoah Valley Campaign in 1862, fighting at the

Battle of Bull Run ("Second Manassas" to the Confederates), Antietam, and Fredericksburg, among others. He fought at Gettysburg in 1863 and defended Richmond from the approaching Union troops in 1864. At Spotsylvania, Virginia, he was taken prisoner and held in Fort Delaware, then was released three months later in a prisoner exchange. Wounded earlier at Shenandoah, John Thomas Carson suffered a mortal wound fighting under General Jubal Early at Winchester, Virginia, in 1864.

Back at his Macon County plantation, his wife, Susan Sophronia, was warned of Sherman's advancing army. She scattered the cows and buried the silver and put on all her petticoats and skirts so the Yankees couldn't take them. According to a story told by her daughter Lula (the writer's grandmother), the plantation was spared, supposedly because Joseph Carson, John Thomas's elderly father, gave a Yankee officer a Masonic sign. Family stories say that a very young Carson nephew perched on the fence post in front of the house while the Union forces marched by, thrilled that the soldiers said hello to him. After the war, John Thomas Carson's widow undertook a concerted effort to retrieve her husband's body so he could be buried on the Reynolds property. Friends were able to find his "body servant," a term for a kind of enslaved valet, who helped retrieve John Thomas's body for burial. (It was uncommon, during and after the war, for a family to put time and effort toward an uncertain end, into searching for their loved ones and bringing their bodies home.) Susan Sophronia paid $1,500 to erect a monument to John Thomas in the Carson graveyard on the plantation grounds, where his brother James, who had also died in the war, was buried.

Carson would have learned this from her grandmother, who passed down other stories about her relatives' Civil War exploits. A great-grandfather with a war history like John Thomas Carson's, with a $1,500 monument on his grave? It's impossible that Carson—who bore his name—was not told of his heroic exploits in the war. Not only was her great-grandfather a Confederate hero, but her ancestors enslaved people, as did roughly one-third of antebellum Southern farmers. John Thomas was recorded as enslaving eighteen in 1869; the 1860 census showed that his father, Carson's great-great-grandfather, enslaved twenty-six; and a great-grandfather on her father's side enslaved twenty-one, also in 1860.

Carson never commented, at least for any record, on her family's Civil War history or their enslaving past, even though much of her life was bound up with the grim history of race in the United States. But she would later draw on family stories in portraying the reactionary and racist Judge Clane in her 1961 novel, *Clock Without Hands*. The judge is a former congressman whose life dream is to restore the South by a scheme in which the government would redeem Confederate money. In the years she spent working on this novel, Carson often said she would be weighing in on the South's reaction to the civil rights struggles and victories of the 1940s and '50s, especially the landmark Supreme Court decision *Brown vs. Board of Education* (1954), which held that segregation in public schools was unconstitutional. *Clock Without Hands* and three short stories written in her last year were her only literary contribution to that conversation, but she often referred to racial issues in letters to friends and family and in her posthumously published autobiography, *Illumination and Night Glare* (1999). She told a friend that the South had an evil quality that scared her. She left no doubt that she was talking about race in directing her friend to follow news discussions of the poll tax. These taxes restricted African American voting. Southerners, she said, were passing laws like this that conflicted with the Constitution. The Fifteenth Amendment, enacted in 1870, had granted the right of Blacks to vote, but states like Georgia were doing their best to take it away.

Certainly Carson's maternal grandmother knew of her father's exploits during the war. Lula Caroline (sometimes listed as Tallulah in Georgia records), born in 1858, was the last of John Thomas and Sophronia's three children. Because her father died when she was six, Lula would live for most of her life in an informal guardianship set up by her brother Robert. Robert was said to have walked barefoot thirty miles to Columbus carrying his shoes (to prevent wear and tear), where he found work at a wholesale druggist's firm. (Many of Carson's extended family were druggists, either wholesale or retail; she would draw on their experiences in creating a pharmacist protagonist, J. T. Malone, in *Clock Without Hands*.) Robert married the boss's daughter and became a partner in the firm, subsequently emerging as a pillar of the community: president of the school board and a deacon in the First Baptist Church.

Carson stated in her autobiography that her first love was her grandmother. "I slept with her," she added, "and cozied in the dark"—indicating that she associated love with "cozying" or physical contact (*ING,* 6–7). (Carson favored much bodily contact with friends, intimates, family members, and so on—a very large group.) By then, her grandmother, Lula Caroline, was the widow of Charles Thomas Waters, who died in 1890; the couple had five children, including Carson's mother, Bébé. Charles Thomas was the son of Elam Waters, another dynamo, said to have made and lost fortunes "on a grand scale." He owned a cotton mill in Potterville and a second home in Reynolds (where he would have met Lula Caroline) besides his establishment in Columbus. When he was an executive with the Central Georgia Railway he traveled all over the state in a private railroad car, always clad, according to an early McCullers biographer, in a "white linen duster."

Charles Thomas Waters was an alcoholic; he was said to be "tended by a strong man-servant who could control his sudden [fits]" (*ING,* 21). He died in 1890, before he reached thirty; his two brothers also died young, their deaths usually said in the family to be alcohol-related. Charles Thomas once shot the family cow in a fit of rage; his future son-in-law, C. Graham Johnson, remarked, "He got to where he loved whisky better than anything on earth." He died two months before the birth of his fifth and last child, Vera Marguerite, or Bébé—Lula Carson's mother.

Bébé was raised by a single mother, in the way such establishments worked in the late nineteenth century. Two uncles, Robert and Alphonso (Lula Waters's brothers), had moved to Columbus from Butler, Georgia, a town midway between Macon and Columbus. Alphonso became a prosperous lawyer, and Robert established a wholesale and retail druggist concern. Lula's father-in-law, Elam Bertram Waters, bought Lula and her children a large, narrow frame house, trimmed with gingerbread, on the corner of Thirteenth Street and Fifth Avenue, near her brothers' establishment and also the First Baptist Church.

Robert made many decisions for Lula and her children—he was appointed guardian of the latter—which Lula didn't always appreciate.

Her circumstances were difficult. As McCullers researcher Margaret Sullivan wrote, "Her family lived comfortably, but economically. . . . She was quiet about her misfortunes, and the townspeople respected her for . . . her skillful management of what she had." The family was not immune to these tensions, however. "Within the family, where the stoic attitude was not such a necessity, there was worry and sometimes bitterness over the straitened circumstances." Lula's was a well-known and respected family in Columbus, but she was definitely a poor relative.

Bébé's older siblings died young. The only one who stayed in Columbus was Martha Elba (known as Mattie), who married a pharmacist, C. Graham Johnson, another alcoholic who died young. Aunt Matt (sometimes known as Aunt Tieh) was the Smith children's favorite aunt; she was a kindergarten teacher, and the Johnson children were frequent companions of Bébé's brood.

According to Virginia Spencer Carr, Carson's biographer, Bébé showed no interest in going to college or taking up an occupation, but she had an active imagination and was known to be a riveting storyteller. She also had a near-photographic memory and would recite the first chapter of *War and Peace* to whomever would listen. Lillian Smith (no relation) later described Bébé as a "vivid" individual, a rebel when young. Eventually, no doubt prodded by her mother to earn a living so they could be free of Robert's supervision and financial aid, Bébé went out and got a job, finding one in a retail jewelry shop, Schomburg's, a successful concern on Broad Street, where she met the retiring, gentle watch and jewelry repairman Lamar Smith.

The Smiths, Carson's paternal ancestors, were said to be of English and French Huguenot ancestry. On the English side, they were descended from Colonel Thomas Scott, who emigrated to Virginia's Prince Edward County from Cumberland, England, in the seventeenth century. His great-granddaughter Ann married into the Gachet family; her husband, Charles Gachet, left La Rochelle, France, for Santo Domingo, now Haiti. After Gachet's first wife was killed in a slave uprising in 1790—differing and sketchy accounts of this event survive—he left the island for Savannah, Georgia, home to an active Huguenot community. There he married another Ann, whom he had met on board the ship that brought him to Georgia. The Gachets— Charles was a physician—were prosperous, enslaving twenty-one in 1860. The couple resettled in Louisville, then the state capital. One of their five children, James Edward Gachet, was Lamar Smith's grandfather. James Edward was a colonel in the Confederate Army who after the war settled near Union Springs, Alabama. His daughter, Mary Louise (known as Molly), married William Hooker Smith, an Alabaman who had served in the Alabama Third Regiment, Company D, in the Civil War as a very young man. Penury threatened when Smith lost an arm in an accident with a cotton gin around 1887. He moved to Tuskegee to look for a job and became the tax assessor for Macon County.

William and Molly had ten children. William apparently earned a fairly good living, as he sent all five of his daughters to college. But few of the children remained in the South, and most of them (except two daughters, who married local men) migrated to the same place, Detroit. Lamar, Carson's father, was the seventh child; he stayed in the South, where his own father remained as well. After a brief stint as a telephone lineman, Lamar turned to what he was best at: repairing things, working for a jeweler in Tuskegee. He boasted of being able to fix anything with moving parts. In Columbus, Lamar is first listed in the city directory in 1910, at the age of twenty-one, giving "watchmaker" as his occupation. Failing to find much business on his own, he offered his services to jewelry store owner Fred Schomburg, who hired him at $20 a week ($500 a week now). It was there that he met Bébé. After a year, Lamar proposed. Bébé departed for Miami for a long stay with an old friend. As she made her way north again, Lamar showed up in Jacksonville, where he persuaded her to marry him right then and there. The *Columbus Enquirer* reported their Jacksonville wedding on February 14, 1916—Valentine's Day. Their first child, Lula Carson, named after Bébé's mother, was born almost exactly one year later.

People had a soft spot for Lamar Smith. A Columbus friend called him "an easy, good country boy who'd do anything for you." A niece came up with a vivid description: Lamar was "like a great, big, sweet collie dog who was affectionate and loved for his family to show him affection." He was "slouchy" and loped when he walked, traits he would pass on to his first daughter. He was said to be very funny when he talked, which wasn't often. Virginia Storey, Carson's cousin, said, "He was a quiet unassuming man with a keen sense of humor. We all adored him." When Carson was just one, Lamar left Schomburg's and opened his own jewelry store, in the Murrah building on Twelfth Street, later moving to 1131 Broad Street, in the lobby of the Grand Theatre. The father of the autobiographical heroine in both *The Heart Is a Lonely Hunter* and *The Member of the Wedding* has a jewelry business. Carson suggested her father preferred repairing jewelry and watches at his bench in the back of the shop to dealing with the public. At other times, she claimed he spent his spare time inventing—what, she did not say. In *The Heart Is a Lonely Hunter*, Mick Kelly says of her father, "He felt like he wasn't much real use to anybody." (Lamar, however, was not the type to complain about such things.) Carson wrote that novel when she was twenty-two, and it's notable to imagine a daughter that young intuiting that her father felt that way.

After their marriage, Lamar and Bébé moved in with her mother into the big house on Thirteenth Street, where Carson (then Lula Carson) was born. A son, Lamar Jr., who came to be known as "Brotherman," followed in 1919, and a sister, Margarita Gachet, called Rita or "Little Pretty" (she was the pretty daughter), was born in 1922. Carson later admitted being wildly jealous when Lamar Jr. had an operation (for undescended testicles) at the age of three. Visiting relatives would add a coin to a growing pile of small change in his hospital room, and Brother-man could have anything he wanted to drink—chocolate milk, lemonade—anytime he wanted it. Carson was wild to stay in the hospital with her brother and mother and, according to her later account, yelled and carried on.

She told another, darker story about sibling rivalry in a piece she would write for *Mademoiselle*. One year not long before Christmas, when the children were quarantined with scarlet fever, their nurse told them a story about her son Sherman. The boy had put his baby brother down on the hearth to play and then forgotten about him. A spark caught the baby's nightgown, and he was fatally burned. Carson remembered the story, and on Christmas Day, feeling "hostile," she took her baby sister out of her playpen and put her on the hearth. After an interlude of play—Carson got into the family's supply of fireworks, which the Smiths traditionally set off on Christmas night, and fired a Roman candle for her awed brother—Carson found that her bad feelings had vanished, and she remembered her sister. She ran to the living room to lift the baby from the hearth and found she had crawled off. The baby was headed for the Christmas tree, and watching this, Carson felt the first surge of love for Rita, her "heart cleansed of jealousy" (*TMH*, 243).

The siblings themselves seemingly accepted the idea that Carson had been marked out for great things since birth, and a friend noted that Carson was fairly humble about it. "She never lorded it over the others," the wife of one of her cousins later said. "Little Lamar and Rita saw her as her mother did." Bébé Smith was her eldest child's "most ardent admirer and supporter," said Virginia Storey, suggesting not only the extravagance of her support but introducing the slightly weird idea of a mother *admiring* her child. In her toddler period, Carson "was different from the normal four-year-old. We thought she was a born lady. . . . And everyone just accepted the fact in the family that Carson was different and set aside," said Storey. Similarly, one observer noted that Carson "as a child played alongside of other children, never with them." If this sounds a bit lonely, readers of *The Member of the Wedding* will recall that Frankie, the autobiographical heroine, is both an insider and an outsider at once. In fact, only in putative adulthood could someone like Frankie have enough perspective to realize that one *could* be both at the same time. It was out of this place, in fact, that Carson could have written Frankie's story so insightfully and meaningfully.

Church was an important part of the lives of the Smith family and their offspring, largely because it had been for Bébé's mother and her siblings. They were congregants at Columbus's First Baptist Church on Twelfth Street, just a block away from Lula Waters's home. Founded in 1829, the church is housed in a large brick Greek Revival structure built in 1859. In the early twentieth century, six enormous Doric columns were added to the front; Carson's granduncle Robert, a deacon, entirely underwrote one column. Accounts differ, but it would appear that Carson began attending church on November 29, 1925, and was baptized the following May. (Most children joined at around age nine. It's said that Carson was so small that the preacher had to hold her up for the ritual.) When she first started Sunday school, she was troubled to learn that Sunday was a day of rest. She asked the teacher what would become of her father, who *had* to go into work on Sunday—to wind the watches and clocks. It's notable that while Carson attended Sunday school for seven years, her parents, after the death of Lula Waters, by and large stopped attending church, although Lamar Sr. walked Carson to the church every Sunday morning. And when Carson developed a visceral dislike of organized religion, around the age of fourteen, she, too, would withdraw completely from the church.

In the meantime, Bébé doted on Carson, dressing her in home-made smocked dresses. She paid particular attention to Carson's (then) blond, straight hair, patting lilac cologne into it and, on special occasions, putting it in rags to give it some curl. (Her daughter would later stay far away from curled hair and perfumes—and even dresses. If she had to wear a skirt, she preferred a suit.) Bébé was "like a stage mother," observed a family friend.

Carson may have been an extraordinary young girl—and an extraordinarily spoiled specimen—but aspects of her childhood were quite typical. With Brother-man, for instance, she built a tree house, and they persuaded the cook to send up their lunches in a basket. She and her best friend, Helen Harvey, read a range of book series written for juveniles: Tom Swift, the Bobbsey Twins, the Rover Boys, and Marjorie Maynard. They also loved Robert Louis Stevenson's poems for children and knew them "almost by heart." Because just two full days separated Carson's birthday from George Washington's, her family gave the four-year-old "a Washington-based extravaganza" that was written up in the local newspaper. The children pinned a hatchet on the hand of an image of Washington, and the girls who won prizes for this and other games received a box of cherry candy, while the boys got a "large hatchet." A full *forty-eight* children were invited—a large number by any standard, even if not all of them attended. "The surnames of the [invited] children read like a 'Who's Who' of Columbus society," noted a city observer. Not bad for the daughter of a small businessman.

⟨≋⟩

Columbus, where the Smith and Waters families had situated themselves, was settled and planted in cotton after the Creek Indians were
infamously "removed" in 1836. Cotton interests used the river to ship
their crops; when railroads took over such functions in the 1850s,
businesspeople in Columbus looked to harness the waterpower of the
Chattahoochee River. Mills began to appear on the riverbanks, as com-
panies used the force of the water to power machinery that produced
textiles; there were as well significant numbers of lumber mills and
gristmills. Columbus had boomed throughout the antebellum period,
and with the Civil War, its economy leaped ahead. The city became a
leading manufacturer and supplier of whatever the Confederate Army
needed, from shoes to iron. The city is said to have been "divided" over
secession, though the state legislature eventually voted for it. Sherman
in 1864 did not get as far as Columbus, but Wilson's Union raiders laid
waste and torched some manufacturing areas of the city; they unknow-
ingly struck a week after Robert E. Lee had surrendered.

After the war, the city rebuilt, and the textile industry continued
to expand, often at the expense of other manufacturers. In the early
twentieth century, a progressive mayor, L. H. Chappell, was responsible for opening a city waterworks to make the river water potable,
for modernizing the downtown, and for persuading military brass to
open the training camp known today as Fort Benning (a setting Carson would borrow for her 1941 novel, *Reflections in a Golden Eye*). By
1920, Columbus had 31,125 residents.

But the area surrounding Lula Waters's house on Thirteenth Street
and Fifth Avenue, where the Smith family lived until Carson was eight,
was no longer thriving. Construction of a viaduct, one of the South's
longest, over Twelfth, Thirteenth, and Fourteenth streets, was almost
complete; it would greatly reduce the number of accidents between
motorists and the railroad. As the mills along the Chattahoochee
expanded with the growing economy, workers needed housing close to
the mills. Shotgun-style frame houses were built for laborers, many of
them African American. They soon outnumbered the plantation-style
mansions and Victorian piles that had been built, often by mill owners,

near the river, and many of the owners of the latter homes decamped. The downtown business district around Broad Street (today, confusingly, called Broadway and referred to as "uptown") was still thriving. Lamar Smith's jewelry business, now in the lobby of the Grand Theater of Broad Street, profited from the steady foot traffic of the moviegoing public. Bébé Smith, who had bought her sister and brother out after their mother left the property to the three of them on her death in 1925, was proud that, even though the neighborhood had declined, she was able to sell the house for $10,000 more than Robert Carson had paid for it. It was this money and more that had come to Lula and her children when Robert died in 1914, that allowed Bébé and Lamar Smith to become homeowners.

Columbus, then, was a small place, but like some other Southern cities (Memphis and New Orleans, for instance), it was more cosmopolitan than the countryside around it. Columbus was ethnically mixed. Greeks, Italians, and Jews were shopkeepers or ran modest restaurants and businesses. Mostly working-class whites and African Americans worked in the textile mills, and upper-middle-class whites were in the professions or business. A vibrant Black culture was in place as well, as indicated by the career of Columbus native Ma Rainey, the pioneering blues singer, who established a theater in town that drew some of the country's top jazz and blues artists, including Louis Armstrong. All this just blocks from where Carson was growing up.

Jim Crow was firmly in place in Columbus and racism was out in the open, but the city was rigidly divided along caste lines as well, and members of one stratum who made their way up into a higher one worked hard to stay there or rise further. Columbus was very much a *respectable* city, and families like the Smiths, solidly middle class, would not be dislodged easily, however eccentrically people like Bébé and Carson behaved. But despite its fairly rigid class lines, Columbus was also a complex environment in which individuals from many different groups interacted daily at a fairly intimate level. The Smiths, and especially the curious Carson, would have known about Ma Rainey's theater, for instance, even if they would not visit it. *The Heart Is a Lonely Hunter* is built on this kind of communication across class lines. People of different backgrounds, like Mick Kelly, Jake Blount, and Dr. Benedict Mady Copeland, who as an African American physician confounds barriers of class and race, interact with the deaf-mute John Singer and sometimes with each other. They also find common ground in Biff Brannon's coffee shop, the ironically named New York Café.

Columbus would provide the backdrop for all of Carson's novels, appearing in close-ups in some, other times in a wide-angle view. While she wrote about the Georgia countryside and her suburban backyard (and kitchen), what caught the writer's eye most often in the landscapes inspired by Columbus was poverty: poverty, suffering, and—in Carson's observation—loneliness. In *The Heart Is a Lonely Hunter,* she describes a "fairly large" town whose downtown featured

> several blocks of two- and three-story shops and business offices. But the largest buildings in the town were the factories, which employed a large percentage of the population. These cotton mills were big and flourishing and most of the workers in the town were very poor. Often in the faces along the streets there was the desperate look of hunger and of loneliness. (*HLH,* 6)

Another feature of the city that left its mark on Carson was the short distance between the Waters home on Thirteenth Street and Phenix City, Alabama, reachable by the easily walkable 720-foot Fourteenth Street Bridge. Phenix City was already the embodiment of iniquity, known for its bars and brothels, no doubt an irresistible draw for Carson, though perhaps not until her adolescence.

Newspaper editor Ralph McGill, who knew Carson over many years, later remarked that she "could see the poetry and terrible sadness in the drab and ugly," noting the "rows of company-owned shacks on unpaved streets, outdoor privies and no drains." Carson remembered a visit she and her grandmother made "to the mill section" at Christmastime. There she caught a fleeting glimpse of the inside of one of the homes: "I saw a baby sitting on a chamber pot by an open door in a cold, two-room house with only a puny blaze in the fireplace." Though many years had passed since she made this observation, she wrote, "The degradation and desolation of that single scene have never left me." Recognizing emotions like that requires sensitivity and imagination—good qualities for a future writer.

In 1923, when Carson was six, her beloved grandmother, Lula Waters, died. (Lamar's mother had resettled in the north, either in Buffalo or Detroit, and Carson did not know her well.) Carson called her grandmother "Mommy." Lula Carson Smith—who would drop her first name, Lula, at age fifteen—called her mother "Bébé," as did almost everyone else. In turn, Lula Waters doted on Carson, whom she called her gray-eyed grandchild. The girl's eyes reminded her, she waxed lyrically, of her husband's gray eyes, the same husband, she said, who was raging in the back room without alcohol. "Come kiss me, child," she ordered Carson (*ING,* 13). Carson remembered the scent of lemon verbena around her grandmother; she recalled the treats her grandmother surprised her with, telling her to look in a top bureau drawer, where she would find a cupcake or, most memorably, kumquats.

Lamar Sr., like far too many of his relatives and like his wife (and, as it would turn out, both his daughters), was a drinker, probably an alcoholic. Family members seemed to accept this philosophically, and there is no record until Carson's generation of anyone trying to stop drinking. A favorite story about Carson's grandmother concerned the visit that some ladies from the Women's Christian Temperance Union (WCTU) paid her. It was immediately after her husband's alcohol-related death, and she knew exactly why they had come: they wanted to place WCTU purple and gold emblems over her husband's corpse; perhaps he had recently "taken the pledge"—or perhaps he did so often. Lula Waters wouldn't have it, insisting, "I come from a long line of drinking men. My father drank, my son-in-law [Lamar Sr.] who is a saint drinks also" (*ING,* 7). Moreover, she stated, she drank as well, and Lamar fixed her a "toddy" every night, which she enjoyed. Lamar came into the room at this point, and Lula asked for a toddy right then and there, and he offered toddies to the WCTU members as well. (The Smiths and McCullerses all used the term *toddy*—a fond and harmless-seeming way to refer to a drink that in most of their cases was anything but innocuous. It could include anything from sherry warmed up with tea to straight bonded bourbon.)

Carson and the rest of the family relished this story. But in an unpublished autobiographical fragment, Carson rehearsed the scene with the temperance ladies and added some other, darker observations on her grandmother's sense of what was behind the exchange with the WCTU ladies. She remembered Lula's husband frequenting the credenza on which the liquor was arrayed. It caused Lula everlasting pain, and she constantly offered up prayers about his drinking. The drink had him, she mourned. It was a compulsion; the compulsion came from dark forces.

Though overdrinking may well have brought misery and anguish during Carson's childhood, it could feed as well into a kind of good-natured exuberance that people associated with the Smith household. In its general informality, Carson's family was different from those of her more strictly raised friends. And the Smiths were on their way up, it seemed; in 1925, having acquired a car, they moved eastward out of the city to what was then a suburb, Wynnton. Wynnton was situated in the hills east of Columbus, where the air was thought to be more salubrious than the original settlement on the Chattahoochee.

The Smiths rented a house at 2417 Wynnton Street. Almost as soon as they moved there, they noted that the street was getting to be a busy thoroughfare. They wanted to own their home, so in 1926 they found a property they could buy: a craftsman-style stucco bungalow at 1519 Stark Avenue in a quieter neighborhood. The one-story house had a deep front porch, low rooflines, and high ceilings; it boasted a breakfast nook, a new feature common to the craftsman vernacular. A garage was set farther back on the plot, and an alley ran behind the garage. Rita remembered camellia japonica shrubs in the front of the house and along the fence in the backyard; there was also a holly tree, as tall as the house, that the Smiths liked to remark was perfectly symmetrical. Carson became alive to her surroundings and grew to love the Smiths' suburban yard. She loved visiting her cousins, Aunt Tieh and Uncle Gray (who she said were "richer" than her own family), and sitting under the scuppernong arbor, eating her fill of the sweetish

Carson's childhood home, 1519 Stark Avenue, Columbus, Georgia

fruit. Supper was often fried chicken, and watermelon was often the dessert, served very cold, Carson noticed.

The house was far more modest than the big Victorian house where they had lived with Lula Waters, as if the Smiths were taking their proper middle-class place. It was, to be sure, a solidly middle-class neighborhood, with similar families living in similar houses and lots of kids around for the Smith children to play with. As the Depression settled in, few people were buying jewelry from Lamar Sr., but his repair business picked up as more of them tried to make do with what they had. With the proceeds of the sale of Lula Waters's house, the family was not doing badly. Carson, a child of the Depression, would look back at the 1920s and observe that the family was well-off, but hardly among the town's rich. She knew, for instance, that her family could not afford the horse she wanted.

The move to Stark Avenue necessitated a change in schools, and Carson, now in third grade, transferred from the Sixteenth Street School to Wynnton Elementary, just a block from her new house. Though obviously intelligent and an enthusiastic reader, Carson was never very interested in school—at least in the academic side of things. Most of her doings were extracurricular, so much so that most of her memories didn't involve school at all. She had a dramatic streak, for instance, and organized the staging of several plays, using the sliding doors between the Smiths' two sitting rooms at Stark Avenue as a curtain. As the oldest sibling, Carson designated herself the impresario and star. The children fashioned costumes out of the household tablecloths and sheets, and after the show, they offered the guests lemonade in summer, cocoa in winter. The shows ended when Carson began to take the drama more seriously. After reading Eugene O'Neill, she wrote a three-act play that was simply impractical to stage in a sitting room and gave a reading instead (*TMH*, 249–50).

Her talents were so many, it seemed, that she could choose which to pursue. Their multiplicity meant that on her skinny shoulders rested the considerable weight of carrying the family along with her—not financially but into a hoped-for future. Many years later, Carson told a friend, she had been acting as the head of the family, financially and otherwise, and felt it as a heavy responsibility. "Carson always said that she was going to be rich and famous because when you were famous you could have everything you want," said a friend of a slightly older Carson.

Because she was marked out as special, she felt herself somehow outside the sphere of normal childhood. But she also felt the burden that comes when others vicariously invest in a person's achievements and that person becomes an object of hero worship. This emerges in two early short stories, "Sucker" and "Wunderkind." "Sucker," written when she was around seventeen, is about the burdens of hero worship. An older boy lives with his younger cousin, called Sucker, who idolizes the narrator. Sucker's adoration comes to grate on the older boy, especially when rejection by a girlfriend leaves him angry and resentful, and in the penultimate scene he sets out to destroy Sucker verbally. He tells the younger boy that his company is unwanted, and furthermore he taunts him for not being smart enough to understand this. "You're too dumb," the narrator says. "Just like your name—a dumb sucker" (*TMH*, 17). It works. Sucker changes (and people start to use his real name, Richard); he is no longer an acolyte. The pendulum swings so far the other way that the narrator sometimes catches a look in his eyes "that makes me almost believe that if Sucker could he would kill me" (*TMH*, 19).

The virtuosic story "Wunderkind" draws on deeper feelings about talent and the special ways it complicates the shift from childhood to adolescence. It's about what it's like to be a wunderkind, a condition that is by definition fleeting: the child grows up. In the story, Carson imagines a piano-playing heroine who confronts the wunderkind's greatest fear, that her talent has left her. The heroine has not only aged out of the description but has lost her ineffable passion. "Her hands seemed to gum in the keys . . . and she could not imagine the music as it should be": "'I can't,' she whispered. 'I don't know why, but I just can't—can't anymore'" (*TMH*, 85–86).

Carson herself seemed destined for a brilliant career in music and was sensitive to the pitfalls and tragedies that threatened along the way. In the parlor of her grandmother's house on Thirteenth and Fifth was a beautiful rosewood flattop piano that had been passed down through several generations. Carson's grandmother did not play, but her guests did, so the instrument was in frequent use. Bébé did not play either, but she vowed that her daughter would. During the next few years, Bébé and Lamar Smith built an excellent record collection, mostly of classical music, principally for their eldest daughter's delectation.

Relatively quickly, they decided that she would become a concert pianist. Most children do not begin piano lessons until they are between six and eight; earlier, their hands typically aren't large enough to play chords. A prodigy, however, might be expected to begin earlier, and Carson began to play at the age of five, on an upright piano that Lamar bought for her in 1922.

Several stories detail Carson's first performance at the piano. In her truncated autobiography, *Illumination and Night Glare*, she wrote that she sat down immediately and began to play "a tune I had made up," then "swung into" the popular "Yes, We Have No Bananas." To her parents, Carson later recorded, "This seemed a miracle" (*ING*, 12–13).

Helen Harvey, Carson's neighbor and first real friend, told a similar story differently. She and Carson went to a silent film, where they heard the accompanist play the then-popular "On the Wings of an Angel." They went back to Stark Avenue, where Carson sat down at the piano and promptly played the song from memory. This recollection probably conflates Carson's first performance at the piano with an occasion when she and Helen heard "On the Wings of an Angel," after which Carson played it at home. (The song, then called "The Prisoner's Song," was not recorded until 1924, two years after Lamar bought the piano.) Whatever the circumstance, Carson was soon signed up for lessons with Alice Kierce, a friend of Bébé's who had studied at Columbus's Chase Conservatory of Music.

Despite the fact that she went for a single half-hour lesson a week, she made considerable progress—perhaps because she practiced all the time. She later said that what existed beyond the impulse to eat, drink, or sleep was music; it was one of the foundations of her life. Often Mrs. Kierce would let her stay after the lesson and continue playing on her Knabe grand piano, sometimes for several hours. She pestered Mrs. Kierce until her teacher taught her Liszt's Second Hungarian Rhapsody, a showy and difficult piece that requires technique and skill unlikely in a young pianist. (It would often be used in cartoons, as the ultimate in grandiose classical music.) Mrs. Kierce thought Carson played it "extremely well," even putting aside her age—she was ten.

Told repeatedly that she had an illustrious career before her on the concert stage, Carson went along with it, and this gradually became her ambition as well. Nobody seems to have considered the possibility that she might prefer to be a composer—not just to play Beethoven but to be another Beethoven. With the usual caveats about reading fiction for the writer's life, her first novel, *The Heart Is a Lonely Hunter* (1940), suggests the trajectory Carson saw for herself. One of the four strands of the novel follows Mick Kelly, an adolescent coming of age who is consumed with a love of music. One summer night, walking outdoors in her town, Mick hears Beethoven's Third Symphony coming from a radio in the neighborhood. (Beethoven was German, she learns, and "spoke in a foreign language and lived in a foreign place—like she wanted to do" *HLH,* 117.) She is tremendously moved; this was different from anything she'd ever heard: "She sat with her arms held tight around her legs, biting her salty knee very hard. It might have been five minutes she listened or half the night. . . . She listened in a quiet, slow way and thought the notes out like a problem in geometry so she would remember. She could see the shape of the sounds very clear and she would not forget them" (*HLH,* 118–19).

Mick finds that at the piano, she can "arrange bunches of notes together until the sound came that she wanted. . . . She made up new music too. That was better than just copying tunes" (*HLH,* 161). She learns how to read music, and soon she is spending her evenings not on her schoolwork but on the music she makes up: "Mostly she had written just little tunes—songs without any words and without even any bass notes to them." Carson adds, "There was so much she didn't know about how to write music." She gives her compositions names; one she particularly likes is the aptly titled "This Thing I Want, I Know Not What," which she characterizes as "a beautiful and marvelous song— very slow and soft." She pledges a future for herself:

Later on—when she was twenty—she would be a great world-famous composer. She would have a whole symphony orchestra and conduct all of her music herself. She would stand up on the platform in front of big crowds of people. To conduct the orchestra she would wear either a real man's evening suit or else a red dress spangled with rhinestones. . . . It would be in New York City or else in a foreign country. Famous people would point at her. (*HLH,* 240–41)

Not in music but in literature, Carson would indeed present her art before "big crowds of people," appearing either in a rhinestone-spangled red dress, she imagined, or in a "real" men's evening suit, metaphorically speaking. The details might differ, but she saw herself, even then, on a great stage.

2

That Rainbow Youth of Mine

In 1930, packed off to her first day at Columbus High School in a pink wool suit, Carson admitted the experience was "scary." Her fears were borne out that first week when, in a momentarily quiet hallway, a bigger girl grabbed her and threw her to the floor, demanding that she say "fuck." Rubbing her face into the floor, the girl made her say it three times before letting her get up. Carson never told her mother.

She managed to convince herself that because she was to be a concert pianist, school was not as important as her new enthusiasm, practicing the piano. She seemed to have no difficulty convincing her parents as well, later writing loftily that she didn't believe in school but did believe in training in music. She added that her parents agreed with her, as if she had been calling the shots—which she may well have been, even at that young age (*ING*, 12). A classmate, Norman Rothschild, had the impression that Carson showed up in high school only at exam time. "She was haughty as hell," he remembered, and "looked down on" her teachers. "Carson was smart and she knew damn well she was smart."

She later acknowledged that she may have missed certain social experiences by keeping herself apart but claimed it "never" bothered her (*ING*, 12). Well, yes and no. As a reading of *The Member of the Wedding* suggests, she was not asked to join certain of her schoolmates' clubs and felt almost existentially excluded and alienated; the sense of being an outsider would be the source of some of her best writing. She was, however, a member of at least one club, the Loud-Mouth Dancers, in the fifth grade and of the club's high school iteration, Let Me Dance. But Carson felt—and a comment that another member made to a Carson biographer would seem to bear this out—that she was invited only because of her piano-playing ability, a valuable asset in a club devoted to dancing.

It did not help that she changed her name. Nobody in her family called her Lula; they wouldn't have dared, calling her "Sister" instead (Lamar Jr. was "Brother-man"). But they called her Lula in school, or often Lula Carson, using the double name in Southern fashion, and she hated it. When she was a sophomore in high school, at fifteen, she legally took the name Carson and dropped the Lula altogether. "Carson Smith" could well have been a boy, the gender ambiguity no doubt being part of the point. Her looks were androgynous enough that if she wanted, she could pass as a boy.

With puberty, she shot up in height, achieving her full 5 feet 8½ inches. She said, perhaps only half in jest, that she started smoking to stunt her growth; remarking on her appearance years later, her piano teacher Mary Tucker wrote, "She was *so* tall, and had a graceful awk-

Ten-year-old Lula Carson in coat and tie, c. 1927

wardness, or an awkward grace. She loved to leap over things—hedges, bicycles, any sort of obstacles, with [limbs] flying in all directions." Without being pretty, she projected a very eccentric kind of charm, and observers noted especially her "sunny smile." As she and her classmates matured, she kept a certain girlishness that would remain with her all her life while other girls became more womanly. With her lanky limbs and large mouth, Carson looked ungainly, different. She sometimes cut her own hair, and it showed. And she was refining her fashion sense. She preferred trousers to skirts and settled on men's oxfords for footwear, often with knee socks or crew socks—when the other girls were wearing stockings—and oversize men's shirts. She often wore boys' knickers despite the fact that few boys wore them anymore.

Carson's goal was not to be indistinguishable from her peers; if they wouldn't have her, she *wanted* to stand out in some way. Perhaps she knew she was not pretty enough (or short enough) to blend in with the other girls, so she had to use her somewhat odd looks to advantage, by calling attention to herself. This required courage—or gall—and was especially unusual in an adolescent of that time and place.

It was also dictated by Carson's emerging gender awareness and, following close on the heels of that, her sexuality. Though her new name was gender nonspecific, as an adolescent she mostly dressed like a boy. It is hard to tell from what source this drew—most likely not any true gender dysphoria, which would have been more pronounced in these years. She was a tomboy. She thought boys' clothing was more comfortable and more liberating; she could leap, climb, slouch, and dance without fear of showing her underclothes. Dressing as a boy marked, as well, what was undeniably Carson's nascent feminism. Mick Kelly, the autobiographical heroine in *The Heart Is a Lonely Hunter*, might have been speaking for Carson when she told her friends that she chose not to look like them, saying, "That's why I wear shorts. I'd rather be a boy any day."

She did not believe girls should have to wear confining and impractical clothing, just as she was discovering that most girls were expected to marry and reproduce to the exclusion of a career or creative work. She might have been exempt from this because of her plans to be a concert pianist, but she would have known that no females were ever truly free of the mandate to marry and reproduce. She was also out-raged that society held such expectations in the first place. Easiest to act like a boy, dress like a boy, and maybe pass as a boy. McCullers's several autobiographical heroines resist expectations in just this way. Mick Kelly, in response to her sister's complaint about her "silly boy clothes," asserts that she wears shorts so she won't have to wear her sisters' hand-me-downs: "I don't want to be like either of you and I don't want to look like either of you. And I won't" (*HLH,* 42). The unconventional Miss Amelia in *The Ballad of the Sad Café* wears overalls and gum boots and has "bones and muscles like a man" (*BSC,* 4). And Frankie Adams in *The Member of the Wedding* not only dresses like a boy, wearing "blue black shorts, a B.V.D. undershirt, and she was barefooted"; she has a boy's nickname and a boy's haircut, although it has grown out so anarchically that it has no part (*MW,* 2).

Carson, like Frankie, had an undetermined sexual trajectory at this point in her life. Like many adolescents, she was a morass of inchoate longings. Carson's cousin and close friend, Jordan Massee, observed that she had "extraordinary needs," as we might expect in a creative person or someone very motivated toward one end. "But," he added, "she had a tremendous capacity for love." He did not mean that she wanted primarily to be loved, though of course that was there as well, but rather that she had "the capacity for loving others." Simply put, she believed that being in love was her natural state, and for most of her life she was.

In early and mid-adolescence, Carson studied the piano with Mary Tucker, a local musician. Mary Sames Tucker was born in 1894 and grew up in Texas; recognizing her talent, her parents moved to Boston so she could attend the New England Conservatory of Music. Afterward she gave up her dreams of becoming a concert pianist to marry Colonel A. S. "Tuck" Tucker and raise their two children, Virginia ("Gin") and Buddy. Colonel Tucker took up his post as the command-ing officer at Fort Benning, the military base in Columbus, and in August 1930 the Tuckers moved into a house at the base, on Austin

Loop. Columbus residents soon knew of the talented presence in their midst, and parents began sending their children to Mrs. Tucker for piano lessons.

Carson was twelve or thirteen when she and her mother first heard Mary Tucker perform in a recital. The older woman's playing moved Carson, as it always would. Bébé, also impressed, set up a meeting for Carson and herself with Mary. Carson played for Mary, fast and furiously, her special piece: Liszt's Second Hungarian Rhapsody. Mary was impressed not so much by Carson's talent as by the outsize emotion with which the girl played, and by her determination and stamina in learning and playing a difficult piece. Carson began taking lessons on Saturday mornings at the Tucker house at Fort Benning. She became friends with Gin, just months younger than she, and as their friendship developed, she came to regularly spend the rest of the day at the Tuckers', alternating between practicing on the piano and gossiping with Gin.

The lessons continued over the next four years. Often Carson's mother dropped her off at the base early Friday morning and picked her up the evening of the next day. If she was lucky, she arrived early enough to hear Mrs. Tucker playing Bach. "To me you were the descendant of Bach," Carson told her, "and his solitary appointed votive." Carson's playing greatly improved, and she seemed on a path to attend a music conservatory or school, perhaps Juilliard, at the proper time. (She also talked of going to Budapest to study under the piano master Ernö Dohnányi.) She practiced for hours every day, and more on weekends, intent at once on pleasing her teacher and on working toward a future that would take her out of Columbus. She practiced to the exclusion of all else, including school—in which as a teenager she lost interest.

As Carson spent more and more time at the Tuckers', she and Gin became close. Gin later remembered Carson as "a tall, slender, active young woman [who] . . . had a kind of uncertain grace. . . . She had . . . a kind of Peter Pan quality." The Tucker home was near the fort's stables, and Gin and Carson rode horses many afternoons. Both imaginative girls, they spent hours together speculating on the riches and fame they would someday enjoy. They fantasized over which artist they'd most like to marry, each passionate about her choice. Carson later recalled for Gin the tiffs they'd have over what seemed to be hugely significant artistic matters. They visualized Carson's debut as a pianist at Carnegie Hall and what she might wear.

Like Frankie and Mary Littlejohn in *The Member of the Wedding*, Carson and Gin shared and argued over their enthusiasms: Carson thought Rachmaninoff's Second Piano Concerto was the best piece of piano music in the world, while Gin argued for Brahms's First. They loved Michelangelo. Still clumsy adolescents (Gin was, at five foot eight, a half-inch shorter than Carson—another bond), they longed for grace and elegance. They were devastated to learn that they were probably too tall to be classical ballerinas. Undaunted, they discovered Isadora Duncan, and danced interpretively wearing loose clothing. They founded their own School of the Dance, which they kept going "by strategy and bribes," Carson noted, and for a good week they had "a whole gang of sweaty children draped in sheets and hopping hopelessly around the back yard." The girls were equally moved by Duncan's autobiography, published in 1927, which passionately argued for free love, and by Duncan's own sad story: the drowning deaths of her children, and her own tragic end on the Riviera at the age of forty-nine, when her long silk scarf became entangled in the wheels of her car. Carson told her father that she intended to follow in Isadora's footsteps and run away to Paris, where she would support her family (even then, seeing herself as the family's mainstay) by dancing.

Carson later told Mary that the Tuckers were what she remembered best from her childhood, and that every detail about each family member was etched onto her consciousness. The Tuckers were her real family, she told Mary, to whom she was becoming ever closer.

Mary later recalled Carson between the ages of thirteen and seventeen as being "as vigorous and active as a young colt, a picture of lean, muscular strength." She was speaking twenty-seven years after the lessons ended, as if that talented, headstrong girl were standing before her.

Carson's relationship with Mary Tucker began, naturally, with music. Mary later said she was not sure Carson had the talent to "reach the top" as a concert pianist, but she kept any such doubts to herself because Carson "was easily discouraged by criticism." What she instilled in her student was discipline. The girl who played "loud and fast" needed to slow down and learn her music. The strategy seemed to work; Mary acknowledged that Carson developed "a crystal-clear, pellucid style." She worked on several Chopin études and Bach's English suites in A minor and D minor. The Bach "settled her down," Mary thought, weaning her away from her preference for "big music that used all her energy." When the lessons came to an end, Carson was learning the Chopin Piano Concerto No. 1 in E Minor. In the middle of this portentous period, Mary arranged a landmark event in Carson's life: she took her to see Sergei Rachmaninoff play.

Carson almost had to cancel. A sickly child, she seemed to pick up, into adolescence, every passing cold and flu, and in December 1933 she was quite ill with what turned out to be pneumonia. But Rachmaninoff was performing in January in Rome, Georgia, and Carson fully intended to go, illness or no. Bébé drew Mary into the kitchen for whispered consultations about Carson's health; when she wanted to telephone the teacher, she did so from a neighbor's house so Carson wouldn't overhear her conversation. Finally, Bébé cleared her to go. Mary also brought along a friend, Edwin Peacock, a young man who worked at a civilian job at Fort Benning. Carson and Edwin formed a bond on the ninety-mile road trip to Rome. (He remembered the concert being in Atlanta, not Rome.) They stopped in Pine Mountain to pick wildflowers. Mary, Carson, and Edwin would all remember going to hear the great Rachmaninoff as a milestone in their lives.

Carson recovered from this particular illness, but Mary next fell ill with a rare bloodstream infection and was bedridden, so many of the conversations the two remembered were held with Carson sitting at the foot of her bed. Mary said she told Carson she would get her a full scholarship at the Juilliard School.

During Mary's illness, however, her husband received word that he was being transferred to Fort Meade, Maryland, and Mary told Carson of their impending move. Carson felt hugely betrayed. At some point she told her family, Mary, and pretty much everyone else—the sequence is not clear—that she was giving up music for writing. She broke off all communication with the Tuckers, so Mary felt betrayed and abandoned as well.

In later years, Mary, reporting to biographers, tried to minimize her emotional investment in Carson for the sake of propriety, but this much is clear: she wanted to preserve her position as wife, mother, and musician, as well as her social standing. However, in a later account she acknowledged she had erred in "making our association too closely confined," an admission she did not explain. She said that her determination to enroll Carson at a music school was sidetracked and delayed by her illness and Carson's, but "it was not laid aside til she said she proposed to be a writer and not a pianist. . . . There was no breach, no recriminations, no apology, and our good by [*sic*] was affectionate." She continued:

> We were sorry, but we had had a fine four years. It is so easy to see from 32 years of retrospective thought, that [Carson] was deeply hurt, and I was rather dangerously hurt—let's admit it—in my self-esteem. For one thing what did I do wrong? rang in my mind like a tolling bell for years and years.

What really happened between her and Carson is shrouded in mystery—perhaps as it should be, because no one else can speak with any authority about what happens when two people are alone together. But these evasions and fuzzy descriptions obscure the fact that between them there had been not only love but physical attraction.

It is also safe to say that neither had had sex with a woman before and that they likely had no sexual contact. Carson would tell Mary Mercer, her therapist and, later, companion, that Mary Tucker tried to caress her, but Carson slipped away. Mary Tucker loved her, she felt, just as she loved Mary—though she never told Mary of her feelings. She was too afraid. If Mary hugged her, Carson would extricate herself. Giving in to the physical attraction at the time would have been extraordinarily difficult for two sexually reticent and inexperienced Southern women. They were constrained as a teacher and a pupil whose work together was very important; as a woman of forty and a teenage girl; as a mother and her daughter's best friend. Equally important, this happened in the 1930s, when lesbianism was not spoken of in almost any context.

For these reasons, too, their feelings came as a surprise to both, and understandably they withdrew from the physical attraction as from an electrical shock. While lesbian longings may not have been unfamiliar to Carson, her youth must be factored in here; the beginnings of sexual attraction can be unsettling to an adolescent, even traumatic, and perhaps especially so when the attraction is to someone in authority. The same-sex aspect of the attraction may have been new to Mary as well. She later said to a mutual friend of Carson's, Dorothy Griffith, "I could never quite understand lesbianism," whatever subterranean place it might have in her own makeup: not unusual for a woman of her time and place. The taboo nature of homosexuality at that time made it impossible for Mary to admit what was going on, to herself or, later, for the most part, to anyone else.

Finally, Mary, like Shakespeare's lady, would protest too much, revealing years later the nature of the interlude while trying to minimize or deny it. On the one hand, she aimed to downplay her role in Carson's life by insisting that there *was* no relationship: "I'm an old friend and music teacher and that's it." Mary continued,

> I can't bear it for biographers or critical writers about Carson to overemphasize the four years of her music study. It would be silly to deny it was important, but it would be outrageous to put too much weight on the period & imply all sorts of emotional involvements, mysterious influences & pressures and all sorts of goodness-knows-what eccentric or aberrational motivations.

But Mary herself, apparently fearing that biographers and scholars would tire of this evasiveness, and feeling conflicted within herself, went back to the relationship over and over like a dog with a bone. She would veer to the other extreme: "I was a disaster to her," she flatly, and a bit cryptically, stated to Margaret Sullivan. Sometimes talking about it made her feel better about her role in the affair. It "helped so much to soften and release me from that penitential interval when it seemed that I might have been so utterly mistaken in my association with Carson," she told one biographer. Mary bobbed and weaved, only revealing her own feelings of shame and guilt. At the same time, she wanted acknowledgment of the important part she played in the well-known writer's development. And she may have simply enjoyed the attention she was getting from the chroniclers of Carson's life. Even so, in every account she gave, it is clear that she could not, even to herself, acknowledge what she was feeling.

Mary was almost always hard on herself about the time. "I was ashamed of it now, was ashamed of it then," she wrote to Sullivan, adding, however, perhaps with a sigh, that it was "such a wonderful period." And she allowed herself a little latitude, once in a while, to think back on the experience fondly. Writing about Carson twenty-five years later, she mused, "She had a lovely body, her skin was like ivory."

Carson's relationship with Mary Tucker, her first experience of being in love, transformed her. Because she felt Mary "betrayed" her by moving away, she came to associate love with betrayal. The one time she talked about Mary Tucker in psychiatric treatment, years later, she told the doctor how Mary had tried to caress her, then went right on to describe how betrayed she felt when the Tuckers (not just Mary) left. In that account, in fact, betrayal, not love, was predominant. Yet Mary Tucker represented her awakening, physically (her sexual feelings), emotionally, and musically. And the awakening was what she recalled, with the distance of time. In a letter to Mary when the two women made contact again, in 1950, Carson, then thirty-three and seemingly relieved to be able to talk freely, tried to trace the dimensions of that awakening. The Tucker family, she said, was the source of most of the happy memories of her youth. By way of example, she recalled the first time she stayed for lunch with the Tuckers after one of her Saturday piano lessons. The maid served artichokes, which Carson had never seen before. She was horrified, she admitted, but she watched Colonel Tucker start in on his artichoke and followed suit. In the same letter, she called up the mixed feelings of the last year of her lessons. She burst forth that she had loved Mary, beyond normal limits, and was unable to comprehend these emotions involved. She was left feeling, she said, a strange guilt and sadness.

To Carson at a young age, love and loss seemed inextricable. But with time, she was able to fashion the emotions into art. Music transformed her life and informed her writing. Mary Tucker thoughtfully observed to Margaret Sullivan that *The Heart Is a Lonely Hunter* was a fugue—Carson was always impressed by counterpoint in fugue composition, she remembered—and *The Member of the Wedding* a sonata. Many years later Carson said *The Member of the Wedding* was originally "just [a story of] a girl in love with her piano teacher" (*ING,* 32). She told Mary that she was sure the novel would "speak to" her. If it had not been for her experience with Mary and her family, she wrote, the book would not have been written.

Besides being heartbroken, Carson may simply have felt misunderstood. She had wanted to be a composer before wanting to be a pianist, but nobody seems to have listened to her. Perhaps nobody who was part of her world in Georgia had any idea how a child, and especially a girl, trained to become one. She later told Mary, perhaps with a sense of grievance, that she was glad she hadn't chosen a career as a concert pianist, because she was born to make art, not analyze it. But she did not forget her early ambition when she sat down to write her first novel a few years later; Mick Kelly's dream is to be a composer.

Mary Tucker later questioned if Carson's illness in 1932, just before they separated—on top of many other episodes in childhood and adolescence that had compromised her health—also made Carson wonder whether she had the physical stamina for a professional music career, with the result that she chose to write.

The idea of being a writer was not totally new to Carson. She told Helen Harvey that she had first thought about it when she had pneumonia in 1933. Her first writing efforts date from 1934, when she was sixteen. Perhaps the impulse to create something with words began with the plays she had staged in the Smiths' front parlor. Her earliest effort was a play with the inauspicious title "The Faucet," set, oddly enough, in New Zealand. At the time her dramatic idol was Eugene O'Neill, a picture of whom she displayed on the mantel. She later described the plays she wrote at the time as "harrowing" and this seems accurate, for "The Faucet" was, according to one account, about revenge and incest. When it was finished, she sent it off to an address she found for O'Neill; she never heard anything, and the play has disappeared.

Her efforts stepped up after she graduated from high school in June 1933. She had no thought, apparently, of going to college. Her grades had been mostly Bs and Cs, and no teacher singled her out or encouraged her. Her language teachers remembered her best; she took French, Spanish, and Latin, and they noted that she seemed to be playing with words.

She threw herself into preparation and study after announcing her decision to give up music. Her cousin Virginia Storey, Aunt Tieh's oldest child, was working at the Columbus Public Library, a Carnegie library located downtown. Carson told Virginia about her plans for herself and said she wanted to read the great books of Western literature. Virginia remembered her cousin reading the ancient Greek classics, especially the dramas. She devoured the Russian realists, who were to become very important to her; Tolstoy and Chekhov were her passions. Her reading was not programmatic—the only modernist she mentioned later as an influence was D. H. Lawrence, especially *The Rainbow* (1915) and particularly the last third of the novel, when Ursula Brangwen seeks emotional and sexual fulfillment. Carson would have noted Ursula's lesbian love affair and the overall sexual frankness of the novel, not to mention Lawrence's short story "The Prussian Officer" (1914), a frank and unsettling account of same-sex relations in a military setting. She read and admired Baudelaire, especially the twinning of sex and death in his *Fleurs du Mal* and his lesbian verse. Enid Starkie's biography of the poet provided one blueprint for a life in art—irresponsible, dissolute, but dedicated to literature that addresses the twin concerns of love and death—not exactly what Carson envisaged for herself, but close.

Bébé, so instrumental in teaching Carson that a life in art was

Bébé in the Stark Avenue house

her destiny, provided a social context for such a future. Carson's mother was a charming and cultivated woman who had very little formal education and the tendencies of an autodidact; that is, she had a number of empty spaces in her body of knowledge. She could recite poetry at any time (in addition, of course, to the first chapter of *War and Peace*) and prided herself on keeping up to date in literary affairs. She liked Southern folk legends and lore. She was a kind person.

The writer Lillian Smith, a later friend of Carson's and author of *Killers of the Dream* (1949), voiced some of the feelings Carson may have shared about growing up white in the South. Smith was a great admirer of Bébé, seeing her as a sometimes hapless and feckless mother hen in a shambolic household. Smith compared Bébé's family to the family in *You Can't Take It with You*, the 1936 hit Broadway play about a family of eccentrics and their bemused struggles with money and other aspects of the conventional world. Bébé was a "vivid woman who was a rebel when young," Smith wrote, who somehow "pulled everything awry"—that is, made everything more interesting—to the point where Carson could sometimes be embarrassed by her flamboyance. She was also a kind of stage mother, all her ambitions concentrated on her oldest daughter and her career. Bébé dominated the field around Carson, as Smith saw it, but without being domineering. Others felt Bébé crossed that line. Mary Tucker, for instance, found Bébé's "ebullience" hard to take, while Mary's daughter, Gin, was a fan. A few Columbus people thought Bébé had "affectations," or "liked to play the grande dame."

As Carson got older and began bringing friends home, Bébé came into her own as a hostess. Helen Harvey liked the informality of the Smith household; the family "lived in a different world where you could do wild things and have the best time imaginable." Writing about a slightly later period, Bob Walden, then a soldier at Fort Benning, said of the Smith house, "The Stark Avenue home and its inhabitants were something to which I could relate and I was there anytime that I could get away from camp: for friendship, for family, for food, for music—guests listened to records and to Carson playing Bach, Scarlatti and folk songs—for reading and being read to, and just sitting."

Bébé was always well informed, well read, and generally au courant. In the 1910s and '20s phonograph ownership soared, as the machines became more affordable. The Smiths had amassed an impressive record collection, almost all classical music. Carson brought friends like Edwin Peacock over to listen to and talk about music, such that Bébé could have been said to preside over a kind of salon—Columbus, Georgia, style—with young people convening at 1519 Stark Avenue a couple of evenings a week. Edwin enjoyed evenings at the Smiths' very much; they were in no way glamorous, he later said, but Bébé was very warm and welcoming. Once he picked flowers along the way from Fort Benning to Stark Avenue—a long trek—to present a bouquet to her.

Edwin and Carson had become close in the period after Carson's graduation, close enough that he felt part of the family. Edwin had been born in Thomasville in southern Georgia in 1910 and left there two years after graduating from high school to take up a Civilian Conservation Corps job in Columbus, followed by a civil service job at Fort Benning. Her first (known) gay friend, Edwin rented a garage apartment on Wynnton Road behind the Women's Club that became a haven of sorts for Carson, especially after he furnished it with a spinet and phonograph; with friends, they formed a group called the Record Club. Edwin was well read, with strengths in areas that were uncharted territory to Carson. He introduced her to Marx and Engels and to the literature of social protest, pointing her toward the work of writers like John Dos Passos. It is impossible to overstate this turn in Carson's development. She was for a time passionate about Marxism, the source for the fiery speeches that the Black doctor, Benedict Copeland, delivers in the *The Heart Is a Lonely Hunter,* which reveal Carson's relatively sophisticated understanding of the subject.

Growing up in a region still under the thumb of Jim Crow, she had an awareness of the color line that is perhaps easier to trace. Carson located a turning point in her orientation at a moment when she was about eight or nine. The family had a succession of African American domestic servants: from Nursey, a childhood nurse, and Cleo, who replaced Nursey, to Vannie Copeland Jackson (the only one whose last name we know), Lucille, and Della; most only worked part-time. Carson remembers looking on with her brother, Lamar Jr., when Lucille telephoned for a cab to take her home after work one day. When the taxi arrived, the driver said, "I'm not driving no damn nigger." Carson describes Lamar's and her own response to witnessing "Lucille's embarrassment and the ugliness of the whole injustice." Lamar hid in the dark crawl space under the house, and Carson, after calling the driver "You bad, bad man," joined him there, where they held hands to comfort each other, "because there was nothing, nothing else we could do" (*ING,* 54–56). Lucille had to walk the mile or so home.

The incident captures the humiliation a child can feel *for* someone she loves when she sees that person humiliated. The humiliation and the impotence ("there was nothing, nothing else we could do") marked Carson, like many another Southern white child, indelibly. Lillian Smith, who had so admired Carson's mother, experienced a nearly identical incident, which she would write about in *Killers of the Dream.* Not that Carson did not have a long way to go to overcome her native racism, to the extent it could be overcome in her time and place. But she knew at an early age that something was fundamentally wrong with the system in which she was growing up.

Conditions were not good in Georgia in the 1920s and '30s for anyone, Black or white. The boll weevil had decimated the state's cotton crops beginning in 1915; cotton prices also declined steadily through the 1920s. A three-year drought beginning in 1925 left rural Georgia reeling, only to be followed by the worst drought in recorded history in 1930–31. The Great Depression hit the state hard. Despite conditions in the agricultural sector, however, Columbus was able to carry on. Because of its textile mills and iron manufacturing, it was not heavily dependent on the farming economy. The continued presence of Fort Benning helped. But no local economy was immune to the effects of the 1929 stock market crash and its aftermath.

The New Deal relief measures, undertaken starting in 1933 by the administration of Franklin Delano Roosevelt, brought gradual relief to much of the country, though in the South, especially for African Americans, the picture remained bleak. In fact, Georgia provides a remarkably succinct example of the New Deal's intersection with Jim Crow. The state's newly elected white governor, Eugene Talmadge, who found the New Deal a "communistic experiment" in "wet-nursin'," managed to prevent the newly formed Civilian Conservation Corps, the very group that employed Edwin Peacock, from signing up African Americans. Roosevelt, with an interest in the state engendered by his regular visits to Warm Springs after he was stricken by polio in 1921, ordered Talmadge to induct Black Georgians into the corps, vowing that no further CCC funds would reach the state as long as the governor stalled. The overt crisis passed, but the CCC inducted very few African Americans and segregated the work camps. As was the case nationwide, it would take another world war before Georgia recovered economically and grievous conditions abated for most. African Americans continued to leave Georgia en masse for Northern cities.

Edwin Peacock did not write, but he was an enthusiastic reader, and he was willing to plow through Carson's earliest writing efforts. He remembered an early novel called "A Reed of Pan" or "Pan's Pipes"— which proved intractable; he was unable to finish it. Gin Tucker found some of Carson's early efforts "pretty awful."

Edwin opened her eyes to the literary scene and the wider world by introducing her to *Story* magazine, a forum for the best new (and established) writers. Getting published in *Story*, Carson could tell, even from the sidelines in Georgia, was the most promising and perhaps realistic goal for a writer starting out.

Story was launched in 1931 by the expatriate journalist and editor Whit Burnett and his wife, Martha Foley. Originally published in mimeograph form in Vienna—dedicated, according to Burnett, to "noncommercial" stories—the magazine moved, first, and briefly, to Majorca, and then to New York in 1933. Though it flourished in the 1940s and beyond, finally folding in 1967, the 1930s were the decade of its greatest influence, reflecting growth and change in the literary world. Richard Wright, James T. Farrell, J. D. Salinger, and William Saroyan were introduced in its pages, and anyone from the early 1930s on who was interested in serious new fiction by American authors read and discussed the work they encountered there. Edwin and Carson devoured and talked over the latest issue of *Story* whenever it made its way to Columbus, perhaps by Edwin's subscription.

Unlike Edwin, however, Carson knew she had to get away.

In September 1934, Carson made the first of several trips from Columbus to New York. A lot about this trip is shrouded in mystery, none of the several accounts of her stay totally convincing. It is not even clear whether her family was sending her off to be a writer or a pianist, calling into question whether she had been decisive enough in announcing her goal. She evidently told her parents that she would enroll at Juilliard *and* take writing courses at Columbia University. The family agreed that Lamar Sr. would sell an emerald and diamond ring Lula Waters had left to her granddaughter to raise money for tuition (to which school is not clear), an amount to which the Smiths were able to contribute as well.

Everything about the 1934 trip to New York trip sounds strange, ill thought out, and tentative, in fact. Word went around Columbus about her plan. Where would she live? A local young woman who would be taking some classes at Columbia offered Carson a bed in her apartment over a linen shop. Lamar Sr. took Carson to meet the young woman, said he didn't like the look of her—her hair looked dyed—and Carson held her breath. But in the end, her father agreed to let her go anyway (*ING*, 15).

She took a steamship north from Savannah. In those days of poor roads and cars that were not reliable for long distances, and before interurban buses were widespread, one took either the train or the steamship for such routes. But the Central of Georgia Railway Company went into receivership in the early years of the Depression, throwing interstate passenger service in the area into confusion. Later Carson would make the trip by steamship one more time; otherwise, she would rely on Greyhound buses to ferry her back and forth between Columbus and Manhattan. She was delighted to go by boat because she would see the ocean for the first time.

Carson, at age seventeen, found New York awe-inspiring and humbling, but about her movements after arriving there in September, we know little. The absence of letters home or to friends like Edwin (he evidently didn't save any) makes clarity impossible. She may have deliberately cloaked the whole thing in mystery. Somehow she lost the money her family gave her: she entrusted it to the roommate, who lost it, or it was stolen from Carson, or she lost it on the subway when her purse was stolen. In any case, the apartment didn't work out—Carson claimed a man assaulted her in the building's hallway—and she went looking for another place. She later said that she took a room in a brothel, but there is no evidence for this. She also said she had a string of jobs, some more interesting than others: working for *More Fun* and *New Comics,* two comic magazines ("Me, a tragic writer, editing the funny papers," she later wrote [*ING,* 16]); serving as an accompanist for dance classes, sometimes at a settlement house; waitressing; walking dogs; and working as an "improviser" for dancers, whatever that might be. The most likely sounding job was as a clerk for a real estate firm. Her employer found her reading Proust at her desk, she said, and promptly fired her.

Eventually, Carson registered at Columbia for writing courses, probably in time to go home to Columbus for Christmas. By February 1935, by any reckoning, she was definitely enrolled in creative writing classes. One of her teachers was Helen Hull, the author of several novels that received widespread recognition in the 1920s and beyond, *Quest* (1922), *Islanders* (1927), and *Heat Lightning* (1932), the latter selected by the Book of the Month Club. Hull, who held a PhD from the University of Chicago, had a lifelong female partner; Carson would not necessarily have been aware of this, however. Her other teacher, about whom scarcely more is known, was Dorothy Scarborough, an Oxford-educated Texan who held a PhD from Columbia and was a respected folklorist. Scarborough was best known for her 1925 novel *The Wind,* the basis for the 1928 movie with Lillian Gish. Carson never referred to either woman again; her writing teacher the following semester, Sylvia Chatfield Bates, she occasionally mentioned, but not often.

In time, though perhaps not until the spring semester, Carson found a safe and even congenial place to live. She threw herself on the mercy of a Columbia dean, who recommended the Parnassus Club, a boardinghouse for young women situated on West 115th Street, up by the university campus, and housing mainly Juilliard, Barnard College, and Columbia students from the nursing program, as well as young musicians, writers, and artists. Founded by Florence McMillan, a retired accompanist to three celebrated opera stars—Enrico Caruso, Louise Homer, and Leo Slezak—the focus of the club was music. The Parnassus Club charged sixteen dollars a week for room and board and had a "strict" curfew of eleven p.m. However congenial, Carson soon moved to the Three Arts Club, a similar boarding establishment recently built at 340 West 85th Street "for women students of the drama, music, and the fine arts." Perhaps she preferred to be some distance from school; perhaps she ran afoul of the Parnassus Club's strict curfew. She used the Three Arts Club as the mailing address for her first writing submissions. A year later, when a story was accepted for publication, Carson had the magazine sent to the housemother of the Three Arts, Edith Markloff, and to Carolyn Bilderback, a friend who also lived at the club and who went on to become a successful modern dancer, teaching at the Manhattan School of Movement for seventeen years.

Carson may have needed some time away to come to a decision about her career before finally giving up any musical aspirations. She also needed exposure to New York to see what kind of future was possible for a talented woman from the Deep South. But then, little was settled about Carson Smith's life as she entered her twenties. She may not have been confident that she knew the answers to any number of important questions—whether, for instance, she had the talent to become a writer. She knew she wanted to create, and she knew she did not want to stay in Columbus, Georgia; she may have even known that a big city would be more hospitable to her sexual preferences (though they were as yet undefined). She knew very little.

In the meantime, Edwin was barraging her with letters about a new friend, a corporal at Fort Benning whom he had met either at a drawing class or at the public library. (Edwin told different stories to different people.) Independently, the corporal had met (at the library) Carson's cousin Virginia Storey and was dating her. Edwin had brought his new friend the corporal over to the Smiths' one evening, where the newcomer found a warm welcome. The Smiths and Edwin seem to have been in agreement that Carson had better come back to Columbus to meet Reeves McCullers.

3

Charming the Skin Off a Snake

By all accounts, James Reeves McCullers was a man of immense charm; indeed, in first-person descriptions the word *charm* occurs repeatedly. "He could charm the skin off a snake," said his cousin, Vernon McRae. The Smiths, Edwin Peacock, and the odd guest at Bébé's salon on Stark Avenue thought he was an ideal match for Carson, solely on the basis of his charm. A Reeves partisan (much, much later, Carson and Reeves's friends would fall into two camps, Reeves people and Carson people) described him as a "buoyant, seldom-morose, and lovable person." Reeves, according to his brother, "never lost his poise." Carson often said he was the most handsome man she'd ever met, and others agreed. She told Gin Tucker that his face was "sensitive." Beneath unruly blond hair he had gray eyes and a somewhat sharp chin and nose. She added, with satisfaction, that he was three-quarters of an inch taller than she and quite trim. More important, she found he had an exquisitely subtle sensibility.

Reeves McCullers had unlikely beginnings, though something set him, his siblings, and their mother apart; at least they shared a wider field of vision, as they all made their way, eventually, to New York City. He was born on August 11, 1913—four years before Carson—in Wetumpka, Alabama, the seat of Elmore County in the eastern part of the mid-state region, not too far from the Georgia state line. He was born at the home of his paternal grandfather, James "Wiley"

McCullers, who was a clerk at a dry goods store. Reeves's father, known as Bud, moved the family to Jesup, Georgia, the Wayne County seat, in the southeastern part of the state, when Reeves was still an infant. Bud seems never to have amounted to much, but it is hard to tell, as a serious accident, incurred on his job as a brakeman on the Atlantic Coastal Railroad, left him with a crushed leg and a modest settlement from the railway in 1923, when Reeves was ten. Along the way, Bud McCullers had worked as a telephone lineman, a guard at the Valdosta State Prison, a farmer whose farm (belonging to

James Reeves McCullers, born in 1913

his father-in-law) failed, and a clerk in a drugstore—thus joining the many members of Carson's extended family who worked in the pharmacy business. After his injury, he made a couple of stabs at earning a living, but he also began to drink even more heavily. He left the family around 1930.

His wife's family thought she deserved better, though technically both families were from the aspiring middle class; Reeves's parents became part of the lower because of Bud's bad luck and his likely alcoholism. Jessie McCullers was born a Winn, and her father was the proprietor of Winn & Company, selling farm implements and horses, in Jesup. Later, Jessie and her children would rely on financial support from the Winns.

Because family finances were so precarious, the older McCullers children often lived with relatives. Reeves, between the ages of ten and twelve, spent his summers in Wetumpka with Ida McCullers Lancaster, his aunt, and her husband, John, who was president of the town bank. In 1925, at twelve, Reeves moved to Valdosta and lived with his paternal aunt Emma Rose and her husband, Vernon McRae. It was a particularly happy time for Reeves, as his cousin, Vernon Jr., was just

Eighteen-year-old Reeves by the side of a Columbus road, c. 1935

a year younger. He was the one who said Reeves could charm the skin off a snake, and he was cheerful about the fact that Reeves was better than he was at almost everything. But Reeves had a propensity to drink even then; at fourteen he got drunk enough that he borrowed and crashed the McRae car. Aunt Emma was cheerful about the fact that Reeves's stunt cost the McRaes five hundred dollars—"but he was sweet," she added.

Reeves and Vernon both joined the Boy Scouts, Reeves enthusiastically enough that he became an Eagle Scout at thirteen, said to be the first in Lowndes County. This is scouting's highest honor, reserved for a very small percentage of boys who have shown great achievement, measured not only by the number of merit badges a boy earned but also by his potential for leadership. The distinction is attested to by a contemporary *Time* magazine headline, "How Eagle Scouts Have Made Their Mark on America." Over the years, Eagle Scouts have included Steven Spielberg, Sam Walton, L. Ron Hubbard, and Gerald Ford.

Reeves's years with the McRaes were comfortable, as Vernon Sr. owned a drugstore. For his senior year in high school, he returned to Wetumpka and his prosperous Aunt Ida and Uncle John Lancaster. There he was a high school star, a football hero, a member of several clubs, a talented actor, and a B student, equally popular with the girls and the boys. Though only five feet nine, he was wiry, strong, and tough, unafraid of fighting—thus his success in football. But it was a small school, and its standards were likely not very high. Though it was to become the Wetumpka High School in 1932, when Reeves attended it was still called the State Secondary Agricultural School. The students were expected to become farmers.

Reeves purportedly graduated in November 1931—and not the following spring, as would be expected. It is unclear why, and the unusual circumstance gives some credence to the belief of Andrew Lyndon, a later friend, that Reeves never finished high school. Sometimes Reeves is said to have attended college for a year, though this probably refers to occasional college classes he attended later in his life. What we know for sure is that in April 1932, Reeves, at eighteen, enlisted in the army at Fort Benning, five months after his school years came to an end.

Reeves had previously harbored ambitions to go to West Point, which would have given him a college degree and a clear career path. For whatever reason, both he and a friend, John Vincent Adams, were stymied in their attempts to get there. One observer said his parents' divorce might have contributed to his failure to get into the military academy. West Point admission requirements were constantly evolving. Perhaps Reeves and his friend were thwarted at getting into the military prep school that preceded West Point, which would have been a regional program, or perhaps their efforts to get into the academy itself, after participating in a preparatory program in high school (like the modern ROTC), came to naught. It is hard to imagine in what areas Reeves would have fallen short, unless he failed to secure a nomination. Perhaps, as would happen often in the future, his ambition faltered.

If Reeves's formal education was cut short, however, he proceeded on the course of the autodidact, diving into a range of subjects that appealed to him without any kind of overarching plan—with the result that he acquired an impressive body of knowledge that was riddled with holes. He devoured whatever he could find in the way of modernist literature, from T. S. Eliot to Faulkner, and he read great swaths of philosophy and history. Like Edwin Peacock, he made a study of Marx and Engels until his critique of capitalism was, he felt, unimpeachable. He filled numerous notebooks with philosophical observations, notes on whatever he was reading, and literary efforts. The time he spent scribbling in what was becoming a towering pile of notebooks convinced many people—perhaps Edwin and, for a time, Carson—that he was already a prolific writer with a brilliant future before him. Yet for all we know he never showed anyone anything he had written.

Earlier, when Reeves moved in with his aunt and uncle in Valdosta, he found a town whose population had been about 10,000 in 1920, as compared to the 31,000 Columbus boasted at the same time. The downtown business district was growing along with the economy, but the residents were mostly still dependent on agriculture—again unlike Columbus, which had expanded into industry. At this time an infamous series of events left its mark on the town. Reeves appears never to have written or spoken about the Valdosta lynchings of 1918, seven years before he arrived in the town, yet he would have been part of many a conversation about it, at least until he left the South in 1940 and probably beyond. He and Carson almost certainly would have discussed it.

What happened was this: On May 16, on a plantation near Morven, Georgia, an African American farm worker, Sidney Johnson, shot and killed his boss, the planter Hampton Smith. He also shot Smith's wife, but she survived.

Johnson was a convict laborer, a fixture of the Jim Crow South. Unable to find willing workers for the wages he wanted to pay, Hampton Smith, like many other planters, essentially leased convicts from the local jurisdiction, paying their fees and providing them room and board in exchange for labor. Because the demand for cheap labor in the South was sorely felt, white legislators enacted laws making criminal a host of small infractions, giving those convicted a choice between a stiff fine or a jail sentence. (Sidney Johnson's "crime" was playing dice, for which he was charged the—for him, exorbitant and impossible—fee of thirty dollars.) Thus the planters and the justice system ensured a steady supply of convict laborers who were, in effect, enslaved; they were forced to work, and their movements were controlled. It is not surprising that the planters who availed themselves of this system were not model employers. Smith, the planter whom Sidney Johnson killed, was known to be an abusive boss who beat Johnson repeatedly, one time for saying he was too sick to work.

After the shooting, Johnson ran, hiding out in nearby Valdosta. Next day the white citizens, enraged that they could not locate him, began the lynchings. On the first day, the mob killed two Black men in two different counties. By the time Johnson was caught on May 22, a total of thirteen African Americans had been lynched. The most infamous deaths were those of Hayes Turner, a farmhand who had also incurred Hampton Smith's wrath, and his wife, Mary. Hayes, arrested because of his history with Smith, was supposedly being transferred from one jail to another that Saturday when he was lynched, his body left to hang from a tree until it was taken down on Monday. Mary, who was eight and a half months pregnant, spoke out against her husband's killers, denying his guilt and asking that the lynch mob be arrested. But the mob tied her up and poured gasoline on her clothes, which they then ignited. Naked, her skin blistered and charred, Mary Turner's belly was then slit open with a knife, the baby spilling to the ground and reportedly uttering two cries. One of the mob crushed the baby's skull with his heel, and the crowd then shot Mary Turner full of bullets.

When the police found Johnson, in a Valdosta house, a shootout ensued, and the fugitive was killed. The mob outside seized his body, castrated it, and dragged it behind a car to Morven, the town where Smith had been killed. There they hung the body from a tree and burned it.

After the lynchings, at least five hundred African Americans fled Valdosta and the surrounding towns. At the same time, white employers threatened to kill any Black workers who attempted to flee. The contradiction in terms was unerringly typical of life in the South during Jim Crow. It was not a good time to be Black in Lowndes County.

Reeves McCullers was five at the time of the lynchings, and he likely grew up hearing about them. The story, with all its gruesome details, would have fascinated small boys in and around Valdosta. Reeves would almost certainly have known members of the white mob who were responsible for the lynchings. He might have known some of the African American victims as well. He might have seen Sidney Johnson playing dice on a Valdosta street corner.

Carson, given her fundamental quarrels with Southern life, especially its treatment of Black people, would have wanted Reeves to talk to her about the lynchings. By the time she met him in 1935, Valdosta was infamous among Georgians. As would-be writers and students of human nature, Carson and Reeves would likely have been most interested in the motivations, however crude, of those involved: Hampton Smith, Sidney Johnson, and certainly Mary Turner, the pregnant woman who protested the lynching of her husband and paid for it with her life and her baby's. It is hard to know about Reeves, but Carson would have found a certain grim fascination in the darkly specific details. Neither wrote about it directly—which does not mean it did not leave a mark. The incident reveals a new ugliness and pathology that the term "Southern Gothic," so often used to describe Carson's writing, only hints at.

When Carson met Reeves, they were immediately attracted to each other. It was late May or June 1935, when Reeves was in his fourth year in the army, at Edwin Peacock's garage apartment. They seem never to have stopped talking. Reeves's charm and good looks and his articulate volubility on any number of topics that interested Carson ensured his appeal for her. It speaks to his discernment that he found her distinctive but unusual looks attractive, not to mention the slow drawl with which she voiced outrageous views or made biting remarks. Like all those who loved her, he believed Carson was marked out for great things. Like Bébé, he offered her unconditional love; because she was the recipient of this love, Carson had the confidence to believe she was attractive to anyone she was attracted to.

She was bound and determined to become a writer, her confidence in her future unshakable. She had already written a semester or two's worth of stories and came across as quite the professional, talking about word counts and the literary marketplace. Reeves took heart from her example and set his sights, which until then had been concentrated on college courses in journalism and philosophy, on becoming a writer himself.

Carson, eighteen, fell in love. It was important to her that Reeves was liberal politically, which she found especially significant, given the benighted towns he had grown up in. She and Reeves and Edwin spent whole days talking. Carson occasionally worried about her absence from home, but her parents seem not to have minded, as they had been charmed by Reeves as soon as he walked into their house. He cemented the connection by bringing classical music records when he visited the Smiths. Though Reeves's immediate family was lower in status than the Smiths, the McCullers extended family was better off; in any case, social class meant little to Lamar Sr. and Bébé.

But the journey to sexual relations, which Reeves and Carson thought they wanted, was bumpy. Carson's only experience with sexual feelings had been with Mary Tucker, feelings that she may by now have regretted she had not acted upon. The first time Reeves held her hand, Carson professed herself "shocked," and told her father about it. She feared it might "disturb" their friendship, a worry she expressed even more vociferously when Reeves tried to kiss her in a car. When he asked her what on earth *that* was about, she explained earnestly, "Well, our intellectual and moral relationship would be disturbed if you kissed me."

A little later, however, Carson recalled, she and Reeves were sitting on the front porch long after her parents had gone to bed. Reeves came right out and asked her whether she was a lesbian. She was confused by the question. Who knows? she said. She had loved Mary Tucker, she said, but she had never told her so, always keeping herself apart. What are lesbians like? she asked Reeves. What do they do? In answer, Carson later said, he undertook a kiss that he explained as the one Baudelaire had given to his girlfriend. That is, Reeves began to perform oral sex on her. Early on he paused and asked her if she liked it. Carson answered that she thought so.

But she was preoccupied by the fear that her sleeping parents might wake up and see what she and Reeves were doing on the darkened porch. Between that and marveling that Reeves had not shed a single article of clothing, including his coat and tie, she was slow to give herself over to the experience. Afterward, when he asked again if she liked it, Carson said she had. Then Reeves told her he did not care whether she was a lesbian or not, he still loved her, and he wanted to know when they would get married. It would be another year, however, before they had unclothed, penetrative sex.

⁓

In the meantime, they talked. That summer Carson was reading George Sand, Rousseau, Descartes, and Pierre Loti, and they discussed her reading as well as the theories Reeves had imbibed from his study of political thinkers like Marx and Engels. They spun visions of the future, of life in New York City and lots of travel. Carson told Reeves of her abiding romantic desire to see snow.

They talked and they drank. Drinking was central in the Smith household and always had been. Whatever the location of the line between heavy drinking and alcoholism, this much is known: Carson's grandfather died from drinking (at the age of thirty, with concerted effort). Her grandmother said that pretty much every member of the Smith family drank. If a Smith traveled, the other Smiths made sure he or she had access to alcohol on the trip to stave off the DTs. When Carson was ill with pneumonia, Bébé allowed her to go to hear Rachmaninoff in Rome, Georgia, sending her off with a jar of equal parts cough syrup and whiskey. Carson was slightly drunk when she met and shook hands with the master after his performance.

Reeves and Carson, in the first year of their acquaintance, drank beer almost exclusively, and they drank a lot. Over the next twelve months, when Carson wrote to her New York friend Emma DeLong Mills, she often would be drinking "Bock beer," even in the morning, usually pleasantly high, she confessed. The couple moved on to sherry, which would remain a favorite tipple of Carson's; she mixed it with tea or passed it off as tea. In her fragmentary autobiography, she noted that Reeves sometimes drank whiskey; she didn't—yet. She wouldn't have recognized alcoholism when she was that age, she wrote, credibly enough. But she referred only to Reeves's drinking and not to her own—he had an amazing physique and temperament, she said. Rita and Reeves, the only two family members who would eventually seek help from Alcoholics Anonymous, were the designated alcoholics of the extended Smith clan. Nothing about Lamar Jr.'s drinking habits is known, but those of Lamar Sr. and Bébé—especially Bébé—indicate problems with alcohol as well. And with regard to Carson, whom her family considered a creative genius, a pattern was established early: no one criticized her or confronted her about her drinking, ever.

One of Carson's earliest efforts was "Instant of the Hour After," an interesting story that doesn't quite work. But it provides a riveting picture of her relationship with Reeves, their exchange of ideas with an Edwin Peacock figure, and the centrality of drinking in their relationship. The story opens with a couple waking up, hungover, in their host's apartment. Philip, the Edwin character, is absent that morning,

From left to right: Edwin Peacock, Carson,
Reeves, John Adams in front; mid-1930s

and the couple's exchange about the night before reveals an ominous hostility between Marshall, clearly based on Reeves, and the unnamed narrator, the Carson figure. She worries about her hangover, finding all the objects in the room unfamiliar and strange; she doesn't remember much from the night before. She contemplates taking an Alka-Seltzer but doesn't feel up to the effervescence involved. Marshall is a "claustrophobic," and the narrator's relationship with him is "mutually loving but mutually destructive." Marshall explains to the woman, " 'It's this—' he said in a voice drained of all tone. 'My love for you, darling. At times it seems that—in some instant like this—it will destroy me' " (*TMH*, 62). The whole story, in fact, is claustrophobic.

Reeves was a bright, inquisitive, and determined learner, but he had what Carson would later call a "lost quality," which one friend or another noticed over the years, and which was tied to his inability to write. (Not a scrap survives, except well-written and vivid letters.) Whether this problem preceded his drinking or not, alcohol would exacerbate every problem he encountered and would compromise his functioning, though his charming, articulate, and brilliant side would win him plenty of respect and love. For Carson, it was different. She could and did function, writing in top form while nursing a thermos of tea and sherry. With notable exceptions, those who knew her denied that Carson was ever drunk. There is no doubt, however, that alcohol was central in her problems with Reeves, especially when it loosened her tongue and unleashed the sarcasm, bitterness, and sometimes meanness that lurked below the surface.

In the months after their meeting, however, they were deliriously in love. They took fifteen- or twenty-five-mile bicycle rides or walks into the countryside. In one letter, Carson says she and Reeves had walked twenty miles in the county to see a friend. (They got a ride back.) Edwin remembered them cycling thirty miles into the country, where they ate a boxed lunch and went swimming.

A lot was going on that summer. For several weeks in June, Carson worked for Columbus's daily newspaper, the *Ledger-Enquirer*, although scant record survives of her employment—if, that is, she held a paying job there. A woman editor at the paper remembered Carson exclaiming that she would rather "starve to death" than be a newspaper reporter, but otherwise no trace of her work there remains. She didn't mention the job, in any case, to Gin Tucker, to whom she wrote that summer, telling her that she was interested in starting a magazine with a young student she knew, who was also a theater critic who cannot be identified: perhaps someone she met at the *Ledger*. She also alluded to a chance to get her first novel, most likely "A Reed of Pan," published, but upon looking it over, she realized just how "wormy" it was.

That summer a tragedy was narrowly averted: the Smith home almost burned to the ground. Bébé had been out at the A&P when the fire began, and Carson, temporarily sidelined by a bad case of athlete's foot, was at home reading Dostoyevsky. According to Carson's (perhaps embellished) account, the next thing she knew, Lamar Jr. was telling her to get out, but she told him to stop bothering her while she was reading. Rita shouted that she heard the fire engines coming. Carson reluctantly got up and "hobbled" out of the house. Smith family lore holds that two of Bébé's stock of excellent holiday fruitcakes were saved. Legend also holds that Carson talked her way into temporary quarters provided by family friend Jim Woodruff in his family's recently vacated home on Second Avenue. There the Smiths lived while the Stark Avenue house was being repaired, a job that took half the summer. There is no record of what caused the blaze.

The summer no doubt flew, leaving both Reeves and Carson very determined to be together—and, in Carson's case, to write. Reeves had reenlisted in the military in 1934. In part because Carson was fixated on New York City and was returning there in the fall, he looked into taking college courses at Columbia University in philosophy, psychology, and his relatively new interest, writing. But he was still at Fort Benning when Carson left for New York for September classes.

That fall she switched gears and studied at Washington Square College, the downtown campus of New York University, otherwise located at University Heights in the Bronx. She was drawn to a teacher there, the novelist Sylvia Chatfield Bates, probably on another student's recommendation. No doubt she looked up Bates's work, which included editing an important anthology of twentieth-century short stories published by Houghton Mifflin in 1933. Bates's latest novel, the 1934 *I Have Touched the Earth*, was described by *Kirkus Reviews* as a story about a "small town girl" who "find[s] an outlet in friendship with another girl and that winds up morbidly psychological, in the Faulkner vein." Had Carson seen the book, she would have found much to interest her.

Bates's class absorbed all of Carson's attention. Students wrote and submitted stories, and Bates commented on their work in writing. Her comments are preserved with Carson's early stories: "Residuum"; "I Want, I Want"; "Wunderkind" (the only one of these stories published in her lifetime); "Instant of the Hour After"; "Dear Mr. Brahms"; "Court in the West Eighties"; "Like That"; and "Poldi." Often Bates's comments reflect an ongoing dialogue with Carson. Her comment on "I Want, I Want" begins, "I don't know why you think I will demand more structure." About "Wunderkind," she wrote, "We disagree on your stories for I like this one." She was frank about her preferences, commenting about "Residuum," "It is of course a very morbid story, but I don't mind that" (*TMH*, 87). She was almost always encouraging. Closing her comments on "I Want, I Want," she wrote, "The story is not all it should be. . . . You have a story but it has not quite come through," then added, "It is as good as I've seen printed in the 'little' magazines." Many of Bates's comments were simply workman-like, however, aimed at helping her students master the conventions of published short stories in commercial and literary periodicals: "And by the way, certain parts are not printable in a magazine, Joyce or no Joyce" (*TMH*, 63).

Bates's best students had the chance of a reward beyond a good grade, and the last words of Bates's comment on "Wunderkind" suggest what it was. Bates put out a mimeographed collection at the end of each year containing the best stories written for her classes. She then submitted them for the *Story* prize, which included publication in *Story* magazine. "Please return for my files," Bates wrote in her critique of "Wunderkind," "i.e., submit for Mss 1936 and STORY prize" (*TMH*, 87). Carson would have been overjoyed.

Reeves, for his part, was casting about for ways to get out of Columbus. His hitch in the army would not be up until 1937, and his only option was to buy his way out of it. Providentially, a death in the family in January 1936 made it possible for him to do so. His aunt Ida died, leaving him three Alabama Harbor Bonds, which he redeemed for $1,500, enough to pay back the army, and in August 1936, he was finally a civilian again. He wasted no time making his way to New York, where he moved into a small apartment on West 43rd Street and promptly enrolled in classes at Columbia in journalism and anthropology.

Carson was already back in the city; she had returned to Columbus briefly after finishing Bates's class in the spring semester, then had quickly turned around to take a summer class with *Story*'s Whit Burnett himself. Burnett accepted two of her stories for publication in *Story* in December 1936: "Wunderkind," the autobiographical piece about a young female piano prodigy that Bates had liked; and "Like That," about a young girl who watches her sister, newly adolescent, become interested in boys and resolves never to grow up if it means acting "like that." (For some reason, this story did not appear in the magazine.) *Story* paid twenty-five dollars a story, equal to about $230 today.

That fall Carson signed up for another class with Bates, but early on she became very sick with an illness that forced her to drop out of school. She lay ill for over a month. It was the first time poor health had really interfered with her plans.

Different observers, and Carson herself, locate the beginning of her health problems at different stages in her life, partly because no one caught what was really wrong until later, when she developed serious heart problems. Carson believed the trouble started in the fall and winter of 1931–32, with the pneumonia that nearly kept her from attending the Rachmaninoff concert.

A definite answer is impossible to find without knowing exactly what Carson was ill with four years later. An early biographer speculated that her ill health might have begun in 1936, with a bout of tuberculosis. TB in those days, before the advent of the antibiotic streptomycin, was thought in most cases to sooner or later cause the patient's death. Treatment could involve surgery but almost definitely would require a stay at a sanatorium, where fresh air and rest often brought sick patients back from the brink.

In January 1937, Carson, writing from Columbus, told a friend that she was having a rest cure at home rather than in a tuberculosis hospital. She regretted that she was not able to write stories or even letters. In February she wrote that she was still under observation and was going for regular X-rays, but she did *not* have tuberculosis in her lungs, and anything else she might have was negligible.

She was a free woman, she crowed.

But something else was wrong as well. In 1936, Carson was very sick indeed. Either at this date or back in 1932, she seems to have had an undiagnosed strep throat infection. Because antibiotics did not yet exist, however, the disease could continue unchecked, even with a proper diagnosis, and in some cases it could lead to rheumatic fever. The latter causes joints to ache and swell and almost always scars the heart valves, causing the organ to work harder at pumping blood. When the valves are not working properly, blood can pool in the heart and clot, which in turn can lead to a stroke.

The relationship between strep infections and stroke was totally unknown in the 1930s. Strep was likely not preventable and was definitely not treatable. But Carson, knowing none of this, was simply happy when she was able to return to normal life. She wrote Gin Tucker that the 1935–36 school year had been pretty much a wash. At the end of the previous summer, she explained, she had had a "chest ailment" that probably began after a case of pneumonia. So from September 1936 until the spring of 1937 she'd had to take that rest cure. But after that she was once again a "husky," healthy human girl, she wrote confidently.

⁓

In 1935, in one of Sylvia Bates's classes at Washington Square College, Carson had made a good friend in Emma DeLong Mills, who at forty-one was twenty-three years Carson's elder. Emma had had a colorful past as a "farmerette," a woman who worked the farms of soldiers while they were overseas during World War I, and later as an army nurse. The two formed a strong bond, talking and corresponding at length about their writing careers. Emma produced four full-length stories each semester. In her freshman year, she roomed with Mei-ling Soong, who in 1927 married Chiang Kai-Shek, the Chinese general and autocrat. Emma's interest in all things Chinese had been developing since then, and she would spend the rest of her life raising money and working for the Chinese Nationalist Party.

While Emma's letters to Carson have not survived, Carson would write almost twenty letters to her friend over the next four years, which follow her development into a serious writer and the beginnings of her life with Reeves. Emma often gave her presents, particularly when Carson was leaving on trips (almost always to Columbus and back in those days), and Carson's letters usually began with effusive thanks. She told Emma what she was reading and how her writing was going, congratulated Emma when a story was accepted, and commented on the "spunky" behavior of "your friend" Madame Chiang, who fascinated Carson (along with the rest of the United States).

In a 1936 letter, Carson wrote that she very much hoped Emma and Reeves would meet soon in New York. He was a genius, she wrote proudly, and had a fascinating mind. Reeves, who had been living with

Reeves and Carson in Columbus before their 1937 marriage

Vincent Adams (who also sprang from the army), was again taking classes at Columbia in the spring of 1937. Adams had rented a property in suburban Westchester, in Goldens Bridge, still a somewhat rural community on the Croton River. Reeves joined him there and asked Carson to come live with them.

Perhaps because Goldens Bridge was almost fifty miles from Manhattan, Carson knew she could hardly go to live with Reeves without telling her family—and, not so incidentally, informing them that she was sexually active, and that she and Reeves were very serious about each other. She wrote Lamar Sr. and Bébé bluntly that she was going to Goldens Bridge to live with Reeves. If she were to marry him, she wanted to make sure they got along in bed. A young bride should not be ignorant of sex, she said. But Carson's father protested that most girls knew little or nothing about sex when they married. Carson replied that she was different, reminding them of her adoration of Isadora Duncan and the free love Duncan espoused. Marriage? She poohpoohed it. The whole exchange, Carson later said, left Lamar agape.

At this point, Carson had written nothing about her feelings for women, in letters or elsewhere. It is not clear that she was even aware of such feelings, though Reeves's explanation for cunnilingus indicates that both were aware that lesbianism existed. At this stage of her life, she was focused on Reeves, probably to the exclusion of any lesbian feelings—which she would seldom write about at this time, in any case.

Reeves had made himself comfortable at the Goldens Bridge house, which had a studio for his use. But Carson remained too sick to travel until late March. When she finally arrived, he promptly dropped his Columbia classes to devote himself to their life together. They spent two months presumably testing their sexual compatibility and making forays into the city, each showing the other favorite places and discovering new ones together. They discussed getting married at length. Carson later said that she told Reeves she didn't think she could marry him if he didn't have a job. Fair enough, Reeves said—he would go south and get one.

And so he did. That summer Reeves went to Charlotte, North

Carolina, on the promise of a job at the *Charlotte Observer*. The job went to someone else, and Reeves had little hope of finding any work on a newspaper in the South: "Someone will have to die or stay drunk for a month for me to get a decent job on one." He still hoped to work on his own writing, but he was, for the moment, discouraged. "I still study and read a bit," he wrote Vincent Adams, "and have foolishly high hopes about my particular star, but things get a little thicker every day."

Reeves soon landed an Atlanta job with the Retail Credit Company, founded by Cator and Guy Woolford in 1899. The company, which would eventually become Equifax, one of the three giant U.S. credit bureaus, assessed the creditworthiness of individuals and businesses. Most likely Reeves's job was evaluating applicants for auto or life insurance. (Eliot Ness, the FBI agent whose "untouchables" helped bring down Al Capone, held the same job with the company at roughly the same time.) In the midst of the Great Depression, it was a dispiriting and even ignoble occupation. Moreover, the company paid Reeves by commission, which meant he could eke out a living, but barely, Carson confided. (He later received a salary of twenty-two dollars a week.) Otherwise, she said loftily, Reeves was not sympathetic to the mission of Retail Credit. The only good thing about the job, she said, was that he was outdoors most of the day. Soon enough, however, he was forced to buy a car for the work, a used Chevrolet that Carson condemned as a gas glutton. And he was shortly transferred to a branch in Charlotte, a city roughly twice the size of Columbus.

The job was steady enough that Reeves thought it was time for them to marry. During the third week of September, he showed up in Columbus with little notice. They hadn't been prepared to marry so suddenly, she said. She and Reeves made arrangements for a wedding at noon, with the immediate family, Aunt Tieh and her children—Carson's cousins—and Edwin Peacock in attendance. Edwin was responsible for the music, the adagio movement of Bach's Concerto for Two Violins in D Minor. The ceremony, with Dr. Frederick Porter, pastor of the First Baptist Church, officiating, was held in the Stark Avenue living room, after which the couple posed for informal photos in the side yard of the house. Carson wore a tailored suit (which her cousin called her "traveling suit") with knee socks (a new fashion) and what were known as Girl Scout oxfords, sturdy mannish lace-up shoes. About the wedding, she thought it was lovely, Carson wrote Emma. The next day they left for Charlotte.

4

———

A Young Knight

The previous year had been a bust, Carson wrote Gin Tucker on October 10, 1937, resolving to accomplish a lot in the coming winter. She noted that she had embarked on a new writing project, a kind of fantasy. Whether this marked the beginning of her first novel, *The Heart Is a Lonely Hunter,* is not clear, but soon enough, as of November, she was referring to a book that she had underway, complete with a hero and a symbolic character, a deaf-mute. She had written forty pages, she told Emma DeLong Mills, her friend from writing class, and reported that her excitement was buoying the writing along.

Carson's letter to Gin followed her receipt of a long-hoped-for letter from her friend, which, she wrote, made her walk up and down the room in a frenzy of happiness. Gin had told Carson about her recent marriage—for which Carson sent her heartfelt congratulations and a recording of Brahms's Fourth Symphony—and Carson told Gin about Reeves. Even though she was trying to confine herself to the barest details, the letter ran to ten typed pages describing her new husband and their plans. She emphasized their insistence on culture: the art on the walls, the music they listened to. And their books: Reeves was adamantly against storing any books in the attic and meanwhile kept buying more, with the result that the bookshelves were jammed. Every surface was piled with books, and books and papers were stacked against every free wall. Carson genuinely loved Gin, her closest female friend, but she also wrote out of curiosity about Gin's mother, Mary Tucker. After asking about each member of the family, she told Gin she'd love to hear about them or, better yet, to hear *from* them.

She told Gin about an encounter, or rather a nonencounter, with Mary and her husband two years earlier, and a year after the Tuckers had moved away. There was one thing that she could not understand and that puzzled and hurt her. One morning she had been out walking in Columbus with a cousin when she saw Gin's parents drive by; they did not stop, though they did wave to her. Carson hurried home, certain that since the Tuckers were in town, they would call, but they never did, though she stayed by the phone all day. She ranked the experience among the worst things that had ever happened to her, she wrote, seemingly without self-consciousness or guile. It was a miserable puzzle, she wrote, one that she could not figure out.

Carson would go back to this puzzle, reliving what she saw as Mary's rejection of her, again and again in her life and work. It was inexplicable to her that she could love someone yet her love would be unreturned. Carson would never understand, even as she grew up and fell in love with other people, how Mary had been unable, on many different levels, to respond.

In Carson's imagination, love was a joint experience between two persons—but the role each played, and the emotional impact of each on the other, was quite different. "There are the lover and the beloved, but these two come from different countries," she later wrote in her novella *The Ballad of the Sad Café*, the work that most directly addresses this theme. If she was right—and her relationship with Mary seemed to confirm this observation—the experience of being in love meant great loneliness, because being the beloved or the lover means being emotionally apart from the other person. The beloved, of course, has the confidence and satisfaction of being loved. But Carson did not experience love in the way of the beloved. She might, of course, have been an object of romantic love without her knowledge; she might have dismissed some would-be lovers almost unconsciously. But more often, and from her perspective, tragically, she was the lover.

The single greatest exception in Carson's life was Reeves McCullers. His love for her was boundless. In their relationship, she was emphatically the beloved, in the face of Reeves's love. In the beginning, she tried and often succeeded in matching it, but the imbalance worsened over the sixteen years they were (intermittently) together, and it caused them both great joy and great misery.

Carson and Reeves derived much satisfaction from setting up a household and work schedules and plans. When they moved into their first apartment in Charlotte, at 311 East Boulevard, near downtown, she wrote a flurry of letters, but these slowed to a trickle, especially the following year, after they moved to Fayetteville, North Carolina. Were she not buried in her work—she was laboring full-time on her novel—she might have been miserable. For someone as bright and ambitious as Reeves, these years mired in the South canvassing for a credit company must have been particularly deadening. Increasingly, Carson and Reeves drank. One of their first purchases in Charlotte was a gallon of wine for fifty cents. It tasted like some awful sweet medicine, Carson wrote Gin. They apportioned a little more in their budget to replace the bad wine with gallon jugs of "mediocre" sherry. Actually, Carson told Gin, they hoped the first gallon they bought would last the winter. It's hard to tell whether Carson was fooling herself or trying to fool Gin.

In letters to Gin and Emma, Carson re-created their first apartment in Charlotte, in a house that looked remarkably like the Stark Avenue house in Columbus. They had one very large room and a tiny kitchen. Books were everywhere. They'd hung

The newlywed Reeves at the kitchen table, Charlotte, c. 1937

reproductions of Renoir, Brueghel, de Chirico, and Picasso. They also had a small Donatello reproduction that she especially prized because it had had pride of place on the mantel in Columbus, and a bronze "plaque" of Saint Cecilia; these sculptures were to stay with Carson through many moves. They had one large eating and working table. Until they got Reeves a reading light for his side of the bed, they comically managed to tie a table lamp to the headboard. She wanted to describe the way the sun illuminated some favorite blue Chinese bowls, casting sunlight across the entire apartment, she wrote Gin. They hoped to rent a piano for Carson.

The couple budgeted $3.50 a week for food. (They assumed traditional gender roles around the house; Carson did the food shopping and cooking.) The results were pretty dismal. Carson described a vegetable fat they cooked with that looked like lard, which sounds unmistakably like Crisco. After a few days of this, they would splurge on Schrafft's candies—Carson had a sweet tooth—and often gave up and went to the S&W restaurant downtown, the flagship of a chain of inexpensive restaurants in the South. Otherwise, Carson would buy a cut of meat at the butcher shop and ask the butcher how to cook it. One night she cooked a chicken; she plucked the pinfeathers on the bird but did not clean it, so the terrible smell of baked innards greeted Reeves when he came home. Carson hadn't noticed (*ING*, 18–19).

Reeves and Carson moved from their first apartment in Charlotte to a larger but cheaper one, and in the spring of 1938 they decamped to Fayetteville. By this time they cared less and less about domestic life, as Carson grew more deeply engaged in her work. They settled on their writing plans fairly quickly. For the time being, Reeves was working and supporting them both; they would alternate years, each spending a full year working while the other wrote and studied. Carson wrote Emma about their intentions: After Reeves had worked for a while, she would find a job and take over while he wrote, and they would continue to switch off working. Somewhere along the way, however, the plan changed such that Reeves remained in charge of making money beyond the prescribed period, while Carson continued to write. Probably the change emerged as the novel advanced. They decided that if Carson could publish her stories and, most important, her novel, their money problems would be solved, and they could both devote themselves to writing. Reeves had become as invested in the novel as was Carson.

Reeves seems to have realized fairly quickly that he could not, at this stage of life anyway, write full-time—he had nothing on paper that he could show to anyone. Before marrying Carson and taking the job at the Retail Credit Company, he had written on the side, filling notebook after notebook with journal entries and writing attempts, according to Carson, but none of them have survived. In November 1936, Reeves had written Vincent Adams that he hoped to sell a collection of essays that he thought might bring him "gas money" to visit his friend in New York. But he no longer wrote in his downtime. Instead, he mused about the sort of job he could take that would offer him some kind of fulfillment. He considered teaching, writing publicity materials, and covering European news from France. Emma Mills was taking a course with Nathaniel Peffer, the Far Eastern correspondent of the *New York Tribune,* and that appealed to Reeves. He was beginning to show a capacity for leadership, and for a time he volunteered as a scoutmaster, spending his spare time teaching campcraft and other skills to boys who reminded him of his younger self. He did have potential as a writer, his letters show, but he could not shape his words into any kind of formal structure. He might have made a successful corporate executive— a position so bourgeois he would never have considered working toward it. As it was, he flailed, both professionally and personally.

He did, however, devote a significant part of his spare time to talking to Carson about her work and editing it. In years to come, rumors circulated that Reeves really wrote Carson's books. (Another such rumor held that her mother, Bébé, wrote them.)

Reeves helped Carson write a detailed outline for her novel. Together they devised a pedantic but tantalizing précis, about five thousand words, for a story whose main character would be a deaf-mute. She later described herself as having seen her story "illuminated"—Carson's word—in the pattern of a carpet in the Columbus home (recalling, perhaps, Henry James's metaphorical "figure in the carpet"). Suddenly she saw that it would center on this character, whom she would name John Singer. Everything then fell into place.

Carson would never again work from an outline; usually, she would start with a character and let the story build around him or her. Her outline for *The Heart Is a Lonely Hunter,* the one exception, begins with these thoughts:

> The broad principal theme of this book is indicated in the first dozen pages. This is the theme of man's revolt against his own inner isolation and his urge to express himself as fully as possible. Surrounding this general idea there are several counter themes and some of these may be stated briefly as follows. . . . There is a deep need in man to express himself by creating some unifying principle or God. . . . Human beings are innately cooperative, but an unnatural social tradition makes them behave in ways that are not in accord with their deepest nature. . . . Some men are heroes by nature in that they will give all that is in them without regard to the effort or to the personal returns.

The next paragraph begins, "Of course these themes are never stated nakedly in the book" (*ING,* 163).

This is indeed a smart explanation of the ideas that would inform the novel, but the words are unmistakably not Carson's. She seldom spoke or wrote on such an abstract level; when she did, it was confined to a sentence here and there. More likely, the voice behind the outline is Reeves's. He could have been describing himself in the opening pages when he invoked "[man's] urge to express himself as fully as possible." It was to his marriage that Reeves referred when he wrote of those who "will give all that is in them without regard to the effect or to the personal returns." He was helping Carson fashion the (over) articulated structure on which her writing would hang.

From this awkward beginning, with Reeves's help she went on to describe in some detail each character and how his or her nature would be revealed: Biff was shaped by his sexual past while Jake met issues of social justice head-on. The strong impression is that Carson thought out the characters and Reeves helped her formulate what they stood for, or were based on, or symbolized. Carson would do the later, most important work: she would set the machine of a plot, or several plots, in motion and endow the story and characters with the peculiar narrative logic and individuality that were her special genius.

As it emerged, *The Heart Is a Lonely Hunter* told the story of four characters who revolved around John Singer, a deaf-mute in a small Southern city much like Columbus. Biff, who owns the New York Café frequented by the novel's characters, himself has a tragic story. Dr. Benedict Mady Copeland is an African American Marxist physician whose family has a sad trajectory. Jake is an alcoholic and socialist who tries to organize the workers at a local carnival. Mick Kelly is an adolescent girl with musical ambitions who efficiently loses her virginity over the course of the story; she must take a job to support her family, dashing her musical hopes. Singer himself is in love with another deaf-mute, who has been taken away to an insane asylum; when he learns of the friend's death in the asylum, he commits suicide. The center, it seems, cannot hold, and all the characters are left alone. The title, suggested by Houghton Mifflin's Hardwick Moseley, was drawn from "The Lonely Hunter," a poem by a man who wrote as a woman. William Sharp, a Scottish editor with a mystical bent, was his "truest self" in the poems he wrote as Fiona Macleod. The poem reads, in part, "But my heart is a lonely hunter that hunts on a lonely hill." Its title and the poet's gender-ambivalent identity would have appealed to Carson.

Reeves and Carson drew up the outline in the winter of 1937–38, when they were living in their second apartment in Charlotte, at 806 Central Avenue. Emma had sent Carson a flyer with word of a competition she might be eligible to enter. The Houghton Mifflin Literary Fellowship Award, open only to writers who had not published books, awarded the winner $1,000 and book publication. Carson decided to apply and asked Sylvia Bates and Whit Burnett to recommend her. Then she and Reeves went to work typing up the chapters she had written and composing and typing the outline; they sent copies to Burnett and Bates. Burnett, Carson reported to Emma, was mean about it. He evidently had a beef with Houghton Mifflin for using his name without permission on the flyer for the prize, which had caused him a good deal of trouble. He therefore refused to write a letter of recommendation for Carson. He did tell her that he liked the chapters and outline and that if Houghton Mifflin did not give her the prize, she should send them to him for publication by *Story* magazine's book imprint.

Burnett's explanation, which Carson relayed to Emma, may not have been the whole truth. It would have been petty—and unlikely—for Burnett to punish Carson for what the publisher had done to him. Evidently embarrassed at writing a letter of recommendation when he had been quoted in the circular advertising the prize, he couldn't afford to be criticized for doing so—in which case he could have informally endorsed Carson's novel to Houghton Mifflin (though there is no record of this).

Sylvia Bates, Carson said in the letter to Emma, was her hero. Once she heard about Burnett's refusal to write Carson a letter—according to Carson, just a few days before the deadline—Bates appealed to a colleague, William March, a writer of psychological fiction who was then best known for a World War I novel, *Company K* (and later for his novel about a murderous child, *The Bad Seed*). March agreed, as did an editor at *The Atlantic* whom Carson did not name in her letter to Emma. Visions of what to do with the cash prize crowded her imagination, Carson wrote Emma, adding that she would be happy if Houghton Mifflin agreed to publish her book and pay her one hundred dollars.

The last month in Charlotte had been a hectic time for Carson, getting the outline and six chapters of the novel typed and mailed to her recommenders and to Houghton Mifflin. They were leaving for Fayetteville: a relocation to Asheville, which he and Carson were enthusiastic about because it was a bit of a cultural center, did not transpire. The move to Fayetteville was a promotion, because Reeves would no longer be paid by commission but placed on salary. But the couple would have seen it as simply a delay in their plans to get to New York City, which was surely among Carson's "visions" for that thousand-dollar prize. Perhaps the prize money could even pay for Reeves to quit his job to study and write.

As they hatched their plans, Reeves and Carson were also avidly following the looming crisis in Europe. Fascism was spreading across the continent. Hitler had annexed Austria in 1938; just ahead, in September, the 1938 Munich accord would allow Germany to annex the Sudetenland from Czechoslovakia, leading British prime minister Neville Chamberlain to declare "peace for our time." And in Spain, Franco's nationalists were winning against the Republicans. All this was happening as the couple was packing up and making the move from Charlotte to Fayetteville. The world picture, Carson told Emma, made everyone live in a state of dread.

The radio was on nonstop, and the news depressed and worried them. Both were idealistic and committed to working for change (even if mostly in theory), and their inability to do so in the Deep South, in the 1930s, was frustrating to them. They talked about getting jobs as foreign correspondents in Europe, although that seemed beyond them at this point. Too much of their energy was taken up by their marriage, Carson's literary plans, and Reeves's determination to turn his job into something more fulfilling.

Not surprisingly, they found it difficult to muster enthusiasm for the move. Fayetteville seemed familiar territory, though it was even farther from family and friends than was Charlotte. (Carson and Bébé knew the bus schedule between Charlotte and Columbus well.) But the small city, more rural and dependent on farm prices, was even more depressed than Charlotte or Columbus. Carson was happy with their new home at 102 Rowan Street: it occupied the wing of a house with its own private yard and minuscule front porch. While the kitchen was tiny, the house had a large room downstairs and upstairs a bedroom and screened porch. The accommodations were a bit odd, Carson said. There was no hot water, and she and Reeves had to duck their heads (perhaps an exaggeration) to get through the doorways. After a few days, they found that the walls were thin, and they could hear all their neighbors' movements in the adjoining apartments.

Reeves had high hopes for the Fayetteville office of the Retail Credit Company, which he established himself in the Stein building. In 1916 the Steins had erected the first skyscraper in Fayetteville, a five-story building housing Stein's Department Store. But the economy had affected the business; nobody was buying insurance or real estate, and no one was interested in buying credit information. The nearby presence of Fort Bragg didn't help the local economy much, at least not during the Depression. Reeves put in ten-hour days, often bring-ing work home with him. He even worked on Sundays. In the spring of 1938, Carson wrote a letter to Emma from the company office, on paper with the letterhead Credit Bureau, Inc. She typed on the curious office typewriter, which printed only caps, big and small. There had been winds and rain all day, she wrote, but that evening the scent of spring was all around her.

They were biding their time until Carson heard the results of the competition. In the meantime, life in the South was becoming impos-sible, Carson told Emma. In a later letter, she compared herself to a dog that had bloodied itself straining against its tether. All there was to do was drive around the countryside drinking wine; they sometimes went to the ocean beach in Wilmington. She and Reeves had plans, Carson said, to travel around the world, spend a year in Tahiti and one in Paris, travel to the Soviet Union, Holland, the Scandinavian countries, and so on, then make their way to New York City, always the goal. She pleaded with Emma to visit. Periodically Carson would write that she had frequent dreams of her friend, whom she was unable to reach in the dream. To their delight, when Emma had to make a trip to Norfolk in February 1939, she did pay a short visit.

By then Carson was finishing her book, fleshing out the elabo-rate outline she and Reeves had concocted. "The Mute" (her early title) did not win the Houghton Mifflin Literary Fellowship Award. But Houghton Mifflin did accept it for publication, offering a $500 advance (about $10,000 today). Evidently the publisher was convinced by the six chapters she had sent but also by the outline, which made a strong case that she would have no trouble completing the novel. In fact, her submitted materials convinced them that she would finish soon, so they scheduled publication for the spring of 1940, just a year off. Carson had her work cut out for her, and she wrote steadily all though the fall and winter.

She later told a friend that Houghton Mifflin had offered her a $250 prize that she refused: a pure invention. She also claimed that the publisher wanted her to make changes in the text, which she had refused to do. While her early correspondence with Houghton Mifflin is not preserved, arguably the publisher had qualms about two elements of the story: Mick Kelly's sexual initiation (a rather graphic scene), and the homosexual relationship between the two deaf-mutes, Singer and Antonopoulos (although there is no reference to sex between the two men).

Carson was unlikely to turn down the offer of publication over such changes. She was too eager to get her work in print and launch her career, not least because the plan to move to New York City hung on the money. Next, she was complaining that Houghton Mifflin was dragging its heels in delivering the second half of her advance, which had been due on delivery—the publisher claimed the novel had dim commercial prospects. Reeves had put in a request with his employer to be transferred to New York, but he and Carson intended to go whatever the answer, once the second half of her advance came through, when they would have the cash they needed for the move.

When they received the $250 payment, however, they decided it wasn't enough to finance the move. Moreover, the Retail Credit Company was willing to transfer Reeves to Savannah but not New York. They elected to stay where they were, although Carson made a brief trip to Columbus just after she sent in her novel in April 1939.

Carson was nonetheless energized by her achievement and immediately began a new piece, unsure whether it would turn into a short story or a novel. Initially, it was titled *Army Post* (later, *Reflections in a Golden Eye*). Carson later told a researcher that she was looking for something fun to do, given her temporary sentence to life in Fayetteville, where their circumstances were barely civilized. Through the thin wall, she was treated to a drama between a sadistic father and his sick child; when the child cried, the father would hit him on the head to keep him quiet, a dynamic that seemed to feed into the characterizations in the story she was writing. The germ of the story was Reeves's report of a story he had likely heard at Fort Benning during his time there in the army. It was about a voyeur at the army camp. Carson took this and constructed a story about a Private Williams and his interaction with Captain Penderton and his wife, Leonora. Williams takes to spying on Leonora in her bedroom at night, while Penderton is consumed with lust for Williams. Meanwhile Leonora is having an affair with Major Langdon, whose wife, Alison, has been so undone by the death of their infant daughter that, bizarrely, she cuts off her own nipples with garden shears; she relies on her friendship with their homosexual houseboy, Anacleto, for solace and distraction. Carson later said that the novel was strongly influenced by D. H. Lawrence's story "The Prussian Officer." Certainly Penderton's feelings for Williams are far more overtly sexual, even graphic—though no sexual act is described—than the deaf-mute Singer's love for Antonopoulos.

This was harsh stuff, but Carson told the story straightforwardly, simply, and deftly. It's nothing more than a fairy tale, told simply and with the barest authorial voice, she said—meaning, presumably, that she told it like a fable. That being the case, it is not that hard to understand how she could comment that from the outset it promised to be fun. She wrote four or five pages a day and wrapped it up in two months. Wisely, she decided not to submit her new novel to Houghton Mifflin or any other house until *The Heart Is a Lonely Hunter* came out: not due to anything intrinsic to the manuscript but so as not to muddy the waters for the progress of her first book. Indeed, when Carson tried to tell her editor at Houghton Mifflin about this new book, he told her to focus on one matter at a time.

It was a time of extraordinary fecundity. Once *Reflections in a Golden Eye* was finished, Carson began thinking about and making notes for another new novel, about a girl who feels left out of her brother's upcoming wedding; tentatively, she was calling it "The Bride and Her Brother." All this activity suggests that completing *The Heart Is a Lonely Hunter* bolstered her self-

Carson's first novel was published on June 4, 1940.

confidence. It also suggests she very much liked the writing itself—something not true of all writers.

The changes in Carson's and Reeves's lives played out in front of an ominous backdrop that saw Nazi Germany take over the rest of Czechoslovakia in March 1939, then join forces, shockingly, with the Soviet Union in a ten-year nonaggression pact. When Germany and the USSR invaded Poland in September, Britain and France declared war on Germany, and World War II was underway. Americans hung on every word from Europe, though Washington was officially determined to stay out of the conflict; even at this date, that seemed possible. Carson was perhaps a little less engrossed in these developments than Reeves, partly because as an ex-soldier, he followed military news, but both began to talk more seriously of going to Europe as war correspondents. Since this would have required better language skills and journalistic connections than either of them had, however, they began instead to discuss taking in a refugee child from Germany. But this, too, was unrealistic; the United States, unlike the U.K., had no official plans to bring refugee children over, and even if it could be arranged, taking in such a child would be neither simple nor easy.

The fast pace of Carson's work and the development of her plans for future writing were matched by the speed at which events moved after *The Heart Is a Lonely Hunter* appeared on June 4, 1940. Even she felt whiplashed.

Carson had had terrible trouble with Houghton Mifflin after she sent in the manuscript in the spring of 1939. She heard nothing from them for a long time—and then no mention of the $250 of the $500 advance, which was due her on delivery of the manuscript. Over the next year, she corresponded with the publisher regarding editorial matters, but long silences were the rule. At last they set a publication date for May 1940, and they wrote to Carson about promotions they were planning, beginning that month. When Carson protested that she had no way of getting to New York until she got the $250, they sent her the check and announced that they would move the publication date to June 4. Finally, she and Reeves saw their way clear to move to New York.

But out of left field, Reeves was given the opportunity to sail a boat to Nantucket with his friend Vincent. He wanted to go. Carson decided she would go to New York by herself on the bus, the cheapest way, and Reeves would join her after he reached Nantucket. She hurriedly asked Emma DeLong Mills, her friend from writing classes, if she could put her up until she found a place to stay. Emma said yes, and then found Carson quarters in a boardinghouse where in total isolation she passed the day of the book's publication (*ING*, 20).

After that Tuesday, the reviews began to appear. By the following weekend, when Reeves arrived and the couple rented a walk-up apartment at 321 West Eleventh Street in Greenwich Village, the book's critical success was assured.

Among the first notices was May Sarton's on June 8 in the *Boston Transcript*. With this book, "something has been added to our life," Sarton wrote. "It is hard to think that we shall have to wait a year or two before we can expect another book from this extraordinary young woman." A review the same day in *The Saturday Review of Literature* also remarked on the accomplished author's startling age, adding, "but the more important fact is that it is an extraordinary novel in its own right, considerations of authorship apart." Critic Clifton Fadiman, in a not entirely positive review in *The New Yorker,* called *The Heart Is a Lonely Hunter* "a sit-up-and-take-notice book for anyone to write, but that a round-faced, Dutch-bobbed girl of twenty-two [*sic*] should be its author makes hay of all literary rules and regulations." Richard Wright, the young African American writer whose controversial *Native Son* had appeared just three months earlier, ignored Carson's age and wrote a considered assessment in *The New Republic*: "Miss McCullers's picture . . . is perhaps the most desolate that has so far come from the South. Her quality of despair is unique and individual, and it seems more natural and authentic than that of Faulkner."

Wright's reference to Faulkner would have resonated for many readers, and not just on regional grounds. Five years earlier two white Southerners, Erskine Caldwell and William Faulkner, had developed a genre that was distinguished by darkly romantic Southern settings;

bizarre characters, even freaks; and plots that hinged on motivations that were at once tragic and comic. In their hands, the South was a haunted place ruled by primal loves, hatreds, and obsessions, the id to the rest of America's ego. An awareness of race and the tragedy of slavery underpins many such works, with varying degrees of success.

In this new genre, Carson McCullers seemed a worthy successor to Caldwell and Faulkner, redeeming its somewhat pejorative aspects, and critics seemed delighted, not surprised, by the fact of Carson's age and gender. Two of Southern Gothic's other defining practitioners were female but not yet on the scene: in 1940 Eudora Welty, forty, had published one short story, and Flannery O'Connor was fifteen. In fact, Carson was perhaps more acceptable as a distinctly female Southern voice because she was twenty-three and had published a novel, thus seeming a natural heir to the two older men. A unique constellation of critical responses rose to greet *The Heart Is a Lonely Hunter,* then, and Carson was poised to reap the rewards.

Houghton Mifflin got behind the novel, launching an unrelenting flow of publicity. On June 16 the publisher ran a large ad in *The New York Times* (whose reviewer, that day, said, "She writes with a sweep and certainty that are overwhelming"), calling her book "the literary find of the year" and "a perfectly magnificent piece of work." Carson went to Klein's and in the overheated pandemonium of the store bought herself a summer suit (*ING,* 20).

It was impossible to miss Carson, all of twenty-three, in the summer and fall of 1940. Photographs of her were ubiquitous, if not all to good effect. Back when she was still writing the novel, she had asked a Columbus photographer to take an author's portrait, and the results were unfortunate. The best photo of the series, used on the book's back cover, showed a plain Carson, with pouchy cheeks (a feature that often showed up in her photos), bangs and the rest of her hair pulled back, wearing a man's shirt and blazer, and holding a cigarette. Carson later referred to it in a letter to her editor at Houghton Mifflin as "the old horror" she'd provided as an author photo for her first book.

Her distinctly odd, androgynous, intelligent looks were not easy to forget, however. Several observers left their impressions. A newspaper reporter thought she had "the look of a young knight." Her

For dearest Cousin Jordan
devotedly
Carson

Publicity photo by Louise Dahl-
Wolfe, 1941

gray eyes looked at you "search-ingly." Another observer, noting her "green skin" and "huge shad-ows under her eyes," said she was "a charming Southern girl, but she was odd-looking." She looked "slightly unhealthy," he went on, adding, "But she was animated and charming." She was almost always dressed in men's clothes, down to the shoes, but also wore well-made women's suits. She went through a vast quantity of men's tailored white shirts; the poet John Ciardi noted that at a liter-ary conference Carson changed her shirt three times a day so it would always be crisp; one friend remembers her preparing for a party at her Village apartment and tell-ing Reeves imperiously, "I want you should go down and get me a fresh shirt from the Chinaman." The shirts had to be crisp and white, worn either buttoned to the neck or with collar splayed over the lapels of her suit jacket. Though she might seem at first glance the antith-esis of fashion, she was actually quite thoughtful about what she wore and enjoyed clothes. Her look might be seen as an exaggeration of the prewar look, which, with its emphasis on padded shoulders and suits, was itself masculine. Much later she grandly bragged about her time in the city, that she had been one of the most fashionable young women in New York, knee socks notwithstanding. Her confidence in her own looks and fashion sense made her walk tall; she was thus able to carry off even the oddest getups.

When *Vogue* decided to feature her in its September issue, they sent the fashion photographer John Rawlings to get a better image than her author photo. The result was felicitous. A smiling Carson, her clean and shiny hair styled with bangs in a pageboy, again wears a man's shirt and blazer. She leans on a stack of books and holds a cigarette that she looks entirely too young to be smoking. It's a very flattering picture, but it does not look much like Carson. Superior images weren't taken until 1941, when the pioneering fashion photographer Louise Dahl-Wolfe took a series of pictures in Central Park, including the iconic image of Carson in a man's shirt with the top button fastened, her arms behind her head, cigarette in hand. The photo showcases her intelligent, frank gaze and suggests her eccentricity; this is not a typical ingenue.

Unfortunate author photo or not, *The Heart Is a Lonely Hunter* was popular with New Yorkers and admirers of literary fiction, though it did not make the *New York Times* or *Publishers Weekly* best-seller lists. Magazines sought her out to contribute to their pages. The editors of women's and women's fashion magazines took special note, for they published some of the very best new fiction in their pages, as Carson was by now well aware. Not long before her first novel was published, Maxim Lieber, not yet a well-known literary agent, had taken on the task of sending "Sucker" and "Court in the West Eighties" to a string of magazines, without any luck. Now *The Heart Is a Lonely Hunter* caught the attention of George Davis, the fiction editor at *Harper's Bazaar*. He kept up with new fiction not only because he saw the mission of the magazine as publishing cutting-edge work but also because he was a novelist himself and had been a literary sensation, like Carson, in 1931, when his *The Opening of a Door* was published to much acclaim. (He had been twenty-five.) Davis wrote a letter to Carson asking if she had any fiction she might want to publish in his magazine, and if she'd like to meet him for drinks and discuss it.

A pivotal figure in Carson's life at several junctures, George took to Carson immediately, as she did to him. At thirty-four, he was urbane, green-eyed, and handsome, if a little pudgy, a charming and brilliant man. Born in Canada, his father a pharmacist who became a doctor, he grew up, one of five boys, in Michigan. His brother brought home a French bride from the First World War, and under her wing, George became fluent in French. After gestures in the direction of work and college, George, at twenty, joined the rush to Paris by Americans with a hankering for a literary career. His upstairs neighbors in Saint-Germain-des-Prés were the writers Janet Flanner and her companion

Solita Solano. Through them, he met Paris's expatriate writers, those whom Gertrude Stein had dubbed "the Lost Generation," from Ernest Hemingway to Djuna Barnes. Unlike many of this group, George knew French literary Paris as well, including André Gide, François Mauriac, Paul Éluard, and André Breton; he translated Colette and Jean Cocteau, both of whom were friends. He was photographed by Man Ray. He met W. H. Auden and Christopher Isherwood in London, valuable contacts for future contributors to his magazines, along with Virginia Woolf and the Sitwells. In 1931, Harper published *The Opening of a Door,* a novel set in the American Midwest, a goodbye-to-all-that renunciation of what he felt to be the false values of middle America. It sold well and garnered much praise. Clifton Fadiman called it "the most unfirstish first novel I've read," while *The New York Times* deemed it "a high achievement in creative literature . . . a work of beauty."

Broke at twenty-seven after spending the advance for his second (never published) novel, George was forced to return to the United States in 1933, where, despite having no magazine experience, he landed a job at *Vanity Fair* as articles editor. Moving on, from 1936 to 1941 he was fiction editor at *Harper's Bazaar,* publishing such writers as Jane Bowles, Woolf, the Sitwells, and Auden. The connections he made in the U.K. were especially important; lacking a personal connection to an editor like George, most British writers could not even think of publishing their work in a fashion magazine. What writers found in him was not only a finely honed literary sensibility but also considerable charm and wit. Ben Hecht called George "the funniest man in America," and Auden went further, claiming that he was the funniest man he'd ever met. Janet Flanner described George as "a sulky, ultra-sensitive brilliant character," noting especially his "deadly wit." In short, he was just the sort of sophisticated, outspoken editor who could be expected to be drawn to the quirky universe Carson created in her writing, with its sexually ambiguous characters and complex social settings.

When George approached Carson about contributing to *Harper's Bazaar,* she did not immediately think of her new work, *Army Post;* she assumed it was too long. (Somewhere along the line the novel was renamed—it's not clear by whom—*Reflections in a Golden Eye,* after a line from the T. S. Eliot poem "Lines for an Old Man.") But George rifled through her old work, mostly short stories, until he came to the novel. He was willing to gamble on running the piece in two parts, evidently sure that the dynamic story line would prove gripping enough to drive readers to buy the magazine two months in a row. He ran an ad announcing the forthcoming work in the September 1940 issue, and the editor's note in October welcomed McCullers, saying he would describe her as "a *Wunderkind*" except that the term "sounds too trivial or condescending." Instead, he announced that she was part of the group "we call writers' writers—Hemingway, Katherine Anne Porter, and others." The first of two installments of the novel began beneath Dahl-Wolfe's arresting photograph of Carson in Central Park, with her hands clasped high behind her head.

The timing of the appearance of *Reflections in a Golden Eye* was inspired for all parties involved. *Harper's Bazaar* got the latest effusion from the literary star du jour, and George's cap got a feather. Houghton Mifflin received the benefit of free advertising for her second book. Ordinarily, the publisher might have been reluctant to publish an author's second novel so hard on the heels of the first, fearing it would cannibalize the sales of the former. But in this instance they not only reaped free advertising, they landed a second novel by their sensational young writer without any coaxing. In turn, they needed to publish quickly to take full advantage of the novel's appearance in the magazine, which worked to Carson's benefit, for she wanted not only the money from a second book but also the appearance of forward momentum. And of course Carson enjoyed the satisfaction and boost to her self-confidence that came with being a prolific, white-hot arrival on the literary scene.

5

—

Flowering Jazz Passion

In 1940, George Davis performed the great favor, indirectly, of introducing Carson to the person she would fall headlong in love with.

The story actually began years earlier, when George had made a fiction-scouting trip to London for *Harper's Bazaar.* There he befriended novelist Christopher Isherwood and poet W. H. Auden. George had inhaled the heady freedom of Europe in the 1920s, when the nightlife in Berlin was lively and gender and sexuality preferences fluid. Auden, Isherwood, and Davis all made important connections in Berlin in those years, notably with the two eldest children of the renowned writer Thomas Mann. Erika and Klaus Mann, born just one year and nine days apart, celebrated their birthdays together "like twins," and both were talented artists, known as the literary Mann twins. Klaus Mann was a risk-taker; his outspokenness about the Nazi regime led to his flight from Germany for Paris and Amsterdam. He co-founded a literary magazine out of Amsterdam, *Die Sammlung,* whose editorial policies so upset the Nazis that in late 1934 they stripped him of his citizenship. He left for the United States in 1936. Klaus met George on a visit to Paris, "when [George] was frail and young and composed his first novel."

Erika was an actress but made her mark with a cabaret show called *The Pepper Mill* (in which Klaus sometimes participated). The group's material was risqué but also antifascist. She appeared as a kind of emcee wearing a white clown costume. This got her in a lot of trouble as Hitler came to power; she was threatened with the loss of her citizenship when the troupe began to satirize the Nazi regime. When it became clear that she would be stateless, she fled to Switzerland, from there writing to Isherwood asking that he marry her so that she could become a British subject. Isherwood referred Erika to his friend Auden, whom he had known from boyhood. Auden wired "DELIGHTED" and married her upon her arrival in the U.K. Despite differences over Britain's involvement in World War II

Erika Mann, about thirty, shortly after she wed W. H. Auden in a marriage of convenience, 1935

(Auden, a pacifist, was at this time against British entry into the war), the two became friends. In 1939, Auden and Isherwood, friends who were intermittent sexual partners, sailed for the United States.

On their arrival in New York aboard the *Champlain* in January 1940, George Davis met them at the harbor. Isherwood described George at the time as "small, plump, handsome, sparkling." George shepherded them everywhere in New York, from Coney Island to the Rainbow Room. They soon reconnected with Erika and Klaus Mann. Erika was making an unsuccessful tour of the States with *The Pepper Mill,* and Klaus was planning a new literary magazine, *Decision,* with contributors William Carlos Williams, W. Somerset Maugham, and Nancy Cunard. In his diary, Klaus recorded that he had met Carson, the "strange, new" author, and her "equally strange" husband. "Strange, primitive, naïve and simple creature. Possibly very talented," he noted. When he read *The Heart Is a Lonely Hunter,* he said he found it "arresting, in parts." He noted "an abysmal sadness, but [found it] remarkably devoid of sentimentality." Carson herself, he wrote, was a mixture of retirement and wildness, "morbidezza" and "naiveté." As it turned out, she became a loving and supportive friend, telling him, "You are brilliantly gifted, and I believe that almost anything is possible to you. . . . I value our friendship more, perhaps, than you realize."

Erika Mann and Carson met, according to Carson, when she wrote to Erika seeking advice about her third novel, which at this imagining was about someone Jewish from Germany. Late that June, Carson learned that Erika was staying in the Bedford Hotel, where, coincidentally, her Houghton Mifflin editor, Robert Linscott, was also staying. She arranged a meeting of the three of them in Erika's room. They were discussing Carson's plans for the novel, the subject of which she abandoned shortly afterward, when a strange woman entered. She had blond hair cut like a man's and, Carson later wrote, "a face that would haunt me to the end of my life" (*ING*, 21).

Annemarie Schwarzenbach was born in Zurich in 1908, the daughter of a wealthy Swiss businessman who made his money in textiles. Her mother came from the German aristocracy: the daughter of a Swiss general, she was bisexual, had a passion for horses, and dressed Annemarie in boy's clothes. Annemarie determined early on to become a writer but continued with her schooling until she received her doctorate from the University of Zurich in 1931, the year she published her first novel. At odds with her family, who she felt had Nazi sympathies, she traveled ceaselessly, writing several more novels as well as travel books. In 1935 she married, in Iran, a French diplomat, Achille-Claude Clarac—both were homosexual—to obtain a French diplomatic passport for easier travel. An outspoken antifascist, Annemarie sought out other writers who were distraught by the rise of Hitler. She met Erika Mann in Berlin in 1930 and fell in love with her, but Erika soon fell in love with another woman, the actress Therese Giehse. Annemarie also befriended Klaus Mann, with whom she traveled around Europe and to a writers' conference in Russia. In 1935, Klaus introduced Annemarie to morphine, and by 1938 she was an addict.

Annemarie was thirty-two when she met Carson. She dressed boyishly, as she had since childhood. Much photographed, she seldom appears in images in a skirt but almost always in pants, often in a man-tailored shirt with a tie. With her close-cropped hair and "dark and slow-moving" blue eyes, she resembled, according to one admirer, a Donatello head of David. Klaus and Erika called her their "Swiss child"; Klaus described her as "delicate and ambitious," comparing her to a "pensive page," while the French novelist Roger Martin du Gard said she had "the face of an inconsolable angel." Sensitive and highly strung, "she never went to sleep before dawn," said her friend Ruth Landshoff. She clearly had an arresting presence, so warmly was it described, despite her habits, both narcotic and insomniac. R. L. York remembered:

In 1940 Carson fell in love with Annemarie Schwarzenbach, a Swiss writer and world traveler.

> She was an enormous success with people, though she was not brilliant and often did not talk at all, but just sat and listened or thought some thoughts of her own. Her beauty was not brilliant either, but angelic and lovable and most people who met her immediately felt concern about her. When she was not about, they said "We hope Annemarie is well and happy." But they knew all the time she was not, and that she needed many friends to help her and to console her.

York was trying to capture the protective instinct that Annemarie aroused in her friends; she seemed to them vulnerable and unhappy, even tragic. Carson was no exception. Her attraction to Annemarie was immediate, and she vowed, "I will dedicate all my work to her, forever." Less taken by her personality—her conversational silences revealed a withdrawn, private person—or even by her beauty, Carson responded so precipitously because Annemarie was the first straightforward lesbian Carson had encountered—and certainly the first lesbian to whom Carson was sexually attracted. Her overwhelming erotic attraction to Annemarie perhaps also brought Carson's sexual orientation, which she was at the time unable to see clearly, into sharp focus. When she met this beautiful, androgynous lesbian, something snapped into place. That Annemarie was a world-class beauty never fazed her; because of her mother's abiding, total love for her daughter, Carson never questioned whether she was attractive enough, physically or mentally, to be worthy of such a partner. This was part of Carson's appeal, in fact: she was special and never doubted it—as her mother had made her feel from birth, in or out of her presence.

Carson later told the story of her love affair with Annemarie to the writer Kay Boyle, a good friend. The air between them, she told Kay, was thick with feeling, intolerably so. She had never felt the same way in her marriage to Reeves, the marriage being very much on her mind, just after her move to New York with him. While she claimed she and Annemarie spent the "strange green" month together, it seems more likely they were "together" less than a week, a romantic couple only in Carson's fantasy. Among other circumstances, both of them were living with others, Carson with Reeves and Annemarie with her lover, Margot von Opel (a German actress who had married into the carmaker's family). Carson remembered one day when the erotic attraction seemed mutual. "We walked around the streets together," Carson said, "and did not have anywhere to go." They had no place to be alone, so they ducked into alleys and parks hoping to satisfy their hunger for each other. They "decided," Carson said—implying they made the decision together, though it was probably Annemarie's choice—to separate for two months. Carson wasn't going anywhere except possibly to Columbus for a visit, while Annemarie was leaving the city altogether to join Margot at the von Opels' house on Nantucket. Annemarie and Carson may have corresponded while they were apart, but no letters from those months have survived.

Those scant days with Annemarie sparked jealousy in Reeves, and one night he questioned Carson closely about what they'd been doing. ("Just talking," said Carson.) Was she in love with Annemarie? he demanded. When Carson said she didn't know, Reeves slapped her face and, when she was picking herself up off the floor, slapped her a second time (*ING*, 22). In her autobiography, she described Reeves's aggression as "quick and powerful as a panther," underscoring how much he surprised and frightened her. As far as is known, he never struck her again, though he scared her several times with violent threats. Emotional turmoil was part of Reeves's psyche, just as surely as were his charm and his loving nature. Carson had come to love him, so she stayed. She did not see staying or leaving him for another woman as a clear choice; circumstances did not make life with a woman seem possible—for now.

Since coming to the city earlier that month, things had grown tense between her and Reeves. He had been unable to find a job and was at loose ends; when he had nothing to do, he drank. Without any skills, as Carson wrote in her autobiography (she passed over his experience with Retail Credit), he hung around the West Eleventh Street apartment, where Carson was writing almost every day, which she acknowledged might have grated on him. Writing much later, she said his lack of purpose made her miserable from the start, and she would maintain that she found something immoral in his absence of direction, which in turn made her feel suffocated (*ING*, 23).

Now Carson's sudden love for Annemarie Schwarzenbach further complicated matters. Notwithstanding their steamy interlude of oral sex on the Stark Avenue porch—the only time Reeves asked her about lesbianism—Reeves did not know until now that Carson was physically attracted to women. Her mannish dressing, her bold demeanor, the sympathy for sexual outsiders in *The Heart Is a Lonely Hunter*—he had not put it together, taking refuge in denial. He did not know what to make of Carson's attraction to Annemarie now, repeatedly telling his old army friend Vincent Adams that Carson was "having an affair of some sort" with Erika Mann and/or Annemarie. "Go see those females," Adams advised, "and tell them to get the hell out of your wife's life," and "pop them on the jaw" if necessary. Reeves proceeded as if Annemarie were just another suitor whose attentions Carson could entertain for a time. But the evidence indicated that Carson was in love with her new friend. Had he accepted Carson's lesbianism at this point, the lives of both of them might have been drastically different.

But he did not want to believe it, and at this juncture Carson did not display the strength of purpose needed for a life choice like this one.

As for Adams's recommendation, Reeves did no such thing, neither confronting the "females" nor to "pop them on the jaw." In fact, he became friends with Annemarie. He quickly realized that she was not exactly a rival because neither she nor Carson was free, or wholeheartedly wanted to be free, to carry on a love affair. Reeves and Annemarie actually consulted about what might be best for Carson—an odd, not exactly propitious development. Annemarie, in a relationship with von Opel and still somewhat in love with Erika Mann, was at most briefly infatuated with Carson, though she cared very much for her welfare and acknowledged there was a bond between them. On her part, however, the bond was not romantic love. Carson either did not realize this or else chose to ignore the problem; either way, the potential was there for great disappointment. As for Reeves, despite the emotional distress that Carson's bond with Annemarie caused him, he made the—for him, inevitable—decision to be supportive of it, just as he supported her ambitions, plans, and even whims.

The details aside, a pattern was establishing itself in Carson's love life. She would repeatedly fall in love with women very much like Annemarie: older, lesbian, dramatic, elegant, and attractive, exuding worldliness and sophistication and generally unattainable, usually because the beloved was involved with another. These women would initially respond to Carson's attention—she was a singular and compelling figure, after all—but then retreat, and the usually unconsummated romance would be over. Time and again, the inexperienced young woman from the small-town South would fail to engage the worldly older woman in a grand passion, try as she might. But she did keep trying.

Although Carson swore that Annemarie was her great love, she felt equally passionate at the beginning of all her crushes, continuing to search for another great love.

She hoped to see Annemarie that summer, when Carson would be attending the Bread Loaf Writers' Conference from August 14 to 28. Bread Loaf had been a much-loved fixture in the literary landscape since John C. Farrar (later of the publisher Farrar, Straus & Giroux) founded it in 1926. It was held annually at what was once a Victorian summer resort in rural Vermont, under the aegis of Middlebury College. Appointed fellows discussed, studied, and read, guided by accomplished writers and publishers, and spent much time socializing at meals and in the evenings. The conference was now run by Ted Morrison, a writing professor at Harvard. Sometime in the early summer, Robert Linscott wrote to recommend Carson, and she was one of six fellows selected for the August 1940 conference. The faculty, who included Wallace Stegner, Louis Untermeyer, John P. Marquand, and most notably Robert Frost, named as the other fellows Brainard Cheney, a novelist; poets John Ciardi and Edna Frederickson; novelist Marian Sims; and novelist and short story writer Eudora Welty. *Reflections in a Golden Eye* was being circulated among the Bread Loaf judges, who were not all enthusiastic. Untermeyer gave Carson special encouragement, but Welty was wary of her, describing her in a letter from Vermont as "an odd little 22-year-old with long hair, bangs, cigarette cough, boy's clothes, & a new pal of Louis Untermeyer." One writer's wife complained, "Untermeyer had a mad crush on Carson; he served cocktails every afternoon made of the worst gin, and Carson would tell us how Negro spirituals were such a pure art form."

The Bread Loaf organizers had noticed Welty, also a Southerner, for her short stories, which had appeared in *The Sewanee Review* and *The New Yorker*, among other places. Her first book, a collection titled *A Curtain of Green*, would be published by Doubleday in 1941. Born in Jackson, Mississippi, in 1909, Welty was eight years older than Carson, though the two were similarly poised at the start of their careers. Carson never commented directly about Welty, and they never became friends, but Welty would dog her steps in the years to come. After the conference, Edna Frederickson dropped Welty off at the train station, and according to Welty's biographer, she was "happy to see the last of [Carson]."

There is no record that either writer felt competitive about being a woman writer from the South. The older woman's disapproval no doubt stemmed in part from differences in temperament—Welty was prim, Carson not—but it also may have concerned Carson's drinking. She was hardly alone in partaking of what one Bread Loaf partici-

Eudora Welty at thirty-one, summer 1940. Though they chose to ignore each other, Carson and Eudora were rivals.

pant called "the alcohol fumes that purified us." Treman Cottage, a dormitory for visiting writers, was nicknamed Delirium Tremens Cottage. Stegner reported on Carson's "drinking straight gin out of water glasses"; he also noted her youth. John Ciardi saw her on the first day and asked a faculty member, "My God, whose 'enfant terrible'?" W. H. Auden and Katherine Anne Porter visited Bread Loaf that summer as speakers—this was probably when Auden and Carson first met—and one participant remarked on seeing her in intimate conversation with him in various corners. Stegner remembered that Auden and Carson drank his last bottle of bourbon on a Saturday, noting with chagrin that the liquor stores would be closed the following day. Carson indeed carried on a flirtation with Untermeyer, though he was more than thirty years older and married; he noted they had "a platonic affair intensified by not-so-platonic embraces." They shared a devotion to music, especially Mahler's *Songs of a Wayfarer,* which Carson heard for the first time that summer. She told Untermeyer that after she left, she whistled melodies from it constantly.

Carson was disappointed that Annemarie did not join her at the conference; she had prevailed on Linscott to ensure her new friend was invited. The invitation may not have been extended officially, but there was room for friends and partners, and Annemarie felt she would be welcome there, as she indicated in a letter to Linscott. She told him that she was called to New York on urgent business in August; she had to see Erika off to Europe and confer with *Nation* editor Freda Kirchwey about the activities of the Emergency Rescue Committee, a newly convened group dedicated to getting artists out of occupied Europe, which interested Annemarie. Moreover, she had a deadline for taking out her first papers for U.S. citizenship. But she "was afraid to disappoint Carson & hurt her." She proposed that they meet in Boston, where they could also see Linscott. Boston was also on the way from Bread Loaf to Nantucket.

Then Annemarie canceled entirely, telling Linscott that she and Reeves had decided that Boston was too far away from Bread Loaf for Carson to get there easily. Instead, she suggested Linscott step in and take Carson to Cape Cod for some time near the ocean. Annemarie's letter to Linscott was heartfelt but perhaps not entirely truthful. "I wish I would be able never to hurt [Carson]," she wrote, of whom she was "deeply fond." She referred to her talk with Reeves somewhat mysteriously, writing, "He is a fair person, and tries hard to 'live up' to his being with Carson." She spoke vaguely about plans to return to Europe and then decide whether to pursue staying in the United States permanently. For Carson—who had no idea that Annemarie, Reeves, and Linscott were conferring about her—the trip to Boston to see her editor, followed by a few days on the Cape with him, was small recompense.

Carson returned to New York, where a persistent heat wave stalled over the city. In the West Eleventh Street walk-up, she was miserable. That summer, however, George Davis introduced her to two new sets of friends: one a lesbian couple, expatriates in Paris, the other a couple important because of their location in a bohemian outpost of New York City.

One day that summer George took her out to Croton-on-Hudson, where the journalist Janet Flanner was spending the season with her partner, Solita Solano, also a journalist. *The New Yorker's* Paris correspondent under the byline Genêt, Flanner was in the United States writing a two-part profile of Thomas Mann, which was giving her great trouble because she found she disliked both Mann and his writing; she asked Carson to read a copy, knowing of her friendship with Erika and Klaus. When Flanner and Solano had known George Davis in Paris, he had been so poor he went everywhere in carpet slippers,

Carson with George Davis, her first New York friend, on the banks of the
Hudson River, fall 1940

and they were pleased to see him now in the United States, well fed
and stylishly dressed, wearing real shoes. The women found Carson to
be "an eccentric of the first water" and "full of the energy of affection."
Though Reeves was not mentioned, George and Carson may have
brought him along with them; at any event, Flanner and Solano soon
got to know him as well and found him charming—not surprising, as
a contemporary who met Reeves that summer found him "glowing."

On weekends, George took Carson out to rural Rockland County,
near Suffern, New York, where the composer Kurt Weill and his wife,
Lotte Lenya, were renting a house. George had known them in Paris
after they fled Germany in 1933. The couple had moved north of the
city in part to be close to Weill's collaborator, the playwright Maxwell
Anderson, who lived on South Mountain Road in New City, near artist Henry Varnum Poor, his wife Bessie Breuer, and their two children.
Bessie, who became an important friend of Carson's, had been a noted
magazine editor and contributor. She had published many short stories
and two novels: her first, *Memory of Love* (1935), had been made into a
1939 movie with Cary Grant and Carole Lombard, *In Name Only*. She
had known George Davis in his Paris days, when she was Paris editor

of *Charm* magazine, a New Jersey–based publication influential in the fashion world. Bessie's daughter Anne remembered meeting Carson when she was "the literary sensation of the moment," whom Anne saw as "a skinny girl in . . . white knee socks."

George knew of Carson's infatuation with Annemarie and her troubles with Reeves. He, too, had romantic problems. He was in love with a French sailor about whom he had heard nothing since the fall of France to the Germans. (George was "incurably self-destructive" due to his preference for "rough trade" and an "insatiable appetite for sailors.") Moreover, that spring and early summer he had clashed repeatedly with the much-admired *Harper's Bazaar* editor in chief Carmel Snow. When Snow demanded drastic cuts to important stories by Glenway Wescott and Katherine Anne Porter, George handed in his resignation. She accepted it, and that August found George without a job and behind in his rent. He wanted a change of scene and thought it would be good for Carson, too, so he proposed that they find living quarters to share. They looked in Rockland County, near the Lenya/Weills and the Andersons, but could not find anything suitable.

In the meantime, as George would claim, he had a vivid dream about a house in a city: not a brownstone exactly, but the same size, situated in a neighborhood where the sky was a vast blue expanse, skyscrapers visible only in the distance. Determined to find the building, which he felt sure existed, he first narrowed his search to areas that fit the description (it could only be in New York) and remembered that he had liked the neighborhood where Auden was currently living, which was Brooklyn Heights. As soon as he came up from the subway, George could tell that the light was right and the sky every bit as wide as it had been in his dream. He poked around the pretty brownstone-lined streets, admiring the views from those close to the bluffs overlooking the Brooklyn Navy Yard, until he found a four-block dead-end street perched on just one such bluff, called Middagh. As he always told the story, a "house for rent" sign magically advertised the building he had imagined, Seven Middagh, a strange Tudoresque Victorian Gothic structure with decorative trim and a peaked gable, surrounded by more traditional flat-roofed Brooklyn brownstones. He called Carson and insisted she come with him to look at it.

Seven Middagh Street in Brooklyn Heights was home to a vibrant artistic community when Carson came to live there in 1940–41.

The building had been chopped up into a boarding-house and left to molder, but George saw potential in the high ceilings, marble fireplaces, carved trim, and expanses of wood, and he had no trouble getting Carson to visualize it as well. The rent was seventy-five dollars per month (about $1,300 today), an incredibly low rent for an entire house, even in somewhat seedy Brooklyn. Even so, if Carson and George were to rent it, they would have to fill it with other people who could help them afford it. They began to envision like-minded friends, artists, writers, and musicians who might be interested in private living spaces with shared common areas: a sitting room, dining room, kitchen, and baths. The arts philanthropist Lincoln Kirstein was a friend of George's and a champion of Auden's poetry. George thought Kirstein might bankroll the venture if Auden were on board. Tentatively they enlisted Auden, who moved in on October 1.

Auden became the informal housemother, collecting rent, organizing the food shopping and cooking, and announcing meals. Wystan (Carson could not manage to pronounce his name correctly and called him "Winston") had an unlined, handsome face, not yet the wrinkled, reserved eminence of the postwar decades. By nature he was witty and dry. Descended from Anglican clergymen, he was the son of a bookish doctor and grew up middle-class; he had planned to become a mining engineer. At Oxford, however, he befriended some young poets, Stephen Spender and Louis MacNeice among them—the nucleus of a brilliant generation of English poets who would dominate the prewar decade—and began to write verse, publishing a volume privately in 1930. In 1937 he was in Spain supporting the Republican side in the civil war; his poem "Spain," issued as a pamphlet for the cause, was widely read and acclaimed. With Christopher Isherwood, whom he had met in Berlin a decade earlier, he visited China in 1938, to write a book on the beginnings of the Sino-Japanese War.

Auden and Isherwood traveled to the United States in 1939, and that year Auden became a U.S. citizen. Many friends took their move as a betrayal; war was imminent, and Auden had made no secret of his pacifism. However, within two months of his arrival in the United States, when Germany invaded Poland, he wrote his well-known poem "September 1, 1939," working out his ambivalence about war in general and this upcoming war in particular. Yet he wanted to stay in New York. At the same time as he agreed to join forces with George Davis and Carson, he met and became romantically involved with the man who would be his lifelong partner, Chester Kallman, himself an aspiring poet (and only a visitor to Seven Middagh). Auden's residence in the house meant that Erika and Klaus Mann were often on hand. Before long, their brother Golo moved in on the fourth floor, which was not much more than an attic. Auden used to practice his German with Golo.

Davis, Carson, and Auden moved in while major repairs were underway on the house. The furnace needed to be replaced, the floors sanded, the walls plastered and painted, the plumbing repaired or replaced, and the wobbly staircases secured. George moved into the two front rooms on the third floor while Auden

W. H. Auden, a housemate at Seven Middagh Street in Brooklyn

took the back rooms, which looked out over the harbor, the Brooklyn Bridge, and the towers of Manhattan beyond. Carson, who temporarily left Reeves behind in their Village apartment, took the room just below Auden's on the second floor, which had a small adjoining dressing room and was painted empire green. George's two cats, Sophie and Roy, wound their way in and out, especially pampered by Auden. Workmen tackled the repairs, cleaning, floor sanding, and painting. Carson was proud of the fact that the house's linens and matching towels were chosen and donated by George's friend Diana Vreeland, the fashion editor of *Harper's Bazaar*.

Perhaps the most flamboyant of the residents moved in later that month: Gypsy Rose Lee, the renowned vaudeville star turned striptease artist. Born in Washington in 1911, Gypsy (née Rose Louise Hovick) had been performing on music hall stages with her sister, June Havoc, from her earliest days. She later found a home with a traveling company, Minsky's Burlesque. Bringing wit and style to stripping, Gypsy didn't take it all off; she was the original performer to make removing a glove a protracted erotic act. When someone in the audience asked her to remove the last scraps of her clothing, she begged, "Please don't ask me to do that! I'll catch cold." Sometimes known as the Literary Stripper, Gypsy was well read and artistically inclined. Some of her paintings graced the walls of her friend Peggy Guggenheim's gallery. She wrote pieces published in *The New Yorker*, a memoir, a play that opened on Broadway, and two novels.

George had originally met Gypsy in a bookstore: Seven Arts in Detroit, where George was manager. Gypsy would have been fifteen or sixteen at the time (she claimed she didn't know her birth date), and he perhaps five years older. George had the wit and presence of mind to recognize that any burlesque performer visiting a Detroit bookstore was worth knowing, and the two became friends. When Gypsy was performing with Minsky's, they saw a lot of each other, and George encouraged her in her ambition to write a book, a murder mystery set at a burlesque, soon titled *The G-String Murders*. When he was looking for housemates, she was riding high, having replaced Ethel Merman on Broadway as the star of Cole Porter's *Du Barry Was a Lady*. But Gypsy

Stripper Gypsy Rose Lee wrote a mystery,
The G-String Murders, when she was Carson's
friend at Seven Middagh Street.

was restless. She and George convinced themselves that the house on
Middagh Street would be a magical place, conducive to writing.

More residents joined them in October. Benjamin Britten, the
British composer, had studied at the Royal College of Music and had
met Auden in the 1930s, when both were working on documentary
films for the General Post Office (GPO) Film Unit in the U.K. Britten met Peter Pears, the British tenor who would be his life partner,
in 1937, when he was twenty-four and Pears twenty-seven. Pears had
been very repressed, but the death of his mother and his friendship
with Auden helped him integrate his homosexuality into his personal
life, according to a biographer. Like Auden and Isherwood, Britten and
Pears were pacifists and left England the same year, the latter two traveling first to Canada and then to New York. Britten was responsible for
the concert grand piano in the parlor of Seven Middagh. (Later, Paul
Bowles would move his upright into a basement room behind the fur-

nace.) Everyone, including Carson, enjoyed playing, though Britten obviously had dibs. The piano figured in some remarks of James Stern, a British writer and translator, who remembered "George naked at the piano with a cigarette in his mouth, Carson on the floor with half a gallon of sherry, and Wystan bursting in like a headmaster, announcing 'Now then, dinner!'"

The only straight residents were Richard Wright and his family, and Gypsy, for the most part—though Carson once said she and Gypsy went to bed together, the only woman, Carson reputedly said, Carson had had sex with. Louis Untermeyer, visiting Carson there, later called the house "that queer aggregate of artists." Alert to the double meanings of words, he recalled an evening at Seven Middagh that was "a gay (in both senses of the word) occasion." In the unfriendly, or hostile, world of prewar New York, the Brooklyn Heights house was a place where lesbians and gay men could forget society's intolerance and be themselves.

Dropping in for a few days to see Auden was the Northern Ireland–born poet Louis MacNeice, who had come to the United States in 1940 for a lectureship at Cornell. He left a vivid description of the Seven Middagh ménage:

> I was staying now in a household on Brooklyn Heights, still being painted and without much furniture or carpets, but a warren of the arts, Auden writing in one room, a girl novelist writing—with a china cup of sherry—in another, a composer composing and a singer hitting a high note and holding it and G[y]psy Rose Lee, the striptease queen, coming round for meals like a whirlwind of laughter and sex. It was the way the populace once liked to think of artists—ever so Bohemian, raiding the icebox at midnight and eating the catfood by mistake. But it was very enjoyable and at least they were producing.

When Thanksgiving came around, the colonists decided to celebrate with a housewarming and a birthday party for Britten, who was turning twenty-seven, on the day after, November 22. Carson went out and bought a turkey that would feed six, but as the guest list grew,

George saw they would need more food and bought a larger bird. The three Mann children were included, as were Seven Middagh's financier, Lincoln Kirstein; the comparatively mature forty-year-old American composer Aaron Copland; Michael and Beata Mayer, the two grown children of musician Elizabeth Mayer and her psychiatrist husband, William (later pressed into service for Carson's emotional and medical needs); Chester Kallman and his father; several of George's fashion magazine friends; and Reeves McCullers. Britten's biographer believes Annemarie Schwarzenbach was present, but this is unlikely: Carson wrote about the occasion and would have noted if Annemarie had been there.

The dinner went off beautifully, lubricated by champagne from a case Carson donated. Feeling that George had unfairly impugned her judgment over the size of the turkey required, she took pains with the chestnut stuffing. After consuming all the food, champagne, and wine, everyone adjourned to the upstairs parlor for cognac, where they played, appropriately, drunken parlor games, including Murder, or Wink, in which a player who is chosen as "it" kills the other players one by one by winking at them; Ghosts, the rules for which were more complicated; and charades. Michael Mayer remembered trying to convey the title of the play *You Can't Take It with You* by somewhat desperately picking up Carson (who was featherlight) and carrying her across the threshold.

Britten played the piano and Pears sang, popular songs or anything anyone knew the tune to. Britten's biographer noted an "improvised ballet": Pears and George performing a mad dance to *Petrushka,* "swinging from curtains and hot-water pipes." Auden was drunkenly trying to speak German with Golo Mann. The hilarity in the room was momentarily silenced by the blare of fire truck sirens outside. Carson sprang up, as did Gypsy: they both loved a good fire, and were accustomed to following fire trucks to their destination. Both glad to have a partner in crime, they raced along the dark streets of Brooklyn Heights, when suddenly Carson stopped, calling to her friend. She grabbed Gypsy's arm, she later said, and out of breath, gasped, "Frankie is in love with the bride of her brother and wants to join the wedding" (*ING,* 32). Gypsy provided her a shoulder when Carson burst into tears, explaining that she was writing a story about Frankie, an autobiographical adolescent in a small Southern town, who felt herself a terrible outcast. The story would follow Frankie through one summer, but Carson had not been able to find the right way to express Frankie's isolation in narrative until that moment with Gypsy. It was what she later called an "illumination," a moment when a creative idea sprang into being—a good one, she thought.

⁂

Carson meanwhile was attempting to see Annemarie, who was undergoing an episode of emotional collapse. She had attempted suicide before, as depression, or perhaps bipolar disorder, compounded her morphine addiction. The winter before she met Carson, she had undergone insulin shock therapy. Because of Annemarie, Carson's early residence at Seven Middagh was miserable. She was as much in love with Annemarie as ever, but she had adjusted to the fact of her friend's relationship with Margot, whom Annemarie credited with getting her off morphine that spring. But when winter threatened, Margot decamped for the von Opels' Palm Beach home. Carson remembered that terrible fall: Annemarie had got hold of a phonograph, installed it in her rented room, and played Mozart day and night. She thought Carson should be writing, Carson later told Kay, and told her to go back to Columbus to do it. That anger and confusion made work impossible. Carson walked the city streets, pausing often to stand on corners and think.

One day Carson heard that Annemarie had been taken to the psychiatric ward of a hospital in Connecticut. She escaped soon afterward and fled to the New York apartment of a friend, Freddy Wolkenberg. Carson had returned from a short visit to Georgia and rushed to see Annemarie at Freddy's. She found her friend sick with pleurisy and emotionally frantic. Annemarie insisted that they should go to the woods and hide together there. Ominously, there was a broken window in the apartment. Freddy explained to Carson that Annemarie had called Margot and begged for morphine. When Margot hung up on her, Annemarie threw the phone through the window. She had been drinking what Freddy thought was water; Carson found it was straight gin.

What happened next is not clear. The version that Carson told Kay two years later was probably fanciful: she and Freddy managed to calm Annemarie down, but for the next couple of days Annemarie insisted repeatedly to her that they must go away together. Carson agreed to take her to the woods, somewhere in Vermont or Maine. They could run away together, Carson wrote Boyle. They would each get better, and they would both write. In this version, Carson's happiness was absolute.

The considerably more disturbing version she later gave her therapist is the more believable one. According to this telling, Annemarie at some point asked Carson to take off her clothes and began touching her. Carson was more than willing; she felt a sort of "flowering jazz passion." At last she and Annemarie were together, and Carson was feeling the physical passion that had previously eluded her. She was wet with desire, she later told a therapist. But suddenly something changed. Annemarie leaped out of bed and found in a little box a pile of clippings. She pulled one out, a gossip column about the house in Brooklyn, and "who is sleeping with who." Specifically, the item made mention of Gypsy, and Annemarie, like many readers, found this detail fascinating. Then she turned mean. She told Carson to bring Gypsy to her. She wanted Gypsy, Annemarie said. She didn't want Carson—Carson was too bony. Bring Gypsy here, Annemarie told Carson. If Carson liked, she could watch.

Elements of this story are probably exaggerated. It does not seem likely that Annemarie and Carson began to have sex in this crazy atmosphere, though the detail of a clipping about Gypsy rings true. Carson did step in gallantly, offering to spirit off a grateful Annemarie. But at a later point, Annemarie said terrible things and rejected her sexually.

Carson, wounded, had further grounds for feeling provoked. In the aftermath of Annemarie's escape from the hospital Carson had telephoned Margot, who had told her in no uncertain terms not to have anything more to do with Annemarie at this time, adding that she had a guard watching her house. Carson also told Annemarie that Erika Mann was staying with Margot. This really galled Annemarie, who had long carried a torch for Erika. Annemarie lashed out, and Carson, not surprisingly, was on the receiving end.

That night in Freddy's apartment was a long one. Annemarie at one point barricaded herself in the bathroom and was silent for a long time. Carson was sure she had morphine with her and thought perhaps she had overdosed. In fact, Annemarie had slit her wrists with a razor, as Carson and Freddy found out when they finally persuaded a confused Annemarie to open the door. In the ensuing panic, Carson ran out to get a doctor, literally going door to door to find one. Freddy called the police. After they arrived, Annemarie, bleeding and in the midst of morphine withdrawal, blurted out her entire story: her love affair with Margot, her nationality, her morphine addiction. Knowing it was unwise to bring up these matters, Carson tried to divert the police, even, oddly, claiming her father was an Irish cop. Eventually, Annemarie's psychiatrist appeared and told Carson and Freddy to hire a German-speaking nurse to stay in the apartment with her. Annemarie again told Carson to go home, go back to Georgia and work, that Carson was too young to be exposed to such chaos and should return to her parents.

After the nurse arrived, Carson left, heading for Seven Middagh. Her housemates believed she was still in Georgia, and Golo Mann was sleeping in her room. When she turned up that night, Auden, seeing how distraught she was, let her sleep in his bed and gave her his diary to read, directing her to Kierkegaard's observations on human suffering. Perhaps resenting the reading assignment, Carson later told her therapist that Auden was a great man, but the great were not always compassionate, she supposed.

Annemarie was taken to Bellevue, and from there to Payne Whitney in White Plains, which provided state-of-the-art psychiatric treatment. Carson tried to reach her via letters and phone calls but without success. Determined to leave the hospital, Annemarie learned that she would be released only if she agreed to be deported. She wrote Carson a heartrending letter saying if her choice was between deportation for lunacy (and drug abuse) and treatment in an American hospital, she chose lunacy. For if she was declared a lunatic and deported to Europe, she could at least join up with the French Resistance. As it happened, the legal formalities meant that Annemarie stayed in Bellevue and

Payne Whitney until February 1942, when she was finally sent back to Switzerland. She did indeed join the Resistance after she returned to Europe, and she again took up writing and traveling—and her drug habit.

At the height of the chaotic scene of Annemarie's breakdown, when she told Carson to go back to Georgia, Annemarie recognized, if Carson did not quite yet, that she had come a long way from Columbus and was really out of her depth. Carson was almost ten years younger than Annemarie, and her sexual experience was as yet very limited; she had a sexual life with Reeves, but she almost certainly had no experience with a woman, pace her fantasies about Annemarie. She had got herself entangled with a mélange (the Manns, Margot von Opel, Annemarie) who were older, more sexually experienced, more worldly. These new friends were from more sophisticated and affluent backgrounds, and they had been intensely involved with one another for some time, in both Europe and America. Carson was in over her head, and Annemarie and friends probably did not take her seriously—even as they admired her new celebrity and the money she made from *The Heart Is a Lonely Hunter*. In the end, Carson was an afterthought to Annemarie, but Annemarie was far from that to Carson.

The level of chaos—and betrayal—that Carson experienced with Annemarie in the fall of 1940 was indeed new and overwhelming to her, her own gift for self-dramatization notwithstanding. The memories were indelible. She would relive for years her horrible time with the dope-sick, suicidal Annemarie in Freddy's apartment and eventually would describe it at length to her therapist, trying to come to terms with her painfully persistent feelings for this woman with the face that was seared into her heart for life. The last time she saw Annemarie, she was bloodied from her suicide attempt, sweating and vomiting in drug withdrawal, and lashing out at Carson in ways that she knew—because she was a sensitive, intelligent woman who in her own way did love Carson—would most hurt her. That Annemarie chose to reject her sexually in their last encounter was the final twist of the knife, for that was the area where Carson was most vulnerable. But Annemarie's failure to love her romantically was also, most likely, a blessing in disguise. Carson was unaware then, and perhaps later, of having dodged a bullet. Realistically, the last thing she needed in her life was an emotionally troubled, self-dramatizing drug addict.

❧

Carson's sexual proclivities drew comment from an unexpected quarter. Shortly after her crisis with Annemarie in the fall of 1940, Carson returned to Columbus for a while, where she was miserably unhappy. In one traumatic episode, which she related to a therapist nearly twenty years later, her sister, Rita, told their parents that Carson was a lesbian. According to Carson, Rita had to explain to Lamar Sr. what a lesbian was. Rita said that Carson was in love with a woman. Rita shared Carson's bed, but she no longer wanted to. To Lamar Sr.'s credit, he immediately said, according to Carson's account, "Sister [Carson] is the best child I have known, and if you are half as beautiful as she is, I'll be satisfied." Not exactly to the point, but a credible show nonetheless.

In a painful sequel, however, the next day Lamar asked Carson whether she had ever touched Rita. Carson, stunned by the question, resorted to humor: Why would I touch her? she asked. Telling this story later, she made no comment about this betrayal on her father's part: he had evoked a heterosexist misapprehension that homosexuals were indiscriminate and promiscuous and were not above making advances on the young, with the added wrinkle of such an approach being, in this case, incestuous. Bébé and Rita stood by, complicit in their silence. As accustomed as Carson was to being the central figure in her family by virtue of her gifts, she felt bewildered and lost.

And where was Reeves in all this? In later years, Carson told and retold the story of Annemarie's dramatic breakdown without reference to her husband, yet he was not far away, living in Greenwich Village. Carson felt that her writing career depended on her finishing her third book, which she argued could happen only if she was at Seven Middagh alone, among other artists. She painted Seven Middagh as a creative experience that was most definitely temporary; when her book was well underway, she would move out to join Reeves and finish it. He was in touch with Carson almost daily and was a frequent guest at Middagh Street, a congenial and charming presence, but evidently no one had remarked on the fact that he was not living with Carson. Finally, when she clashed with her family about her sexuality, neither Rita, nor Lamar Sr., nor Bébé seems to have asked what her love for a woman might do to her marriage. Reeves was, for the moment, forgotten by all.

6

A Bit of a Holy Terror

The year 1941 began ominously for Carson, despite her success with her first novel and the publicity it brought her. In the wake of Annemarie's committal to a psychiatric hospital, beyond Carson's reach, unable or unwilling to answer her letters, Carson was ill off and on. She came down with an ailment in her lungs, an infection of some sort, and was suffering from high fevers and weakness. Bébé was concerned enough that she made her way to New York City, where she stayed with Carson in the Middagh Street house; she enjoyed the array of writers and artists, reminiscent of her small "salon" in Columbus. Carson got physically better but remained emotionally devastated over events with Annemarie. She had begun to worry, too, about what it all might mean for her and Reeves. What Reeves thought and felt at this juncture is not known. Over the next month, Bébé took Carson back and forth to Columbus, and then Carson became very sick indeed.

Her respiratory ailments returned with a vengeance, and now the doctors diagnosed tuberculosis (this time not in her lungs but in her joints, she told Bob Linscott) and a long-standing, dormant case of the "grippe." After a different visit, the doctors said she had virulent pneumonia in both lungs (*ING*, 31). She was not better until early February. As she was recovering, however, she experienced a frightening new set of symptoms. One morning she was up at six to join her father, as she usually did, and was having her usual breakfast of oatmeal with him (*ING,* 131), when she happened to look at the kitchen clock and found herself unable to understand the numbers on its face. Her speech became halting. She was unable to process anything she read and soon suffered from severe headaches. She worried that her eyesight and brain were damaged, and she begged the doctors to tell her it was not permanent.

While the doctors temporized, trying to make sense of this new problem, Carson asked her father to contact her friend Dr. William Mayer, a psychiatrist she had come to consider her unofficial therapist. She had met Mayer through the Seven Middagh circle. The Mayer home on Long Island was a haven for many émigré artists, especially musicians. (The German-born couple had themselves fled Nazi Germany.) Benjamin Britten and Peter Pears were frequent guests, as were Auden and Kallman, Auden addressing Elizabeth Mayer, a well-known translator, as "Dearest and Best of Fairy Godmothers." Elizabeth was also a talented musician and had installed a Bechstein grand piano in the living room. On one occasion Pears sang, accompanied by Elizabeth and Britten on the piano and Albert Einstein, a neighbor, on the violin.

Carson had met William and Elizabeth Mayer the previous fall and had almost certainly contacted him for advice about Annemarie's plight. She may also have consulted him informally about her own emotional distress. She felt immediately that he would become a dear friend, and in the current crisis she was certain he could explain her condition to her. Mayer could not be sure, however: whatever the problem, it was more physical than psychiatric. He felt he could tell her, however, that her symptoms were likely not permanent. Indeed they did go away, gradually, leaving her weak for the rest of February and all of March.

The episode indicated serious physical problems, whatever the precise issue. Later, doctors would determine that Carson had suffered her first stroke. She would learn, only much later, that it was the result of a bout of rheumatic fever she had had in the 1930s—either 1932 or 1936—brought on by an untreated strep infection. The rheumatic fever led to rheumatic heart disease, which in many cases brings on heart conditions and strokes. In the winter of 1941, however, Carson's doctors were still telling her that she had tuberculosis and/or pneumonia. When a skin rash began to plague her that spring, bringing with it flu-like symptoms, they dismissed it as hives. Only later would it become clear that she suffered from erysipelas, a serious skin condition also related to her long-ago, untreated strep throat.

In the midst of her illness came the happy occasion of the publication of *Reflections in a Golden Eye*. Carson wrote her editor that she found her copy stunning—it had a distinctive typographical design on the cover—and said mildly that she hoped it would sell. Her lack of enthusiasm no doubt stemmed not only from her physical condition but also from the fact that the book had already appeared in serial form in October and November 1940 in *Harper's Bazaar*. The manuscript had been circulating the previous summer, when she was at Bread Loaf. Added to this, Carson had finished writing it back in the spring of 1939. With a seriously ill author, Houghton Mifflin scrapped any author-related publicity plans they might have had in mind.

The timing of the novel's appearance was suspicious to many. Linscott had wanted to hold it back for a while, but Carson had insisted Houghton Mifflin bring it out as scheduled. It was not entirely a surprise when one reviewer suspected that it was either a first novel that had been put aside, or "over-hastily written." Another reviewer, in the *Boston Transcript,* used her review as an occasion to comment on Carson's youth and early fame. She cited as well McCullers's attraction to "the morbid and bizarre," holding that *Reflections in a Golden Eye* was not the second novel the public had awaited.

Critics and reviewers commented on what they saw as bizarre elements in the plot: homosexuality (a married officer is in love with an enlisted man) and voyeurism (the same private spies on the officer's wife). Reviewers might well have been put off as well by two distinctly unpleasant images: a live kitten dropped into a mailbox, and a woman who, while unhinged, has cut off her nipples with garden shears. It's difficult to see how homosexuality and voyeurism might constitute the "genuinely horrible situation" that unmistakably unsettled the Boston reviewer. Clifton Fadiman in *The New Yorker* took issue with the novel's "feverish concern with distorted and neurotic types," as well as the author's "grotesque and forced hallucinations." Robert Littell criticized the "inversions, mutilations and nastinesses" that "stick in one's mind like burrs." But the author of an unsigned review in *Time*—usually a fairly conservative weekly—evidently in tune with the novel's sensibility, approved *Reflections* as a story told with "simplicity, insight, and a rare gift of phrase," commenting that the novel represented "the Southern school at its most Gothic, but also at its best," adding, "It is as though William Faulkner saw to the bottom of matters that merely excited him, shed his stylistic faults, and wrote it all out with Tolstoyan lucidity." Overall, however, critics disapproved of the novel's "bizarre" elements even if they otherwise liked or admired it. Almost comically, none of them could bring themselves to mention explicitly the kitten or the nipples. One gets the distinct sense that Carson would have enjoyed their discomfiture.

In her autobiography, Carson noted that Columbus reviled the novel because of the clear implication that the army post in which it was set was Fort Benning. At the post, Beatrice Patton, the wife of Brigadier General George S. Patton, Jr., then staging training exercises with the Second Armored Division, reportedly canceled her subscription to *Harper's Bazaar* when it published the novel. George C. Marshall, Patton's mentor, who had once served as assistant commander of the Infantry School there, had met a young Carson through the Tuckers; he later told them that after *Reflections in a Golden Eye* came out, he wondered whether "the whole post had gone to pot" since he had lived there. Soon after the book was published, Carson later said, she received a threatening telephone call from someone who said he was with the Ku Klux Klan. It is not clear what he was threatening to do or why. She called her father, who came home early and talked with the police, who then placed a guard at the Columbus house. In a later recollection Carson said that she had been so sick at the time that her memory was hazy and that she had asked her father about a related memory of him and two policemen rooting around in the shrubbery (*ING*, 31). Certainly the implication of homosexuality and voyeurism at Fort Benning, a bulwark of the Southern military tradition, its presence a source of local pride in Columbus, would have been subversive and suspect. It is not hard to believe that the Klan would have singled her out and threatened her.

But in early 1941, Carson's mind was elsewhere. She made her old claim to an interviewer that *Reflections in a Golden Eye* was a simple kind of fairy tale. She was amazed, she said, that the book was taken seriously. She was being disingenuous: on the eve of World War II, she had chosen to write a disturbing story describing homosexual impulses among men living in close quarters on an army base, and the commingled desperation of the women in their lives. This was radically new subject matter in serious American fiction, taking themes usually found in pulp novels and giving them treatment that subverted the carefully maintained layers of hierarchy in military life and perhaps in life beyond the base as well. As such, the book is a milestone in gay and queer fiction.

And as Tennessee Williams pointed out later, in many ways the novel was an advance on her first. He felt she had succeeded in creating a world of its own, and that rather than the succession of tragedies of *The Heart Is a Lonely Hunter,* this novel was characterized by a more wide-ranging and "distilled" tragic sensibility. He felt it was a mature work, showing "the gift of mastery over a youthful lyricism."

When *Reflections in a Golden Eye* came out, Carson had put aside the manuscript of *The Member of the Wedding,* the story about Frankie, the adolescent outsider, which she was now calling *The Bride and Her Brother.* Instead, she was writing what she spoke of as another "tale," which she called "The Ballad of the Sad Café." It was a strange book. Another kind of fairy tale but filled with ardor and passion, she told her editor. She thought it her best work so far, in terms of the quality of the writing. It was an odd, fable-like tale of the vivid, fiercely independent Miss Amelia and her love for her supposed cousin, a hunchbacked dwarf, and her just-returned husband, fresh from the penitentiary.

After spending January and February in Columbus, Carson decided not to go back to Seven Middagh, which she found delightful but not conducive to serious work. Instead, she hoped she and Reeves could get a "quiet place" together in Greenwich Village. She was so unsure what to do that one time she packed her bags and got halfway to the train station to embark for New York before changing her mind. She told a friend that she thought Reeves didn't actually want her to move in with him just now, and she confessed she was thinking of decamping for Hollywood to write for the movies. Robert Linscott dissuaded her from such a course.

In March, Reeves, aware that Carson doubted his steadfastness, came down to Columbus to retrieve her and bring her back to the city. They took up residence again in the apartment on West Eleventh Street, even though George Davis was keen for Carson to return to Seven Middagh. Carson was at loose ends. Husband and wife were drinking too much again, though they had vowed to live more soberly on their arrival back in New York.

Several years earlier, when she was studying writing at NYU and Columbia, Carson had met the aspiring poet Muriel Rukeyser, four years her elder, and the two women had immediately formed a bond. Rukeyser was a politically committed poet who, as a student at Vassar, had covered the 1932 Scottsboro trial for the Communist-affiliated college newspaper. In 1936, as the Spanish Civil War was breaking out, the London journal *Life and Letters To-Day* sent her to Barcelona to cover the People's Olympiad, an event mounted by the Catalan government to protest the 1936 Berlin Olympics. (The Olympiad never took place.) In Europe, Rukeyser crossed paths with Klaus Mann, and in New York she became his assistant on a journal he founded in 1941, *Decision: A Review of Free Culture.* An influential organ for its brief life, *Decision* published such exiled authors as Franz Werfel, Stefan Zweig, and Klaus's father, Thomas Mann. Others associated with *Decision*, either as contributors or as board members, included Sherwood Anderson, Somerset Maugham, Vincent Sheean, and Stephen Vincent Benét. Carson, close to the Manns in these years, became friends with Rukeyser, as did Reeves—later, in fact, Rukeyser and Reeves had a brief affair. Carson later alluded to her own outrageous behavior on the night she and Rukeyser met, which Carson did not define. Muriel was married briefly and had a child; she also had lesbian relationships.

Sometime in May, Rukeyser gave a party and invited the couple.

Also attending was the composer David Diamond, and his meeting with Carson and Reeves proved momentous.

Born in Rochester, New York, in 1915, to Austrian and Polish immigrants, his father a carpenter and his mother a dressmaker, David taught himself the violin as a child. He received his formal musical education at the Cleveland Institute of Music and the Eastman School of Music in Rochester and studied in Paris under Nadia Boulanger. He became reacquainted in Paris with Maurice Ravel, whom he had met in Rochester; his 1937 *Elegy in Memory of Maurice Ravel* was much admired. David eventually settled in Rochester but spent the late 1930s on Jane Street in the Village, where he made connections with the artists Willem de Kooning and Arshile Gorky. Though he was receiving prestigious commissions and building a reputation, he was forced to work at a soda fountain and at a janitorial job to make ends meet. But in 1941, the year he met Carson and Reeves, he had been awarded a second Guggenheim Fellowship, and the New York Philharmonic premiered his First Symphony. David was twenty-six at the time.

David Diamond, composer, about 1941, when he met Carson and Reeves

He was a nice-looking young man, with curly red hair that he tried to comb backward from a high forehead. He was a natty dresser and believed he was first noticed by his idol, Ravel, himself given to eccentrically colorful combinations in dress, because of his purple turtlenecks. Primarily homosexual, David did not hide his orientation. He later described himself as known to be a "problem person," adding, "I was a highly emotional young man, very honest in my behavior."

Certainly he seemed so to Carson that night at Muriel's. She had heard about him from

Britten and Pears and was of course intrigued to meet another composer, given her childhood ambition. It was Carson who made the initial impression on David. They talked about Yaddo, the artists' colony in Saratoga Springs, New York, that she was thinking about visiting; David would be there that summer. Carson admired a ring he was wearing, and he promptly took it off his finger and presented it to her. Returning home that night, David wrote dramatically in his diary, "I have met Carson McCullers, and I shake as I write." It was her loneliness that made such an impression, he said, describing her as "this lovable child-woman." Of her and Reeves, he wrote, "As we share the days together, I'll know more about them. I wonder what my destiny is in regard to Carson."

Two evenings later Carson and Reeves gave a party for Bessie Breuer and her husband, Henry Varnum Poor, and there David's attention was drawn more to Reeves. There had been a lot of drinking. A friend of David's, the British musician Geoff Harvey, offered to help a drunk Reeves home, but the two got into a tussle. The partygoers pulled them apart, and David took Reeves to a nearby bar to calm him down. That evening David wrote in his journal that his "destiny lay not only with Carson, but with Reeves as well." On the twenty-fifth of May, he noted "the way Reeves looked at me"; he added that they were all extremely drunk that evening. The next day, after Reeves left the apartment, David crawled into bed with Carson "and held this child, this so tender, this so great artist in my arms." He wrote in his journal that Carson had announced, the night before, "Reeves, David is part of our family. I love him."

That same day, however, he wrote more definitively that the object of his romantic and/or sexual attraction was not Carson but her husband. "Thank you, dear God, for bringing me to Reeves," David wrote fervently. "My feelings and thoughts are so full of love for this sweet, gentle man. I have almost everything I need now—and Carson is so fine about it all." The next week the three spent almost all their time together, though the sleeping arrangement on the one night that David came home with them indicated that any further physical relationship would be between Reeves and David. The two men spent the night in Reeves's double bed, while Carson took the apartment's single bed, where she often slept even when she and Reeves were alone. Carson played the piano for David, Bach inventions that he thought she rendered "beautifully."

In David's diary, he described how his relationship with Reeves, whom he called his "sweet gentle lover," was progressing. The two went to social gatherings together, without Carson. Describing a party at art dealer Kirk Askew's for the composer Virgil Thomson, David wrote, "We were so in love we even forgot where we were and were kissing all over the place much to the annoyance of everybody." Through Seven Middagh, Thomson (if not Askew) was very much a part of Carson's social circle, and sooner or later she was bound to hear of this evening.

David also observed the tensions in their marriage and witnessed frequent noisy battles between Carson and Reeves. As time went on, he was often involved. On May 30 the situation seemed overwhelming to a drunken David, and he started to jump out a window. Both McCullerses, equally drunk, leaped on him; Carson hit him with her fists like a boy's, and Reeves hit him so hard, he knocked him out.

Carson told David that she rarely had sex with Reeves because of her health. Though David was hardly a disinterested party, he, too, felt that there was little substance in the marriage. Carson's attention was elsewhere: her interest in David—and in Reeves—flagged as she grew more and more caught up in her growing celebrity. David later looked back quite critically at her behavior at that time, observing:

> Carson did not even seem aware that she had rejected Reeves to the extent that she now was losing him. She appeared far more interested in everything else going on about her, in the celebrities she was meeting, in the hangers-on, in her pseudofriends who swarmed about her. Although her work, of course, took her away from Reeves, at least 75 per cent of it was caused by *people*. Charmed by a smile, adulation, or [a] kind remark, Carson at this time loved almost everyone she met.

Carson did go to Yaddo that summer, which only intensified this tendency, for the artists' colony gave her further opportunity to add to those friends in the artistic community whom she had already met through Seven Middagh, among them Lincoln Kirstein, the Manns, *Mademoiselle* writer Leo Lerman, writer Gore Vidal, and others. The identity of the "hangers-on" or "pseudofriends" about whom Diamond was so vehement is nearly impossible to fix. Celebrities aside, Carson thrived at Yaddo.

Yaddo was by this time perhaps the most famous artists' and writers' retreat in the country. It had its beginnings in 1881, when financier Spencer Trask and his poet wife, Katrina, bought an old Queen Anne house in upstate New York, 160 miles from New York City. It burned down in 1891, by which time the Trasks had lost all four of their children, two of them to diphtheria. Nonetheless, they rebuilt, putting up a mansion with fifty-five rooms, turrets, a great hall on the main floor, and all manner of lavish Victorian decoration. They entertained on a large scale and welcomed friends' extended stays. In fact, since they had no immediate heirs, the Trasks began to lay plans for the conversion of their estate, after their deaths, into a haven for writers, artists, and musicians, providing the solitude—and sociability—that many artists want or need. Their plans were by and large underway when Spencer Trask was killed in a railroad accident in 1909. Katrina's health worsened. She recovered enough to marry a business partner of her husband's, George Foster Peabody, but she died shortly afterward, in 1922.

Four years later Yaddo was up and running as an artists' retreat, boasting four hundred acres, the fifty-five rooms in the old stone mansion, three smaller houses, and an array of studios for daytime use by residents. In 1899, Trask had presented his wife with beautiful gardens, studded with marble statues, four lakes, a rose garden, and less formal plantings, including a rock garden, beyond the terraced beds around the house. It was a lovely, serene place to work. The fifteen to twenty invited guests, who stayed from a week or two to a whole season, worked between ten and four o'clock, enjoying lunches left at their doors, and were free in the late afternoon. They gathered for a sociable dinner before whatever was on for the evening: more work, for some of them; for others, more drinking and gaiety. Often the Yaddo station wagon was commandeered to take guests into nearby Saratoga Springs, where they frequented such bars as the New Worden and Jimmy's, the latter a smoky dive on Congress Street in the African American part of town.

Yaddo was overseen by Elizabeth Ames, a capable woman who had lost her husband in World War I. She got her job after a visit to her sister Marjorie Waite Peabody, who worked for George Foster Peabody, Katrina Trask's second husband. George, who was born and raised in Columbus, would eventually adopt Marjorie—she was much younger. She and Elizabeth, the Knappen sisters of Minneapolis, brought some youthfulness to the spirit of the old property.

Yaddo had found an excellent leader in Elizabeth Ames. She was a somewhat intimidating but warmhearted woman who had just the right degree of flexibility to accommodate the wildly varying needs and desires of an unruly bunch of artists. When residents infringed any of the few rules, Elizabeth Ames would notify them in a letter on blue stationery that they learned to dread. Just as she knew when to bend the rules, so, too, did she know when to enforce them, and she could be formidable. A slightly mysterious woman and a devout Quaker, Ames was called "a truly angelic woman" by one guest, and "strange, disturbed . . . disliked by most people" by another. She was said to be "devoted" to Carson.

The ease with which Carson struck up a friendship with both Marjorie and Elizabeth was hardly remarkable. As David Diamond said, Carson loved almost every person she met. She had been buoyed by a support system of family and friends as far back as she could remember. Bébé Smith had given her daughter the assurance of total love. She never wavered in her belief that her daughter was a genius and that the way for her to fulfill her destiny was for Bébé to smooth her path. But some mechanism also left Carson needy, and she sought to construct a support system made of other people who loved her unconditionally. Once they were in place, she tried to cement them in like stones in a wall, to ensure that she was never alone, never cast on her own devices.

Elizabeth Ames became, for a long time, part of Carson's stone wall.

Arriving on June 14, Carson found her fellows at Yaddo that summer very intriguing people. Katherine Anne Porter, by virtue of having lived there for almost a year, seemed the queen bee. Eudora Welty, who had failed to hit it off with Carson at Bread Loaf, arrived in June. Eudora and Katherine Anne had been exchanging complaints about Carson, calling her latest *Reflections in a Golden I.* Welty remarked bitterly that the *Time* reviewer had pronounced that "that little wretch Carson" represented the high point of Southern writing. David Diamond reported in his diary that Welty hated the ground Carson walked on.

Carson herself, meanwhile, made friends with the composer Colin McPhee, the short story writer Edward Newhouse, and the critic Newton Arvin. She had the third floor south room, she told her correspondents, and her study, big enough to skate in, had twelve windows. Her bedroom looked out on a "marvelous Henry James lawn." (Perhaps she was imagining tea on the lawn in the opening chapter of *The Portrait of a Lady*?) She told her editor that she was thriving there, loving the quiet and getting lots of work done. Yaddo reminded her a little of *The Magic Mountain,* and her stay was definitely salubrious for her, as she gained six pounds that summer, which she needed after her illnesses. Certainly the food was as wonderful as she had heard it was, all the vegetables fresh from the Yaddo kitchen garden. By the end of the summer of 1941, she could say that she had made great progress on *Ballad* and had written two short stories she sold to *The New Yorker,* "Correspondence" and "Madame Zilensky and the King of Finland." On top of these achievements, she told Muriel that she had walked so far and danced so often that she'd raised blisters on her feet.

Carson stayed at Yaddo twice that year, first from June 14 to August 2, and then a short visit in September. Her stays were like visits to decompression chambers, opportunities to check out of her problems, among them her relationship with Reeves, her relationship with David, and all permutations of the relationships among the three. She was getting letters from Annemarie from various corners of the globe, and though both spoke of future meetings, none was imminent. Yet in Carson's fantasies, bolstered by the warmth of Annemarie's letters, the love affair continued.

By the summer of 1941, Reeves had moved out of the West Eleventh Street apartment, but it was not clear where he had gone. He simply fell silent, and Carson received no letters from him at all.

While Carson still believed she was in love with David, she knew her sexual desires were, for the most part, for women. With Reeves, she never found the aching tenderness she felt with Annemarie, with whom she found "tension"—a code word in her lexicon for sexual desire. But she also told Kay that she had never had sexual relations with anyone but Reeves. Leaving aside the questions of how she defined "sexual" relations and whether she was telling Kay the truth, this statement is difficult to interpret. She made it at the end of 1942, which would rule out as sexual partners Mary Tucker, Annemarie, and—already unlikely—David Diamond.

David had a Yaddo residency that summer, arriving in early July and leaving at the end of that month. Sometime after he left, he evidently expressed some dissatisfaction and anger at what he saw as Carson's refusal to be clear with him about her feelings. Understandably, she balked; David was sleeping with her husband, and she had discovered she liked women—what feelings was she not being clear about? She replied at, for her, great length: She didn't know why David wanted more than a platonic friendship with her, she said. She didn't want another passionate relationship—she had had enough of that with Annemarie. That kind of love inevitably led to misery, and she was through with that, having suffered a narrow escape. But her letter then edged off into ambiguity. She recognized a strong and intense bond with David, and she felt she and he had very quickly reached an emotional high point. David may have asked her to live with him, or for all three of them to live together. Maybe if she hadn't married Reeves, she replied, she might be able to. And living together was the only step she saw beyond "brotherly love." Sexual intimacy seems to have had no place in the ménages she imagined.

And what about Reeves? she continued. She had no idea what their relationship was with each other. Neither he nor David had told her anything about it, she added, and she would not ask. Something told her to pull back, however. At a low point in their marriage, before they moved to New York, when they were not having sex, she had asked Reeves about it. He said flat out, because she asked, that he was not a homosexual and that was not what was going on with David. As with Carson, it is not clear how Reeves defined homosexuality—whether he meant sexual acts with men or just romantic connections with the same sex. He said that David was the first man he was attracted to.

We do not have any correspondence between David and Reeves, and Carson was not getting any mail from Reeves, so it is uncertain how his affair with David proceeded. Reeves came up to Rochester in July for an extended visit with David. David's brother-in-law found Reeves a job at Samson United, a Rochester manufacturer. He took the job very seriously, later saying that he thought the skills he'd acquired there in production control and time and motion studies would be a lot of help in finding other good positions.

Not surprisingly, David asked Reeves what Carson thought of the move to Rochester and his plans, and Reeves confessed he hadn't written her for a long time. He was deeply divided and did not know what to say to her. He worried that he had "abandoned" her, unable to acknowledge that, emotionally, she had abandoned him. "I miss Carson terribly, so much so that I can hardly bear it," he told David. David's journal entries reflected further troubles. "I do love sleeping with Reeves but somehow I feel that I am holding on to Death," he wrote, noting Reeves's obvious depression and self-destructiveness. David also revealed in his diary that he had opened a letter from a female nurse to Reeves, which revealed they were planning a date—at the same time he and David were talking about sharing an apartment.

Things got worse. While Carson was at Yaddo that summer, she was not receiving checks that she had been expecting. Since West Eleventh Street was her New York address, she concluded that Reeves was receiving the checks but not sending them on because he couldn't write the letters he felt must accompany them. In reality, for Reeves, it was a short hop from withholding her checks to forging her signature and cashing them, which he began doing around June. He forged her signature on a $400 check from *The New Yorker* for her story "The Jockey," which appeared in July. He forged her signature on royalty checks from Houghton Mifflin, some of them even at the publisher's New York office, presumably claiming his right as a husband. At some juncture, her father wrote to Carson from Columbus that her bank in Columbus had told him that Reeves had forged a check for $300 from Carson's account. Meanwhile, as David later noted in his diary, Reeves was suicidal; worse, he wanted David to kill himself with him. On a Rochester bridge, Reeves repeatedly urged David to jump with him, so insistently that David was frightened.

Carson, horrified, described these awful developments to Bob Linscott. While angry, she decided not to prosecute Reeves over the checks because of the publicity it would attract; otherwise, she might have. She did not know what to make of his actions, calling him mentally ill. Later she called this period crazy and sick. It is worth noting that when she heard about the checks, she immediately consulted lawyers rather than asking Reeves for an explanation. She wrote to David summarily that "obviously" she had to divorce him. Why "obviously"? Why "had to"? Why not see that he got help, especially if the forgery indicated some "mental sickness"? But Carson wanted to move on. After speaking to a lawyer about a divorce, she went off on a trip to Quebec with Newton Arvin and Granville Hicks and his wife, a welcome diversion. On her return to New York, she filed for divorce on grounds of adultery (presumably naming David Diamond), which was the necessary condition for a divorce in New York State.

David, years later, tried to put Reeves's sexual preferences and the check forgeries into perspective. "Reeves, I still say, was *not* homosexual even though *we* had a fulfilled relationship." He did not mention how long the relationship had been "fulfilled." Heterosexual men, he wrote,

> often function in bisexual roles when they are attracted to certain men who are sympathetic to them. I don't think Reeves would have gone to bed with me *only for sex*. He truly loved me but was

incapable of [using?] the love constructively while being tortured by guilt for the forgings and abandonment of Carson.

"It's a complex, subtle problem," he concluded.

David was right about the complexity, and Carson was no doubt correct that Reeves was mentally ill. Certainly he had been drinking heavily and barely knew what he was doing. He might have rationalized (or wished) that he and Carson held their money jointly and that he was entitled to it. The forgeries seem to have been committed not so much out of financial need as desperation, an indication that something in him was breaking down. His actions also suggest despair over the future of his relationship with Carson on account of his affair with David, what the affair might say about his own sexual nature, and Carson's evident indifference.

In another letter to David, Carson waxed philosophical, deploying a lovely and deceptively cheerful analogy about the difficulty of categorizing love: In the same way that jam is jam, she said, love is love. There's all kinds of jam: quince, strawberry, even spoiled jam. In fact, some jam has a fly or two jammed up in the jar. Love is love, but it's all jam.

Maybe, just as jams had to be labeled and sorted out, so, too, did love. How or why that might happen is not clear; also unclear was whether that was a desirable outcome. Did she really want her love for David and her love for her husband labeled and sorted into different categories? And what about her love for Annemarie?

The blithe tone of the analogy is misleading as well. Though she may have seemed indifferent to Reeves, the triangle caused Carson great pain. She was forced back on herself, to look at her needs and desires in the light of day and evaluate her feelings for David, for Annemarie, for a passing ballerina (her current crush), and for Reeves. For Carson, self-knowledge was often elusive, but she assessed around this time how impossibly needy she was, telling David that she had been feeling awfully clinging, made so by a kind of dread that crept over her. This made her so demanding, she said, that she didn't know how those who loved her could stand being with her. She felt this kind of temperament and emotional neediness was that of a child. She didn't know if this would ever change, she said. She needed constant reassurance that she was always loved.

It was a hard-won realization, but also a statement of intractability. The situation would likely never change, Carson concluded. She would probably always be needy beyond reason. She was like a child, she said, who probably would never grow up.

It was hard to see what others—Carson and, later, Truman Capote—found appealing in the meek and retiring Newton Arvin, but a few minutes of conversation revealed his charm as well as his critically deft mind. Holding a bachelor's from Harvard but no further degree, he joined the faculty at all-women Smith College in Northampton, Massachusetts, in 1924, at the age of twenty-four, and would stay there for over thirty years. He wrote prolifically about both literature and politics: left-leaning, he followed closely the trial of the anarchists Sacco and Vanzetti, for instance. He read seven languages. He put himself on the map of literary criticism with his book-length study, *Hawthorne,* published in 1929, and maintained his place with later critical biographies of Whitman (1938) and Melville (1950).

Carson's friend Newton Arvin, literary critic and Smith College professor, 1951

Newton was a modest-looking man, prematurely balding, complete with gold-rimmed glasses; he was also a stylish dresser with a considerable interest in fashion. He had closets full of expensive suits and kept linen shirts and cashmere sweaters in great Gatsbyesque stacks. In fact, he and Carson often talked about clothes. In one letter, she said she was eager to see him because she had five new dresses. She described one in detail: it had a short jacket and was a dark ash color, but the darlingest detail was that the jacket's lining had a red and white stripe, revealed when the jacket fell open.

The two met at Yaddo. Newton had been going there for years and was now a trustee; he was one of those on whom Elizabeth Ames smiled. He and Carson found common ground in the evenings at the boîtes in Saratoga Springs, delivered there in the Yaddo station wagon more nights than not. Newton was enamored of Oskar Seidlin, a young poet and émigré who taught in the German department at Smith. (Carson made the happy discovery that Oskar worked as an assistant to Klaus Mann on *Decision* magazine.) She told Newton about the situation with Reeves and David Diamond, though she probably didn't yet know of their romantic involvement. She described her role in the triangle and confessed hyperbolically, "Newton, I was born a man." Perhaps that seemed the only explanation.

Even as the triangle hung fire, and perhaps hungry for some more drama, Carson sought out intrigue at Yaddo. She decided she was in love with Katherine Anne Porter, whom she had met the previous summer when Porter spoke at Bread Loaf. This summer Porter was the object of much admiration among the Yaddo residents. She was acclaimed for her 1930 short story collection, *Flowering Judas,* and in 1939 she had published a collection of three novellas, *Pale Horse, Pale Rider,* that secured her reputation as a prose stylist. She had risen from humble Texas beginnings and had led a colorful life since, scraping by as a reporter and a writer. At fifty-one, nearly twenty years older than Carson, she was dramatically beautiful, with a striking head of white hair.

The previous summer Porter's then-husband, Albert Erskine, had read *The Heart Is a Lonely Hunter* and declared, "Katherine Anne, that woman is a lesbian." Porter had ignored his statement, hoping that Carson would turn out to be a protégée, more in the mold of Eudora Welty. But when she met Carson at Bread Loaf, she found her to be "tiresome to what a degree," as she wrote Erskine in exasperation. She thought she wouldn't take Carson up; the new literary sensation wasn't "a hopeful youngster" but "rotten to the bone already"—strong words

Carson pursued writer Katherine Anne Porter at
Yaddo in 1941.

indeed. Carson did not forget what Katherine Anne said to her when
they first met, clearly designed to draw blood: "Lots of youngsters
write a novel and then never write another."

Nevertheless, soon after Carson's arrival at Yaddo, she spoke up and
announced, "I love you, Katherine Anne," adding, somewhat desperately, "You're the only famous writer I have ever known." According
to Porter biographer Joan Givner, Carson's "mooning passion" for the
older writer "horrified" Katherine Anne. "She had always had a revul-
sion for lesbians and she became seriously disturbed." (Most of Porter's
male friends, on the other hand, were homosexual.) She complained
to Elizabeth Ames that Carson's presence made her uncomfortable,
and Ames somewhat curiously suggested that Porter eat all her meals
in her room for the duration; it's not clear why Ames confined Porter
to her room rather than Carson. Porter still felt threatened, however,
and moved to another building, North Farm, where she was joined by
her friend Welty. There the two felt their bond strengthened by their
shared antipathy toward Carson.

Carson continued her pursuit regardless. According to Porter, "The only difference [her move] made to Carson was that she had to walk some little distance to find me." One day she knocked loudly and long at the doors of North Farm and eventually got inside through a window. She then pounded on Porter's door. Porter ignored the racket. Hearing nothing for an hour or two, Porter thought it safe to go over to the mansion for dinner. But when she opened her door, Carson was prostrate on the doorsill. What she did next became the flourish on a favorite Yaddo story: without saying a word, she stepped over her admirer's prone body and went on her way.

Carson seemed to have a boundless capacity for personal crisis, and that season at Yaddo she needed it. By midsummer, she was telling Newton about Reeves's check forgeries and her decision to divorce him. She made two trips down to the city to meet with lawyers; she also consulted her friend William Mayer, whom she had come to think of as her personal (unpaid) psychiatrist. She seethed all the while. On her trip to Quebec with Granville and Dorothy Hicks, with their daughter and Newton along, it was all she talked about, Hicks said. She railed against Reeves, "how he had forged her checks . . . had beat her, pushed her into the hall naked, tore up her clothes, etc." Hicks noted that all these stories were suspect because *both* Carson and Reeves liked "melodrama." This kind of behavior was common enough (though certainly extreme) in drunken fights between two volatile people; for the moment, it was just as well for them to be apart.

Her other relationships seemed nearly as fraught. Newton was recovering from his divorce from a woman who had been a student of his, Mary Garrison. On the trip to Quebec, for which Newton and Carson fortified themselves with gallon jugs of sherry as well as bottles of brandy and whiskey, the Hickses were mildly surprised to see their friends register at the hotel as Mr. and Mrs. Newton Arvin. Perhaps it was because Carson liked physical closeness, or perhaps to save money, or both. The next day, however, they re-registered in separate rooms. Hicks speculated about an unsatisfactory sexual encounter. Whatever the explanation, their friendship remained solid when they left Quebec.

Newton returned to Yaddo after a few days in Northampton with

Carson. She then went back to the city by way of New City, in Rockland County, where her friends Henry Varnum Poor and Bessie Breuer were building a house. She also saw Kay Boyle and her assorted friends and family in tow, four children and two stepchildren. She had just settled in nearby Nyack, where Bessie had found them a house. After a meeting in New York with her lawyers, Carson returned to Yaddo.

But she was at Yaddo only briefly that September. She spent three weeks that fall in New York City hotels, first the Bedford on East 40th Street, then the Brevoort in the Village, which she much preferred. She signed more papers relating to the divorce, had some dental work done, and saw editors and friends, including Bob Linscott and George Davis. She intended to go back to Georgia, she said, and would stay there a year or until *The Bride* was finished. In the meantime, she launched a flurry of letters to friends and acquaintances, as she had decided to apply for a Guggenheim Fellowship. In an undated letter written early that fall, she told Newton she needed him as a sponsor because he was a respected academic. She also thought of Ted Morrison (from Bread Loaf), Granville Hicks, Louis Untermeyer, and later, Kay Boyle.

Before she left for Georgia, however, she had at least one more set of toes to step on. In several letters to Bessie Breuer, she mulled over her sponsor choices—perhaps an unwise move, for Bessie may have felt *she* should be asked for a letter of recommendation. Bessie does not seem to have raised any of this with Carson, perhaps out of pride. But that December, after Carson left New York, Bessie tried to start an epistolary quarrel with her, objecting to being passed over for Carson's farewell party on the eve of her departure from the city. Carson protested that it had been a working occasion with friends who were helping her get organized to move, adding, inscrutably, that she couldn't believe Bessie would ever think she needed to be invited in such a situation. Did she expect Bessie, somehow learning about the party while it was going on, simply to show up? It was all just "foolishness," Carson added, further insulting her friend.

Toward the end of her life, looking back on this time, Carson would say that she had become a well-known fixture on the literary scene when she was too young to know what she was doing. "I was a bit of a holy terror," she commented. She wondered how she could warn future artists away from such behavior. Of course, it wasn't that simple; her personality, and her sense of drama, captivated people as talented and intelligent as David Diamond and Newton Arvin at the same time as they were driving others away. But neither was all this merely an episode in a young writer's personal development.

7

I Feel That Book with Something
Like My Whole Body

Watching the war unfold in Europe, and nervous that Japan's alliance with Italy and Germany would pull the United States into the conflict, Carson, Reeves, and their friends felt their domestic world almost eclipsed by world events. The war news, Carson wrote a friend in New York, took up residence in the corners of rooms and made them all feel dreadful.

France had fallen to the Germans in June 1940, and by July the air war known as the Battle of Britain had commenced. Meanwhile Mussolini had carried the war into North Africa, where Italian troops were marching toward the Suez Canal. Though aid to besieged Britain did not have universal support, with the signing of the Lend-Lease bill in March 1941, the United States became the "Arsenal of Democracy" in the war against fascism. Yugoslavia and Greece surrendered to the Axis powers in the spring of 1941. In June, Germany launched a massive invasion of the Soviet Union, tipping American public opinion in support of U.S. entry. A peacetime draft began in September. When Carson last saw Reeves in April, he had been enthusiastic about becoming a soldier again, though he was unsure how or when to join. Now she thought he was probably back in the service but did not know for sure. The world seemed to have gone crazy, and the United States was about to become part of the madness.

The war news aside, Carson was in retreat from all the pressing news in her life: from the hopes and dreams of her first couple of years in New York with Reeves, from the great love she still felt for Annemarie, and from the shards of her broken marriage and Reeves's check forgeries. She crept back to Columbus in the fall. Bébé was happy to enfold her in her arms. Her brother, Lamar, had recently married a young Columbus woman, Virginia Standard, and lived now with his wife's family. Rita was off at the University of Miami until Christmas. The business about the divorce undid Carson completely, and from her hotel room, before she fled to Columbus, she had to send for William Mayer to assure her that she was not going insane.

She had great plans for her time in Columbus, however, mainly working on *The Bride*. She was physically committed to that book, she told Newton. Somehow, she said, she hoped to re-create in the twelve-year-old Frankie a character who embodied the crazinesses and passions of her own childhood. She had resolved to stay in Columbus until the summer of 1942 and finish the book, after which she hoped to return to Yaddo. (To Ferris Greenslet at Houghton Mifflin, she said she planned to be in Georgia for a year or more.) She dreamed of travel, she told Newton, but she'd just have to saunter along whistling a tune until she was done.

She was determined to make the most of life on Stark Avenue. She traded in the family's old upright piano for a new Gulbransen forty-inch spinet, for which she paid $300, and began a daily routine of work on her book in the morning and piano practice in the afternoon, a long walk, and tea with sherry at the end of the day. She embarked on a massive effort to eat so that she could gain, as the doctor ordered, twenty pounds, promising Newton that after a few months she would be as robust as a prizefighter.

But soon after Thanksgiving, she got sick. First came a strep throat and an ear infection, which soon devolved into double pneumonia and pleurisy. In December she was in the hospital for several days and was attended by a professional nurse at home—so sick, she told Bessie and Newton, that she came close to dying. She was barely aware of the Japanese attack on Pearl Harbor, so that when she slowly got well, it was to a transformed world: her country was at war. Muriel Rukeyser told her that Reeves had joined the Coast Guard, at which news Carson professed indifference, and which in any case turned out to be wrong.

Bébé nursed the convalescent, getting her well and then keeping her so. She cooked all Carson's favorite foods: boiled onions, stewed tomatoes, and mashed potatoes. She and Lamar avoided references to Reeves, but Carson did learn that Reeves had borrowed money from Bébé. It was money her mother had set aside for Rita's college expenses and that she was unlikely to see again. Bébé and Lamar had considered Reeves family, but no longer. Her family now viewed Reeves as an enemy, Carson told Newton, and when she learned he had shaken down her mother for money, she felt the same way.

Much as Bébé and Lamar Sr. liked having Carson at home in the absence of her siblings, her mother knew that there was a limit to how long she could shelter her adult daughter. Carson, too, began to itch to get away. Columbus had changed—it was packed with thousands of soldiers stationed at Fort Benning. But she stayed for the entire winter of 1941–42. She had no friends in Columbus, she told David Diamond, and lived like a tiny creature hidden in her mother's capacious coattails. Life in New York would be hard without Reeves, she admitted, but living by herself, learning to be an independent adult, wouldn't hurt her. Bébé herself thought she should leave, Carson told David in another letter. Her mother wanted her to lead a happy life, she said, and didn't understand that it was impossible.

Everything changed again in March, when she learned that she had been awarded a Guggenheim Fellowship. Suddenly she felt vistas open before her. Travel to Europe was impossible, but she wanted a foreign setting, reminding David that the only time she had spent outside the United States had been her trip to Quebec the previous summer. She resolved to go to Mexico. She expected David to counsel her not to and anticipated resistance from him. But he should recognize that she hadn't had the experience of traveling and living abroad that David had enjoyed. She'd always wanted to, but when she first left home at seventeen, she had been so worried about finding a job and having money that she did not feel "free." When she left for good, it had been with Reeves. So she could say she never had been free.

She was dead set on Mexico, she said, though she didn't know a single person there and had no idea which towns might be hospitable or indeed anything else about the country. She acknowledged the difficulties in going there so ill informed, so she resolved to ask Henry Moe, the Guggenheim official she had been communicating with. In a graphic figure of speech, she told Newton, a little orchestra was tuning up its instruments in her gut. She was so excited that she was uttering hosannas.

Henry Moe advised her that thus far Mexico had not turned out well for Guggenheim fellows, so on second thought Carson resolved to stay in Columbus for the time being and get more work done on *The Bride.* But the prospect of a summer at home depressed her. *The Bride* took place over a Georgia summer, and that season, she told Elizabeth Ames, was like a bad dream, To Newton, she quoted her own manuscript, in which she described the small-town Southern summer as "a silent crazy jungle under glass" (*MW,* 1), the hot, cloudless days in Georgia horrifically torrid.

Actually, Carson was thinking about going back to Yaddo. Perhaps forgetting what a roller-coaster ride her previous summer there had been, she felt certain that if she could return, she could finish her book by fall. She wrote several letters to Elizabeth Ames, feeling her out on the subject. She wondered whether it wouldn't be a little greedy to hold a Guggenheim and stay at Yaddo at the same time. She reasoned, however, that the Guggenheim gave her the wherewithal and Yaddo the place to work. She assured Elizabeth that she was completely recovered from the double pneumonia and absolutely fit for sustained work should she be allowed to visit. She felt she was all cured, and her nerves in better shape than they had been even as a child. She got up with the sun and worked steadily until the afternoon, when she practiced the piano. Her parents were pretty much the only people she saw. It was a weird existence, she acknowledged, but the writing was getting done.

To her great relief, Elizabeth agreed—though Yaddo was retrenching in response to the war, accepting fewer applicants and closing parts of the estate. Evidently Carson didn't need to make a formal application, as Elizabeth replied to her query immediately. Carson was delighted to learn that she would be there at the same time as Newton and David; she could not have hoped for more. She and Elizabeth settled on July 2 as the date her residency would begin, and she determined to go straight to Yaddo from Columbus, without stopping in New York City.

Perhaps her happiness about her immediate future, or perhaps her sense of distance from her marriage, made it possible for her to sit down and write one of her best (and most loved) stories, "A Tree. A Rock. A Cloud." A man in a café hails a boy of about twelve and begins to talk to him, launching into what is at first an enigmatic story. His wife of one year left him twelve years ago, he says, breaking his heart. With time and reflection, he says, he has developed a "science" of love. Falling in love with a person is way too complicated, he says, "start[ing] at the wrong end of love." You must start small, he says. With "a tree, a rock, a cloud." Since the man understood this science, he tells the boy, he sees a street full of people, a bird in the sky, a traveler on a road, and he can love them all. "Now I am a master, son. I can love anything" (*BSC*, 150–51). Like the man's "science," Carson's story is deceptively simple. The reader understands what the man does not say, that it is extremely difficult to love again after a major heartbreak, often not for years. Even then you have to start with objects. The man is still not able to love another human being, or does not dare try. But you are living with love in your life again, and that makes all the difference, he says.

⁓

Carson had no word from Reeves or about him. He had left Rochester, but she didn't know when; only the rumor about the Coast Guard reached her. In June, as it turned out, she did stop in New York on her way to Yaddo, because her Houghton Mifflin editor would be in town and wanted to see her. Among the other friends she saw was Muriel Rukeyser, who told Carson about a letter she had received from Reeves in May. He had enlisted in the army at Camp Upton, far out on the north shore of Long Island, in Yaphank. He would not join a combat division for some time and soon shipped out for Fort Jackson, South Carolina, before heading to Officers Candidate School. He did not mention Carson and referred to the immediate past only obliquely, writing, "All my bridges are blown up and I seem to be healthy and well." For the time being his plans were unclear. He did not know whether he would leave for Michigan to join a division to be activated in September 1942, or stay in South Carolina with his present division, the Second Battalion of the Rangers, which he believed was headed for Africa.

Reeves's letter to Muriel, with a check enclosed for repayment of a loan, could be construed as a communication for his ex-wife. The letter's passive-aggressive tone ("Write to me, dammit") suggests that he hoped Muriel would show the letter to Carson. He knew Muriel would not write him back because on a recent New York visit she had refused to meet him for lunch. ("You wouldn't spare thirty minutes for lunch with me.") Carson does not seem to have taken the bait, though later letters indicate that she communicated with Reeves before February 1942, when she heard directly from him. For the time being she was focused on her work. After seeing Linscott, Janet Flanner, and Bessie Breuer, she was off to Yaddo.

That summer the Yaddo board had taken the step of integrating the colony. Newton Arvin wrote Langston Hughes offering him a residency; another African American at Yaddo that year was the Canadian composer R. Nathaniel Dett, presumably also invited. According to Hughes's biographer, Carson was his "best friend" that season. They always ate breakfast together, and Hughes joined Carson and whatever colonists were along on visits to the New Worden bar in the evenings. Though Yaddo was forward-looking in inviting African Americans at this date, their behavior, especially if they were males, was closely scrutinized. Hughes found Carson, as a Southerner, fairly sympathetic to African Americans' troubles; he quoted a remark she made about a Georgia segregationist with relish. People like this man, she said, "Their hind brains don't work." That summer they wrote a joint postcard to Ralph Ellison, urging him to come to Yaddo.

Carson stayed at the colony from July 2 to January 17 of the next year. She spent time with Newton, though his stay was short, and with their mutual friend the writer Helen Eustis, who had married her English professor at Smith, Alfred Fisher. Fisher and Eustis came to Yaddo at different times that summer, so that one of them could stay home with their child. Biddy, as Helen was known, was working on a roman à clef murder mystery set at Smith; it would be a literary sensation when it was published as *The Horizontal Man* in 1946. That summer Elizabeth assigned Carson the mansion's much-coveted tower room, which had been Katrina Trask's bedroom. Carson found she did not like the large space; its size, she said, spooked her. Biddy had the room on the other side of the connecting bathroom, and so the two traded.

One of Carson's most regular correspondents during her stay was Bessie Breuer, who with her husband Henry Varnum Poor had become one of Carson's closest friends. Henry had known Carson for a long time, perhaps earlier than 1940, when he painted her portrait. He was among the first artists to make their home in Rockland County, on South Mountain Road, where, starting in 1920, he built Crow House, a remarkable and beautiful structure made from red sandstone and chestnut beams fashioned from trees on the property. Self-taught as an architect, Poor would go on to build or redesign houses for his neighbors, including Lotte Lenya and Kurt Weill, John Houseman, Maxwell Anderson, and Burgess Meredith. He married Bessie in 1925, and they had three children, Anne, Josephine, and Peter. A talented ceramicist, he made a blue mug for Carson, which she used for the next fifteen years for her morning coffee.

Henry had begun to see a lot of Carson when George Davis became his friend in 1940, and Bessie first met her at Crow House the same year. One wintry Sunday, George brought her and Reeves out to New City along with Weill and Lenya. Bessie remembered "a dark tall girl with haunting eyes, white shirt, and grey flannel pants . . . and her husband, a slight young man with fine features." Carson took an immediate writerly interest in Bessie when she noticed her typewriter on a tour of the house. Carson made numerous visits out to South Mountain Road that year, with and without George and/or Reeves. Bessie would pick her up at the Spring Valley bus stop, clutching a bottle of Vat 69 whiskey.

In late June 1942, Bessie performed the office of a great friend: when Carson's train from Georgia arrived at Penn Station, she met her train, which Carson very much appreciated. Carson told her to come to Yaddo for a stay that summer. Bessie thought that she could manage only a week because of the children. Most guests stayed longer, so Bessie probably did not end up applying.

Along with Bessie, Kay Boyle had become an important friend, despite the seventeen-year age difference between them. Kay had lived in France for almost twenty years, married first to a French student (with whom she had a daughter). She had then married bon vivant Laurence Vail, Peggy Guggenheim's ex-husband, and had three children with him. She published several volumes of award-winning short stories beginning in 1929. By the time Carson met her, she had written eleven novels and was a published poet as well; she was considered one of the best writers of the 1920s and '30s. When Carson first became friends with her, she had left Vail for an Austrian baron fleeing Austria, Joseph von Franckenstein. She was an unconventionally attractive woman, extremely thin and with a prominent nose: she had a marked intensity and was a lifelong social activist. She and Carson were seldom in the same place at the same time; this held true in 1942 as well. Kay was living in Nyack, while Carson was shuttling from Reeves's

Novelist Kay Boyle in 1941. She had a brief
but intense friendship with Carson.

Greenwich Village apartment to Columbus and Yaddo. Carson saw Kay mostly in New City, when she was visiting Bessie and Henry.

Carson described her Yaddo quarters at great length to Bessie. That summer she did not get as much writing done as she would have liked, so in the fall she moved to a cottage on the property, Pine Tree Studio. She was in a small cabin in the woods, entirely by herself, she announced to Bessie. She had a great big table, and there was a red rug on the floor. In the evenings she went back to the main house for dinner and any after-dinner activities. The solitary condition suited her just then.

On December 1 terrible news reached her: Annemarie Schwarzenbach had died in Switzerland on November 15, following a bicycle accident on the sixth that sent her into a coma three days later. All Carson had at first was a cable from a Therese Giehse, whom she did not know. Only later did she learn the details. Klaus Mann wrote about the event in his diary:

> A bicycle accident, they're telling me now it was. Yes, an ordinary bicycle that bolted like a wild horse. In Engadine there are very steep roads with many sharp curves—that's how it happened. Our Swiss child lost control of the contraption, and it threw her into a tree, in Switzerland, and her head—her dear, beautiful head with her "lovely face of an inconsolable angel"—smashed into it in the most abominable way. She did not die straight away.

Carson poured her heart into a twelve-page letter to Kay Boyle in which she related the whole saga of Annemarie's breakdown in the fall of 1940, when Annemarie had rejected her so completely. She left out the sexual aspect of the rejection, but she did seem to realize that Annemarie had loved her, if at all, only briefly, and thought of her more as a kid brother. She knew, she told Kay, that somehow or other she would lose Annemarie.

A nervous collapse was expected of Carson, she seemed to believe, but it never came. She had always spoken rather melodramatically about Annemarie, and now she did so to the fullest. She had to work and live like a monk, she told Elizabeth Ames. Annemarie existed now only in the souls of those who loved her, including Carson. Given that, she had to live and conduct herself so as to be "worthy." Carson was proprietary about Annemarie; even if her love was not reciprocated, she took comfort in the fact that she had loved her friend as much as she was capable. Because Annemarie lived now only in her friends, Carson thought, and because she loved Annemarie the most, then Annemarie's spirit resided in her more than in anyone else. *Her* feelings were somehow more special than anyone else's, including the family and friends Annemarie had known long before Carson. As a writer, Carson could recognize and write effectively about this kind of reaction, but as a person she was blind to it.

Carson was always hyperbolic when describing her feelings for others. She invariably spoke of love, even to those she had just met, and those she met in a professional context, and those she knew to be committed to or involved with others. She always addressed letters to "Precious" or "My darling." Love, or loving, was her default emotion. Some of this was, no doubt, Southern. She had been telling nearly complete strangers that she loved them from earliest childhood— *tenderly* was the word she most often used. But the habit, tendency, or predilection seems to have run deeper than that. All her theorizing and philosophizing about the lover and the beloved masked a profound insecurity and a matching defensiveness. If Carson loved and was not loved back, she was secure in her position. That such rejection could cause emotional pain she did not quite understand. In this scheme of things, she left no room for the impossible: that the love she felt would be returned. The writer and critic Alfred Kazin, who would come to know Carson in the months ahead, wrote in his journals that Carson seemed to "long to give 'love,' to effect an instant embrace." He sensed in Carson the outsider whose only response is to love and to become close to everyone within reach.

A later friend, Hortense Calisher, noted this quality in Carson's body of work. Among the so-called Southern Gothic writers, Calisher wrote,

> Only McCullers, more naïvely honest than any of them, more lyrically endowed than any and with an asexual mobility which could

seem both childish and adult, wrote of "love" as undifferentiated sex. Whether or not her vague or weak sexual orientation made her sound the more "universal," she had the ego to write large.

Usually, Carson's correspondents—and not just the Southern ones—used similarly expansive, overblown language back at her. They, too, "embraced" her "tenderly," spoke of how much they loved her, gathering that this was what Carson expected. Annemarie had been one of the most extreme on this score. Her letters to Carson over the past two years were always signed, "Your Annemarie." "Don't forget my tenderness for you," she wrote in October 1941 from the Congo. (Carson so enjoyed telling her friends about Annemarie in the Congo.) "My dear, dear little Carson," she opened another. "I live with the intense wish of love and friendship towards you,—and the feeling that you live, and love me." She spoke of "friendship," too, and in the same letter she said she loved Carson as if she were her sister, but closed, "I kiss you—Your Annemarie."

The last letter Carson received from her, however, ought to have given her pause. Carson's success with her writing evidently ate at her Swiss friend. An extraordinarily talented woman, Annemarie had received her doctorate at twenty-three. As a journalist she had filed more than a hundred stories, many of them accompanied by expressive photographs that she took. She published several books, though most were not translated into English in her lifetime. She was a world traveler and a brave idealist engaged in fighting fascism when she died. Yet she was thirty-four to Carson's twenty-five. She was a morphine addict. She had suffered several breakdowns and attempted suicide more than once. She was struggling to find her way, and Carson's example made her somewhat bitter.

Carson's success was different. She was a novelist, first of all. Annemarie had written one work of fiction, a novella. The other book-length works published in her lifetime were travelogues-cum-memoirs. She was a gifted, sensitive writer, but Carson, in America at least, was overnight a literary lion. She seemed to distill her work effortlessly from her imagination. More than that, Carson was enjoying success

American style, which meant being photographed, interviewed, sought out—becoming a celebrity.

American success had eluded Annemarie. She could not get her work published in the United States—neither articles nor books. A photographic tour of the South and Appalachia had yielded brilliant work, yet she had not been able to place the resulting photo essay with an American publisher. To her, she wrote, the United States meant only a "terrific & painfully hurting defeat." Her only hope for recognition there, she came to feel, lay in Carson's dedicating *Reflections in a Golden Eye* to her. She had known Carson was going to do so, but it was not until she actually received the book that she became excited. "If this book, *Reflections in a Golden Eye,* should be printed, & dedicated to me, it will most probably be the only trace I leave in the U.S." The book, she said, "will make up for me, and my defeat." She hoped Carson would let her translate the novel. "Carson remember our moments of understanding, and how much I loved you."

She said nothing about the novel itself. It is not hard to discern bitterness as well as a note of passive aggression in Annemarie's response to the book, whose value for her apparently lay mainly in its usefulness to her American reputation. She was moved to scoff at fame in another letter. In the United States, she wrote, she "earned no fame. . . . Fame and brilliant careers are only the reverse of failure. . . . And both, Carson, are not for us." She urged her young friend not to rush her writing. "Even if . . . you can't write for a long time, this doesn't matter. . . . Inaction, if our soul is pure & open, is not bad, and even better than any wrong action." Luckily, Carson's talent was not diverted by anything Annemarie said.

It took her "several whiskeys" to sound out George Davis about returning to Seven Middagh that December. As she told Kay, she couldn't seclude herself at Yaddo forever, much as she might like to. She loved her cabin in the woods, but it belonged to Yaddo, and to regard it as any kind of home was misguided, she knew. She had some money saved from the Guggenheim and a thousand-dollar advance from Houghton Mifflin. George let her know that she was always welcome at Seven Middagh, and she was delighted at the chance to forgo the effort of finding a place in the city.

She feared she had caused George nothing but a headache. Though they really had started the household together, with Auden quickly joining up, she had moved out a little more than a year later, complaining that too many people were around the house, and the telephone rang nearly nonstop. Then she had come back, and then she'd left again, which she felt drove George crazy. The house was different now, she found on a visit in November. It was divided into what were really separate apartments, though the residents still shared the kitchen and a living room/dining room. Richard Wright and his wife had the first floor and part of the second, set designer Oliver Smith the top floor, and George had the third. Louis MacNeice was in residence only on his trips to the United States, and Benjamin Britten and Peter Pears had gone back to England, which left only Auden and Chester Kallman, who remained in their rooms on the second floor. The room next to George's, where Carson had lived before, was untenanted, and between the two there was a hall that could be made into a small kitchen. George had completely redecorated the room and kept it unoccupied for Carson. The walls were painted a saturated greenish blue. It was large enough for a grand piano and an alcove for a desk. Because Middagh was a short dead-end street and thus very hushed, traffic noise was far off and muffled. George seldom brought friends home, Richard Wright's family lived very quietly, and Oliver Smith led a monkish existence. Perhaps because she thought the somewhat buttoned-up Newton had formed a wrong impression of the house, she added, in a handwritten note, it wasn't as "campy" as during her previous stay there, and she felt the residents lived more respectably. She noted the view of the New York skyline, the muted noises of the harbor, and the faint scent of salt air.

Best of all, she said, George wanted her to move back. When she got to New York on January 17, the same day she left Yaddo, she found that George had not expected her until February and was storing his things in what he called "Carson's" room while his quarters were being painted. She was able to move in but quickly came down with a nasty cold and stayed in bed for ten days. George's friends were all pitching in to get his rooms finished, and she did some painting herself, finding she couldn't get any writing done with her room in such disarray.

Seven Middagh had definitely changed. The Wrights were a stabilizing presence. George had met Richard Wright back in 1940, when *Harper's Bazaar* published his story "Almos' a Man." After Wright published his review of *The Heart Is a Lonely Hunter* (*Native Son* came out the same year), he and Carson kept missing each other. She signed his copy of *Reflections in a Golden Eye* with a note, "Dick, I have wanted to see you for a long time, but you are so exclusive." By the time she moved back to Seven Middagh in January 1943, Wright was a friend. He and his wife, Ellen, with their two-month-old daughter, Julia, had Carson down for a Southern breakfast: that included rice and ham and baked apples, Carson told Elizabeth Ames. There was some unpleasantness about Wright and his white wife; the African American furnace man refused to work in a house where a Black man lived with a white woman. Auden told the worker to get out, and Carson was indignant. A few times someone threw stones at the Wrights' windows.

Carson ventured out seldom in January; she was sidelined first by the cold and then by mushrooming dental problems. She ran into the photographer Walker Evans, an acquaintance; hearing she was in pain, he immediately sent her to his dentist, Sam Neikrug. It turned out that Neikrug was an old friend of Leonard Ehrlich, a writer who was Elizabeth Ames's boyfriend. These connections became a problem when Neikrug, pulling a back molar, cracked her jaw. Carson did not have it tended to promptly, and a nasty infection set in, requiring further dental work and a tactical shift to a different dentist. She kept telling Elizabeth that it could have happened at any dentist's—and insisted that she not tell Leonard about it. The dressing for the infection had to be changed daily, necessitating a trip to Manhattan. She also saw Biddy Eustis, who had left her husband, Alfred Fisher. Carson had been trying for some months to help Biddy find a job and had taken the train down from Yaddo in November to speak to Gus Lobrano, a fiction editor at *The New Yorker,* about her friend.

After the pain abated, she took tentative steps toward some kind of social life. In January she had gone to Manhattan to meet Bessie and Henry, who were having drinks with John Steinbeck and his second wife, Gwyn. Steinbeck was still flush from the huge success of *The Grapes of Wrath* (1939). Inevitably, she told Elizabeth, a big crowd of friends and strangers formed, as it always seemed to do in New York. She left soon afterward. The following weekend she went out to Crow House in Rockland County to visit Bessie and Henry. She was also happy to report that she had run into Leonard Ehrlich, who had recently joined the army. They had met by chance at a concert by the harpsichordist Wanda Landowska that Carson went to by herself. Leonard was there with David, Muriel, "and a whole little group from Yaddo." William Mayer was coming out to see her the following night, she told Elizabeth, on one of his quasi-professional visits.

Just after Carson moved in, she met a woman who won her heart again—or at least reawakened her erotic feelings. They met at the dentist, talking in the waiting room. Cheryl Crawford was a theatrical producer who at forty-one was fifteen years older than Carson. A thoroughgoing professional, Cheryl appeared shrewd, forceful, and

somewhat stern, but friends found her intensely domestic—she collected antiques and designed dream houses—and sympathetic. Carson was willfully ignorant, for a time, of Crawford's life outside the dentist's office: the older woman lived with her partner, Ruth Norman, who was a cookbook writer and restaurateur.

Carson went into detail about her feelings in a letter to Elizabeth in midwinter. She had met someone, she wrote, who in a short time had become dear and "precious" to her. She acknowledged that her attraction to Cheryl was lesbian without voic-

Carson had a crush on theatrical producer Cheryl Crawford, shown here in the 1940s.

ing her sexual feelings explicitly—no mean feat. There was a thick tension between them, Carson explained. Specific factors were keeping them apart—probably a reference to Cheryl's partner, Ruth. She did say to Cheryl that the "tension" in the relationship that distinguished it from her friendships with other women didn't necessarily mean sexual tension. Because of the circumstances that prevented their becoming closer, Carson anticipated that the physical experience she sought was not to be. She supposed at some point she would find herself alone and decided a sexual love affair was to be denied her. It seemed to her that God had in mind for her a solitary path.

This suggests that Carson had made an advance (or two) and was deflected. In a letter to Crawford after going to Columbus in late April, she acknowledged her mistake and hoped it would not hurt their friendship. She regretted the physical pass she had made at Cheryl. But she couldn't deny the intense tenderness she felt, which seemed to her could only be expressed physically. She was like a stupid child who tried to grasp what she could not have, she said. She explored her emotions and concluded that a fulfilling sexual relationship was not to be. Yet she persisted in looking for it. Whenever she reached out for it, however, she only hurt herself and sometimes those she loved, she told Crawford. Though she had accepted that an erotic physical relationship with a woman was not for her, she tried nonetheless to defy this fate. But she had also sought acceptance of her solitary state and believed she had found it.

This was, of course, not true: she did suffer from this quandary. But she also managed to preserve her friendship with Crawford, which was tactically wise, given Crawford's role in the theater world and Carson's long-standing interest in writing plays. Crawford would prove to be a good friend over the years: she loved, she later said, Carson's "quirky" sense of humor, her "formidable directness" (Carson had no small talk), and her enthusiasm for people as well as for books and music. What she did not like was Carson's "necessity to devour her friends." Crawford used the term *leech* repeatedly. But she also had a clear picture of Carson's sexuality and may have understood her on that score better than almost any of Carson's other friends. Carson "did have strong homosexual feelings," she said, "regardless of how physical they turned out to be." Perhaps it did not take any great insight to understand this, but Crawford's straightforwardness on the subject was rare at the time.

Two levels of reticence surrounded Carson and sexual preference: the reticence of those around her, and her own. Both were informed by the South, where the word *lesbian* was never used—ever. In such a setting, the Southern Gothic strain gave misfit artists like Carson the freedom to write about all kinds of taboo subjects, usually race but also homosexuality and any other topic deemed freakish, often with great sympathy, and even to make them the stuff of fine literature, as long as no one—the writer, her characters, or the critics—directly named the taboo. The refusal to do so was part of what made the whole enterprise gothic, in fact.

The other level of reticence concerned the real constellation of prejudices, harassment, discriminatory laws and ingrained customs, secrecy, and general homophobia that characterized American society in the first half of the twentieth century—even the literate and cultured world Carson moved in. Carson seldom had to grapple with these prejudices directly. But she was aware of them, and her awareness would have fed into her thinking about relationships and about her own sexuality. In those times, a person in Carson's situation had to come to terms with homosexuality rather than to revel in it or even feel good about it.

Carson referred a few times to herself as an "invert," which was the accepted term for lesbians and gay men in the 1930s and early '40s. Inverts were generally thought to be born that way; many believed homosexuality was genetic. Back when she first met Edwin Peacock and Reeves, Carson appears to have been aware that the lot of many twentieth-century American lesbians was to live in a homophobic society. Carson probably first got an inkling of this in 1935 or 1936, when Reeves told her what the scientific community, as embodied in sexologist Havelock Ellis, had to say about "inversion." Back then—until 1937—only a medical doctor could purchase Ellis's magisterial seven-volume *Studies in the Psychology of Sex*. Volume two, "Sexual Inversion," was especially pertinent. When Reeves was at Fort Benning, he managed to persuade a librarian at the Columbus Public Library to let him read the work, and he probably shared his findings with Carson. Later, when Bébé Smith idly asked what gay men did in bed, Reeves offered to locate for her the first four volumes of Ellis. (Bébé said that she did not want to learn any more.)

Carson told David Diamond in 1941 that she was reading Havelock Ellis's 1939 autobiography, *My Life*. Ellis's wife, Edith Lees, had been an "invert"; Ellis wrote of her, "Whatever passionate attractions she had experienced were for women." After their honeymoon, Ellis and Lees lived together only in the summers, and both pursued affairs with women. It is possible that their marriage was not consummated. Edith was diabetic—then a condition difficult to manage—and almost definitely suffered from bipolar disorder; she tried to commit suicide toward the end of her life. She was in the same position that Edith was, Carson wrote. For all of Havelock's greatness, he couldn't in the end help his wife, and she went mad. Carson seems to have taken away some thoughts on her love for women, her marriage, and the marriage's future. Like Edith Lees Ellis, Carson sought in her union with Reeves a kind of relationship that was marked by what Ellis said he had in his marriage: "the deepest sympathy possible with all chance to remain an individuality." Which might or might not include sex.

Reading Havelock Ellis would have impressed Carson and Reeves differently, Carson because of Ellis's acceptance of his wife's lesbianism. Yet she would have also read in *My Life* about how much pain his wife's affairs actually caused him, however much he accepted them in theory. Reeves had taken to calling the women Carson fell in love with her "imaginary friends"—a startling locution, as both knew they were in fact very real, *not* imaginary—and it is likely that her liaisons caused him distress. But Ellis's acceptance of his wife's "inversion" convinced Carson that, on balance, he didn't mind Edith's affairs—if true, a self-serving conclusion if there ever was one. Perhaps she tried to convince Reeves to rise above any jealousy. For his part, Reeves appears to have held out the hope that Carson was sexually attracted to men as well as women—telling himself that their union could be sexual, not just a kind of supercharged friendship or companionate marriage.

But Reeves may have taken away some other ideas as well, perhaps more theoretical than those he picked up in his earlier reading of

Ellis. Like Carson, he would have been comforted by Ellis's liberalism and his plea for public tolerance of homosexuality. Heretofore sexologists like Krafft-Ebing had written that homosexuals were outcasts, the "stepchildren of nature." As Ellis's biographer writes, Ellis "was the first heterosexual investigator to grant them dignity as complete human beings." But Reeves may have hoped to find in Ellis some endorsement of bisexuality, of the man who had sexual impulses toward (and experiences with) people of both sexes. And what if he was predominantly heterosexual? Could this experience be other than confirmation of bisexuality? Not until Alfred Kinsey's *Sexual Behavior in the Human Male* (in 1948) did the public begin to grasp how common it was for men to respond to other men sexually. Reeves's inability to find some validation of his feelings in Ellis's pages or elsewhere may have contributed to his own emotional troubles and tendency toward serious depression.

Carson was receiving mixed messages, too, and not only from Havelock Ellis. In her case, society's disapproval of homosexuality (which Reeves would also experience), however indirectly she felt it, may have been one of the factors that prevented her from expressing her own sexuality. For the most part, however, Carson found milieux in which all kinds of sexuality were accepted. Societal disapproval did not prevent her from initiating romantic sexual relationships with other women. But she had a pattern of throwing herself at women who were for whatever reasons inappropriate for her. The result was that she never had such a relationship with a woman, probably until the last years of her life. The absence of romance in the life of someone who was as obsessed with love and loving and who herself was as loving as Carson is regrettable.

In such a context, it is hardly surprising that Carson's feelings were so confused. In a letter to Newton Arvin in June, she told him that she had met and liked Cheryl Crawford, whom Newton knew, and that soon her feelings had somehow gone awry. Cheryl had no idea of a sexual friendship with Carson, which Carson understood. But a certain tense misery had crept into the relationship as well. As she had told Cheryl, she thought she had outgrown those kind of feelings, but a little demon inside her threatened to emerge from time to time.

8

Practically Paradise

As Carson was mourning the loss of the woman she loved, Annemarie, and was coming off an abortive romance with Cheryl Crawford, she got a letter from Reeves. It was the first she had heard from him directly in almost a year and a half. Reeves's reappearance in her life at this juncture seems extremely ill-timed. Carson, however, did not view it as such—perhaps even seeing it as a solution to the "demon" in her that she had naïvely thought she had outgrown. Sometime in late February 1943, as Carson wrote Elizabeth Ames, she received a letter from him that she found moving. She had returned Reeves's first letter to her unopened. The second one she opened and, presumably, read; at any rate, she preserved it. He professed his continued love for her, and in a gesture that seems to have won her over, he offered to start paying her back for the forged checks. "If you can use any money," he wrote, "I would be glad to repay some I owe you by having some sent from Washington each month. There are no strings attached to that offer and if you have all you need well and good." Reeves had a flair for drama and spoke movingly about war, fear, and the upcoming "baptism of fire."

Carson later learned that Reeves had enlisted about a year before, at Camp Upton on Long Island. He had gone from there first to Fort Jackson, South Carolina, and then on to Officers Candidate School at Fort Benning. He was now at Camp Forrest, Tennessee, where he was training with the Rangers, an elite U.S. Army corps meant to be the American answer to the British Commandos, trained for amphibious assaults, long-range reconnaissance, and attacks. The Rangers were required to show initiative, common sense, and sound judgment. To complete the training, candidates had to be in excellent physical condition and capable of great stamina. Certain skills were especially in demand: map reading, self-defense, marksmanship, scouting, mountaineering, and so on. Reeves, with his Eagle Scout expertise, his experience as a scoutmaster, his native intelligence, and his fine physical condition, was a natural candidate. Early on his superiors noted his clear leadership skills and marked him for advancement.

After returning Reeves's first letter unopened, Carson opened and seems to have responded to all his subsequent communications. She had ample time to read them over and think. We don't know, however, exactly how she answered him because no letters survive from Carson to Reeves from the period of their separation to Reeves's shipping off to England at the end of the year. In a letter he wrote Carson in November, Reeves told her he had burned her letters for the last nine months, prior to his embarkation overseas. While this was eminently sensible, in that keeping the letters with him during wartime was unwise, it is not clear why he had not instead returned her letters to her, or entrusted them to his mother or his siblings for safekeeping. Perhaps he wanted to downplay the likelihood that her letters would reveal his check forgeries.

That spring Reeves seemed to anticipate, recognize, and answer Carson's skeptical questions. In one of those first letters, she told Elizabeth Ames, Reeves had said he was grateful to her for allowing him to "atone" for that awful time when he was "sick." She was so relieved, Carson told Elizabeth, that the period of mental illness was over. A few months later he referred to his "expiation" early in the year. To Newton she wrote that Reeves's awful sick period was over. She told Elizabeth that it seemed to have disappeared without a trace.

Reeves's having acted as he did as some kind of "illness," then, was the reality they agreed upon, quite the opposite from the assumption she had made back when he was forging checks: that he was a bad person. Now, without any explanation, she seems to have decided it was all an illness and in the past. In the spring, she wrote magnanimously to Newton that she was sure that Reeves's soul was safe. She called the letter in which he said he wanted to atone for his actions highly moral and quite wise.

In April or early May, when Carson was still in Columbus, the two agreed to spend Reeves's upcoming five-day leave together. Reeves proposed a meeting at an Atlanta hotel. Carson balked; she preferred to see him in Columbus. "I will feel very strange going back to Columbus but if you say it is all right then I will be at ease," Reeves answered. He made a reservation at Columbus's Ralston Hotel.

Evidently the interval went well; Reeves thought it went extremely well. They visited Bébé and Lamar, who treated him like family again. He thrived, telling stories about life as a Ranger, radiating pride in the men under his command. "There have been few days in my life that were so soothing, calming and satisfying," he later said. Whenever Reeves talked about an occasion when they might meet in the ensuing months, he emphasized that their meetings should be calm and quiet, an antidote to their "mixed, hectic and insecure" relationship before they split up. He imagined sitting with Carson in sidewalk cafés, drinking and talking. "Can we have calm, pleasant hours together drinking and talking about the present and the future?" he asked. On their last day, she brought him a blue sweater that he cherished, bringing it overseas with him, wearing it "all the time," he said.

Reeves conveyed that he would do anything to win Carson back. As he saw it, she had cast him out and begun divorce proceedings; now here she was, eager to forgive him for the forged checks. And he was doing something about his drinking. He had stopped for good, he convinced her (and perhaps himself). His many references to drinking as central to their companionship in the future (his evocations of drinking in sidewalk cafés) suggest otherwise.

Carson was amply aware of his problems with alcohol. The two drank together. But it was one of the hallmarks of their relationship that Reeves was the only one who was acknowledged to have a drinking problem. Now and then he admitted it, acknowledging as well that he had abused drugs. In one letter, Reeves referred to his bad dreams but hastened to add, "But I don't take anything" and "I won't ever do that again." What he "used" instead, he wrote, was brandy.

Reeves may well have first been exposed to drugs at Seven Middagh. Auden was a notorious drug user, albeit a high-functioning one. He discovered amphetamine in the 1930s, which he ingested through Benzedrine inhalers every morning. He took Seconal every night to go to sleep. Auden called speed a "labor-saving device." He thought these drugs deserved a place in the pantheon of substances, or what he called "the mental kitchen," near to hand for writers, along with alcohol, tobacco, and coffee. Auden continued what he called "the chemical life" for twenty years with little apparent ill effect.

Sedatives, amphetamine, and other such drugs were easy to come by—Benzedrine could be bought at a drugstore—and their use was not usually considered criminal or dangerous in any way. Current thinking about addictive behavior aside, common sense says that if Reeves had a problem with alcohol, it was not a good idea for him to sample drugs, for he would likely develop a problem with them as well. If addiction was the "illness" that Carson thought had led him to forge checks, it had not gone away, though he and Carson both hoped it had either vanished or become manageable by the time of his wartime military career.

During Carson's stay in Columbus in the late spring of 1943, alcohol was on her mind for another reason. Her father, she discovered, was drinking a quart of whiskey a day, she reported to Elizabeth Ames. He said he wanted to stop, and Carson persuaded him to dig and plant a vegetable garden with her, as they had enjoyed it so much the year before. They both got excited about the prospect of tomatoes. But later that spring, Carson found Lamar Sr. in very bad shape again; she essentially had to dry him out on this visit, as he was shaking uncontrollably when she first saw him. She described for David how she would give him alcohol drop by drop, and he would swallow them, sitting at the table in his bathrobe, trembling. Another day he might get dressed in a suit and tie and sit at the table, trembling, drinking the liquor that his daughter doled out. He was in a lamentable state. To Elizabeth, Carson wrote sadly that he was seemingly not long for this world. The family could find nothing to combat his hopelessness. By the end of August, the tomatoes had withered and rotted.

But Carson was in Columbus only briefly before she packed and went off to Yaddo, arriving on June 8. The guests for the summer of 1943 included the writers Morton Zabel, Jean Stafford (with whom Carson shared a bathroom), and Agnes Smedley. Langston Hughes arrived with the African American writer Margaret Walker, who later commented, "Both Langston and I loved Carson—she was a little genius, she sure could write." That summer Carson and Hughes "threw dice for money" and ate fried chicken and drank champagne at a Black establishment in Saratoga Springs, probably Jimmy's. Another writer, Alfred Kantorowicz, became a close friend of Carson's and, soon afterward, Reeves's. Just arrived on American shores in 1941 after interment by the Vichy regime, "Kanto" was a prominent German intellectual and anti-Nazi, who, Jewish and a Communist, had been forced to leave the country after Hitler took power. He had helped to hold together the German exile community in the 1930s and fought in the Spanish Civil War. He had numerous supporters and friends in the United States, including Thomas Mann and Ernest Hemingway, but his Communist affiliation put him in a bad light with the authorities, and after the war he would return to Germany. In the years before American entry into the war, however, Kanto and his wife, Frieda, were well-loved figures both at Yaddo and in New York.

Jean Stafford, the wife of poet Robert Lowell, was a talented writer who was just finishing the novel that would make her reputation, *Boston Adventure* (1944). She was intensely curious about Carson, reporting to a friend of Lowell's that she was "by no means the consumptive dipsomaniac I'd heard she was, but she is strange." Like the other residents at Yaddo that summer, Stafford complained, Carson was leftist in her politics. (Stafford and Lowell at the time were not.) "Perhaps the most irritating of them all is Mrs. McCullers who, although she is a southerner, passionately hates the South," Stafford added.

As always, Carson's heart was an open book. The previous fall

Alfred Kazin, who became fond of Carson, had been on the same New York–bound train from Saratoga Springs, and made some remarks in his journal that explain part of her appeal:

> Carson was pure sensibility, pure *nerve* along which all the suffering of the South and the Smith family passed. She was all *feeling*, an anvil on which life rained down blows. . . . Tremulous elfin, self-pitying charm. Always problems of *identity*. Internality of the American Dostoevskian sort without the slightest political sense of the word. . . . The southern *isolato*.

On the train, Kazin said, she had a thermos of sherry that she poured into a paper cup. She was taken with some rambunctious soldiers on board and shared her sherry with them until Kazin told her to stop. He commented on what he saw as her ongoing trouble with sexuality and general sexual identity. "Love—loneliness—the silent cry of the fortress, the love of the abnormal," he remarked. "The boy-girl Reeves—David Diamond—Newton Arvin." Referring to the gardens at Yaddo, which were open to the public, he posed a question to himself: "Do you remember how she pranced around in the garden at Yaddo imitating a lunatic in front of those visitors who wondered what the place was?" As Langston Hughes well knew, Carson could be a lot of *fun*.

Carson was trying to focus. And not to concern herself with money—on top of the Guggenheim, she had a $1,000 grant ($16,000 today) from the American Academy of Arts and Letters. Not to think much about Reeves or her sexual preferences. Not to dwell on thoughts about her father. She had been working on *The Member of the Wedding*, which she was still calling *The Bride and Her Brother*, or just *The Bride*, since early 1941, and it was commanding most of her attention. On breaks from work on *The Bride*, she had written other major fiction, producing "A Tree. A Rock. A Cloud" and the remarkable novella *The Ballad of the Sad Café*. But until *The Bride* was finished, she told David Diamond, she felt like a cur chained to a stake. Indeed, she worked as hard as a dog—and yet had so little to show for it. To Bessie, she compared it to making pastry: "It is like making and cooking the pastry of an apple strudel flake by flake and then piecing it together. When

it must read so simply, like a coup de main," a surprise attack. It is a lovely simile and conveys the great care she was taking and the pride she felt in how she constructed and shaped it.

The first paragraph was so good that she could not resist showing it to people and reading it aloud. The first sentence she was especially proud of: "It happened that green and crazy summer when Frankie was twelve years old." She powerfully evoked the feel of a Southern deep summer day: "In June the trees were bright dizzy green, but later the leaves darkened, and the town turned black and shrunken under the glare of the sun. . . . The sidewalks of the town were gray in the early morning and at night, but the noon sun put a glaze on them so that the cement burned and glittered like glass. . . . The summer was like a green, sick dream."

She told Bessie that it was a piece of writing that was comparable to a poem, in which the smallest slip could be fatal. It had to be done carefully and beautifully, because if it were not like a poem, there wasn't much point to it. She compared it as well to a ballet in its intricacy, and in a moment of drama, she likened the project to invoking God on a desolate plain.

The novella *The Ballad of the Sad Café* appeared in *Harper's Bazaar* in 1943 but was not published in book form until 1951.

She was getting good news about her other writing. George had found *The Ballad of the Sad Café* among her papers and persuaded her to send it to *Harper's Bazaar*. (He had since moved on to *Mademoiselle*.) The magazine accepted it, and it appeared in August 1943, just before Carson left Yaddo for Columbus. The payment would take care of her living expenses for the next five months, she told Elizabeth. Once again her story was about love unevenly felt between eccentric outsiders. In this case Miss Amelia, "a dark, tall woman with bones and muscles like a man," who runs a general store in a small Southern town, falls in love with a hunchback dwarf, Cousin Lymon, who claims to be a distant relative. Her love is reciprocated for a time and she flourishes, adding a popular café to the store. She and Cousin Lymon live together in relative harmony for six years. Then her ex-husband, a handsome ne'er-do-well called Marvin Macy, to whom she had been married for only a matter of days, drifts through town and takes up with Cousin Lymon. After a physical battle between Miss Amelia and Marvin, he and the dwarf trash her property, stealing whatever they can and destroying the rest. She boards up her building and never appears in public again, though the townspeople know she still lives there because of the lights in her upstairs apartment. The reader is left with the ashes of the characters, and the story is imbued with sadness and loneliness. It ends with an evocation of a nearby chain gang and its "both somber and joyful" song (*BSC,* 71). But few readers were convinced of its "joyful" nature.

All was not well with *The Ballad,* for shortly after its publication, Carson received an anonymous letter (among other letters that were positive) accusing her of anti-Semitism. The relevant passage was on the second page of the piece and concerned Morris Feinstein. One character says of the hunchback, "I'll be damned if he isn't a regular Morris Feinstein." The townspeople, says the narrator, "nodded and agreed" with this assessment; Morris Feinstein had lived in the town "years before," says the narrator. "He was only a quick, skipping little Jew who cried if you called him Christkiller, and ate light bread and canned salmon every day. A calamity had come over him and he had moved away to Society City. But since then if a man were prissy in any way, or if a man ever wept, he was known as a Morris Feinstein" (*BSC,* 9). When the townspeople conjured up Morris Feinstein, it was less as a Jewish person than as a person possessed of a certain sensitivity carried to extremes. It is not clear how calling someone who is Jewish oversensitive is an anti-Semitic slur, but it could conceivably be taken that way.

At the time the story was published, the summer and fall before America entered the war, anti-Semitism was downright common in the United States. (Whether the writer can be given a pass for this kind of prejudice is another issue.)

The letter writer addressed himself "to [Carson,] the distinguished young writer I started to read but at the bottom of the second page you poke fun at the Jew." He made reference to "your friends Mr. Lewis [labor leader John Lewis? Writer Sinclair Lewis?] and Hitler perhaps too." Carson's defense was about the intent: she might be said to have "poke[d] fun" at the Jewish man, she said, but she didn't spare any of her characters on this score. (Perhaps the townspeople are guilty in a different way from Morris Feinstein, for thinking it "over-sensitive" to respond to being called a "Christkiller.") She felt, she told Alfred Kazin, "as Swift would have felt if somebody had accused him of actually cooking the babies." In fact, she sent a blizzard of telegrams and letters to Kazin, who described himself as "intensely Jewish" and who was currently looking ahead to *The Walker in the City,* his book about being the son of Jewish immigrants in New York. David Diamond got a similar blizzard of letters. She tried to put Kazin in touch with Diamond, presumably to mount some kind of Jewish defense of her story.

This is not to say that her distress at being accused of anti-Semitism in *The Ballad* was not genuine. She could barely sit still for trying to do something about it or to respond in some way—which was difficult, as the letter indicated it was from "An American," without giving the writer's name. She questioned Kazin, Diamond, and Newton Arvin about a possible response—prevailing on *Harper's Bazaar* to publish a letter—or perhaps something more, for writing such a letter would require a long disquisition about the ethics of aesthetics or how there was no room in her life or her art for prejudice. Interestingly, she was concerned about being unable to respond to her critic directly, perhaps based on her sense that the accusation of anti-Semitism was made on shaky grounds. She did not change the story between the *Harper's Bazaar* publication and the version finally published in book form as *The Ballad of the Sad Café: The Novels and Stories of Carson McCullers* in 1951. Nor was it changed when Martha Foley collected it for *The Best American Short Stories of 1944* in the interim. The letter would have shaken anyone, but it especially disturbed Carson.

In late May, after their five-day sojourn in Columbus, the tenor of Carson and Reeves's relationship changed. His letters from 1943 and 1944 supply a truly remarkable record of his intense, determined campaign to win her back. In the months to come, he wrote her about every two days. Even with the army's confused mail service, she got a steady stream of letters throughout the war. She wrote back, but not as often, and her letters are somewhat muted, if loving. A typical letter closes with a mild wish for his safety; she asked that Reeves take special care of himself. She would go for a walk in the cold, monochromatic winter landscape, she said, and think of him. She signed her letters, "Your, Carson."

Reeves, on the other hand, was an extremely compelling letter writer; even the most ignoble descriptions of, for instance, the dull daily routine of army life sparkle. His eloquence reached its highest points when he told Carson how much he loved her. It was not just that he told her so literally, though he did that, but rather that he "told" her in rhetorical turns that showed how much he understood her and loved her, with all her faults (though he did not see them as such) as much as her strengths. He was brilliant in naming and describing those strengths. He propped her up, and he seems to have meant it. His letters are full of the grit of camp life, but he also took it upon himself to be positive—if realistic—about what lay ahead. In one letter he wrote about the whippoorwills, the swifts, and the nighthawks but closed somewhat meditatively: "My life is as ordered as the times and circumstances allow. I am confident of my ability in my work and respect my job. I have the faith and trust of the people I work with, and I have the goodwill of the person I love most. Bullets and injury will never wreck these," acknowledging that "only death" could do that.

In the first of these letters, Reeves remembered something Carson had said to him about *The Member of the Wedding:* that Frankie "was the expression of [her] failure." He took great exception to the statement: "To me you are not and have never been a failure as a person. You were the best wife a man could have—coming home from work, in the evenings, in the bed, of hurried early mornings, at the market, in times of trouble. You were the most considerate, lovely and compatible person I could ever hope for as a life companion. . . . As long as I am alive you must *never* feel lost and lonely and cut off from anyone for you will always be the first and most dearest person in my life." The show of support must have comforted Carson, especially as her father declined and his death grew imminent.

Reeves conveyed that he would do anything to win Carson back. His very identity rested on her, on being her husband, on nurturing her talent. The problems that would arise from his so defining himself, from seeing her as the essential element of his being, were not far in the future. But even if he was aware of them, Reeves kept his head down and concentrated on seducing Carson anew.

We can assume that Carson was heartened by his letters and inclined to reconciliation; we can also assume that she used the word *forgive*. Reeves, too, used this locution and logic. "You know . . . how I feel about marriage," he wrote her in October 1943. "You know how I felt about our trouble. When we were no longer friends and were almost entirely apart I was almost destroyed." "Our trouble" was just a kind of hiccup in their relationship, Reeves implied. Both of them began to believe it.

Reeves's letters teemed with ideas for the future, after the war. Some were specific: he really wanted to work in China, for instance, where he said he had a friend and a promise of a job. He thought seriously about staying in the army and making a career of it. As early as mid-May, he was remarking that he had found out "new, good things about [my] self" but was hesitant about applying them until he saw the postwar world. He liked leading men and was good at it. He disliked inaction and wasting time. These qualities would put him in good stead later, but who knew what civilization would look like after the war?

In a later letter, Reeves expressed his eagerness to talk over plans with Carson. He had come to realize that he did not want to start life again in the United States. Carson was not to consider this "escapism," he cautioned, and continued with a strikingly astute self-examination that indicates how far he had come in those early months in the army. He wasn't fleeing anything, he wrote:

It is only that I seem never to have fully identified myself in America. I love deeply so much of this country but I have never found a place in it, mostly because of an uprooted home in youth and a wild adolescence with no security. There was also a complete lack of personal love until I knew you. After I was with you I coasted on your identity until I became alcoholic that year in New York. But the shock of our being apart straightened me out quickly and I have been of right mind since last spring.

Reeves felt himself reaching a new maturity in the army this time around. Perhaps he felt the military had finally recognized his potential—and allowed him to realize his potential. Carson wasn't to think the China plan had been discarded, he told her, but he had a "contingent plan." He might stay in the army and work in the AMG—the Allied Military Government for Occupied Territories—and work in "rehabilitation." He didn't define that word; presumably he meant reeducation and postwar support for those in occupied territories, Allied sympathizers, or enemy combatants. At this stage, it was probably not anticipated that the presence of U.S. forces in Europe would become a great point of controversy and, later, a political football. Every issue connected with the AMG would be challenged, not least the concept of "rehabilitation" that had attracted Reeves.

Or he would find work with a newspaper or magazine—or with some "commercial concern," he wrote. He was studying German and French, he told Carson. Whatever future he chose, he considered her essential to any plans. "I would like to think of us being in Europe together in whatever country my job might carry me. . . . This plan isn't by any means a daydream—I think of it very often. Would you like that? Our being together, being near each other?"

That fall they began to seriously consider remarriage. It was Carson's idea; she wanted to be as close as she could be, legally, in case Reeves was wounded or killed. She expressed reservations, probably related to sex—she may have been viewing theirs as a companionate marriage, without sex, while Reeves was probably not. But Reeves expected Carson from whatever direction the wind blew, and he reassured her that a traditional life together, married or not, was not for him.

Carson and Reeves spent his last leave before going to sea at the Fort Dix Officers Club. They took two trips into New York City, staying a couple of nights at Seven Middagh, where George Davis gave a party for Reeves. They saw David Diamond and friends for a night on the town; David, seemingly oblivious to Reeves's single-minded campaign to get Carson back, still had hopes for his relationship with Reeves, writing in his diary that Reeves had taken his hand in the taxi on the way back to Brooklyn the night before "and held it so tenderly." The evening, David wrote, left him "emotionally exhausted." Reeves agreed to see David before he sailed, but it is not clear whether such a meeting took place.

Though Carson and Reeves had thought their remarriage would take place on this leave, they decided they would not get married just then—not for any particular reason except the cumulative reservations they still had. One glitch was sex. Carson told Elizabeth that they were not having it and that she was happy about this: Now that Reeves was well, they loved each other as friends, with less of the tension that seemed to characterize a physical relationship. This point meant a lot to her, she said, possibly indicating her desire that the marriage exclude sex. By December, however, they had resolved *not* to remarry. She hoped Reeves would fall in love and get married, and that she would act as godmother to every one of his passel of eight children.

Further evidence of such misunderstanding centered on their thoughts about children. In one of the letters he sent while he was on board the ship taking his battalion to England, Reeves wrote, "We can't have children but we love them and when we are older we can certainly get one if we wish." A slew of uncertainties surrounds this juncture in their relationship. It was not clear what Reeves meant by *can't*. Were they unable to conceive a child, or had they been advised that doing so would be medically or emotionally unwise? It's not clear what Reeves meant when he said that they could "always get one" if they wished. Presumably he referred to adoption, but this is the first and only time the option comes up in correspondence between them, or between either of them and others. Finally, it's not clear what Reeves meant when he referred to a time "when we are older." Was he responding to some acknowledgment on her part that she was too young or that they were not mature enough to take the step? Whatever the case, they clearly were not seeing eye to eye on this important point—judging, at least, from the record of their correspondence. The only record of what Carson felt about children is an exchange she had with the writer and Nyack neighbor Hortense Calisher, and it seems fairly casual, not least because Hortense recorded it in Southern dialect: "Hortense, did you *want* yo chi'drun?" Carson asked, according to Calisher. "Ah didden. Ah always felt they would innafere with my work." If true, it is significant that in her dialogue with Reeves on the subject of children and their future, Carson's career was not mentioned.

No matter, Reeves said. "I certainly feel and am closer to you than any husband has been to a wife. You are constantly in my thoughts, even in dreams, but you must know that I love you in a real way as you are in the bright light of day." He felt strengthened, he said, by Carson's love and by her faith in him: "If it were not for the renewal of our love and friendship . . . I would not be the soldier I am now or have faith in the peace and the new world as I do."

In early 1944 Carson, like the rest of the country, was consumed by what was happening at Anzio. The town had become the focal point of the German resistance as the Allies fought their way up the peninsula on their way to take Rome. After three Ranger battalions landed safely, Axis forces responded, and the result was a bloody, prolonged deadlock. Because of the Ranger involvement, Carson became convinced that Reeves was at Anzio, and as reports came back of Ranger fatalities, she was nearly frantic.

At the same time, Carson was trying to get a job as a foreign correspondent and grew more and more upset by her failure. She wrote a number of letters to *Time,* and when they did not respond as she had hoped, she wrote to Clare Boothe Luce, the much-admired and multitalented writer, currently a congresswoman, who was also married to the publishing magnate Harry R. Luce. Her first letter received a form rejection, but then she became hopeful, hearing that Boothe Luce interceded. Carson's own lack of experience made it impossible for her to secure a foreign correspondent's slot, and she wrote a personal letter to Boothe Luce saying she understood. But she took it as a rejection. She had also wanted to join one of the armed services, but her doctor told her that no one with her history of lung problems would be accepted. Carson was frustrated. It must have seemed, behind a lot of this sense of rejection, that she was not getting what she wanted—which in fact happened very seldom.

This, on top of the news about the Rangers at Anzio, precipitated what she called a nervous attack, which she described as very frightening. Little else is known of how it manifested and whether she received treatment for it.

Finally a series of letters arrived from Reeves, who was not at Anzio. He was still in Britain, where he had been sidelined with a broken wrist, sustained when he fell off a motorcycle. He was given what he called a "staff job" and said he hated being away from his men. He had, it seemed, fallen naturally into a leadership role; coming back from a weekend off, he wrote Carson that although he had "the manner of a stern grandmother with them," the men were glad to see him on his return. That week they would be making a three-day trek of eighty-two miles. "My stoicism seems to be a comfort to them when the going gets rough and serious," he wrote. "I never grumble and neither do they."

On the eve of D-Day, Reeves sent Carson a remarkable letter from a craft bobbing in the English Channel, part of the huge armada making its way to the beaches of Normandy. He had been up late sipping Scotch, saved for the occasion, with the ship's skipper, nervous about the rough seas. He fully expected the coming days and nights to be "horrible, terrifying, miserable," he wrote. His company was to take Pointe du Hoc, with one company landing on Omaha Beach Charlie and going after enemy positions at Pointe de la Percée. A military account noted that "Lieutenant J. R. McCullers managed" to get a boat filled with crucial munitions and supplies near the shore. A newspaper article quoted Reeves as a member of that "Crazy Ranger Gang," struggling to gain a foothold near Pointe du Hoc, saying the Germans "aren't so perfect soldiers. If they were, they would have driven us out overnight. We were badly outnumbered; we were in a constricted position and we had no mortars." But, added Reeves, "Nobody had an intention of quitting and that was just too much for the Germans." Nearly two weeks after D-Day, on June 25, a telegram arrived saying Reeves had been "slightly wounded" in action. In context, that was good news, as it sidelined him for a few days—he spent time visiting with the returning inhabitants of Cherbourg and drinking strong coffee laced with cognac or the local calvados: "something like applejack, only better." He then rejoined his company as they made for the port of Brest, as part of the Allies' strategic objective of securing Atlantic ports so that critical materials could get through for their forces. Reeves then slogged through two miserable months in German-occupied territory trying to secure the ports; he had been able to visit liberated Paris for a day.

That summer Carson went to Yaddo with a slightly lighter heart. The retreat was only informally open; in residence were Elizabeth Ames, Agnes Smedley, Carson's friend Biddy Eustis, and the Ehrlichs: Leonard's brother Gerald and his family. Yaddo guests seldom had guests of their own, but that summer Reeves's younger brother, Tom, visited Carson there in fulfillment of a promise he had made to Reeves. Even more handsome than Reeves, blond-haired, hazel-eyed Tom, a homosexual who became somewhat open about it, had enlisted and gone overseas with the Air Corps. For unclear reasons that may have had something to do with his homosexuality, Tom was sent to a hospital in England, where Reeves visited him twice. "He is supposed to have done something wrong but I never did find out what and am not really interested," Reeves told Carson. Tom's visit in the summer of 1944 remains mysterious.

Carson was making little progress on her writing, caught up as she was in the war news. She was eager to go to Europe and made further inquiries about getting a position as a foreign correspondent or even joining the WACs. She soon realized that given her physical condition, both, especially joining the service, were impossible. Though she and those around her—including her doctors—were unaware that her history of rheumatic fever made heart problems and even further strokes likely, they knew that she was susceptible to every imaginable lung problem, especially pneumonia, which might in turn affect her heart.

Bébé Smith was alert to Carson's physical health—when she could turn her attention away from her ailing husband. In the summer of 1944, Bébé, then fifty-four, made a trip to New York to attend to her daughter. She was eager to see her other daughter as well, for Rita, who had graduated from the University of Miami the previous May, had also moved to New York City, getting an

Carson, about age twenty-three, and her sister, Rita, about eighteen, early 1940s

apartment on Bleecker Street. Rita—Skeet, Carson called her—was launched on a promising career as well. In her senior year, she had been a member of the *Mademoiselle* college board, a precursor of the guest editorship that Sylvia Plath would win in 1949 (and would use in her novel *The Bell Jar*), which introduced her to all aspects of magazine production. Rita was also making a name for herself in writing. Her story "White for the Living," published in *Mademoiselle* in June 1943, won an O. Henry Prize and was included in the same volume of prize stories as her sister's "A Tree. A Rock. A Cloud." For whatever personal reasons, which may have included financial ones, Rita decided to pursue a career in women's magazines. George Davis called in some favors—though Rita hardly needed help—and she interviewed around town, eventually taking a job at *Mademoiselle,* where she would rise to fiction editor.

Bébé returned to Columbus in July, and the Smith daughters hurried home when they received word that Lamar Sr. had died, on August 1, at the age of fifty-five. In the preceding two years, his life had taken an unmistakable downward path, consumed by depression and drinking. He seems to have shot himself at his workbench, with *The New Yorker* and *The Nation*, ready to take home with him, along with his hat, by the door. These preparations led family and friends to believe (or to claim) that he had died suddenly, but Lamar almost surely committed suicide. The survivors' prevarication about the cause of death increased the strain felt after the funeral; on the other hand, it might have helped the family to keep at a distance the guilt and sorrow that might have arisen around Lamar's real cause of death. No doubt they all felt that they could have done something to prevent his suicide, but Lamar's poor health would have killed him soon enough. Carson could comfort herself with the reminder that she had shown her father plenty of love in his final months; indeed, there was seldom any shortage of love in the Smith household. She would have remembered, for instance, the vegetable garden that she and Lamar had put in a year earlier and their talk of tomatoes.

Reeves wrote that he was "deeply shocked and grieved" by her father's death; he had probably been told the real cause. "He was such a kind and gentle man. No man loved his family as he did," Reeves wrote with palpable sincerity. Carson told Newton that she felt more grief than she had expected and found the death terribly unsettling. There were "swarms" of details for Bébé to deal with well into the fall, and after thirty-one years of marriage, she was desolate. Under the strain, she collapsed and was hospitalized for a few days. She decided that she could not continue living in the Stark Avenue house. After the family got a good lawyer who could help them with the finances, the Smiths were able to rent out the house in order to meet the mortgage payments on it until they could sell it. The jeweler's business had to be sold, Lamar's insurance collected, and the estate otherwise settled. By September 1, just a month after Lamar's death, Carson and Bébé had moved to Nyack, New York, to a rented apartment that Bessie Breuer found for them in a building owned by Helena Clay, a local landowner who became a friend.

Bébé moved north in part because she wanted to be near her daughters. Rita was more or less established in New York City, though her heavy drinking had by then crossed the line into alcoholism. She had also developed a full-blown fear of elevators. (Friends noted that she worked in an office on a high floor and walked up the fire stairs rather than take the elevator.) Rita planned to come out to Nyack every weekend.

Bessie not only found them their apartment but told them what bus to take to Nyack, then met their bus. She had gone to her Nyack neighbors Ben and Rose Hecht; they were away, but she picked armfuls of flowers in their conservatory, which she put into vases and bowls in the Smiths' new Nyack home. At the bus stop, Bessie met Bébé for the first time, finding her a "distinguished rather slender woman" who was "restrained, cultivated in manner." (Perhaps Bébé *seemed* restrained in comparison to the effusive Carson.)

The apartment did not have enough space to accommodate all three Smiths and their household effects, so Bébé started looking for a house to buy. She loved the area, especially after finding a Carnegie library right downtown; she was an "omnivorous" reader, especially of detective stories and murder mysteries. (Carson was more drawn to what is today called true crime.) Bessie Breuer and Henry Poor of course lived nearby, in New City, on distinctly bohemian South Mountain Road. Nyack was a similar community, with beautiful

Bébé bought the house at 131 South Broadway, Nyack, in 1945.

old buildings and houses overlooking the Hudson, close to a charming downtown that was the commercial hub of Rockland County. Incorporated in 1872, the town, an "inner suburb" of New York City, lies nineteen miles from the northern end of Manhattan, just over an hour's drive. It was known for its resident artists, theater people, and writers. Edward Hopper was born in Nyack and grew up there. When Carson lived there, its most widely known residents were Charles MacArthur and his wife, Helen Hayes; and Ben and Rose Hecht. MacArthur and Hecht were successful playwrights and screenwriters whose collaborations included *The Front Page* (1928) and *Twentieth Century* (1932), as well as the recent films *Gunga Din* and *Wuthering Heights* (both 1939). The actress Helen Hayes insisted on being called, locally, Mrs. MacArthur. The slightly tattered, bohemian aspect of Nyack appealed to Bébé, Carson, and Rita.

Carson was happy in Nyack, absorbed by war news and her correspondence with Reeves, mostly, but also working on *The Bride*. She'd never been in a place so quiet, she exulted to Newton—it was a veritable Eden. From time to time, she also busied herself with essays and reviews. *Vogue* published two of her wartime pieces: "Night Watch over Freedom" on January 1, 1941, calling for solidarity with Britain; and "We Carried Our Banners—We Were Pacifists Too," appearing on July 15, 1941, concerning the sad necessity of abandoning earlier principles for the pragmatics of fighting fascism and America's attackers.

Excited by the proximity of interesting neighbors, Carson made some social forays into Nyack and New City. She had dinner at Henry and Bessie's place on South Mountain Road; Bessie served an impressive veal roast and, in honor of Carson, two Southern dishes, collards and sweet potatoes. An evening with Ben Hecht and his wife, with Henry and Bessie also guests, went well until Rose Hecht, in a discussion about Black civil rights, said she thought that Southerners knew best how to treat Black people—as children, handled kindly. Carson ignored the nod to the South, and though she responded "with restraint," according to Bessie, her "dismay and anger" were visible, and Bessie knew the Hechts and Carson would not become friends. For Thanksgiving, Carson and family went to a dinner hosted by Kay

Boyle, where Luise Rainer was a guest; Carson brought Al Kantoro-wicz and his wife. Carson loved it all: the proximity of new and old friends, the accessibility of the village vis-à-vis Manhattan, the situation on the Hudson River, and the comfortable feel of the town.

Ensconced in the Nyack house, Carson received a letter from Reeves dated September 17, 1944, from the battle at Brest, that related a troubling brush with the authorities and a transfer to a new company. Reeves said it was a long story that really began in the States, summing up: "The old man and I had a falling out finally and lesser authority bowed to higher authority." The "direct reason" was "very sad and tragic":

> It involved patrols sent out from my company. I took a patrol in one direction and Meltzer in another. We were to return at a certain time at the point of departure. There was one place that was a hot spot and everyone was told not to go there. . . . I told Meltzer specifically not to go near this place but being eager and impulsive he barged in. He and four of the men were killed. I spent eight hours getting to them to see if any were only wounded but they were all dead. Three of us were wounded slightly doing this. . . . The offshot [*sic*] was that someone had to be the goat and I was elected. The old man asked that I be transferred for "not properly disciplining my officers."

Many soldiers and officers felt he had got a "raw deal," he said. It was hard to leave his old battalion, with whom he had lived and fought for a long time. It was especially hard to lose Robert Meltzer, in civilian life a Hollywood screenwriter and the one close friend he had had "in years." They had made all sorts of plans in New York, Reeves said, and Meltzer had been especially keen on meeting Carson.

What exactly happened with Reeves and "the old man" is difficult to decipher, but if he was demoted, it was not by much. He remained a combat officer, and in a November 8 letter to Carson, he spoke of men he had been with "for over two months" (*ING*, 91).

In December Carson was terrified by news of the fighting in the Ardennes and at the Battle of the Bulge. On December 3, Reeves wrote her a long letter from a "rest hospital" in Belgium, where he had gone after weeks of fighting. He also wrote Muriel Rukeyser a long letter on December 4, detailing his activities in Europe since D-Day. After a brief pause in the fighting in a quieter sector in Luxembourg, he told Muriel, he had spent three straight weeks fighting in rainstorms after "wallowing in muddy foxholes and ditches—dodging all German ordnance in the book." Then "I began to poop out. It seems I am not getting any younger and living in the mud, rain, and cold so long gave me a touch if rheumatiz in my hips." He was sent to the rear to rest for two days, then hospitalized. He thought everything in the hospital was wonderful: "They seem to understand just how a man feels coming out of battle and that it takes only a few simple normal things to put the light of life back in his eyes." It was heartrending to see the men brought into the hospital, he said. Those with cases of battle fatigue were, if possible, worse than the badly wounded.

On December 6, Reeves, eager to rejoin his men, was sent back to his company. But three days later his hand was "smashed" in a barrage, and he learned he would have to be hospitalized for six weeks to three months. He had been diving for a dugout and broke several bones in his left hand and received a rear end full of shrapnel, which was easily enough removed. He was evacuated by plane from Paris to England, where he awaited either reassignment to a desk job or a transfer to the States.

In the hospital, Reeves had word that his old battalion—the one he had commanded before the disciplinary incident—had been "completely annihilated" near where he had left them. He was especially sorry to hear about the death of a sergeant, a Polish man from Rochester, "who sort of looked after me for nearly three years." At D-Day, while Reeves was coming ashore, his foot had caught under a vehicle; the sergeant had got him loose, saving him from drowning. In Brest, Reeves and three others had been pinned down by machine-gun fire. The sergeant made his way around the Germans and routed them from behind. Worse, the sergeant had hoped to transfer with Reeves in September, but Reeves had talked him out of it. He probably would have been alive if he'd made the move (*ING*, 117). Such was the news Reeves had to digest during the "days of limbo"—as Carson called them—while he waited to return from the U.K.

Reeves finally shipped back to the United States in February 1945, though he officially remained in the military while further work was done to repair his hand. But his time in the war was over, along with the possibility of injury or death, and the elation he felt offset any lingering depression. Carson, too, was overjoyed.

9

Our Love for Each Other Is Like a Sort of Natural Law

Reeves and Carson were married again on March 19, 1945, in a courthouse in New City, Rockland County. After the ceremony, they went to Crow House on South Mountain Road to notify Henry and Bessie. A week later Reeves wrote to Edwin Peacock to ask for the blessings of their oldest friend. They missed Edwin playing a Bach concerto on the gramophone, as he had at their first wedding. "But we were happy again anyway," Reeves added.

Reeves is cut from a different cloth than most people, Carson told her friend Kay Boyle. Not everyone understood him. Her admiration for her once-again husband was genuine. She believed, and others agreed, that he was one of the smartest and most talented (at what was not yet clear) men she had met, that he had read almost everything and was often summarily sure he was right in arguments, although the latter does not seem to have put anyone off.

Carson seems to have believed from their first meeting that she and Reeves were bound to each other for life, more profoundly than other couples, and despite their troubles, she still believed it or at least accepted it. They loved each other in an elemental, essential way, she wrote Reeves in November, in a way that was beyond their control. They had a touching respect for the institution of marriage as well.

Both of them had treated it as a foregone conclusion that once the difficulties between them were cleared up, they would remarry.

Only because Reeves was in the army did they need a legal marriage, Carson said. Presumably once they were married, there would be less confusion about his allotments and his legal address. Carson explained their thinking to Newton Arvin shortly afterward. She reminded him that they had had long talks about Reeves when they were last at Yaddo, when Carson thought Reeves could well die overseas. The time apart had allowed them both to think about their relationship. Even when Carson had resolved to stop loving Reeves—after the check forgery—she found she couldn't. They were simply attached. Since that was the case, they resolved to remarry.

Both of them, while they were apart, had been involved with members of the same sex. In deciding to remarry, they overlooked these matters or at least were content to take refuge in deep denial. Reeves seems not to have committed his thoughts to paper. But Carson's letters to Newton and to Elizabeth Ames clearly and specifically differentiate her feelings about Reeves from her feelings for Annemarie and Cheryl. Her relationship with Reeves was chaste, she insisted. Once remarried, she never said another word on the subject of their sexual relations, so it is hard not to conclude that they did not resume then.

Another wrinkle in the fabric of their relationship would quickly come to prominence: Reeves's ambition, as a writer or otherwise. He spent several months in a military hospital in Utica while his doctors debated a bone graft operation on his wrist. He continued to press for an appointment in the AMG; he felt sure he would get one, though he feared it would be in the Pacific rather than Europe, where he and Carson dreamed of going. He made several trips to Washington, D.C., to try to nail down a position; he also spoke to some people there about a possible intelligence job. In July 1945, however, the doctors at Utica judged him permanently disabled and recommended him for "permanent limited service," sending him to Camp Wheeler in Macon, Georgia.

Reeves was furious. He had no interest in staying in the army if it was only to train the "shoe clerks and ribbon salesmen" reporting for service in the South into peacetime troops (*ING,* 148). While he acknowledged to Carson that the infantry was his first love, and that he liked leading men in battle, he had no interest in bossing trainees. He would be resubmitting his papers for assignment to the AMG, but he feared it was little use. If he had any future in the army, however, he would have to stick with his assignments.

Thus he was in Macon for much of 1945. He and Carson debated whether she would join him in a little apartment there. He told her in November that he thought his best career plan might be to return to Germany for work of some kind, but he would take a job in the United States in "factory management" if he could get one, presumably drawing on his experience in Rochester in 1941. If Carson would not join him, he said, he would not go back overseas. He would move heaven and earth and do the impossible for her: "I have no intention of allowing us ever really to grow old." She decided not to move to Macon and in fact does not seem to have visited Reeves there. Perhaps the prospect of Georgia brought back painful memories.

In the months that followed, Reeves looked into other possibilities, including becoming a doctor or perhaps a psychiatrist. The free or low-cost tuition guaranteed by the G.I. Bill appealed to both him and Carson, and he looked into accelerated programs leading to an undergraduate degree, preparatory to medical school, in two years. He spoke to a dean at Harvard, who was encouraging, and when Reeves missed an application deadline for the program there, he and Carson asked Newton to find out about such programs at Amherst, which was just down the road from Smith. Reeves hoped to enroll as early as that June.

He continued exploring options for medical school for many months. When he visited Newton at the beginning of February to learn more about the program at Amherst, Carson wrote Newton that Reeves had been full of beans when he left Nyack. In March he went in person to Harvard, hoping he might work something out despite the missed deadline. The veterans' adviser there told him he could take a test later that month to qualify for admission in June. But two deans at the medical school conveyed some sobering truths. At Reeves's age, thirty-one, he would not be able to practice medicine for nine years.

He was older than most veterans availing themselves of the G.I. Bill, probably too old for protracted schooling, especially as he had no undergraduate credits to apply toward a degree.

Reeves had managed to take numerous leaves from the Utica hospital and from Camp Wheeler. Now, he and Carson were getting used to a new home. With the help of their landlady, Bébé had managed to find a house for sale that was right next to the building where she and Carson were renting. The house at 131 South Broadway, which Bébé bought for $9,000 (she had sold the Stark Avenue house for the same price), was a handsome three-story, shuttered and white clapboarded Second Empire–style Victorian with a mansard roof, adorned with all manner of Victorian details, including decorative friezes, bracket cornices, and generous porches with views of the Hudson. The house had been divided into apartments. Bébé installed a bathroom on the third floor, where Reeves and Carson would live, and moved into an apartment on the ground floor, which had access to the garden and room for Rita, who would join them on weekends. Carson loved her new home. She often asked friends whether they thought, as she did, that the house looked as if it belonged in the South. As indeed it did, recalling the wooden Victorian houses with large and welcoming porches that she was familiar with in Southern cities.

Reeves spent his leaves in Nyack, cleaning out the basement and painting and sprucing up the attic apartment. He had to return to the South soon, and in the meantime Carson was eager to get moving on *The Bride,* which she had brought into the home stretch. She decided she would like to go to Yaddo again. Because of the war, there likely was no formal application to make for residency; she simply cabled Elizabeth Ames that she would arrive on June 26 and stay until August 31, 1945.

The Yaddo mansion remained largely unused, so the few artists and writers in residence, all friends of Elizabeth Ames, stayed in the outbuildings. Carson, however, was allowed the tower room. The colonists included Leonard Ehrlich, his brother Gerald, and Gerald's family; the writer Jerry Mangione, author of *Mount Allegro,* a successful 1943 autobiographical novel; Howard Doughty, a Smith English professor and friend of Newton's; the painter Eitaro Ishigaki and his journalist wife,

Ayako; the composer Alexei Haieff; and the writer Eleanor Clark, who had been a frequent guest at Seven Middagh Street.

Carson had few distractions that summer, and she was determined to finish the manuscript before fall. She put Elizabeth, who had agreed to read it, through draft after draft and finally sent it on to her agent, Ann Watkins, who had been representing Carson since 1943, referred by Watkins's client Kay Boyle. Even then, she was not finished. Kay gave it a thorough read and was for the most part extremely positive, but she objected to a scene in which twelve-year-old Frankie meets and drinks with a soldier in a café who talks her into going upstairs to his room with him. When he makes a move, Frankie hits him with a glass pitcher; later she is unsure whether she might have killed him. Kay thought this didn't fit. The soldier is a generic character, she said, and were Carson to flesh him out, the tenor and focus of the book might change. She also felt Frankie's brother Jarvis and his bride, Janice, were cardboard characters; she wanted Carson to make them fully rounded, especially because Frankie wishes so terribly to join them on their honeymoon. Carson was so affected by Kay's comments that she asked Ann Watkins to return the manuscript so she could work on it further, but in the end she didn't act on either suggestion.

Carson promptly turned to a new friend, a remarkable Southern writer several years younger than her, Truman Capote. Two years earlier Truman, a prodigy like Carson, had walked into the *Mademoiselle* office with a story and had been given an audience with George Davis and Carson's sister, Rita. That first story didn't appeal to Rita, but *Mademoiselle* published "Miriam," an eerie tale about a malevolent little girl and the trouble she wreaks, in 1944. Rita brought Truman up to Nyack to meet Carson sometime in the spring of 1945.

Carson gave Truman her manuscript to read, and he said he loved it. He didn't agree that the soldier should be cut, arguing that the introduction of this new and dangerous character throws the whole story into a very effective imbalance. A mutual friend noted that Carson "was enchanted with [Truman] and regarded him as her own private little protégé." She sensed a kindred soul and determined to help him in his career. He had not yet published a book, and Carson was keen to get his work in front of editors who could change that. First, Rita helped her find him a literary agent, Marion Ives, who had worked with Rita at *Mademoiselle.*

Carson no doubt wished she could send Truman to her editor, but on this subject, confusion reigned. The previous year Bob Linscott had moved to Random House, taking many of his authors with him. Now that *The Member of the Wedding* (the new title) was finished, he hoped that Random House could publish it. But Carson had enjoyed a productive meeting with Houghton Mifflin's Hardwick Moseley and Ann Watkins. Moseley, not

Truman Capote, c. 1949

strictly speaking an editor, involved himself in many aspects of book production and was familiar to Carson from her good experience with the publication of *The Heart Is a Lonely Hunter.* (He had thought of the title.) She decided to stay at Houghton Mifflin.

Linscott was appeased by Carson's new discovery and took Capote on, signing a contract with him for a novel, which would turn out to be *Other Voices, Other Rooms.* When it was published in 1948, the author photo, showing Truman prone on a sofa, aiming a boyish, seductive gaze at the camera, caused a huge stir and made publication a much-talked-about event. It was Bob Linscott who picked the photo.

Clearly Truman and Carson, two literary wunderkinder from the South, would either become great friends or great enemies. Part of Carson's appeal to Truman was in fact the South. "Carson's family were wildly Southern," noted Phoebe Pierce, who once visited Carson and was subjected to "Brother-man"—Lamar Jr., up for a visit with his new wife, Virginia—playing the piano extremely badly, summoned back again and again by cries of "Play it again, Brother-man." Truman was also attracted to Carson's eccentricity, elements of which he shared:

odd looks, a glowing reputation as a prodigy (and a corresponding childishness in demeanor), and a fondness for drink.

He was drawn to Carson from their first meeting:

> The first time I saw her—a tall, slender wand of a girl, slightly stooped and with a fascinating face that was simultaneously merry and melancholy—I remember thinking how beautiful her eyes were: the color of good clear coffee, or of a dark ale held to the firelight to warm [Carson's eyes were gray]. Her voice had the same quality, the same gentle heat, like a blissful summer afternoon that is slow but not sleepy.

Carson and Truman never did become great friends—possibly because they were so alike, or because they both had outsize egos, or because each saw the other as a competitor.

⟨⟩

Another important figure in Carson's story entered her life that year. Carson and Bébé found his return address on a card he sent for Christmas 1945, and on January 9, Bébé wrote a letter to Jordan Massee, asking him and his friend Paul Bigelow to come to Nyack for dinner. She and Carson had wanted to contact him for at least a year, she said, but hadn't known how to. Carson had learned Jordan was in New York City four years before, while she was living at Seven Middagh, and a soda jerk in Brooklyn Heights had introduced her to Paul Bigelow. Paul recognized her name, and the two of them fell on each other like old friends. Yet they did not exchange addresses and phone numbers and had no way of reaching each other.

Jordan was probably equally pleased to have word of Carson. He and she shared a quasi-mystic bond based in the belief that they were some kind of cousins, or barely missed being each other's cousins. Before either was born, Jordan's father, Jordan Sr. (known as "Big Daddy," and he was indeed a model for the character with that name in Tennessee Williams's *Cat on a Hot Tin Roof*) and Mabel Carson, Bébé's cousin, fell in love with each other but did not marry because their families disapproved of the familial connection and forbade it. Early in Carson's friendship with Jordan, the two spent a good deal of time figuring out just how they were related (and how they *would* have been related had Jordan married Mabel). Finally, Carson said that trying to figure it out gave her a headache, and they agreed they would always say they were double first cousins. (Jordan believed they were actually third cousins.)

Carson was immediately devoted to Jordan and Paul. Jordan, whose father was a hugely successful entrepreneur and businessman in Macon, grew up privileged, rich, and homosexual, dubbed by an adoring nanny "King the Beauty," a nickname Carson loved—though more often she called him "Boots." He was supportive of her and defensive on her part without being uncritical; she liked his sharp tongue, even at her own expense. Three years older than Carson, Jordan had moved to New York in 1941, after spending the previous decade shuttling back and forth from Europe. He brought something of the South into Carson's life; she liked to have Southerners in her orbit. He also kept detailed diaries over the years, noting which meals Carson took with him and Paul, who else was present, and so on. He was equally protective of Bébé, whom he loved, he said, quite as much as he did Carson, and he was adamant about Bébé's importance to her talented daughter. "Without that mother," he stated

categorically, "the genius of Carson McCullers could never have survived and flourished." Furthermore, he observed perceptively, Bébé fit like a glove into the more cosmopolitan world that both her daughters now inhabited in New York. She "moved from a narrow and provincial background into the broader sphere to which Carson as a free soul, and as a celebrated writer, had gravitated, and moved with a grace and an adaptability that still amaze me."

Carson's honorary cousin and close friend Jordan Massee, undated

Jordan was perhaps the only one of Carson's relatives and close friends who did not like Reeves, maybe because he was aware of the pain Reeves caused her. Still, he probably never told her of his dislike and tried to be fair: "There was no time, until the final break between them, when I did not fully appreciate his importance to Carson," he recalled. Jordan was delighted to be in touch with Carson and her family.

Carson delivered *The Member of the Wedding* in its final form in November or December 1945. As with *The Ballad of the Sad Café,* *Harper's Bazaar* was publishing it first, and quickly, in its January edition. The novel's book publication date was moved from February to March 19, perhaps because of a change Carson insisted on making in the jacket flap copy. Originally it compared Frankie to Mick Kelly of *The Heart Is a Lonely Hunter,* but Carson felt strongly that this novel should not be promoted as a rehash of the earlier one. Frankie had to be unique, she said, or there was no point. Both Hardwick Mosley and Houghton Mifflin editor Dorothy Hillyer agreed with her.

Carson had worked hard to distinguish Frankie not only from Mick but from herself. It is impossible to overestimate how much she had riding on this book, which is not directly autobiographical. Carson had never wanted to run away with Lamar Jr. and his wife; she had never picked up a soldier or cold-cocked him with a beer bottle; she had never formed a bond with a very young neighbor boy as Frankie does with John Henry; and she had two parents, not one bewildered father. But even with these particulars, there are plenty of small parallels between the artist and her art. Frankie's father, for instance, is a jeweler who spends all his time at his workbench, just like Lamar Sr. Apart from these factual points, the feeling of the book seems consistent with Carson's emotional landscape—most prominently, her feeling that she was an outsider, a member of no group.

Carson was trying to capture the essence of her awkward adolescence. "In a bungling way," she later said, "I was trying to combine the freshness and the poetry of my own childhood but it seemed formless. . . . I was faced with the task of communicating a vision of life with the poetry and passion of a 12-year-old child." Over the five years she took to write it, interrupted constantly by the war, by Reeves's travails, by her loves and infatuations, and by her incessantly nomadic life, she put excruciating care into each word. Years later, when a Houghton Mifflin employee asked her to name her favorite piece of her own writing, she answered like a shot that it was the first paragraph of *The Member of the Wedding*. According to the Houghton Mifflin employee, Carson "went on to say that she had worked on this one [paragraph] for two weeks before it finally satisfied her, and that perhaps the best single sentence she had ever written was the book's opening line—'It happened that green and crazy summer when Frankie was twelve years old.'"

The Member of the Wedding, published in March 1946, did not get the reviews Carson had hoped for.

The roots of *The Member of the Wedding* in Carson's own life and imagination went deeper. Before she had the "illumination" that she should want to "join" her brother's wedding, "Frankie was just a girl in love with her music teacher" (*ING*, 32), Carson later wrote. In the final version of the book, no trace of the girl or her teacher remains. But the feelings of a love—like hers for her piano teacher Mary Tucker—that cannot connect with its object, a vague free-floating emotion that the lover cannot even name, and the sense of inexplicable loss when nothing existed in the first place pervade the novel, the source of its bittersweet mood. The emotions Carson felt when she was just such a girl suffuse the novel. More relevant, they anchor it in Carson's psyche; she and *The Member of the Wedding* were one. So the issue of its critical reception was momentous. Carson expected nothing less than raves.

She did not get them. The notice in *Kirkus Reviews*, coming out in mid-January, two months before the publication date, was grudging: "An odd, unhappy little story with the bizarre, neurotic atmosphere [she] achieves." At the time, *Kirkus* notices were available only to industry professionals, and Houghton Mifflin might have kept this one from Carson. The earliest commercial and literary reviews, appearing on March 24, were mixed. Virgilia Peterson in the *New York Herald Tribune* praised her earlier work but found this novel lacking in "breadth." Sterling North in *Book Week* noted Carson's success in creating "an uncomfortably unforgettable" protagonist, but he found flaws in Frankie's motivations. The novel got a near-rave in *The New York Times Book Review,* however; Isa Kapp criticized its static quality but concluded, "Rarely has emotional turbulence been so delicately conveyed. Carson McCullers's language has the freshness, quaintness and gentleness of a child." But Kapp's review appeared on page five, was just two columns long, and had no illustration.

The reviews that appeared a week later, on March 30, delivered more of the same qualified praise. George Dangerfield, in *The Saturday Review of Literature,* tagged Carson as "a suggestive rather than an eloquent writer, but often seems to present us less with a meaning than with a hit," though he called her "both a mature and fine writer." *Time,* the following day, said the novel was "strictly limited by the small scope of its characters" but was "often touching." The reviews were mostly favorable, but were hardly raves.

Edmund Wilson's review in *The New Yorker* proved devastating to Carson. *The Member of the Wedding,* he wrote, "has no element of drama at all." Two things happen in the novel, he noted: Frankie tries to go on the honeymoon with her brother and his bride, and she "gets over it a little later, when she finds a sympathetic girlfriend." That's all that happens, he wrote, "but it takes her 65,000 words." He criticized the "formless" quality of the "interminable conversations," though he praised Berenice's speech as "perfect." Overall, he wrote, in the review's most damning pronouncement, "The whole story seems utterly pointless."

Wilson was at the top of the critical heap, and Carson prized *The New Yorker* above almost all other venues. She vowed never to read her reviews again. It is an understatement to say that her conception of herself as a writer changed at this point. She would not publish another novel for fifteen years, and she never spoke as glowingly and fondly of any of her work as she did about *The Member of the Wedding.*

All she could cling to, after the book's reception, was the perfection of the novel's first paragraph, of the first sentence.

Even the favorable critics, in a way, missed the point of the book, partly by failing to understand how it reflects the way children see the world, where *everything* is drama, including many things that are lost to adults. The novel quickly became one of her most warmly received works in part because of its profound portrayal of childhood and in part for its exquisite language. The rest of the novel lives up to that first paragraph.

The lowest point may have been an evening almost two months later, after the reviews had had plenty of time to sink in, when the Houghton Mifflin editor Hardwick Moseley visited her in Nyack. Carson evidently got drunk and started crying like a baby, blaming him for her bad reviews, especially Wilson's. Her letter to him the next day was full of apologies, though she said she wouldn't make excuses. She then proceeded to excuse herself on the grounds of her generally poor health and the "disturbing" month before. The previous evening, she said, had been part of one long party with friends that began early that day. When drinking goes on too long, she acknowledged, it becomes "fatal" and, in her case, doubly fatal.

Luckily, she had been at Yaddo when the reviews actually arrived. It helped to be around empathetic fellow writers. Newton proved a comfort, as did Howard Doughty, the writer and Smith professor with whom Newton was then romantically involved. After Newton's departure at the end of the month, Doughty was a good companion. He made Yaddo tolerable, Carson told Newton. Of course she loved Elizabeth Ames and Leonard Ehrlich, but there's no trace of fun misbehavior about them, she found—she was sure Newton would agree.

No sooner had Newton departed than a new influx of guests provided plenty of the "naughtiness" Carson desired that spring at Yaddo. Among them was Marguerite Young, the author of two books of poetry and *Angel in the Forest*, a strange study of the New Harmony commune in Indiana, where her mother lived. Young's supposed riposte to an amorous Carson is said to have been: "Well, Carson, if I did love any woman, it would be you." That taken care of, Young became a friend.

Truman Capote took the train up from New York City on May 1

with another Yaddo resident, writer and Condé Nast editor Leo Lerman. The latter remembered Carson with "a cup of tea in one hand and sherry in the other, putting them down now and then and writing a few lines of verse." He also recalled playing the game of Murder, a pastime of the Seven Middagh residents, and passed some evenings dancing. Katherine Anne Porter was at Yaddo again that summer, reminding Leo of a Southern belle, "most like Bette Davis playing Fanny Skeffington." One evening Lerman wrote in his journal that someone put some rhumba music on the phonograph, and Katherine Anne "jumped up and did what looked like the shimmy."

Carson and Truman became—for this spring, at least—inseparable. One observer was transfixed by the sight of the two of them dancing one night in the gigantic Yaddo kitchen: "McCullers, the taller of the two, jouncing mannishly while the tow-headed, bottom-heavy Capote spun around her, inventing clever pirouettes." Capote's biographer notes that Carson rifled through his wardrobe that spring, borrowing his crisp white shirts and even his shoes. In one drawer she found a piece of paper giving his legal name, Truman Streckfus Persons. When she threatened to call him that in front of the other residents, he countered that if she did so, he would call her Lula Mae. Shortly after Carson left, Newton arrived and became Truman's first important lover. Carson was delighted, writing to Newton that she loved anyone who cared for him.

Reviews aside, the news from the outside world was not all bad. Carson had been awarded a second Guggenheim Fellowship. She and Reeves—he visited her three times while she was at Yaddo—laid plans for a trip to Europe, beginning with Paris. They were encouraged to come by an American expatriate, John L. Brown, and his French wife, Simone-Yvette L'Evesque. Her Japanese friend from Yaddo, Ayako Ishigaki, had given her Brown's name and an enthusiastic recommendation. A polymath with a doctorate in medieval studies and comparative literature, Brown had worked with the OSS during the war and was, among many other things, the European editor for Houghton Mifflin. He wrote Carson in April with a query about French translations of her books; though he was himself a translator, he would facilitate the work rather than undertaking it himself. *Reflections in a Golden*

Eye was a natural for translation into French, Carson replied. *The Heart Is a Lonely Hunter* would be more difficult, she thought, because it was written in at least four separate voices. She was especially protective of *The Member of the Wedding,* which she thought was inextricable from its language and was best treated as a poem, not a novel. The wrong translator could ruin the book, she said. Brown reassured her in warm terms, and when the two couples met in New York several months later, they cemented their epistolary bond.

A central piece of Carson's career and her personal life was put into place that summer of 1946, when she met Tennessee Williams. Six years older than Carson at thirty-five, Tennessee was born in Mississippi, where he spent his early childhood with his mother's family; his grandfather was an Episcopal priest. When Tom (his birth name was Thomas Lanier Williams III) was eight, the family moved to St. Louis, where his father, previously a traveling salesman, became an executive at a shoe factory. Locked in a loveless marriage with the neurasthenic Edwina, Tom's father drank; their three children included a troubled sister, Rose, whose emotional problems developed into schizophrenia in adolescence. Evidently once her madness took hold, she became overtly sexual in her action and speech, and her parents institutional-

Carson and Tennessee Williams, c. 1950. The playwright was perhaps her closest friend.

ized her, allowing her to be given a lobotomy (then thought a promising treatment). Tom, a talented writer since childhood, settled on writing plays after a turbulent period attending various colleges and holding menial jobs. It was not until *The Glass Menagerie,* loosely based on his family's emotional dynamic and the troubled sister he so loved and missed, was produced in 1944, moving the next year to a long run on Broadway, that his career was launched.

Tom, by now known as Tennessee, had read *The Heart Is a Lonely Hunter,* which he hugely envied, writing to Bennett Cerf in 1940, "It is so extraordinary it makes me ashamed of anything I might do." Sometime in the spring of 1946, he read *The Member of the Wedding* and was again greatly impressed, enough so that he wrote Carson a fan letter, emboldened when he learned that his good friend, theater maven Paul Bigelow, was a close friend of Carson's "double first cousin," Jordan Massee. Tennessee said he couldn't think of any modern novel that had moved him as much, comparing her work favorably to that of Katherine Anne Porter, Christopher Isherwood, and Eudora Welty. But his letter won her over when he said he particularly admired her creation of Berenice. In response, he told her about his African American nurse, Ozzie, whom he had deeply loved, and who packed up and left the household suddenly one day, which Tennessee believed was because he had called her a nigger. The guilt he suffered remained with him his whole life. The story struck a chord with Carson. Into her portrait of Berenice went her love of several Black nurses, including Lucille; the moment when a cabdriver hurled the same epithet was a defining memory of her youth. She and Tennessee shared the conflicted nature of open-minded white Southerners, and this may have been the first signal that they had found rare friends in each other. It was an acknowledgment, perhaps, of this strange Southerners' bond that Carson would call him "Brother," that most Southern of gestures.

Tennessee rented a cottage on Nantucket for the summer, setting up housekeeping at 31 Pine Street with his current partner, a Mexican called Pancho Rodriguez, whom he had met in New Orleans. Somewhat at loose ends—he later said he had gone to Nantucket "to die" after a frightening operation (he was a self-confessed hypochondriac)—he invited Carson to come visit him on the island for as long as she wanted. He later said that he wondered what on earth he had done as he waited for her ferry, but the moment passed when he saw Carson coming down the gangplank, a tall woman in slacks and a baseball cap with "a radiant, snaggle-tooth grin." Settling into the modest cottage, its wooden shingles grayed by the elements, Carson, in a rare fit of domesticity, went out and bought paper flowered curtains, candles, and a red-and-white-check oilcloth for the kitchen table. Over the next couple of weeks, she impressed Pancho and Tennessee with homemade mayonnaise (learned from Bébé), clam chowder, green pea soup with hot dogs in it, and a creation they dubbed "spuds Carson," an unlikely combination of potatoes mashed with cream, olives, onions, and grated cheese. She cut blue and white hydrangeas to put in the fireplace, and when she brought in some flowers from the yard, she and Tennessee fashioned a makeshift altar, complete with a photograph, consecrated to the actress Laurette Taylor, star of *The Glass Menagerie*—who also had a place in Carson's heart.

Just before her arrival, a big storm had blown out several downstairs windows on the north side of the house, allowing a pregnant cat to get inside and deliver her litter in the downstairs bed in which Carson was to sleep. She would not think of having the mother and her five kittens disturbed, she said, which won over Pancho, who tended to be jealous. He confided that he was glad, when he first met her, that she was, as Tennessee had thought from her work, a "gay girl." The three often rode bikes to the beach. At night, Carson played Bach and Schubert on an old upright piano, and she and Tennessee talked about books. Both of them could recite yards of Hart Crane, a particular favorite. He told her that she should think of dramatizing her work, starting with *The Member of the Wedding*. Carson, remembering Edmund Wilson's remarks about her nonexistent sense of drama, began to think it over. She knew very little about the theater, having attended few if any plays as an adult, but she may have recalled the plays she staged in the Stark Avenue parlor in Columbus, her reading of O'Neill and Ibsen, and especially her play "The Faucet," perhaps her first finished piece of writing, which she had confidently sent to O'Neill.

Tennessee was trying to work on his play *Summer and Smoke* during Carson's visit, but he was hard put to get much done. Hoping to busy his high-maintenance guest and encourage her in what he genu-inely felt would be a worthy exercise, he managed to get hold of a typewriter and set it at one end of the dining room table opposite his own, sitting her down in front of it. He worked on his play—he later said, "Carson is the only person I've ever been able to stand in the same room with me when I'm working"—while she set about hers. Later, looking back on this time, Tennessee reminded Carson of their work at the dining room table, proposing that they again try to work together "in adjoining trances." According to Carson, they read the day's work to each other over after-dinner drinks (not, of course, the first of the day). Carson took to the process well. By the time she left in August, after almost three weeks, she had a working draft of her stage version of *The Member of the Wedding*.

There were a lot of extracurricular activities, aside from drink-ing. They might join Pablo on the beach in the mornings and bicycle around the island in the afternoons, depending on how their work was going. And they had an active social life. Tennessee remembered Carson conceiving a huge, unrequited crush on someone in Nantucket whom he did not name, and drowning her sorrows every evening. He'd leave her sitting downstairs with a bottle of Johnnie Walker, "mooning over this romance in her head," and when he came down in the morn-ing, he would find the bottle empty.

Who the object of Carson's attentions was that summer is not clear. One possibility is the actress Rita Gam, who had become a friend of Tennessee's on the island. Both Pancho and Carson claimed that Gam was one of the most beautiful women they had ever known. Pancho later said that Carson met a "charming" husband and wife at a party given by friends of the artist Elisabeth Curtis. Carson fell in love with both of them, said Pancho, but "especially" with the wife. "Carson went wild and raved about her beauty, poise, and elegance." But the wife was more interested in Tennessee, Pancho added.

Carson's new beloved may also have been the celebrated stage actress Katharine Cornell, who had a so-called lavender marriage with director and producer Guthrie McClintic; the two were staying in their house on Martha's Vineyard. Carson, Tennessee, and Pablo took the ferry over one afternoon for tea. Cornell knew that Tennessee was "feverishly" working on a play for her and was very receptive to her guests' attentions. Cornell was much older than Carson, fifty-three to Carson's twenty-nine, but Carson's crushes tended to be on older, worldlier women. The impulse passed, such as it may have been, and when she was back in Nyack, Carson wrote a thank-you note to Cornell and her husband for the wonderful Nantucket afternoon. The note also said that she had a very pleasant trip back with Nancy Hamilton, another actress and Cornell's younger lover: another candidate, possibly, for the object of Carson's affection.

Tennessee wrote, "Finally Carson began to keep company with a baroness. Then there was no more mooning over her unrequiting [*sic*] lover." It is unlikely that this interest was romantic, however. The baroness was Margot von Opel, who had been Annemarie Schwarzenbach's lover; she and Annemarie had escaped together to the von Opel home on Nantucket during the first few months of Carson's passionate attraction to Annemarie. Margot and her husband, Fritz—the carmaker's grandson—had been arrested in 1942, accused of being enemy aliens. Margot was not held, but Fritz was interned for the rest of the war, possibly on account of his expertise in rocketry.

Margot was back in Nantucket with her husband, released in that summer of 1946. In a therapy session years later, Carson remembered how she and Tennessee shanghaied Margot to read Rilke for them, which she did very well. Subsequently they ate several meals at the von Opel house, as Margot was an excellent cook, and by this time Carson was saying they "never had a square meal" at the Pine Street cottage. Inevitably, she and Margot talked about Annemarie. Margot had "suffered like a dog," she said, during her monthslong love affair with Annemarie, a turn of phrase that struck Carson, since, she said, only dogs suffer like dogs. Neither woman was jealous anymore. Margot asked Carson's forgiveness for not letting Annemarie go to her in the summer of 1940. Carson had actually liked Fritz, whom she had known in New York. The best evidence for Carson's strictly platonic feelings for Margot is, in fact, the transcript of the 1958 therapy session, for she likely would have mentioned any sexual attraction then.

She left Nantucket in the first half of August. Tennessee had the house through September, so she promised to come back, agreeing, with his encouragement, to bring Reeves with her. In late August Tennessee made a quick trip to New York City to deliver what he hoped was the final version of *Summer and Smoke* to a typist, and he stopped to see Carson in Nyack to find out how her play was progressing. Carson had given it to Ann Watkins to circulate among theater producers. Around Tuesday, September 10, Reeves, Carson, and Tennessee went to Nantucket to stay at Pine Street for several days.

They were back in Nyack that Friday and went into the city for a party given by George Davis in his East 86th Street brownstone apartment. The guest of honor was one of George's new writers, Ray Bradbury. In a letter to a friend, Bradbury described the "quite neurotic" Carson, whom he waltzed "wildly" around George's place: "McCullers is a fey, pale, pouty, stocking-gawky girl with a bang-fringe hair-do and ploppy ways." Though Carson was known to cut her own hair as often as not, she prided herself on her wardrobe, however her getup (especially the knee socks) struck other people. As always, she radiated the utter self-confidence that was the result of the nearly magical quality of the love given her unstintingly by her mother.

In February 1946 Reeves had been promoted from first lieutenant to captain, which, since the war was over, had the sole effect of raising his pay. On March 16 he had officially been discharged from the army. He had received two decorations: a Purple Heart and a Silver Star. But a future in the army, for the second time in his life, seemed closed to him. His future was cloudy.

Soon after his discharge, Carson and Reeves plunged into preparations to go to Europe, a prospect, Carson told Newton, that had her somewhat overwhelmed. She was trepidatious beyond the usual novice traveler's nervousness. That was no surprise: she was putting an ocean between herself and her support system, namely Bébé and her sister, Rita, but also Newton Arvin, Elizabeth Ames, and Bessie Breuer. For such an independent thinker, Carson lived in a web of dependency and perhaps feared that with her people an ocean away, she would have a hard landing. So she tried to line up other friends who she hoped could form a support system in Europe. Kay Boyle was going over at about the same time as Carson; Rita gave a bon voyage party in Nyack not only for Carson and Reeves but for Kay and her brood and Kay's new husband, Joseph von Franckenstein. She and Carson laid elaborate plans that promised to put them in each other's company far more often than in the States. Carson was also declaring her tenderest love for John and Simone Brown, the expatriate couple with whom she had corresponded in May.

After the war, many Americans who could afford it were eager to visit Europe, perhaps for a protracted stay. Such plans were often optimistic and forward-looking, reflecting a postwar and post-Depression desire for new places and new experiences. Living there was cheap, too, and attracted a lot of Americans they found simpatico, like Tennessee Williams, Truman Capote, and John and Simone Brown. The fact that commercial air travel was just becoming available, with more frequent transatlantic flights, no doubt contributed. Reeves, his hopes for a medical career frustrated, thought he might find a place for himself in Europe, working for the army (he still held out hope), a multinational corporation, or a new nonprofit like UNESCO. He had hoped to attend, before they left, a Berlitz school on the G.I. Bill to learn French and German, but as the date for their departure loomed, he was reduced to cramming on his own. Carson, too, spoke loftily of her plans for Europe. For instance, she told John Brown that the quality of the translation of her works into French was especially important to her because she believed that Paris would be *the* capital of postwar Europe. Carson and Reeves met the Browns in New York in October, and Carson immediately cast them in the role of beloved support staff.

Carson and Reeves, who had settled on Paris as the place to start their travels, were concerned about where they would stay, both in the long and the short term. Earlier that year Carson had befriended Henri Cartier-Bresson when he came out to photograph her in Nyack, and the French photographer wrote to his sister Nicole, who lived in Paris, to see if she could put them up or knew of a place to rent. He also suggested Carson contact Claude Leroy, a French poet who had been a prisoner of war, escaped, and joined the Resistance. Carson and Reeves don't appear to have followed up, but they did arrange to stay for a week in the coming winter with the Cartier-Bresson family. They also got in touch with Ira and Edita Morris, a meatpacking heir and his Swedish writer wife, who had a house sixty kilometers outside Paris; Carson had met the Morrises during the war at their house in Rockland County through George Davis. The two couples became friends, though the Morrises were considerably older.

Reeves and Carson, in typically disorganized fashion, failed to line up any housing before November 22, which was the sailing date of their ship, the *Ile de France,* and they made nervous jokes about sleeping in the Luxembourg Gardens. John Brown stepped into the breach and volunteered to make them a reservation at the Hotel California in the rue de Berri, "which is semi-requisitioned by the Embassy for visiting Americans and which consequently is . . . extravagantly heated." He warned them that food prices were high and supplies scarce; they would do well to bring coffee, chocolate, and sugar. More important, without being asked, he told them he would be meeting their train when it arrived in Paris on November 29 and bring them to their hotel. He would be very happy to see them again because he felt that "our conversation has just begun."

10

Like a Broken Doll

Reeves and Carson were staggered by Paris. Reeves said, somewhat opaquely, that the experience was "almost like being born." He marveled at "the flower markets with every kind under the sun, the beautiful full-bosomed, twitch-tailed Parisian girls . . . the oystermen, the sea-food women, the pretty prostitutes, the sidewalk cafes, the nice people in bars who exchange drinks with one, the Seine fishermen, the Seine itself with its thirty-seven bridges!" Carson, less effusively, marveled at "the elegance, the sense of space, the beauty of this place," declaring herself *bouleversée,* overcome.

Carson, Reeves said, "rather took literary Paris by storm." In letters to the United States, she complained of the many interruptions—the phone and people dropping in. Inadvertently, meeting one such visitor, she agreed to deliver a lecture on American literature compared with French literature at the Sorbonne. She understood what she had done only when Kay Boyle turned up with an announcement of the upcoming event, and Carson realized she was meant to deliver her lecture in French. She turned to John Brown, who as an erstwhile U.S. cultural attaché had lots of experience helping Americans out of tight spaces; he enlisted two professors to sit onstage with Carson and discuss the announced subject (in French, of course) with a smiling Carson, who, as arranged, spoke up only once, to recite one of her poems in English.

The Ballad of the Sad Café and *Reflections in a Golden Eye* were selling well in France. André Bay, her editor at Éditions Stock, held a book launch for the French edition of *The Heart Is a Lonely Hunter* at his country home with over a hundred people attending, spirited away from Paris in private cars. Carson was cashing a lot of checks, but also spending money she didn't have. She later told Jordan Massee that she and Reeves spent $11,000 the year they were in Paris; Bébé told him it was more like $14,000 (about $130,000 and $160,000 today). They took up residence in an elegant suite of rooms in the Hôtel de France et Choiseul in the rue du Faubourg Saint-Honoré, where Kay and her children also lived. Carson must have boasted to Tennessee—at this date, not as used to literary success as she—for he wrote his friend the writer Donald Windham about how much he admired Carson for "living on her foreign royalties," her books selling "as well or better than here. And she is living in style in Paris in a hotel suite with gilt chairs, rose wallpaper and a big fire-place." In Europe, writers were treated "like princes," Tennessee informed Windham, a bit grumpily.

From Italy, Natalia Danesi Murray, Janet Flanner's new partner, wrote to Carson and Reeves, inviting them to visit her in Rome. They intended to go, but in the meantime new friends, Monique and Valentin Cotlenko, both doctors and Russian refugees living in Paris, invited Carson on a family skiing trip to the Tyrol. The very idea of all that snow would have drawn her; actual skiing would have been the realization of a young girl's fantasy. Her visit to Rome was memorable for a tweed suit Natalia insisted Carson have made by Natalia's own tailor, Ciro Giuliano. Carson wore the resulting pantsuit for the rest of her visit and would still wear it over five years later. Natalia had remarked on Carson's appearance in Rome in her old peacoat and some "absolutely awful" boots. Tennessee for years claimed Ciro had taken her for a "street-beggar" when Carson showed up at his shop.

When Carson and Reeves—he had joined her in Rome—returned to Paris, it was spring. They had by all accounts been drinking heavily in Italy, and time passed in an alcoholic fog. Murray had noted Carson's drinking and her consequent short temper, but in these relatively early days "everyone loved her anyway," Natalia noted, "and said that she must come back when she could stay." André Bay, her French editor, told a disturbing story of arriving at Carson's Paris hotel room to take her out to lunch, only to find her still in bed drinking cognac. He claimed he had to carry her out of the room and to the restaurant in her nightgown. More convincingly, he said that Carson "always seemed to be in something of a fog, as people who drink constantly from morning till night sometimes are." Apparently the cognac was an ominous sign; Carson and Reeves drank the often-potent after-dinner drink before, during, and after most meals.

Kay Boyle noticed that things were not right with the couple. She had often remarked in letters to friends how much she liked Reeves, so this was something of a new wrinkle. She confided in Bessie Breuer that she didn't think things were going very well: the three rooms the pair occupied in the hotel made her think of "prison cells." Her heart went out to them, but there was little she could do: "They belong in America. They are lost and lonely and unhappy here."

That summer Carson had a misunderstanding with Kay, which spelled the end of their friendship. Ira and Edita Morris, their wealthy friends from Rockland County, had offered Carson and Reeves the use of their place fifty kilometers from Paris. Carson described the house in Nesles-la-Gilberde as a beautiful, half-wild country estate, calling it another Eden in a letter to Elizabeth Ames. But Kay believed she and her family had been promised the château for the same time period.

Later that year Kay learned that Reeves had slept with her oldest daughter, Bobby, then twenty. The friendship was over. She told Bessie that she thought Carson had got into "a personal dead end" in Europe. "Reeves—so much that is unforgivable has happened that I simply can't think or talk about it anymore. Our break has been so complete that there can be no mending of it, for it involves so many others besides myself. So—a finis must be written to that friendship, or whatever it was." Kay's fifth child, Faith Carson Franckenstein, was Carson's goddaughter, but the bond between these two intense and talented women could not withstand the strain.

Another of Carson's close but tumultuous relationships was with Janet Flanner, twenty-five years her senior. Carson had first met her

Janet Flanner was a good friend to Reeves and Carson and an advocate for Reeves when their marriage collapsed.

around 1940, through Erika Mann. George Davis brought her out to Croton-on-Hudson, where Janet was staying with her then-partner, the writer and critic Solita Solano, at the Tumble Inn. Janet was one of the first visitors to Seven Middagh; comically, she had understood George to say that they were living in a "bawdy" house rather than a boardinghouse. Janet and Solita admired Carson's great reserves of "energy and affection." But Janet was also unafraid of being critical; while she was supportive, she was outspoken in her disapproval of some of Carson's behavior. When Carson first met and was romantically drawn to David Diamond, a friend of Janet's, in 1941, Janet urged her to "face facts": David was homosexual. Further, Janet warned David not to get involved with Carson and Reeves, presumably because they were so disruptive.

Janet, now with her second partner, Natalia Murray, read *The Member of the Wedding* in 1946 and registered an immediate and oddly emphatic dislike. The book "terrifies me," she wrote Natalia. "To think that such disorder, physical and mental, resides within her perpetual juvenility," she went on, "is an alarming sight to see in print." She seems to have identified a sexual subtext in the book that disturbed her profoundly; at the same time, she marveled at the novel's astute portrait of adolescence:

I am moved by its record of accuracy in juvenile female suffering, but aghast at the sordidness of so young a nature and body, with such free grossness—so like the young, lacking conscience or experience—as to leave one bereft of comment. Puberty is the worst period even in one's memory, and to have to participate in someone else's puberty, in print, now, at this time of the world, seems unbearable.

These remarks say as much about Janet's deep aversion to adolescence and to that period's rampant emotionality, such an unavoidable part of Carson's nature, as they do about the book. But she was genuinely and profoundly concerned about her young friend. In the months to come, Janet in Paris and Natalia in Rome, where Natalia was working for Carson's Italian publisher, Mondadori, would be mature anchors for Carson and Reeves.

But in the summer of 1947, everything changed. Carson was staying alone at the Morrises' place in Nesles—Reeves was at the American Hospital in Neuilly because a wound on his leg had become infected. One night she awoke feeling thirsty and got out of bed. She fell to the floor, where she found herself paralyzed. She lay there, fully alert, until Reeves came home eight hours later. Doctors told her she had suffered a stroke. Later they would call this her second stroke, noting that its probable immediate cause was an embolism that she had thrown off on her skiing trip to the Tyrol. The first stroke was held to be the episode in Columbus in 1941 that began with her unable to read the numbers on the kitchen clock's face. The second stroke left her left side partially paralyzed; the right side of her face was numb, and she lost lateral (peripheral) vision in her right eye. These changes might or might not be permanent, said the doctors at the American Hospital, where she remained for several weeks. Most of them did abate, at least partially, in the weeks ahead.

After her release from the hospital, she and Reeves, unable to stay at the Morrises' because of the quarrel with Kay Boyle, moved into a strange little house in the rue Claude Bernard near the Luxembourg Gardens, separated from the street by a building with two courtyards—and thus no street noise, but also with no indoor toilet or stove. Now, once settled, she could begin to work, she told Bessie Breuer: she had to.

That summer in Paris, Richard Wright, who had become a French citizen in 1947 after leaving the United States the year before, made a record of his dealings with Carson and Reeves. Visiting her just after her stroke, Dick found Carson alone and looking poorly. After the stroke, Robert Myers, the doctor at the American Hospital in charge of her care, had told Carson that she could not drink "at all." So she cheerfully informed Dick, that late summer day, after pouring them each a cold beer. Four beers later she brought out a bottle of cognac. Reeves wasn't there, and as the day wore on, Carson felt increasingly anxious about where he might be. As she and Dick drank through the afternoon, Carson confided her anxiety about Reeves's emotional state. He drank too much, she said, and perhaps was using drugs. He believed people were staring at him all the time. She told Dick about Reeves's efforts to devise a way to make a living, which were increasingly fitful. In March he'd told Edwin Peacock that he had a job with General Motors "in my pocket," and later he told Bessie and Henry Poor that he was "still fishing" with the United Nations and UNESCO. In June he was pursuing a position working with refugees.

Richard Wright, Carson's Middagh Street housemate, became a friend in Paris, undated.

Dick, shocked to see that it was eight in the evening, rose to leave, but Carson begged him to stay. He was horrified by her condition and her stories about Reeves, but also grimly fascinated. Finally a neighbor looked in and said she would stay with Carson until Reeves got home, allowing Dick to leave. Carson and Dick were in telephone contact all the next day, for Reeves did not turn up until the following evening, considerably the worse for wear.

Dick remembered thinking, after witnessing this drunken afternoon and evening, that Carson would die soon.

He confided, somewhat cryptically, in his journal, "Why does she repel me so? The more I talk with her the more I feel that there is something in her that I cannot like; and she is one person whom I want to like."

Several nights later, another disordered occasion gave Dick further cause to worry. While driving Carson and Reeves to a party, he kept looking at Reeves, sitting in the back seat with Ellen Wright, to see if he showed any sign of being on drugs. Evidently Reeves did not. At the party, Carson continued to voice her worries about her husband, especially his inability to find work. Dick offered to introduce Reeves to Claude-Edmonde Magny and some other well-connected French writers who could perhaps help him.

Late in the evening, Ellen told Dick she needed to go home but that he was welcome to stay. Reeves went down to put her in a taxi, returning soon afterward to continue drinking. When Dick got home, after midnight, Ellen, still awake, told him that Reeves had made a drunken pass at her, trying to climb into her cab. She had easily fended him off, but Dick could not shake his anger at Reeves. In his journal, he wrote, "I've been trying to find a job for Reeves, but can you help a man when he molests your wife?" He resolved that he would give Reeves no further help and "keep away" from both McCullerses.

Soon afterward the Wrights moved into an elegant large apartment near the Bois de Boulogne on the avenue de Neuilly. But they were uncomfortable in such a luxurious place so far from the city center, so they moved into a hotel. They sublet the apartment to Reeves and Carson. The arrangement did not last long.

After almost a year in Europe, Carson and Reeves were making plans to return to the United States, writing to Bébé and Rita on October 24 that they had booked passage (first class) on a Dutch ship, the *Nieuw Amsterdam,* due to arrive in New York on December 1. But soon after November 1, Carson developed a kidney infection that sent her back to the American Hospital. Her third stroke followed. This time the entire left side of her body was paralyzed, and it was also extremely painful. Dr. Myers did what he could to relieve the pain and reduce the paralysis, but the best place for such treatment was the Neurological Institute in New York City. Because of Carson's need for immediate treatment, travel by ship was not an option, so Reeves booked an Air France flight, arriving in New York on Sunday, November 30. Carson's fear of heights, so severe that they had had to move out of the Hôtel de France et Choiseul because of their top-floor rooms, was overlooked at this juncture.

Bébé and Rita were at LaGuardia to meet the plane with an ambulance to take Carson to the hospital. To their surprise and distress, *both* Carson and Reeves were taken off the plane on stretchers. During the long flight, Reeves had suffered a seizure as a result of the DTs. Bébé told Jordan Massee and his partner, Paul Bigelow, that back in Nyack, Reeves suffered two more "convulsions."

Soon after their return to the United States, he wrote Dick and Ellen Wright his version of the journey. His symptoms had started in Newfoundland, where the plane stopped for fueling, about two hours from New York. The first sign of the attack was an impression, or, more likely, a hallucination, that the plane on takeoff had barely missed a hangar full of gasoline, which was apparent only to him, the flight attendant, and the pilot. Later his condition became markedly worse:

> I went into sort of a coma and did not regain consciousness until two days later at our home in Nyack. Carson was conscious but could not move or say anything. So we were both carted out there via ambulance. Within a few days I was coherent, ambulatory and much better. The 7–8 doctors Carson and I have had in for each of us diagnose my trouble as an eplectic [*sic*] seizure, the second I have had since I was 8 years old. If I maintain good general health, drink very little, smoke less, avoid emotional nervous excitement it will not recur.

While the focus was on Carson and the sequelae from her stroke, Reeves faced a crisis all his own.

Only one other person ever mentioned epilepsy in connection with Reeves. Andrew Lyndon, a Macon resident and friend of Jordan Massee, met Reeves in the fall of 1946 and later said that at the time they met Reeves suffered from some sort of "attacks," which Andrew believed were epilepsy. But Andrew's account was vague, and he may have got the dates wrong. Others believed Reeves manufactured his "attacks" out of a need for attention.

It's likely that Reeves made the epilepsy story up out of whole cloth, and that Carson, Rita, and Bébé knew very well that he had. Whether this was Reeves's first attack of the DTs, we don't know, but all indications are that he knew all about the consequences of alcoholism. He had probably been initiated into such matters by Carson's sister, Rita, who was aware of her own problem by this point. Rita was attending meetings of Alcoholics Anonymous by now and likely told Reeves about the program if he had not become aware of it on his own. She would later become a good friend of the so-called First Lady in AA, Marty Mann, as did Reeves.

No precise dates can be applied to any of this because of the "anonymous" nature of AA. No records show exact dates for the history of the organization, just as no records exist for individuals' "membership." AA dates back to 1935, when Bill Wilson, one of its two founding fathers, first got sober. Wilson knew only that talking to other alcoholics worked—and thus AA took off, a group "whose primary purpose [was] to stay sober and help other alcoholics achieve sobriety." Women began to join after Mann went public about achieving sobriety in 1939.

Certainly by 1947, when he was carried off the plane, suffering acute alcohol withdrawal, Reeves knew what was wrong with him. Most likely, he had previously investigated AA and perhaps had gone to some meetings before he and Carson went to Europe. But soon after this attack of the DTs, Reeves did stop drinking. How long this period of sobriety lasted we don't know, but for the time being, as AA recommended alcoholics do, he was concentrating on his own plight. Getting sober and staying that way had to take precedence even over the condition of his stricken wife.

Both Carson and Reeves realized that they needed to separate again.

In an early 1948 letter to Tennessee, Carson announced what seemed to be the end of her marriage, complaining that Reeves needed her emotionally and financially, and that it was painful to think about how he would get along without her. But the marriage could not survive, she told Tennessee, referring to Reeves's escapades and philandering the previous year in Paris. To stay in it would require that she tolerate a level of dishonesty she found impossible. Tennessee, who was in Rome, in turn told Paul Bigelow that "Reeves is . . . a sick person and a very pitifully maladjusted one who needs help"—just as did Carson, he said. He cautioned Paul not to take Carson's word for her emotional situation, for she was too ill.

Carson's realization of Reeves's shocking dependence on her followed on the heels of her growing understanding that, given her strokes and paralysis, *she* was now almost wholly dependent on others and would probably continue to be so for some time. Her doctors at the Neurological Institute were doing what they could to reduce the pain in her paralyzed limbs. Slowly, she was regaining some movement and ability to walk with a cane. But it was a bleak winter. Christmas came and went with little notice. Snowstorm after snowstorm buffeted Nyack, and a huge blizzard hit on January 23, the worst snow in sixty years. In February, Reeves moved to an apartment in the city and began looking for work.

Carson was languishing as well with a puzzling and inappropriate crush on Robert Myers, her doctor in Paris, whom she was pursuing by letter. Beginning with her long illnesses as a child and adolescent, she had long been susceptible to anyone who physically touched her, even in strictly therapeutic ways, and who cared for her welfare. Given that Myers was married, the crush was capricious but no less insistent; that it was hopeless only added to Carson's depression. In early 1948 Tennessee, on the heels of *A Streetcar Named Desire,* his second Broadway hit after *The Glass Menagerie,* was on his way to Europe and, foreseeing health crises like the hypochondriac he was, asked Carson to recommend a doctor in Paris. He consulted Myers, who did not impress him, writing to Carson, "I did not like that doctor of yours one bit!"

Dr. Myers, who seems not to have felt bound to confidentiality, had only glum things to say about Carson, telling Tennessee he didn't think she'd ever walk again and that further attacks would follow. Perhaps Tennessee was blaming the messenger for the message.

Carson quickly wrote back, saying that her feelings for Myers vanished when she heard that Tennessee did not like him; she couldn't love anyone he did not like, she said. As the winter rolled on—it kept on blizzarding—Carson told Tennessee of a week that had been "utter Hell," as they were snowed in, not that she could do much outside the house. She complained that she was unable to eat or sleep.

Perhaps forgetting her condition, Tennessee had asked her to join him in Europe. The only thing that kept her going, Carson replied, was imagining the two of them swimming in the warm waters of the Mediterranean. She wanted to travel together and even share a house, and asked whether Tennessee thought that was a possibility. While she was bedridden, Rita brought home a copy of *Life* magazine with a story about Tennessee, including a photo of the playwright with his lobotomized sister, Rose, who happened to be in a facility in Ossining, just across the Hudson from Nyack. Tennessee's love for his sister considerably informed his love for Carson, who was now nearly as helpless and ill as Rose. Carson came to love the idea of Rose—and, when she met her, Rose herself. She looked forward to occasions when Tennessee brought Rose to visit, delighting in her confused utterances, which she professed to understand. She had dreams of Tennessee freeing Rose from the institution and bringing her to live with the two of them. At any rate, the story and photograph in *Life* moved her to write a letter to the editor, which appeared in the March 8 issue: "Tennessee Williams is not only an extraordinarily great artist, a genius, he is also one of the wholly beautiful human beings I have ever known." (She and Tennessee always talked this way.)

Tennessee tried to redirect Carson's attention to other matters, among them himself. "This is to assure you that I am feeling a lot better," he amiably began a letter in January, having recovered from whatever ailment had sent him to Robert Myers. He seldom said anything about her condition, in fact, but smoothly assumed a future for her—which might have been the best he, or anyone, could have done.

Tennessee prevailed on her to leave her agent, Ann Watkins, whose efforts to get *The Member of the Wedding* produced had not been going well, and to sign with his agent, Audrey Wood, who was a close personal friend and indeed an emotional mainstay in his life. On his advice, Audrey went to see Carson in Nyack on March 6, giving Tennessee a vivid account of how she found her. Carson was "in bed in a little boy's pink woolen pajamas," with her mother, sister, and friends and neighbors, even Reeves, clustered around her:

> The only thing she could discuss over and over again was MEMBER OF THE WEDDING—and Tennessee Williams! The climax of the afternoon came when with adoration in her eyes she asked us whether we wanted to hear you recite a poem on a record. . . . It began and though I listened as hard as I ever have in my life not one word was understandable. As this monotonous voice droned on, McCullers leaned forward with great ecstasy and . . . said, "Isn't that the most beautiful poem you have ever heard?"

Amazingly, Carson had gone back to work soon after her plane landed the previous November. Ann Watkins, now phased out in favor of Audrey Wood, whose tenure as Carson's agent would be short as well, had told her around that time that the Theatre Guild had agreed to produce the theatrical version of *The Member of the Wedding* if Carson was willing to collaborate with an experienced playwright. Ann suggested another client of hers, Greer Johnson. By now Carson had been in touch with Johnson and was working on the script. Reeves had bought an electric typewriter, which was then quite unusual—it was sensitive enough to the touch that she could typewrite with her good right hand and the disabled left. Hearing about all this from Carson, Tennessee thought it sounded like a good plan, and his support, as always, meant a great deal to her.

Carson's attention, meanwhile, was caught by a piece of fan mail she received via *Life,* a response to her letter to the editor about Tennessee. The writer, Sidney Isenberg, was an intern at the Medical College of Virginia in Richmond, training to become a psychiatrist. He had been drawn to Tennessee by the psychological complexities of his work. With the feature in *Life,* he became interested in Williams's life as well, and seeing Carson's letter, he had sought out her work. He sent her a special delivery letter.

Carson wrote back, telling Sidney that his letter had been a great source of encouragement to her. She explained that her friendship with Tennessee had begun with a letter in which he asked her to visit him on Nantucket in the summer of 1946. She filled in her correspondent on the features of her life that day in late February 1948. She had not been well for several months, feeling, she confided, like a beat-up doll that had been flung aside and forgotten by a spoiled child. Noting her work on the script of *The Member of the Wedding,* the original of which she had written at the same table with Tennessee the summer they met, she told Sidney about Greer Johnson, with whom things were not going well at all. She found his material impossible to use, she wrote, and now Johnson was suing her for violating the terms of their contract. She closed the letter saying she was going to forward Sidney's letter to Tennessee, and she asked him to write her another one to replace it. Then Carson fell silent. Not until April did she write to Sidney again, pointing out the irony that his profession was psychiatry, given that she had spent the intervening weeks at Payne Whitney, in the psychiatric ward.

At the time of Audrey Wood's visit, Carson was overwhelmed by her sorry physical state, the seeming failure of her marriage, and the professional quagmire she found herself in. Progress in relearning how to use her left side, to walk, and to use her hand was very slow. However much Carson loved attention—and confined to her bed in Nyack, she now had her mother's almost undivided attention—she didn't like being an invalid and was not good at it, she told Sidney. She felt herself a victim, like that doll, cruelly thrown from her own life into what sometimes seemed the backwater of Nyack, where she hardly got up from her bed.

In fact, however, she also played the part of the spoiled child who had flung the doll—or that part of her life—into a corner. The woman who once described her young self as "a bit of a holy terror" recognized this side of herself. It was not only that Carson was headstrong enough to jeopardize her recovery by being a "bad invalid." Part of her feared she herself might be responsible for her condition, and that her paralysis might all be in her head.

This scenario would haunt Carson for the rest of her life. Her paralysis was neither total nor constant; sometimes she could use her arm and hand, and sometimes she could walk fairly easily. For some unconscious reason, she often worried, she might have willed her paralysis, and she couldn't get free from this condition until she understood what had impelled her to prostrate herself. At various times a friend might suggest this sort of explanation to Carson, who was willing to entertain the possibility.

At other times Carson would vehemently resist this argument. She had, after all, suffered a stroke, a medically recognized condition with immediate physical consequences. Hardly a classic malingerer, she would have been aware that her illness—or her response to it— had a psychological component. Sometimes being an invalid seemed the path of least resistance, and she would spend day after day in bed because she did not want to get up and face what lay before her.

She had one of these moments in mid-March, when it all seemed too much to bear, and she cut the inside of her left wrist with a razor. She terrified her mother and Rita when they heard a crash from the bathroom—Carson, her wrist slit, had fallen. Bébé, understandably upset and worried about doing the right thing, arranged for Carson to be taken to Payne Whitney in Manhattan, convincing her that she needed a rest. Evidently William Mayer, Carson's psychiatrist friend, whom she considered her doctor, was not available, because Bébé moved very fast and Carson was ensconced in what she called "Bedlam" by the third week in March. Bébé knew that Carson was "bitter" about what her mother had done, but she felt she had no alternative.

Payne Whitney, founded in 1927, offered what it claimed to be state-of-the-art psychiatric treatment. Its interior resembled a handsome private home, featuring fine wood paneling, chandeliers, and comfortable chairs and sofas. Carson would stay for three weeks. She told Newton Arvin that the psychiatric ward felt like a labyrinth with no exit.

As in many such institutions, patients were "promoted" from one ward to another, offered more freedoms as they improved—or behaved themselves better. Carson was not sick enough to be subjected to such common procedures as electroshock, insulin therapy, or psychosurgery; her treatment was most likely some form of talk therapy, though patients like her were more often thought to be in need of the "rest" that Payne Whitney's comfortable environment provided. The authorities took away her glasses, outraging her. It is difficult to understand what their reasoning might have been, but the fact that they also took away her stub of a pencil gives a clue as to their motives. Though she did find a competent doctor on her assigned ward, she clashed with the head doctor, whom she somewhat cryptically dismissed as a "Swiss peasant." He had no understanding of creative people, she said. He saw writing, using what she saw as faulty logic, as neurosis, telling Carson that she was on the ward because she was not facing her illness and disability. She insisted that writing defined her, trumping her condition, but he believed that she was evading the truth. Weeks afterward she expressed her fundamental mistrust of psychotherapy for creative people: Art grows out of the artist's inner life, neuroses and all. Even if her conflicts made her suffer, she did not intend to seek treatment and risk having her inner landscape tampered with.

Carson was indeed in denial about her emotional problems. She could not explore her feelings about her poststroke condition, which might have helped her find a way to function and be happy within her limitations. Unpacking her neuroses would prove to be an extremely complicated task, which would take more than facing her stroke's sequelae. She worried what treatment of these problems would do to her creative gift, fearing that it would leave her a well-adjusted invalid fixated on her medical condition, without a thought of writing fiction. Moreover, as long as she was at Payne Whitney, she could not have physical therapy or visits from medical doctors who might address her physical challenges. More immediately and most important, she wanted to get back to her work.

William Mayer, her friend and protector, visited her in the hospital, passing on his recommendations to Bébé. He told Carson that she would never improve in the hospital, that the doctors could not understand her well enough to help her. Carson, Bébé, and Mayer had to remove Carson against medical advice. They simply walked out, all three enjoying the drama. The experience effectively mended any rift between Carson and her mother over what she had seen as Bébé's betrayal in having her committed.

Purely by coincidence, Sidney Isenberg and Hervey Cleckley, who had been Sidney's mentor in medical school at the University of Georgia, were hatching a plan to bring Carson to the annual meeting of the American Psychiatric Association that May in Washington, D.C., although for what specific purpose is not clear. Cleckley, who in 1956 would become known for coauthoring *The Three Faces of Eve*, a best-selling novel and later a movie about a woman with multiple personalities, was drawn to the conjunction of creativity and nonconformity, the emotional complexity, of Carson's work. Isenberg had sent his friend her recent letter, written before her hospitalization, and the older doctor received it "with interest but also with amazement. . . . The startling lack of formality and the immediately personal details in her letter to you make me wonder if, by some inward sort of genius, she has succeeded in side-stepping the artificialities . . . that keep most people living in the shadows and, so often, merely going through rather emaciated motions of living." The two doctors swapped slightly unsavory quips about their "poetess" and "mysterious lady," and they were thrilled when Carson wrote Sidney that she and her mother would like to meet them at the convention. There they had a pleasant lunch with him, Cleckley, and two other psychiatrists. True to form, Carson formed lasting friendships with both Sidney and Cleckley. She derived some pleasure from what she took to be their endorsement of her mental health.

There was good news on other fronts. She was delighted to hear that Reeves had found a job—and a job he liked. In early spring, he began work as an accountant at the New York radio station WOR. (The station's mix of music, news, and talk bore no resemblance to its later right-wing talk format.) It was a miracle, she told Sidney. Reeves had somehow found a footing. He took an almost childish pride in his new position, which involved a secretary and a tape recorder for taking dictation. She did not pretend to have much faith in the future of their marriage, but her hopefulness was palpable. Reeves seemed to have sworn off all alcohol. To Edwin Peacock and John Zeigler, she said that Reeves had become his old self, sensitive, supportive, and a great support for Bébé, Rita, and her. He had started coming out to Nyack on the weekends. Before long he was reinstated and moved back, commuting to his job in the city.

Reeves's turn for the better may have made it easier for Carson to refocus on her writing after returning from Payne Whitney. While her play hung fire, she brought out some old short story manuscripts and sketches and began reworking them. To her delight, *The New Yorker* bought the sketch "April Afternoon" for future publication. She was even more pleased to receive, in May, a so-called first reading contract, which gave the magazine the right of first refusal on anything she wrote. While many writers considered such a contract almost a heaven-sent sign of their success, it did not commit the magazine to much except financially. In fact, the editors extended the contract to Carson at least in part because they had got wind of her situation and wanted to encourage her to keep writing. In 1950, when the magazine finally rejected "April Afternoon," editor Katherine White wrote to Harold Ross: "I read it when it first came in and as I remember we thought it just might work if she improved it, and we knew she was sick and hoped it might encourage her if we bought it." The magazine paid in full and up front for the unrevised story because it knew she was struggling with hospital bills. She fully appreciated it, she told Tennessee.

In hindsight, it is possible to see that Carson's best work—with some exceptions—was behind her, whether because of the two strokes—or, more precisely, the changes in her life that her physical condition required—or because of a series of emotional conflicts that manifested in her increasing drinking and her problems with Reeves. Tennessee Williams, who knew how crucial his approval was to Carson's physical and emotional recovery, worried that he was unable to give it and had a terrible time not being honest with her. Carson "is a continual problem, however lovable," he told his friend Donald Windham. He'd been reading her stories, and they were "not quite stories and she's 'hypersensitive.'" He got the impression they had all been written years earlier, perhaps ten years earlier, for "the quality is so immature." He did not know what to do: "It is terribly upsetting." What he did do was to say nothing, just encourage her. Anything else would have been devastating to his still shaky friend.

11

The Jigger Got Bigger and Bigger

With the new year, Carson was charged with a determination to set her life in motion once more. To that end, in early 1949 she left Nyack for New York City. Her year-long residence in the South Broadway house had begun to pall, and she hoped to avoid the cabin fever that had set in the previous winter when she and Bébé were housebound by a succession of snowstorms. She decided to join Reeves at his apartment in the city, not so much to try to reconcile as to visit a longtime friend who could perhaps help her figure out what to do next. As it happened, they picked up their marriage as if there had been no break, moving on as a couple who had been together—one way or another—since they met in 1935.

Reeves, still working for the radio station, had a small railroad apartment at 105 Thompson Street, south of Washington Square, in a mostly Italian Greenwich Village neighborhood. Carson was almost completely happy to be back in the thick of things with Reeves. Unfortunately, the apartment was a fifth-floor walkup, difficult for her with her weak left side. Reeves agreed that it was too dangerous for her to go down the stairs on her own. This meant that during his day at WOR, Carson was confined to the apartment. She occupied herself by writing letters and fiddling with the manuscript of the stage version of *The Member of the Wedding*. When Reeves was home, they happily spun fantasies of getting a place in the country, perhaps with an apple orchard, where they could live most of the year, spending the rest of the time in Europe. Realistically, this would have made employment for Reeves difficult, but they were happy to be together, imagining such scenarios. Carson wrote Tennessee that Reeves was being his best, most considerate self and looked after her with great sensitivity. He returned every day for lunch at home, a meal that he prepared, just as he shopped for and cooked their dinner at night.

In the month or so she lived in the Village with Reeves, Carson made overtures to two distant friends. She had known Paul and Jane Bowles briefly through her friends at Seven Middagh; the Bowleses spent a year there beginning in 1942, but Carson had by then left. Paul, born in New York City in 1910, was a writer just completing his first novel, *The Sheltering Sky*, which would be published later that year to critical acclaim and a spot on the best-seller list. But Carson would have been especially drawn to him because his first love was music, and he was also a composer: her own childhood ambition. In the 1930s he had traveled back and forth to Paris, studying with Aaron Copland in France, and often collaborated with others on music for stage pro-

Writers Jane and Paul Bowles, c. 1939. Carson was interested in Jane, though they were neither lovers nor rivals.

ductions in New York. He spent most of his time in Tangier, which provided the setting for his novel. In July 1948, Tennessee summoned him back to New York to write the music for his new play, *Summer and Smoke* (which he dedicated to Carson).

Carson was also very interested in Paul's wife, with whom she had much in common. Jane Auer, two years older than Carson, grew up Jewish on Long Island, met Paul Bowles in 1937, and married him the next year. They had been living in Tangier since 1947, where Jane had fallen in love with a Moroccan peasant woman, Cherifa. Jane had published a novel, *Two Serious Ladies,* in 1943, and was working on a play. She and Paul ceased having a sexual relationship after a year and a half of marriage; both were bisexual and felt free to have affairs.

Carson and Jane formed a bond over the plays they were working on. Jane was writing what would become *In the Summer House.* Oliver Smith, whom they both knew from Seven Middagh, was going to produce Jane's play, Carson excitedly told Tennessee. Smith wanted to produce *The Member of the Wedding* as well, though he needed to find the right director before moving forward. Carson was setting the play aside to focus on other work. *Mademoiselle* bought two stories from her in January, "Art and Mr. Mahoney" and "The Sojourner."

"Art and Mr. Mahoney" is about a morbidly sensitive man who claps prematurely at a piano recital and fears he has thus lost his good reputation in his social circle. "The Sojourner" concerns the relationship between the protagonist and his ex-wife; he recalls "the fiber by fiber (jealousy, alcohol and money quarrels) destruction of the fabric of married love" (*BSC,* 121). She also wrote "Home for Christmas" and "Loneliness: An American Malady," two uneven short essays that she published in December 1949 in *Mademoiselle* and *This Week,* respectively. She published similar short essays over the years, most of them negligible, though her takes on seasonal topics, like "Home for Christmas," in which she called on memories from her Georgia girlhood, were not without charm.

But Carson was restless; the apartment was small, and she quickly grew tired of the cold. In a letter to their Columbus friend Edwin Peacock, Reeves broached the possibility of Carson's making a trip south. Edwin had recently opened a bookstore in Charleston, South Carolina, with John Zeigler, a native of Manning, South Carolina, whom he had met just before the war. Carson "feels constricted in New York," Reeves wrote to Edwin, "and needs country air and green, growing things near her." He could not accompany her because of his job, but they planned a trip together in late spring to Sullivan's Island, a small patch of land at the mouth of Charleston Harbor where Edwin and John had a second house. Carson had been away from the South for four years and needed to examine "some roots." An idea for a new novel that would likely become *Clock Without Hands,* a story she had been mulling over about race and the South, required her to again immerse herself in all things Southern. She was thinking, Reeves said, of going on to Georgia after Sullivan's Island, to Columbus for a few days, and to Macon to see Jordan Massee and Paul Bigelow. *The Member of the Wedding* was hanging fire, and Carson was determined to pick up the thread of her life and work despite her physical condition. The South promised, more than a backward look, inspiration for the future.

Rather than going first to South Carolina, Carson decided to travel directly to Georgia, perhaps because her mother was going with her. Bébé and Carson left on March 13 for Columbus, where they stayed with Kathleen Woodruff. She had been one of Carson's pupils in 1937, when Carson assembled a course in music appreciation for some Columbus matrons; Kathleen was an older woman who had regaled Carson with stories of life in Paris in the 1920s. But Carson wasn't very interested in reacquainting herself with either Columbus or its residents. Instead, she immersed herself in rereading Baudelaire's *Fleurs du Mal* and Isak Dinesen's *Out of Africa,* to the dismay of Kathleen, who had scheduled social events for Carson and Bébé. Jordan noted that Carson "was able to cut herself off from all personal contacts, except with . . . the Woodruffs." On her next-to-last day in town, she asked her hostess to give her an at-home permanent wave treatment called a Toni, a procedure previously available only in a beauty salon. Not only was the resulting hairstyle unflattering, but Carson was evidently allergic to the chemicals in the preparation, and her face swelled up with hives. She was mortified when Jordan came to Columbus to drive her and Bébé to Macon. Jordan, however, was struck by something else, noting in his diary how changed in appearance was *Bébé*—not Carson—after the "terrible strain" of caring for Carson since her return from Europe.

Bébé stayed only a couple of days in Macon, going on to Brunswick, in southern Georgia, to visit Lamar Jr. and his wife, Virginia (known as Jenny). They had recently adopted a baby boy they named Lamar and called Bill. Carson stayed behind, meeting some of Jordan's friends and spending a lot of time with his parents. Tennessee and Carson averred that Jordan Massee, Sr., was "the best raconteur they had ever encountered," said Jordan Jr., who claimed that Carson stole some of the older man's most entertaining stories outright. On this visit, she won Jordan Sr. over by telling him he was just what she expected the father of "King the Beauty" to be.

Carson and Reeves had originally planned to travel south in May, when Reeves had two weeks' vacation from his job, and Carson may have hoped they would spend an extended time in Macon with her newly discovered cousin. But Jordan's diaries indicate what a tiring guest she could be, pace Reeves, who had told Edwin Peacock how easy it was to " 'do' for" Carson. "Carson requires constant attention," Jordan wrote, "which is exhausting," adding, however, that it was "a labor of love." He summoned family members and friends who were eager to meet her, and others who wanted to renew friendships with her. Night after night he stayed up late talking to her, ceding her his room while he slept on a staircase landing. Carson may well have found this "constant attention" tiring; at any rate, she missed Reeves.

While Carson was in Macon, she received upsetting news from Alfred Kazin about Elizabeth Ames. The press had reported that a longtime Yaddo resident, the writer Agnes Smedley, was a Communist, prompting the FBI to investigate. Smedley was a close friend of Elizabeth. The poet Robert Lowell, who was then at the artists' colony, claimed that Elizabeth was a Communist sympathizer and asked the board of directors to fire her at once. Carson immediately telephoned Newton Arvin, who urged caution—he was a member of the board—

but she insisted on supporting Elizabeth in some way. Jordan helped her write letters to Elizabeth and to the board, but she grew so frantic that she left for New York early, on March 25.

By that time, the brouhaha had died down somewhat; at any rate, Carson no longer felt she had to rush up to Yaddo. Within days the board decided to support Elizabeth, though they also took the occasion to curtail what Carson had described to Jordan as her imperial style, giving her less control over the admissions process, among other things. The board censured Lowell, who in any case was just days away from hospitalization for his first manic breakdown. Ames, who told Carson the affair had been devastating, was hospitalized for a rest.

As soon as Reeves's vacation began on May 13, Carson and Reeves set out for the South again, stopping first in Charleston to see Edwin Peacock and John Zeigler. In 1946 they had opened the Book Basement, a used and new bookshop, which would become a long-lived cultural mecca and a favored spot of Charleston's arts community. The store was on the ground floor of an antebellum mansion at 9 College Way, quarters the two men shared with John's aunt, who owned the property.

After visiting Edwin and John in Charleston, Reeves and Carson went off with them to their beach house rental on Sullivan's Island. Edwin and John invited another long-standing gay couple, Edwin Newberry and Robert Walden, whom Reeves and Carson knew from Fort Benning days; they took along with them Harry Woolfolk, a friend from Charlotte. The ocean was still a little too cold for swimming, but most of them braved it. Besides Newberry and Walden, Edwin and John had a wide circle of friends visiting the island, and apparently it was a wild time; one night, after much drinking, Reeves asked Harry Woolfolk if he would like to come to bed with him and Carson. Woolfolk said no, without anyone being too embarrassed. Perhaps Reeves was operating in the spirit of his and Carson's emotional triangle with David Diamond; perhaps as well he was acting on sexual feelings that David had awakened in him. Since the entire incident was distorted by the copious alcohol consumed, it was not difficult for Carson, Reeves, Woolfolk, and the assembled guests (if they knew) to move on and try to forget it.

Carson and Reeves's itinerary called for them to continue from Charleston to Macon to see Jordan, Carson hoping Reeves and Jordan could get to know each other. But she began to feel ill while at Sullivan's Island. Reluctantly, she cut short her visit south just as she had the earlier one, explaining to Jordan that she feared another stroke or similar attack.

Jordan Massee was outspoken in his devotion to Carson, but he complained that their friendship wasn't characterized by the exchange of ideas he found necessary in a true friendship; she was all emotion. As a child, he said, he had longed for a brother, and Carson was "in a way" like a brother to him. But his diaries portray a woman entirely dependent; he writes often of having to go downtown to buy envelopes for Carson, beer for Carson, whiskey for Carson, flowers for Carson to take to his mother.

Perhaps most remarkable was the alacrity with which he adapted himself to her needs. He refers in his diaries to "the long procedure that finally leads Carson to bed and to sleep." It is not quite clear when the pattern got underway, but she needed an elaborate bedtime winding-down ritual that involved ministrations by others. As Jordan later said,

> It took a long time from the time Carson got up to go to bed to the time she closed her eyes to go to sleep; [it] was a lengthy period and of all the duties of that household, that was the most difficult—to finally get her to be willing to go to sleep, and I don't think she would ever have gone to sleep had it not been for that—without the alcohol.

In these early years, Jordan got Carson into bed and ready to go to sleep with a last beer.

By 1949 Carson's drinking was so excessive that her doctors were concerned—any alcohol use, in fact, was thought to be unwise for a stroke victim, as for anyone seriously ill. In May 1948, just after her second stroke, Carson reported to Sidney Isenberg that she had consulted Cheryl Crawford's doctor. She was terribly upset by what the doctor said, she wrote, for he proscribed coffee, cigarettes, and alcohol.

To Tennessee, she wrote that Cheryl had prevailed on the doctor to allow her three cigarettes a day, a cup of coffee, and a glass of sherry. So distressed was Carson that when she got home, she called her friend Dr. Mayer, "and he said I didn't have to give up those things."

Ten months later, however, Carson was back to a regimen prescribed by doctors who were experienced in the care of stroke victims. They said that each evening she could have two cans of beer (one of which she made part of her bedtime ritual) and "one large drink—or two small ones," Jordan recorded on March 21. "Unfortunately, they didn't define 'large' or 'small,'" he added, "and the jigger got bigger and bigger." Perhaps not on this trip but on most future trips to see Jordan, Carson and Bébé drank cheap dry sherry, often all day long, which they bought (or, rather, sent Jordan to buy) in gallon bottles, the cheapest possible; he remembered a jug cost $1.98.

Alcoholism reached far back in Carson's history, beginning with her grandfather Charles Thomas Waters. According to Carson's grandmother Lula, Lula's father drank, her husband drank, her son-in-law drank, and she drank (*ING*, 7). Carson's father, Lamar Sr., was more often drunk than sober in the year or so before his death. Bébé certainly was a tippler, though most observers agreed with Jordan that she "would get herself into a state of euphoria, without ever getting drunk." She never slurred her words; "she was just in a calm, happy state." Truman Capote remembered (perhaps unreliably) Bébé drinking Guinness stout for breakfast, citing its "nourishing" properties. Sometime during the period in which she lived in Nyack (1944–55), she was hospitalized for malnutrition, which often accompanies overdrinking.

With two heavy-drinking or alcoholic parents, the Smith children were at risk for alcoholism. Rita Smith identified as an alcoholic and attended AA meetings from the late 1940s on. At *Mademoiselle* she could not afford relapses, and for the most part she seems to have avoided them. She did slip in the beginning and often drank until passing out. On such occasions, Bébé would confide to witnesses that they worked Rita so hard at the magazine that "when she gets home she just collapses" and had to be carried upstairs.

Little is known about the drinking habits of "Brother-man," Lamar Jr., probably because his sisters had only minimal contact with him in

A family plagued by alcoholism: Rita, Bébé, and Lamar Smith in Nyack, late 1940s

adulthood. Lamar always had trouble in school, suffering from what appears to have been severe dyslexia. Reading and writing were difficult for him. He was, however, Carson told Jordan, a "mathematical genius" and was sent to Georgia Tech to study engineering. But he could not keep up there and dropped out. Eventually, he found employment in tool and die work, a job he loved, "since he can do anything with his hands," Carson told Jordan.

Coming from such a thoroughly alcoholic family, Lamar Jr. would have been lucky to dodge the bullet. Alcoholism has been called a disease of denial, and Carson's family and close friends rarely discussed drinking. Bébé's insistence that Rita was exhausted when she was in fact dead drunk could be explained in two ways, Jordan told an interviewer. Either Bébé was too naïve to know what was going on, or "she knew precisely" how drunk Rita was and made excuses as "a pretty nice Southern way of passing it off." Jordan felt, "in some complicated way" he couldn't explain, that both interpretations were valid. Certainly old-school Southerners like Carson and her family, in their coy reticence, took particularly well to denial.

Jordan detailed how Carson would make sure that the two drinks she was allowed would last; she refused to give her glass to him to refill, asking him instead to bring her the bottle. "Her idea of a drink in the old fashion[ed] glass was some drink," he said, bourbon with just "a little bit" of water." But Jordan also stated flatly, "Carson was never at any time in her entire life an alcoholic." The statement, in itself a great feat of denial, fit all too well into the well-established pattern in the lives of Carson and those close to her. The general, unstated assumption, in adulthood as in childhood, was that Carson was a genius who must be granted the latitude to realize her gift as she pleased. Surrounding herself with family members who shared this assumption ensured that she could continue to behave exactly as she pleased. "Enabling," allowing the alcoholic access to the substance and often tacitly endorsing or encouraging drinking, is a staple of the contemporary literature of addiction. Carson surrounded herself with enablers.

This was especially hard on Reeves, who was trying to get sober himself. Edwin Peacock remembered that Reeves went to an AA meeting when at the beach in South Carolina in the spring of 1949. Part of the reason for his move from Nyack back to New York City may have been to gain access to AA meetings, which were likely sparse or nonexistent in and around Nyack. Cheryl Crawford noted that the chore of fixing Carson's drinks often fell to Reeves. He, too, seems never to have criticized or even remarked on Carson's drinking to others.

Both Reeves and Rita had trouble achieving sobriety in 1949 and 1950. Rita relapsed in rather spectacular fashion. Her life was busy but not particularly happy. While her letters speak of an otherwise unidentified boyfriend, Dan, a construction worker with aspirations to write, the family's Nyack neighbor, Bessie Breuer, talked of "the wreck of Rita's love life," insinuating, somewhat nastily, that it was Carson's fault. Rita kept writing stories but found it hard to juggle her job as an editor of quality fiction in the women's slicks with an aspiration to publish quality fiction in the same magazines. Jordan, who was close to both sisters, described Rita, who was in analysis with a certain Dr. Franklin, as the "sweetest, gentlest, quietest" woman, "full of neuroses."

As an early member of AA, Rita was an insider, her social life consisting mostly of fellow alcoholics like playwright William Inge. She was now important in Reeves's recovery as well. He pronounced himself sober for most of 1949, though he was drinking a robust amount of wine. Like many alcoholics at the time, he believed that only "spirits" counted, not beer or wine. By most definitions, then, Reeves was not sober during this period. By the end of the following year, however, Carson could report that Reeves was committed to AA and did not drink. She hoped their bad times were over.

During the second half of 1949—and for the next year, really—Carson was consumed with the stage version of *The Member of the Wedding.* The problems with her erstwhile collaborator, Greer Johnson, came to an end; his suit for $50,000 in damages, claiming that he had the right to half of any proceeds, had failed. Carson boasted that she did not even have to pay a lawyer, which was unlikely. Tennessee, she said, was by her side in court throughout and was a bulwark of support. His testimony—he could attest that Carson had written the play herself on Nantucket with him back in 1946—was wonderful. It was unlikely, however, that the suit was ever heard in a court, and Tennessee's "wonderful" testimony was a figment of Carson's imagination.

In the end, she revised the script herself. In August she could report to Tennessee that the play's future was exciting. The Theatre Guild, largely because of the fallout from the lawsuit, let its deadline for a production expire, so once again the play was offered to producers. Audrey Wood, who was now Carson's agent, sent it to Robert Whitehead, later known as the Gentleman Producer, who was just beginning his illustrious career. Two years before, he had mounted an award-winning, highly successful staging of Euripides's *Medea,* starring Judith Anderson and with John Gielgud as Jason, the text adapted by the poet Robinson Jeffers. Whitehead would not have trouble raising funds for *The Member of the Wedding* with his co-producers, Oliver Rea and Stanley Martineau.

Overtures had been made to Joshua Logan, who was riding high with the successful wartime drama *Mister Roberts,* but he had to bow out because of another commitment. Harold Clurman was then tapped for the job. Clurman, one of the most familiar figures in the New York theater, had been a founder of the Group Theatre in the

1930s. Along with Cheryl Crawford, he had assembled an array of talents in the depths of the Depression that included actor-director Elia Kazan, playwright Clifford Odets, and actors John Garfield, Luther Adler, and Stella Adler. They added a passionate left-wing element to the American theater that brought it up to date with the miseries and rage of the economic collapse. The fashion for left-wing theater faded by the end of the decade, but many of the Group's alumni went on to successful and influential careers, particularly Stella Adler, who would train generations of actors, from Marlon Brando and Montgomery Clift to Robert De Niro and Harvey Keitel. Clurman, in the 1940s and '50s, was perhaps the most visible of the Group veterans, directing a string of successful plays while holding down positions as drama critic for *The New Republic* and later *The Nation.*

Clurman was reportedly dubious about the commercial viability of *The Member of the Wedding*—until he met Carson. Prior to their meeting, Whitehead warned Carson that the director would probably want revisions, but afterward, writing to Tennessee, she reported that Clurman was enthusiastically on board and didn't want any changes. She felt he "got" the play, even recognizing the contrapuntal structure of the work and naming Frankie's desire to belong: somewhat dreamily, she compared the play to a rondo.

Both Clurman and Whitehead indeed "got" the play, if their early stabs at casting were any indication. Early on, Whitehead approached Ethel Waters to play the part of Berenice.

Waters was that rare performer in the days of segregation and Jim Crow, an African American actor and singer who was a luminous star in her own community and a popular figure among white audiences as well. Starting out as "Sweet Mama Stringbean," a gangly singer and musical comedy performer in the 1920s who specialized in sultry songs full of witty innuendo, she moved through the 1930s and into the '40s into matronly roles as she gained in girth. She was in the cast of the seminal all-Black movie musical *Cabin in the Sky* in 1943 after starring in the Broadway version, singing the indelible "Happiness Is a Thing Called Joe." Six years later she played the mother of a young woman passing as white in the landmark racial drama *Pinky.* On both productions, she had worked with top-flight directors, Vincente Minnelli and Elia Kazan, respectively, and by the time she was approached about Carson's play, she was used to negotiating the tense relationships between Black and white characters in their roles. She had also become a devout Christian.

Waters, though she was in dire need of money, turned the Theatre Guild down, complaining that Frankie, whose alienation and (ambivalent) desire to be part of a group power the play, swore and otherwise used bad language. Worse, the character of Berenice did not square with her religious beliefs. Berenice drank, smoked, and had "lost her faith in God" (*ING*, 45). When Bob Whitehead showed Waters a revised version, she complained, "There is still no God in this play." After Clurman agreed that she could add a couple of religious lines to her part, Waters signed on (her biographer claiming that she demanded "top billing *above* the title").

A further piece was added to the puzzle when Carson saw Julie Harris act. Nyack resident Helen Hayes had mounted a local production of *The Glass Menagerie,* with twenty-three-year-old, five-foot-three-inch Harris playing Laura. Carson was struck by her performance. Independently and separately, Whitehead and Clurman, too, were smitten by Harris, and she won the part of the nine-years-younger, tomboyish Frankie, with a self-administered boyish haircut. (Just before the opening, Harris had all her hair cut off.) Finding someone to play the seven-year-old, preternaturally sage John Henry was not as easy. Fortunately, someone remembered that Fritz de Wilde, the actor playing the bridegroom, had a son about the right age; the untutored Brandon was promptly cast.

The production came together rapidly in the summer and fall of 1949. Rehearsals began on October 28, though the part of John Henry was cast only at the last minute. Brandon could not yet read, but he proved a quick study, his parents reading the play to him often enough that he knew everyone's lines. The dubious and often disapproving Ethel Waters provoked some concern until she noticed that the production people and anyone watching the rehearsals found her readings funny, which encouraged her. Clurman later commented, crudely, that directing her "had been more like training a bear than directing an actress."

Carson went into the production knowing "next to nothing about the theatre"; according to Clurman, she took to the experience. Tennessee had advised her about the script and no doubt contributed ideas about the casting and staging, but there is no indication that he went to rehearsals with her or saw the play before its out-of-town opening.

Carson had to put her novel out of her head. She told *New York Times* interviewer Harvey Breit that she loved seeing her play come together during the Philadelphia tryout. "It all had to spring from another medium. It was fascinating. The play has to be more direct. The inner monologue has to become the spoken word. It has to become more naked emotionally, too." She tremendously enjoyed helping to assemble the production and watching Clurman work his alchemy on the stage. No doubt she was gratified that everyone around her was focused on her work: on her, by extension—but also on something larger than her. Though Julie Harris noted that it was clear "everyone was her slave," Harris liked Carson anyway—and Carson does not seem to have been disruptive or demanding throughout the tryout.

After the play was licked into shape and reduced, in a painful process, from a four-hour running time to two, it opened at the Walnut Theatre in Philadelphia on December 22. It was a tense occasion—Waters was still fumbling with her lines, and De Wilde had a bad case of stage fright that evening. Carson was backstage drinking one whiskey after another. Jordan and Paul were there for opening night, but Tennessee, engrossed in finishing *The Rose Tattoo* in his new Key West home, let his boyfriend, Frank Merlo, represent him at the opening.

The Philadelphia critics, for the most part, loved *The Member of the Wedding*. Positive reviews appeared in the *Bulletin* and the *Daily News*. The *Bulletin* noted the skill of "Miss McCullers" at the creation of characters rather than of a "unified drama," but said that she showed herself "a mistress of true talk and literate writing as well as having a flair for moving climaxes to the eight scenes in the three acts of her play." *The New York Times,* reporting on the twenty-fourth, quoted those reviews, and all the omens seemed positive for a success on Broadway.

But after the nine-day Philadelphia run, Carson was unexpectedly sidelined by pregnancy. At thirty-two, she had not been feeling well in

Philadelphia and had checked herself into the hospital, attributing her condition to her strokes and related illnesses. Routine tests revealed that she was pregnant.

Bébé was in Georgia, visiting Lamar and his family when she received word of Carson's hospitalization and the pregnancy; she rushed north to be with her daughter. Neither Bébé nor anyone else thought it wise for Carson to go through with childbirth. Reeves, who had attended most of the rehearsals and the opening in Philadelphia, left no record of how he felt, although he commented, rather strangely, about the play, "Neither of us has ever had a baby but this was about the closest thing to it that I can imagine." It is unlikely that either he or Carson even entertained the notion that she might have the child or, indeed, had any desire for one. This was the last time she would come this close. She had a medical abortion in the hospital over Christmas.

Carson described the experience differently in her unfinished auto-biography. There she wrote that after opening night she felt ill and tests showed she was pregnant. Bébé, who was already in Nyack in Carson's account, told the doctor in no uncertain terms that Carson could not

The Member of the Wedding opened on Broadway on January 5, 1950, with Ethel Waters as Berenice, Julie Harris as Frankie, and Brandon de Wilde as John Henry.

have this baby. The argument so upset Carson that she had a miscarriage, which went so badly that she had to be hospitalized and nearly died from loss of blood (*ING*, 46–47). The two versions of this episode do not reconcile well; the outcome of this pregnancy remains obscure.

Meanwhile, as the opening of *The Member of the Wedding* on Broadway, January 5, 1950, drew nearer, advance word continued to trickle out into the press. One story a few days before announced that the company had arrived in New York from Philadelphia. Another pointedly described the play as "the entire handiwork of Mrs. McCullers," making clear that it was produced by Oliver Rea, Robert Whitehead, and Stanley Martineau—and *not* the production previously contemplated by the Theatre Guild, which had been co-scripted by Greer Johnson.

Carson was too nervous to attend opening night, instead going early to one of two after-parties, ostensibly to help out. This party, given by two producers' wives, was held at the Martineaus' apartment near Broadway; Rita hosted the other at a borrowed apartment. At one or the other venue, probably the latter, the reviews began to come in. The first one, in the *New York Herald Tribune,* was not enthusiastic, citing the lack of drama in the play and recalling Edmund Wil-

At the opening night party given by producer Stanley Martineau, Ethel Waters, Carson, and Julie Harris in characteristic poses

son's damning remarks about the novel's lack of dramatic tension. But the *Daily News, World Telegram,* and *Daily Mirror* reviews were very positive. All three focused on the reactions of the audience, the *News* noting the "loud, honest cheers" at the curtain call; the *World Telegram* citing attendees cheering "as if with one voice" the appearances of Waters and Harris at the play's end; and the *Mirror* describing a "spellbound" audience. There was much to celebrate, all of which a less-than-robust Carson found somewhat overwhelming. An evocative photograph shows Carson, looking troubled and weary, on a couch at the Martineaus', nestled on the capacious bosom of an accommodating Ethel Waters. A boyish Julie Harris is draped over the sofa armrest, having a cigarette and drinking a cup of coffee.

Two important reviews would not appear until the fifteenth. A rave from Brooks Atkinson in *The New York Times* praised the writing and acting. He cited, again, the lack of "dramatic movement," deciding, however, that *The Member of the Wedding* "may not be a play, but it is art." The powerful critic praised the show's "incomparable insight, grace, and beauty." Wolcott Gibbs in *The New Yorker* singled out the "magnificent performance" of Ethel Waters and the "remarkably spirited" acting by Harris and young Brandon de Wilde. He cited the play's "queer, fantastic wit" and a script that "reaches something very close to poetry."

As for audiences, Waters in particular would electrify them, night after night, with Berenice's resonant wisdom, her combustive relationship with Frankie, and not least, her fervid rendition of "His Eye Is on the Sparrow," a gospel hymn that she had offered Clurman and Carson in place of the Russian lullaby that was in the script. "The hymn brought more God into the show," Waters said approvingly. A luminous, intense Julie Harris was launched on a long and celebrated reign as a Broadway star. De Wilde would go on to a busy career until his death in a car crash in Colorado at the age of thirty.

The Member of the Wedding received several nods in the coming award season. Sadly, as an adaptation rather than an "original play," which the competition called for, it was not eligible for the Pulitzer Prize, which went to *South Pacific.* On April 8, however, the play won the coveted New York Drama Critics' Circle Award, receiving seventeen of twenty-five votes. Two weeks later the Theatre Club presented Carson with the gold medal for the best play of 1950. And on May 1 it was announced on national television that *Member* had won the Davidson award for best play of the previous season and best first play by an author to be produced on Broadway. Clurman was cited as best director and Brandon de Wilde for best supporting performance by an actor. The best female performer award, however, went not to Ethel Waters but to Shirley Booth in *Come Back, Little Sheba*.

Carson's play would run for 501 performances, closing on March 17, 1951. It grossed $1,112,000 during its run; to her take from this was added a percentage from any future productions after the Broadway run was over. When screen rights were sold for $75,000, Carson received 60 percent of that—about $482,000 today. Her immediate financial worries were over. For the rest of her life, Carson would try to write plays or relaunch some of her stories and novels for the stage. She knew a theatrical production wasn't an easy or quick venture for her or anyone else, but *The Member of the Wedding* went off so spectacularly that it seemed like magic.

Those around her stressed the hard work involved in the mounting of the play. Reeves, who described himself as only a "waterboy" on the project, told John and Simone Brown that "it was certainly harder work and strain than I ever experienced in the United States Infantry." An overstatement, to be sure, but he was amazed at just how much it took out of him physically. Overall he was elated, telling friends it was a "real treat" just to be associated "with such a thing of beauty. . . . Besides being a critical and artistic success and a financial success for Carson," he enjoyed as much as she did the reaction of people who every evening filled the house and went away "crying and laughing and tell[ing] their friends about it."

The critical success of the play was also a vindication of sorts, because the original novel had received such a mixed reception. The play made no major changes in narrative, theme, or portrayal of the characters. As a play, it was not particularly dramatic. This quality was, ironically, much more forgivable to drama critics than it had been, for instance, for Edmund Wilson, who found that the novel had "no element of drama at all" and damned it because of it. *The Member of the Wedding* was enough of a drama to be a hit on Broadway.

Carson's friends—and later, her biographers—would (mis)remember Tennessee attending the opening of the play and both after-parties. At one of them, David Diamond said, he had talked to Tennessee about his commission to write incidental music for *The Rose Tattoo*. But Tennessee remained at his new house in Key West until mid-February. The success of Carson's play pleased him very much, and he greeted it with a great sense of relief. Actually, he "blushed" at "how little faith [he] had in its success." Later he was surprised to recall that he had actually thought it would be "dangerous" for Carson to have her play produced. Tennessee always, and rightly, saw Carson's existence as precarious, whether romantically, professionally, or emotionally, and he worried about the effect an outright artistic failure might have on his friend. To Paul Bigelow, who knew Carson well, he confided that the play's success had revealed to him "the existence of a Providence of some kind." He hoped that when she settled down, she would enjoy the enormous "psychological benefit" of the play's triumph and return to her writing. Getting down to brass tacks, he told Paul, "If I do not say that I hope she will immediately sit down to write another play, I trust you will understand my reasoning in the matter." As Paul well knew, while Carson's writing of the script and her involvement in the production of her play had been magical for her, it had been a trial for those around her. She had behaved like a diva. She was too smart to think the play had revealed her to be brilliant, but her vanity suggested to her that those around her were only now appreciating her talent. They treated her differently, and not surprisingly, she came to behave differently, entitled and too often petulant. Friends like Tennessee had hoped the play would give her an emotional boost, but they hadn't bargained for success.

12

I Am an Invalid

With *The Member of the Wedding* a hit on Broadway, Carson was riding high professionally. But she was consumed by business problems, worrying that she had signed one too many agreements about her play. The old lawsuit by Greer Johnson, though settled, was nagging at her; without any apparent cause, she feared that if he saw the production, he would claim the writing was his. And in March she was appalled to hear from Houghton Mifflin that they would be receiving 15 percent of her play's proceeds. Her back immediately went up, as her publisher seemed to have become one of many who wanted to be part of the play's success.

The more she thought about it, the angrier it made her. She had not heard a peep from Houghton Mifflin over the past two years, when she had suffered so from physical woes. She zeroed in on Hardwick Moseley, putting a personal face on what she felt was a betrayal. She wrote to Hardwick that Rita had suggested he might not have heard of her illnesses. But that was impossible, she continued, since her good friend in Paris, John Brown, who served as Houghton Mifflin's European editor, knew her physical condition well and would have informed Moseley and the Boston office about it. She could only conclude that he had heartlessly stood by and that he had contacted her only because he wanted to capitalize on her success. Though they hadn't been in touch with each other for over two years, she wrote, she knew that he had heard of her terrible health problems and yet did nothing to help.

Carson's argument sounded several different themes. The strongest was the most commonsense: The publisher had nothing to do with the play. It had had no plans to publish her play; indeed, it's not clear whether anyone there had read it or seen it or even knew she had been writing a play. Yet her contract with Houghton Mifflin specified that it would receive 15 percent of the proceeds from any theatrical adaptation. Over several letters in March and April—before both sides called their lawyers in—Carson's grievances came to settle on three major circumstances. First, in 1939, when she was expecting the second $250 of her advance for *The Heart Is a Lonely Hunter* to finance her and Reeves's move to New York City, Houghton Mifflin had left her high and dry (she claimed, melodramatically, that she had actually gone hungry). Second, over the years Houghton Mifflin had provided her with only the barest of income. Finally, the way she saw it, her publisher had not helped her in any way in her efforts to turn *The Member of the Wedding* into a lucrative dramatic property.

Author and publisher were forced into negotiation. Carson brought in Floria Lasky, a lawyer with Fitelson and Mayers, a firm that often worked with her agent, Audrey Wood; she came to Carson by way of the Theatre Guild and the Greer Johnson lawsuit. Lasky would become an important friend but at this point, she stepped in to ask Houghton Mifflin to settle for 5 percent of the proceeds from *The Member of the Wedding*. In return, Carson—who likely had little desire to stay with her publisher—agreed to let them see a selection of short stories for publication. Remarkably, it had been more than five years since she had sent new material to the publisher. It was eager as well to see part of her new novel-in-progress, *Clock Without Hands*. Lasky explicitly stated that subsidiary and dramatic rights to the novel or any short stories would not be granted.

The upshot was that Houghton Mifflin got a piece—though just 5 percent—of the money her play was making, including, evidently, from any further productions. The immediate result was far more positive: Carson gathered, for the collection her publisher wanted, short stories and a novella that had previously appeared only in magazines. The result, which Houghton Mifflin would publish the next year, was *The Ballad of the Sad Café and Other Stories,* a volume that would boost Carson's writing income—and her reputation.

Though all figures are not available for the financial profit Carson made on the play, a sketchy impression is that in its first nine months, investors received $112,500. When the screen rights were sold to Stanley Kramer's production company for $75,000 plus a share of the profits, Carson received 60 percent of that—about $40,000—but none of the profits. Her daily life may have changed very little, but Carson was able to buy the Nyack house from her mother.

⁂

As her financial situation improved, Carson had yet to address the realities of her physical condition, which was not good. She vacillated between acting as though her infirmity was nothing major and describing it as crippling. To Moseley—someone she wanted to view her situation as dire—she wrote that she'd had a cerebral hemorrhage and as a result was an invalid. She was paralyzed on the left side; she was barely able to walk and couldn't type or play the piano.

As an "invalid," however, she was full of plans, including making a visit to Ireland and then to France. These open-ended plans presupposed that she would be able to get around like a fully able person. In fact, her paralysis differed in degree sometimes from day to day, lending weight to a suspicion in some quarters that her infirmities were under her control—perhaps voluntary or imagined.

This opened a window for cruelty. Maria St. Just, a Russian British actress who had recently become a friend of Tennessee's, took an instant dislike to Carson, transparently because she considered Carson a rival for his affections. She exultantly gave Carson the nickname "Choppers" because "her cheeks looked like two lamb chops." She told a catty story about Carson's ability to control her paralysis. "Deeply mistrustful" of Carson's left hand, Maria described it as "like a little hook." "Choppers," when presented with a piano, Maria said, sat down and with alacrity, "before you could say Jack Robinson," played "like Schnabel." "I told you so," Maria said to Tennessee. And indeed, Maria went on, "The music abruptly stopped. As abruptly, the hook reappeared." It is difficult to imagine such a cleverly diabolical response to Carson's plight, but Carson's condition and her failure to behave consistently like an invalid left her open to such remarks.

When Carson resolved to go back to Europe, beginning with a visit to Ireland, she said, not surprisingly, that it was for her health. But the plan to visit the continent was long-standing. She and Reeves planned to go to Europe that summer for an indefinite stay; now that Carson had the wherewithal, they were seriously thinking of buying some property and spending at least part of every year there. This suggests that she was traveling not so much for her health as in spite of it, or more likely, that she felt her mental health depended on getting away for an extended period. Since the play's opening just after New Year 1950, she and Reeves had been staying in New York City in a succession of borrowed apartments, Reeves having relinquished his Thompson Street walk-up, whose four flights of stairs made it impractical for Carson. In March they were staying at Cheryl Crawford's apartment on the Upper East Side, though they soon left to stay in a sublet at the Dakota on West 72nd Street. Carson seems to have felt it was not emotionally healthy to stay in Nyack—a suburb, after all—with her mother, who was all too ready to cater to her daughter.

Sometime that month Stuart Preston, the iconoclastic and flamboyantly gay art critic of *The New York Times,* introduced Carson to the Anglo-Irish writer Elizabeth Bowen, who was then passing through New York. Carson was immediately fascinated by her. At fifty-one, Bowen was a handsome woman—not beautiful—with "delicate coloring," pale blue eyes, high cheekbones, a large nose, and a high forehead, her reddish gold hair held in a bun at her neck. So noted May Sarton, a friend from those years and, briefly, a lover; Sarton's biographer describes Bowen's "cat eyes" and "glamour." She was at the height of her comparatively modest fame, known for her collections of stories and her seven novels; the latest, *The Heat of the Day* (1948), a tale of espionage in a domestic setting, powerfully evoked wartime London after the Blitz.

Carson was drawn to Bowen not because of her fiction—she never

Anglo-Irish writer Elizabeth Bowen hosted Carson at her Irish estate in 1950.

said anything about Bowen's writing, which was dissimilar to her own—but because the older woman was a current sensation in literary circles, and because Carson herself liked to identify as "almost pure Irish." Bowen was married to Alan Cameron, a kindly red-faced Brit with a walrus mustache, but she carried on her romantic life as if she were single. Most important for Carson, Bowen was widely and accurately said to have had affairs with women.

Carson would have picked up on any indication of this. As usual, she was eager to fall in love, preferably with a woman, and Bowen was a romantic figure—complete with a (presumably palatial) estate in Ireland, in Kildorrery, near Cork. Bowen had published a book about the house, *Bowen's Court,* in 1942, and it had figured prominently in one of her novels. Casually meeting Carson in New York, Bowen issued a breezy invitation to come visit sometime, and Carson seized on it, convincing herself that Bowen's Court held the promise of restored health, productive work, and even love.

Carson got the wrong idea completely, about Bowen, about Bowen's Court, and about what a stay there would be like. She called Bowen from the States, friends later recalled, unmindful of the time difference. The butler on the other end of the line told her it was four in the morning and advised her to call back the next day. It was likely Bowen's husband who answered the phone; she had no butler. Actually, Bowen's Court was hardly the aristocratic estate Carson envisioned. One scholar writes that it "was maintained by Bowen primarily as a writing retreat and as a place for friends and other writers to visit and enjoy quiet, intimate soirées," but it was "dilapidated." Sarton noted that it was "austere," with little furniture and few rugs. It was remote rather than bucolic. Bowen had recently put in modern plumbing. The great shutters on the house were closed every night to keep out bats and moths, rendering it depressingly gloomy. It was hardly the marvelous mansion Carson described to a reporter from Georgia.

Dreams die hard, and Carson, who arrived the third week in May, represented Bowen's Court in letters home as the Irish country estate she had envisioned. She looked out on a great expanse, an emerald green "demesne" (she helpfully provided a definition and noted that it was pronounced to rhyme with *domain*) with stately trees where sheep grazed. The gardens were lovely, she said, noting that Edmund Spenser had written parts of *The Faerie Queene* at his nearby estate, which was now in ruins. The approach to the house was indeed impressive; it sat in what Sarton described as "a bowl of rough grass," and one drove downhill to the house, which Sarton called "gaunt, many-windowed, rather forbidding."

When reality set in, Carson felt somewhat lost. Bowen did not seem to want a closer relationship with her, romantic or otherwise. She was available to Carson at meals and for an hour after breakfast, when she went out to pick flowers; beyond that, her visitor was on her own. While Elizabeth was holed up in her study, Carson wrote a friend, she read or sometimes roamed around the yard. She was writing some poems, she said. In the evening, if a neighbor looked in, there might be drinks by the library fire; Carson specified, rather forlornly, that this fireplace was "public," presumably not the intimate setting she had hoped for. Increasingly, Carson drank.

Years later Bowen would speak critically of Carson, poking fun at her ways. Carson had, it seems, disagreed with friends like Jordan Massee over what would be appropriate to wear at Bowen's Court. Jordan and Paul Bigelow had not wanted her to bring her maroon slacks and most definitely not her blue jeans. Soon after her arrival, she "confessed" to Jordan and Paul that she had worn the slacks and that Elizabeth had told her that many Irish women wore trousers. The older writer praised her blue jeans, Carson noted waggishly, but Elizabeth later told writer William Goyen that on Carson's first night, she had been taken aback to see Carson descend the stairs for dinner wearing tennis shorts.

After a week, failing to penetrate Bowen's reserve—Tennessee wrote Paul Bigelow that Bowen had got herself out of a delicate situation, suggesting that Carson had made a pass at her hostess—Carson sent a telegram to Reeves, summoning him to meet her in Paris. She was mulling over where to live, and her visit to Bowen's Court, which lasted a little more than a week, strengthened her resolve to find something resembling a home. She was thinking of relocating to Virginia, where her old piano teacher, Mary Tucker, lived. Tucker, who had contacted her and come back into her life after the success of her play, was encouraging Carson to move near her and her husband. Carson had found one house in the area in particular that set off a train of thought. She and Reeves didn't want to continue paying rent and living in a succession of places that were never home, Carson wrote Mary. Though she led Mary to believe she was close to a decision to move to Virginia, she was inclined toward her other dream, buying a house in Europe, preferably France, and dividing her time between there and Nyack.

Carson and Reeves checked into the Hôtel de l'Université in Saint-Germain-des-Prés, a Left Bank hotel near the center of Paris. When they contacted a few people they knew to say they were in town, many responded; Carson's reputation had been shined up by the success of *The Member of the Wedding* on Broadway. John and Simone Brown, their expatriate literary friends, promptly invited the McCullerses to Clairefontaine, their country house in Brunoy, about twenty kilometers southeast of Paris. The couple responded with alacrity, but first they spent several days in Paris seeing other old friends.

Paul and Jane Bowles, they discovered happily, were staying in their hotel; they shared several breakfasts in Carson's room, and she thought she and Jane would wind up being friends, Carson told Tennessee, but the rivalry between the two women persisted. A few years back Jane had said, "She's one year younger than I and has done much more." To her husband, however, she dismissed Carson, first damning her with faint praise: "Certainly [she] is as *talented* as Sartre or Simone de Beauvoir but she is not really a serious writer," adding, "I am serious." She went into some confusing detail about the differences between

Carson's freaks and her own. While Carson was adept at portraying them, "her freaks aren't real," Jane said.

Tennessee, who was in Paris briefly before decamping for Rome, devoted an entire letter to Paul Bigelow about the behavior of the Bowleses and the McCullerses. Carson and Reeves came to his hotel for the afternoon, when they were joined by the Bowleses. Jane "was so nervous that she drank half a bottle of vodka." Carson received a phone call from Florence Martineau, the wife of Stan Martineau, one of the producers of her play. Stan had fallen off the wagon, Florence told Reeves and Carson in turn. The McCullerses were full of advice, telling Florence about Reeves's great success with sobriety—he was drinking "only wine." Tennessee added, "And here was Reeves reeling about the room like a storm-wracked schooner."

The afternoon was difficult, as Tennessee wrote, reminiscent of Carson's bibulous hotel visit with Richard Wright on her visit to Paris in 1947. Neither she nor Reeves got along with Paul Bowles. A jolly Reeves addressed him, "Well, son, how does it feel to be a published writer?"—a bitter, passive-aggressive remark. Paul "looked like a Moroccan camel with a mouthful of the spiniest and most indigestible plant that grows on the desert," Tennessee observed. As the afternoon wore on, Carson said three different times that Tennessee did not like her play. The playwright responded cleverly, "When have I ever not liked anything you have ever done?" for which remark he was given a kiss on the lips. The company soon parted, not before exchanging embraces in the spirit of Carson's tender kiss. Paul, on the other hand, couldn't stand physical contact, or as Tennessee put it, "Paul is terribly squeamish about any physical contact with anything not Arab and not under fifteen." He moderated his bitchiness, closing the letter by declaring the Bowleses "a pure delight" and that he could say the same about Reeves and Carson, "although quite naturally in a dissimilar fashion."

The McCullerses' visit in Brunoy with the Browns was the polar opposite of Carson's stay in Ireland. The Browns had "streams" of guests, and Carson sounded aggrieved in describing the dinners with multiple courses, complaining that she got bored. Nevertheless, she assured the Tuckers, she and Reeves just loved the Browns. Reeves didn't know how to describe Clairefontaine, "a beautiful villa, chateau, estate, propertie [*sic*]." The house was on four acres bordering the Yerres River, with vegetable and flower gardens, freshwater ponds, and a grotto. Reeves thought he and Carson might strike out and look at country properties, though their thoughts about where to live were changing; "We don't think it wise to try to settle in Europe," Reeves told the Tuckers. Yet they resumed their search.

Conversations with the Browns and some frank stocktaking led the McCullerses to decide definitively that, regardless of where they settled, their needs demanded a live-in couple. Though Carson had managed several households and cooked, she told the Tuckers, her present physical condition meant that they needed someone who could run a household. The logistics were formidable. If they hired a couple in Europe, where she felt they could find a couple they could afford, and then bought a house in Virginia, Carson wondered what she was to do with the servants in the interim. Board them somewhere in the States, she supposed. She needed to find out what the prevailing hourly wage was in Nyack. And there was the language barrier: Carson spoke French "badly" and Spanish "not at all." The Browns recommended a trip to Basque country, where they could find a Basque couple; they were said to be "sturdy, industrious and dependable people." The problem was that neither of them spoke *any* Basque.

Expatriate writer and editor John Brown was a good friend to Carson and Reeves in Paris.

They planned for a few weeks off and on at the Browns', despite the possibility of more six-course dinners. But they found Europe "hot and crowded" and impossible to navigate unless you had a car, which they didn't. Reeves airily described the "weeks" they would spend at the Browns' and added, "We may go back to Ireland for a month before returning to the States," evidently projecting a stay at Bowen's Court.

Before Carson left Bowen's Court, her host had extended a casual invitation to her to come back "any time," little expecting to be taken up on it about six weeks later. It is almost comical to imagine her face on getting word that Carson meant to take her up on her offer of a second stay—and that she was bringing her husband. Elizabeth filled the house with visitors, whether by coincidence or to spread the burden of entertaining Reeves and Carson is not clear. Two of her guests were from the literary world: the English author Rosamond Lehmann and the writer Frank O'Connor, known primarily for his short stories, many of which appeared in *The New Yorker*. Lehmann was best known for her first novel, *Dusty Answer* (1927), whose heroine, a Cambridge student, is attracted to both male and female lovers. Other guests at Bowen's Court included Audrey Fiennes, a family friend, and Dudley Colley, a cousin known for his stable of racing cars, about which he wrote a witty memoir. It was a fairly lively bunch, but Carson did not shine in this company either. She and Reeves arrived late in July and left within a week.

Bowen later assessed her relationship with Carson, prefacing her remarks with a throwaway phrase that probably sums up best the person she got to know: a "terrible handful. . . . I always felt Carson was a destroyer." She went on to say, "For which reason I chose never to be closely involved with her." That statement stands in sharp contrast to the "close friendship" Bowen enjoyed with "that other great Deep-Southerner," Eudora Welty. As Bowen's most recent biographer has pointed out, Bowen almost certainly had an affair with Welty in 1951 and intermittently until Bowen's death in 1973. As for Carson, "she remains in my mind as a child genius, though her art . . . was great, somber, and above all, extremely mature." Bowen said, "I remember her face, her being, her bearing with a pang of affection—and always shall."

How was Carson a destroyer? The one person who could have prompted Bowen's observation was Reeves. Bowen had taken a liking to Carson's husband, who charmed her as surely as he did everybody. But Reeves was drinking again and no longer just wine. Bowen held Carson responsible for her husband's plight, which increasingly seemed a headlong rush to self-destruction.

The 1950 visit to Europe, kicked off by Carson's difficult sojourn at Bowen's Court, was an odd, abortive affair, in part intended to help her—and Reeves—find a new and better environment for themselves. But their stay merely underscored how confused they were and how poorly they fit in with many of the people Carson hoped would be their friends. On top of that, because Reeves was again drinking, they could not, for the moment, get along, however much she needed him. They decided to separate on their return to the States.

The telephone call Tennessee witnessed in Paris, between the McCullerses and the Martineaus about Stan's relapse, indicates just how near Reeves and Carson were to people in AA who could help. Carson shouted into the phone, "Get Marty Mann!" Reeves, who appeared drunk to Tennessee, shouted, "Get Marty Mann! Tell her to get Marty Mann!" Later he heard, "Honey, get Marty Mann and she'll pull you out of this thing!"

Marty Mann, born in 1904 to a well-heeled Chicago family, was no less than the First Lady of AA, a pioneer in the organization's early days, considered the first woman to get sober in the new program. In 1944 she founded the National Committee for Education on Alcoholism (NCEA), meant to be the educational arm of AA, "thereby making possible recovery for millions of alcoholics and relief for their families, employers, and communities," according to her biographers. The organization, under her direction, became the enormously influential National Council on Alcoholism (later the National Council on Drug Dependence).

Marty Mann was also a lesbian. After a brief marriage (she took back her maiden name) and a number of affairs with women when she was still drinking, she entered a relationship with Priscilla Peck, a *Vogue* editor, and they became lifelong partners. It is perhaps misleading to say that Marty was closeted, for she and Priscilla were part of a vibrant homosexual subculture; they were, for example, longtime summer residents of Cherry Grove on Fire Island, then an almost exclusively gay enclave. On the other hand, Marty, as a member of AA, and particularly as she took on a leadership role in the group, was very much closeted. Gun-shy of anything that would compromise the image of AA in any way, as she advanced in the ranks and became a director of the National Council on Alcoholism, she was ever more at pains to conceal her sexuality. Thus she always called herself *Mrs.* Marty Mann.

When Carson knew her in the early 1950s, Marty, thirteen years her senior, was a tall, beautiful, self-assured, and elegantly dressed woman, a debutante from Chicago, established in her work and settled in her personal life. Whether it was middle-age discontent, or the emotional demands of her profession, or simple susceptibility to a whim or weakness, Marty was at a vulnerable point when she met Carson. They had known each other since before Carson left for Ireland and France in May. When Carson returned from Europe on July 31 and she and Reeves separated, she went to stay part of the time with Stan and Florence Martineau in Glen Cove, Long Island, and partly in Cherry Grove with Marty and Priscilla. This appears to be when they shared some physical intimacy. A letter Carson wrote to Marty on June 26 refers to one she had received from Marty written three weeks earlier. Marty's letter, she said, had hurt her deeply, because Marty had criticized her relationship with Stan Martineau. Carson was quite enmeshed with the Martineaus, dating from January, when *The Member of the Wedding* opened; in fact, Florence later said that it was Carson's habit to call her "many times daily—and often through the night," to discuss her worries.

Marty's June 5 letter, which no longer exists, also hurt her, Carson said, because Marty seemed to be drawing back from their intimacy. All month, Carson complained, Marty had been wary of her talking about their relationship. Marty had told her she wished Carson would not even touch alcohol, making her one of the very few people who dared speak to Carson about her drinking. Somewhat predictably, Carson evaded the issue, accusing Marty of trying to cover up her "guilt" over their friendship. Carson would take the "blame" (her quotation marks) for her last day with Marty, saying that what happened between them that day, clearly some kind of lovemaking, was one of the happiest experiences of her life. She understood, however, her friend's "distress," most likely based on Marty's fear that Priscilla would learn about what had passed between them. Carson promised never to kiss or touch Marty again. She understood, she said, but it was "agony" for her to deny her "craving" for the older woman. She could not live without some friendship with Marty, she stated adamantly. She hadn't told anyone about matters between them, she said, not even Reeves.

Two days later, however, Carson wrote again, this time more confidently, suggesting that her feelings were not entirely unreciprocated. It is a love letter; when Marty came into a room, Carson said, Carson was transformed, made strong and joyful. She had been planning to go back to Cherry Grove, but she didn't think it wise, she said playfully, because she couldn't vouch for her ability to keep her hands off Marty.

Yet she had many reservations, anticipating Marty's objections and arguments and suggesting some worries of her own. She needed Marty desperately but did not know what she had to offer the older woman. She was an invalid, with one arm "spastic," barely able to walk, often spending the day in bed. Without Marty's letter, it's impossible to know for sure, but the strong impression is that Marty had told Carson that there was to be no further relationship between them, but not decisively enough to keep Carson from clinging to a fantasy. She'd always felt that Marty could foresee a life with Carson, but now she knew that even so, that was not possible. She closed by telling Marty she wished Marty's arms were around her making all of Carson's unhappiness and tears go away. Falling in love again brought with it, as always, terrible fears of abandonment and vulnerability.

On September 4, Carson mailed in one envelope three separate passionate letters to Marty. She promised she would be back in Cherry Grove soon. She had finally gone down to Virginia to look at the houses Mary Tucker had picked out, even if buying one was less and less likely because of the McCullerses' separation and Carson's involvement with Marty. She waxed rhapsodic over the beautiful music she was treated to at her erstwhile piano teacher's house—by nine a.m. the morning she arrived, she said, Mary was playing Bach.

Carson, mindful of Marty's need for secrecy, described a system of penciling the other's name on a folded letter, but not in red pencil, which for obscure reasons would give the game away. She chided Marty for thinking her capable of indiscretion. She felt sure, she said, that any romantic misunderstandings were in the past. She wrote out "our" Rilke poem, "Love Song" ("All that touches us makes us twin / Even as the bow crossing the violin / Shows but one voice from the two strings that meet"). Marty shouldn't worry that their relationship would cause any distress to Carson. She implored Marty many times to pray for her.

But the correspondence breaks off there. Notes that Jordan Massee made in his journal on October 21 reveal a long-simmering, murky brouhaha between their friend Paul Bigelow and Carson that involved Marty. Paul had made some "indiscreet" remarks about her to Marty, who in turn passed them on to Carson. The gist was that Carson alienated her friends, such that everyone eventually deserted her—except for Jordan, Paul reportedly said, because Jordan was Carson's cousin and could never see her clearly. Earlier that summer, when Carson was still in France, Marty had demanded that Carson stop seeing Paul because of things he had said about *her*. Jordan's interpretation was that Paul had made some remarks about Carson that he thought were funny, but Marty had taken them as serious judgments.

Jordan, turning from his (not very clear) account of what happened, recorded his own thoughts. Why did Paul make facetious remarks about people? he wondered. And "why in the name of God would Marty ever have repeated such remarks to Carson?" He suspected Marty of being humorless. But nothing accounts for her passing on these remarks except bad feelings between the two women. Marty's biographers, who write as AA insiders eager to protect Marty's reputation, say that she "was able to sidestep a serious involvement." They claim that Carson "continued to write passionate love letters to Marty despite Marty's insistence that she stop," though letters that document such insistence have not survived.

In the next year, Marty "succumbed" to a serious love affair with Jane Bowles. The relationship between the two women, one a sober alcoholic and the other an active one, was serious enough to threaten Marty's life with Priscilla. A photograph shows Jane and Marty poolside, Marty's arm around Jane, who is wearing a strapless bathing suit.

Marty's hand is resting possessively atop Jane's right breast. Carson would certainly have known about this involvement, which began sometime in late 1950—just a month or two after Carson and Marty were exchanging prayers and Rilke's love poetry—and did not end until mid-1954. What Carson felt about it is nowhere recorded.

13

Harder Than Marble

Over the holidays at the end of 1950, Carson had a warm exchange of letters with a new friend, the poet Edith Sitwell. The two writers met at a party given by Tennessee at his East 58th Street apartment on Halloween; also in attendance were the poet and publisher Jay Laughlin, Gore Vidal, the writer/editor Leo Lerman, the writer Oliver Evans, Bébé and Rita Smith, and the director Daniel Mann, along with a further sampling of writers and theater people. Jordan Massee recorded his impression of the famously eccentric English poet:

> Sitwell arrived very dignified and very grand, but with the natural grandeur of royalty, no pose. And yet, very simple, despite a topaz ring the size of a hen's egg, and a huge gold bracelet, oriental, I think. She wore English walking shoes, with low heels, a long black dress, and a long black cape, both to the floor, which she kept on, and a rather peculiar hat.

Carson perched on the sofa next to Sitwell, talking for what Jordan thought was a long time. "Sitwell treated her gently," Jordan observed, "as one treats a small, nervous child." They promised to send each other their books after Sitwell returned to the U.K. Sitwell invited Carson and a group that included Tennessee and the poet Marianne Moore to a rehearsal of her reading of Lady Macbeth at the Museum of Modern Art, a controversial performance whose high (or low) point was Sitwell's interpretation of the sleepwalking scene in *Macbeth*.

What Carson saw that night at the party was an outlandishly dressed yet oddly elegant Sitwell, then sixty-two, six feet tall, with a prominent nose and aristocratic mien, another outsider who did not quite fit in. Sitwell was not a lesbian, though her closest relationship was with the woman she lived with; nor was she conventionally heterosexual, despite her lifelong, passionate love for the gay painter Pavel Tchelitchew. A wit later said that at her death she was like a letter "returned unopened."

For those unacquainted with her work, Sitwell may have presented an easy target, but she was undeniably a major force in English poetry. Many thought her heyday was in the 1920s, when she devised the entertainment *Façade,* a recitation of her poems to music by William Walton. Her work may have seemed conventional, even sentimental, but in fact it was thoroughly modernist, and she became a touchstone for innovative poetic technique. Over the next ten years she wrote a number of reviews and critical articles, bringing her much-needed cash and establishing herself as a doyenne of the English literary scene. In 1937 she published a novel, *I Live Under a Black Sun,* based on the life

English poet Edith Sitwell met Carson in New York City in 1955.

of Jonathan Swift. She returned to poetry when the war broke out, though her new efforts were less highly regarded than her earlier work, and she had become ever more a provocative, avant-garde icon: an established eccentric.

When Carson was writing at all these days, she was writing poetry—which may have helped draw her to Sitwell. In 1951 her attention was absorbed by an ambitious long poem, "The Dual Angel," which pleased her enough that she used an excerpt as her message in her Christmas cards that year. The poem opens, like an epic, with an "Incantation to Lucifer"; unfortunately, Carson, an extraordinarily poetic writer in prose, had little versifying talent, and her rhymed stanzas are wooden and lifeless.

Of Sitwell, Carson spoke in superlatives. In an early letter she pledged eternal love in her most treacly Southern manner. She compared her new friend to T. S. Eliot, Milton, and Shakespeare: She was simply the greatest living poet. Sitwell's letter touched her deeply, and she was so grateful that Sitwell loved her, too. Their friendship made Carson tremendously happy, she said.

When Carson sent Sitwell her first two novels, the poet responded in kind: "You are a transcendental writer—there cannot be the slightest doubt of that. . . . What a great poet's mind and eye and senses you have." Carson told Sitwell not only about her current physical challenges but also about her forced stay at Payne Whitney in 1948. The hospitalization touched a nerve in Sitwell, as it was no doubt intended to do; she was pained, she wrote, "to know what you have suffered in that terrible house where you found yourself locked up. How *could* anyone have done such an appalling thing to you. . . . And the horror of being told that nothing one does, says, or thinks, is 'normal.'" On the latter point Sitwell especially sympathized: "Naturally, a genius does not think in the way in which an ordinary person thinks."

Carson was feeling forlorn that fall and winter. In late December she had an appointment with a new doctor, who she believed could treat her weakened, painful left side and banish her paralysis, making walking possible without a cane. Alas, the doctor had no such good news and in fact told her that her condition was permanent. What had she done to bring this suffering on herself? she asked. Her new friend saw her as unmistakably Christlike: "You say what have you done to deserve it. I think sometimes that a noble and great soul is called upon to bear anguish as some sort of redemption for the world—as the greatest who ever bore flesh suffered anguish. I don't know, but it seems so to me."

Even beyond her usual joy at discovering a kindred spirit, Carson, separated from Reeves and recovering from the debacle with Marty Mann, would have welcomed an ally in her corner at this time: more so, given Sitwell's position in the British literary establishment. Carson was aware that she might do well to cultivate a readership in England; she also had the American writer's awe of the seemingly lofty nature of British literary circles, in which Sitwell was an éminence grise. Her little taste of this world on her visit to Bowen's Court the previous year much impressed Carson; always mindful of her literary reputation, she saw an opportunity. She decided a visit to England was in order.

Carson was treading water in the early months of 1951—treading water and cashing checks, that is. She sold the film rights to *The Member of the Wedding* to Hollywood producer Stanley Kramer for $75,000—about $737,000 today—plus a percentage of the profits. In the meantime, the stage version closed on March 17, a profitable fourteen-and-a-half-month run. After a week it went on the road, traveling first to Boston and then to northern cities in the United States and Canada. Carson's royalties from the play alone had been, in 1950, around $75,000 net. After the movie rights sold, her lawyer, Floria Lasky, set up an allowance for Carson out of funds from her investments.

These were not good months for Carson, however, a time of dashed hopes as far as her health was concerned. David Garnett, a novelist and denizen of Bloomsbury who met her that spring in New York City, left a devastating description of her appearance. Sitting on a sofa at a party, she presented "a crumpled figure with short rat-eaten orange hair. . . . Her eyes were dark and full of pain. Her complexion was that of some overcooked grey vegetable tinged with poison. Doesn't soda sometimes discolour food so that it becomes unpalatable?" He drew a causal connection between her physical condition and her drinking habits, not-ing, "She was in continual pain. She drank to alleviate it—not because she was an alcoholic." Amazingly, given the ill feeling his description of her suggests, Garnett counted himself a great fan of Carson.

He was not wrong about the pain. Carson suffered greatly both physically and emotionally. Perhaps to compensate, in the weeks and months that followed and over the space of two continents, she seemed constantly in motion: never in any one place for very long, acting on a string of impulsive decisions, alternately charming and driving away one would-be friend after another. She was working very little and drinking incessantly. Increasingly, and ominously, people found it easier to indulge her and then distance themselves rather than assume the seemingly impossible task of intervening. When she could, she dragged Reeves along as a drinking companion; when they were sepa-rated, he became an object of stray aggressions.

David Diamond became reacquainted with Carson and Reeves around this time. He noted that Reeves was "so much better since join-ing Alcoholics Anonymous" and that Bébé, too, had stopped drink-ing. Carson's alcohol consumption, on the other hand, he found more damaging than her physical ills that spring: "She has several highballs daily before dinner and a bottle or two of wine after." As usual, those around her excused this behavior because she was in such pain. "As long as [Carson] lives in the alcoholic haze so much of the time (and she does not realize it!)," David wrote in his diary, "it will be impossible to *really* have a healthy, mutually gratifying relationship. She can *take* only. Reeves now gives and takes."

What she inflicted on others went double for Reeves. His sobriety was shaky—sometimes he allowed himself beer, sometimes wine, which even in the 1950s would mean that he was not sober. Janet Flanner, a loyal friend, observed, "Perhaps his part in the war had led him astray, destroyed his resistance to ordinary life, to rationality, and the patterns of living without excitement and without authority." He had not lost his charm—their neighbor Henry Poor's daughter remembered Reeves from about this time as "glowing." But he was increasingly unstable, and those around Carson saw the "danger signals," according to Ten-nessee's friend Oliver Evans: "Reeves would alternate between fits of abusive violence, during which he would threaten [Carson's] life—and his own—and spells of abject remorse during which he would beg her forgiveness." He had long talked about suicide, more than once threatening, when drunk, to go out the nearest window. David remembered the scene on a Rochester bridge when Reeves tried to convince him that they should jump off the bridge together. It had been the beginning of the end of their doomed relationship.

Catastrophically, Reeves started drinking in earnest again in June 1951. He slipped into a major depression, exacerbated by heavy drinking. It looked like end-stage drinking, and family and friends, especially Marty Mann, rallied around him to convince him to get help. He checked himself into Doctors Hospital on East End Avenue between Eighty-seventh and Eighty-eighth streets, which was known in part as a haven for the troubled rich.

What happened next is riddled with uncertainty. Carson and Reeves had planned to sail for Europe on the *Queen Elizabeth* on June 28. Her family seem to have assumed that Reeves, in treatment in Doctors Hospital, would not be accompanying her. But the two decided that Reeves would join her on the ship somehow, and they bought first-class passage on the ship, as the manifest shows. (Among Carson's papers are two receipts for the tickets signed by the purser.)

What followed was a chaotic welter of events, out of which nobody—except, briefly, Reeves—looks good. Rita and Bébé evidently had no way to convey Carson from Nyack to the pier on Manhattan's West Side where she was to board the ship. Carson refused to take a bus because she felt people stared at her on public transportation. Perhaps her luggage was an impediment—the McCullerses had taken seventeen pieces of luggage on their previous trip to Europe (putting the lie to Carson's indifference to clothes).

Even though Reeves was launched on the treatment program that they had urged on him, Bébé and Rita agreed that Rita, who had an apartment down the street from the hospital, would visit Reeves and ask him to check himself out for the day. He would then drive Carson and her luggage to the embarkation point. His recovery, evidently, was not a concern for the Smiths.

Reeves usually complied with the family's treatment of him as a lapdog or flunky—he often cast himself in this role. But this time, at least initially, he would not. When Rita visited Reeves in his room, she told Andrew Lyndon, a Southern friend, she found him surrounded by empty bottles of beer, smuggled to him by a nurse. But this time he put his foot down and refused to go along with Rita's scheme. (It interfered, as well, with the plans he had previously made to join Carson on board.)

In some fashion—Reeves did not drive her there—Carson was transported to the ship and conveyed on board. Somehow Reeves managed to get on board, too, presumably after checking himself out of Doctors Hospital. He did not intend to stay in England long, only a week. All this is redolent of a plot conceived in an alcoholic haze by one or both of them.

Carson and Reeves continued to keep the Smiths in the dark about his accompanying her to England even after the ship sailed. It took a while—a week—before Bébé and Rita noticed that Reeves was gone, despite the proximity of the hospital to Rita's apartment. When they did, the Smiths finally showed some solicitude for him. Jordan Massee recorded in his diary for August 2, "Rita called very late. She was frantic. After Carson's departure, Reeves disappeared."

Eventually, either Carson or Reeves or both put out the story that Reeves was a stowaway on the ship, boarding without her knowledge and making his presence known only when the ship was well underway. One apparent purpose of the stowaway story, whether conscious or not, was to absolve Carson of any blame for Reeves's return to drinking and the irresponsibility that went with it. She had no intention of leaving him behind. She wanted him around; the relationship, in complicated fashion, worked for her, and a drinking Reeves was a known quantity. His support, however clumsy, was very loving and thus was important to her, the potential damage to her troubled husband notwithstanding.

On the last day aboard, Carson wrote to her publisher, on RMS *Queen Elizabeth* stationery, with marked equanimity, that she planned a leisurely, relaxing visit to old friends like the Sitwells in England, and then to France and Venice, sailing back home in September.

Carson and Reeves plunged into the London literary scene. Reportedly Carson relished telling a story about Reeves disgracing himself at Edith Sitwell's. After a lot of drinking, while Carson and Edith were enjoying animated talk, he suddenly slipped to the floor, where he stayed, for another hour. Neither his hostess nor his wife paid any notice. About another incident, Rosamond Lehmann, who had met Carson at Bowen's Court, noted that "a very drunk Carson with her no less drunk husband" presented themselves at Lehmann's house in the country. Lehmann saw that a social visit was "out of the question" and sent them packing. Later, she recalled, Reeves, "unable to cope," returned to the States.

Reeves did indeed depart on August 7, flying back to New York. Carson immediately wrote him, in a letter that manifests the latest emotional weather between them. She addressed him with endearments as usual, stating that she already missed him. Both of them, it seems, had decided that he would devote himself to sobriety on his return. Reeves had to take as his one object getting well and staying that way—the latter calling to mind Reeves's dramatic slips. She had faith in him and knew he would not let her down. He was to devote himself to work, she said. Soon, however, Reeves, forgetting his Doctors Hospital sobriety program, decamped for the familiar Smith household in Nyack, despite the fact that Bébé and Rita had been less than helpful of late.

Back in London, Carson's companion and partner-in-crime was the poet David Gascoyne. A year older than Carson, he had risen to prominence in the 1930s with the assistance of Edith Sitwell, who classed him, Dylan Thomas, and George Barker as the best of a generation of young poets loosely grouped as the New Romantics. Sitwell most likely had a hand in Gascoyne's presenting himself as Carson's unofficial host. He was greatly interested in the Surrealist movement before the war, and his work continued to spring mostly from the Surrealist vision. A fragile, intense, and boyish thirty-four-year-old, he was certainly not the rock that Carson needed at this troubled time; he was already showing the signs of instability that would land him in a psychiatric hospital with a serious amphetamine psychosis. After Reeves left, David asked Carson to stay in his elegant flat at Grosvenor House, at 25 St. Leonard's Terrace. Carson described the accommodations to Reeves as a boardinghouse, making no mention of her host.

David was mostly homosexual, but the two appear to have formed a strong bond, perhaps encouraged by their mutual love of poetry. It may have been David's influence that prompted Carson to return her attention to her long poem, "The Dual Angel," in these months. In any event, she was delighted to share the space with him. David's protector, Sitwell, had already been very hospitable to her, and Carson was eager to repay Edith with a party of her own, which David agreed to host.

Among their guests was Rosamond Lehmann, who had already had a taste of Carson under the influence. Rosamond was one of three talented siblings, the others being John Lehmann, a writer and powerful editor, and Beatrix Lehmann, a celebrated stage actress, always called Peggy. Known especially for her performances in Eugene O'Neill's plays, Peggy had a buoyant personality and a caustic wit. Boyish in aspect, she had joined the Boy Scouts during the First World War. (They took up such wartime tasks as messengering and stretcher bearing.) Her bisexuality, as well as her radical politics—she was an ardent Communist—made her an outsider, despite her success in the theater. Not surprisingly, Carson developed a crush on her.

On this and other social occasions, however, Carson did not shine. The British in general were not taken by a Southern accent and syrupy effusions of love. But everyone noticed her drinking, and it put people off. Carson answered every invitation that came her way, and if the ones she wanted did not materialize, she and David were apt to show up anyway. Her publisher, Cresset Press, gave a party for her, hosted by the director, Dennis Cohen, and his wife, Kathryn Hamill Cohen, a psychiatrist. The Cohens were a handsome and talented couple who had built themselves a significant modern house at 64 Old Church Street, showcasing furniture of Dennis's design. He had bought Cresset Press in 1927; originally a publisher of limited editions, Cresset had expanded its list and now prided itself on prestigious fiction titles like Carson's.

In the midst of this round of activity, Tennessee came to town.

While he resented Carson's neediness and manipulative bent—traits he himself had in plenty—the two were still close. Indeed, their bond had been strengthened the previous spring when she met his sister Rose, rendered forever docile by a lobotomy, when Tennessee brought her to Nyack. Carson, with characteristic generosity, told Tennessee that Rose could stay and live with her. He remained fierce in Carson's defense when it mattered.

Tennessee was nevertheless chagrined to see Carson doing so badly in London. David Gascoyne, he said, was "a youngish and very seedy sort of mad poet, and I mean really mad." Tennessee's first sight of Carson was on a sofa at her lodgings with a cigarette and a "nearly empty" bottle of sherry, "stupefied." "A fish couldn't drink so much without sinking. . . . This all day and half the night drinking will lead to disaster," he wrote to his then-boyfriend Frank Merlo. "She needs psychiatric treatment worse than anyone I know, even myself, and it is heartbreaking." In letters to friends, he wrote that Carson was always threatening to move in with him, confiding that the prospect terrified him.

Carson was briefly involved with Kathryn Cohen, her therapist and the wife of her British publisher, Dennis Cohen of Cresset Press, in 1956.

Tennessee was greatly relieved to find that Kathryn Cohen, "on whom she had one of her immoderate 'crushes,'" was literally on the case.

Kathryn was an elegant woman with an interesting past, just the sort who drew Carson. Born in New York City in 1905, before the age of forty she was a successful actress and a performer with the Ziegfeld Follies. She married Dennis Cohen in the late 1930s, and when war broke out, she enrolled at Cambridge to study medicine, graduating with a degree in genetics. Regardless, she became a psychoanalyst with St. George's

Hospital, an eminent teaching hospital then located in Hyde Park. She often had affairs with women. The writer Patricia Highsmith was most recently her lover, and Cresset Press went on to become the British publisher of Highsmith's psychological thrillers.

When Kathryn saw the shape Carson was in, she immediately arranged for her to be hospitalized at St. George's, proposing as well that she treat Carson's physical condition with hypnosis. She held that there was no reason why Carson couldn't walk and move freely. Rosamond Lehmann took it upon herself to write to Reeves, telling him Carson was "exhausted from seeing too many people, drinking too much, and thrashing about in a welter of plans and projects with which she could not cope." Carson described what had brought her to St. George's in an eight-page letter to Reeves postmarked September 23. In the preceding days, she wrote, she had fallen into a deep depression, seeing only misery in every direction. Her old demons came back to haunt her—with a vengeance. She couldn't sleep for three days, despite dosing herself with Luminol (phenobarbital). She was unable to eat or walk.

In Kathryn, she felt she had found what she dreamed of in a doctor: one who didn't go away, leaving her alone with her sickness and feelings of abandonment. If this seems a lot to ask, it's important to remember that doctors played an outsize role in Carson's life. For long periods, they were likely the only people (except sometimes Reeves) who touched her body, and she was bereft when doctors left her. Carson became convinced that Kathryn could effect a cure. The early hypnotic sessions seem to have gone well, enough for Carson to continue. But what was most therapeutic, Carson told Reeves, was the love she and Kathryn shared.

Carson told Reeves all this, down to the last detail, and more. Her letters to him that summer and fall are documents of cruelty, blueprints for the worst way to treat a loved one. She was in a good deal of pain, physical and emotional, but the question remains as to why she felt the need to hurt someone else, as if there were an economy of suffering. She wrote her first, September 23 letter, from the hospital, opening with a detailed description of the psychic state that sent her there in a despair out of Kierkegaard. But everything had changed, she continued, changed so suddenly from bleak misery to a beautiful and loving universe that she was reminded of a kaleidoscope they had in Nyack and the miraculous *change* it effected with just a small turn of the wrist. The reason was Kathryn; she reminded Reeves she had told him about her. She and Kathryn had become friends, she wrote.

At this point Carson broke off, telling Reeves she could imagine his reaction, settling in with perhaps a ginger beer at his elbow, a nod to his sobriety, wondering when their usual drama would commence. She made abundantly clear that they were back on all-too-familiar territory.

Indeed they were, and once again Carson reported that she had a new "imaginary friend": Kathryn Cohen. The concept of a friend or lover who was both imagined and real was by now a familiar one, and it referred to Carson's lesbian loves. In a recent letter, Reeves had told Carson that "the great fear" was that an imaginary friend would come between them. In the heterosexual world they shared, these homosexual lovers were not "real"; the term "imaginary friend" effectively neutralized them.

But this time, she told Reeves, her imaginary friend was *real*. Carson always felt compelled to include Reeves in her affairs, although to what end is unclear. She understood, she wrote, why Reeves would be afraid of an imaginary friend, feeling he might be left out as a result. But that would not happen this time, she assured him, for neither she nor Kathryn would ever leave him outside their embrace. Unless— and here she not so subtly began to place the blame on Reeves—he made their relations impossible, undermining himself as he had done so often in the past and bringing about an unhappy ending through his own agency.

The letter then takes a vindictive turn. She described how beautiful Kathryn was. She'd long feared finding her greatest imaginary friend, Carson wrote, because chances were she would be absolutely hideous. She could have borne that, she supposed. But the opposite was true in this new friendship: Kathryn was heart-stoppingly beautiful. She thanked Reeves for the wisdom and tolerance he showed, making it possible for her and Reeves to have this "conversation."

Finally, she attempted to turn the whole affair into a challenge to Reeves's character: if *he* was big enough, *they* could survive this. Kathryn was leaving for a conference in the Netherlands, she wrote, but she was fine about it: Carson was secure in her knowledge of Kathryn's return. She drew a contrast between her secure confidence with Kathryn and Reeves's "frenzy" on learning that she would be going somewhere—like Europe—without him. His frenzy, she finally said, was the fault of his lack of understanding and acceptance of his wife's independence. Carson sent her best to Bébé and Rita and asked Reeves to lavish (French) kisses on their recently acquired French boxer Kristin (named after Kristin Lavransdatter, the heroine of Sigrid Undset's Norwegian trilogy).

When Tennessee appeared in London in the early fall of 1951, he was caught up in revisions to *Summer and Smoke* before its London premiere. He reported to Audrey Wood on Carson's drinking, adding that she was "brooding and mooning over John Lehmann's sister, the middle age one on the stage who is said to be dikish [*sic*]." He really hoped Carson would get psychiatric treatment. In October he went on at some length: "Confidentially, I have never seen her in quite such nervous disorder." In that month, he said, the "female hypnotist" had got her into a nursing home in the country.

Kathryn had tried to hypnotize Carson, with some success, though she realized that alcohol complicated any attempt to treat her patient. When she had to go off to a conference in the Netherlands for a few days, she checked Carson into the quaintly called Old Plaw Hatch (the reference is to an old hunting preserve), near East Grimstead in Sussex. From the continent, she wrote Carson two letters, one quite affectionate, the other more distant. The first asked Carson to straighten "those broad, beautiful shoulders, strengthen your long, slender legs and stride with your head high." She hoped Carson was getting some rest: "writing, eating, sleeping and not taking too much 'fluid,'" meaning alcohol. By this time, any romantic or physical relationship with Carson was over, despite the warm advice she gave her.

As of the end of October, however, Carson had left the country "home" against doctor's orders and come up to London, hoping to move in with Tennessee at his hotel. He was relieved to be able to say he did not have room, but he took responsibility for her by asking a New Orleans friend, Valentina Sheriff, to intervene. Sheriff, a Russian by way of Shanghai who had married a rich man, managed to get Carson a room at the Ritz and conveyed her there. A quarrel between Carson and Tennessee developed, however, probably because Sheriff took Carson's side in an argument, rousing the ire of both Frank Merlo and Tennessee. Merlo told her off, which ended up straining relations between the two men and Carson.

In the midst of this tension, Carson was trying to throw the best light on her situation. In a wire to Reeves sent on September 29, she conveyed the notion that Old Plaw Hatch was a salubrious country retreat. Two letters followed, which she may have sent in one envelope. These letters are intricately cruel, painful to read. In one of them, she expresses her disappointment at not having heard Reeves's reaction to her bombshell about Kathryn, the letter in which she talked of her imaginary friend. Why had he not replied? Evidently, her announcement of her new love affair meant little if it did not provoke a response from her husband.

First, she writes that she is proud of Reeves for trying to turn his life around. Somewhat condescendingly, she counsels him to find a vocation—perhaps the inclination he'd shown, back in 1945, to be a doctor. She thinks of this, she says, only because Kathryn went back to school at thirty-seven. Then Carson rattles off Kathryn's professional credentials (she had an impressive medical career, Carson said), implicitly comparing Kathryn's accomplishments to his sorry life.

Here the letter devolves into an imperious list of items she wants Reeves to send her. First, her "elegant" robe, the quilted velvet one. Also her "sturdy," hand-knitted dark blue sleeveless sweater. And he should send her finest cold-weather clothes, which she did not pack, not realizing the weather would turn. She also wants her "collected works," a matter of some urgency. The other item Carson requests is a piece of jewelry. She asks that Reeves buy it for her, a commission that sounds impossibly complicated. What she wants is a ring with a watch on it, for she has bought herself a beautiful bracelet, but her watch looks odd with it. The watch on the ring must be large enough to be functional. Priscilla Peck gave her partner, Marty Mann, a similar item, and Carson suggests that Reeves consult Marty about it—forgetting, seemingly, that Marty was a recent "imaginary friend."

The ring would cost $55 or $60, she says, and Reeves should get the money from Floria. Of course, Reeves will not know what size the ring should be. So Carson suggests, first, that he go by the size of his own wedding ring. But then another possibility suggests itself. She thinks, she told Reeves, that she left her wedding ring at home. Reeves must understand that her doing so was in no way revealing or symbolic. He should not read too much into it, for she left the ring in the midst of the craziness of embarking on her trip. But he can measure her ring size from her abandoned wedding ring. Perhaps he will have to pay more than $55 or $60, she writes, urging him to go with Bébé to Cartier's and check prices. She closes the letter impersonally, stating that she is going back to writing her poem.

It is difficult to say what purpose this seemingly whimsical request for a piece of jewelry served beyond upsetting Reeves. In his shaky condition, he did not need to know any more about her imaginary friend, perhaps least of all this person's professional accomplishments. Nor did it help him for his absent wife to suggest that she had wanted to make her trip to Europe as an unmarried woman—which he intuited as the reason she left her wedding ring behind.

We do not have Reeves's letters back to Carson to let us know what he made of all this. He did, however, write two surviving letters to Rosamond Lehmann as a designated point person for Carson's stay in England. He was relieved, he says, when Carson began treatment with Dr. Cohen, for he knew about and approved of Freud's use of hypnosis, which he thought would be easier for Carson to take because of her love for Kathryn. In one letter he acknowledges that Rosamond might not have formed the best impression of him when he and Carson made a drunken appearance at her country house, but he guesses she knows he is a better person than that.

Rosamond might have lost track of Carson after her hospitalization; if she did, it was probably with some relief. But Reeves's letters seem to prod her to ask Kathryn Cohen for further information. Kathryn wrote to Rosamond on November 27, two weeks after receiving her letter. She washed her hands of Carson, she said, after her patient decamped for the Ritz. Within a week, she wrote, "all the gain of my treatment was lost." Carson had talked wildly of further destinations—Paris, China, New Orleans—but Kathryn saw "she wasn't fit to travel anywhere" and advised her to go home. Her efforts to treat Carson had "failed completely." Carson had been impossibly needy and difficult. She hoped she and Carson had parted friends, but she was not sure.

Carson told Tennessee she wanted to continue her travels after her stay in England. That was a very bad idea, he told Audrey Wood. He offered to see her off on the plane to New York, "to which the female hypnotist had persuaded her to return," but she declined. She flew home on October 25.

In summing up his impressions of Carson at this time, Andrew Lyndon stressed that she was not a "monster." She was a genius with a strong sense of self-preservation in the midst of her seeming self-destruction. In this context, she could often be "firm," or insistent on turning events to her advantage. He mentioned this interpretation to Tennessee, whose response was passionate. Pounding on the table in front of him, he exclaimed, "Firm? She is harder than this marble!"

14

Grappa Rather Than Gin

The writer William Goyen, a new friend in the early 1950s, left several fascinating descriptions of Carson, all informed by his basic sympathy for her. "She had a lot of talent and I loved her very much," he said succinctly. He had met her as one of Robert Linscott's writers, although Linscott had left Houghton Mifflin, and Carson, for Random House in 1944. That "nest" of talent, or so Goyen called it, included Truman Capote and Gore Vidal, either of whom might well have introduced Goyen to Carson. He admired her work and her sensibility: "Her writings are a sort of fairy-tale, a strange and marvelous world. Carson McCullers truly invented a literary genre," he said in a *Paris Review* interview:

> [She] had great vitality and she was quite beautiful in that already decaying way. She was like a fairy. She had the most delicate kind of tinkling, dazzling little way about her . . . like a little star. Like a Christmas, she was like an ornament of a kind. . . . She said far out, wonderfully mad things, that were totally disarming, and for a while people would say, "I'll go wherever you go." She'd knock them straight out the window.

Those reactions, however, were changing, and while Goyen did not specifically link the change to the early 1950s, it seems to have been happening after he met her in 1950 or 1951. Instead of saying, "I'll go wherever you go," people now had an altogether different reaction, Goyen said: "She had an eye for human frailty and would go right to that; that's why people fled her. They thought, who needs this? Why be around her?"

⋙

After Carson flew back from her disastrous trip to England at the end of October 1951, she and Reeves simply floundered. Rather than settling back into the household in Nyack, where Bébé would have met most of their daily needs, they embarked on further travels. Their first stop was New Orleans, possibly urged by Carson's friend Valentina Sheriff, who lived there. Reeves told Rosamond Lehmann that when Carson came home, she was "not very well" and that they went to New Orleans to "recuperate." He put quotation marks around the verb, suggesting something other than physical woes. The trip did not turn out as planned, in any case, as Carson came down with a respiratory virus that turned into bronchial pneumonia and pleurisy. When she ran a fever of 105 degrees, Reeves took her to a local hospital. Antibiotics did their work, and she got back to Nyack safely.

There, Reeves wrote Rosamond, they embarked on a "quiet, domestic life" now that Carson was over "the emotional involvement with the Doctor in London." They'd hired a cook/housekeeper who was working out very well, and "life is composed and peaceful for us." He was working in New York City, at what is not known—possibly returning to a recent job with Bankers Trust—and Carson was working on the poems she'd written in England. Reeves did not mention to Rosamond that he and Carson were thinking of moving to Europe in the new year. In fact, in the same letter, he remarked, somewhat curiously, "I won't be back in Europe for several years."

But with the impulsiveness that characterized most of their joint decision making, they bought fourth-class passage for Naples on the SS *Constitution* on January 20. They were headed to Rome, traveling with their car and their French boxer, Kristin, because they hoped to make the move a permanent one.

❧

In the months before they sailed, Reeves once more tried to stop drinking. Earlier, when Carson wasn't torturing him with her love for Kathryn Cohen, she had urged him to get sober. In an undated letter from London that fall, she practiced positive thinking, writing that she expected him to get better and to stay better: she believed, she said, waxing vaguely threatening, that he would do it because he had to. When he met her on her arrival back in the States, she said, she needed him to be well—she simply couldn't take his self-abuse any longer. She promised that she still loved him and thought their marriage could work. Carson did not refer explicitly to drinking or alcohol in her letter; she and Reeves preferred not to name the problem. They had returned, it seemed, to believing the marriage could heal them.

On the ship to Naples, they were happy to see someone Carson had met at Yaddo and liked. Marguerite Young, Midwest born and bred, was a moderately acclaimed writer who had published two books of poetry, one of them a prizewinner; she was the recipient of a Guggenheim and a Newberry Library Award. Beginning in 1944, she was writing the epic novel that would become the bulky and reader-resistant *Miss MacIntosh, My Darling.* Contracted for in 1944, it would, notoriously, not be published until 1965.

Young had noticed Carson reading Proust on deck, wearing unusual sunglasses with blue lenses, and identified herself. Carson immediately bonded with her. Once on the midnight watch, Carson got up from her deck chair and addressed all the sailors and attendants and stargazers, "Ladies and gentlemen, I want to introduce you to America's most beautiful of all prose writers. . . . She is angelic." She then murmured something privately to Young about saying something like that only to people who couldn't read, which Young felt perfectly illustrated Carson's fiercely competitive nature.

Competitiveness aside, they got on well enough that Carson and Reeves suggested that Young join them—and Kristin—on the drive to their common destination, Rome. There all three had reservations at the fabled Hotel d'Inghilterra. Once there, Young recalled, Carson sniffed that the hotel was not elegant or fashionable enough for her and wanted to move to a more luxurious establishment.

The snobbishness that Young noticed in Carson's dissatisfaction with the Inghilterra extended to her impression of the Italian social scene. On the voyage over, Carson had told Young that she and Reeves were sorting the letters and cards of the writers in Rome who wanted to meet them. When Carson asked how many such appeals Young had received, she said she had none. Unperturbed, Carson said she expected to see her new friend at many gatherings in the months ahead.

A cosmopolitan and often crassly commercial artistic scene permeated Italy in the postwar years. Rome in 1952 was a thriving metropolis, and American expatriates were drawn there, many working in the movie industry, which was then undergoing a renaissance. Rome in the 1950s was hardly Paris in the 1920s, but the *miracolo italiano,* the postwar economic boom, was transforming the country, bringing waves of migrants from the countryside into the cities and producing a new culture of consumerism. The ancient city was becoming modern—and it lured multitudes of Americans. The movie business attracted key members of Carson's literary cohort, including Capote, Vidal, and Auden, as well as Marguerite Young. Ensconced in Rome, they took frequent trips to such spots as Taormina and Ravello.

As they had in Paris on their previous trip, Reeves and Carson wanted to find an apartment, feeling that living among Europeans—people who were profoundly different from the Americans they knew, more tolerant, more discerning—was the best way to travel. In an apartment, they could remove themselves from the tourists who came looking for monuments and palaces—not their style at all—and make room for their work. They were flush with money but planned to get by on Reeves's army pension, about $350 a month, and an allowance Carson received by way of Floria Lasky.

They got some help finding an apartment from David Diamond, who was now living in Rome on a Prix de Rome scholarship and subletting their mutual friend Natalia Murray's apartment. They had written him the previous December, asking him to be on the lookout for a place for them to stay in Rome. Still very much in their thrall, he had asked some American friends, George and Tina Lang, to help with the hunt.

The Langs came up with a place that immediately appealed to Carson and Reeves: an apartment in Castel Gandolfo, a picturesque village on Lake Albano, about thirteen miles south of Rome. The village's centerpiece was the Apostolic Palace, which was for centuries a summer residence for popes. The apartment was modern and quite comfortable, but its decorative flourishes did not suit Carson. She and Reeves extended an invitation to David and his new companion, Ciro Cuomo, to visit them on a day trip on February 11, the day after they moved in. They ferried David and Ciro out from Rome in their car.

David detailed their visit in his diary, noting, "All day Carson groans, and sips highballs." She complained about the apartment and about Italy, declaring she was ready to leave for Paris anytime. Reeves drove David and Ciro back to Rome at midnight. David marveled that this "sullen" Reeves bore little resemblance to the man who had once so obsessed him. Reeves and Carson would remain in Italy until the end of April and would live there off and on for the remainder of the year, but David and Ciro would not see them again on that visit. David would not see Carson again until 1956. Perhaps his disaffection was reciprocated.

Carson was introduced to a number of Italian writers, some of whom became friends, including Alberto Moravia, Carlo Levi, and Ignazio Silone. She made an important acquaintance in her translator, the Italian Irene Brin, and Irene's husband, Gaspero del Corso. Brin and del Corso ran L'Obelisco Galleria d'Arte, an influential art showplace, and Brin was notable as a cutting-edge Italian fashion icon and a contributor to *Harper's Bazaar,* what might today be called an influencer. Carson was duly impressed. But it was Brin's translation of *Reflections in a Golden Eye* that most affected her. The first of her books to appear in Italian, the novel, with its edgy quality and attention to the nature of authority, sexual anxiety, and social class, appealed to an Italian sensibility that was in revolt against the militarism, authoritarianism, and traditionalism of the prewar fascist regime.

The week that Reeves and Carson arrived, Carson asked Young

if she'd received an invitation to a soirée given by Princess Marguerite Caetani. Young said no and discovered that Reeves had not been explicitly invited either, for whatever reason. Since he would not be escorting Carson, he proposed to Marguerite that they go exploring in a horse and buggy. Young enjoyed what she called a "divinely beautiful" day.

The princess had exalted social connections, but it was in her role as a patron of literature that she formed a connection with Carson. Born Marguerite Chapin to a wealthy family in Connecticut, she had married the composer Roffredo Caetani, prince of Bassanio, at a young age. She moved to Europe, settling with her husband first in Paris and later in Sermoneta, an Italian hill town. She started a literary journal, *Commerce,* drawing on the couple's extensive circle of friends in the arts. After moving to Rome in 1945, the princess had started *Botteghe Oscure* ("Dark Shops," the name taken from a Roman street), a literary magazine published twice a year in five languages that enjoyed considerable cultural currency. In the late 1940s and '50s, it published writings by Dylan Thomas, Elsa Morante, Adrienne Rich, Georges Bataille, and William Carlos Williams. Poet Robert Lowell called the princess "a mad, sympathetic aristocratic" version of Yaddo's Elizabeth Ames.

Eugene Walter, the princess's American secretary, was a Southerner from Mobile. He later described an occasion—possibly the soirée from which Reeves and Young were excluded—when Blanche Knopf came to visit the princess, bringing Carson with her. Walter was not immediately responsive, because Blanche's dress and makeup struck him as excessive for a daytime occasion, a reaction he attributed to his Southern upbringing. Carson looked a little sickly but impressed him once she started talking: "There was this little mousy thing with green skin and huge shadows under her eyes and looking like a lemur sitting next to me on the sofa. If I were casting a sharecropper film, I would cast her. She looked slightly unhealthy. But she was animated and charming; she was one of those cats and monkeys."

Marguerite was very taken with "The Dual Angel," the poem Carson had written in her months in England, and arranged to make room for it in full in *Botteghe Oscure*'s first issue of 1952; *Mademoiselle* would publish it that July. Sometime in the next few months, Marguerite also committed to publishing a piece of Carson's work in progress, *Clock Without Hands*. Carson had had the germ of the novel—and the title—in mind since the 1940s; when asked by reporters for her views on race, she often said she was going to address those issues in her next novel, *Clock Without Hands*. She had always felt that as a Southern writer, she had a special imperative to address race, especially in light of the mounting civil rights battles there. The novel as she imagined it at this point revolved around Judge Clane, a retired congressman and racist whose hopes for the new South turn on the revaluation of Confederate currency, and a young blue-eyed African American man whose purchase of a house in a white neighborhood sets off a tragedy. Carson had talked to Jordan at length about race and the novel-in-progress one evening in March 1949. She described the character she would introduce first, J. T. Malone—a postman at this date, later a pharmacist—and the young black man, then called Prince and later Sherman. Because the judge was based in part on Jordan's father, she asked Jordan "hundreds of questions" about the Ku Klux Klan in Macon and "the attitudes of second and third generation Southerners after the Civil War."

"The Dual Angel" appeared in *Botteghe Oscure*'s 1952 issue as promised, but Marguerite warned Carson that she needed the extract from the novel by that summer, at least. Thus Carson pulled out the manuscript, which she had carried to Europe with her, and worked the first chapter into some kind of shape. J. T. Malone, now a druggist in a Southern town, learns he is dying of leukemia and tries to make sense of his life and his seemingly meaningless looming death. The marble pestle he used to compound drugs in the back of his store becomes a symbol of constancy and meaning when things that are not so real and hard threaten his equilibrium and his sense of order. Thus the title, "The Pestle," which Carson used for the selection, also published in *Mademoiselle* in July 1952.

No doubt her progress on *Clock Without Hands* gave Carson confidence during her initial weeks in Rome. She was heartened to learn that she had been elected as one of fourteen new members to the National Institute of Arts and Letters, along with Tennessee Williams and Newton Arvin, Louise Bogan, Jacques Barzun, and Waldo Frank; also chosen was her old bête noire, Eudora Welty. Carson would not travel back for the induction ceremony, but the honor recognized her as part of a larger literary community. Then, too, she could (and probably did) brag.

Tennessee, however, feared that Carson's stay in Rome represented little more than a change of scenery. He doubted, he told Maria St. Just, that they would see a real transformation in her: "I fear it is [only] to be 'grappa' rather than gin." They spent the last winter months huddled around their fireplace. In their first two months, Reeves wrote a friend on April 13, they were sick "off and on." They enjoyed a noisy Easter because of the pope's presence in Castel Gandolfo, with bells ringing and "nuns running around all over the place." With the advent of better weather and better health, they hoped to leave Rome and travel in Austria and Germany, then to Paris "for an indefinite time."

The only traveling they did, as it turned out, was in Italy. They were in Florence in April and Venice in May, where they were joined by Cheryl Crawford and her partner, Ruth Norman; the four of them photographed each other feeding pigeons in the Piazza San Marco. From there they drove to Milan, where Carson met her Italian publisher, Leo Longanesi. Her interpreter and champion was Mario Monti, also a translator of Tennessee Williams. He later said he would never forget Carson's white socks.

They arrived in Paris in May 1952 in their car, with their dog, and no place to stay. As always, they preferred an apartment rather than a hotel. They finally phoned John and Simone Brown at Clairefontaine, their home in Brunoy. The Browns assured the McCullerses that they had room to put them up. The invitation delighted Reeves and Carson, for they had set their hearts on buying a property in the French countryside and could use Brunoy as a base.

The stay with the Browns went bad quickly, however. Years later John talked about the visit, not mincing any words. The primary problem was alcohol; these were "people so drunk they were no longer in control of themselves." Reeves was trying yet again to stop drinking; Carson had "ordered him to," according to John. But as usual, he seems not to have stuck with it. Brown saw with "dismay" the arrival of a case of wine Carson had ordered. "Don't worry, dear John, it's only wine," she told him.

"She couldn't make head nor tail of the mess her life was in," John later said, nor of "her very disabling illness, her desire to write, her impossible life with Reeves, her dependence on alcohol." His assessment of their marriage was devastating, noting that she would invite friends over but refuse to make any preparations; when they arrived, she would refuse to leave her room to welcome them. In the face of this behavior, "Reeves was at a loss. So he got drunk." Brown provided one of the most devastating descriptions of their marriage at this time: "These two had an abominable, cannibalistic relationship. But she was the vampire. With him she threw tantrums. She wanted him to wait on her, to attend to her every need. She had a colossal power of destruction." Carson and Reeves had intended to stay for a month, but after a few weeks, the Browns had to ask them to leave, in part to spare their young children the display.

At this perhaps unlikely juncture, Carson and Reeves found the country property they had been looking for, in Bachivillers, a sleepy place with about 150 residents. The ancient stone house was next to the village's only church, L'Église Saints-Sulpice-et-Lucien; it had once been the residence of the *curé* and was known as L'Ancien Presbytère.

Carson and Reeves bought this house an hour from Paris in the village of Bachivillers in 1952.

Carson later described it as possibly the loveliest bit of real estate she had ever seen. Plums, pears, figs, and walnuts grew in an orchard. Fortuitously, a recent American owner had renovated it, even installing central heating, then rare in rural France. She and Reeves each had a bedroom, she remembered; the house also boasted a guest room (*ING*, 43).

The town was fifty-six kilometers north of Paris, or about an hour's drive. The stone house, in the shadow of the church and its graveyard, was surrounded by picturesque stone walls. Perhaps most important for Reeves and Carson, the land—about an acre—included a sunny spot that had been a vegetable garden. Among Carson's dearest memories of the Stark Avenue house in Columbus were the garden her father tended in the last years of his life and the delectable tomatoes they grew there together. Between the fruit trees and the vegetable garden at their new home, Carson and Reeves believed they would be nearly self-sufficient. A favorite fantasy of theirs was enumerating the ingredients they would need for gumbo, vegetables they dreamed of harvesting in their own backyard: okra, tomatoes, celery, and onions.

It was already June when they bought the house, a bit late in the season, but Reeves hurriedly planted the already-prepared plot. Meanwhile they concentrated on the fruit trees, which didn't need much attention at that time of year. Carson wanted to grow not only the ingredients for gumbo but also flowering plants for a Southern garden. "I've got to get me some lantana seeds and some four o'clock seeds," she told Eugene Walter. But she didn't want the bright pink flowers or the ones "all speckled and spotted." Eugene sent home to Mobile for seeds for the pale pink lantanas and pure white four o'clocks that she wanted. Jordan was quietly amused by Carson's recounting the glories of their new country house; she put him in mind, a little bit, of Marie Antoinette.

They paid less than $5,000 in cash for the property, an extremely low price (about $52,000 today), especially given that it had central heating and modern plumbing. The house came with a gardener and a French couple, the Jofferses, who cooked and took care of the house. "In true French fashion," Carson wrote in a kind of reverie, the couple fed them soup and a soufflé, followed by a main meat or fish course and salad, followed by fruit. Carson never forgot, she said, Madame Joffers's extraordinary vegetable soup and tried in vain to find the recipe (*ING*, 43). It isn't clear why the Jofferses left, but Reeves's temper, Carson's spotty French, and their quarreling when drinking might have been factors; both McCullerses were hard on servants and found it difficult to keep them. A Russian housekeeper followed the French couple, who claimed to be "a direct lineal descendant of Genghis Khan," Reeves said. Carson could do hardly any housework and cleaning, and Reeves was taken up by the grounds and repairs. They didn't know the area or the neighbors. They planned to travel off and on, using L'Ancien Presbytère as a base, so household help was a necessity and required their careful attention.

But caught up in their own activities and their own drama, and disabled by alcohol, Carson and Reeves had no further attention to give. As it turned out, their proximity to Paris was both a blessing and a curse. Even that summer, when they wanted to stay put in their new house, they found themselves going back and forth to the city. One reason was eminently practical. Because Reeves was a veteran, they could get all their food and supplies from the Paris PX (Post Exchange) for half of what it cost in the United States. Largely because of the PX, Reeves believed they could live in France for a third less than in the States, reducing the amount Floria Lasky sent Carson each month. Unfortunately, the PX also carried liquor.

Their finances were in excellent shape. Their accountant told them their estimated income for 1952 was $43,800, about $427,000 today. He reviewed their situation: they had paid off their mortgage on the Nyack house, they now owned a house in France outright, and they had added a portfolio of stocks—"unquestionably" a good idea, said the accountant. With these assets to back them up, Reeves had the financial space to write or do whatever he wished, Carson noted. Unmentioned was the fact that she had made all the money.

They were in Paris later that June when Tennessee Williams came up from Rome to consult with Elia Kazan over the Broadway production of his play *Camino Real;* his presence may have brought them there.

"She and Reeves came to Paris, both in terrible shape," he reported in a letter to Oliver Evans. "He was on liquor and sleeping tablets, she was on liquor. . . . He had been threatening to kill himself." Waxing especially cynical in a July letter to Maria St. Just, Tennessee described Carson as hardly "one big bundle of sheer animal exuberance." She was no fun to be around.

Tennessee and the McCullerses were all staying at the Hôtel Pont Royal. One night Tennessee got a panicked call from Carson, asking him to come *down* to their room right away. He had thought they were on an upper floor, but they'd moved to a room lower down, Carson said, because Reeves was threatening to jump out the window. A leap from the window of their new room did not interest him.

That night Tennessee answered the summons, finding in their room a pale and frantic but not on the face of it suicidal Reeves. Evidently he had been casting about for reasons for his continued misery. What was the matter? Tennessee asked. "I am homosexual," Reeves said with deathly seriousness.

Tennessee burst out laughing, and Reeves eventually joined in. "Lots of people are that," Tennessee answered, "without jumping out of hotel windows." Carson, however, remained solemn. Tennessee was torn; he needed to leave for a meeting with Anna Magnani about the role he hoped she'd play in *Summer and Smoke*. But he didn't want to leave Carson alone with her distraught husband. He took the gamble, promising to talk after he returned. Somehow, Reeves was deflected from self-destruction that day. But Tennessee felt guilty about leaving Carson and Reeves in such a state. A couple of weeks later he invited himself to Bachivillers but never did visit there, despite Carson's entreaties.

The day after that scene, Carson told Tennessee that Reeves was going to admit himself to a clinic, presumably to dry out, and that they were going to sell L'Ancien Presbytère. But if Reeves got treatment, in the summer of 1952 or the next ten months they were in Europe, it is nowhere recorded. If he did go into a clinic, it is unlikely that he stayed. At times he tried valiantly, attending AA meetings in Paris—as of 1950, there was only one English-speaking meeting. But he was seldom sober during their attempt to start a new life in France.

For a period at Bachivillers, Reeves seemed to spend his mornings in the room designated his studio, where he was working on his writing, having decided that he had been neglecting his true vocation, literature. But he would show up at lunch a little drunk. Carson paid no attention until she remembered that his studio was right over the wine and liquor cellar, only a staircase away (*ING*, 43).

They passed a thoroughly miserable summer. One bright spot was their introduction to a young intern, Jack Fullilove, at the American Hospital in Neuilly, which Carson visited regularly because of her paralysis and generally shaky health. He was one of three doctors involved in her care; the others were her old crush, Robert Myers, and Neal Rogers, an internist who had a range of celebrity patients, among them the Duchess of Windsor. Carson sometimes checked into the hospital for a couple of days, where she would be waited on and otherwise given the attention she wanted. The growing unpleasantness of her company shrank her circle of friends in Europe, but the doctors and nurses at the American Hospital seemed by contrast a warm surrogate family.

Reeves found friends there as well—and medical help. He visited Carson often enough that his condition was known to the staff. It is entirely possible that he, or Carson, or both of them appealed to her trio of doctors for help. At one point that summer, one of them prescribed Antabuse, which Reeves took intermittently over the next year and a half. Antabuse was a new drug taken daily by alcoholics trying to stay sober—it causes violent illness if the user drinks. Approved by the FDA the previous year, Antabuse promised to remove the burden of decision making from alcoholics who took it—not a huge number. Of course, they could also decide not to take it and then, after the few days needed for the drug to leave their systems, drink again. But Reeves was motivated—indeed, often desperate—which boded well for his sobriety with the help of the drug. Antabuse worked well for him, at least at first.

In mid- to late summer, Carson received bad news from home. Bébé was not well. Back in May she had suffered a severe heart attack, falling and breaking six ribs. Carson and Reeves had flown to New York then, perhaps fearing she was near death, but two weeks later, when Bébé was no longer in danger, they had returned to Paris. In this latest crisis, Carson learned that Bébé had suffered a pulmonary embolism, a potentially life-threatening condition. She flew home, alone this time, and once again saw her mother through the scare. But she and Rita decided that Bébé could not live alone in Nyack, even with Rita, still working at *Mademoiselle,* coming out for weekends; and Bébé was lonely and unhappy without Carson and Reeves. After much consultation and planning, Lamar Jr. agreed to take her in. He and his wife and their adopted son, Bill Lamar, had lived in Brunswick, Georgia, since 1945, but it was decided that Bébé would be happier in Columbus, so Lamar uprooted his family and made the move. Bébé joined them in August. When Carson flew back to Paris that month, mother and daughter missed each other terribly.

In the meantime, Reeves's mother, Jessie, who had long since left Georgia and was living in Greenwich Village near her son Tom, bought a paint store in Nyack for her daughter, Wiley Mae, and Wiley Mae's husband. In Bébé's absence, Jessie, Wiley Mae, and her husband moved into 149 Broadway, Jessie filling in for Bébé as landlady. When construction began in March on the Tappan Zee Bridge, which would span the Hudson River, connecting South Nyack on the west bank with Tarrytown on the east, hordes of construction workers descended on the area looking for housing. Jessie happily rented to them, ensuring a steady income for the three years it took for the bridge to be built.

Soon after returning from the States, Carson again left L'Ancien Presbytère, this time with Reeves. Through Truman Capote, she was invited to come to Rome to work on a screenplay, her first venture into that form. The project was a film by the Italian director Vittorio De Sica, who had received international acclaim for *The Bicycle Thief* (1948). Carson was hired not by De Sica but by David O. Selznick, one of the producers. Selznick, whose biggest financial success had been the 1939 *Gone with the Wind,* was bankrolling the film for his wife, actress Jennifer Jones. Capote later claimed that he had been offered the job originally but had deliberated so long that Selznick gave the job to Carson. The film, to be titled *Stazione Termini,* would follow Jones as a married American woman alone in Rome and her affair with an Italian, played by Montgomery Clift. She decides to break off the affair and return to the States, but the Italian pursues her around Rome's Terminal Station trying to get her to stay—unsuccessfully.

Carson described herself (and Reeves) as working nearly around the clock, all through October, on the screenplay. Reeves wrote a cheerful letter on November 3 to Edwin Peacock and John Zeigler describing the work that *both* of them were doing on the script, but other indications are that he was too drunk to work. Carson told Jack Fullilove that Reeves, having evidently stopped the Antabuse a few days before their flight from Paris to Rome, began drinking on the plane and had not really stopped. Now he was taking sleeping pills during the day to get enough rest to go out all night drinking. When he and Carson crossed paths, Reeves threatened, again, to commit suicide.

Capote painted an extremely nasty picture of the McCullerses during this time in a letter to Cecil Beaton. Riffing on "Sister Woman," the family nickname that Tennessee commonly used for Carson, he referred to Carson as Sister and Reeves as Mr. Sister: "Sister (the famous Carson McCullers, you remember *her*?) and Mr. Sister are frequently to be observed *staggering* along the Via Veneto, where they are now established members of the movie crowd (she is writing a movie for David Selznick); but of course Sister and Mr. Sister are too exalted, and usually too drunk, to recognize my poor presence."

Meanwhile Carson was constantly hounded for rewrites. She worked mostly with line producer Wolfgang Reinhardt, whom she found reasonable enough. But eventually she had to submit the script to Selznick, who was in Paris. In October Selznick showed up in Rome, and though Carson thought she could rework the screenplay to meet his exacting standards—or the fantasy film in his head—she could not, and she was fired. Capote came back on board.

In the meantime, according to his friend the novelist William Styron, Capote had perfected an imitation, in his best Georgia accent, of a drunken Carson searching her hotel room for an overdue script Selznick was demanding: "Well, just a minute, David, Ah seems to find, Ah'll hunt under the bed . . . it's around heah somewhere . . . daggone if Ah know where that script is." Capote pulled out all the stops, Styron recalled.

On the other hand, as Marguerite Young (whom Truman called, unbeknownst to her, the Cow) later commented, Truman was himself drinking a lot at the time. He would often show up at Young's apartment in the morning with a bottle of gin or vodka and shepherd her around the city in his car. On one such outing, Young said, Capote spotted Carson standing on a traffic island, her silver-handled cane at her side. "Ahhh," he hissed to Young, only half in jest, "now I can get her! I can just brush past her and knock her down and kill her!" Young dissuaded him, warning that their friends would surely know he did it.

Truman professed to adore Carson, but relations between them were always tense, even more so since his novel *The Grass Harp* had appeared the year before. Gore Vidal said Truman "plundered" Carson's work in his first book, *Other Voices, Other Rooms*—and that was just the beginning. Indeed, her especially fine story "A Tree. A Rock. A Cloud" is easily traceable in a passage from Truman's *The Grass Harp* that hangs on a character's insight into love:

> A leaf, a handful of seed—begin with these, learn a little what it is to love. First, a leaf, a fall of rain, then someone to receive what a leaf has taught you, what a fall of rain has ripened. No easy process, understand; it could take a lifetime, it has mine, and still I've never mastered it—I only know how true it is: that love is a chain of love, as nature is a chain of life.

It was not the wording, of course—though the cadence is almost identical—but the concept, the kind of plagiarism that could leave the "plundered" author dejected and hollow. Carson said Truman was like a baby that you've taken to your bosom to suckle who then bites you. Bébé called him "a little crook."

Certainly Truman was no help to Carson as she floundered in her career, her marriage, and her psyche. In the aftermath of their experience with the film and Selznick, Reeves characterized it as "hectic," but said that when it was all over, there was no "ill will," adding that he and Carson had achieved their objective: "some crisp, green, American money." He was, as usual, buoyant when sober, but Carson was exhausted and wound up in a clinic attached to Salvator Mundi Hospital in Rome for close to a week before she and Reeves fled back to Bachivillers.

The following year Jack Fullilove would be the person closest to Carson and Reeves. The young intern—he was ten years younger than Carson—often came out to L'Ancien Presbytère on weekends and was reliably present for holidays. After the Jofferses, a Russian cook supplanted a Turkish one; not long afterward Carson and Reeves were able to rehire the Jofferses, who had been with the house in the beginning; they took care of the property during the McCullerses' absences. On Thanksgiving Jack and some colleagues from the American Hospital went to Bachivillers for an American meal, the ingredients coming, of course, from the Paris PX.

That Christmas Carson and Reeves stayed in Jack's apartment at the American Hospital. It was a pleasant time, and the three of them, Southerners in Paris, decided to observe it by going to see *Gone with the Wind,* which by some happy logic was showing in a Paris movie theater at Christmastime. Later, in Jack's apartment, Carson, probably drunk, invited Jack to come to bed with her and Reeves. (He declined.) It was not the first time she had asked another man to share their bed—nobody ever took her up on it except perhaps David Diamond—and it seems to have arisen out of an impulse to assuage Reeves's unhappiness.

Sometimes Reeves said, as he had to Tennessee, that his trouble was that he was homosexual, and Carson thought he might be happier if he could act on those feelings. If alcohol was involved—always likely—she might have had no idea what confusion she was spreading, or that her clumsy attempt to help only made things worse, both for Reeves and for herself and Reeves as a couple. On the other hand, Carson's behavior in England the previous summer and fall makes clear that she was perfectly capable of consciously subjecting Reeves to a kind of emotional torture. Asking Jack to join them in bed could also be interpreted as a purely malicious gesture designed to complicate their relationship with Fullilove and to make his friendship with Reeves— Jack was one of the few friends Reeves had in Rome and Paris in 1952—impossible, by tangling it in the homosexual urges that caused Reeves such confusion and torment.

15

A Colossal Power of Destruction

At the end of 1952, hard on her unsatisfactory experience with the movies, Carson became enmeshed in a high-profile but potentially dispiriting theatrical project: the dramatization of Anne Frank's *The Diary of a Young Girl*. The project was dispiriting not just because of the grim subject matter but because of how badly the whole affair was handled.

The Diary of Anne Frank is one of the most powerful literary documents of the Second World War. A Dutch Jewish girl and her family and another went into hiding from the Nazis in what they called the Secret Annex, in a commercial building in Amsterdam. Anne was thirteen when she started her diary, fifteen when the Nazis discovered them in August 1944, and going on sixteen when she died, probably in 1945, probably of typhus, at the Bergen-Belsen concentration camp. Otto Frank, her father, survived the camp. His daughter's diary was saved by a family friend who had aided the Franks throughout their time in the Annex. They gave it to him in July 1945. Aware that he possessed what was, among its many other qualities, a priceless, emotionally transformative document, he arranged for German, French, and English translations. Doubleday published it in the States in 1950 after editor Judith Jones had plucked it from a slush pile.

When Carson and Reeves met Otto Frank in 1952, theater people were seeing great dramatic potential in the diary. Carson's friend

Cheryl Crawford had written her on November 13 advising her to consider adapting the work and saying that she had arranged for Doubleday's European editor, Francis Price, to give her a copy of the diary. Carson read it and said she was interested, and Price set up a meeting with her and Otto Frank. Anne's father very much liked Carson, finding her "a sensitive and lovable creature . . . very, very sympathetic," although he thought she was frail, noting that she walked with a cane and, curiously, was "unlucky to look at." Carson in turn told Mary Tucker that Otto Frank was one of the most extraordinary individuals she had ever met—he reminded her of Gandhi.

Soon afterward Cheryl Crawford and Barbara Zimmerman, a Doubleday editor, met with Frank, then in New York, to discuss the possible play. They were sure that Carson was the right person to dramatize it, recalling Frankie in *Member of the Wedding* and her adolescent discontent: the sensitivity, wit, and pathos of a young girl growing into a woman and who feels herself an outsider, much like Anne in her diary. Surely the creator of Frankie Addams could bring to the diary the receptivity and emotional intelligence necessary to fashion a successful play. Cheryl assured Anne's father that Carson had "an uncommon understanding of adolescent girls."

A week after receiving Cheryl's letter of November 13, Carson wrote her back rather formally to say that she was engaged in writing *Clock Without Hands* and dramatizing two of her own works, *The Heart Is a Lonely Hunter* and *The Ballad of the Sad Café,* but an Anne Frank script was a departure from those projects that she was very excited about. The following week, Reeves told Crawford that Carson "wanted to try" turning the diary into theater, though she was intimidated by what she called its greatness. Reeves enclosed with his letter to Crawford a copy of one Carson was mailing that day to Otto Frank.

In her letter, Carson poured on the Southern charm. She opened by announcing, disingenuously, that she didn't know what to say about the diary; she had been crying over it, but now she needed to write, and she was at a loss. It had emotionally flattened her.

Pulling out all the stops, she compared Anne to Keats, Mozart, and Chekhov, who all died young, saying that the diary of the adolescent girl was an extraordinary, unprecedented gift to the world. She had been playing the posthumous sonatas of Schubert and thought of them as "Anne's music." She closed by saying that her heart, and her husband's, were "filled with love." The last sentence represented Carson at her warmest. She was generous and expansive, wanting to share the happiness of her new home with a friend she felt was a companion of the heart and who, for the time, had no real home of his own. He should think of their place as his French home, complete with music, books, three dogs, and an excellent cook.

To sweeten the deal, Crawford had promised Carson an assignment to write an introduction to an edition of Anne's stories. But in her letter to Frank, Carson had explicitly not said anything about the play or Anne's short stories. She was responding only to the diary. In fact, she and Reeves were nervous that another party stood between them and Carson's adaptation. Meyer Levin had contacted Otto Frank months before and received a verbal agreement that he would write the play. Levin was a novelist struggling to make a living from his writing, though much of his work was critically praised. When he read Anne Frank's diary, he became obsessed, resolving that he would not rest until the diary was adapted as a stage play. After he reviewed the book glowingly in *The New York Times,* producers finally saw the potential in the dramatization he had been trying to sell them.

Then Levin read in the newspapers that Carson McCullers would be adapting the diary, and he was outraged that a "novelist" had been chosen to write a play. (One of the many mysteries in this story is why Levin, the author of six novels and as yet no plays, felt he could seize on this particular point—and in spite of Carson's hit play.) He had, he told Carson in an early November letter, "a moral right to do the dramatization." Soon enough it became clear that Levin based this on the fact that he was Jewish and she was not.

In the early 1950s, this issue was not called "cultural appropriation." Rather, the situation raised a different question, as to whether Anne's story was specifically Jewish or was universal. The latter would mean that it spoke to the human condition rather than that of any smaller group. To Levin, this was an either/or question, and his answer, emphatically, was that it was a Jewish story. In the same letter, Levin said he "would not be honest" if he did not say that, as a Jewish writer, he felt "a certain sense of wrong" that "others" could interpret such a work. He'd objected in a similar vein, he said, when John Hersey, who wasn't Jewish, wrote a novel set during the Warsaw Ghetto uprising, *The Wall* (1950).

The issue hung fire over the holidays. As the winter weather blew into Bachivillers from the English Channel, snowing them in several times, Carson and Reeves were stewing over it. Otto Frank visited them at L'Ancien Presbytère for a few days, according to a letter Carson wrote to Mary Tucker, but it is not known what they discussed. Carson voiced no doubts over the issue of whether she could capture the specific experience of a Jewish family trying to survive the Nazi terror. The protagonists in her work are in fact culturally particular; nor were their lives necessarily hopeful. On the other hand, even with the best intentions, it would not be easy for her to capture the specifically Jewish flavor of Anne's life. Her Southern sensibility wouldn't help much.

A letter from Cheryl Crawford dated January 3 told Carson that the "Anne book" was "free" now, and she'd like to have a play written and ready to go by the summer. Crawford had officially turned down Meyer Levin's script. Eager to nail down her appointment, Carson called a supporter in the States, Janet Flanner, urging her to wire Otto Frank that the project was now viable and to prod him to make a decision. Crawford and Frank must have hoped that Levin would no longer thwart their project. Meanwhile Flanner, after hanging up with Carson, imitated her for Natalia Murray: "When I kept reading [Anne's] book and saw her po' l'il face and then Ah looked at Cheryl's photo then Ah jus' thought mah heart would never forgive me ef Ah did'n do thet play."

After the phone call, Carson cabled Crawford "demanding" action, though she was in no position to make demands. "I say to the devil with threatened suits and commercial hazards with subject matter." In other words, ignore Levin and further claims he might make. "Otto Frank and I believe in it and want it. I think it is a good idea for a powerful play."

But Crawford did indeed fear continued legal pressure from Levin if she produced the play, and if Crawford were not the producer, then it seemed Carson would not be the playwright. Levin continued his importuning and further muddied the waters in innumerable ways. Everyone who had had a stake in Carson's adaptation dithered and delayed before choosing various outs. Carson herself pleaded ill health; "When I was reading the book," she elaborated six years later, "I was so upset that I broke out in a rash on my hands and feet, and I had to tell [Otto Frank] that under the circumstances I could not do the play" (*TMH*, 278). Cheryl Crawford's excuse for bowing out was colored by her protectiveness toward Carson: "[She] is so fragile and I have always been her protector so I must be very wise and certain about the right thing to do," she said. Crawford had a further out: she was hard at work on Tennessee's *Camino Real*, and "I don't want to do another somber play now. . . . I have a comedy I like a lot."

The project knocked around until it was finally given to Frances Goodrich and Albert Hackett, authors of such screen fare as *The Thin Man*, *It's a Wonderful Life*, and *Father of the Bride*. The husband-and-wife team wrote the play, which was different from the sort of adaptation that Carson, with her introspective Southern sensibility, would have written, and it also deviated dramatically from Levin's specifically Jewish vision. It was a triumph of idealism as embodied in a "funny, hopeful, happy Anne." Kermit Bloomgarden ended up as producer, and Garson Kanin as director. The play became a Broadway hit and won Goodrich and Hackett a Pulitzer Prize in 1955. The Levin saga nonetheless continued: he sued Otto Frank, which, a friend of his said, was the public relations equivalent of suing the father of Joan of Arc.

Carson's abortive dramatization of Anne Frank's diary would be just another one of the innumerable stories of a theatrical might-have-been, except that it came at an increasingly desperate time for her. It was the only project on the horizon that might have allowed her and Reeves to get outside themselves long enough to escape the cycle of alcoholism and emotional abuse that was threatening to pull them down.

Carson's physical limitations meant that when her left side, including her hand, seized up, she couldn't feed herself. William Goyen described just such a scene: Reeves "had to feed her like a baby because of her paralyzed hands." Almost inevitably, "when he spilled some food, she would become furious." Carson was not always unable to eat, but when she was, and needed Reeves to help, she was bound to resent it. The same applied to bathing and dressing, tasks that fell to Reeves during the many periods when her condition was worse. But her real dependence was more intangible, larger, unwieldy, and even more likely to breed resentment. So often in the past Reeves had been abusive, but now he took care of Carson, making sure she had the right conditions for working, that her teacup wasn't too often topped off with sherry or bourbon, that she felt emotionally well enough to function. That last was not impossible as long as Carson felt loved. She may not have loved Reeves exactly—though this summons up innumerable knotty questions about what the word means—but she very much needed him to love her.

"Yes, Reeves is a grand boy," Bébé wrote expansively to Mary Tucker in 1950. "And it comforts me that she has him. She is his whole existence! So patient, gentle and understanding." This was the problem, for Reeves came to think he had no existence apart from Carson. Bessie Breuer recalled that Reeves, "who despite his defects, loved her above all," had once told her, felicitously, "We are drones, Bibi [sic], Rita and I, and our mission is to serve her, our Queen Bee." Janet Flanner, another friend of Reeves's, looked at the situation in the spring of 1953 and wondered what would become of Carson out in the country as she was. Not to mention her husband: "What will happen to him if he does nothing all day long, for idleness (except when he is bathing and dressing her) is what drives him to drink every so often."

But Reeves made sure Carson felt loved, for his love never stopped. As he had in his letters to her during the war, he kept finding new ways to express how he felt. Like the writer he aspired to be, he explored the ways language could convey it. One letter, to "Butter Duck," closes with a declaration: "Whether we are divorced or not—it makes no difference in my deep love and feelings for you."

Not surprisingly, the same letter contains a protestation that he is not drinking, has in fact stopped drinking. That may or may not have been true, and if true, only for the moment. When he was drinking, they quarreled, and Reeves often threatened suicide. Ominously, he began to urge Carson to die with him.

Reeves's persistent misery surfaced and became dire in 1952 and 1953. Assessing what undergirded it is difficult, as the scrim of alcoholism is extremely difficult to penetrate. But it's useful to look at which of his qualities predated his drinking days: not the good ones, which were many, but those that seemed most defining and hardest to dislodge. He found it difficult to apply himself to a vocation. He wanted first of all to write, keeping copious notebooks and endlessly reading, as all writers must do. Meeting Carson encouraged this ambition; they would write together, they vowed. When her career appeared to be taking off, Reeves seemingly abandoned his own writing ambition to further hers. The one aspect of her career that gave him any trouble was financial, as she brought in, over the years, most of the money in the marriage. Usually, when he was especially aware of it, he renewed his efforts to find remunerative work. Otherwise, he adapted to it, telling Floria Lasky that financially Carson "wants to be entirely independent of me or anyone else." Of course, Carson might have meant that she did not want to be Reeves's financial support.

Truman Capote read the situation wrong when he said dismissively of Reeves, "He should have been running a gasoline station in Georgia, and he would have been perfectly happy." (Capote may have been on firmer ground when he said, just before this remark, that there was nothing wrong with Reeves "except her.") Reeves may have come from humble beginnings, but along with every other member of his family, he had migrated to New York City and environs, seeking something better for himself. He had always wanted more. Five years later, in Carson's preface to *The Square Root of Wonderful*, a play she wrote about a failed writer and the woman who had loved him, Carson said, of the character based on Reeves, he "wanted to be a writer and his failure in that was one of the disappointments that led to his death" (*SRW*, vii).

Most of Carson's and Reeves's friends agreed; it was only in the war that Reeves had functioned well. On the other hand, Janet Flanner felt he'd never recovered from the war, that ever since he had seemed to operate under profound "disorientation." Perhaps the war had "destroyed his resistance to everyday life." She remembered a dinner at Carson and Reeves's when the hosts drank profligately, Carson pouring a steady stream of sherry into a teacup and Reeves excusing himself often to refill a glass with straight gin. Dinner was delayed for hours until a drunken maid emerged from the kitchen with a burnt roast. Still, Flanner admired "the grace with which [Reeves] carried his liquor." To her, "he was the incarnation of the southern gentleman—composed and tactful, brave and kind." William Goyen found him "seductive," "strange and just as ill [as Carson]."

Jordan Massee felt that he got a pretty good idea of how things were progressing from Carson's letters from France. At first, he said, it was all "Reeves and I," about their search for a house, the excitement of finding it in Bachivillers, and then "an awful lot" about the vegetable garden. Then as there were fewer references to Reeves, she began to harp on Jordan's visiting and on how much he would love it there. She implored him to visit, saying she was alone so much of the time because Reeves was always in Paris "looking for work." Later, she would continue to plead great loneliness, supplying no explanation for why she was alone in the countryside.

In the midst of this, Rita and Lamar Jr. accused Carson of neglecting their mother. Bébé's health had not been good for some time. The pulmonary embolism of the previous year had damaged her heart, doctors believed. With congestive heart failure and arteriosclerosis, she needed to be cared for. She was enjoying life with Lamar and his wife, Jenny, especially getting to know her grandchild, Bill. But Lamar let Carson know in no uncertain terms that Bébé felt neglected: she "meets the post man every day in hopes to get a letter from you." Lamar also noted that Bébé was diagnosed with depression and an "anxiety complex." When the only response to Lamar's intervention was a check and a letter from Reeves, Jenny wrote for Lamar, telling Carson to take ten minutes "at least once a week" to write her mother.

After Carson and Reeves bought L'Ancien Presbytère the previous summer, Bébé had anticipated joining them and making a home for them there as she had in Nyack. Carson's health, they all knew, often made her dependent on others for her daily needs, physical and emotional, and the family were well used to Bébé filling that role. But as Jordan explained later, Carson did not explicitly invite her mother to France. While Bébé saw the "necessity" of going to her daughter, she didn't feel she could go without an invitation. By the spring of 1953, it was too late. "Carson did not know what the situation would be, from one day to the next, or if there would be a Reeves there," Jordan said. Carson could see the writing on the wall, that she would have to give up the country house she had so quickly come to love.

By that time, Jordan said, "Carson and Reeves['s] relationship was such that Carson was afraid." Reeves was threatening suicide again, coupling it with the suggestion that Carson die with him. Reeves spoke of little else, and it began to seem he might force her if she would not comply. In the spring of 1953, she told Tennessee, Reeves became fixated on the little orchard on their property. He tried to hang himself from a pear tree, but the limb to which he'd attached the rope broke. Thwarted, he gave up. In the aftermath, Carson tried to shrug it off, joking with others about Reeves's ruining her trees. But the jokes fell flat, as those close to the couple knew how desperate Reeves's self-destructiveness had become—even as they looked the other way, seemingly hoping someone else was taking care of it.

Not long afterward, Reeves dragged Carson out to the same orchard and pointed to a cherry tree from which they could both hang themselves, from different boughs. He gestured toward two lengths of rope at his feet. Carson recoiled in horror, no doubt fearing Reeves might force her. She was trapped with him in the little house in the countryside.

When she stayed in Paris, it had always been with Reeves: in their friend Jack Fullilove's apartment in the American Hospital or Robert Myers's place. Valentina Sheriff, the colorful Russian who was Tennessee's friend, had a place in Paris as well, where Carson sometimes stayed by herself. Carson liked Sheriff well enough that they had planned a ten-day trip to Vienna and talked of a cruise among the Greek islands. (The plan fell through.)

Mostly, though, it was Reeves who spent whole nights in Paris, some presumably given over to all-night drinking in cafés or at the apartment of whoever he went home with, other nights with Jack or Sheriff. To Carson, he referred to "an AA friend" with whom he stayed on weeknights. He was not welcome at the Browns', though he stayed in touch. Carson had finally had enough of careening alcoholically around Paris with Reeves.

Moreover, Reeves was running up big bills that only Carson could pay. She got around $700 per month from her investments, or around $6,800 today, which she had learned did not make her rich, especially given that a writer's financial future was uncertain and that money must be stretched to cover the fallow times. But Reeves liked to live large and ran up bills in Paris restaurants and the hotels where he would have had to stay from time to time. He made extravagant travel plans. And the house in Bachivillers, however up to date the heating system (she was thrilled to find the windows had screens, rare as hen's teeth in Europe), seemed to eat money.

At L'Ancien Presbytère, Carson watched time go by. Reeves would take their car, so she was stuck there and at his mercy. He could return anytime, drunk or not, either to stay or just to pick up some clothes or papers. Often she would drink with him, and they would fight. Janet Flanner wrote to Natalie Murray, "I am sick of their drinking and quarrels. They are so tragic and destructive."

In that same April letter to Murray, Flanner described a phone call from Carson in the spring of 1953. Carson, in Paris, was headed back to Bachivillers and asked Flanner whether it would be proper to ask

Carson with her boxer, Kristin, in Bachivillers, 1953; she is about to leave Reeves.

the hotel maid to bathe her—usually Reeves's domain—and pack her things. Flanner told Carson she would come over and pack for her, pointedly ignoring the bathing request. Carson was "very calm," she noted, and touchingly confessed, "I am homesick for my house." She was not "drinking badly" on that occasion, said Flanner, "but enough," four or five whiskies. In an aside, she told Murray that these days Carson was going through, per week, four or five bottles of bourbon as well as a bottle "or so" of gin for "before-luncheon consumption."

Getting Carson off to Bachivillers meant not only packing for her but ordering her a bowl of soup, waiting for the friends who were going to drive her, and helping her downstairs—"she can hardly move alone, with surety." As Janet and Carson approached the elevator, Reeves suddenly appeared; it was the middle of the afternoon and he seemed, said Flanner, "to have dropped from the ceiling of the corridor." He wanted to talk to Carson, saying that he had "hard words" to say to her. He asked her to sit down with him in the hotel bar to "settle things." "Certainly not," Flanner told him. "You are not going to settle the remainder of your marital life in any bar." Before Flanner bundled her off, Carson asked Reeves, "What is it you resent so?" Describing this episode, Flanner told Murray, "I am so tired of arguments, people's voices and the pitiful spectacle of Carson and Reeves that I hope I see neither of them soon."

Tennessee reported to Audrey Wood—who was no longer Carson's agent, now that Floria Lasky had come on the scene—that when he talked to Carson on the phone in late June, she was "in great distress" over Reeves. Reeves had never stopped drinking, Carson told him. She "desperately" wanted to talk to Tennessee about it and pleaded that he come out to L'Ancien Presbytère. The situation was "apparently insoluble," Tennessee told Wood. "I don't think there is anything anyone can do about it. Short of devoting your life to Carson, I don't see how you can help her, though she certainly needs help." He felt guilty about not visiting her, but he was leaving for Rome the next day.

According to Tennessee and other friends, Carson hurriedly flew to New York, after a dramatic incident that rings emotionally true though it does not seem totally accurate in its details.

Reeves was driving Carson, she told Tennessee, from L'Ancien Pres-

bytère to the American Hospital in Neuilly, just west of Paris, for a
doctor's appointment. Reeves insisted again on their committing a
double suicide. She saw on the car's floorboard the same two lengths
of rope that he had produced in their orchard a few weeks before, and
she panicked, fearing that this time he might physically overpower her
and force her to hang herself. She resorted to the "subterfuge" of telling
him to stop and get them a bottle of wine. Reeves pulled up to a place
where he could buy a bottle, and while he was inside, Carson jumped
out and hitched a ride toward Paris. She went straight to the American
Hospital, she said, and never saw Reeves again.

Probably Reeves did propose double suicide in the car, and probably that did tip Carson over and make her resolve to leave him immediately. But beyond that, the details of the story do not hold water.
If she had fled to the American Hospital, Reeves would have found
her immediately, as that was where they had been headed. If she had
resolved on the spot to fly to New York, she would have had to return
to L'Ancien Presbytère, if nothing else for her passport (and Reeves
would also have looked for her there).

She may, however, have fled immediately after that, going straight
to the airport to find a flight. She told friends she lit out with only
the clothes on her back. She flew out of Paris on July 23. When Floria
Lasky picked her up at the airport in New York, she had on a flimsy
dress and no stockings and was carrying a lightweight valise, containing only what she'd written of *Clock Without Hands*.

The drama wasn't over when she got to New York. First, Carson
needed her belongings from L'Ancien Presbytère, which meant coordi-
nating with Reeves. Her friends stepped in to negotiate so she would
not have to deal with him. Shortly after Carson's arrival, Rita wrote
to the Browns, giving them a rough accounting of what she wanted
Mme. Joffers—who had not been paid for some time—to assemble
for shipping. But Reeves inserted himself almost immediately, writing to Carson on the fifth day after she left. It was a "dreary, bleary"
time without her, he said. Ever since she left, he had been playing
their favorite pieces of Schumann and Schubert. "Nothing in life that
I experience," he wrote, "will be good unless you share it with me." He
asked her plaintively, "Is it all gone, or, can we have a life together?" He

thought she might say it depended on him, that unless he changed his behavior, there was no hope for a future for them. But unless she cared, it was useless. *He* certainly cared enough. "My blood, fingernails, soul and bones are yours," he said, in one of his typically novel avowals of love.

Without Carson, Reeves would be hard pressed to live as extravagantly as he had in the months before. In fact, he barely had any money at all. For some time he had (once again) been forging her checks; around the time she left, he had forged a rather large one to a "money changer"—a shadowy figure named Alvin Blick, presumably a foreign exchange broker—who cashed checks written in dollars for francs at a favorable exchange rate. Because this person enjoyed favor among the expatriates in Paris, Reeves's forgery of the large check had led a number of her American friends in Europe to break with him and turn cold to Carson. It caused bad feelings as well between Carson and Princess Caetani, who had introduced the McCullerses to Blick. The reason Carson left Paris "so precipitously," Truman cattily told Newton, was her refusal to honor the debt Reeves had incurred with this person. Now Carson's friends were being "hounded" by her creditors, Truman said, probably an exaggeration. Reeves, he said, "might well be arrested"—that is, "if alcohol hasn't killed him off in the past 24 hours." Letters from Floria Lasky to Carson indicate that Carson sent a check for $300 to Princess Caetani to be given to Blick; she noted the "urgency" surrounding the payment.

Reeves was receiving supportive letters from his mother, Jessie, who was still living in and managing the Nyack house, though she saw the writing on the wall and was making plans to move. She went from addressing Carson and Reeves as "my precious children" in early July to warning Reeves about his wife after Carson arrived back in Nyack at the end of the month. He should be very careful about what he said when he wrote to Carson, as she could and did say "some weird things." The Nyack house, Carson told Jessie, was hers; Reeves owned no part of it. Jessie admitted that Floria Lasky spoke to her after some of the checks Jessie was writing were turned down, but she told Lasky that her son had not written any checks, adding, "I have done what I know is right and I don't think they can give me too much trouble."

She was reluctant to tell Reeves everything, she said, because she did not have any address for him except the house in Bachivillers, which she knew was going to be sold. In a September letter, Jessie told Reeves that she understood he felt that he could not live without Carson, but that he could in fact live "in peace and be happier" if he would just stay away from her for a while. Like her son, she thought this was just another flare-up in the endless face-off that the marriage had become.

At summer's end, Jack Fullilove and Valentina Sheriff drove out to see Reeves in Bachivillers, finding him vacant and depressed. Jack noted that he had lost probably thirty pounds since their first meeting the previous summer. Reeves had no money; all he had was Carson's car, which he badly needed, driving between Paris and Bachivillers. Sheriff took the lead in checking him into the Hôtel Château-Frontenac at 54, rue Pierre-Charron—an excellent, even luxurious establishment— telling the proprietor that she was assuming all financial responsibility for Reeves's stay, then and in the future. The police were looking for Reeves because of the bad checks. By now, he had the sympathy of most of Carson's friends in Paris. "Reeves was simply trying to survive," said Janet Flanner, "for Carson had abandoned him completely."

He appealed to Carson one last time, on September 6, a Sunday afternoon, writing from Bachivillers. Ostensibly he was letting her know about some correspondence with her agent in England that he had taken care of, unasked. He had recently had a crash in Carson's car, which the insurance company was paying for. As soon as that was taken care of, he said, he was turning the car over to Russell Porter, a Paris-based lawyer whom Floria Lasky had retained, who would sell it as Carson directed. He was working with the Browns to get her baggage and household effects sent, but it was taking some time. Everything about the house had been seen to. The Jofferses were still there and sent their love. Reeves couldn't pay them but kept the larder stocked with food and drink from the Paris PX. And as to her request, via Rita and Simone Brown, for her typewriter and phonograph and records, Reeves asked that he be allowed to keep the typewriter. He had paid for it, he said, and it would be very expensive to buy a new one in France. If Rita bought a new one in the United States, he would gladly pay for it.

Addressing Carson with the mysteriously derived nickname "Butter Duck," he asked again whether, if he paid all their debts and was sober, they "might pick up the spark of old love again. Or is it all gone?" In the final paragraph, he brought up divorce. "If and when" she wanted one, he said, he would cooperate fully. "Whether we are divorced or not," he wrote, "it makes no difference in my deep love and feelings for you. I cannot possibly have any personal life without you, and, whether we are together or apart I will think of you the first thing in the morning and the last thing at night." In a postscript, he reiterated, "I will do everything possible in the interests of your property here, I am sane, sober, fully dressed and in my right mind: I will do anything, anything for your ease and peace of mind. I love you."

It is impossible to tell, of course, how sincere Reeves was, or whether Carson was considering taking him back one more time. He was spiraling downward, forgoing the Antabuse and drinking suicidally. Throughout the fall, the Browns and others tried to arrange with him the shipping of Carson's trunks and other belongings, but the effort seemed disorganized on all sides. The Browns told her in October that Reeves was drinking too much but had been sweet to their children. In early November, Reeves telephoned Janet Flanner, calling himself "the man from across the River Styx." On November 18 he phoned Simone Brown and Bob Myers and said he was "going West." He asked Jack Fullilove to have dinner with him that night. Jack was on call and asked to meet Reeves the next evening. That would be too late, said Reeves—he was "going West" tomorrow.

Reeves's body was found in his elegant room at the Hôtel Château-Frontenac, still paid for by Sheriff. He had taken an overdose of barbiturates on top of alcohol and choked on his vomit, dying of asphyxiation. On November 19 he had "gone West"—perhaps in search of Carson.

❧

When Carson received word of Reeves's death, she was on the road, working on a journalistic assignment that must have seemed a godsend at the time. She had been in Nyack for three months, living almost in seclusion. She had involved herself in two projects. First, she was adapting her short story "The Sojourner" as a television play for the *Omnibus* series, to be performed and filmed in December; the Ford Foundation was the source of funding, and Carson prized the connections she had made there. The other project was a commission from *Holiday* magazine to write a feature on Georgia. No doubt Carson took this on because of the pay. She was getting $1,500 (over $14,000 today).

In pursuit of the *Holiday* piece, Carson had invited herself to the home of a friend in Clayton, Lillian Smith, the white author of the 1944 best-seller *Strange Fruit,* about an interracial romance. Smith was outspoken on race and a supporter of the nascent civil rights movement, and in profiling her as a Georgia author, Carson was courting controversy. The two women were cordial but not close; Reeves had formed his own friendship with Smith, once arranging to come visit her in Georgia with a male friend, though he never showed up.

Carson had descended on Lillian on November 20 distinctly *not* invited; a letter to Lillian had just arrived announcing Carson's arrival. The night Carson got there they drank and talked about Reeves far into the night; Carson was "tearing him down with every breath," Lillian recalled. In talking about her husband, "she did not realize that she was really exposing herself," though Lillian did not specify how. Late that night the phone rang, and Lillian picked up. It was Rita Smith saying Reeves had died. Lillian spoke casually to Rita in front of her guest, deciding on the spot that she would not tell Carson right away.

Lillian had her partner, Paula Snelling, give Carson the news the following morning. That whole day Carson was on the phone, passing on the news to friends and family and probably to Reeves's family as well. She made the phone calls from her bed, distraught. Lillian said she drank a fifth of scotch over the course of the day. Carson occasionally let Lillian or Paula make calls for her, but she usually grabbed the phone away in order to convey what she wanted in the way she wanted it said.

After much deliberation, Carson made preliminary plans for the funeral, including the music she wanted to be played: Bach's Double Violin Concerto in D Minor. She had one request that Lillian thought curious: Janet Flanner was to approach the coffin during the ceremony and kiss the corpse on both cheeks. The body was to be laid in the American Legion cemetery in Neuilly. Every detail of these plans was arrived at after much discussion with several people.

At one point the telephone service went out: providentially, for Lillian and Paula. The delay meant panic for Carson, and she decided to leave right away. With great effort, they persuaded her to stay the night and take a seven-thirty a.m. bus from Clayton. Somewhat oddly—she didn't know him all that well—she went to visit Dr. Hervey Cleckley in Augusta. Cleckley was the psychiatrist colleague of Sidney Isenberg; Carson had befriended the two men back in 1948, just after her hospitalization at Payne Whitney. For whatever reason, she decided not to return from Lillian's to Nyack to be with Rita and Bébé; perhaps she felt the presence of a psychiatrist would be comforting. That night she fell into bed, exhausted, free of Reeves and mercifully drunk.

16

Endings Are Knives

FOR J.R.M.

You named me when I had forgot, offered identity
and

When I was lost—what image tells?
Nothing resembles nothing, yet nothing was not blank
It was configured Hell:
Of noticed clocks on
winter afternoons
Malignant star, demanding furniture
All unrelated and with air in between

The terror. Was it of space? Of time?

—Carson McCullers, "When We Are Lost," 1948

Everyone knew and no one knew. *The New York Times* reported on November 27 that Reeves had died in Paris on November 18. Its account left the impression that his death was *not* a suicide: "Several weeks ago, Mr. McCullers suffered severe injuries in an automobile accident. It has not been determined if the accident was the cause of death." This information no doubt came from Robert Myers, Reeves and Carson's doctor friend, who was likely casting about for details to provide the French police. Reeves had barely been scratched in that accident (though he nearly totaled the car). Carson, significantly, knew that Reeves had died from an overdose of barbiturates combined with alcohol.

But she did not know that just before his death he had sent her a telegram in Nyack, telling her what he was doing: that is, a suicide note. As of December 18, a month after his death, Carson had still not been shown this telegram or even told of its existence. That day Rita wrote to Floria Lasky saying that she, Jordan, and Bébé felt that Carson should be told what the telegram said. They had kept it from her, Rita said, until they felt she was strong enough to sustain the facts. Too many people, in Paris and New York, knew what it said, and if Carson learned about it from someone else, she would never forgive any of them—or Floria. The telegram was sufficiently ambiguous, Rita argued, that Carson was "far more likely to take it as a declaration of his love for her than proof of his suicide—which indeed it is not." Suicide notes reveal only intent; even so, it is hard to believe the room for interpretation left by the telegram would have made Carson feel any better.

She did not seem to be grieving. In fact, her predominant emotions seem to have been anger and relief. Those who loved her shared this view. "At last Reeves is outside the disorder of living," Bébé scrawled on a scrap of paper. Reeves's action, said Janet Flanner, "seems to me to have been decided in the favor of dignity which his life no longer offered." Another friend of Carson's had a charming memory of Reeves: "It comes back to me sorrowfully—that evening in May . . . and how much we liked your husband, how delightful he was to lead us to you and our midnight talk—an evening to me always to be loved. I remember too the rose he picked for us from the vine above your door. Endings are knives, sharp or dull." Natalia Danesi Murray made some grimly pointed comments: "In the disappearance of Reeves there is a measure of greatness because it has been the supreme gift of deliverance, of liberation from a destructiveness that was engulfing you both." His suicide, she wrote, was "the one important and positive gesture of a weak soul." It was, she concluded, "the supreme gift to a genius": that is, to Carson.

Carson wouldn't discuss Reeves or his death with anyone. She would banish Reeves from her thoughts, she told Newton Arvin firmly when she wrote to him before Christmas that year, and he could not damage her further. In fact, she went on, she felt better than she had in some time—freer, happier.

Almost immediately she was criticized as cold and unfeeling. Her closest friends accused her of deserting Reeves in France, leaving him in turmoil at the worst possible time. "Reeves died, ultimately, out of great love for Carson," said Tennessee. "His was a desperate loneliness. Without her, he was an empty shell." Bob Myers, a good friend to both, was defensive on Reeves's part, telling Carson, "All of us here feel badly about the whole matter, in spite of the troubles Reeves gave this year. Don't forget, they were real problems to him, too. He was mentally sick, and we must all look at it from that angle." No one seemed to grasp that Carson had been through Reeves's crises many times before, that she had taken him back formally as her husband once and informally time after time, believing him when he said that he had stopped drinking, that he was drinking only beer, that he would stop seeing other women, that he would stay within a budget, that he would pay back money he'd borrowed on her name, that he would stop kiting checks, that he had changed, that he was mentally ill and so was not accountable for his behavior, that things would be different.

More concrete criticisms concerned Carson's deserting him financially. During his time in France, the $350 monthly check from the army had been enough to live on when coupled with the allowance Floria Lasky sent Carson every month from the earnings on her investments, but Reeves's check alone wouldn't support him. When Carson left him in France, he had nothing except the car and his meager possessions in L'Ancien Presbytère, which was owned by Carson. His sudden poverty had moved Valentina Sheriff to pay for a room at the comfortable, even elegant Hôtel Château-Frontenac, which gave rise to rumors that he was partying elaborately at Carson's expense after her departure.

Carson directed Bob Myers, John Brown, and Janet Flanner to take care of the logistics for the funeral and the disposition of Reeves's body. This was a vexed issue for Carson. She looked into having the body shipped home, perhaps for burial in Georgia, which would be very costly. Reeves's family—his mother, Jessie, who'd recently moved back to New York City from the Nyack house; his sister, Wiley Mae; and his brother, Tom—supported that option. Cheryl Crawford thought this was what Reeves would have wanted, and with some other friends she raised money toward this end. When Carson opted not to fly his body home, these friends and the McCullerses grumbled that she did not want to pay the costs involved. But she was trying to make plans from the United States, and the logistics were intimidating. This, too, excited more comment, but from a medical point of view alone, she could not possibly handle flying over to see to the arrangements herself.

Carson thought that Reeves would have preferred to be cremated, and she decided his ashes would be buried in the American Legion Cemetery in Neuilly-sur-Seine. A small ceremony was held at the American Church, where John Brown delivered some remarks about Reeves. This was where the Bach was played, and where Janet Flanner kissed Reeves's waxy cheeks. The ceremony at the gravesite was more impressive. A knot of soldiers were present, among them a bugler and a drummer, and the American flag was much in evidence. Three volleys were fired, and the bugler played taps for Captain James Reeves McCullers. John Brown read the Twenty-third Psalm. Present were Bob Myers and Jack Fullilove, Richard and Ellen Wright, Monique Cotlenko, Odette, Monica Stirling, and Truman Capote. Truman and Monique cried throughout, and Truman was heard to gasp, "My youth is gone." Janet Flanner saw that photographs were sent to Carson.

Arrangements for the funeral and burial were mixed in with the logistical details of getting both Carson's and Reeves's possessions home, including the contents of the Bachivillers house; dismissing the servants there; and selling the car and the house. The boxer, Kristin, was shipped to Nyack, while her puppies, Nicky and Antonne, were sold. Everything was that much more complicated because Carson was on the other side of the Atlantic. Details of shipments had already dominated her correspondence months before Reeves's death, following her return from France, and they continued for months afterward, with the Browns and with Carson's Paris lawyer, Russell Porter. Among their belongings was a life-size painted wooden sculpture of an angel or perhaps the Virgin Mary, which they had proudly positioned outside L'Ancien Presbytère; Reeves and Carson were especially fond of it, having bought it together in France. (It ended up happily claimed by Bob Myers.)

"A lot of animosity" flew around these arrangements, remembered Jordan Massee. Their friends seemed to find it easiest and most satisfying to blame Carson, both for Reeves's death and for not properly honoring it afterward. The person who disapproved most was the one whose opinion perhaps mattered most to her: Tennessee. "The only thing Carson did that I did not like," he later said, "was casting off Reeves as she did and showing no feelings for him or his memory. She spoke of him in the most unkind terms, and it always upset me. Reeves died for her, and she refused to admit it." It is unlikely that he told Carson this. There was no breach in their friendship, but Tennessee's unconditional love, which was so important to her, was severely tried.

Carson lay low for a time in Nyack, then fled. The holidays were bleak, and the winter long. In her correspondence from this time onward, no substantive references to Reeves appear, and friends and acquaintances did not record anything she said about him. It was as if he had never existed, and Carson made clear that was what she wanted for the time being.

She left Nyack in mid-February. Edwin Peacock and John Zeigler had given her an open invitation to their quarters in Charleston, in the antebellum mansion where they operated their bookstore. It was a wonderful place, wrote a Charleston historian: local writers and readers came in to browse, sit by the fire, have tea, and on Saturdays listen to the Metropolitan Opera on the radio. Visiting cultural luminaries, such as Maurice Sendak and Langston Hughes, dropped in, too. Carson liked to sit on a stool next to a little pantry off the store, where Edwin or John would fix her iced rum drinks; sometimes she would talk to students who came in, other times she just read.

Edwin and John felt she needed to see people, and Carson humored them. She met Charlestonians Laura Bragg, director of the Charleston Museum (and the first female museum director in the United States), and Gordon Langley Hall, the child of two servants at Vita Sackville-West's and Harold Nicolson's Sissinghurst Castle and a prolific writer. Hall—later a woman, Dawn Langley Simmons—remembered Carson as "shrunken and birdlike," dubbing her "the Snow Princess of the North." Edwin Newberry and Bob Walden came from Charlotte, North Carolina, for a weekend and campaigned for Carson to visit them after she left Charleston. And Edwin and John gave her a big party on the patio outside the bookstore, with her reluctant consent. She enjoyed herself nonetheless, meeting a visiting couple who would become very close to her in the years ahead, Robert and Hilda Marks. Hilda was a refugee from Nazi Germany and Robert a Charlestonian, a writer; they now lived in New York City. With Robert, Carson talked about ideas and writing, while with Hilda, she was, by Hilda's account, girlish and "purely unintellectual."

Edwin and John thought Carson's visit was doing her so much good that they took the extraordinary step of going over her head for her own welfare. They wrote a formal letter to Floria Lasky asking whether Bébé might join Carson in Charleston for several months, returning to Nyack in September. "The simple life of this quiet town seems to be agreeing with her," they wrote. "She is much more rested, and less nervous, than when she arrived." Expenses would be considerably lower than in the North, and the rent Carson and Bébé could collect on Bébé's apartment in the Nyack house would more than cover what was needed for servants and living expenses. The only disadvantage they could see was that Carson and her mother would be quite far from Rita and their friends, but it would only be for a short time.

Carson was "emphatic," Edwin and John wrote, that she did not want to "press this upon her Mother." Of course they would make sure that she talked it over with Rita and Bébé, but she had asked that they let Floria know about it "so that you can give your own good advice." In other words, Carson wanted Floria to break the ice and muster all necessary arguments to convince Bébé. John evidently thought twice and sent Rita a copy of the letter with a note he scribbled at the bottom; it was best to enlist her beforehand. There can be no better proof of the two men's love for Carson and their concern for her welfare—or of her power over them—than this carefully mounted campaign.

But the plan was dead in the water, for just as Carson was gathering strength from her Charleston sojourn, Rita called and told her that Bébé, now sixty-two, had fallen and broken her hip. The Smith children mobilized as best they could from afar, but they were defeated by hospital rigmarole. They had to wait a week before Bébé could even get her hip pinned, the standard treatment. Lamar and Jenny twice sent fifty dollars for Bébé's medical bills; Lamar was working an extra job to cover the expense. They wrote that they hoped the matter hadn't created too big a burden for Rita, as it was on her shoulders that the burden fell; she stayed in Nyack supervising Bébé's care up to the operation and her transfer afterward to a nursing home. "We certainly do appreciate your looking after everything. It's such a big responsibility for one person," Jenny wrote. Unasked was the question of what Carson was doing to help. Coming on top of what Lamar if not Rita believed was Carson's "neglect" of Bébé during her two previous health scares, Carson's silence this time was earsplitting. Bad feelings lingered from Bébé's heart attack and its aftermath in the summer of 1952, when Lamar and Rita had to put their heads together to see to their mother's care and Reeves had sent Rita an unsigned check, which she had to return to him.

This time Lamar and Rita had their mother's situation pretty well sorted out, except that Carson could not seem to decide whether her presence was required in Nyack or whether she could go straight on to Yaddo, as she was thinking of doing. Rita wrote, perhaps somewhat peeved, that she couldn't help Carson with that decision. But Carson decided that her presence wasn't necessary as long as Rita was managing the particulars of Bébé's care. Rita had long since made peace—of a sort—with her big sister, reconciling herself as well to her own place in the family dynamic. But the confusion and bad feelings following Bébé's accident were hints of just how badly the children might function as a group in their mother's absence.

Carson simply did not want to return to Nyack yet. She loved being the center of attention among her gay male friends, who treated her as a kind of mascot or minor royalty. When Bob Walden and Edwin Newberry—Bob knew Carson from Columbus days, and the pair always saw her on her Charleston visits—again invited her to visit them in Charlotte, she agreed, ending her monthlong stay in Charleston. She was most intrigued by Edwin's description of the house he had designed for himself and his partner. It was one enormous room, with one alcove for sleeping, one for a library, and an open-plan living area—a novel concept then—that was spacious and welcoming, with an enormous stone fireplace. Because it was really one big room, Carson slept on a couch next to the fireplace, the men in the bedroom alcove. It might have been crowded, except that Bob and Edwin were gone all day at their jobs.

In their absence, Carson stewed, drinking too much. She received a letter from Bob Myers accompanying the "forms" that some of her friends had filled out at Reeves's funeral, replete with criticisms of her and how she had handled the whole affair. She made long-distance calls all day long, many about the house at Bachivillers, when and how to sell it, and who might handle it. Though she did not go into any detail about Reeves or her marriage, Bob and Edwin noted that she seemed deeply unhappy.

Bob and Edwin wanted Carson to meet their Charlotte friends and neighbors, and she made her first appearance at the luxurious home of the Cannons, of the towel fortune. It was not a propitious debut, according to their friend Harry Woolfolk, another acquaintance from her Charleston visits. She came in bedroom slippers—evidently with no explanation—and was sullen throughout, talking to no one and asking to leave right after she arrived. Woolfolk did not like Carson or, rather, felt compelled to bait her, out of a curious impulse. It's worth recalling that it was Woolfolk whom Reeves had asked to go to bed with him and Carson when visiting Sullivan's Island in 1949. Like several acquaintances in the past few years, he got it into his head that Carson was merely faking her physical limitations—curling her left hand into a claw and walking with a cane—and he called her on it, telling her that he found her sinister and didn't think she needed a walking stick. He could not later remember Carson's reply, only that it was "very sharp and unladylike" and that he immediately regretted offending her.

One day Carson came across a book in her hosts' library that captured her attention for a few days. It was written by the novelist William March, who had recommended her for the Houghton Mifflin award back in 1937. She devoured *The Bad Seed,* a mesmerizing popular novel about a mother who comes to the realization that her eight-year-old daughter, Rhoda, is a self-centered sociopath who will murder a classmate almost on a whim, if her victim has something she wants. Rhoda then murders a peripheral character who might expose her. Carson would have been fascinated by the young girl, who was a misfit or freak much like a McCullers heroine but with no sense of right or wrong. *The Bad Seed* was both a popular and a critical success, an overnight best seller, and a nominee for the 1955 National Book Award. Carson noted as well that one of her Rockland County neighbors, Maxwell Anderson, was adapting it for the stage. Ever since the success of *The Member of the Wedding,* Carson had been alert to what seemed to her the ease of producing a Broadway hit. She liked *The Bad Seed* so much that she wrote a letter to William March declaring herself a fan.

Her theatrical interest piqued, Carson spent a good deal of her time in Charlotte working on a musical adaptation of *The Ballad of the Sad Café.* This was at Bob's suggestion; he could clearly see musical overtones in the novella. Just one example was the coda, a lovely scene describing the long days of convicts working on a road crew and the mysterious song—or noise—they raise up. Bob understood the novella and tried to understand Carson, but in the end she wore on him and Edwin, and he secretly wrote to Rita, asking her to invent a pretext that would require Carson to return to Nyack.

It wasn't necessary, as Carson had devised a plan to return to Yaddo. In the months after Reeves's death, she felt keenly the absence of any real home. Generally, she loved to travel, but not to sightsee, sample foreign culture, or discover unfamiliar foods; rather, she wanted to live in another world, immersing herself in the quotidian. But without Reeves, she simply could not manage it, either physically or emotionally. A visit to friends was all that was possible for her, like the trip to

Charleston to be with Edwin Peacock and John Zeigler—friends she could count on to feed and bathe her should it be necessary, as Reeves had done.

Nyack was no longer her home, now that Bébé was in a nursing home and no one was there to take care of her. Rita couldn't do it; she worked all day, as did Jordan Massee, someone else she might have called on. All spring she had been thinking about Yaddo, where she'd spent so much productive time from 1941 to 1946. She had recently heard from her old friend there, the director, Elizabeth Ames. In fact, Rita had initially written to Elizabeth that spring, perhaps opening discussion of a visit; she might have written further to Elizabeth after Bob Walden asked Rita to arrange to have Carson called up north. This was not as underhanded as it perhaps sounds. With Bébé unavailable to wait on Carson in Nyack, and Rita's resources stretched thin, Yaddo was a good solution for all concerned—except for Rita, who was saddled with Bébé's care. Carson left North Carolina on April 19 and made her way directly, avoiding Nyack, to Saratoga Springs, where she would stay until July 3.

Elizabeth was shocked to see Carson after their long separation, she later recalled. Her friend's health had obviously declined drastically. She would come to believe that Carson's personality had changed, too, a development she attributed to some kind of organic brain damage; the strokes "had affected not only her brain, it seemed, but her personality as well. Her temperament was more irascible." More reasonably, Elizabeth believed Carson's drinking had changed her and blamed it for everything from her "bloated look" to her behavior with her fellow colonists. "She was much less tolerant, especially when she had been drinking, and she was more liable to make an unpleasant remark about someone at the dinner table, or goad someone in an irritating manner." But Elizabeth returned to the aftereffects of her strokes: "She was very lame then and depended heavily on her cane. Her hand seemed withered and her speech thick when she had been drinking, nor could she control her tongue. I attributed that to the stroke. I am afraid she was a terrible handful." Elizabeth had not been surprised, she said, when Rita had contacted her that spring, hoping a place could be found for Carson at Yaddo. Rather than give her a cottage on the grounds or a room in the mansion, Elizabeth put her up in her own residence, Pine Garde, where she could give Carson the extra help she needed.

Guests at Yaddo had strange memories of Carson that spring. Granville Hicks, who, along with his family, had been her companion on that intense and eventful trip to Quebec thirteen years before, was shocked when he saw her on a quick visit to Elizabeth, concluding that she would die within the year. Another resident remembered her appearance: she usually wore a summer dress or a housecoat, "drooled a good deal," and had a "speech impediment." Such observations were anomalous and were most likely based on short acquaintance.

Some colonists that spring were more sympathetic to Carson. Leon Edel, the literary critic and biographer of Henry James, provided a more considered and nuanced view of Carson on this Yaddo stay. He appreciated knowing her, he said, even for so brief a time: "Carson had a great deal of warmth, and a picturesque mind—a mind in which its fancies leaped and plunged and offered always the unexpected. . . . Her inventions were always startling and often delightful, like some surrealist painting." He referred kindly to her drinking as finding "solace at the cocktail hour," and he noted only her childlike apology for behavior at one such party. It was this girlishness, so odd and yet so appropriate in this thirty-nine-year-old woman, that particularly struck him, an ambiguous quality. He remembered her apologizing for her behavior at the party, "dropping a little-girl curtsy in the process." She read some of her poems to the colonists, and he remembered the work displaying "tender feeling and much of the childish wonder that she had kept intact within her; and she could be, in a group, very lively and witty." Like a child, too, however, "she could be attention-demanding, and there was a certain pathos in her pleading look, those large, liquid eyes that asked the world for love." He had a thoughtful, almost Jamesian "read" of her nature:

One always felt the burden she carried—a kind of sense of doom which she eased with the comedy of her mind and her devotion to her art. She shaped and reshaped her fancies and her "case"—a little case—is poignant in its accomplishment, in the face of her life-denying demons.

Edel's and other residents' memories leave the distinct impression that Carson neither enjoyed nor provided the fun she had on past visits to Yaddo or the artistic camaraderie the colony encouraged. Rather, her stay at Yaddo that spring was difficult at best.

❧

When Carson returned to the States after Reeves's death, she had resolved to find some means of bringing in income, given that her writing at the time did not promise any immediate profit. Surely the impetus came from someone else—Floria Lasky, perhaps, or another knowledgeable friend—but Carson sent out feelers to institutions or venues at which she could deliver a talk or give a reading or appear "in conversation." She would have mounted any such campaign with a certain grimness; she hated appearing in public, or before large groups of people. Her first such engagement was at Goucher College in Maryland, which held her to a grueling schedule: an appearance at an English department tea on the day of her formal lecture that evening, and two workshops the next day, one in the morning on fiction writing, and another in the afternoon on drama. It went off quite well, and she made other dates, among them an appearance at the Philadelphia Fine Arts Association. She suggested to Newton Arvin that they appear together at Smith College, talking about their shared past.

Usually Carson would speak from what she would later revise and publish as her "Notes on Writing," called "The Flowering Dream." The kernel of her vision was that the meanings of a work of art aren't realized until the work is finished. It's like a flowering dream, she said. "Ideas grow, budding silently, and there are a thousand illuminations coming day by day as the work progresses" (*TMH*, 274–75). Later in the talk, eventually published in *Esquire* in 1959, she explained the origins of the impressive array of eccentric characters in her work:

> I become the characters I write about. I am so immersed in them that their motives are my own. When I write about a thief, I become one; when I write about Captain Penderton, I become a homosexual man; when I write about a deaf mute, I become dumb

during the time of the story. I become the characters I write about and I bless the Latin poet Terence who said, "Nothing human is alien to me." (*TMH*, 276–77)

Writing was "a wandering, dreaming occupation" for her. It was therapeutic, in this time after Reeves's death, to fall back on and try to define her craft. It helped her prepare for the ambitious, and not entirely successful, projects to come.

Carson also agreed to a prestigious engagement at the Poetry Center in New York City, at the 92nd Street Y. She booked it for May 8, right in the middle of her Yaddo stay. New York was in striking distance of Saratoga Springs, and she arranged to stay overnight with Hilda and Bob Marks in their midtown brownstone. As the date approached, however, she became ever more trepidatious and somehow persuaded Tennessee to appear with her. He did not much like public speaking either, and by this point he usually knew how to evade Carson's manipulative behavior, but he had noted his friend's downward trajectory in the last year or two, especially after Reeves's death, and generously agreed. The idea was for Carson to speak—the title was "Twenty Years of Writing"—and for Tennessee to read passages from her work. The inverse might have been less stressful for most writers, but not for Carson. "Carson did not read well at all," Hilda Marks flatly stated.

A pitcher of clear liquid appeared on a small table between them. Disastrously, it was a pitcher of martinis, provided as one of Tennessee's conditions, endorsed by Carson. It may have seemed an odd, even malicious idea for Tennessee to ask for it, when he complained so loudly about her drinking to her and to their friends, and it certainly was that, but also Tennessee was far enough along in his own drinking that he himself felt he needed the alcoholic crutch.

The poet and critic John Malcolm Brinnin introduced Carson, noting that Tennessee would be making a "surprise" appearance; a transcription of a recording of the evening noted, "Audience gasps." What followed was a Southern-inflected calamity. A distressingly long silence followed Brinnin's introduction, said Hilda Marks, and similarly unnerving pauses punctuated the evening. Finally, Carson began to tell stories about her writing history, starting with her youthful adoration for Eugene O'Neill. When she began talking about *The Heart Is a Lonely Hunter*, she asked Tennessee to read the opening paragraph; instead, he read a paragraph describing Antonopoulos in bed in the asylum when Singer goes to see him. It's a lovely passage, but hard to talk about without providing the complicated backstory. It was not possible for Carson to anticipate what Tennessee would read or when. By the end of the evening she was simply befuddled. After reading a passage from *The Ballad of the Sad Café*, she reflected on "this mysterious thing,

> this mystery of creation. I remember about this book, *The Ballad*, the story. I remember when I thought about that. I was playing Berlioz on the gramophone, and a few months before I had seen this little dwarf in a café in New York, in Brooklyn. And suddenly the Berlioz and the dwarf, the hunchback, went together. Why I don't know. And I thought about *The Ballad of the Sad Café*. I had to interrupt *The Member of the Wedding* to write it; although I felt guilty all the time I was doing it. No, I don't know. I wish I did know. I wish somebody would tell me. Doesn't somebody else have some?

In the middle of the program he read her story "A Tree. A Rock. A Cloud" in its entirety. After the audience applauded, Tennessee said, "Well, it's ten o'clock. I don't know how long we were supposed to read, Carson." But they took questions from the audience for at least another half hour.

Tennessee's friend Don Windham was in the audience, and he felt that Tennessee deliberately undermined Carson. He "increased her nervousness by pushing the microphone back and forth in front of her, read passages from her work other than those she asked for to illustrate her point, then leaned back, smoking his cigarette and smiling thoughtfully." The writer Leo Lerman, who came to dislike Carson thoroughly, noted her "monstrous exhibition" in his diary and provided a somewhat idiosyncratic, nasty description: "Carson witch-like with a silver-headed stick—disjointed, her depravity open, again proving that the best crooks show their hand all the time and charm their victims into applause." But he also admitted, "The packed house loved it."

Donald Spoto, later a Williams biographer, also found the evening difficult, but he was perhaps more objective, observing that the pitcher of martinis "resulted in a strange event." It was a spectacle, two of the most famous writers in the country spending an evening in front of strangers, "interrupting one another, stumbling and slurring over their words, perversely relishing one another's boozy humor as much as they were oblivious to the uncomfortable audience." It wasn't so much what either one said—though Carson did tell a longish, utterly inexplicable joke about a woman who runs a theater showing foreign films—as their giggling, lethargic manner of speech, broken by lengthy silences.

It was a long time before Carson could tear herself away from the crowd who clustered around afterward, asking her and Tennessee for autographs, making remarks, and asking questions they assumed the two authors would welcome. Though many in their audience could tell Carson was not in top form, both writers had such a reservoir of goodwill to draw on that neither registered much damage to their reputation. For Carson, the evening inserted itself neutrally into the procession of boozy days and nights when she vaguely missed Reeves, trying to get past his suicide and the guilt she felt but unable to find her way.

She took the train up to Saratoga Springs for the remainder of her Yaddo stay. She was desperate to take up her work again. Time and again in her last months and years with Reeves, she had tried and failed to resume work on *Clock Without Hands,* and she was eager now to at least go through the motions. She had made some progress on the novel in the winter of 1953, when she and Reeves were more or less snowed in at Bachivillers, but Reeves had rightly pointed out to Floria at the time that Carson's work was "not such that it can be turned on and off like a thermostat." Rather, "she must have long periods of tranquility behind and in front of her to create." Carson was also thinking over Bob Walden's proposal that they work together on a musical adaptation of *The Ballad of the Sad Café*. And she was working up an idea for a new play, in which the heroine, struggling with a failed-writer husband whom she had married twice and who has killed himself, now seeks love with a "normal" man. This sketch of a story makes clear that Carson was not entirely unwilling to confront her long, tragic relationship or to consider how to transmute it into art—even if she refused to discuss it with anyone.

Still, Carson did not have the drive she had on earlier trips to Yaddo. "I don't believe she worked much—her heart wasn't in it," Elizabeth Ames observed. Not surprisingly, she felt unwell after her speaking trip to New York City, and a Dr. Swanner was called in. Elizabeth wrote Rita that the doctor thought Carson should stay where she was a little longer, so her time at Yaddo was extended to July 3. Her blood pressure was a bit high and her pulse was too fast, though the medication prescribed was clearing up what seemed to be an infection.

Elizabeth had once again aligned herself with Rita, and the two were in frequent correspondence. Dr. Swanner, Elizabeth told Rita, "is trying to prevail on Carson to drink less," because it did no good for her physical condition. She was careful not to let Carson know they'd been in touch, and she hoped Rita would be similarly careful. She suggested Rita ask Carson, either when she visited her at Yaddo or after Carson returned to Nyack, how much she was drinking "and then caution her." They should both "do as much for her as we can." But Elizabeth closed the letter with a warning: "Do let me repeat: Dr. Swanner's concern with how much Carson drinks is strictly confidential—it must not be mentioned to her."

Why not? Carson's habit was serious enough that a doctor was talking to her about it. But Elizabeth's remarks suggest that either she or Rita or both may have intervened before, and the result had not been good. Rita had been a member of AA for years and credited it with her own sobriety. Reeves had attended AA meetings in his last years, albeit with less success, and both knew AA luminaries like Marty Mann who presumably could help. Yet it does not appear that Carson ever attended a single AA meeting, and Rita likely never broached the subject with her. Carson was a genius, after all—or so her friends and family had always reasoned. The upshot was that when it came to drinking—a problem that was as formidable as her physical condition if not more so—she did not get the help she needed. Of course, nothing would help unless Carson had the desire to stop drinking.

Carson returned to Nyack and Bébé, who had now recovered from her broken hip, but soon decided to take advantage of Tennessee's vacant East 58th Street apartment, which Leo Lerman remembered as "disheveled, unloved, transitory." Having lunch with Carson and Rita there in late July, Lerman thought Carson somehow "ma[de] even greater disorder" in the noisy apartment. She responded strangely to a remark Rita made, perhaps about Rita's eight-year psychoanalytic treatment with a Dr. Franklin. "My neurosis is as important as yours," she told Rita. Lerman, whose dislike for Carson perhaps made him a less-than-reliable observer, chalked this odd statement up to Carson's covetousness: whatever anyone else had, like a dress, she wanted.

But at that lunch Carson seemed to resent the attention Rita was getting for her emotional problems. Rita had an abundance of amusing stories about her various neuroses in action, any of which she might have produced for their guest. But Carson could have seen a psychiatrist or therapist if she wanted; those around her would likely have been relieved had she done so. But the amount of attention available at lunch was limited; Carson wanted it and felt she deserved it. Lerman recorded that later that afternoon Rita said, "Sister needs love. She can't live without love." The operative word was *need*. "Sister" had enormous needs, and love sounded better than attention. The attention she got for her needs she—and Rita—characterized as "love." Unfortunately, love was not forthcoming, except from her staunch loyalists Bébé, Rita, Tennessee, and her cousin Jordan.

In August, Carson wrote two letters to people she now chose to regard as her dearest friends, Newton Arvin and the Browns. She overlooked the fact that her most recent exchanges with John and Simone had been tense and testy, letters about getting her belongings shipped back from France. Now she wanted her friends to share in her good news. She had just met the Chilean poet Gabriela Mistral, who had been awarded the Nobel Prize in 1945. Mistral had taken a liking to Carson and told her that she had written to Stockholm nominating her for a Nobel Prize. Carson said that she didn't imagine she would get it, especially since she would be up against such worthies as André Malraux, Edith Sitwell, and E. M. Forster. Nevertheless, she asked the Browns whether the French reviews of her work could be readied in the event the committee needed them. The news gave her a decided boost. Although she and her mother had both recently been sick, she told the Browns, they were feeling better, and she hoped that "the *Ethan Frome* atmosphere will soon lift." She was resting and regrouping, and this expectation of professional recognition made her more determined to get her professional life back on track.

The rest of 1954 was quiet, with Carson still putting a new life together, or trying to, in the wake of Reeves's death. She made another of the public appearances she had planned with such optimism earlier in the year, but her speech at the Philadelphia Fine Arts Association in October was the last such appearance she would make. Then in December, Carson's beloved aunt Mattie (or Tieh), her mother's sister, died suddenly. The family worried that Bébé would take her death hard, but it was a blow to Carson as well, because Aunt Mattie and her children were fixtures of her childhood memories.

In the wake of this loss, Carson went ahead with a Christmas party she had planned with her mother and sister. Leo Lerman had a driver take him, playwright William Inge, and British writer Lesley Blanch up to Rockland County for the evening. Inge was a good friend of Rita's; they had met in AA, and he likely knew Carson fairly well. Lerman left a vivid account of the drive from the city to Nyack "in the deep, intensely grass-green twilight," the churches lit up with Christmas lights. At the house on South Broadway, they found Carson on a "dowdy" sofa, "glower[ing] evilly," not at all pleased to see them. A television set blasted a football game upstairs the entire time. It was, he said, the "most un-party party" he had ever attended.

17

I Seen the Little Lamp

Carson's single closest friend outside the family (Jordan Massee was considered family) was Tennessee. Despite his disapproval of her refusal to mourn Reeves's death and take responsibility for her husband's funeral, theirs was a tight and lasting bond. From about 1952, notes of criticism began to creep into his letters and remarks to others, but he was at the same time fiercely loyal to her. It was "a unique friendship," Cheryl Crawford noted, "and I think her special qualities of craziness appealed to him." As always, Tennessee saw Carson in the same light as he saw his damaged sister, and Carson fully endorsed his desire—and need—to make Rose a part of his life. When, after the opening of *The Member of the Wedding* on Broadway, Tennessee gave Carson a ring that had belonged to Rose, she took it in the right spirit, saying she would treasure it until the "blessed" day would come when Rose was better, when she would return it.

A blessed time, indeed, when a lobotomized woman with schizophrenia gets well, but Tennessee and Carson successfully made themselves believe it could happen. He told an interviewer, in a frenzy of hypochondria, "My fondest dream was to own a ranch in Texas and have my sister Rose, my grandfather, and Carson, and we would all live together, all of us invalids."

In the spring of 1955, Tennessee was riding high. *Cat on a Hot Tin Roof,* directed by Elia Kazan, was opening on Broadway. Carson was at his side for the casting and rehearsals, cheering him on and wishing him well at every juncture, seemingly not a whit jealous. She was at the opening in Philadelphia on May 7, where Christopher Isherwood (who didn't much like the play) encountered her. She kissed him when they were introduced, and he noted a brace on her arm, which he called "quite unnecessarily repulsive," adding in his diary, "and she really ought to powder her nose."

When Tennessee invited her to fly to Key West with him just before Easter, Carson gladly accepted. He had bought his place there, at 1431 Duncan Street, in 1950, partly for the sake of his grandfather, who had hugely enjoyed wintertime visits to the unique resort town for several years; he'd put in a pool in part for his grandfather's enjoyment. The spring of 1955 was bittersweet, as his grandfather, at ninety-seven, had died not long before the opening of *Cat on a Hot Tin Roof.* Tennessee had for as long as he could remember enjoyed a special bond with this man, whose love, he felt, was unconditional, much like Carson's. He was eager for her visit.

Carson and Tennessee arrived in Key West around April 10, and Carson stayed until the twenty-seventh. Tennessee was working hard on his manuscript of the play, as his publisher, New Directions, wanted to put it out as soon as possible. Carson was well into the writing of her new play, in part about her marriage to Reeves, so they intended a working vacation along the lines of their summer on Nantucket nine years earlier. As a break, they planned on going to Havana to meet Ernest Hemingway, Tennessee wiring him in advance. There was some misunderstanding, however, and when Tennessee and Carson showed up in Havana, Hemingway wasn't there.

But Tennessee had invited to Key West the new French literary wunderkind Françoise Sagan, who had had nice things to say about Tennessee during a recent press conference. Her sensational novel, *Bonjour Tristesse,* about a young woman's coming of age, had just been published in the United States to considerable praise and consternation. Sagan's literary debut was an out-of-nowhere triumph like Carson's, and the two women were eager to meet. Little of substance passed between them while they were Tennessee's guests, however.

Sagan wrote an account of her friendship with Tennessee and Carson in her 1984 memoir, *With Fondest Regards*. She was struck by Carson's thinness and by her blue eyes, mentioning the latter three times. (Carson's eyes were gray.) Tennessee and Carson shared, she wrote, "the life of the outcast and the pariah, the life of the scapegoat and misfit, a life familiar at that time to every American artist and non-conformist." Carson was "poor, sick, tired," Sagan wrote somewhat overheatedly. "All the poetry, all the suns of the world proved incapable of lighting up her blue eyes, of animating her heavy eyelids and gaunt body. But she kept her laugh, the laugh of a child forever lost." Sagan was most moved by the way Tennessee and Frank Merlo tended to Carson: "putting her to bed, getting her up, dressing her, entertaining her, warming her, loving her." More particularly, they "carried her up to her bedroom, laid her against her two pillows like a child, sat at the foot of her bed and held her hand until she fell asleep because she was afraid of nightmares."

Tennessee wrote a letter to Maria St. Just on April 27, complaining about "Choppers's" visit. Somewhat predictably—Maria brought out the worst in him—he borrowed Maria's crude nickname for Carson. Carson had spent the whole time "swilling my liquor and gobbling my pinkie tablets," he wrote. His supply of the latter was dangerously low, and Carson required two every night, but he was able to replenish his hoard in Havana without a prescription, he reported.

At the time of Carson's Key West visit, her left hand and leg were in danger of atrophying, but she could still get around well, usually, with her silver-topped walking stick. She liked being treated like an invalid—or perhaps like a child. Already in 1949 Jordan Massee had taken note of the elaborate and lengthy process required to get Carson off to bed and to sleep. Reeves had performed these tasks as well, in addition to feeding her and dressing her when necessary. It goes without saying that Bébé was familiar with Carson's difficulties at bedtime and the measures needed to address them. Those who loved her best treated her, in effect, like a child, at least as concerned daily routines. But Carson was a strong-willed woman, and this was how she wanted it.

Tennessee was frustrated by her drinking and her inability to work on her play. After she left, he told St. Just that he had asked Frank to take her to the Key West airport and put her on a plane to Miami. He assuaged his guilt by paying her travel expenses both ways. He knew what he was doing, telling Maria, "It is much easier to give money than love." Carson demanded attention and constant expressions of love, her needy behavior seemingly exacerbated by Reeves's death. Tennessee asked Maria to visit her in Nyack, explaining, "She needs every little bit of attention or affection, real or make believe, that anybody can give or pretend to give her."

Carson had been home for a month when she received a grievous blow: her mother died. On the morning of June 10, Bébé told Ida Reeder, the recently hired housekeeper, that she was not well and would be staying in bed that day, an unusual turn of events. After she took a phone call, she asked for Ida and told her she felt as if she were going to die. Ida telephoned all over town, to a doctor, for an ambulance, and to the hospital. She called Hilda and Robert Marks, at whose Manhattan home Carson was then staying, but Carson was elsewhere and did not get the message for some time. Almost immediately Ida had to repeat most of the calls to say that Bébé was dead. She had vomited blood and died in Ida's arms.

Carson heard the news later that morning from Jordan, and then either he or Carson called Lamar Jr. and Rita, who was in a hospital recuperating from an appendectomy. Rita was only narrowly prevented from getting up and leaving the hospital, so appalled was she at the thought of Bébé lying dead at the funeral home with no family present. It took Hilda Marks two full days to get Carson out of the apartment and up to Nyack, Hilda recalled, so reluctant was Carson to face her mother's death. Carson insisted that she could make all the funeral arrangements herself from the Markses' apartment, in absentia, just as she had done for Reeves when she was a full continent away. But she couldn't. Rita left the hospital early, against medical advice, to go to the Nyack funeral home and make the arrangements, then to Oak Hill Cemetery in Nyack to buy a plot. By then, Lamar and his wife had arrived.

Carson eventually did get there, and the funeral and the wake afterward at the South Broadway house went off without any glitches. But bad feelings about Carson's shirking of her responsibilities were exacerbated when the will was read in September. Bébé had written it in 1949, before the Broadway success of *Member of the Wedding*, when Carson had had nothing but piles of doctor bills in front of her; accordingly, Bébé left her estate to be divided up equally among the three children. Lamar and Rita felt the will was out of date. Carson had abundant assets at the time of Bébé's death, so they felt their shares should have been larger. Carson was in a position to even matters up by transferring assets, or money, to her brother and sister. Furthermore, dividing the total assets among all three made each portion smaller; the pie to be divided was already small as Carson had recently bought the Nyack house from Bébé. This interpretation was another development that followed the drawing up of the will. The arguments back and forth grew passionate, and Carson threatened to have Lamar and Rita removed from the premises if they did not leave on their own without further objections.

Her mother's death left thirty-eight-year-old Carson in poor health, deeply lonely, and painfully alienated from her brother and sister. The loss of Bébé resonated on any number of levels in her life, from the practical—she had lost a lifelong caregiver—to the more intangible. Bébé had defined the universe for Carson as a child, imagining a world apart for herself and her children. She had invoked legends and folklore to reinforce the family's specialness, and they had taken on little rituals of their own.

The writer William Goyen witnessed a striking example. Bébé had introduced the children to the 1922 Katherine Mansfield story "The Doll's House," about a family who are given a wonderful doll's house with a charming, distinctive interior. The youngest daughter is enchanted in particular with a little lamp in the house; "the little lamp is real," she marvels. Against all odds, a poor child in the village at last gets to inspect the legendary doll's house that she has heard so much about. The afternoon is unpleasant, but afterward she turns to her sister and gives her "a rare smile": "I seen the little lamp," she whispers.

Goyen once went with Bébé to meet Carson's plane. When Carson alit, Bébé joyfully repeated for Goyen that little girl's line. Goyen wanted an explanation, so Bébé again delivered the line, this time to Carson, who burst into tears. Carson explained to him how the little girl in "that beautiful story" sees the glowing little lamp and says reverently, "I seen the little lamp." The sense of ineffable mystery and the secret, triumphant joy it evoked were a kind of secret language among Carson, Rita, and their mother to convey a special happiness that only a lucky few, the Smiths among them, shared.

The sense of an intimate, shared, joyful secret, of a privileged distance, encapsulated in the romantic story of "The Doll's House," just this side of sentimental, was part of what sustained the family: especially Carson, whose physical woes put her in need of a place of refuge, however conjured up. Little things bound the Smiths together. Leaving their apartment in the Nyack house, one exited into the back garden and climbed up a little hill to reach the street, ducking under tree branches to do so. When Rita left the house at the beginning of the work week, which she would spend in the city, she would hang her coffee cup on a tree branch on her way out, indicating she would be back. The little ritual reinscribed the specialness of the house and its inhabitants. In this kind of eccentricity, characterized by a passionate fondness for difference, is found not only the genesis of the so-called freaks of Carson's fiction but also the ruling principle of her emotional existence. Without Bébé, Carson was without direction. For the past few years, she had been wandering, distraught, alone, or lonely, fueled too often by alcohol; she needed to come to rest. But without Bébé, she had no rest.

So often that it could be called a habit, in periods of distress Carson looked around frantically for someone to love. After her mother's death, she zeroed in on an unlikely candidate: a gay male theater producer, Arnold Saint-Subber. In 1954 Carson had interested him in a very early draft of her new play, *The Square Root of Wonderful*.

Saint—as he was known—was a year and a day younger than Carson, something they both made much of. Born in New York to theater ticket brokers, he hung around the stage from a young age, signing on as an assistant stage manager for the 1938 revue *Hellzapoppin'* and as assistant to the producer of a musical staged at the 1939 World's Fair. While working as a stagehand on *The Taming of the Shrew,* starring theatrical veterans Alfred Lunt and Lynn Fontanne, he came up with the idea for *Kiss Me, Kate,* which he produced. Through his friend Montgomery Clift, Saint met Cole Porter, whom he convinced to write a score—and he had a bona fide hit on his hands, running for over a thousand performances from 1948 to 1951.

Carson may have met Saint through Truman Capote, as he had produced a theatrical adaptation of *The Grass Harp,* though that 1952 production flopped. Carson said that starting in the spring of 1955, Saint came to the Nyack house every day, goading her to finish her play, which at the time was little more than a jumbled mass of notes. Carson began spending all her time with the producer, even speaking of being in love with him. One morning she called Cheryl Crawford to tell her that Saint had proposed to her and she had accepted. Carson was "so excited," said Cheryl, who nevertheless took a cynical view of the matter: Saint "got what he wanted out of it," a play. Carson knew, she said, that Saint was gay, but she seemed to think he was making an exception for her. Cheryl was fond of Carson—and probably not so much of Saint, a professional rival—but other onlookers commented more cruelly. Bessie Breuer said—to Cheryl, as it happened—that she regretted she had had no news of Carson, "whose dream of marriage to Saint Subber hasn't happened yet!" Some friends were kinder, and their comments were probably closer to the target. "She really thought she was in love with Saint," Hilda Marks said, "and talked about how much she wanted to marry him. . . . But I really think Saint was petrified of Carson sexually. . . . She used to scheme about how she might get him to marry her."

But Carson's friends might have underestimated her. Though she was capable of dogged persistence in impossible relationships—with, for instance, Marty Mann—no doubt on some level she knew what was going on and that she and Saint would not marry. She was, however, caught up in what appeared to be a mutual infatuation, not necessarily romantic on either part. Their relationship lasted for over two years, the time it would take to mount *The Square Root of Wonderful*. Long afterward Saint recalled how alike they were, as evinced by their birthdays; he said, perhaps believing it, that they were born on the same day in the same year. He and Carson lived in their own world while they worked on the play, he suggested, conveying the intensity of that world: "No two people ever gulped life as we did, ever ate as much as we did together, smoked as much, believed in God as much, read the Bible as much as we did together."

Carson fell in love with Saint Subber in 1955, when he agreed to direct her new play, *The Square Root of Wonderful*.

At the same time, it was "a terribly depressing period in both of our lives." Saint felt Carson was constantly comparing him to Reeves. She knew how to argue with him, to get under his skin:

> There was not one trick I didn't use, or that Carson didn't use, to make a point. I know as many twists and turns of hers as anyone, yet I dare say there were that many more in reserve. . . . Carson was the most innocent angel in the entire world and also the reddest, most bitchy devil. She was the most sweet-mouthed person in the entire world, yet no sailor could curse as she did, and no degenerate descend to her low level.

In the main, however, he thoroughly appreciated their time together:

> [Carson] was a powerhouse. There was nobody stronger in the world. She was enormous. She staggered the imagination. She was the iron butterfly. Yet, Carson was both the giver and the receiver. One could not tolerate it if she were just a taker. She enriched my

life, beautifully enriched it. *The Square Root of Wonderful* was not only my biggest failure, but also my greatest success.

All indications, indeed, pointed to success on Broadway. Both Carson and Saint had good—if short—track records on the stage. Carson could not forget how much she had loved being involved with the production of *The Member of the Wedding*. "Writing a play can be among the most satisfying experiences of an author's life," she wrote in her introduction to the published script of the new play. "If he is lucky, the production, with the constellation of artists involved, can heighten and give the fullest dimension to the script and the audience serves to intensify the experience and to make the author feel yes, that's it" (*SRW,* ix). She hoped for another critical and financial hit like *The Member of the Wedding*. And of course Saint wanted the same thing. He needed a bona fide hit to set next to *Kiss Me, Kate* and to follow the failure of *The Grass Harp*. In this respect, Cheryl's statement was accurate, if too reductive: he wanted to get a hit play out of Carson.

In 1958 Houghton Mifflin published Carson's play, a thinly fictionalized retelling of Reeves's suicide.

Where did *The Square Root of Wonderful* go wrong? The answer must lie in Carson's original draft, though it went through many changes before the final version of the play was published by Houghton Mifflin in 1958. Carson was extremely invested emotionally in the story, the most autobiographical she ever produced, drawing on the failure of her relationship with Reeves, Reeves's suicide, and her difficulty moving forward creatively. The two main characters each combine elements of their originals. The drama concerns the love of the heroine, Mollie Lovejoy (Anne Baxter), for a new man in her life, John Tucker, an architect (his name a salute to Carson's first love, Mary Tucker). Mollie, a housewife with bohemian tendencies, is still married to Phillip—she married him twice, as Carson did Reeves—the blocked author of one successful book and a couple of failures; he returns over the course of the play hoping to marry her a third time and soon afterward kills himself. Mollie has a young son, Paris, and visiting her at the time of the play's action are Phillip's mother, the seemingly oblivious and largely comic Mother Lovejoy, and Phillip's sister.

The problem was that Carson's emotional involvement was all over the place, so that while *Square Root* is autobiographical, it doesn't fictionalize her life in any disciplined way. Details of her life are abundant and scattered throughout, perhaps deployed by Carson to inject some authenticity. So, for instance, the play is set in Rockland County; Mother Lovejoy talks of traveling to hear Rachmaninoff perform in Georgia, as Carson did; Mollie's family lived near a military camp, as did the Smiths; and Phillip is a genius, a great pianist who gives the piano up to become a writer, as did Carson.

Mollie Lovejoy is now blissfully in love—perhaps the autobiographical parallel to her high hopes for a future with Saint—but she still must attend to the failure of her marriage to Phillip and, later, her guilt over his suicide. The occasion for her guilt appears in heartbreaking fashion in the last scene in the play. The echo of Carson's last moments with Reeves, when she left him alone in Bachivillers, is unmistakable. Mollie says: "I had packed in the night, and he saw me packing. When one person leaves another person after fifteen years, and he sees them packing . . . Don't you see how I was responsible [for his suicide]?" (*SRW,* 152; ellipsis in the original). She tells John, whom she is shortly to marry, "If I had truly helped him, he would be alive today. . . . I nursed him, I lived with him, I loved him, for fifteen years, so let me alone, leave me to my grief" (*SRW,* 153). Carson had been with Reeves for just over fifteen years.

Phillip, not Mollie, is the writer in the family, but Reeves is clearly present in Phillip's extravagant talk of love and the couple's perfect, separate world: "Without you I am so exposed, I am skinless," he says (*SRW,* 49), and "Between the rest of the world and us there's always been a curtain—like a Pullman curtain" (*SRW,* 47). It is Mollie who makes a comparison that would have been resonant to husband and wife: "We have been like children, Phillip, primitive like children" (*SRW*, 115).

Carson was invested in Phillip the writer perhaps more than she was in Mollie. Phillip delivers, in dialogue with Mollie, virtually all of Carson's poem "When We Are Lost," which earlier had been untitled, only marked "For J.R.M." It explores the meaning of Reeves's suicide. Phillip calls Mollie "Butter Duck," Reeves's nickname for Carson. Phillip, in the last lines before he leaves to commit suicide, says that he is crossing the River Styx—as did Reeves. And Phillip voices one of Carson and Reeves's most dearly held fantasies when he describes for his son what life would have been like had the couple lived on the apple farm they had long dreamed about, buying a cow, growing vegetables— "tending the green curled lettuce, the dusty summer corn, the eggplant and purple cabbages," just as Reeves had poignantly tended the garden he so loved at L'Ancien Presbytère in the months before his death.

On some level, Carson was trying to answer unvoiced questions that her friends and family had been pondering about Reeves's suicide. But her need to provide answers led her to write into her play not only Phillip's suicide but also Mollie's imminent marriage to a virtual stranger, John Tucker. Those seeking keys to the riddle of Reeves McCullers's suicide would be left in the dark; the play is all over the place, at once too close to Carson's own experience and inexplicable in the characters' motivations and conclusions. Simply put, we don't see enough of Phillip either to understand his suicide or to understand and forgive Mollie for her role in it or for falling in love with and running off to marry a man she's known for only ten days.

Writing several years later, Carson seems to have known how out of control her autobiographical hand was in *The Square Root of Wonderful:*

> The play was about a writer who had married a foolish woman. . . .
> The unsuccessful writer was an extension of all my own fears of fallowness and failure. I was particularly hard on him as I sometimes get very hard on myself. He combined all the most unloving traits that were in me. My selfishness, my tending to gloom and suicide. In fact, he was a thoroughly bad actor.

She concluded, "Why I wrote this crap is hard to realize; of course, I had no idea it was so bad" (*ING,* 50).

Getting the play onto the stage occupied Carson and Saint from March 1955 to the fall of 1957. It was not a good period for her, despite their closeness. They took the play apart and put it together innumerable times. Early in 1956, Carson sat down with the text, borrowed the story of Phillip, his failed writing career, and his suicide, and crafted it into a powerful short story, "Who Has Seen the Wind?" which Rita shepherded into the September 1956 issue of *Mademoiselle.* It tells the story of Ken Harris, a blocked writer married to an editor, Marian, who is at the end of her rope with her almost constantly drunk husband. We're very much inside Ken's head, and the surroundings look a lot like Reeves's. "The war had come as a relief to Ken," who was stuck with a manuscript and nearing a divorce; the war, "surely . . . the great experience of his generation," put an end to all that (*TMH,* 185). Carson had a fine eye for drunkenness and suicide attempts; at a penthouse cocktail party, Marian finds Ken alone, about to throw himself off the terrace, fifteen floors up. This is nothing new to her; indeed we learn of a dramatic moment in a bathroom with a bottle of Lysol, among other melodramatic but no less desperate measures. Marian persuades him to leave the party, but he then insists on going alone to another one, despite a snowstorm building in intensity. Back in their apartment near dawn, Ken and Marian have a quarrel—after first indulging in the apple farm fantasy Carson and Reeves shared— with Marian reminding Ken that she is his "bread and butter" but believes his career is worth it. They review some options they'd previously fought about: that he might get a job writing ad copy or try his hand again at writing television scripts. But she admits to being afraid of him, which is new, as it was when Reeves frightened Carson so profoundly in Bachivillers. Ken assures Marian, in tones that might have been Reeves's, "Why, I wouldn't touch your smallest eyelash. I don't even want the wind to blow on you" (*TMH,* 198). But when he picks up a pair of scissors, she leaves; Ken walks out, too, into the new-fallen snow on his way to self-destruction—whether now or later.

If there's a weakness in the story, it's Marian's character; we don't understand why, beyond some residual charm of his, she stays with

Ken. But Carson deftly slices and dices what she had been through with Reeves and molds it to fit into two characters who don't correspond neatly to herself and Reeves. The impasse in Ken's career is Carson's. At the time she wrote the story, she was struggling to come to terms with her future as a writer as well as with Reeves's failure, drunkenness, and suicide. Ken gets floridly drunk on the evening the party takes place. That is nothing new; Marian has told him to quit several times, just as she has urged him to get psychiatric help. Significantly, Marian is not an alcoholic like her husband, but the alcoholic character has elements of both of them. The story rehearses many of the trajectories that her relationship with Reeves followed at different times, but in the end Carson writes of the inevitability of his self-destruction and her survival.

The story is paced brilliantly, so that we fear for the characters; Ken might go off the terrace, might stab Marian with a pair of scissors, might die, drunk, in a snowbank. It brings Carson's talent to bear beautifully on the tragedy of her marriage, with not a wasted syllable. But try as she might, when she turned again to translating her story back into *The Square Root of Wonderful,* it wouldn't come right. In the play, complicating the story of Mollie's relationship with Phillip is her love for a new man, John, the architect. Phillip arouses our sympathies, but only intermittently; his suicide has none of the tragic inevitability of Ken's in "Who Has Seen the Wind?" His death is a device necessary to drive the plot, but it fails to engage the reader or the playgoer.

Even after writing this assured, near-perfect short story, then, Carson was still down in the weeds with Saint Subber, grafting her by now ridiculous hope for romance onto her attempt to channel her emotions into the play. As Saint said, "We battled such as no two people had before. . . . I also was forever comparing myself and being compared to Reeves." There was no such thing, he noted, as remaining detached when helping Carson in her creative struggle: "To know Carson well . . . was an occupation that took 100 per cent of your time. Even going to the bathroom was something you shared with her, as you did every intimate detail. You shared not only what was on your mind, but also what you were thinking, all your fantasies." His life with her was, he said, "a kind of marriage."

Alcohol fueled their relationship, but Saint was fortunately able to pull back and concentrate on his author's plight. According to the man who eventually became the play's director, Albert Marre, Saint talked Carson into taking "a long rest" at Doctors Hospital in the spring of 1956. For her to begin intensive work with Marre, Saint told her, she needed some time away from alcohol. Carson could not admit, even to herself, that drinking was part of the problem. She chose Doctors Hospital, which Reeves had entered for his abortive drying-out back in 1951, but since she feared others might make the association, it was said that she was going in for a rest, not for an alcoholic "cure." Moreover, she doomed the effort from the start when she insisted that she be allowed to drink in the hospital whenever she wanted. Saint went along, hoping that once she was admitted, the doctors would know how to handle such resistance.

Marre claimed that he never thought she drank that much. "In spite of the talk that had always abounded about Carson and her drinking during most of her lifetime, I knew that she was doing relatively little of it then. She wouldn't start drinking until five or six in the evening, and she wouldn't drink at all during the day. Of course, she could polish off a whole bottle of sherry in the evening, but she was no kind of alcoholic." Carson's way with a bottle of sherry alone would have strongly suggested the opposite, and most likely Marre had no real idea how much she was drinking. Carson presented the episode, in fact, as one in which she put something over on Saint. For as Marre discovered when he visited her at Doctors Hospital, Carson had no intention of actually drying out:

> There she was, sitting up in bed with a tumbler full of bourbon. . . .
> It was early in the day . . . and I said to her, "What in the hell is that?"
>
> "Oh, it's a riot," she said. "The people here think I'm some sort of wild drinker, and so they bring me a drink at nine in the morning, and then again at two and six—and I'm getting absolutely

stoned, sipping like this. But if you dare tell Saint Subber, I'll kill
you." She was mad at Saint Subber for arranging the whole thing,
and she was going to get even. It amused her that her "rest" was at
his expense.

Not surprisingly, Saint began to pull away from Carson around the
time of her hospitalization, and it was Marre who picked up the slack
in the early summer of 1956, when Saint brought him in to direct.
Thirty-one years old, he had an MA from Harvard and a recent Tony
award for Enid Bagnold's thriller, *The Chalk Garden*. He and Carson
came to be friends as the play went through revision after revision.
It survived six scripts, Marre later said, and tinkering went on all
the while. Marre's time with Carson was limited, however—and so
perhaps was his patience. He was directing a revival of *St. Joan* with
Siobhan McKenna in a limited run on Broadway from September 11
to November 27; he couldn't have known ahead of time that *St. Joan*
would return on Christmas for another two weeks. As a result, he
largely disappeared for those months and wouldn't really devote his
time to Carson and *The Square Root of Wonderful* until the summer of
1957. The play was effectively postponed for a year.

Carson spent the fall and winter of 1956–57 quietly. Jordan Massee recorded a November overnight to Nyack in his diary and noted
Carson's stay with him at his West End Avenue apartment in New
York later that month, when she attended a meeting and a dinner at
the American Academy of Arts and Letters. On Christmas, Tennessee
visited overnight, bringing his sister, Rose, who had just moved to a
new facility on the Hudson, relatively close to Nyack. He wrote about
it in a letter to St. Just, this time refraining from using the nickname
"Choppers" for Carson. He had given Rose a wonderful Christmas
present, $250 in clothes, over which she was "in raptures." Carson loved
Rose immediately and asked her, "Rose, precious, come here and kiss
me." To Tennessee and Carson's hilarity, Rose said, "No, thank you. I
have halitosis." And when Carson asked if Rose wanted to undress her
before bed, Rose flatly said no.

Tennessee greatly appreciated this visit for Rose's sake; bringing
together these two women in his life, both of whom he at once pitied

and loved, was important to him. Not long before he had told St. Just, "Laughing at Choppers is too easy, but when you remember the poetry of her work, you feel differently about her, appreciate her isolation and her longings, and you forgive her selfishness." Carson's relationship with *her* sister was no doubt strained since the quarrel among the siblings over Bébé's will. With the deaths of her husband and her mother, Carson had lost the two people who understood and loved her best. Tennessee was all she had left.

i trust you

Carson had thrown all of her by-now-limited literary energy into *The Square Root of Wonderful;* she was no longer working on her long-gestating new novel. For over two years, she had devoted herself instead to the play and fixed her ambitions on her return to the theater, even surviving a hopeless infatuation with its producer—only to have the venture fail utterly.

The play was to open on Broadway at the end of October 1957, but things started to fall apart the summer before. Director Albert Marre was passionately committed to the play, but once again he had a scheduling conflict. He was on the West Coast directing a Jean Anouilh play, *Time Remembered,* when Saint Subber let him know that it was time to cast *Square Root* and begin rehearsals. Marre's schedule would not be adjusted to allow him to continue directing the McCullers property, and after so many delays, Saint would not even consider adjusting *his* schedule.

Saint's schedule, in fact, was so sacrosanct that Joseph Mankiewicz, whose company, Figaro, was producing the play, jumped in to help until a new director could be found. Mankiewicz and Carson exchanged different versions of the play and conferred by telephone, but they could do little without actually meeting. Sometime that summer the casting was finalized; Anne Baxter, the thirty-four-year-old actress who had won an Oscar for Best Supporting Actress in *The*

Razor's Edge (1947) and a further nomination for *All About Eve* (1950), was tapped to play Mollie Lovejoy, Carson's autobiographical stand-in.

Desperate to get his cast rehearsing the play, Saint turned to José Quintero to direct. Already much admired as the founder of the Circle in the Square Theatre in 1951, Quintero had begun a long association with the plays of Eugene O'Neill, directing both *The Iceman Cometh* and *Long Day's Journey into Night* in 1956. He made a valiant effort with *The Square Root of Wonderful,* attempting yet another rewrite of Carson's script. Carol Matthau, Baxter's understudy, said the word was that Quintero couldn't direct stars; Mankiewicz, who had brilliantly directed Baxter in *All About Eve,* was a hard act to follow in that respect. Quintero was drinking and was unable to save the play. When it opened at the McCarter Theatre in Princeton, New Jersey, on October 11, Quintero knew, as did everyone else involved, that he had to leave the production. Jordan Massee said later that Quintero started drinking because he knew the play was a failure but did not want to let down Carson, to whom he had become close. Reportedly, she met with the cast and crew after the last Princeton performance and gave them the opportunity to leave the production. She didn't know anything about directing, she said, but as the playwright, she understood her characters and could help the performers if they stayed.

George Keathley, recommended by Tennessee Williams, was called in to take over directing. The play was rewritten more than once while it was in Princeton and, three nights later, in Philadelphia. One whole act was excised. Anne Baxter said later that she knew everyone was watching her to see if she stayed with the play, but a complex of factors, not least her fondness for Carson, kept her from leaving. Carson later wrote, in hindsight, "Nobody seemed to realize it was just a bad play and so all the frenzied hiring and firing went on . . . till the opening in New York" (*ING,* 50).

As a rule, Carson did not go to openings. (As the only other opening she did not attend was *The Member of the Wedding,* this tradition, in the manner of Broadway, may have been invented on the spot.) That first night John Leggett, a Houghton Mifflin editor, took her to dinner, she later wrote. She was wearing a "stunning," specially made dress, he remembered, but she looked barely able to attend the performance even had she wanted to: "She was a wraith, green-white in color and so thin and tiny she seemed made of sticks." In Carson's telling, she "skulked around the theatre waiting fearfully for news" (*ING*, 50).

She did go to the producers' party afterward, where, she said, Saint Subber cried, the producers cried, and when the *New York Times* review was read, "they all cried double" (*ING*, 50). Tennessee was at the party when the reviews started to come in, all negative except the *World Telegram and Sun,* where the best Frank Aston could manage was to describe it as a "sturdy entertainment." In the *Daily News,* John Chapman said the play might be called "a trauma in three acts." As an audience member, he had felt like a psychiatrist listening to strangers telling him everything, he said. "Since I did not know or particularly care for these strangers, I was uncomfortable." Carson turned to Tennessee: "Tenn, help me out of here." It wasn't easy to get to the door, with well-wishers and crepehangers on every side; he later called it an "agonizing exit."

Other reviews were no more favorable. Harold Clurman, the director of *The Member of the Wedding,* reviewed it in the November 23 *Nation,* calling it a "dud." Wolcott Gibbs, in *The New Yorker,* tried to say good things about Carson while dismissing the play. About some particularly bad dialogue, he said he preferred to think that she had not written it, but rather "some skulking littérateur in the ranks of the management." (He may have been right.) But the lines were "delivered loud and clear on the stage of the National." With each of them, "the poor play collapses more helplessly into absurdity," Gibbs's review concluded. Unfortunately, advance ticket sales had been so brisk—because of Carson's name—that the National had been booked for eight weeks, so the company dutifully performed *The Square Root of Wonderful* to the bitter end.

Floria Lasky had a perceptive, if extreme, observation on why the play failed. It simply wasn't a play: "It was a posthumous argument with Reeves." When *Square Root* was published by Houghton Mifflin the following year, Carson wrote an introduction in which she argued the play puzzled audiences by being at once tragic and comic. Alternating comic and tragic scenes had confused the audience—though people can respond to situations "with both laughter and tears." The precarious balance required by tragicomedy had been one ingredient in the success of *The Member of the Wedding,* and she had sought that balance in her second play as well. It had eluded her.

☙

"Carson . . . was a hysteric paralytic, you know. Her arm did not work and it was slowly atrophying." So Anne Baxter stated after observing Carson over the five or so months she knew her, joining a small crew of observers who suspected it was all in the sufferer's head. But regardless of whether her paralysis was "hysteric" or had a physical basis, its consequences were very real, and the muscles in her arm and leg were atrophying. In 1958 she began a series of operations aimed at reversing the process and making her left side less painful.

All this was still shrouded in mystery and confusion, however. Neither Carson nor her doctors knew, in 1958, the true etiology of her strokes, their basis in the rheumatic fever she had as a child. Perhaps because the strokes were so surprising in such a young woman, different people saw her condition differently, and many were confused or just in error about what was wrong with her. In 1954, for example, when they observed her at Yaddo, several residents advanced opinions about Carson's condition. Elizabeth Ames felt Carson's personality had changed. Someone claimed she drooled and had a speech impediment. Another believed she had a metal hand.

Some believed that to varying degrees, Carson had control over the physical effects of the stroke—namely, the paralysis of her left side. Tennessee's friend Maria St. Just believed it was entirely voluntary, commenting that Carson could play the piano one minute while in the next her hand would contract into an unusable hook. Harold Woolfolk believed Carson was faking and called her "sinister" because of it.

The "hysterical" explanation of Carson's paralysis had received a thorough airing during her 1951 visit to England, when Kathryn Cohen administered a series of tests to determine if a course of hypnosis could roll back her paralysis or at least suggest what was causing it. Her tests found there was no organic cause for Carson's paralysis, that it was what was then known as a conversion reaction—today called a conversion disorder, referring to emotions or conditions that are converted into physical symptoms—and that a course of hypnotism might solve the problem. But hypnotism failed.

Baxter's designation of Carson's condition as hysterical paralysis was not far off, if we discount the negative connotations of *hysterical*, with its roots in the Latin word for uterus. The term has long summoned the image of a sorely neurotic woman manufacturing physical complaints with no basis in fact; the term *conversion disorder* was introduced partly to avoid the negative and sexist connotations of *hysterical*.

It is not clear how much of this diagnosis Carson understood, but likely she felt that whatever the source of her condition, she should be given the special treatment accorded a paralyzed woman, treatment that she had come to desire and that had in fact come to be essential to her well-being. Julie Harris, who had played Frankie in *The Member of the Wedding* and was a neighbor of Carson's in Rockland County, remarked in the 1970s, after Carson's death, that she was "really sold" on Carson's work and mourned the writing she might have produced in the absence of her physical ills—or as Harris bluntly put it, "had she chosen not to cripple herself." Harris believed that Carson's medical problems could have been avoided and that she deliberately manipulated her environment to get what she wanted. "It was a pity she couldn't free herself from this problem," she commented.

Carson had put herself in a kind of box: she desperately required someone to tend to her daily needs, yet her neediness put off anyone who was not paid help. She could find no one to take the place in her life that her mother had occupied far into Carson's adulthood, loving her unconditionally, anticipating her every desire, and providing absolute faith in her genius—not to mention seeing to her physical care. Nor could Carson find a replacement for Reeves, who had played a similar role, someone capable of his devotion, indeed his absolute love and desire for her. As might be expected, her response was to further infantilize herself: asking her friends, for example, to see her off to sleep with comforting rituals—a last alcoholic drink, laxatives, sleeping pills—and even to carry her into her bedroom.

With many neurotic conditions such as conversion disorders, after a certain point it becomes more useful, and more humane, to look beyond the etiology and instead treat the patient's symptoms. There was no sense in blaming Carson. Later in life, after she'd begun the series of operations designed to alleviate the pain of her atrophying muscles, Truman Capote told Jordan Massee that he thought Carson "enjoyed" ill health. Jordan nearly took his head off: "Truman, Carson could have maintained the status of an invalid after the stroke in Paris, enjoying all the privileges of a writer of universal acclaim and distinction, without enduring the dreadful pain resulting from the subsequent operations undertaken to restore some limited use of the arm and leg on the paralyzed side." She endured those operations voluntarily, Jordan said. "Why? Because she enjoys illness? There are people who enjoy the *results* of illness, but I have never known *anyone* who enjoyed illness." But Jordan could not always be there to defend Carson, and without a defender, she was not always treated charitably, adding to the considerable physical and emotional ills she suffered coming off the failure of *The Square Root of Wonderful*.

Bentz Plagemann, a writer in the neighboring town of Palisades, had become a friend of Carson's over the years, though he was closer to Bébé and Rita; he had also known Reeves fairly well. In his 1990 autobiography, Plagemann was a little sheepish in admitting to having had several gossipy conversations with Kay Boyle about Carson. But he was also genuinely concerned about her direction, or lack of it: "She wouldn't stop drinking," he wrote. "She greeted . . . guests at the door of her house with a welcoming drink in hand, bourbon and branch, and saying 'Have a toddy for the body.'" Looking back, he observed, "It saddened me to see her so indifferent to her own welfare, rushing toward, or so it seemed to me, her own self-destruction." Her writing was proving to be a source of anguish rather than the bulwark it had once been. *Clock Without Hands* was stalled, she feared permanently. Sometimes she thought it was because of the death sentence her principal character, J. T. Malone, lives under; he has leukemia, and the book follows him through the last year of his life. Perhaps writing Malone's story brought her into too close contact with death, something all too familiar to any invalid. In any case, she had not managed sustained, substantive work on the novel since before Reeves's death in 1953.

Carson's friends took up the idea of getting her some kind of psychotherapy. The prospect was not unfamiliar to her; Rita had been seeing Dr. Franklin for years, and Carson had to acknowledge that it had helped her, not least in maintaining Rita's sobriety. More important, Carson had undergone a kind of therapy with her friend William Mayer, the psychiatrist she had known since the days of the Middagh Street ménage. But the last time Dr. Mayer had been in touch with her was about a month before Reeves's suicide and a couple of months after Carson's flight from France, and he had died in 1956, at the age of sixty-nine. His death was unacknowledged in Carson's letters, although there's plenty of reason to suppose that his disappearance from her life might have been one of the engines of her despair, given her propensity to fall in love with her doctors—and attempt to make them fall in love with her.

Another psychiatrist friend, Ernst Hammerschlag, was instrumental in finding Carson a psychotherapist in 1958. A friend of Janet Flanner and Natalia Danesi Murray, Hammerschlag, who as an internist saw to Sigmund Freud's medical needs before moving to the United States and training as a psychoanalyst, swiftly became Carson's friend as well. Unsurprisingly, she often dreamed about marrying him. (They often discussed it, Carson later claimed, repeatedly asking Ernst, who was gay, how they would handle their extracurricular affairs.) But because it would be difficult to convey Carson to a therapist in New York City, they looked for someone local. Hammerschlag came up with the name Mary Mercer, a psychiatrist who specialized in treating children who was also a resident of Nyack. The irony of sending Carson, who understood the emotions of childhood so well and often seemed to want to retreat into childhood herself, to a child psychiatrist would not have been lost on anyone concerned.

Mary E. Mercer came highly recommended. During Carson's residency at Payne Whitney in 1948, Mary had actually caught a glimpse of her in a group of patients in a garden. She was "so noticeable," Mary later said, "her face unforgettable." Born in 1912, Mercer was from Ansonia, a mill town in Connecticut, and graduated from Simmons

College and the University of Colorado School of Medicine. Later she said that she, like Carson, had been raised to leave her hometown and "take a prime seat at life's feast." In 1951, at the age of forty, Mary married Ray E. Trussell, MD, a medical administrator who would eventually become commissioner of hospitals for New York City. Trussell had three children from a previous marriage (Mary was his third wife of five), all of them adolescents or younger during the ten years he and Mary were together.

Mary probably agreed to see Carson as a favor to Hammerschlag. Perhaps she was curious to meet a well-known neighbor, or a well-known writer, though she had never read any of Carson's work when they met. She also may have intended only to meet Carson and pass her on to a colleague.

Carson arrived at the basement office of Mary's modern house at 5 Tweed Boulevard, about a mile from her home at 131 South Broadway, on February 2, 1958. It was a dramatic modern structure, cantilevered out over the Palisades. After struggling with the screen door for several moments, Carson was out of breath when she came face to face with the doctor, whom she had been surprised to find, she later said, one of the most attractive women she had ever known. She dressed elegantly and had dark hair, very white skin, and blue-gray eyes. She carried herself beautifully. And she always wore a single strand of pearls (*ING,* 74). Carson noted the small gap between Mary's front teeth, like the Wife of Bath—an association that connected the feature with lustfulness.

Carson later told Mary that the first time they met, she was overcome with fear. (Carson typed her letters to Mary in these early years in all capitals, taking less care for misspellings and typographical errors than usual.) When Mary asked what had brought her there, Carson answered that she had lost her soul; Mary suggested it was only mislaid. Carson suspected, she later said, that psychiatry had no use for the soul—which she believed her stay at Payne Whitney ten years earlier had borne out. What had immediately brought her to Mary, she said, was her inability to finish *Clock Without Hands*. After so many fitful and unsuccessful interruptions, she felt fitful and unsuccessful herself, and did not think she could ever write again. Carson behaved as

Carson began psychotherapy with
Dr. Mary Mercer in February 1958.

if it were the most natural thing in the world to write such letters to her psychiatrist, despite the fact that she had sessions with the doctor twice a week. Her letters while she was in treatment amplified or drew on things she had said in her sessions. When the formal course of therapy was over in May, Carson continued to write all-capital letters to Mary about her most intimate thoughts and emotions. Probably Mary did not comment on the letters during her treatment of Carson, for Mary was a traditionalist and concentrated on what was said in the sessions. But she would keep the letters for the next fifty years.

At her first meeting with Carson, Mary asked her whether she dreamed; the next day Carson wrote Mary a letter dutifully relating her dreams the previous night. The first one replayed very accurately, she thought, and it was not at all spectacular—that is, it was not "surrealist" at all. She dreamed that she was easy and self-assured during the session, but at the end of it she had struggled terribly to get into her coat. Thereafter the dream turned strange, she wrote. Mary (always Dr. Mercer in these early months) asked her if she liked oyster stew, adding that whole milk was better for you than skimmed milk. Carson was still struggling with her coat, and once it was on, she tried to run, but she was able to move only in slow motion; exiting, she found the screen door that had given her trouble when she first arrived still recalcitrant and more frightening than it had been in reality. We don't have Mary's interpretation of this dream, but Carson added her own: She thought the dream was about money and the worry over money, as she thought oysters were symbolic of riches. She somehow thought milk was the first success in a child's life. She recounted another involved dream featuring another doctor, her French friend Monique Cotlenko, whom she was trying to find in some weird way underwater, often the setting for her dreams. The scene switched to skiing in the Alps with Monique—which gave Carson occasion to tell Mary about her lifelong love for snow.

"i trust you," Carson wrote Mary after their first meeting, this time using all lowercase letters. After the second meeting, when leaving Mary's office, she fell, tripped up again by the doors. Besides Carson's creative work, these early sessions touched on her childhood, though rather less than might be expected—perhaps because, as she said soon after, she was at the outset fearful that somehow Dr. Mercer would take her life away from her, including what she called her "rainbow youth." Inevitably, the subject of Reeves came up, and Carson regretted that the doctor couldn't know him and thus understand the great magnetism and charm that made so many people love him and, more important, that had kept her close to him for so long, what she called "the shine and beauty of his young days" (*ING,* 76).

Also at their second meeting, she fell on the stairs leading up to the office. At the end of the third, wrongly believing the doctor did not want to continue their meetings, she bade Mary goodbye and collapsed into the taxicab on the way home, suffering an agonizing pain in her chest, and begged the driver to take her to the hospital. Once at Nyack Hospital, she was diagnosed with acute heart failure and pneumonia and put in an oxygen tent, her condition described as serious. She was eventually moved to the Harkness Pavilion at Columbia-Presbyterian Medical Center in New York.

Mary Mercer visited her in the hospital almost daily, but Carson could not see beyond the oxygen tent. She did not register Mary's presence, but in her delirium she believed a certain good-looking and friendly nurse was actually the doctor. Marielle Bancou, an attractive French neighbor who visited Carson often, finally understood what Carson was doing and told her that the nurse was *not* the doctor—which plunged Carson into delirious despair, feeling she had again lost her way. The following day at twilight, Mary, informed of the situation, turned on the light in Carson's room and told her clearly that she was there. Then, Carson said, she was back to reality and their work together could continue.

Carson's hospital stay marked a turning point in her life, and not just in her therapy—and relationship—with Mary Mercer. When she was out of the oxygen tent and recovering in her hospital bed, she learned that Mary, as a medical doctor, had been asking questions. The doctors at Columbia-Presbyterian finally were able to explain Carson's medical condition to her and how strep throat in her childhood had led to rheumatic heart fever, leaving her vulnerable to a series of disabling strokes. Carson was immensely cheered. What she had lived with all those years as a stroke victim, she told Mary, was a constant fear that her strokes had damaged her brain and that brain damage was what caused her severe writer's block. Happily, another stroke was extremely unlikely in her case, the doctors were able to tell her. In a patient who has had rheumatic heart disease, growths called "vegetations" spring up around the valves, fragile masses that can break off and travel to the brain, where they can plug an artery and cause a stroke. Because the doctors could see no vegetations around Carson's heart valves, they said, it was almost certain that she would not have another one. Furthermore, some of the effects of her paralysis—the painfully contracted fingers, hand, and arm, as well as the left leg— could be mitigated by surgery. The first operation, to lengthen her left biceps and tendons to make the elbow more flexible, was scheduled for late May.

Carson returned from the hospital to South Broadway sometime in early May and took several weeks to recuperate, cared for mostly by her African American housekeeper, Ida Reeder. Originally hired in 1954, when Bébé was recovering from her broken hip, Ida had soon taken over the cooking; by the time of Carson's hospitalization in February 1958, she had proven herself indispensable to the running of the household. She and Carson referred to each other as "Honey," "Darling," and "Child." Ida told a reporter that on empty afternoons they gave themselves a party, dressing up for the occasion and eating ice cream and cake.

Mary Mercer continued to visit Carson frequently in March, and at some point they discussed her taking up Carson's therapy again. The doctor asked Carson to consider certain questions that would shape their early sessions, among them the role in her life of romantic love. This drew Carson back into the throes of her romance with Annemarie Schwarzenbach, especially the nightmarish period at the end of 1940 when Annemarie rejected her sexually.

In two letters written to Mary in these weeks, Carson dwelled on the question of romantic love in general. She appears to have registered incredulity that her friends really loved her; when Mary responded that she could not believe this, Carson began to tentatively explore the possibility that she *was* fundamentally lovable. Similarly, Carson seems to have referred to someone in her emotional orbit as "vicious"—possibly the Reeves who had forged her checks—because the doctor said she could not believe Carson would love anyone vicious, to which Carson responded in a similarly tentative and happy manner.

Carson's financial picture was gloomy. She had banked on profits from a successful Broadway run of *The Square Root of Wonderful,* which had failed to materialize, and she told Mary she could only pay ten dollars a session. Mary's usual fee was at least twice that. Around this dilemma, the doctor and patient spun a not-entirely-unrealistic fantasy that they could collaborate on a best seller: an account of Carson's therapy based on transcripts of their sessions.

Carson initially floated the idea. She may have been motivated by a desire to forge a closer bond with the doctor, to whom she was increasingly attracted. She also wanted the sessions recorded but was unsure how to propose it. In a letter to Mary after her formal therapy was over, in just over a month, Carson gave an explanation for each of these impulses, referring to "A Flowering Dream," the personally important essay she had rewritten that spring, with Mary's help, about the sources of her creativity. Carson had hopes that the sessions, recorded on a Dictaphone, not only would allow her to "control" her treatment in some way (which was clearly very important to her) but could also be the basis for a book about the therapy sessions.

Much later, Carson's agent Robbie Lantz wrote to Mary about this plan to tape and transcribe the sessions. The purpose, he said, was to get Carson to talk more during her hour: "Then you had the inspiration to tell her to treat the sessions as 'literature,' gave her a Dictaphone, had transcribed the tapes that she recorded." It's not clear how Lantz would have known this, or why he constructed such a scenario. Was he accusing Mary of something? In response, she pooh-poohed this "mute Carson" theory, adding, "You are too wise and experienced not to realize that a recorded conversation between a patient and a psychiatrist is not literature, even when the patient is Carson."

Carson could wax playful about the scheme to produce a book, in one session telling Mary that introducing humor into the therapy was a wise move, as the transcripts had to have a lighter, humorous side or she would never get an advance from her publisher. The doctor needed to set some ground rules, however, since using a Dictaphone and transcribing sessions would test if not violate psychiatric protocol. First, they agreed that Carson was to transcribe the sessions herself: perhaps not ideal from an accuracy standpoint, but it meant that fewer parties would be involved in the practice. Further, Mary stipulated that there only be two copies, one for Carson and one for herself, and that Carson was to use them only as a "resource" for a future book. Even so, word got out, and to Mary's colleagues, no less. When Mary asked Carson about it, she admitted that she had talked about the tapes and even played some, probably for Ernst Hammerschlag or Hilda Marks, because she hadn't seen any harm in doing so. Mary reiterated the need for secrecy.

Rumors surfaced that the tapes existed and were fodder for a literary project, and before long Harold Hayes, an editor at *Esquire,* contacted Carson, inquiring about the "journal" she was keeping of her analysis. He lived in Ossining, he said, and could easily drop by after work one day to see the journal. Carson made a notation at the bottom of the letter to tell him she wasn't keeping a journal but hoped perhaps to base future fiction on the transcriptions.

But the business at hand was therapy, taping the sessions just a new wrinkle. The first meeting taped was an April 11 appointment, which in the transcript was called the initial "experiment" with the Dictaphone. Carson ranged widely in her sessions, invoking Baudelaire and Poe, for instance; the latter brought her to an unsettling story splashed all over the pages of the New York *Daily News,* the tabloid that Carson read avidly. (*The New York Times,* delivered daily, was often untouched.) It was about a celebrity murder: movie star Lana Turner's daughter, Cheryl Crane, had confessed to the murder of her mother's boyfriend, a mobster named Johnny Stompanato. Overhearing a violent fight between Turner and Stompanato in Turner's bedroom, Crane rushed in with a kitchen knife, and Stompanato walked right into the blade. When the police came, Turner tried to own up to the murder herself. Crane was eventually exonerated when the court ruled the killing a justifiable homicide. Love letters between Turner and Stompanato were read out in the courtroom, and Carson found them fascinating, comparing them in her session to those of Heloise and Abelard, a pair of tragic lovers from medieval times. With relish, she noted, the daughter felt the knife going into Stompanato.

She also told a long story about seeing a male visitor to Gypsy Rose Lee at Seven Middagh, slipping a thousand dollars under a carpet, evidently as a tip to Gypsy for services unknown to Carson. The doctor had heard the story from Carson before, and the transcript reveals her and Carson conferring about how to tell the story. The correction gives the transcripts the feel of collaboration.

But the main subject in that first session was Carson's response to therapy and her mental state. She made a point of discussing her smoking and drinking with a touch of defiance. She had once asked Elizabeth Bowen, who smoked "like a chimney," what she would do if she had been told, as Carson had been, to give up smoking and drinking. Bowen replied, according to Carson, that if she were Carson, she would be smoking and drinking as if there were no tomorrow— because there might not be. The night before the session Carson had a kind of panic attack, during which she felt she was having a stroke. Before starting therapy, she said, she would have drunk a whole bottle of alcohol to quell her panic, whereas this time she had just one drink—"really just a few sips"—before calling Dr. Mercer at five a.m. When the doctor reminded her that she had admitted to drinking two or three bottles of champagne with a recent visitor, Carson changed the subject to her inability to blow out the candles following the visit; she hadn't had the necessary breath. From there it was on to her inability to write letters to friends.

That spring Carson and her therapist made Dictaphone recordings of a total of nine sessions on successive Fridays. The Lana Turner
murder came up several times. Carson talked about her experiences at
Payne Whitney, remarking more than once about Mary having caught
sight of her there. In the second taped session, on April 14, she cozily
told Mary that she'd planned for not only the doctor but the doctor's
husband and three stepchildren to come with her to Europe that summer, and that she'd informed her old friend Elizabeth Bowen (whom
she planned to visit) that the doctor's family would be with her. Once
again, Carson was attempting to rapidly attach herself to someone she
felt was sympathetic and who might perhaps care for her; not surprisingly, she was also falling in love.

19

That Green and Glowing Spring

She was once again feeling joyful, Carson wrote to her psychiatrist on April 4. Her novel was with her, every day, like a breathing thing. With this arresting image she conveyed perhaps the most important news of all about her emotional well-being. She was back at work.

Clock Without Hands had been gestating as early as 1942, when Carson was still hard at work on *The Member of the Wedding* at Yaddo, her head filled with ideas for another book. However, she did not really turn to it in any concerted way until 1950, distracted by the dramatic version of *The Member of the Wedding* and slowed down by her 1947 stroke. By 1950, however, Reeves, evidently during one of the periods in which he was managing her career, could write to Hardwick Moseley that Carson had written ninety longhand pages of the novel, now titled *Clock Without Hands*. That same year she reported to Moseley that this new novel was complex, the whole enterprise ambitious.

In the fall of 1951, she put in a sustained period of work focusing on the novel's central character, the pharmacist J. T. Malone, which she shaped into "The Pestle," the excerpt published in *Botteghe Oscure* and *Mademoiselle* two years later. She was writing well in France in the early 1950s, but Reeves's death brought composition to a grinding halt. The next four years were swallowed by the writing and staging of *The Square Root of Wonderful*. When she wanted to return to *Clock Without*

Hands in 1958, after the play closed, her writer's block brought her to Mary Mercer's door seeking psychiatric help.

Carson was finally able to return to the manuscript that spring. At first, she was dismayed by the shape her novel was in. She wrote Mary describing the traumatic day on which she went back and read the first six chapters. She was stunned, exclaiming that the new work was close to garbage. But she began again to write: first letters to Mary but gradually *Clock Without Hands*. She could type with only one hand. For a time, with permission, she arranged to work in Mary's living room. Ray Trussell, Mary's husband, encountered Carson there almost every day and marveled at her concentration. "One could walk into the living room and find her staring at the one page she had punched out with one finger during the day and she would never know you walked through," he said. The manuscript came slowly but surely. In the same letter to Mary in which she described her work as possibly garbage, she was able to write that she worked on her novel every day and that, amazingly, she thought it contained some of the best writing she'd ever done.

Carson's therapy never addressed issues of creativity or writing strategies specifically; she seldom referred to them, instead ranging widely over a variety of topics. The nine transcripts of Carson's 1958 therapy sessions glow with her droll charm and quick wit, which enliven what might otherwise have been rather flat accounts of childhood hurts or triumphs and present-day problems and daydreams. One day Carson came into the session announcing an out-of-the-blue plan to present a theatrical version of *The Ballad of the Sad Café,* staged by Carol Reed, the British director known for such films as *Odd Man Out* (1947) and *The Third Man* (1949)—whom Carson had once met—and starring Anna Magnani as Miss Amelia. For the next two sessions, she talked at length about what she boasted was a brilliant idea, speculating about Reed and how best to approach him, composing a letter that closed with her note that she was sending along her current favorite book, Isak Dinesen's *Out of Africa.* (Nothing came of her idea.) Other concerns and preoccupations included Lizzie Borden; Carson's adolescent passion for Mary Tucker; a childhood memory of Lamar and setting off a firecracker indoors; her sense of sartorial style as a young woman;

and relationships with the occupants of Seven Middagh, especially Auden.

Reeves came up almost out of necessity. Since his death, Carson had seldom mentioned his name, much less looked back on their history. In therapy, she remembered his giving her a purse with ten $100 bills for her to join him in New York City, saying that they could take writing classes together. She remembered announcing to her parents that she was going to stay with him in Goldens Bridge and that she was sleeping with him, arguing that doing so let both partners know whether they were compatible or in tune sexually. (Why this would have been in question was not asked or addressed.) She remembered Reeves's war experience with the Rangers and how fulfilled he felt then. And she told the long risqué story about Reeves performing oral sex on her on her parents' porch in Columbus, coyly describing Reeves's "kiss" as the kind Baudelaire gave his mistress—did Dr. Mercer know that kind of kiss? Carson asked.

Carson said comparatively little about her childhood. She talked only obliquely about her parents, with one significant exception. In her session on May 5, she related the story of Rita's informing their parents that Carson was a lesbian, and her father's asking whether Carson had ever "touched" Rita. She made no specific comments on how the episode might have traumatized her. She didn't have to.

A great deal of time in her sessions was given over to the topic Mary had asked her to think about: her experiences with romantic love. She spent a session recalling Mary Tucker, their music lessons together, Carson's friendship with Mary's daughter, Gin, and her feeling of betrayal when Mary moved away. She confessed that Mary Tucker did try to "caress" her. Yet Carson seems to have acquired a new, more mature perspective on the relationship, understanding that the affection they shared was erotically charged, even though neither of them could act on or even acknowledge it at the time. Telling the story to a trusted psychiatrist may have helped her to see that the piano teacher she adored had not "betrayed" her—despite her having *felt* betrayed when Mary left town abruptly in 1934 after her husband's transfer.

In therapy, Carson returned over and over to her great love, Annemarie Schwarzenbach, but in somewhat curious fashion. She did not describe their earliest time together—the very brief time when Annemarie seemed to reciprocate her passion. Nor did she talk about the pain of their ultimate separation and Annemarie's letters to her from the farthest reaches of the globe. She said nothing about receiving the letter telling her Annemarie had died after a bicycle accident. Instead, she told Mary in minutest detail the harrowing story of Annemarie's escape from a mental institution at the end of 1940 and her taking refuge in the apartment of her friend Freddy, the surreal episode that ended in her slashing her wrists and being taken to Bellevue. What Carson dwelled on was Annemarie's explicit sexual rejection of her: ordering Carson, cruelly, to bring her Gypsy Rose Lee instead, for Carson was too "skinny" for her tastes.

Mary's remarks are also preserved in the transcripts; as one would expect from a self-avowed Freudian, they are few and far between and often classically Freudian. In one session, Carson told a story dating to when her brother was in the hospital as a child and her mother often off visiting him there; Carson and a friend went to a drugstore owned by an uncle and ordered ice cream cones and all manner of candy, telling the fountain clerk to charge it to her uncle. Dr. Mercer jumped in at this juncture, saying,

> There are the threads of your being left by your mother when she took your brother to the hospital, and in the small child's mind the possibility she loved him more than you, which is always painful. . . . And what about the meaning of deserts [sic] and sweets in life? They are the things one earns only after eating one's vegetables. And you needed the sweets because they substituted for love.

More often, however, Mary's remarks were supportive and encouraging. When Carson berated herself for her handling of the police the night of Annemarie's attempted suicide, she replied, "You had to act under that much pressure. You could act. That is heroism." At another moment, she noted what she interpreted as Carson's accomplishment in surviving, in choosing life over the death instincts of some people she was close to: "That is what I see in you as a writer and as a person, and that is why I think your future is so glorious. You stand at the threshold of really coming into your own, and I would say it is about time." Mary's language was often high-flown, and she had a tendency to announce insights with obvious excitement. When Carson related her experiences with Mary Tucker, mentioning the latter playing Mozart "magnificently," Mary intervened: "And when you really face your despair and cope with it, you too can play, now with words, just as magnificently. Don't you know that[?]"

Carson had therapy with Mary five times in April and four times in May—at least according to the transcripts. There is nothing in them, however, that indicates the sessions came to an end with the one on May 16. But Carson was scheduled to go into the hospital on May 18 for surgery. She was a patient in Columbia-Presbyterian Hospital's Harkness Pavilion from May 18 through 30, and the operation was enough of a success that Carson scheduled more surgery for September to fuse the bones in her wrist.

She wrote two letters to Mary in May 1958; the next was dated June 30. In it, she related a dream: she was embracing and kissing the doctor, who somehow seemed unmoved. Carson felt she couldn't express her love. Mary maintained her professional distance through this period, later claiming the therapeutic relationship was over in nine months, which would bring the treatment up to December. But the formal sessions were over by June.

Sometime in June or early July, the relationship between Carson and Mary assumed another dimension. It is difficult to determine exactly when their romantic relationship began in that "green and glowing" spring, in part because of Mary's strict observance of psychiatric ethics. Long after Carson's death, she issued a blanket refusal to all McCullers scholars and biographers, saying she couldn't talk about a patient—though their therapy sessions had ended almost ten years before Carson's death. Also, she was still married in 1958; both she and Trussell enjoyed some stature in medical circles, and Mary would not have wanted any scandal. It was still the conformist 1950s, and in the New York City suburbs—however "bohemian" the town—adultery was judged harshly, and lesbianism was still a shocker. Carson's effusiveness as a letter writer, too, makes dating the change in the relationship difficult. She used the word *love* to describe many relationships, not just romantic ones, including everyone from family members to hired workers to idols she "loved" from afar. Finally, Mary was a private woman who, though open-minded on social issues, publicly observed the proprieties.

Mary was probably afraid not only of having it said she had lesbian sex but also of actually having lesbian sex. Carson was "so much more sophisticated and worldly than she," Mary said ten years after Carson's death to Margaret Sullivan, a prospective biographer. The interviewer noted, "Sure, Mary had read about this and wilder cases but Carson had experienced it." "One period—yes," Sullivan noted, and then wrote in her interview notes, in brackets, "[probably all lesbian or bisexual]." Sullivan also wrote, "C introduced these things to Mary?" adding, "Yet C far beyond earlier experimental phase." It is not clear what "the wilder cases" that Mary had read about were, or what Sullivan meant by "one period." It is also important to note that the interviewer is speculating in most of these remarks. Clearly, Mary would not be pinned down to specifics, and in fact she would remain reticent for the rest of Carson's life and beyond.

By the summer of 1958, Mary and Carson were a couple.

Carson first alluded to their new relationship in a letter dated July 11. First, she informed the doctor of her resolve to cut down on her drinking, specifically, not drinking wine with dinner if she had had whiskey before. Drinking too much had triggered what she and Mary called "sleep talking," when Carson called Mary in a blackout and said things she did not remember afterward. Carson used to be able to command a lot of willpower and self-discipline, and she thought she could summon it up again. But whatever she had said the night before, Carson wrote that her love with Mary was her final love, and it was as genuine and passionate as her first love. Harking back to how Mary Tucker had imposed the discipline she needed back in the days when Carson stormed through the Hungarian Rhapsody, she assured Mary Mercer both that she could discipline herself again and that her love was tender and heartfelt. Pledging lifelong love may have been part of her courtship of Mary, but it may also have been a frank statement of fact; Carson knew she was unlikely to meet any more available love interests, and that in any case she was not well enough to do much courting. Her *first* love was of course Mary Tucker, whom Carson had extolled to her psychiatrist. Annemarie gets no mention here, perhaps because Carson now liked to see her love life as a journey from one Mary to another.

At the end of July, Mary went to Puerto Rico with her husband for a vacation. Carson, who was battling a fear of abandonment, had a hard time letting her go, but she was consoled by a ring Mary gave her before she left. She got up with the sun, eager to make one last phone call to Mary before Mary's trip. But when she finally called, at eight, the phone just rang and rang. She had waited too long, and Mary had already gone. Bereft, she happened to look down on her hand and saw the ring Mary had given her. She felt an enormous sense of comfort, for Mary had allowed Carson to share a piece of her while she was away. Bestowing the ring marked a turning point, when Mary let Carson know her love was reciprocated.

No great declarations were made, no futures were upended, no marriages were abruptly dissolved, nobody moved in with anybody. Carson and Mary continued as friends quietly, but increasingly in love. Carson did tell some friends, but they were well used to the word *love* whenever she met someone new, whether her interest was romantic or not. Some, when they realized she was serious, arranged to visit Carson and meet Mary. Few of them commented; Janet Flanner and Natalia Murray were exceptions. They would come to dislike Mary, resenting how protective a gatekeeper she could be. But Tennessee, who visited Carson as often as ever, never said "boo" about Mary. Nor did her gay friends in the South, or Jordan. Rita was closemouthed on the subject.

At about the same time, Carson made a new friend in Nyack, who lived in a neighboring apartment building until a major fire burned her out in 1959, when she rented an apartment in Carson's South Broadway house. Marielle Bancou, born in France in 1921, was an artist who ran a successful fabric design business in New York City. Marielle would come to feel that she, too, was edged out by Mary, but she knew how needed and welcome the therapist's attention and care were:

> Mary was a very organized person with a practical mind, and she put order into Carson's chaotic existence, her parade of nurses, secretaries, and so on. Carson was very dependent. She needed almost constant assistance even for the seemingly simplest things, which her paralysis made it impossible for her to do alone.

For her entire life, Carson had been used to placing such matters in the hands of another—first her mother; then Reeves, who on occasion took over all her correspondence, business and otherwise; and when necessary, Tennessee, Jordan, and other male friends, albeit in piecemeal fashion. Whether a degree of practicality figured into Carson's growing attachment to Mary is difficult to say. Certainly she was smart enough to see the quotidian advantages of such an arrangement. But Mary's organizational skills were not what Carson loved her for.

Most important, Mary helped Carson get back on her feet professionally, both in the writing of her next novel and in resuming participation in events that got her name before the public. In May, Carson undertook the recording of excerpts from her three novels, poetry, and the dramatic version of *The Member of the Wedding*. Jean Stein, the daughter of the founder of the media conglomerate MCA, was in charge of the project for MGM Records, which also included readings by William Faulkner, whom she had just interviewed for the *Paris Review*'s "Writers at Work" series. Stein said later that she had registered how difficult the task seemed for Carson, who choked up when reading from the play (Frankie's lines about her brother and his bride, who together were the "we of me"). In general, she read so slowly that Stein had to edit out pauses not just between sentences but sometimes between words and even syllables. Jordan said she forgot to bring copies of her poems to read from and instead simply recited what she could remember. The resulting LP was well received; the *New York Times* reviewer cited Carson's "occasional waywardness with the text, her emotional involvement in what she is reading, the break of her voice in certain passages" that gave the recording its unique quality.

In July, Carson gave a reading at Columbia University with a new friend, Peter Feibleman, whose first novel, *A Place Without Twilight*, had just appeared; she had met him through Lillian Hellman. Feibleman would be reading passages from his own work as well as passages from Carson's. This compromise meant she did not have to appear alone and speak before an audience, which remained a great source of anxiety for her. Hellman was in the audience, and after the reading, Rita and Tennessee joined Peter, Lillian, and Carson at the White Horse Tavern, where they drank Wild Turkey and black coffee, "talking about nothing," according to Feibleman, until late, when Carson, Rita, and Tennessee were driven back to Nyack.

That same month Carson made an anomalous and somewhat bizarre appearance on *Lamp unto My Feet*, a television show. It is not clear how the engagement came about; probably it was a favor to someone in TV, either a Nyack neighbor or a friend of Rita's associated with the show. *Lamp unto My Feet* was a well-known, long-running (1948–79) ecumenical religious program that aired Sunday mornings on CBS. Still photographs from the episode display Carson perched on a couch next to another guest, presumably in a talk show format and probably reading from her work. While up-and-coming actors like William Shatner often appeared on the show for the money ($75 per episode) and probably the exposure, Carson was unlikely to have made the trip into the city except as a personal favor, since appearing in public unnerved her so. When Mary, away in Puerto Rico, heard that Carson had to climb up three flights of stairs to the television studio, she was "incensed."

The summer was unsettled as Carson again felt solid ground beneath her feet and began to harbor some hopes for her writing future and for better health and mobility. In what would suggest a change in mood, she dyed her hair. The result was disastrous—her hair turned a pale shade of orange. On July 20 she wrote Mary that Rita was trying to arrange for her hairdresser to dye it back, no mean feat in those days.

One of those who commented on Carson's orange hair also noted the "incredible disorder" in her bedroom, "of medicines, tranquilizers, sleep masks, lights, ash tray overflowing with scarcely smoked cigarette butts." Besides Carson's strange hair color, the observer made some other not exactly charitable comments: "She smokes endlessly, and steadily sips a tumbler of *vin rouge*. She is still pale, partly paralyzed, and so incredibly thin that she reminds one of prisoners of Dachau: pipestem legs, skeletal arms, the fingers of the paralyzed left hand clutched coldly together like a dead bird's claw." This account places Carson squarely in the summer of 1958, after the first of her two scheduled surgeries, yet her left arm and hand still appeared paralyzed.

In early 1959 the opportunity to meet a longtime favorite author of Carson's presented itself, which triggered a fortuitous chain of events and a lunch party that gave her enormous pleasure.

Carson had been introduced to Isak Dinesen's 1937 *Out of Africa* by John Zeigler and Edwin Peacock when she visited them in Charleston in 1938. She couldn't put it down, and in a typical locution, she declared, "Because of *Out of Africa* I loved Isak Dinesen" (*TMH,* 270). Dinesen became a kind of "imaginary friend," she said later, availing herself of the term Reeves had invented for her lesbian attachments, and she formed the habit of reading the Danish writer's memoir of her adventurous life in 1930s Kenya once a year. She came to love Dinesen's African dogs, the locals, her friends, Carson said; when reading Dinesen's book about "that great and tragic continent, her people became my people and her landscape my landscape" (*TMH,* 270).

Carson had made a habit of attending the annual meetings of the American Academy of Arts and Letters and the attendant festivities ever since she became a member in 1943. She learned with great excitement that Dinesen—whom she knew to call the Baroness Karen von Blixen—was to be the guest of honor at the January 21 meeting and give the keynote address. During cocktails before the event, Carson asked the academy's president, Mark van Doren, whether she could sit next to Dinesen at the ensuing dinner. She was beside herself when she learned that Dinesen had asked to sit next to *her*, and the two embarked on dinner with much mutual admiration.

In an essay published a year later, Carson remembered that when she first met her, she was very old and frail, but when she spoke, "her face was lit like a candle in an old church" (*TMH*, 271). Almost seventy-five when Carson met her, the Danish writer was strikingly thin—dangerously so, for she would die of malnutrition—and dramatically dressed in furs and a turban, black kohl heavily lining her large eyes, in which she had put drops of belladonna (to dilate the pupils, for an arresting gaze). She was craggy and frail but exuded vitality. On her first and only trip to the United States, she was much in demand as a dinner guest, photographed and fêted by the intelligentsia and the fashionable world. Despite her age, she had considerable energy, and on her return to Denmark in 1959, she turned out what would be her last book, a collection of African stories called *Shadows on the Grass* (1960).

Carson learned that Tanya—her friends' name for Dinesen—wanted to meet four people on her visit to the United States: Carson, E. E. Cummings, Ernest Hemingway, and Marilyn Monroe. Cummings had escorted her to the dinner that evening, and Hemingway was out west at an unknown address. But Carson thought she could arrange for the Danish writer and the actress to meet. She had known Monroe since 1954, when they both were staying at the Gladstone Hotel on East 52nd Street in New York, Carson on Tennessee's dime. Though she was clearly bowled over by Monroe's looks—Tennessee remembered her "looking down the declivity of Marilyn's breasts"—Carson was very fond and protective of Monroe. When one of the tenants at 131 South Broadway remarked that he wondered how Arthur Miller could have married someone so "vulgar," Carson sprang to

Monroe's defense. She knew Miller through the academy; in fact, he was seated at the next table over at the same January 21 academy dinner, and when Carson asked him, he agreed to escort Monroe to the lunch, on February 5.

Marielle Bancou and Jordan helped her prepare for the occasion. Reporters surrounded the house that morning, which greatly worried Carson on Monroe's behalf; a reporter had been killed in a car accident covering her wedding to Miller, and she feared Monroe's reaction to the crush of press. When the guests arrived, forty-five minutes late, Marilyn jumped out of the car before it had fully stopped and, hugging Carson, told her she was "shaking" in anticipation of the event and asked for a drink. En route, she and Miller had picked up the baroness and her companion, Clara Svendsen. As the two elderly women made their way carefully down the steps to the entrance of her house, Carson worried the frail Dinesen would fall.

Carson served champagne, white grapes, and oysters—the only items in Dinesen's diet, except asparagus, which she substituted for

In February 1959 Carson gave a lunch party at the Nyack house.
The guests included Marilyn Monroe, Isak Dinesen, and Arthur Miller.

Carson greets Marilyn as she arrives at the 1959 lunch.

oysters when they were not in season—and a cheese soufflé for the other guests. Miller questioned this diet, and Dinesen answered that it agreed with her: "I am an old woman and I eat what agrees with me."

Over lunch, Dinesen, displaying her vaunted flair for storytelling, held forth about the killing of her first lion, the skin of which she sent to the king of Denmark. The tale took up most of the lunch. Marilyn broke up the ensuing quiet with a funny story about trying—and failing dismally—to make homemade pasta for Miller's parents. There was ice cream for dessert, the guests lingering over coffee and brandy, as Dinesen told yet more stories. Carson later said that she put on some records, and that Marilyn and the baroness danced with her on the marble-topped table, but given Dinesen's infirmity and her own, dancing atop furniture was unlikely. Dinesen later compared Monroe to a lion cub; "she radiates at the same time unbounded vitality and a kind of unbelievable innocence." About the lunch, Carson told Mary Mercer, who was in St. Croix, that it had all gone very well, but she was glad it was over. She regretted that Mary hadn't been there, for it would have been something they could have talked about for years. And Carson and Dinesen shared a bond until the baroness's death in 1962.

In a letter to Mary Mercer at the time of the lunch for Dinesen, Carson recalled Emily Dickinson's magnificent poem about suffering and grief, "After great pain a formal feeling comes," which for her evoked the aftermath of pain, the stiff, numbed coming to life again. "This is the Hour of Lead—/ Remembered, if outlived, / As Freezing persons, recollect the Snow—/ First—Chill—then Stupor—then the letting go." When we live beyond such pain or grief, we remember it as those once frozen remember the cold. The "letting go," the return of warmth, is inversely as blissful as the cold has been intense; only then do we understand how great the suffering that came before.

Writing on February 9, Carson referred again to the poem. She didn't know what would become of her once she'd experienced the "letting go," but somehow it had miraculously occurred without pain. How does one define what happens afterward to the person who has known pain and suffering for so long? What is the miracle? Art, Carson says, though not in so many words: art is the miracle that comes after. After the muteness and misery stretching back for years, she could say, simply, that she was writing once more.

20

Insatiability for Living

In the early 1960s, Carson returned many times to an idea she had hatched at the start of the decade: an "In Spite Of" book. She had started a list of people who succeeded or even "merely" carried on "in spite of" having a disability: Rimbaud, Helen Keller, Sarah Bernhardt, and Cole Porter, to name a few. She seems never to have explained why she wanted to make her list into the basis of a book, but quite possibly it was because she took note when the words were applied to her life and work. It wasn't entirely a bad thing, in her estimation. The phrase "in spite of" made the artist special in some way—always welcome in Carson's world—and so it made sense for her to own up to being an "in spite of" person. If you're given lemons, make lemonade.

Carson wasn't at all surprised, then, when *The New York Times* called to arrange an interview for an article about her finishing *Clock Without Hands,* timed to just precede publication. Appearing on September 3, 1961, the article was titled "Carson McCullers Completes Novel Despite Adversity." The subhead: "She Overcomes Ill Health to Write First Book Since '46." Nothing here was either patronizing or overstated: the article viewed it as a considerable accomplishment on her part to have summoned the energy and imagination to keep going, when her multiple surgeries had helped only a little if at all; when she was an invalid and with few exceptions confined to her house in Nyack; and when most of her interactions with the outside world consisted of receiving guests.

The *Times* reporter noted Carson's curious attire: she was dressed in a white gown, all white down to her "spotless tennis shoes." This had become a uniform of sorts, which she wore almost all the time. She was trying to make the best of a bad hand, and she reasoned that if she were to see friends almost entirely in her home, she ought to make an impression. She chose to look the part of a mysterious recluse, behind whose disabilities lay a romantic story. A mysterious recluse dressed all in white: the figure who comes to mind is Emily Dickinson, whose poem on suffering Carson had just recently written out for Mary Mercer. William Mayer, for so long her doctor and "protective angel," had devoted several years to a book about Dickinson, and Carson had heard much about the housebound poet from him before his death in 1956. Perhaps she wanted romantic myths to spring up about her in Nyack as they had around Dickinson in Amherst. That Dickinson was likely America's greatest poet would have only encouraged her in this bit of image-making. The white tennis shoes were a distinctly Carson touch. More traditional footwear made it too hard to get around her apartment, and as long as the sneakers stayed spotlessly white, they complemented her costume, became part of the look. Drawn by fashion since her arrival in New York twenty years before, Carson would remain interested in clothes until the end. She understood that what she wore could broadcast a look that contained clues to her identity: so the men's brogans, Italian suits, and crisp white men's shirts of earlier years. In the 1960s, she was again trying to announce an identity through costume.

Much of 1960 she had spent struggling to get *Clock Without Hands* finished. In February, Carson had complained that she did not feel any sign of life in the book, and that she felt like Sarah, Abraham's wife, "still barren" at the age of seventy-nine. But she wrote reams in the next couple of months, so that in April Mary could report that Carson had "raced ahead" with the novel and now mostly needed to revise. Then she got stuck again, Mary told Marielle, "bogged down" by a number of issues including an "inept" secretary. (Carson was trying dictation.) Mary thought that with better secretarial help, she could work out the parts of the novel that displeased her.

Carson was also upset by her relations with her publisher, Houghton Mifflin. In late January her old friend editor Hardwick Moseley visited her in Nyack along with a colleague, Sam Stewart, and it was to them that she voiced her unhappiness. Hers were familiar complaints, but they had gathered force, and by now they stretched back to the beginning of her career, when Houghton Mifflin did not pay her the $250 she felt she was due from her advance, at a time when she and Reeves badly needed the money. There had been another rough patch when her editor, Robert Linscott, left for Random House; he would have liked to take Carson with him, but after some deliberation, she stuck with Houghton Mifflin. The relationship had been damaged again over the dramatic version of *The Member of the Wedding,* when the publisher had expected a share of the royalties on the production. A year later, however, in a letter to another editor at the house, she drew two hearts pierced by an arrow, designating one "CMcC" and the other "HM Co."

Carson may have reviewed this history in 1960, when she decided to ask to be released from the agreement with Houghton Mifflin that gave them an option on her next book. On February 9, Moseley wrote Carson that they would have to hold her to the contract. This does not seem to have registered, however; soon Robbie Lantz wrote again to Houghton Mifflin about the contract. The publisher understood, Moseley replied, that Carson needed money; he suggested that she submit the eight pages of the novel she had in hand for another part of the advance. Lantz replied that Carson would never submit a partial manuscript and scolded the publisher again for forcing a writer to stay with a publishing house "which, no matter how distinguished it is, is not the one that she would choose at this time."

Mary related to Marielle Bancou that she and Carson had been scrambling to gather up old stories to group with newer ones so that they could fulfill the Houghton Mifflin contract's requirement of a "full-length book." Nothing came of it, because Carson did not have enough new stories to fill a collection.

Houghton Mifflin was not going to give up, however, if internal memos are any indication. One such memo referred to Carson as "poor crippled and boozy," but Lovell Thompson, Houghton Mifflin editor and executive, saw the situation in a more promising light. "I think the climate of appreciation for Carson McCullers could scarcely be better. Her tragedy and her silence are known to most of the critics. . . . I think the world is waiting for proof of her magic." The publisher had recently lost Philip Roth and Wallace Stegner, Thompson noted, and he recommended that Carson be offered an advance of between $25,000 and $50,000, high figures at the time. "As between some loss of advance and the loss of McCullers' name, the lesser of the evils is probably the loss of money," Thompson wrote. She was actually given an advance of $15,000, about $140,000 today.

It's not known whether Carson received the advance Thompson advised. She finished a draft of *Clock Without Hands* in October and sent it to Houghton Mifflin. The manuscript then went, according to the usual practice, to an internal reader, identified as "D de S," likely Dorothy de Santillana, whose report is preserved in the Houghton Mifflin archive at Harvard. She thought it not only a "major novel" but "a triumphant vindication of a major talent." Of Carson's portrait of the elderly Southerner Judge Clane, the reader thought she had devised "a marvelously realized character, and he bears in his person the full weight of what Carson wants to say about the white Southerner and his built-in feeling toward the Blacks. What she wants to say is something terrible and urgent," which she says "as a Southerner, never with that shrill reformer's voice of the Yankee integrationist." The reader does not reveal where she sits on adjudicating between the attitudes of white Southerners and white Yankees about "the Blacks," but the message is that Carson, in her new book, is conveying something deeply perceptive and of pressing importance about the largest issue facing her country.

While the novel had gestated a long time, it took shape along with the civil rights movement, dating to President Harry Truman's desegregation of the armed forces in 1949. But Carson began her final push on the novel around 1955, when fourteen-year-old Emmett Till was murdered in Mississippi and Rosa Parks refused to give up her seat to a white passenger on a Montgomery, Alabama, bus. Early in 1960, when Carson was close to finishing the novel, four young African American men had sat down at a Woolworth's lunch counter in Greensboro, North Carolina, and refused to leave. A month after Carson turned in her draft, six-year-old Ruby Bridges became the first Black child admitted to a segregated New Orleans grammar school. Her entrance into the school, surrounded by federal marshals, inspired Norman Rockwell's iconic painting titled, with wry but urgent irony, *The Problem We All Live With*. Carson had been promising for years that what she had to say as a white Southern antiracist would be this novel. It is not surprising that it took her this long, given not only her poor health but the seismic events that had intervened.

While Houghton Mifflin's reader did not recommend any revisions, others at the publisher might have; their reports were not preserved. Such recommendations as there were must have been easily addressed, for Carson was able to send in the revised manuscript just after New Year's.

As *Clock Without Hands* wound its way through editing and production, her friends became more and more worried about the shape the novel was in. Jordan Massee was caught between two loved ones, his father and Carson, over the portrait of Judge Clane: the character was based in part on Jordan's father. Jordan Sr. objected particularly to Carson's retelling some of the best stories in his considerable repertory, which he had carefully gathered and honed over many, many years. He got specific in a letter to a friend named Watson: the story of "Uncle Jack and the goose girl" would have to be dropped, lest people think he had lifted it from Carson's book, when it was really the other way around. Nor did Jordan Sr. like the book any better when it appeared, a fact his son kept from Carson.

While Houghton Mifflin forged ahead with publication, some of Carson's friends felt the manuscript needed more work. Jordan thought the last quarter of the book was too hastily written and not properly edited. When the galleys came to Carson in January 1961, Mary, Rita, and Jordan plunged into the business of going over corrections and edits with her; after only a few chapters, however, she said she didn't want "any more criticism." Her friends persevered. Jordan's diary entry for February 11 says he worked on *Clock Without Hands* from ten-fifteen in the morning until eleven that night.

Carson had yet another operation on June 20, after the galleys had gone back; the surgery necessitated a ten-day stay at Harkness Pavilion. Despite "a very bad night" after the surgery, according to Jordan, she looked good the next day, when he brought her a new book about Lizzie Borden. (Carson was a passionate follower of the Borden case; Jordan didn't think she'd like the book because it argued that Borden was innocent, while Carson thought the ax-wielding woman was thoroughly guilty of killing her parents.) Just after this visit, Carson's friends found themselves busy worrying about a letter from Tennessee belatedly weighing in on the galleys, which he had just read. He thought the book should be withdrawn from production and rewritten or at least revised. (Rita Smith remembered his objections coming in even later, after "the first bound copies had been printed and distributed.")

Though Tennessee's letter has not survived, Jordan made clear that he had begged Carson to halt publication until she was well enough to make significant changes in chapter four, which introduces the character Sherman Pew, a young, blue-eyed Black man. It is not readily obvious what Tennessee's specific objections were. Sherman is a darkly comic character, but no more so than the judge's grandson, Jester Clane, who is his white counterpart and foil (and a little in love with Sherman). Halfway through the chapter, however, Sherman reveals to Jester that he was "boogered" by his adoptive father, Mr. Stevens. Jester does not know what "boogered" means, and Sherman clarifies, "I was sexually assaulted when I was eleven years old." Jester, speechless, says he didn't know that a boy could be sexually assaulted and promptly vomits (*CWH,* 78).

While it is not unusual for the eccentricities of McCullers characters to have their roots in childhood traumas, the connection is nowhere else as explicit as it is in Sherman's case, and nowhere else in her fiction is a sexual assault spoken of so directly. Whether or not this episode was the reason for Tennessee's objections, Carson's friends and those around her disagreed as to how seriously to address his reservations: specifically, whether to hold up publication for Carson to do so. Robbie Lantz and Floria Lasky were adamant that nothing should hold up the book's appearance. Rita had "doubts," while Jordan said he tended to agree with Tennessee, though he, too, was against a delay. He thought Carson, who hadn't yet read the letter, would not agree with Tennessee. And he thought Tennessee had no idea how ill Carson was, or how crucial publication was to her recovery and well-being.

Jordan seemingly had no compunction about keeping the letter from Carson. His only fear was that, if the changes were not made, Tennessee might raise the issue on a visit to Nyack. Such a confrontation never took place, however; Sherman Pew and his "boogering" were left unchanged, and publication proceeded without a delay.

The next month Joyce Hartman of Houghton Mifflin visited Nyack bearing thirty-five copies of the novel to be signed and a case of Liebfraumilch. She reported to editors Paul Brooks and Craig Wylie that Carson provided a "lovely soufflé lunch" and that they drank champagne all afternoon while Carson signed books. "She is very lonely," observed Hartman, and "very much in need of someone from HM to just plain talk to her and reassure her." She "eats nothing, drinks a lot, and looks like an Auschwitz inmate." Hartman compared the afternoon to "being impaled in the second act of a Tennessee Williams play," but Carson won her over completely.

In the decade since she had last published—minus *The Square Root of Wonderful*—Carson's stature had only grown; hers had become a significant and seemingly timeless literary name, perhaps without her knowing it. The result was a pent-up demand for her new novel. In that supposedly buttoned-down postwar decade, much of the literature, theater, and film that struck a cultural chord with audiences seemed to concern misfits and rebels. People were drawn to characters who were living on edge or not fitting in; the work of Tennessee Williams, William Inge, Truman Capote, and Jack Kerouac was full of them, and James Dean, Marlon Brando, and Montgomery Clift embodied them in the movies. The literary world had caught up with Carson, and in the early 1960s, she seemed like the progenitor of a lot of the newer talent. People continued to read her, and critics treated her as part of the canon.

The publication date of *Clock Without Hands* was September 18, but by September 3, when Nona Balakian, an editor at *The New York Times Book Review*, interviewed Carson, the novel was in fifteenth place on the paper's best-seller list, and by publication day it was number six. The reviews were mixed, but the positive ones were rhapsodic. Charles Rolo in *The Atlantic* called it "masterly," and since it contained little of the "Gothic grotesquerie" found in Carson's earlier work, he thought readers who were not fans of "abnormality" might find this one "the most impressive of her novels." Rolo closed by calling it "a strong contender" for the National Book Award. Dorothy Parker, writing in *Esquire*, did not like the novel much (Carson has not "written a perfect book") but underscored the author's stature: "She has been called the best writer in America and even if you flinch from superlatives, you must believe she is well up close to that." Parker also remarked, rightly, "Lord, what lovely titles she always finds!"

But Irving Howe was dismissive in his prominent *New York Times Book Review* piece: remarking on "the novelist mechanically going through the motions," he called *Clock Without Hands* an "unadorned and scrappy scenario for a not-yet-written novel," an observation that must have galled Carson, given how long she had spent writing it. An unsigned, wounding review in *Time* acknowledged her as one of the leading lights of Southern literature but called *Clock Without Hands* "a novel without direction or much visible point except as a tame foray into race relations." But the reviewer detected "the special McCullers gift: the moment of high emotion when a lonely soul rapping on the wall of his imprisoned self hears an answering knock." Whitney Balliett in *The New Yorker* found

Carson's final novel, *Clock Without Hands,* went into four printings and made the *New York Times* best-seller list before it was officially published in September 1961.

the prose "rumpled and gossipy." Praise in the U.K.—of a decidedly ambiguous sort—came from an unexpected source. Gore Vidal, who was otherwise much given to mean quips about Carson ("Fifteen minutes in the same room listening to one of her self-loving arias and I was gone"), wrote in *The Times Literary Supplement,* "Her genius for prose remains one of the few satisfying achievements of our second-rate culture." And Rumer Godden's prominent review in the *New York Herald Tribune* called it "a marvel of a novel."

Clock Without Hands, though not otherwise comparable to *The Heart Is a Lonely Hunter,* returns to the panoramic structure of that novel; it's an ensemble piece giving a 360-degree view of a community. The works that Carson wrote between these two titles (*The Member of the Wedding,* for instance) were more sharply focused on one or a few characters. Those who inhabit *Clock Without Hands* are among her richest creations. Sherman Pew, for instance, the blue-eyed, light-skinned Black man with no known antecedents ("the sober, ice-cold truth," he says, is that he was found in a church pew), dwells on his good fortunes, travels, and high living. Showing his new home to Jester Clane, he boasts that his bedspreads are "pure rayon silk," and he offers him "Lord Calvert's, bottled in bond," which he buys because of "The Man of Distinction" in the whiskey's ads. Jester, until recently Judge Clane's obedient grandson, is drawn to Sherman, though his sexuality is emergent and tentative. He comes to see what he had in common with his father, an idealistic lawyer drawn to the civil rights struggle, on the side of integration, whom the judge drove to suicide. Judge Clane, who mourns the lost Confederacy, is a comic villain, nearly undone by his feelings for his dead son and his hopes for his grandson.

Despite these rich characters, Jordan was right when he said the last quarter of the book is ragged and loses intensity. Carson seems to have been unable to bring together the kind of statement about the South, Jim Crow, and her characters' lives that had been her ambition. She had been able to pull off that kind of achievement in her earlier work.

All told, however, the novel's favorable reception seems well deserved. It was still within Carson's power to create distinctive characters and elaborate and fascinating worlds for them to inhabit, with hopes and dreams that, however familiar, her readers could understand

and embrace. After more than a decade, Carson had produced another inimitable work.

Seemingly satisfied with her achievement in finishing this ambitious book, for once she paid little attention to reviews. She was happy to let the book make its way in the marketplace, which it did very smartly. It went into four printings even before publication day and sold 45,000 copies in advance as of September 10. With Mary, Carson cheerfully attended a dinner party given for her by Houghton Mifflin on September 22, at the Carlton House on Madison Avenue. But after the publication flurry, she regarded the book as a closed chapter. Mary asked her what she would like as a present for finishing her first fiction since *The Ballad of the Sad Café and Other Stories* in 1951. After much thought, she asked for a crystal chandelier for her dining room. She was as pleased by the chandelier as she was by any reviews or parties.

By the time *Clock Without Hands* appeared, Carson, forty-four years old, was spending most of her time when outside the house in a wheelchair. After surgery in June on the fingers of her left hand, she seemed progressively weaker. While this and her previous operations had aimed to make her stronger and better able to function, and Carson remained hopeful, the arduous and debilitating surgeries seemed to cancel out any improvements. But as Jordan put it, "There was never any promise on anyone's part that she was going to be up and about and playing ball or even very active again." The goal of the surgery was to make her more "comfortable," to lessen her pain; the effort often must have seemed, on balance, questionable.

Her bad habits persisted, thanks in part to her dedicated circle of loving enablers. When she needed a refill of her drink, Jordan recalled, she preferred that he bring her the bottle so that she could pour her own. And the drinks were hefty. When she was in the hospital, a bottle was smuggled in. However much alcohol she consumed, Jordan emphasized, "there was absolutely no visible effect—none," although that was not what others observed.

Mary felt strongly that drinking "helped Carson a great deal," mostly by easing her pain. She was "delighted" that Carson had alcohol, she said. Similarly, she refused to let anyone tell Carson seriously to stop smoking. Carson went through several packs of cigarettes a day and had one burning constantly, but she rarely took a puff, and when she did, she didn't

On public occasions, Carson customarily opted to wear a suit.

inhale. In general, Mary had "complete faith" in Carson's instincts, which extended beyond drinking and smoking to eating. Many people "fussed" (Mary's word) over Carson's eating habits—mainly, how little she ate—but Mary thought Carson had excellent intuitions about what would be good for her, and she usually followed Carson's lead, heedless of any professional responsibilities.

Everyone tried to keep an eye on Carson's sleeping pills, however, which were not supposed to stay by her bed but kept drifting back there. She took them every night, the cornerstone of her bedtime routine, which these days took an hour or longer. Guiding her through it was usually Jordan's responsibility when he was in Nyack, but any visitor might be pressed into service. Mary thought Carson would have thrived "with a corps of people around the clock to soak up that insatiability for living."

Clock Without Hands, a best-seller, brought Carson's writing a good bit of renewed attention. Though she had no new novel or play in progress, others wanted to film or dramatize her work. Thomas Ryan, a *Collier's* reporter now writing screenplays and hoping to direct, bought the film rights to *The Heart Is a Lonely Hunter* and was looking for a studio to back it. Mary Rodgers, daughter of Richard Rodgers and herself the composer of the 1959 Broadway musical *Once upon a Mattress,* worked with Carson for about three years on and off on a musical version of *The Member of the Wedding.* Rodgers, writing the music, later said Carson's script and lyrics were amateurish; she had seen few musicals and did not really understand the form. But Carson considered it "a marvelous collaboration," she told Mary Tucker. Once again Carson seems at least in part to have been trying to revisit the old magic of the Broadway play, complete with financial success. She thought a musical might succeed because John Henry and Frankie, in her book and play, did a lot of singing and dancing around the kitchen. Still, she said, "It would be simply awful if Berenice Sadie Brown went into some elaborate tap dance number with pots and pans." She did complete a script; indications are that she wanted to call it "F. Jasmine Addams," the name twelve-year-old Frankie adopted thinking it much more glamorous than "Frankie."

Another project excited Carson even more, and it was moving ahead more assuredly: Edward Albee's stage version of *The Ballad of the Sad Café.* The thirty-two-year-old playwright had quickly established himself as a leading if controversial figure in American theater with his one-act plays *The Zoo Story, The American Dream,* and *The Sandbox.* He wrote to Carson in 1960, saying he had long admired her novella and detected dramatic possibilities in it. Carson was busy with her new relationship with Mary and finishing *Clock Without Hands,* but she said she'd look at a sample scene. In September she read what Albee had written and gave him the go-ahead.

Albee was friends with an important figure from Carson's past, David Diamond. Albee's longtime boyfriend, the composer William Flanagan, had been a student of David's, who composed the score of *The Zoo Story;* in fact, Albee's biographer believed that David set Albee's career in motion with referrals and recommendations. In January 1961, Albee wrote David that he was staying quiet since beginning work on *The Ballad,* "for the simple reason that I can't work when someone

While collaborating with Edward Albee on a dramatic version of *The Ballad of the Sad Café,* Carson visited the playwright several times on Fire Island in 1962 and 1963.

wants to look at every page, every day." He had a hard enough time, he said, convincing Carson that the production should not be a musical. Elsewhere he was more charitable, telling David that Carson "gave me carte blanche" and was happy with the result thus far. For her part, Carson wrote in an early letter to Albee saying, "I have a feeling we are going to be very good friends."

Albee looked to cement their relationship by taking frequent working holidays with Carson and Mary. In the summer of 1961, the women, accustomed by now to going on almost all their trips together, visited Albee and his current companion, the playwright Terrence McNally, in a house Albee had rented on Shelter Island, off the North Fork of Long Island. That winter Albee found a house on Water Island, a hamlet on a secluded part of Fire Island; he holed up there, without electricity, to finish the script for *The Ballad.* Mary and Carson were his guests on Water Island in the summer of 1962, Albee reading to his guests each evening. The first night he read Beckett's *Happy Days,* and on the second, his recently finished *Who's Afraid of Virginia Woolf?;* they ate dinner early to make time for the long play. The following night he read the first act of his script for *The Ballad.* No one reported how that went, but Carson wrote to thank him for "the sun . . . the suntan, not to mention Virginia Woffe [*sic*] and all the fun, *Happy Days* and 'our' *Ballad*."

A warm friendship had begun. Carson and Mary met Albee again during his residency at Washington and Lee University in Lexington, Virginia, in February and again in May. They would make another visit to Water Island, but they caught indications of some unpleasantness between Albee and McNally that the women found offensive. "I wouldn't like to have had her as an enemy," Albee later said of Carson. "She could be vicious and terribly selfish, but she was very bright and a good friend. I enjoyed her company."

At about the same time as Albee first contacted her, Carson renewed her friendship with Mary Tucker. After Reeves's death in 1953, their correspondence had sputtered but never really died. In a brief letter after she finished *Clock Without Hands*, Carson told Mary about Albee and *The Ballad*. Asking about Mary's family—their health and fortunes—she told Mary that she had an undying tenderness toward her and sent her a kiss along with love to the rest of the family.

She was eager for the two Marys in her life to meet. Perhaps she had exorcised her early hurt over Mary Tucker in therapy; perhaps she felt newly secure, emotionally speaking, in her relationship with Mary Mercer. And especially after Mary's husband Tuck died in February 1962, the women enjoyed an intense three-way friendship.

Both Marys first met when they all convened in Washington, D.C., after the holidays in 1962. They traveled almost frantically back and forth for the remainder of the year, often combining visits to Mary in Virginia with visits to Albee during his residency at nearby Washington and Lee University. They traveled so often that Carson designated a tiny room on the third floor of the Nyack house—what Mary Tucker believed was usually called a sewing room—for her when she stayed. For many months, Carson shared with Mary her decorating plans (all shades of blue) of "her" tiny room.

A visit to Mary's house, Tuckaway, later that spring, when they again met with Albee, revealed that all was not well, despite the good feelings. Carson had recently found a lump in her breast. She did not want to tell Mary Mercer about it, sure that the doctor would insist on an immediate biopsy, jeopardizing their trip. Then Carson evidently made some kind of scene that disturbed the household at two o'clock on a Sunday morning.

Never had she seen "Carson as unstrung" as she had been at Tucka-way on that trip, Mercer wrote Tucker afterward. "I realized that there are many things in our relationship in need of repair & I intend to bring it to pass." The next day she left Carson with Tucker at Tucka-way, while she went home to see patients. Gin, Mary Tucker's daughter and Carson's childhood friend, agreed to look after their guest. That night Carson went to sleep without incident, but after a trip to the bathroom in the middle of the night, she began to cry hysterically. When Gin came to see what was the matter, Carson kept repeating, "I don't like people to patronize me!" Gin guessed that she was referring to the day's visit with Albee. Gin reassured Carson and settled her in to go back to sleep, but it wasn't easy: Carson called her back to kiss her good night four times.

As before, and as always, Mary Tucker was obsessed with what-ever injury on her part might have prompted the teenage Carson to drop music for writing. But her deeper motive in going over and over this ground (although she never said this outright) seems to have been lodged in the sexual feelings she and Carson might have had long ago for each other. She seized on her friendship with Mary Mercer and Carson as a way to atone for what she called her "betrayal." But Mer-cer reassured her in an early 1962 letter that Carson had resolved any emotional conflicts in her writing, most notably in *The Member of the Wedding*, which was originally just a story "about a girl who is in love with her piano teacher."

After Mercer and Carson's spring 1962 visit, Tucker seems to have told Mercer something she didn't want to hear. The information Tucker passed on, Mercer said, gave her "a bad jolt." It was impossible to answer the letter right away—she had tried, three or four times—and she wouldn't be sharing what Tucker said with Carson, "because I doubt it would help." She wished that she and Tucker could talk about this in the future "in an unhurried way." No other trace of evidence, then or later, points to what the "information" was that so disturbed Mercer. Quite possibly it was made up, whatever it was. Tucker seems to have conducted herself with friends like Mary Mercer and Carson at a fever pitch, all situations and events fraught with emotional weight. Her letter may have been calculated to raise the temperature.

The lump in Carson's breast was a real matter of concern, however, and on hearing the news, Mary Mercer swung into action. She took Carson to a specialist—probably an oncologist or surgeon—who thought Carson could wait to have the biopsy done until the next in her succession of hand surgeries, scheduled for June 6. After Carson was anesthetized for the surgery, the lump would be removed and biopsied. If it was malignant, the breast would be removed during the same operation; Carson would have to go under the anesthetic not knowing whether the breast would be there when she woke up. This was common practice in breast cancer treatment at the time; breast reconstruction, however common today, was still extremely rare and was almost certainly not presented to Carson as an option.

Jordan later said that it was a mystery to him why a double operation would be undertaken, judging from "the looks of Carson, of the seriousness of those [surgeries], on anyone in that condition." The doctors kept Carson in the hospital "to fatten her up," he recalled, but he did not think she gained even an ounce; he wasn't sure how they expected her to survive. "How indescribably frail my poor child looks," he thought upon seeing her. "It is as though only the eyes and the spirit remain."

Carson led an active life right up to the surgery in June, however. On a visit to West Point on April 19, she met William Faulkner. A cousin of Carson's, Major Simeon Smith, was writing his PhD thesis at the University of Pennsylvania on her work. He taught at the military academy and invited Carson to the campus during a two-day visit by Faulkner, one of the writer's last public appearances before his death that June. Faulkner was touring the campus and reading from his new novel, *The Reivers,* on the nineteenth. Carson joined her cousin in the audience for the reading. When Faulkner saw her in the auditorium before the event, he came down the aisle and embraced her, calling her "my daughter." Uncharacteristically, Carson recorded nothing about this meeting. Her only comment on Faulkner was an offhand remark in another context altogether: "I have more to say than Hemingway and God knows, I say it better than Faulkner." Despite the snide note, the remark comes across as so offhand that she might have named these specific eminences at random; at another time, she said *The Sound and the Fury* "is probably the greatest American novel" (*TMH*, 280).

Back at Columbia-Presbyterian Hospital on June 6, the biopsy found that the malignant lesion was circumscribed and the lymph nodes not enlarged or suspicious in appearance—but the doctor removed them anyway. Dr. Hugh Auchincloss carried out a radical mastectomy during the same session in which Dr. Robert E. Carroll performed surgery on Carson's hand. Auchincloss and Carson's other doctors were confident that their intervention was successful.

The logistical demands of performing two very different surgeries in a single operation were considerable, requiring exceptional teamwork. The aftermath of the double surgery was, as might be expected, rocky. Mary arrived the next morning to find the nurse unable to get Carson's blood pressure reading; Mary stepped in and found it dangerously low. She and the nurse worked "like trojans" to get it up to a healthy level. That whole day, Mary Mercer told Mary Tucker, "it was touch and go." Only the next day could Mary say that "the fight is over and now it is just the long, slow pull."

A week later she was able to tell Mary Tucker that Carson was reporting less pain in her left wrist. The surgery had physically opened up her hand so that "she can use it to hold on to a rail or a cane!" Considerable physical rehabilitation followed. The radical mastectomy removed the breast, the chest muscles on that side, and all the nodes under the arm, so Carson's right side had to be exercised regularly until she regained use of it. Her left hand had to be immobilized after the surgery as well, so her recovery was prolonged. With the aid of a night nurse, however, she was able to go home ten days after the operation. Neither Mary nor Carson said a word about the loss of her left breast or any emotional distress from it, although such reticence was not unusual for the time.

That summer Carson and Mary Mercer again visited Albee in Water Island, evidence that the adaptation of *The Ballad of the Sad Café* was moving forward, and later that month she received an invitation from the Cheltenham Literature Festival in the U.K. Founded in 1949 in the spa town of Cheltenham, on the border of the Cotswolds, the international festival was already one of the largest events of its kind. It was a prestigious invitation; Carson would be one of three Americans speaking. The talented thirty-nine-year-old British novelist Jane Howard, director of the festival that year, asked Carson to join a panel on October 4, titled "Sex in Literature: A Symposium." Her co-panelists were the American novelist Joseph Heller, fresh from the success of *Catch-22;* the French writer Romain Gary, a dashing former aviator, a recipient of the Prix Goncourt, and an ex-lover of Jane Howard; and the British novelist Kingsley Amis, later to be Howard's third husband. (They met for the first time at the festival.) Carson accepted.

Her appearance at the festival could be seen as a kind of confirmation that her collective work had achieved a new stature with critics and scholars—and that she had gained the status of a literary eminence, something she had not done even at the height of her acclaim in the 1940s. It didn't signal a comeback, exactly, but it thrust her again into the cultural limelight, which she shared with important new British and American talents and an eminent French writer. She found she very much enjoyed it.

Preparations for her trip began as early as August 24, when Mary wrote to Floria Lasky about Carson's requirements. Sending a trained nurse to England with her would have been prohibitively expensive, so a nurse would have to be hired there. Jane Howard asked her secretary, Jackie Gomme, for ideas. Jackie produced her sister, Joanna, who tended to Carson for her entire stay in the U.K. and became a friend.

On September 27, Carson flew to London, where she stayed in a suite at Claridge's. The bill went to the *Sunday Telegraph,* which was in its first year as sponsor of the festival. The hotel, where Carson found flowers from Edith Sitwell and David Garnett, provided a telephone in the suite's bathroom, which Carson saw not as a convenience or a luxury but as an invasion of privacy. That first day she had tea with Sitwell, who was confined to a wheelchair as a result of an accident. Carson arrived in a fur coat and carpet slippers, unsteady on a cane, but looking the "perennial adolescent," as Edith's secretary recalled. Another day she had lunch at Sitwell's with her Nyack friend Marielle Bancou, who came over from Paris for the day. Carson brought a quantity of French champagne and toasted Edith as the "Queen of England," Bancou remembered, and Edith toasted her in turn as "First Lady of America." She also had reunions with Peter Pears and Benjamin Britten, friends from Seven Middagh days; Dennis Cohen, her British publisher, and his wife, Kathryn, Carson's crush during her 1951 visit; the British writer Jimmy Stern, another friend from the 1940s; and the flamboyant writer and activist Nancy Cunard. Either Carson or Joanna wrote to Mary Mercer every day, Carson addressing her as "Heart child" and repeatedly confessing homesickness. The pace must have been a physical challenge for her.

The evening of the panel Carson was carried onstage by a new friend, Tom Maschler, an editor at Jonathan Cape. The event, which began at six, was held at Town Hall in Cheltenham, a grand turn-of-the-century public building, before an audience of a thousand; Carson had rarely spoken before so large a gathering. The panel wasn't scintillating, the four speakers mostly talking about sex by condemning censorship. During the question period, Carson asserted provocatively that Jane Austen was the most sexual writer in English. Amis, trying to draw her out, said that yes, he could see that her novels were a kind of "pecuniary pornography." But Carson faded fast; the program went until eight p.m., and Carson had to forgo the dinner afterward, Joanna reported to Mary.

On the last day of the festival, Carson gave out the annual prizes, including the prestigious Hawthornden Prize (to Robert Shaw for his novel *The Sun Doctor*). She then returned to Claridge's, where she hosted David Garnett in her suite. He found her, despite her infirmities, "as happy as a small child in the early hours of Christmas morning. It was the luxury that most affected her. She declared that she had never stayed in such grandeur, and she even seemed a little afraid that the management would find out that she didn't belong in such surroundings."

On the evening of October 9, she attended a concert in honor of Edith Sitwell's seventy-fifth birthday at the Royal Festival Hall and a dinner thereafter. Arrangements of Sitwell poetry were performed, then selections from Rossini and Mozart. Benjamin Britten was slated to perform but was too ill, and Peter Pears sang an arrangement of *Canticle III: Still Falls the Rain.* Sitwell herself was wheeled onstage to read some of her most recent poems.

Carson stayed in England for a few days after the festival, returning home on October 12. She had not left a sparkling impression on her U.K. trip, judging from the accounts of onlookers. Around this time, her manner of speaking was coming under criticism. Increasingly, she spoke excruciatingly slowly, her Southern accent broader than ever, making it extremely difficult to carry on a conversation with her. Her last stroke had been fifteen years earlier, but she probably suffered minor strokes in the intervening years that affected her speech. The medications she was taking, the alcohol she was drinking, or a combination of both only exacerbated the difficulty—but to the uninformed, drink presented itself as the most obvious explanation. Peregrine Worsthorne, a reporter from the *Sunday Telegraph* covering the festival, noted that a "charming and courteous" Kingsley Amis helped Carson through the ordeal of the "Sex in Literature" panel, but he described her as "mostly incomprehensible, partly because of drink." Joseph Heller gallantly told an interviewer that he thought Carson showed "a great deal of mental zeal" in London and Cheltenham, shopping for antiques and the like, but he noted she always had a nurse with her and "was barely able to speak." On the panel, her remarks were brief "and uttered with very great difficulties, the vowel sounds long, the consonants muffled." His experience with Carson was "both depressing and inspiring."

The cruelest blow, unbeknownst to her, came from an unlikely source: Edith Sitwell. Edith and Carson had long recognized and enjoyed each other's company as distinctly odd ducks. (Sitwell, like Carson, adored Marilyn Monroe, "largely because she was so ill-treated." She resembled, Sitwell said, "a sad ghost.") Edith in a wheelchair, intoning her baroque poems, and Carson speaking almost incomprehensibly, in the company of a nurse: the two had not met since 1951, and neither seemed to have become more conventional in the interim. So far as Carson knew, Edith had shared her delight in their reunion. But soon afterward Edith made a cruel remark in a letter to Maurice

Bowra, an Oxford don known for his wit. "Carson's illnesses had by now affected her brain," she wrote. "She *will* get up suddenly and kiss people and say May I touch you?" At the dinner after the Festival Hall concert, Sitwell put Carson next to a Jesuit priest, thinking she would respect his office and behave. "Not a bit of it! She kept on getting up and asking if she could touch him." Carson would not have known what her friend said, and oblivious to her malicious remarks, she was pleased by the recognition she had received as one of Sitwell's friends.

21

The Sad, Happy Life of
Carson McCullers

Three years after Edward Albee had first approached Carson about *The Ballad of the Sad Café*, the play was finally scheduled to open on Broadway. In January 1963, Carson and Albee wrote appreciative pieces about each other for *Harper's Bazaar*, Carson's titled "The Dark Brilliance of Edward Albee," while Albee described Carson rhapsodically as "Both Child and Sage: Pain and Joy," adding, "She is kind enough to call me her friend." Albee had a hit or two under his belt and was widely considered the future of American theater, and being connected with a brilliant new talent only helped Carson. Her name was kept before the public, and she had a chance to realize a second theatrical success, even after the failure of *The Square Root of Wonderful*—quite a comeback for a bedbound invalid barely able to hold a pen, who could speak only very slowly.

The challenge that met any dramatist of *The Ballad* was first and foremost the shortage of dialogue. Albee later said the novella had two lines' worth, which meant he had "to turn all of that narration into dialogue which sounds as if it were written by Carson McCullers." Asked whether that meant he was speaking in her voice, he replied that he was aiming for something more: "I am using my judgement and whatever craft I have . . . to make the piece completely Carson McCullers."

Perhaps for this reason, Carson seldom bristled at his suggestions or changes. He at least paid lip service to her ultimate authority.

The Ballad of the Sad Café went into rehearsal directly after Labor Day. Colleen Dewhurst was slated to play Miss Amelia; in May she and her husband, George C. Scott, had received Obies for their performances in *Desire Under the Elms*. Miss Amelia's husband was played by Lou Antonio; and Cousin Lymon, the dwarf with whom Miss Amelia falls in love, by Michael Dunn. All were young Broadway up-and-comers. The director was Alan Schneider, who'd directed Albee's *The American Dream* and *Who's Afraid of Virginia Woolf?*, winning a Tony for the latter. Albee had initially asked Carson to be part of the production as a "balladeer," reading passages from the novel, including the well-known passage about the lover and the beloved. He and Schneider solved one problem by taping these bits so Carson did not have to appear in the actual performances, but even then they gave up the idea, perhaps because Carson spoke so slowly. Her readings became lines read by the Narrator, played by Roscoe Lee Browne. Continuing the hands-off policy, Carson attended only two rehearsals, professing total confidence in Albee's script and his theatrical judgment.

When the play opened at the Martin Beck Theatre on October 30, Carson arrived in a wheelchair, wearing a vintage red robe that she said had belonged to a Chinese emperor. The production ran relatively smoothly, but reviews were mixed—though none so bad as those for *The Square Root of Wonderful*. John McLain, in the *New York Journal American*, praised Albee's skill in adapting the "haunting" novella. The playwright, said McLain, showed "exceptional taste and sensitivity and a fine talent for dramatic inventiveness." Howard Taubman in *The New York Times*, praising producer Ben Edwards's set, wrote that "the essential atmosphere stems from Mrs. McCullers abetted by Mr. Albee, whose art and craft have joined to reveal the terrible and dim face of a shattered, unnatural love." Walter Kerr, in the *New York Herald Tribune*, was the most critical. While praising the players (as virtually all the critics did), he found the use of a narrator dulled the drama itself, resulting in "our inevitable detachment."

Possibly the play encountered critical resistance owing to its subject matter: the emotional life of a sexually ambiguous heroine who rejects her husband on their wedding night and falls in love with a dwarf, who in turn falls in love with the woman's husband, all of it ending in calamity. Miss Amelia is left alone in her café, the property maliciously vandalized by the two departing men. She shutters the café and secrets herself in the upper reaches of the old building. The *Times* critic, Taubman, called Miss Amelia's love for Cousin Lymon "unnatural," but McLain went in another direction, reassuring his readers, "There is no suggestion of unnatural sex in the relationships; the wife's affection for the dwarf is that of a girl and her baby brother; the dwarf's feeling for the husband is hero worship for someone who has seen the world and even been in jail." This interpretation would certainly have dismayed Carson and Albee. Miss Amelia's feelings for Cousin Lymon are most definitely romantic, not those of a girl for her baby brother, and Cousin Lymon's "feeling" for the husband is more like lust than hero worship.

Unnatural sex aside, the play ran for two and a half months: not a great run. Carson's friendship with Albee seems to have died with the play. He left the country very soon after it opened, and Carson always thought that if he had stayed in town, he could have worked on the

From left: Edwin Peacock, Mary Mercer, Carson, John Zeigler.
The two couples frequently exchanged visits in the 1950s and 1960s.

script further and turned its fortunes around. Regardless, *The Ballad of the Sad Café* was nominated the following year for six Tony awards: Best Play, Best Director (Play), Best Featured Actor (Play), Best Actress (Play), Best Producer (Play), and Best Scenic Design. While decidedly not a hit, Albee's adaptation was not a failure either.

The opening of the play was an occasion for Carson to see family and friends, arranging for them to get complimentary tickets, an easy way to return hospitality. She invited her old friends from Charleston, Edwin Peacock and John Zeigler. The spring before *The Ballad* opened, she and Mary had stayed with them for a month, and the year before that, they had also visited Edwin and John. The two women had to stay in a nearby hotel because of the steps at the men's place, which Carson could no longer climb.

But Carson was most generous toward Lamar Jr., Brother-man. He was now living in Florida, with a good job in the tool and die business, and he and his wife, Jenny, were proud of their adopted son, Bill. They had settled in Foley, a small town in the northern rural part of the state, so remote that they had no telephone service. They had made vague plans to send Lamar Jr. up to visit Carson and see the Albee play, but they probably could not have afforded it, Jenny told Carson. When Carson sent plane tickets for the whole family, the Smiths were beside themselves with excitement. They bought the youngest Lamar his first suit, writing to Carson how handsome he looked in it. This would be the first time Carson had seen her brother since Bébé died. Lamar kept up after a fashion, writing labored letters, more often to Rita than to Carson. His severe dyslexia made it hard for him to write, so usually Jenny took over the task. In any case, there were only a few letters each year, and sometimes none at all.

Rita was a worry, for she seemed to be struggling with her AA program in the early 1960s; the details are elusive, but Carson noted that she recommended the Connecticut rehab facility High Watch for Rita. Once her situation stabilized, she left *Mademoiselle,* hoping to devote more time to her own writing. A 1961 letter from her brother indicates she was going back to school for an advanced degree, probably a master's; Lamar notes how proud he will be to have a sister "with letters back of her name." She was encouraged when Columbia University asked if she would be interested in teaching a course in creative writing as an adjunct; her own talent for both writing fiction and editing it served her well here. Later, she would also teach in the writers' workshop at the New School for Social Research, downtown. Her magazine job stood her in good stead: *Mademoiselle* was one of a handful of commercial outlets for quality fiction in the country. In its peak years in the 1950s, the fashion magazine published such writers as William Faulkner, James Baldwin, Tennessee Williams, Truman Capote, Albert Camus, and Paul Bowles, and as fiction editor all their manuscripts passed through Rita's hands. Visiting Rita one afternoon, Truman Capote pulled a story of Ray Bradbury's out of the slush pile and gave it to her; *Mademoiselle* published the story, and Bradbury became a lifetime friend. When Sylvia Plath was a guest editor on *Mademoiselle*'s college issue in 1953, an experience indelibly brought to life in *The Bell Jar*, Rita was one of the panoply of glamorous and brilliant editorial stars admired by Plath and the other young women. Joan Didion, a guest editor on the college issue two years later, in 1955, remembered Rita as "the plump, alcohol-splotchy sister of Carson McCullers" (in Didion's biographer's words). "It was the first time I worked in an office," Didion told a reporter, "and Rita Smith was wonderful. Terry Southern was always calling her, and there were always these little crises. Carson McCullers was her sister, so it was just very exciting." Didion imitated Rita saying, in a Georgia accent, "Sistah has ruined my *life!*" Though being Carson's sister was at times extremely difficult for Rita, it was unusual for her to complain as Didion described. She continued to spend the weekends in Nyack, providing or arranging whatever support Carson needed.

Carson, too, was struggling, in a very different way. A month before *The Ballad of the Sad Café* opened, she was hospitalized again, this time for suspected cancer of the cervix. Tests were inconclusive, however, and the doctors decided only to monitor her condition. There followed a string of hospital visits throughout 1964, beginning with a somewhat inconclusive stay at St. Luke's in February for edema of the legs and abdomen (of an unknown cause). She developed pneumonia, and doctors tested the functioning of her heart. In May she broke her hip and shattered her elbow when she got up in the middle of the night to use the bathroom. During the monthlong hospital stay that followed, she developed a blood clot in her lung and, again, pneumonia. In December she was admitted to the Neurological Institute for physiotherapy of her left leg, staying into the new year.

More medical trouble turned the summer and fall of 1965 nightmarish. On June 28 she was readmitted to the rehabilitation clinic at the Neurological Institute for evaluation of her left leg. She was approved for surgery on the tendons in that leg and was moved to Harkness Pavilion on July 1. Surgery was on July 15. There were complications: pneumonia and heart failure. Carson was not discharged until October 13, and then with a full-time nurse.

Complicating Carson's health picture was her early 1960s drug regimen. Available documents range from nurses' notes during hospitalization to notations that Mary Mercer made for her own use to doctors' discharge notes, but reconstructing her drug regimen with any certitude from them is impossible. Neither is it easy, with only these sketchy accounts to draw on, to reach any definite conclusions about either her medical care or her physical and medical condition.

Two different records exist for 1962, dating from her double surgery to remove her right breast and restore the use of her left hand. Mary made a list headed "Notes for Hospitalization" that enumerates Carson's medications: Digitalin, for heart arrhythmia; two different antibiotics, penicillin and achromycin; and Miltown (meprobamate), a tranquilizer. In the evening, she noted, Carson took achromycin; Miltown; and Tuinal, a barbiturate. Mary's notes on Carson's daily use of over-the-counter drugs, her alcohol habits, and her daily routine tell us more. She took only very small "pediatric" amounts of food. She took naps in the morning and afternoon. She needed, before bed, two squares of Ex-Lax. She also required eyeshades and a supply of Kleenex before she went to sleep. (Jordan said Carson and Rita required industrial quantities of Kleenex at all times.)

Most telling, however, are Mary's notes about alcohol; Carson had four and a half ounces of liquor at lunch (from 3 to 4 p.m.); the same amount at dinner (at 7 p.m.); and four and a half ounces again at bedtime (after 9:30 p.m.). A standard drink is about one and a half ounces, so Carson was ingesting an average of three drinks before lunch, again before dinner, and again at bedtime. Even allowing some margin for error in Mary's record-keeping, and even with Carson's habit of leaving drinks unfinished, her alcohol consumption—every day—especially in conjunction with her other medications, can only be described as debilitating. It makes her friends' insistence that she was not an alcoholic all the more incredible.

A record that seems to be a nurse's notes drawn up at discharge after the 1962 hospitalization lists Carson's drug regimen in the hospital. She was not taking Miltown or Tuinal, but she was taking Doriden (glutethimide), a sedative; Darvon (dextropropoxyphene), for pain (it would be banned in 2010 for its addictiveness and for its potentially fatal effects on heart rhythm); Digitalin (digitalis) and Quinidine (quinine), for the heart; and chlorthiazide, a diuretic. Only one note on her nonprescription drug habits is included, milk of magnesia having replaced the Ex-Lax. A significant addition to the list of Carson's medications at discharge was Thorazine (chlorpromazine); in the hospital she had been taking 50 milligrams four times a day.

A similar record exists for 1965, attached to Carson's records for her stay at the New York State Rehabilitation Hospital in March. The list of medications is in the hand of a doctor or nurse (not Mary Mercer), marked "2 week supply." First on the numbered list is Thorazine, 50 milligrams; second is Dulcolax, a laxative; then aspirin for pain; two antibiotics, Flagyl and penicillin; gelatin in capsule form, presumably for brittle bones; Digitoxin, for the heart; hydrochlorothiazide, a diuretic; Valium (diazepam), a tranquilizer; and Doriden again. Presumably this regimen was discontinued after two weeks; it is not clear which drugs she continued taking.

This is a significant portfolio of medications, even for an invalid, heavy on tranquilizers and sedatives. She was probably prescribed Thorazine—a small dose, once a day—to forestall lingering symptoms of alcoholic withdrawal when she went into the hospital. The several tranquilizers were probably prescribed because Carson had trouble sleeping and was anxious about it—which was why she took Miltown and Tuinal at home, as Mary's notes indicate. In the early 1960s, women were commonly prescribed tranquilizers and sedatives, and they did not carry the connotations they do today. The medical community, for instance, had no idea that Valium was as potentially addictive as it is now known to be. By any standard, however, Carson was medicated a lot of the time, an especially worrisome matter when these drugs are taken in conjunction with heavy alcohol use. At the very least, her intake might explain why she spoke so slowly. Such a regimen was not life-threatening, but it did raise questions about its effects on Carson's lingering hopes to continue her writing career.

The inclusion of Thorazine in Carson's drug cocktail is revealing. Her alcohol intake was such that abruptly stopping would likely have brought on delirium tremens, or the DTs, a serious condition in alcohol withdrawal characterized by confusion, shaking, sweating, sometimes hallucinations, and irregular heart rate. Thorazine was first synthesized in 1951 and was in wide use soon after that as an antipsychotic, useful in stabilizing schizophrenic patients. It would become a major factor in the deinstitutionalization of mental patients in the 1950s and '60s. It was also found to calm and quiet patients in alcohol withdrawal. Carson was not psychotic, but she drank enough that when her alcohol consumption was stopped, the DTs were a real threat. Not uncommonly, hospitalized patients would go into the DTs unexpectedly. While this might have happened to Carson, most likely the doctors knew of her drinking and prescribed the drug to forestall an attack.

In and out of the hospital, Carson needed a resilient support staff, which she gathered with mixed success. Mary helped, and Rita pitched in, as did Hilda and Robert Marks. Carson repeatedly begged Hilda to leave her husband and come live with her in Nyack. Her home situation was not ideal for an invalid. Ida Reeder, "the backbone of my house" (*ING*, 73), took care of her needs during the day, but the nights were more troublesome. A system had been in place since before Carson broke her hip; she was supposed to call Mary if she needed to get out of bed in the night for any reason, then call her back when she returned to bed. The system worked fairly well. Once Mary rushed to the South Broadway house and found Carson on the floor of the bathroom. She managed to get her back to bed. For a time, there was an alternate system as well, according to which Carson could ring a bell that let Ruth Wells, her upstairs neighbor, know she needed help.

Jordan later said that he could never understand Mary letting Carson live alone. Perversely, the numerous psychotropic drugs Carson was on increased the likelihood of her falling.

Carson and Mary tried to address the problem in various ways. Not long after Isak Dinesen's death in 1962, Carson wrote to Dinesen's companion, Clara Svendsen, asking her to move in to 131 South Broadway as her companion, assuring her that, with Ida present, the arrangement would not be onerous. Nothing came of this proposal. The situation would have been easier for all concerned if Carson and Mary lived together, but Mary firmly refused, even though she had divorced in 1961 and was living alone. Once a fire broke out at 131 South Broadway—Carson got out safely, and the damage to the house was only from smoke. Afterward Carson had to stay with Mary until the house was habitable again. Rita and Jordan enjoyed joking that Carson had set the fire so she could move in with Mary permanently.

But they liked to think of themselves as a couple with two residences, 131 South Broadway and 5 Tweed Boulevard, making much of their two fireplaces, one in each dwelling. Mary decorated a handwritten letter to Carson when she was in the U.K. in 1962 with her drawings; it shows two different fireplaces, each with a fire in it, noting, "Fires burning day and night in both homes to light your return!"

The letters between Mary and Carson, on the rare occasions they were apart, are rife with similarly witty observations and aperçus, many sentimental in the extreme. There was a special prayer they said when they were apart, though Carson remained an atheist—actually, Mary was perhaps most accurate on this score when she said, "Carson was not a religious person." Mary worried terribly when they were apart but wrote, "I know you promised to take especial care of yourself & I know that you keep your word. So I do not worry." Carson's imagination crept into a letter dictated in 1966 in which she told Mary that in her imagination she kissed Mary's small foot—the left one.

Mary was also taking charge of Carson's financial affairs. Robbie Lantz and Floria Lasky did an excellent job handling investments and keeping track of royalties, but Carson needed someone on her end to keep track of day-to-day expenses and such matters as health insurance. In some years her income included foreign royalties, which Mary

Tucker thought provided her a "fairly steady" income, in addition to her royalties from movie and theatrical sales, but her expenses could be quite high. In a handwritten account for 1960, Mary notes that royalties brought in only $1,000 and dividends $4,800. The rent Carson collected from the other residents of 131 South Broadway provided $3,602; buying the house from Bébé in 1951 and keeping it as both a residence and a rental property had been a wise move. Mary Tucker thought the rents from the four or five apartments (her own small quarters on the third floor were sometimes rented) paid Carson's taxes and perhaps Ida's wages. All the expenses that Mary Mercer could account for—and she wasn't sure of the income tax Carson paid or what she spent on clothing—amounted to $11,601. Total income for 1960 was $12,202, leaving Carson a margin of $421.

Her writing had of course always been her greatest source of income, but it was exceedingly variable. While she earned just $1,000 from her work in 1960, according to Mary, a letter from Robbie Lantz in August 1967 informed Carson that she was due $10,000 for the movie sale of *The Heart Is a Lonely Hunter* and $15,000 in six months as another payment on that property. He also noted that in December, she was owed $8,333 for the film rights to *Reflections in a Golden Eye,* to be directed by John Huston. But Lantz's estimate did not include book royalties or dividends on investments, which she generally received every year.

Concerned in part about the thin margin she was living on, Carson turned again to writing. In 1963 she showed some poems for children to Houghton Mifflin editor Joyce Hartman, who encouraged her to produce more for a children's book. In May 1964 Carson published *Sweet as a Pickle and Clean as a Pig,* a collection of children's rhymes accompanied by charming drawings by the German artist Rolf Gérard. The title rhyme was "When you're sweet as a pickle / And clean as a pig—/ I'll give you a nickel / and dance you a jig." The volume was duly received and reviewed; the *Times* critic thought it "may seem slight and disappointing from so distinguished a pen" but predicted that children would respond to verses about outer space and the nature of air. Carson dedicated the book to Emily and Dara Altman, the young daughters of Floria Lasky, whom Carson much favored. The poems appeal to a child's sense of absurdity and the general weirdness of the world, which we might expect from the creator of *The Member of the Wedding*'s Frankie Addams. One offering asks who put the *d* in *Wednesday*. Another addresses the existential questions raised by the contemporaneous space race, a fascination of many children. Others address paradoxes, like "How High Is the Sky":

> *The sky is higher than a tree I know.*
> *I know it's higher than an airplane*
> *But when at night there is a starry sky—*
> *I wonder which is higher*
> *Stars or sky?*

For whatever reason, however, the book was not blessed with the mysterious alchemy that makes a children's book catch on, and Carson and her friends spoke little of it in the succeeding years.

Seemingly undaunted, she took up fiction again. For some time, she had projected a novel about a subject close to her heart, a civil rights march. She eagerly followed the news of the civil rights movement and the violent response to it in the South, and while she had not spent any prolonged time there since 1954, when she spent a month in Charleston and Charlotte, she wanted to test the subject matter against the model she had developed for her characters and her storytelling. She built a cast of characters much like the odd but strangely compelling inhabitants of her earlier fiction. The march gave the narrative a built-in structure, and she set forth with determination. Soon, however, it shrank from a novel to a story, "The March." The particulars of the march, from the fictional Georgia town of Hilton to Atlanta, brought the narrative some drama through such incidents as the participants' daily search for food supplies, which often ends in violence. But despite her best efforts, the story remains flat and sentimental. The earnest white boy Jim, who discovers his vocation as a doctor over the course of the march, agrees to help his new Black friend Odum talk more like white people do. Jim gets the girl, a classmate who happens to be on the march as well. A prim English teacher and an idealistic Episcopal pastor become engaged. The march might not have changed much, Carson says in the story's last paragraph, but it wrought changes in everyone who participated in it, through love.

Carson was so pleased at producing a long story that she decided to produce two more that, with "The March," could form a collection like *The Ballad of the Sad Café and Other Stories*. She saw the three stories as a trilogy. Again taking race and civil rights as her subject, she turned out the other two, less polished and equally flat. "Hush Little Baby" narrates a day in the life of a Black girl called Nabisco and her first day at an integrated school. Predictably, she befriends a white girl, but the story's real interest is the variety of racist observations made by the adults. "The Man Upstairs" is an interesting character study of Lucilla, a Black woman who does catering for rich whites. The story's subject is her continuing faith in the face of loss. (Her favorite daughter suffers a kitchen fire and is badly scarred, while her wandering husband brings home a prostitute.) The final blow is the death from pneumonia of her granddaughter, Georgia Lee. The weakest part of the story is the last paragraph, in which Lucilla sees Georgia Lee in white robes, flying in heaven in the company of The Man Upstairs. The story's major flaw—and the flaw of the other stories as well—lies in the depth, or lack of it, of her characters. They remain strangely inert and come across as "typical," not at all what they would have been in a classic McCullers story. In her earlier work, her stories seem to develop naturally from her characters; with these late stories, she appears to be fabricating characters to populate a loosely conceived structure—and the results are mostly flat and lifeless.

The worth or quality of the three stories was a subject of some dismay among Carson's friends. Robbie Lantz took on the task of sending them out. He asked Rita, now fiction editor at *Redbook,* whether the magazine would publish "The March," for which he asked $4,000. Rita felt she couldn't say no but sat on the manuscript for weeks, too embarrassed to send it along. The story was rigorously and creatively edited, and duly published in March 1967, advertised on *Redbook*'s cover as "A New Story by the Author of MEMBER OF THE WEDDING."

Lantz was also trying to interest Houghton Mifflin in a volume. Joyce Hartman, who worked most closely with Carson in the 1960s, visited her when Robbie was also present. "Lantz announced, in Carson's beaming presence, that he was sending us the stories which, though they totalled only 70 pages, would make a fine little book," she later wrote. Hartman reported to her colleagues on the manuscript, calling the stories "pathetically bad." What pained her most, she said, "what has moved me to tears is that Carson, that most beautiful of writers, has lost all power to write at all." She was dismayed at the thought of Lantz showing the stories to magazines around town, as Houghton Mifflin would suffer if substandard work damaged Carson's reputation. Instead, she suggested advancing Carson some money until she saw her next payment from the movie, with a "written understanding" from Lantz that he would not show the stories to other houses, nor try to sell them on his own.

The situation was not as dire as Hartman was painting it. The stories needed work, but the basic concept or situation behind each was sound, and the idea of reading the Southern writer Carson McCullers on race at the height of the civil rights battle was compelling. However, it doesn't seem to have occurred to anyone to try to work with her to improve the stories. Luckily, Carson was not enlightened as to her publisher's opinion on her recent work, and the buck was passed for the time being.

At the end of 1965, Carson got the sad news that Tom McCullers, Reeves's remaining sibling, had died. Reeves and Tom's sister Marguerite had died of an overdose of sleeping pills in 1947, at thirty-one. Now Stanton Lee, Jr., Reeves's nephew and Marguerite McCullers's only child, went to see Carson at Columbia-Presbyterian Hospital, where she was recovering from the surgery on her tendons. He gave her the news about Tom, adding that he didn't want her to hear about it in the newspapers. Tom had jumped from the fifth floor of a Greenwich Village apartment building, age forty-three. By all accounts, his life had been a rocky affair. Like his brother, he was good-looking and talented; also like Reeves, he had never found his vocation. He, too, was bisexual and bothered terribly by his homosexual urges. He once told Carson, in considerable pain, "I think I'm homosexual." She responded briskly, "Don't be," he recalled. Carson and her nephew Stanton commiserated over Tom's death and Reeves's. It was too bad that Reeves's two siblings had killed themselves as well, Carson said. Stanton corrected her—*three* of Reeves's siblings had killed themselves—and brought her up to date. Wiley Mae, the third of four McCullers siblings, had died from an overdose of prescription drugs in 1961, at forty-three, like her brother. With the death of Tom, regarded as the baby of the family, all four McCullers children had taken their own lives.

Much had got in the way of Carson's relations with the McCullerses over the years, from her decision to have Reeves buried in France to Jessie McCullers's mismanagement of the Nyack house in the early 1950s. Perhaps the greatest difficulty had to do with David Diamond. When Tom McCullers was stationed in England during the war, he had met Reeves's great friend David, also in the army, and they began an affair. The story is sketchy, but evidently Tom had been under watch on his base on suspicion of homosexuality. When his affair with David was discovered, he was sent to a psychiatric hospital, then back to the United States. Carson and Reeves blamed David, who ought to have known better than to endanger Tom when he was already under suspicion, a candidate for dishonorable discharge. The affair would have disturbed and saddened Reeves, but Carson was plain angry at David, her maternal instincts aroused on Tom's behalf.

Now, in 1965, hearing about Tom's suicide, Carson was depressed, although as always, her physical condition had a lot to do with it. After leaving the hospital in mid-October, she wrote a letter to Mary Tucker detailing her unhappiness. She complained that she had to be turned every hour like a pig on a spit to avoid bedsores. She (surprisingly) confessed to Mary Tucker that she didn't believe in God and that she envied her and Mary Mercer because they did. All she had to look forward to, she said, was physical therapy that might make it possible for her to move from her bed to a wheelchair without great pain. She had even lost her taste for her "beloved Demon-Rum." But she assured Tucker she was coming back slowly.

She lived for friends' visits and her birthday. On that day, Jordan related, she would be up, hair combed, and sitting by the window by eight a.m. (she usually slept until eleven or twelve), waiting for visitors. Tennessee would always try to visit. Once when he came visiting with Frank Merlo, a favorite of Carson's, Tennessee presented her with a cage inhabited by two lovebirds. Carson purported to be delighted. But hours later, as Tennessee was saying goodbye, she pulled him down and whispered, "Tenn, honey, can y'all just take those silly birds with you when you go?" Carson loved presents, both giving and getting them. Buying something to please the chic and elegant Dr. Mercer required much thought and consultation. Soon after the therapy sessions ended, Mary and Carson very much wanted to exchange gifts, but that was strictly prohibited between a doctor and a patient. So Mary promised Carson what she called a "tangible intangible," which in this case was a drive into New York City to see the huge decorated Christmas tree in Rockefeller Center. The trip was a great success.

If Carson's pleasures seem childlike, it was in part because her world had shrunk. Three things gave her a modicum of happiness: food (she loved to talk about it but not so much to eat it), drink (alcohol, which, along with tranquilizers, blunted her affect and kept her desires simple), and physical contact (physical closeness with Mary, whether erotic or not). She read only the *New York Post*, following crime. She disliked whodunits but loved true crime, which revealed in granular fashion the often sordid nitty-gritty of the world of criminals and their victims. She read fiction, old favorites or the classics, almost never contemporary literature. She and Mary read aloud to each other, greatly enjoying, for instance, E. M. Forster's 1905 *Where Angels Fear to Tread*, a lively novel about English travelers in Italy. Joyce's stories in *Dubliners* and *Portrait of the Artist as a Young Man* were among Carson's favorites, as was anything by Virginia Woolf. What she most enjoyed, Mary recalled, was *planning* pleasure; she would lovingly project and then (often with help) cook an elaborate meal involving complicated recipes. It didn't matter if the result wasn't great; once she'd whispered in Mary's ear that she'd prefer a hamburger. It was when there was no pleasure on the horizon, because the horizon was so close that it was no longer a horizon, that Mary knew to worry about Carson's sadness.

As her horizons pressed closer, Carson's physical problems multiplied. In his journal entries pertaining to her, Jordan wrote that 1965 was "a horrible year, with little I care to remember." In September, when she was still in the hospital, Mary wrote, "Carson is the same: thin, weak, spent. I have never seen her so utterly drained." If her condition didn't improve, Mary didn't know how Carson would manage her rehabilitation once out of the hospital.

Back home after surgery, Carson was no longer able to walk but used a wheelchair—when she could maneuver herself into one. She had been working with a physiotherapist about whom she complained, "The apparent purpose of her treatment is to break every bone muscles and tendons in my hip and leg." And just as she seemed to be making progress, pneumonia, her old nemesis, struck in mid-December.

After this low point, a series of chance connections led to one of the happiest experiences of Carson's life: John Huston took on the filming of *Reflections in a Golden Eye* and thus forged a genuine connection with her. Huston had first met Carson briefly in the last months of the war. He had been upstate with friends Paulette Goddard and Burgess Meredith, and they dropped in on her in Nyack. Carson had made an impression on the Hollywood director: "I remember her as a fragile thing with great shining eyes, and a tremor in her hand as she placed it in mine. It wasn't palsy, rather a quiver of animal timidity. But there was nothing timid or frail about the manner in which Carson McCullers faced life."

Nearly twenty years had passed since then. In the meantime he had directed several films that made him a legend, including *The Treasure of the Sierra Madre* in 1948, which won him an Oscar for directing; *The African Queen* in 1951; and *The Misfits* in 1961, along with his share of flops. Producer Ray Stark had wanted to make a film of a McCullers property for years, and he and Huston joined forces and hired a scriptwriter, Chapman Mortimer, to write the screenplay of *Reflections*. Huston sent Carson the screenplay in the summer of 1966 and followed up with a visit on August 5, a very hot day and, incidentally, Huston's birthday. He found her propped up in bed, waiting for him. Ida brought them drinks. There was something "very touching about that reclining figure," he said. She was "so intelligent, so alert, so terribly stricken."

Huston had survived his own struggle with invalidism when he was a boy of around ten. Doctors found a heart ailment they said could kill him unless he stayed in bed, avoided anything like play, and kept to a restricted diet. He spent two years in hospitals and in bed at home before he decided the doctors were all wrong and convinced his parents to let him go back to normal life, which he then did. The experience left him with great compassion for anyone in poor health. This, along with what seems to have been his native benevolence, led him to make another offer to Carson.

Having moved on from talk of the film—Carson said she loved Mortimer's script—the two began talking about Ireland. Huston had recently bought a 110-acre estate outside Galway, St. Clerans, and an old Georgian house that had taken him two years to restore. Huston painted a picture of the place for Carson; they talked about fishing, Ireland and the Irish, and Carson's Irish roots. Huston found himself saying, "Carson, you must come visit me in Ireland." Somewhat to his surprise, she agreed. She immediately realized the obstacles and told him she would need some months to prepare for the trip, which she would make after he finished filming *Reflections in a Golden Eye* in Rome. He extended the invitation to include Ida.

Huston's offer was sincere, and he soon followed up with a touching letter. "Search your mind and Ida's," he wrote, "for notions of things that might add to your comfort." He went further, reassuring her, "You'll see, when you get there, how easy it will be to carry them out." Carson could barely contain her enthusiasm. It was as if she and Huston were both willingly suspending disbelief.

Reflections in a Golden Eye went forward as well, and Carson was delighted that this strange novel was coming to life. Huston had said he could do it as either a low-budget art project or "as a film using the best talent available." She plumped for the latter (*ING*, 65).

"And what a cast!" Carson later exclaimed to Rex Reed, the critic and celebrity journalist who had become a friend. Elizabeth Taylor, Marlon Brando, Brian Keith, and Julie Harris were the headliners in what a later critic called "a hothouse tale of desire and simmering violence." Carson knew Harris from *The Member of the Wedding,* and Brando as far back as *A Streetcar Named Desire.* (Brando wrote Carson that Huston mentioned several times her "desire to get out of that damn bed and get to Ireland.") Taylor wrote to Carson from one of the sets in Rome saying how much she loved the book. What Carson saw and heard about the film—she was sent stills from the production— seemed absolutely on track. Later Huston would say he thought it was one of his best films, a perspective that some critics have come to endorse only very recently.

In the meantime Carson was preparing for the trip, as she had promised. She didn't feel she could sit upright for the flight to Ireland, so she would need to travel on a stretcher. In anticipation, her fiftieth birthday flew by. Ida made her a tree out of a pineapple; on jutting toothpicks she put cocktail onions, cheeses, and cherries. People sent so many flowers that "it looked like somebody had been laid out," Carson said approvingly. Huston sent a thoughtful gift: a set of Irish bed linens.

Mary Mercer and Carson's doctor, Glenn Patterson, were in touch with Huston's doctor in Ireland, Martyn Dyar. Mary took Huston at his word and listed what Carson would need for her to be comfortable. In her room (which Mary said should be "in the thick of things," as Carson didn't want to miss out on any doings), she needed, on her right-hand side, her cigarettes and lighter, an ashtray, Kleenex, Coke or fruit juice, and the silver cup with her name on it filled with bourbon and water. Her food had to be cut up into small pieces.

Patterson, and everyone else concerned, thought it would be a good idea for her to make a practice run, to go away for a weekend with Ida. Stark, the film's producer, entered into the spirit of things and offered to pay for both Carson and Ida to spend a weekend in New York at the Plaza Hotel. The trip went off without a hitch; a hospital bed was arranged, and she and Ida sat around their huge room and ordered exotic drinks from Trader Vic's, "giggling like two debutantes in an old Diana Lynn movie," as Carson told Rex Reed.

After their New York weekend, the trip to Ireland appeared to be logistically manageable. Carson and Ida flew into Shannon Airport on April 2, 1967, Carson on a stretcher; Huston met their plane with

Carson and John Huston began an unlikely friendship when the director was working on a film of *Reflections in a Golden Eye*. Carson's visit to Huston's estate in Ireland in April 1967 was her last venture outside Nyack.

an ambulance. Tired though she was, Carson wanted a tour of the house. She was taken through the rooms with the stretcher aslant. She loved her room, which looked out on green fields with grazing cattle and sheep. Huston had provided an elaborately carved bed from Mexico, over which hung a fourteenth-century Sicilian crucifix. Though she was exhausted, Huston saw something to admire: "Carson was adorable, and brave as only a great lady can be brave." Though it was an adjective nobody had used to describe her in years, she *was* brave; she just needed a challenge to rise to.

Carson did not leave her room for her entire stay, which was meant to be seventeen days. She read, talked with Ida, spoke to a journalist from the *Irish Times,* and slept a great deal. Huston had a stable of "magnificent" horses, she said, and he introduced her to betting on horse races. She loved oysters, and they were served straight from the Irish Sea forty miles away. Huston's cook, Mrs. Craigh, made the best bread she had ever tasted. After dinner, Huston and any dinner guests came to her room for brandy and coffee. Her host was struck by how little she actually drank; she would take a couple of sips from her silver cup full of bourbon and water, put it down, and ask for another. "It was as if a butterfly touched it," he observed. She might have what seemed to be several drinks, but never drank more than a quarter of the contents of her cup. She would make a present of the cup to Huston when she left.

But partway through the visit, Carson became very ill, possibly the result of another small stroke. According to Huston, she turned chalk white and later almost green. Dr. Dyar was "alarmed," as was Ida.

Finally Ida took Huston aside and said, "I think we should go home." Their host was "of two minds" about this; he thought the return trip, with Carson so ill, might kill her. On the other hand, it was unlikely that she would improve if she stayed in Ireland. Finally, Carson announced that she wanted to go home, so the onerous trip back was set in motion and carried off. "I know the trip was hard on Carson," Huston later said. He acknowledged that she might have lived longer by months or even a year or two if she had not made her Irish journey, but he would do the whole thing over again: "It was a fulfillment for her. She saw it as a liberation."

Carson was motivated to make the trip to Ireland not by romantic love or career concerns but simply because she set herself the goal, which Huston's generosity facilitated. This is easier to understand in light of her general health in 1966 and 1967. Following a visit in 1966, Mary Tucker said she could not believe Carson's condition when she last saw her, "more dead than alive." Her speech "comes forth in soundless gasps." Carson came back from this low point, but visitors in these years were shocked by her appearance. Once 5 feet 8½ inches tall, she had shrunk and now weighed barely seventy pounds; she was in danger of starving to death, as her friend Isak Dinesen had.

She was under no illusion that she would walk again. She and friends had hoped that she would be able to get out of bed and sit in her wheelchair, which would at least allow her to move around the rooms in her apartment and even go outside on the porch with its beautiful view of the Hudson. But this was impossible due to the excruciating pain in her left leg whenever she tried to move. By the time of the Irish trip, even the thought of getting into her wheelchair frightened her, as Huston's assistant wrote to Mary Mercer during her stay. Stuart Sherman, a local artist enlisted as a secretary who read to her, described the "perilous journey" from the bed to the wheelchair: "Certain parts of certain bones were extremely susceptible to pain—instant, consciousness-blanching pain—and a bruise acquired through a clumsily maneuvered bed-to-chair transfer could take weeks to clear."

Her doctor began to talk of amputating the left leg to make it possible for her to sit again. Mary Mercer and Drs. Patterson and Bailey exchanged letters on the subject in late June 1967. A letter indicates either Mary or Carson was concerned about the possibility of phantom leg syndrome, in which one feels sensations in the limb even after it is removed: the kind of cosmic bad joke that Carson, on a good day, might have appreciated.

Carson mulled it over for a time. When Tennessee visited that summer, she turned to him. "Tenn, they want to saw off my leg," she said. Tennessee's response was silence, according to Stuart Sherman. While on one level the gothic potentialities of an amputation might have appealed to both of them, in reality it was a horrifying thing to contemplate. But deciding on amputation assumed a crucial fact: that Carson foresaw a future for herself, able to move about her rooms and maybe even travel once she could sit in a wheelchair. She was adamant that she did not want a prosthesis, Mary said; she did not intend to walk and saw no reason to attend to the grueling work of adjusting to the device. Mary thought Carson wanted the amputation 95 percent of the time.

Carson turned to John Huston. Their friendship had lasted, and they talked by phone regularly, Huston calling often from the far-flung places his work took him. (The film *Reflections in a Golden Eye* would come out in October.) Carson asked if he'd visit her in the hospital if she went ahead with the amputation. More than that, he said, he would be there *before, during,* and *after* the surgery. His support helped tremendously; she took to intoning "*before, during,* and *after*" like a mantra. The operation was tentatively scheduled for October 18.

These were difficult days for her, and sometimes she broke down. Mary told friends that Carson would shriek if her plight was too much for her. The pain in her leg could cause a breakdown. So could emotional pain. Once Mary Tucker was visiting, and the two Marys were going out to lunch together. Carson began shrieking, presumably at being left behind. On another occasion, Mary Tucker told a friend that Mary Mercer had a "beau." He was the right age, had a lot of money, and wanted to marry her, she said. How accurate the information was and how serious the entanglement is impossible to determine;

all we know is that Mary Mercer never remarried. Whatever the situation, when Mary Tucker mentioned it, Carson was upset and "went off into hysterics." It was so bad that Ida had to give her a "knock-out pill," perhaps leftover Thorazine. Three hours later, Mary Tucker said, Carson was as "chipper as could be!" She asked Mary to tell her again about Mary Mercer's beau, and Mary agreed to repeat it if Carson promised not to get upset—or Mary would need a "knock-out pill" herself. Carson swore she wouldn't, and Mary Tucker—Carson's first love, who Carson still believed had betrayed her some thirty years earlier—told Carson, for a second time, the painful story about the suitor pursuing Mary Mercer, who was now the love of Carson's life. Charitably speaking, repeating the story to Carson was tone-deaf; less charitably, it speaks to almost pathological passive-aggression, the only question being how conscious Mary was about her motives.

As if she knew her time was limited, Carson began work on two book projects in earnest. She revived her idea of the "In Spite Of" book, about creative people who succeeded in spite of physical challenges. The subjects she always spoke of were Helen Keller, Arthur Rimbaud, Sarah Bernhardt, and Cole Porter. All, with the exception of Keller, had had a leg amputated. The project was dear to her heart, but she seems not to have got beyond making lists; no "In Spite Of" manuscript is among the papers in her archive.

The other project was an autobiography. Carson had local people coming in to read for her; Stuart Sherman read two memoirs, Mary McCarthy's *Memories of a Catholic Girlhood* (1957) and James Thurber's *The Years with Ross,* a memoir of Harold Ross, founder and longtime editor of *The New Yorker.* She liked the Ross memoir, she said, because Ross reminded her of herself: "stupid but a genius."

Memoirs were not as commonplace then as they are today, and she had few other contemporary examples to draw from. So she started right in dictating her own, which she called *Illumination and Night Glare.* "Illuminations" were moments of clarity when an idea for her writing would come to her; the example she uses is her revelation one day back in 1937 when, looking at the pattern in the carpet in her childhood home in Columbus, the key to the central character in her first novel, *The Heart Is a Lonely Hunter,* came to her—he was a deaf-mute. The novel then fell into place. For *The Member of the Wed-ding*, the "illumination" was her realization, while chasing after a fire truck in Brooklyn on Thanksgiving with Gypsy Rose Lee, that Frankie wanted to be part of her brother and his fiancée's new life: a member of the wedding. *Reflections in a Golden Eye* was touched off by Reeves's mention of a Peeping Tom at Fort Benning, She also describes what she calls "unilluminations" or "nonilluminations," when "the soul is flattened out" and the writer cannot write. But she never states what she means by "night glare." Perhaps it was the blinding glare from a bright light at night that prevents us from seeing clearly. What she completed in the book is more illumination than night glare, how-ever: it is a very grounded, if meandering, often lyrical compendium of events in her life, from her love for her grandmother to her house in France. It is tempting to see events in her life as night glare, distracting her from her work. She announces the core of the story in the first, very perceptive sentence: "My life has been almost completely filled with work and love, thank goodness" (*ING,* 3). Her narrative describes an arc between the one and the other.

For example, it is clear to a reader of Carson's autobiography, or any "reader" of her life, that Carson's strongest bonds of love, of erotic and passionate commitment, were with women. Yet Reeves becomes the touchstone of her story. Her marriage to him is the first event not related to her work that she writes about. She lovingly describes their early years, poor and idealistic. (Is Reeves "night glare" or is he "illu-mination"?) She regrets that Mary Mercer, her great love, never knew Reeves and thus cannot understand his role in her life. In a notation to the typescript, Carson reminds herself, "Insert war letters" (*ING,* xvii), the wartime correspondence between herself and Reeves. Com-pared to Carson's blander efforts, Reeves wrote wonderful, inspired letters, describing events with drama, bringing dull army days to life. But what Reeves's letters are really about—their sole subject, really—is his love for Carson. In a life peopled by friends, family, and lovers who were devoted to her, it was Reeves who loved her most.

Illumination and Night Glare ends with a paragraph about Reeves, which begins: "I remember one night we climbed up on the mansard roof of our house just to see the moon. We had good times, and that's what made it so difficult. If he had been all bad, it would have been such a relief because I would have been able to leave him without so much struggle." She then reminds herself how Reeves had helped her when she was writing *The Heart Is a Lonely Hunter* and *Reflections in a Golden Eye*. "I was completely absorbed in my work, and if the food burned up he never chided me. Most important, he read and criticized each chapter as it was being done" (*ING*, 78). That sounds like unsurprising behavior from a writer's spouse, but to Carson it was remarkable; she never found anyone, except perhaps Tennessee, who supported her as a writer the way Reeves did. "Once I asked him if [*The Heart Is a Lonely Hunter*] was any good. He reflected a long time, and then he said, 'No, it's not good, it's great'" (*ING*, 78). His support is everywhere evident in his war letters. On December 3, 1944, he writes, "How I long to sit and have you read some chapters to me—to see how far you have gone and how you have developed." On December 17 he writes, "Try to stay settled and finish the work you are doing. I hope to be home by late spring to read some thick manuscript of yours." Mostly, though, he loved her: in July 1945 he wrote, "I have never . . . loved and yearned more for you than I do right this moment. I have imaginary conversations and think of you all during the day. I shall never get enough of you. Oh, my Darling Girl, how tenderly and deeply I love you" (*ING*, 146). The presence of the letters in *Illumination and Night Glare* bears witness to the remarkable love—from a deeply flawed and troubled man—that was their inescapable bond.

In the economy of the lover and the beloved, set forth in *The Ballad of the Sad Café*, Carson was the beloved and Reeves the lover. Perhaps she dwelled so long on Reeves in her autobiography because she never knew how to be the beloved; in almost all her other relationships, infatuations, and entanglements, she was the lover. In her life with Reeves, the economy was even more pronounced in reverse, because Reeves loved women, mostly—he loved Carson—and Carson loved women. Perhaps there is a key somewhere in this state of affairs to gender identity and sexual preference.

Illumination and Night Glare is a strange, unfinished document: notes toward an autobiography, really. Carson was not finished with the emotional work demanded by the life she described; nor had she decided when to tell the truth and when to lie—or more accurately, to confabulate and exaggerate. But it is an extraordinary document none-theless. Like visiting Ireland, writing her autobiography was a goal she set herself and (roughly) achieved: remarkably, this exercise in autobi-ography was written by a physically diminished woman who kept at it out of sheer will.

"Every day she wrote, but not manually," said Stuart Sherman. "She made up sentences in the presence of a secretary, and the secretary cop-ied those sentences onto paper. On some days sentences came hard and there were only a few of them after several hours' effort. But the effort was always made and some sentences were always produced." She was a writer, and writers wrote. She wanted to establish that once and for all before she died. Rex Reed remembered her smiling her "Raggedy Ann grin" and saying, "I don't know what I'd do without my friends. They are the we of me. . . . The sad, happy life of Carson McCullers. Sometimes I think God got me mixed up with Job. But Job never cursed God and neither have I. I carry on."

As the tumultuous summer of 1967 played out in college towns and in inner cities, Carson continued to dictate her autobiography. She made her way back from the attack she had suffered in Ireland. But on August 15—two months before the scheduled amputation of her leg—she suffered a massive stroke on her right side and became uncon-scious. A tracheotomy was performed on August 19 at Nyack Hospital, but it became clear her speech would be compromised and she would perhaps lose her sight—*if* she became conscious.

Mary Mercer read Carson poetry, hoping to see a flicker of recogni-tion. But Carson did not regain consciousness. On September 28 the hospital called Mary and said a teenage boy had been in a terrible car crash and needed a bed in the ICU. Mary thought Carson would have wanted him to have her bed. "So we moved her down a floor," said Mary. Carson was taken off the machines that were keeping her alive, and she died the next day.

She was fifty.

When she was thirty, Carson McCullers suffered two major strokes that left her partly paralyzed and in increasing pain for the rest of her short life. Steadily declining health from that age on was not a kind hand to be dealt. Carson continued writing, traveled, kept old friends and made new ones, fell in love, and found a life partner, but all of it under a cloud. It is remarkable that she did continue to write, to push through her final novel, *Clock Without Hands,* and to keep pursuing new projects to the last, but what she might have produced had she been mobile and free of pain, we cannot know.

The what-ifs really began in Carson's adolescence, when she came down, fatefully, with strep throat. In the succeeding decades, she had no ability to change the outcome any more than did her doctors. The trajectory of her life was beyond her control. Doomed before the age of twenty, producing her best work before turning thirty, and dying at the age of fifty, Carson lived a life that was in its rough outlines the stuff of tragedy. That she managed to persevere and fulfill herself artistically can be seen as her victory.

Epilogue

Carson was buried on October 3 in Oak Hill Cemetery on a hillside in Nyack, next to her mother. A memorial service earlier that day at the St. James' Episcopal Church on New York's Upper East Side drew a crowd of over two hundred, including Truman Capote, Ethel Waters, Julie Harris, Janet Flanner, *New York Times* theater critic Brooks Atkinson, theater director Harold Clurman, W. H. Auden, and Gypsy Rose Lee—as well as Tennessee Williams, Mary Mercer, Ida Reeder, and Jordan Massee, among others close to her. The music included "Jesu, Joy of Man's Desiring" and "Sheep May Safely Graze," Carson's favorite selections from Bach's cantatas.

Carson's will held few surprises. The bulk of her estate, worth approximately $420,000, went to Rita, Lamar Jr., and Mary Mercer. Bequests included amounts of $1,000 to $5,000 to Floria Lasky's daughters, Emily and Dara; Ida Reeder; Lamar Jr.'s son; and Marielle Bancou and her son. Carson had changed her will more than once, and Jordan Massee was left out of the final version because of a fleeting quarrel.

Carson's literary career was not over yet; there was more material left to publish. Nor, in a sense, was her personal life, as her affairs and her legacy continued to dominate the lives of those who had been closest to her. Rita continued teaching at Columbia after her sister's death and also taught in the creative writing program at the New School for many years. A portion of Carson's papers remained in the Nyack house. Taking possession of them, Rita found she disliked the chores associated with her sister's literary legacy, and she and Lamar eventually turned over the reins to Lasky, who became executor. Rita spent several years gathering previously unpublished material—some of it fascinating, polished work that Carson had written while a student—as well as some published pieces that had never appeared in book form, for a new collection. Houghton Mifflin published it as *The Mortgaged Heart,* in 1971. Soon afterward Rita wrote to Lasky and Robbie Lantz that as far as she was concerned, the next thing to do was to "SELL THE PAPERS, SELL THE PAPERS, SELL THE PAPERS." Lasky did just that in 1976, to the Harry Ransom Center at the University of Texas, Austin, for $45,000. Rita died of heart failure in 1983; Lamar had died in 1981.

Another survivor was Mary Mercer. The year after Carson's death, she bought out Rita and Lamar's shares in the Nyack house, proposing to turn it into a museum, as had been done with Edward Hopper's nearby house, but it was not to be. The best she could do, she said, was to try to rent to artists. Mary held on to a large collection of Carson's papers, most dating to the last eight years of her life, to which Mary continued to add over the next several decades. Immediately after Carson's death, rumors circulated that Mary was writing a novel about her, but no such novel appeared—no trace of one was found in her papers, where can be found other unpublished prose and verse efforts that Mary wrote about her friend, which came to nothing.

After Carson's death, especially in the 1970s, Rita, Floria Lasky, and Robbie Lantz were preoccupied with who ought to write a biography. They seem to have agreed that the estate should name and authorize someone. Various candidates came up: Robert K. Massie, whose 1967 *Nicholas and Alexandra* had been a great success, critically and commercially; Janet Flanner; Kay Boyle (nixed when details of her quarrel with Carson surfaced); and Houghton Mifflin's pick, someone named Phelps. Word reached the estate that Margaret Sullivan, an English professor and Columbus resident, was already hard at work on what promised to be an exhaustive biography. Rita, Floria, and Robbie knew they should go ahead while friends of Carson's were still alive.

They were taken by surprise when word reached them that an academic, Columbus College professor Virginia Spencer Carr, had signed a contract with Ken McCormack at Doubleday and was well along on a McCullers biography. After much consternation, some people in Carson's inner circle, like Jordan Massee and Tennessee Williams, decided to cooperate with Carr, while some, like Rita and Mary Mercer, did not. The biography, *The Lonely Hunter,* appeared in 1975. Carr conducted hundreds of interviews, but that was all she had to go on; none of the papers had reached their institutional homes yet and were not available to her, either because they were not yet organized sufficiently or because their owners did not want scholars or biographers seeing them yet. In the meantime, Margaret Sullivan contracted lupus and was forced to give up her biography, eventually donating her research papers to Columbus State University.

Between 1970 and 1973, Mary Mercer engaged in battle with Floria Lasky and Robbie Lantz over certain personal items among Carson's papers that were left in the Nyack house, most notably transcripts of her 1958 therapy sessions with Carson. Mary heatedly argued that they were her property alone and should not be available to McCullers scholars; anything else would constitute a violation of doctor-patient confidentiality. She steadfastly invoked the doctor-patient relationship whenever she was contacted for information about Carson. She continued to rent out Carson's old house while she lived nearby.

Mary died in 2013 at the age of 101; with her death she donated her collection of Carson's papers—including the therapy tapes and transcripts—to the Columbus State University Archives in Carson's hometown. By that time, the Carson McCullers Center for Writers and Musicians occupied the Smith-McCullers Historic House, which former Columbus State professor Thornton Jordan had donated to the university. As part of the same gift, at her death Mary left Carson's Nyack home, now on the National Register of Historic Places, to Columbus State.

While scholars waited for full access to Carson's papers, her strange and compelling fictional universe continued to draw readers. In perhaps this culture's best index of its popular appeal at the time, *The Heart Is a Lonely Hunter* was an Oprah's Book Club pick in the spring of 2004. *Oprah*'s producers cited Carson's "eclectic band of misfits" and her ability "to give voice to the rejected, forgotten, mistreated and oppressed," adding, "Never have the margins of society been so brilliantly illuminated."

Attention to her novel skyrocketed, and Houghton Mifflin printed 735,000 copies to keep up with the demand. *The Heart Is a Lonely Hunter* was back at number one—briefly—on the national best-seller lists. Sales of her other titles went up as well, reflecting readers' new interest. And in 1999 McCullers scholar Carlos Dews added to the list of McCullers titles by editing and publishing *Illumination and Night Glare: The Unfinished Autobiography of Carson McCullers*. An abbreviated and fragmented but fascinating affair, it contains as well Carson's wartime correspondence with Reeves, which she had wanted included in her autobiography. At the close of the twentieth century, Carson was appearing on numerous "Best Books" lists. *Time* included *The Heart Is a Lonely Hunter* on its list of 100 Best Novels in English from 1923 to 2005, and Modern Library named it one of the Best 100 Books of the Twentieth Century. In 2001, Library of America brought out an edition of her complete novels and in 2017 an edition of her other writings.

Other writers and artists mined Carson's life in their own work, perhaps more than ever. Sarah Schulman's play *Carson McCullers: Historically Inaccurate,* based on her life story, was staged in 2002. In 2020 Jenn Shapland published the acclaimed *My Autobiography of Carson McCullers,* a young lesbian's passionate take on Carson and the role her story played in Shapland's life. The singer and songwriter Suzanne Vega has performed her *Lover, Beloved,* a one-woman show about Carson, in many venues over the years, a film of which was screened in the spring of 2022 at South by Southwest. In 2016 Vega released the album *Lover/Beloved: Songs from an Evening with Carson McCullers.*

Carson had sought dramatic success ever since *The Member of the*

Wedding ran for more than a year on Broadway. While it was her first and only commercial hit on the stage, the play has been produced off-Broadway many times since her death. Fred Zinnemann's film version, which appeared in 1952 and featured Julie Harris's and Ethel Waters's timeless performances, earned Harris an Oscar nomination and enjoys persistent popularity. Moviemakers have been drawn to Carson's work ever since. The film version of *The Heart Is a Lonely Hunter,* its story greatly stripped down, appeared the year after she died. Though Alan Arkin (playing Singer) and Sondra Locke (playing Mick) both received Academy Award nominations, the movie met mixed reviews and is not the favorite that the film of *The Member of the Wedding* has become. A spare and affecting short film of McCullers's best-known (and best) story, "A Tree. A Rock. A Cloud," directed by Karen Allen, debuted in 2017.

John Huston's adaptation of *Reflections in a Golden Eye* had a mixed reception when it appeared on October 13, 1967—just ten days after Carson's death—but has gained greater critical appreciation over the years and is now considered an intriguing and important piece of filmmaking. Carson had read the script closely; the characters came through "exactly as I saw them," she said, and she thought it would be a "great film." She followed the casting as well. First Richard Burton and then Montgomery Clift were slated to play Captain Weldon Penderton, who lusts after a private on the local army base, played by Robert Forster. Eventually Marlon Brando won the role, and Elizabeth Taylor played the part of Leonora Penderton, his adulterous wife. Carson asked Huston to convey to Brando "exactly how right he is for the Penderton part."

Huston maintained to the end of his life that *Reflections in a Golden Eye* was one of his best films. Tennessee Williams thought it succeeded "more perfectly" than *The Heart Is a Lonely Hunter* "in establishing its own reality, in creating a world of its own" (*RGE,* 135). The film does credit to Carson's creepy but compelling, stylized world. A queer sensibility permeates the novel, and Huston's film perhaps best suits her art in this sense, though *The Member of the Wedding* has a claim as well, given its adolescent heroine, broody and moody, who is close enough to childhood to maintain a sense of wonder and possibility.

The otherness that the film of *Reflections in a Golden Eye,* in its best moments, conveys so well has not always worked in Carson's critical favor; she has been faulted for being "preoccupied" with the morbid and grotesque. In response, the critic Patricia Lockwood has written that Carson's fiction was populated by freaks and misfits for a reason: "She wrote from within a body that had been struck down by illness when she was 18; what kind of bodies did they want her to write?" It would be more accurate to date Carson's serious illness from her first major stroke, when she was thirty, but Lockwood is correct that Carson was ill most of her life. Though we cannot know what we lost, it is astounding to imagine the career of a writer not so challenged and of such talent. Therein, in fact, lies the tragedy; Carson was in considerable pain for her last two decades, physical pain that affected her writing, relationships, behavior, and personality. The illness that caused it killed her far too young.

Lockwood reminds us, too, of the nature of Carson's literary legacy: the complexity and the enigma of the outsiders and the alienated who populate her pages. From John Singer in *The Heart Is a Lonely Hunter* to Frankie and Berenice in *The Member of the Wedding,* Cousin Lymon and Miss Amelia in *The Ballad of the Sad Café,* to the blue-eyed African American Sherman Pew in *Clock Without Hands,* and just about every character in *Reflections in a Golden Eye,* she conveys the integrity of spirit of those who are similarly marginalized. The result is a cast of characters and a body of work that readers feel passionate about.

Carson's unerring instinct for the outsider's life informed all her fiction, subtly guiding her to truths that transcend specific characters and their specific circumstances. Hilton Als wrote in 2001 of her characters that "each defines the status quo while existing outside of it," thus her ability to "identify with those unmoored from their surroundings or searching for self in the modern world." Richard Wright, a housemate in Brooklyn in the war years, noted that what impressed him most in *The Heart Is a Lonely Hunter* was the "astonishing humanity that enables a white writer, for the first time in Southern fiction, to handle Negro characters with as much ease and justice as those of her own race." Als credits McCullers with the "Africanism" that Toni Morrison outlined in her 1992 essay "Playing in the Dark," the way in which Blackness—usually in a Black character, but sometimes in a fleeting allusion to race—calls attention, in white writers as diverse as Edgar Allan Poe and Willa Cather, to how race transformed the American literary imagination. McCullers was a genius, Als argued, in creating an Africanist presence—in characters like Berenice in *The Member of the Wedding*—that brought race into her powerful stories, defining whiteness by the inverse presence of Blackness. So Dr. Copeland talks to John Singer, the deaf-mute who is the beating heart of *The Heart Is a Lonely Hunter,* about slavery: those parts of Africa his people were from, those who died on the journey to the coast, those who died on the ships coming to America, and those who were chained and sold at auction once they arrived. Copeland's vivid Blackness throws Singer's whiteness into stark contrast.

One of Morrison's crucial points is that literature written by or about those on the edges of our culture can tell us the most about what happens within that culture, bringing universality closer to hand rather than pushing it away, since everyone feels marginalized at one time or another. "We all of us somehow caught," Berenice tells Frankie in *The Member of the Wedding*. She is caught worse than Frankie, she explains, because she is Black. "But we all caught. . . . We go around trying one thing or another, but we caught anyhow" (*MW,* 113–14). We may or may not be outsiders, but we all have felt ourselves to be, and on this ground we encounter Carson McCullers.

What about Carson's life after death? Lesbian, gay, and transgender writers and artists have found her story fascinating. Critic Sarah Schulman provocatively speculated that if Carson were alive today, she would be a transgender man. Carson once told Truman Capote, "I think I was born a boy," and there's evidence that she tended toward an androgynous ideal, transforming herself from Lula to Carson in high school, and wearing her hair like a boy's. But there are other ways to interpret these facts. "Carson" looks better as a byline than "Lula," and a male-sounding name well situated her to start out in the literary world of the 1940s, which tended not to treat women as serious figures. She found men's fashions more comfortable than women's, she explained, which points to what's been called her Peter Pan syndrome; she clung to her youth, and wearing male clothes allowed her to achieve the kind of agelessness she sought.

One reason for suggesting a transgender Carson may have been her erotic preference for women. But just as we no longer speak of "mannish" lesbians, so we cannot assume that lesbians would rather be men, much less that they would undergo the steps required for a transgender transition, or that afterward they would choose men as sexual partners. Of course, the society Carson lived in demanded she keep her deepest preferences hidden; two of her infatuations, AA spokesperson Marty Mann and Broadway producer Cheryl Crawford, were involved in lifelong relationships with female partners that had to be shrouded in secrecy. And Als points out that another important person in Carson's life suffered the internalization of this stigma: the bisexual—and steadfast—Reeves, her husband twice over.

It is unlikely, however, that Carson would have changed anything about her gender or sexuality, even if she could have. Perhaps "queer" is the term that best defines her. She lived a lesbian and bisexual life—a queer life—entirely in her own way and fairly openly: a remarkable achievement at the time. In her early years she fell deeply in love with two women, Mary Tucker and Annemarie Schwarzenbach; she was also in love with the man she married twice, Reeves McCullers. Marriage to a man was, of course, the "easier" choice at the time and may have facilitated pursuing love affairs, which Reeves never actively prevented. But little about being married to Reeves was easy, and Carson was hardly inclined to choose the easier alternative in any sphere. She wanted what she wanted, and what is remarkable, given the time in which she lived, is that she did not much care how the world viewed her choices. Perhaps in some ways the basic queerness of Carson and Reeves brought them together and strengthened their bond; if she hadn't wanted to marry him, or remarry him, or stay married to him, she wouldn't have, even though the relationship was essentially destructive. Sexual boldness and nakedness were the hallmarks of her life. She could have stepped out of one of her friend Tennessee Williams's plays, her emotional interior completely open to public view.

Queerness was also Carson's defining trait as an artist; when she wrote, she wrote difference, the dangers and ecstasies of otherness. Her intensity could be a mixed blessing, frightening or else repelling those in her path, as with Katherine Anne Porter. She used the language of love constantly and in situations that were not romantic. Her declarations confused and embarrassed many, though perhaps other Southerners, some of them attuned to honeyed language, less so. She tied love explicitly to the creation of her fictional characters: "How can you create a character without love and the struggle that goes with love?" (*TMH,* 280) she asked, as if other writers must start as she did.

She was not naïve about her nature; she realized that otherness often precluded love, though she directly connected her motivations to it. Her theme, she explained, was "spiritual isolation," and love, "especially love of a person who is incapable of returning or receiving it, is at the heart of my selection of grotesque figures to write about—people whose physical incapacity is a symbol of their spiritual incapacity to love or receive love—their spiritual isolation" (*TMH,* 274). In her case, however, she seemed to sense that her demanding emotional nature simply overpowered those to whom she declared her love.

Because of her illness, Carson was physically dependent on others; as she lost strength and stamina, her emotional dependence increased. She tried to turn the situation to her advantage. Presenting herself as all naked emotion and need, she commanded attention—and usually got it. The flip side, also a result of her illness, was that she was never able to be emotionally autonomous. She was a stronger woman than her dependence allowed, but her body ultimately betrayed her, and her most fully committed relationship was one in which she and her husband fed off each other destructively.

Yet she kept trying to find a loving partner with whom she might feel she had transcended otherness—without sacrificing what was special about it. We read Carson's work today because she taps into the universal sense that we are not understood, not loved for ourselves. Carson provides confirmation that our common search means we are less alone. Yet we are no less lonely. Perhaps this was what she meant when she called the heart "a lonely hunter": that the human character, however loving or lovable, is eternally questing. Loneliness, to Carson, is the human condition, and our search for love is without cease. But whatever the odds, whatever the condition that has made us outsiders, in Carson's universe there is a modicum of understanding: at least in the imagination of the artist herself.

With breathtaking irony, such a resolution was precluded for Carson. Doomed to ill health before the age of twenty, producing her best work before turning thirty, and dying at the age of fifty, she lived a life that was in rough outline the stuff of tragedy. That she managed to persevere in her singular exploration of the human soul was her victory. It speaks to her spirit that, despite the constraints of her physical condition, she was able to imagine a world in which the lonely hunter is not alone.

Acknowledgments

Carson McCullers was a great believer in gifts—getting them and giving them. She classified some presents as "tangible intangibles": gestures that are thoughtful and sincere while not something you can wrap up and bestow. An example was Mary Mercer driving her to see the Rockefeller Center Christmas tree. In the writing of this book, I owe a debt to experiences as well as to people, what I'd call "tangible intangibles." A case in point was encountering the Carson family's ancestral home in Reynolds, Georgia.

Records show a plot of two thousand acres was bought by Carson's great-great grandfather Joseph Jefferson Carson on the Flint River in Taylor County, about sixty miles from Columbus, in the mid-nineteenth century. On a hot, clear day in June 2021, I saw the plantation—so family members called it, though the house itself was just one story high and comprised four large rooms. It was a magnificent ruin. The land had evidently been cleared periodically, or the house would have been engulfed by the saplings and other vegetation that had sprung up around and through the floorboards of the wide porches that encircled it. Old oaks sheltered the house. Carson probably never visited the old Carson plantation, which had passed out of family hands before her birth; nor would she have seen the nearby monument to her great-grandfather, Confederate soldier John Thomas

Carson. But seeing the house and the monument gave me a sense of Carson's complex Georgia past. That June visit was a "tangible intangible" in the shaping of my book.

Most of my debt, however, is to tangible human beings.

I owe to my literary agent, Georges Borchardt, a considerable thank-you for nearly thirty years of excellent guidance, friendship, and the correction of French spellings. Thanks as well to Anne Borchardt and Cora Markowitz. My editor, Vicky Wilson, is, like Georges, a publishing legend. Besides her inspired editing and excellent stewardship, I am most grateful to Vicky for the tough questions she asks. Sometimes it takes me a while to formulate the answers, but when I do, I see how necessary—and enriching—they are to my work. At Knopf, thanks as well to Mark Montague, Marc Jaffee, and, especially, Belinda Yong. My friend Debbie Goodsite, a talented and knowledgeable photo researcher, stepped in and finished the thorough assembly of the photographs under a strict deadline.

Three visits to Columbus, Carson McCullers's hometown, were absolutely necessary to the writing of this book. Many thanks to Nick Norwood, director of the Carson McCullers Center for Writers and Musicians, which is located in the Smith-McCullers House in Columbus. A three-week stay in an apartment connected to the house enabled me to sample the center's fine exhibits and library. Another tangible intangible, in fact, was the opportunity to live briefly in the house in which traces of Carson seemed to lurk behind every door. I never saw her ghost, but for some reason I felt her presence most in the breakfast nook.

The Columbus State University Archives and Special Collections was essential to me both for its holdings and for the library staff: director David Owings and archivists Jesse Charlton, Martha Ragan, and especially Tom Converse. The day I arrived, Tom provided an essential tour of Columbus, which proved invaluable for an understanding of the city, along with his considerable knowledge on matters Carson. It was Tom, for instance, who located and showed me the Carson plantation in Reynolds. He has cataloged two of the largest collections in the archive, and he shared his knowledge of where to find Carson-related material across the collections. A talk that Tom gave at the Columbus

Public Library during my first visit, "The Archival After-Life of Carson McCullers," was an inspiration, studded throughout with gems of insight and detail.

The Harry Ransom Center at the University of Texas at Austin is the other main repository of Carson McCullers's papers, and one of its research fellowships made possible a monthlong visit to work in its archives. I'm grateful to Bridget Gayle, Rick Watson, and Kathryn Millan; also to Greg Curtis. Archivist Michael Gilmore helped me with photographs, and Eric Colleary showed me the HRC's collection of Carson's clothes and personal effects—another tangible intangible.

Librarians and archivists at other institutions also immeasurably furthered my research: Carolyn Vega, at the Henry W. and Albert A. Berg Collection of English and American Literature, New York Public Library; Thomas Lannon, Manuscripts and Archives Division, New York Public Library; Peter Monteith at King's College, Cambridge; Genevieve Maxwell, Academy Film Archive, Academy of Motion Picture Arts and Sciences; Kelly Wooten and Elizabeth B. Dunn, David M. Rubenstein Rare Book & Manuscript Library, Duke University; Mat Darby at the Booth Family Center for Special Collections, Georgetown University; Chamisa Redmond, Research Division, Library of Congress; Kate Long, Smith College Special Collections; Aaron Lisec, Special Collections Research Center, Southern Illinois University; Elizabeth Genter and Nicole Westerdahl, Special Collections Research Center, Syracuse University; June Can, Beinecke Rare Book & Manuscript Library, Yale University; Kate Goldkamp and Joel Minor, Special Collections Department, Washington University; Christine Keller, Special Collections, University of Houston; Stuart A. Rose Manuscript, Archives, and Rare Book Library, Emory University; and the Special Collections and Archives Department, Washington and Lee University.

The institution to which I owe my greatest debt is the magisterial New York Public Library, where I had the good fortune to be a fellow at the Dorothy and Lewis B. Cullman Center for Scholars and Writers in 2018–2019. I am most grateful to my colleagues David Bell, Jennifer Croft, Ada Ferrer, Vona Groarke, francine j. harris, Faith Hillis, Martha Hodes, Brooke Holmes, Karan Mahajan, Corey Robin, Marisa

Silver, Kirmen Uribe, Amanda Vaill, Frances Wilson, Lauren Golden-berger, Salvatore Sciabona, and Paul Delaverdac. It was a magical year, not least because of the help given to us by the library staff.

I am, as always, grateful to the individuals at the NYU Biography Center, and also to my fellow biographers Ellen Brown, Lina Bernstein, David Perkins, Steven Swayne, the late Marion Meade, Sydney Ladensohn Stern, and Heather Clark, as well as my Cullman colleagues Amanda Vaill and Frances Wilson. For help with legal questions, thanks to Daryl Jennings of the Authors Guild and Ellis Levine. A special thanks must go to my new friend Carlos Dews, a brilliant McCullers scholar who is currently editing Carson's complete letters. His generosity and good cheer from a great distance enriched my work.

Among those who contributed to this book, directly or otherwise, I am grateful to Peter Elliott, Brent Reidy, Dara Altman and Emily Altman, Peter Poor, Cathy Fussell, Roger Blumberg, Beth Langan, Michael Doherty, Kevin McVeigh, Robin Glenn, Laurie Israel and Elaine Sidney, Keith Nightenhelser, Robert Nedlekoff, Albert Mobilio, Joe Markulin and Lynne Le Brasseur, Blake Perkins, Tina Ruyter, Mary B. Campbell, Lisa Greenwald and Doug Lavin, Tracey Dery, Jeremy and Stacey Coleman, and Randi Parks. Helpful family included Jim Donnelly, John T. G. Dearborn, Ruah Donnelly Dinkelaker, Margery Dearborn, and, more than ever, Eric Laursen. Thanks to Vera Beauvais, the late Martin Hurwitz, Annemarie Monahan, and Deborah Stier for keeping body and soul together.

Buckland, Massachusetts
May 30, 2023

Notes

ABBREVIATIONS

AS   Annemarie Schwarzenbach

BB   Bessie Breuer

BB Papers   Bessie (Elizabeth F.) Breuer Papers, SIU

BSC   CM, *Ballad of the Sad Café*

CD   Carlos Dews

CD Collection   Carlos Dews Collection (MC 175), CSU

CM   Carson McCullers

CM Collection, HRC   Carson McCullers Collection, HRC

CM Collection, EU   Carson McCullers Collection, 1941–1975, EU

CM Papers   Carson McCullers Papers (RL.00868), DU

CSU   Columbus State University, Columbus, Ga.

CU   Columbia University, New York

CWH   CM, *Clock Without Hands*

DD   David Diamond

DU   Duke University

ES   Edith Sitwell

EU   Emory University

HLH   CM, *The Heart Is a Lonely Hunter*

HM Papers   Houghton Mifflin Company Records, Houghton Library, HU

HRC   Harry Ransom Center, University of Texas, Austin

HU   Harvard University

ING   CM, *Illumination and Night Glare*

JM   Jordan Massee

JM/CM Collection   Jordan Massee/Carson McCullers Collection (MC 170), CSU

JZEP Collection   John Zeigler and Edwin Peacock Collection, (MC 182), CSU

KAP   Katherine Anne Porter

KB   Kay Boyle

Linscott Papers   Robert Newton Linscott Papers, MS-MS-ms071, Washington University, St. Louis

MEM Mary E. Mercer
MEM/CM Collection Dr. Mary E. Mercer and Carson McCullers Collection (MC 296), CSU
MEM DU Collection of CM/MST Correspondence, 1959–1976 Mary E. Mercer Collection of Carson McCullers–Mary Tucker Correspondence, 1959–1976, DU
MSS Margaret S. Sullivan
MSS Papers Margaret S. Sullivan Papers (MC 298), CSU
MST Mary Sames Tucker
MST Papers Mary Sames Tucker Papers, DU
MW CM, *The Member of the Wedding*
NA Newton Arvin
NA Papers Newton Arvin Papers, Smith College
NYPL New York Public Library
RGE CM, *Reflections in a Golden Eye*
RM Reeves McCullers
SI Papers Dr. Sidney Isenberg Collection of Carson McCullers Papers (0097), Washington and Lee University
SIU Southern Illinois University, Carbondale
SRW CM, *Square Root of Wonderful*
Story Papers *Story* Magazine and Story Press Records, 1931–1999, Special Collections (C0104), Princeton University Library
TMH CM, *The Mortgaged Heart*
TW Tennessee Williams
TW Collection Tennessee Williams Collection (MS 04535), HRC
TW Papers Tennessee Williams Papers (MS 1354), CU
VSC Virginia Spencer Carr
VSC Collection Virginia Spencer Carr Collection (MC 23), CSU
VSC Papers Virginia Spencer Carr Papers, DU

PROLOGUE

4 "lonely hearts": Lorine Pruett, *New York Herald Tribune,* June 9, 1940.

4 "unique accent": Clifton Fadiman, *New Yorker,* June 8, 1940.

4 "One cannot help": Ray Redman, *Saturday Review of Literature,* June 8, 1940.

4 "So high is the standard": Rose Feld, *New York Times,* June 8, 1940.

5 "another year or two": May Sarton, *Boston Transcript,* June 8, 1940.

5 "ploppy ways": Ray Bradbury to August Derleth, c. September 1946, in Eller, *Becoming Ray Bradbury,* 138. Bradbury said Carson was "a fey, pale, pouty, stocking-gawky girl with bang-fringe hair-do and ploppy ways."

5 champion sprinter: CM to John Huston, November 5, 1966, Archives, Margaret Herrick Library, Academy of Motion Picture Arts and Sciences.

5 "she was a tall, slender wand": Clarke, *Capote,* 96.

5 "I became an established": Reed, *Do You Sleep in the Nude?* 43.

6 "She had a face": Carson McCullers, *Illumination and Night Glare: The Unfinished Autobiography of Carson McCullers,* ed. Carlos Dews (Madison: University of Wisconsin Press, 1999), 21. References in the text to *ING* are to this edition.

7 "assortment of geniuses": Quoted in Presley, "Carson McCullers and the South," 23.

8 "her sad, happy life": Reed, *Do You Sleep in the Nude?* 42.

I. WUNDERKIND

9 "Wunderkind": The story was first collected in *The Ballad of the Sad Café and Other Stories*. See Constance M. Perry, "Carson McCullers and the Female Wunderkind," *Southern Literary Journal* 19, no. 1 (Fall 1986): 36–45.

11 Carson was rewarded: "Elijah Clarke," *New Georgia Encyclopedia,* https://www .georgiaencyclopedia.org/articles/history-archaeology/elijah-clarke-1742-1799.

11 Joseph Jefferson Carson: He was listed in Macon County in 1850, his profession "merchant." See James Lechner, "The Carson Family of Georgia," *Taylor County Tracer* (August 2000).

11 The eldest, John Thomas: For John Thomas Carson, see *U.S. Civil War Soldier Records and Profiles, 1861–1865,* www.ancestry.com/search/collections/1555. His place of death is sometimes said to be Lynchburg, but records show that he died in Winchester City, Virginia.

11 Susan Sophronia: Many of these details derive from James Lechner (whose wife was descended from the Carsons). He tells a fascinating story about tracking down John Thomas Carson's plantation and the effects left behind by Carson and his body servant, Mose, who was evidently enslaved. The plantation, in Reynolds, Georgia, was deserted, but he found a Confederate monument to the major and what he believes is Carson's sword and his signed copy of *Hardee's Infantry Tactics*.

12 her ancestors: For enslavers in CM's ancestry, see Schedule 2, "Slave Inhabitants in Macon County, Georgia," in the 1860 U.S. Census.

13 an evil quality: CM to BB, c. 1943, BB Papers.

13 Carson's maternal grandmother: See Tallulah Carson in the 1870 U.S. Census.

14 "cozying": Carson's "cozied in the dark" with her grandmother may remind biographers and American literature scholars of Djuna Barnes's long incestuous relationship as a child with her grandmother. That was an anomalous situation, and Barnes explicitly described it. (She didn't seem to see anything wrong or even odd about it.) Carson's physical relationship with her grandmother seems to have been different, but her choice of words is interesting.

14 a "white linen duster": Sullivan, "Conversion of Experience," 42.

14 "He got to where": Graham Johnson, "Memories of a Catholic Boyhood," n.d., Folder 2, Box 1, Series 2, MSS Papers. Johnson told the story of Thomas Elam Waters. As an executive with Procter and Gamble, it is unlikely that he shot the family cow or felt this way about whiskey. Anything is possible, however.

15 "Her family lived": Sullivan, "Conversion of Experience," 34.

15 "vivid": Lillian Smith to MSS, March 4, 1965, Folder 5, Box 2, Series 2, MSS Papers.

15 the Gachet family: See application to place Benjamin Gachet's house in Lamar County, Georgia, in the Registry of Historic Places, 1997, https://npgallery.nps .gov/GetAsset/42c9272a1-11a3-4cb2-a501-e647f4e2c7cf. Charles Gachet was said to have emigrated because he broke with his family after giving up training for the priesthood. But that is unlikely as he was a Huguenot. Perhaps he had been threatening to convert to Catholicism. The single best source for McCullers's ancestry is Sullivan, "Conversion of Experience."

16 enslaving twenty-one: See "Slave Schedule for James E. Gachett" in the 1860 U.S. Census. See also William Carter Stubbs, *The Descendants of John Stubbs of Cappahosic, Gloucester County, Virginia, 1652*, no. 2 (1902), 45, https://books.google.com /books?id=BnotAAAAYAAJ&dq=%22Dr.+Charles+Gachet%22+b.+1802&s.

16 William and Molly: It is not clear why the girls in the family went to college, when evidence suggests the boys did not. Perhaps the "colleges" were actually finishing schools.

16 "an easy, good country boy": Jensel Berry and Mrs. D. G. Thomas quoted in Sullivan, "Conversion of Experience," 41–42.

17 "He was a quiet unassuming": Storey quoted ibid., 27.

17 her father preferred: See Carr, *The Lonely Hunter,* 11.

17 she claimed he spent: CM, unpublished manuscript, December 1936, Folder 3, Box 25, *Story* Papers.

17 After their marriage: Though Lula Carson Smith did not become Carson Smith until she was fifteen, I have elected to call her Carson before that date. We at least know that is what she would have wanted.

17 yelled and carried on: Therapy tape 6, April 28, 1958, p. 9, Folder 5-A.6 (a), Box 11, Series 5, MEM/CM Collection.

18 "She never lorded it": Mrs. G. D. James quoted in Sullivan, "Conversion of Experience," 50.

18 "most ardent admirer": Virginia Storey, "Carson McCullers," talk given at Baker High School, September 24, 1964, p. 2, Folder 5, Box 47, CM Collection, HRC. Virginia was a cousin.

18 "was different from": Virginia Tucker, interview by MSS, August 29, 1965, quoted in Sullivan, "Conversion of Experience," 50.

18 "as a child": Sandy Taylor quoted in MSS to Emily Davies, May 9, 1975, Folder 1, Box 3, Series 1, MSS Papers.

19 When she first started: Mrs. J. Dupont Kierven quoted in Sullivan, "Conversion of Experience," 76.

19 homemade smocked dresses: Ibid., 48.

19 "like a stage mother": Lillian Smith to MSS, March 4, 1965, Folder 5, Box 2, Series 2, MSS Papers.

19 "almost by heart": Helen Harvey, interviews by MSS, August 30, 1961, and May 16, 1965, quoted in Sullivan, "Conversion of Experience," 69.

19 just two full days: Bellware, *Muscogiana,* 23.

22 "could see the poetry": Ralph McGill, "Carson McCullers: 1917–1967," *Saturday Review of Literature,* October 21, 1967.

26 Carson told a friend: CM to NA, c. 1944, NA Papers.

26 "Carson always said": Virginia Tucker, interviews by MSS, August 30, 1961, and May 16, 1965, quoted in Sullivan, "Conversion of Experience," 69.

27 In the parlor: Carr, *The Lonely Hunter,* 4.

28 "On the Wings of an Angel": Helen Harvey, interview by MSS, p. 67, MSS Papers.

28 impulse to eat: CM, unpublished ms., Folder 3, Box 25, *Story* Papers.

2. THAT RAINBOW YOUTH OF MINE

30 "She was haughty as hell": Norman Rothschild, interview by MSS, n.d., Cassette tape 1, MSS Papers.

31   With puberty, she shot up: Her passport says 5 feet 8¾ inches. See Folder 2-o, Box 4, Series 1, MSS Papers.

31   "She was *so* tall": Mary Tucker to MSS, September 3, 1965, Folder 1, Box 1, Series 1, MSS Papers. Sullivan quotes this in "Conversion of Experience," 47.

32   "sunny smile": Cheryl Crawford, interview by MSS, n.d., audiotape, Side A, Box 1, Series 5, MSS Papers.

32   "That's why I wear shorts": Carson McCullers, *The Heart Is a Lonely Hunter* (1940; repr., New York: Mariner Books, 2000), 42. References in this text to *HLH* are to this edition.

33   "extraordinary needs": JM's unpublished journal for 1949 is in Folder 21, Box 1, JM/CM Collection.

34   "a tall, slender, active": Gin Tucker to MSS, October 1, 1965, quoted in Sullivan, "Conversion of Experience," 109.

35   "a whole gang": Quoted in Savigneau, *Carson McCullers*, 30.

35   Carson later told Mary: CM to MST, c. 1960, MST Papers.

35   "as vigorous": MST to MEM, June 27, 1961, Folder 6-I, Box 18, Series 6, MSS Papers.

36   "was easily discouraged": Sullivan, "Conversion of Experience," 107.

36   "loud and fast": MST quoted ibid., 105.

36   He remembered the concert: Sears, *Edwin and John*, 12.

37   "it was not laid aside": MST to MSS, April 14, 1966, Folder 2, Series 1, MSS Papers.

37   tried to caress her: Therapy tape 10, May 16, 1958, Folder 5-A.10, Box 11, Subseries A, MEM/CM Collection.

38   "I could never": MST to Dorothy Griffith, October 10, 1973, Folder 6, Box 3, Series 1, MSS Papers.

38   "I'm an old friend": MST to Dorothy Griffith, September 7, 1963, Folder 6, Box 3, Series 1, MSS Papers.

38   "I can't bear it": Therapy tape 10, May 16, 1958, Folder 5-A.10, Box 11, Subseries A, MEM/CM Collection.

38   "I was a disaster": MST to MSS, July 9, 1971, Box 4, Series 2, MSS Papers.

39   Mary bobbed and weaved: MST to MSS, October 5, 1967, Box 4, Series 2, MSS Papers. Some of the efforts of the biographers bordered on the farcical. Both Sullivan and Carr, as it turned out, were lesbians, as were some mutual friends and admirers of Carson's who got caught up in the work. All of them were reticent and/or canny enough to know better than to put anything on paper. Mary Tucker wrote Margaret Sullivan about being in a "panic" lest Virginia Spencer Carr find some correspondence from 1950 (after Carson and Mary's "reunion") that evidently revealed the nature of their relationship: "Am trying not to think about it for fear Carr will get my thoughts through the air waves!" MST to MSS, June 13, 1971. Tucker cut to the chase as soon as she arrived at Mercer's place: "On porch. I asked her point blank. She had been dreading it—wanting it too." MST, interview by MSS, September 25, 1977, MSS Papers. Though she doesn't identify "it" in her notes, the lacuna is not hard to parse.

39   "I was ashamed of it": MST to MSS, March 23, 1966, Folder 2, Box 4, Series 1, MSS Papers.

39   "She had a lovely body": MST to MSS, May 18, 1971, Folder 7, Box 4, Series 1, MSS Papers.

39 The maid served artichokes: CM to MST, c. February 1950 [dated by MST], MST Papers.

40 she was glad she: Ibid.

41 "harrowing": CM, untitled ms. for *Story* magazine, December 1936, Folder 3, Box 25, *Story* Papers.

41 When it was finished: Sullivan, "Conversion of Experience," 135.

42 "pulled everything awry": Lillian Smith to MSS, March 4, 1964, Folder 5, Box 2, Series 2, MSS Papers. See also Lillian Smith, review of Evans, *Ballad of Carson McCullers,* and Smith, unpublished manuscript, Folder 4, Box 2, Series 2, MSS Papers.

42 "ebullience": MST to MSS, September 29, 1929, Folder 4, Box 5, Series 2, MSS Papers.

42 "liked to play": Kathleen Woodruff, interview by MSS, n.d., Folder 7, Box 5, Series 1, MSS Papers. MSS said Bébé "thought highly of herself." Sullivan, "Conversion of Experience," 38.

43 "lived in a different world": Helen Harvey quoted in Sullivan, "Conversion of Experience," 61.

43 "The Stark Avenue home": Robert Walden and Edward Newberry to Rita Smith, c. 1972, Folder 1, Box 48, Series 4, CM Collection, HRC.

45 He remembered an early novel: Sullivan, "Conversion of Experience," 147.

45 "pretty awful": MST to MSS, June 13, 1971, Folder 7, Box 4, Series 1, MSS Papers.

45 editor Whit Burnett: "Whit Burnett, Founder of *Story* Magazine, Dies," *New York Times,* April 24, 1973.

47 she entrusted it to the roommate: Carr tells a different version of this story: the roommate was a young Columbus woman, Claire Sasser, with whom Carson only exchanged letters; Sasser met Carson's ship in New York. It's unclear where she got the name, which works in the favor of this version, as it's unlikely Carr made up the name. Carr, *The Lonely Hunter,* 41–42.

47 serving as an accompanist: She told Leo Lerman she played at a settlement house; it's not clear in what capacity. Lerman, *Grand Surprise,* 25.

47 "improviser": Carr, *The Lonely Hunter,* 45.

47 The most likely: The early biographer Oliver Evans was given yet another version of the early trip to New York City. He says Carson was given the money for tuition at Juilliard and that taking courses at Columbia was part of a backup plan, so when she lost the money, Juilliard was out of the question. Presumably a smaller amount could be raised to pay for classes at Columbia. Evans may have simply speculated when trying to make sense of competing stories. See Evans, *Ballad of Carson McCullers,* 29, 31.

48 Parnassus Club: See Frank da Cruz, "The Parnassus Club," Columbia University Computing History, March 29, 2021, http://www.columbia.edu/cu/computinghis tory/parnassus.html.

48 Three Arts Club: "A Club for Girl Art Students," *New York Times,* May 15, 1904, and "Syndicate Takes West Side House," *New York Times,* November 8, 1952.

48 A year later: CM, List of friends to whom *Story* magazine should be sent, December 1936, Folder 15, Box 78, *Story* Papers. Bilderback had a "lifelong friend." "Carolyn L. Bilderback '38," obituary, *Reed Magazine,* August 2008, https://www.reed.edu

/reed-magazine/in-memoriam/obituaries/august2008/carolyn-l-bilderback-1938
.html.

3. CHARMING THE SKIN OFF A SNAKE

50   "He could charm": Quoted in Carr, *The Lonely Hunter,* 54.

50   "buoyant": Delma Eugene Presley, "The Man Who Married Carson McCullers." I
      saw this in Folder 7.A (2), Box 19, Series 6–7, MSS Papers. It was a copy of a paper
      in which a citation was added to *This Week* 2 (1972), 13–16, but I was unable to find
      this journal.

50   "never lost his poise": Roberta ("Topie") Johnson (later Steiner) to CD, October
      24, 1999, Folder 33, Box 1, Series 1, CD Collection.

52   "but he was sweet": Quoted in Carr, *The Lonely Hunter,* 54.

52   "How Eagle Scouts": Jennifer Latson, "How Eagle Scouts Have Made Their Mark
      on America," *Time,* September 2, 2015.

53   Reeves never finished high school: Andrew Lyndon, interview by VSC, January 8,
      1971, p. 4, Folder 19, Box 2, Series 2, CD Collection.

53   Sometimes Reeves is said: The 1940 U.S. Census identifies Reeves in the category
      "Highest Grade Completed" as "College, 1st year."

57   confused by the question: Therapy tape 5, April 25, 1958, Folder 5-A.5 (a), Box 11,
      Series 5, MEM/CM Collection.

58   go to hear Rachmaninoff: Therapy tape 10, May 20, 1958, p. 6, Folder 5-A.10,
      Box 11, Series 5, MEM/CM Collection.

61   "wormy": CM to Gin Tucker, c. 1935, MST Papers.

62   "small town girl": Sylvia Chatfield Bates, "I Have Touched the Earth," *Publishers
      Weekly,* March 14, 1934, https://www.kirkusreviews.com/book-reviews/sylvia
      -chatfield-bates/i-have-touched-the-earth/.

64   "husky": CM to Gin Tucker, c. 1935, MST Papers.

66   She wrote Lamar Sr.: Therapy tape 7, May 5, 1958, p. 6, Folder 5-A.7 (b), Box 11,
      Series 5, MEM/CM Collection.

66   But Carson remained: CM to Emma DeLong Mills, January 4 and February 24,
      1937, Berg Collection, NYPL, indicate Carson was still in Columbus on prescribed
      bed rest.

67   "Someone will have to die": RM to Vincent Adams, August 29, 1937, quoted in
      Presley, "Carson McCullers and the South," 21.

67   Retail Credit Company: See, for example, "Equifax," *New Georgia Encyclope-
      dia,* https://www.georgiaencyclopedia.org/articles/business-economy/equifax. Bes-
      sie Breuer had the mistaken impression that Reeves was a "file clerk in an insurance
      company." BB, unpublished memoir #1, 1940, supplied to author by Peter Poor,
      October 23, 2018. It is possible that Reeves was simply selling insurance for the
      Retail Credit Company, but he did switch into management by the spring of 1938,
      when he was relocated to Fayetteville, Arkansas.

67   a wedding at noon: Virginia Storey, transcript of "Carson McCullers," talk given
      at Baker High School, Columbus, Ga., September 24, 1964, Folder 5, Box 47, CM
      Collection, HRC.

4. A YOUNG KNIGHT

69   The previous year: CM to Gin Tucker, c. October 10, 1937, MST Papers.

69   She had written: CM to Emma DeLong Mills, November 28, 1937, Berg Collection, NYPL.

73   "gas money": RM to Vincent Adams (November 8, 1937), quoted in Presley, "Carson McCullers and the South," 22.

73   detailed outline: This outline has impressed many scholars of Carson's work. It was included as an appendix to Oliver Evans's biography in 1965; Rita Smith included it in the posthumous collection *TMH;* and Carlos Dews appended it to Carson's posthumously assembled autobiography, *ING.*

75   The title, suggested: Carr, *The Lonely Hunter,* 34n4.

78   Houghton Mifflin had offered her: BB, unpublished memoir #1, 1940.

80   It's nothing more than a fairy tale: MSS, Notes on Goldstein, "Art of Fiction," p. 33, Folder 5, Box 3, Series 1, MSS Papers.

82   "something has been added": *Boston Transcript,* June 8, 1940.

82   "but the more important": *Saturday Review of Literature,* June 8, 1940.

82   "a sit-up-and-take-notice book": *New Yorker,* June 8, 1940.

82   "Miss McCullers's picture": *New Republic,* August 5, 1940.

83   "She writes with a sweep": Rose Feld, *New York Times,* June 16, 1940.

83   "the literary find": T. S. Stripling, *New York Times* advertisement, June 16, 1940.

83   "a perfectly magnificent piece of work": Katherine Gauss, *New York Times* advertisement, June 16, 1940.

83   "the old horror": CM to Robert Linscott, February 5, 1941, HM Papers.

83   "the look of a young knight": "Carson McCullers, Distinguished Novelist, and Her Mother Visiting Relatives Here," *Macon News,* 1949, otherwise undated clipping, Vertical Files, CM Collection, HRC.

84   "searchingly": Julie Harris, interview by MSS, n.d., Folder 7, Box 5, Series 1, MSS Papers.

84   "green skin": Walter, *Milking the Moon,* 163.

84   the poet John Ciardi: Quoted in Carr, *The Lonely Hunter,* 112.

84   "I want you should go down": BB, unpublished memoir #1, 1940.

84   Much later: Therapy tape 6, April 28, 1958, Folder 5-A.6 (a), Box 11, Series 5, MEM/CM Collection.

85   best-seller lists: See "Adult *New York Times* Best Seller Lists for 1940," Hawes, n.d., http://www.hawes.com/1940/1940.htm. This site lists only the top five best sellers each week, but other searches were unavailing and indicate that it never made the top-ten best-seller list in *The New York Times.* See also "*Publishers Weekly* List of Bestselling Novels in the United States in the 1940s," *Wikipedia.*

86   "the most unfirstish": Fadiman quoted in Tippins, *February House,* 12. Much of this information about Davis comes from Tippins.

86   "a high achievement": *New York Times Book Review,* August 30, 1931, quoted in Spoto, *Lenya,* 139.

86   "a sulky": Ibid.

5. FLOWERING JAZZ PASSION

88 "when [George] was frail": Mann, *Turning Point,* 296.

89 "small, plump": Auden, *"In Solitude, for Company,"* 100n13.

89 "Strange, primitive": Quoted in Spotts, *Cursed Legacy,* 165.

89 "arresting, in parts": Klaus Mann quoted in Tippins, *February House,* 20.

90 "You are brilliantly": Quoted in Spotts, *Cursed Legacy,* 167.

90 wealthy Swiss businessman: James Schwarzenbach, a cousin of Annemarie's who considered himself the patriarch of the family, wrote a letter to a Swiss newspaper condemning Erika ("a former member of the German Communist party") and the Pepper Mill as "compromising the neutrality of Switzerland." Spotts, *Cursed Legacy,* 90.

91 "dark and slow-moving": R. L. York, unpublished, untitled manuscript, p. 3, Folder 7, Box 48, CM Collection, HRC.

91 "delicate and ambitious": Mann, *Turning Point,* 187, 278.

91 "she never went to sleep": Ruth Landshoff, quoted in "Annemarie Schwarzenbach," Making Queer History, n.d., https://www.makingqueerhistory.com/articles/2017/5/7/annemarie-schwarzenbach.

91 "She was an enormous success": York manuscript, 5.

91 "I will dedicate": BB, unpublished memoir #1, 1940, supplied to the author by Peter Poor.

93 "Go see those females": Quoted in Carr, *The Lonely Hunter,* 104.

95 "an odd little": Quoted in Marrs, *Eudora Welty,* 66.

95 "Untermeyer had a mad crush": Fannie Cheney quoted in Waldron, *Eudora,* 103.

95 "happy to see": Quoted in Marrs, *Eudora Welty,* 67. VSC maintains that Welty "liked Carson that summer and regretted that she did not know her better." Carr, *The Lonely Hunter,* 111. This was based on a 1971 letter to VSC. Welty was very much the literary politician and unlikely to say anything negative about a still-living fellow writer for the record.

96 "the alcohol fumes": Bread Loaf details from Carr, *The Lonely Hunter,* 107–13.

97 "I wish I would": AS to Robert Linscott, August 23, 1940, Linscott Papers.

98 "an eccentric": Wineapple, *Genêt,* 170.

98 "glowing": Anne Poor to MEM, October 5, 1967, Folder 1-X, Box 5, Series 1, MEM/CM Collection.

98 artist Henry Varnum Poor: Peter Poor, interviews by the author, October 22 and December 10, 2018. *Charm* was a fascinating periodical. A glossy magazine with the unlikely subtitle "The Magazine of New Jersey Home Interests," it was published by Bamberger's Department Store. Yet it had a transatlantic presence. See Dan Turello, "Women, Fashion, and the Transatlantic Avant-Garde," Library of Congress Blogs, September 24, 2014, https://blogs.loc.gov/kluge/2014/09/fashion-in-the-1920s/.

99 "the literary sensation": Anne Poor, "Carson," unpublished manuscript, 3.

99 "incurably self-destructive": Spoto, *Lenya,* 140.

102 Carson was proud: Therapy tape 6, April 28, 1958, Folder 5-A.6(a), Box 11, Series 5, MEM/CM Collection.

102 "Please don't ask me": See "Gypsy Rose Lee," Streetswing, n.d., http://www.streetswing.com/histmai2/d2gypsy1.htm; "About Gypsy Rose Lee," Karen Abbott, n.d., https://www.karenabbott.net/aboutgypsyroselee; and Tippins, *February House,* 81–83.

103 repressed: Powell, *Benjamin Britten,* 127.

104 "George naked": Carpenter, *Auden,* 304.

104 the only woman: See "Conference Panel: Exotic Birds of a Feather: Carson McCullers and Tennessee Williams," *Tennessee Williams Annual Review* 3 (2000): 9. See also "Carson McCullers: A Life of Love and Loneliness," *Lesbian News,* April 14, 2017, http://www.lesbiannews.com/carson-mccullers-life-love-loneliness/.

104 "that queer aggregate": Quoted in Carr, *The Lonely Hunter,* 119.

104 "I was staying": MacNeice, *Strings Are False,* 35.

105 trying to convey the title: Britten, *Letters from a Life,* 2:900–901.

105 "improvised ballet": Kildea, *Britten,* 173.

107 They could run away: CM to KB, December 9, 1942, Kay Boyle Papers, SIU.

107 She was wet: Therapy tape 6, April 28, 1958, Folder 5-A.6 (b), Box 11, Series 5, MEM/CM Collection.

109 Annemarie recognized: Therapy tape 7, May 5, 1958, Folder 5-A.7 (a) and (b), Box 11, Series 5, MEM/CM Collection.

110 Why would I touch her?: Therapy tape 7, May 5, 1958, p. 1, Folder 5-A.7 (a), Box 11, Series 5, MEM/CM Collection.

6. A BIT OF A HOLY TERROR

112 this time not: CM to Robert Linscott, c. January 1941, HM Papers.

113 "Dearest and Best": Carpenter, *Auden,* 276.

113 Elizabeth was also: Tippins, *February House,* 154.

114 "over-hastily written": F. T. March, *New York Times,* March 2, 1941.

114 "the morbid": Margaret Clark, *Boston Transcript,* February 15, 1941.

114 "feverish concern": Clifton Fadiman, *New Yorker,* February 15, 1941.

115 "inversions": Robert Littell, *Yale Review,* Spring 1941.

115 "simplicity, insight": *Time,* February 17, 1941. For Carson's only comments on Faulkner, see "The Russian Realists and Southern Literature" in *TMH.* The adjective *Tolstoyan* would have especially resonated with Carson, as this essay makes clear.

115 "the whole post": Stelpflug and Hyatt, *Home of the Infantry,* 128.

116 "distilled": Tennessee Williams, "Afterword" in *RGE,* 135.

116 It was a strange book: CM to Robert Linscott, c. early 1941, Linscott Papers.

117 a brief affair: Peters, *May Sarton,* 395.

118 "problem person": Kimberling, *David Diamond,* 79; Daniel J. Wakin, "David Diamond, Intensely Lyrical Composer, Is Dead," *New York Times,* June 15, 2005. On Diamond's life, see also his obituary by Bret Johnson in *Guardian,* June 17, 2005.

119 "I have met Carson": DD, "Diary," May 22, 1941, read to MSS, Tape 1, Series 5, Box 1, MSS Papers. Diamond's original diaries at the Library of Congress are sealed. Sullivan read these entries into a tape recorder and did not always specify the entry date.

119 "destiny lay not only": DD, "Diary," n.d., Tape 1, Box 1, Series 5, MSS Papers.

119 "and held this child": Ibid.

119 "Thank you, dear God": Ibid.

120 "Carson did not even": DD, "Diary," May 27, 1941, Tape 1, Box 1, Series 5, MSS Papers.

122 Elizabeth Ames: "George E. Peabody Adopts a Daughter," *New York Times,* May 5,

1926; "Elizabeth Ames, Creator of Yaddo, Upstate Cultural Haven, Dies at 92," *New York Times*, March 30, 1977.

122   "a truly angelic woman": Jean Stafford quoted in Mariani, *Lost Puritan*, 104.

122   "strange": Agnes Smedley quoted in Ben Alexander, "The Lowell Affair," *New England Quarterly* 80 (December 2007): 566.

122   "devoted": Carr, *The Lonely Hunter*, 160.

123   "that little wretch": Eudora Welty to KAP, February 22, 1941, quoted in Waldron, *Eudora*, 113.

123   Welty hated the ground: DD, "Diary," June 29, 1941, Box 1, Series 5, MSS Papers.

123   told her editor: CM to Robert Linscott, c. summer 1941, HM Papers.

123   she had walked so far: CM to Muriel Rukeyser, c. fall 1941, Berg Collection, NYPL.

124   She didn't know why: CM to DD, c. July 1941, Folder 1, Box 1, CM Collection, EU.

125   Maybe if she hadn't: Therapy tape 7, May 5, 1958, Folder 5-A.7 (a), Box 11, Series 5, MEM/CM Collection.

125   the skills he'd acquired: See RM to CM, April 2, 1943, Folder 2, Box 28, CM Collection, HRC.

125   "I miss Carson": Details about Reeves in Rochester are from Carr, *The Lonely Hunter*, 171–73.

125   "I do love sleeping": DD, "Diary," October 29, 1941, Box 1, Series 5, MSS Papers.

126   Reeves had forged a check: BB Memoir, 31, 1940, BB Papers. BB misremembered the year.

126   Reeves was suicidal: DD, "Diary," n.d., Box 1, Series 5, MSS Papers.

126   "obviously": CM to DD, late summer 1941, Folder 1, Box 1, CM Collection, EU.

126   "Reeves, I still say": DD to MSS, November 27, 1977, Folder 3, Box 3, Series 1, MSS Papers; emphases in the original.

127   just as jams: CM to DD, July (n.d.), Folder 1, Box 1, CM Collection, EU.

127   impossibly needy: CM to DD, c. July 9, 1941, Folder 1, Box 1, CM Collection, EU.

128   He had closets: Werth, *Scarlet Professor*, 2.

129   it had a short jacket: CM to NA, August 15, 1954, NA Papers.

129   "Newton, I was born": Quoted in Werth, *Scarlet Professor*, 93.

129   "tiresome to what a degree": Quoted in Unrue, *Katherine Anne Porter*, 180.

130   "Lots of youngsters": JM, "Entries in Jordan Massee's 1949 Journal, #2," March 22, 1949, Folder 16, Box 1, JM/CM Collection.

130   "I love you": Quoted in Carr, *The Lonely Hunter*, 155.

130   "mooning passion": Givner, *Katherine Anne Porter*, 317–18.

131   "The only difference": KAP to MSS, October 24, 1975, Folder 16, Box 3, Series 1, MSS Papers.

131   a favorite Yaddo story: Diamond's diary provides more details on the McCullers-Porter story, suggesting that it lasted longer and was even more theatrical—and that Diamond landed in the middle of it. At first Diamond took Porter's side against Carson, but he soon came to wonder why she "hated Carson so." Porter, herself "so utterly cruel," accused Carson of "great evil."

7. I FEEL THAT BOOK WITH SOMETHING LIKE MY WHOLE BODY

134   took up residence: CM to Emma DeLong Mills, April 19, 1940, Berg Collection, NYPL.

135   She was physically committed: CM to NA, c. fall 1941, NA Papers.

136   a tiny creature: CM to DD, February 11, 1942, Folder 2, Box 1, CM Collection, EU.

136   he should recognize: CM to DD, March 23, 1942, Folder 2, Box 1, CM Collection, EU.

137   Mexico had not turned out well: No doubt Moe was thinking of Hart Crane, who drowned off his ship on the way back from his Guggenheim year in Mexico, almost certainly a suicide.

137   she was all cured: CM to EA, c. spring 1942, Yaddo Papers, NYPL.

139   "All my bridges are": RM to Muriel Rukeyser, May 23, 1942, Muriel Rukeyser Papers, Berg Collection, NYPL.

139   inviting African Americans: McGee, *Yaddo,* 10.

139   "Their hind brains": Rampersad, *Life of Langston Hughes,* 2:48.

139   Helen Eustis: Alfred Fisher's first wife was the eminent food writer M. F. K. Fisher.

140   "a dark tall girl": BB, unpublished memoir #1, 1940, courtesy Peter Poor.

142   "A bicycle accident": Klaus Mann quoted in Savigneau, *Carson McCullers,* 98. This remark is not in the English translation of Mann's *Turning Point.*

143   "worthy": CM to EA, c. January 1943, Yaddo Papers, NYPL. This letter seems to have been written in December, soon after Carson received news of Annemarie's death, but it is not clear why she would be writing letters to Elizabeth when she was staying on the Yaddo property. If she wrote it in January 1943, it is not clear why she had not told Elizabeth sooner.

143   "long to give": Kazin, *Kazin's Journals,* 374.

143   "Only McCullers": Calisher, *Herself,* 379.

144   "Don't forget my tenderness": AS to CM, October 3, 1941, Folder 4, Box 29, CM Collection, HRC.

144   "My dear, dear little": AS to CM, March 20, 1942, Folder 4, Box 29, CM Collection, HRC.

144   The other book-length works: Annemarie Schwarzenbach's bibliographic record is elusive, especially from a U.S. vantage point. It is difficult to ascertain the publication dates of any of her work, complicated by the fact that most of it was written in German and translated to English only after her death, and by the number of her posthumous publications. *Death in Persia* and *All the Roads Are Open* were published in German in the 1930s, as was what seems to be her sole work of fiction, *Lyric Novella.* The three books were acclaimed in the German-speaking world then as now; the rest of her voluminous work in recent years has been as well.

145   "If this book": AS to CM, April 10, 1942, Folder 4, Box 29, CM Collection, HRC.

145   "earned no fame": AS to CM, March 20, 1942, Folder 4, Box 29, CM Collection, HRC. A contemporary observer might contend that Annemarie was "gaslighting" Carson.

146   walls were painted: CM to NA, c. November 1942, NA Papers.

147   "Dick, I have wanted": Quoted in Rowley, *Richard Wright,* 270.

147   the African American furnace man: Tippins, *February House,* 250.

149   "necessity to devour": Cheryl Crawford to MSS, n.d., Folder 21, Box 3, Series 1, MSS Papers.

149   "did have strong": Cheryl Crawford, interview by MSS, n.d., notes, p. 7, Folder 3, Box 5, Series 1, MSS Papers.

150   he managed to persuade: Carr, *The Lonely Hunter,* 168.

151 Bébé Smith idly asked: JM, interview by CD, Folder 22, Box 2, Series 2, CD Collection.

151 "Whatever passionate": Ellis, *My Life,* 218.

151 She was in the same position: CM to DD, July 19, 1941, Folder 1, Box 1, CM Collection, EU.

151 "the deepest sympathy": Ellis, *My Life,* 237.

152 "was the first heterosexual": Grosskurth, *Havelock Ellis,* 187.

152 But a certain tense misery: CM to NA, c. June 1943, NA Papers.

8. PRACTICALLY PARADISE

153 "If you can use": RM to CM, February 23, 1943, Folder 2, Box 28, CM Collection, HRC.

154 training with the Rangers: Black, *Battalion,* xiii.

154 the period of mental illness: CM to EA, c. May 1943, Yaddo Papers, NYPL.

155 "I will feel": RM to CM, May 3, 1942, Folder 2, Box 28, CM Collection, HRC.

155 "Can we have calm": RM to CM, May 3, 1943, Folder 2, Box 28, CM Collection, HRC.

156 "But I don't take anything": RM to CM, October 15, 1943, Folder 2, Box 28, CM Collection, HRC. W. H. Auden was a notorious drug user. See John Lanchester, "High Style: Writing Under the Influence," *New Yorker,* December 29, 2002.

157 seemingly not long: CM to EA, n.d., Yaddo Papers, NYPL.

157 "Both Langston and I": Walker quoted in Rampersad, *Life of Langston Hughes,* 2:73.

157 "by no means the": Quoted in Hulbert, *Interior Castle,* 167.

158 "Carson was pure sensibility": Kazin, *Kazin's Journals,* 374; emphases in the original.

159 if it were not: CM to RM, n.d., quoted in Evans, *Ballad of Carson McCullers,* 100.

159 invoking God: CM to EA, n.d., Yaddo Papers, NYPL.

161 didn't spare any: CM to Alfred Kazin, c. September 1943, Folder 4, Box 24, CM Collection, HRC.

161 "intensely Jewish": "Alfred Kazin, the Author Who Wrote of Literature and Himself, Is Dead at 83," *New York Times,* June 6, 1998.

162 "My life is as ordered": RM to CM, May 16, 1943, Folder 2, Box 28, CM Collection, HRC.

162 "was the expression": Ibid.

163 "You know": RM to CM, October 20, 1943, Folder 2, Box 28, CM Collection, HRC.

164 "It is only": RM to CM, October 16, 1943, Folder 2, Box 28, CM Collection, HRC.

164 "I would like": RM to CM, November 15, 1943, Folder 2, Box 28, CM Collection, HRC.

165 Reeves expected Carson: RM to CM, c. November 1943, Folder 2, Box 28, CM Collection, HRC.

165 "and held it": DD quoted in Carr, *The Lonely Hunter,* 240.

165 Now that Reeves: CM to EA, c. May 1943, Yaddo Papers, NYPL.

165 "We can't have children": RM to CM, c. December 1943, Folder 3, Box 28, CM Collection, HRC.

166 "Hortense, did you *want*": Calisher, *Herself,* 363.

166 "I certainly feel": RM to CM, October 20, 1943, Folder 2, Box 28, CM Collection, HRC.

166 "If it were not": RM to CM, November 15, 1943, Folder 2, Box 28, CM Collection, HRC.

167 "the manner of": RM to CM, May 16, 1943, Folder 2, Box 28, CM Collection, HRC.

167 "horrible, terrifying": RM to CM, c. early June 1944, Folder 2, Box 28, CM Collection, HRC.

167 "Lieutenant J. R. McCullers": Savigneau, *Carson McCullers,* 116.

167 "aren't so perfect": " 'No Stalling' Features 'Crazy Ranger Gang,' " undated clipping, Folder 3, Box 28, CM Collection, HRC.

168 "something like applejack": RM to CM, July 8, 1944, Folder 2, Box 28, CM Collection, HRC.

170 Lamar almost surely committed suicide: While there is no tangible evidence that Lamar Sr. shot himself, Carr wrote that she was convinced of this fact by the testimony of David Diamond and other "intimates" at the conclusion of a symposium at Columbus College (later Columbus State University) marking the twentieth anniversary of Carson's death. Carr, *The Lonely Hunter,* 83, 87n8.

170 "deeply shocked and grieved": RM to Muriel Rukeyser, December 4, 1944, Folder 3, Box 28, CM Collection, HRC.

172 a place so quiet: CM to NA, September 14, 1944, NA Papers.

173 "The old man and I": RM to CM, September 17, 1944, Folder 3, Box 28, CM Collection, HRC.

174 "wallowing in muddy foxholes": RM to Muriel Rukeyser, December 4, 1944, CM Collection, HRC.

9. OUR LOVE FOR EACH OTHER IS LIKE A SORT OF NATURAL LAW

176 "But we were happy": Evans, *Ballad of Carson McCullers,* 101.

176 Reeves is cut: CM to KB, October 14, 1943, Kay Boyle Papers, SIU.

176 had read almost everything: CM to Gin Tucker, c. October 10, 1937, MST Papers.

176 They loved each other: CM to RM, January 6, 1954, in *ING,* 126.

178 "factory management": RM to CM, November 21, 1945, in *ING,* 159.

178 full of beans: CM to NA, February 1, 1946, NA Papers.

179 often asked friends: See MSS, Notes on Goldstein, "Art of Fiction," p. 198, MSS Papers.

180 "was enchanted": JM quoted in Clarke, *Capote,* 97.

181 "Carson's family were wildly": Ibid.

182 "The first time I saw": Ibid., 96. Capote made these very writerly remarks in a eulogy at a memorial for Carson at St. James' Episcopal Church in New York City, "on file" at the American Academy of Arts and Letters in New York, according to Clarke.

183 "Without that mother": JM, "Notes on Carson McCullers by Jordan Massee," "Introduction," p. 1, Box 2, JM Notebooks Series, CM Papers, DU.

184 "There was no time": Ibid.

184 jacket flap copy: CM to Dale [Warren] at Houghton Mifflin, c. early 1946, HM Papers.

184 "In a bungling way": Quoted in MSS, Notes on Goldstein, "Art of Fiction," p. 50, Folder 5, Box 3, Series 1, MSS Papers.

185 excruciating care: CM to NA, c. fall 1941, NA Papers. Note that she was saying this as early as 1941.

185 like a shot: Joyce Hartman to Aaron Latham, May 6, 1971, HM Papers.

185 "An odd, unhappy little story": *Kirkus Reviews,* January 15, 1946.

187 crying like a baby: CM to Hardwick Moseley, May 1, 1946, HM Papers.

187 He made Yaddo: CM to NA, NA Papers. Carson's date for this letter, "The First Day of May, 1946," must be wrong, as she left Yaddo on May 23; probably it was "The First Day of June, 1946."

187 "Well, Carson": See, for example, Meghan O'Gieblyn, "The Most Unread Book Ever Acclaimed," *Paris Review,* September 19, 2018, 3. The line appears in her *New York Times* obituary, November 20, 1995.

188 "a cup of tea": Lerman, *Grand Surprise,* 27–29.

188 "McCullers, the taller": Quoted in Werth, *Scarlet Professor,* 101.

188 When she threatened: Clarke, *Capote,* 101.

188 Carson was delighted: CM to NA, June 26, 1946, NA Papers.

189 which she thought: CM to John L. Brown, May 1, 1946, Folder 64, Box 2, John L. Brown Papers II, Georgetown University.

190 "It is so extraordinary": Williams, *Selected Letters,* 1:278n.

191 "a radiant": TW quoted in Reed, *People Are Crazy Here,* 31.

191 "gay girl": JM diary, March 22, 1949, Folder 16, Box 1, JM/CM Collection.

192 "in adjoining trances": TW to CM, March 1, 1948, CM Papers, DU. This letter is not in Williams, *Selected Letters.*

192 "mooning over this romance": Rex Reed, *Esquire,* 1971, untitled clipping in HM Papers.

192 "Carson went wild": Quoted in Carr, *The Lonely Hunter,* 276.

193 "feverishly": TW to Katharine Cornell, July 31, 1946, in Williams, *Selected Letters,* 2:278n.

193 the wonderful Nantucket afternoon: CM to Katharine Cornell and Guthrie McClintic, c. August 1946, Folder 9, Box 61, TW Collection, HRC.

193 "Finally Carson": TW quoted in Carr, *The Lonely Hunter,* 276.

193 Margot and her husband: See "Post Time: The World War II Palm Beach Takedown of Baron von Opel," *Palm Beach Post,* February 27, 2017; "Fritz von Opel, Industrialist, 71," *New York Times,* April 12, 1971.

193 shanghaied: Therapy tape 6, April 28, 1958, Folder 5-A, 6(a), Box 11, Series 5, MEM/CM Collection.

194 In late August: Williams, *Selected Letters,* 2:65n. John Lahr says Williams went to New York and checked himself into St. Luke's Hospital "in a vain search for pancreatic cancer," 111.

194 "McCullers is": Eller, *Becoming Ray Bradbury,* 138.

194 somewhat overwhelmed: CM to NA, October 28, 1946, NA Papers.

195 she believed that Paris: CM to John Brown, May 1, 1946, Folder 64, Box 3, John L. Brown Papers II, Georgetown University.

196 "which is semi-requisitioned": John Brown to CM, October 29, 1946, Folder 64, Box 2, John L. Brown Papers II, Georgetown University.

10. LIKE A BROKEN DOLL

197 "almost like being born": RM to Edwin Peacock, March 18, 1947, Folder 1, Box 1, JZEP Collection.

197 the many interruptions: CM to EA, c. summer 1947, Yaddo Papers, NYPL.

197 deliver a lecture: Carr, *The Lonely Hunter,* 286–87.

198 "living on her foreign": TW to Donald Windham, January 28, 1947, in Williams, *Letters to Windham,* 194.

198 "absolutely awful": Carr, *The Lonely Hunter,* 289.

198 "street-beggar": TW to Donald Windham, April 8, 1949, in Williams, *Letters to Windham,* 238.

198 "everyone loved her": Murray quoted in Carr, *The Lonely Hunter,* 289.

199 "always seemed to be": Bay quoted ibid., 168–69.

199 "prison cells": KB to BB, May 27, 1947, BB Papers.

199 beautiful, half-wild: CM to EA, June 1, 1947, Yaddo Papers, NYPL.

199 had slept with: Mellen, *Kay Boyle,* 302.

199 "a personal dead end": KB to BB, December 15, 1947, BB Papers.

200 "bawdy": Wineapple, *Genêt,* 170–71.

200 "To think that such": Janet Flanner to Natalia Danesi Murray, April 27, 1946, in Flanner, *Darlinghissima,* 76–77.

202 "in my pocket": RM to Edwin Peacock, March 18, 1947, Folder 1, Box 1, JZEP Collection.

202 "still fishing": RM to Bessie and Henry Poor, June 24, 1947, BB Papers.

203 "Why does she repel me so?": Webb, *Richard Wright,* 270.

203 "I've been trying": Ibid., 272.

203 elegant large apartment: Rowley, *Richard Wright,* 360.

204 "convulsions": Bébé Smith to JM and Paul Bigelow, June 13, 1947, Folder 10, Box 1, JM/CM Collection.

204 "I went into": RM to Ellen and Richard Wright, December 16, 1947, Richard Wright Papers, JWJ, MSS 3, Box 101, Folder 1458, Beinecke Library, Yale University.

205 Others believed Reeves: Andrew Lyndon, interview by VSC, January 8, 1971, notes, Folder 19, Box 2, Series 2, MSS Papers.

206 Reeves needed her emotionally: CM to TW, January 16, 1948, Folder 5, Box 59, TW Collection, HRC.

206 "Reeves is": TW to Paul Bigelow, February 18, 1948, Williams, *Selected Letters,* 2:169.

207 "Tennessee Williams is": Williams, *Selected Letters,* 2:175n.

207 "This is to assure": TW to CM, c. late January 1948, Williams, *Selected Letters,* 2:153.

208 "in bed": Audrey Wood to TW, March 12, 1948, quoted in Williams, *Selected Letters,* 2:179–80n.

209 a great source: CM to Sidney Isenberg, February 23, 1947, SI Papers.

211 like a labyrinth: CM to NA, c. April 1948, NA Papers.

211 faulty logic: CM to Sidney Isenberg, April 14, 1948, SI Papers.

212 friend and protector: CM to NA, c. April 1948, NA Papers.

212 "with interest but": Hervey Cleckley to Sidney Isenberg, April 2, 1948, SI Papers.

213 It was a miracle: CM to Sidney Isenberg, May 6, 1948, SI Papers.

213 Reeves had become: CM to Edwin Peacock and John Zeigler, marked "Probably 1948" by CM, Folder 1, Box 1, JZEP Collection.

213 "I read it": Katherine White to Harold Ross, "McCullers 'April Afternoon,'" Folder 14, Box 1650, *New Yorker* Collection, NYPL. For the contract, dated May 1, 1948, see Folder 3, Box 754, *New Yorker* Collection, NYPL.

213 fully appreciated it: CM to TW, c. 1948, TW Papers, CU.

214 "is a continual problem": TW to Donald Windham, August 19, 1948, Williams, *Letters to Windham,* 225.

11. THE JIGGER GOT BIGGER AND BIGGER

216 being his best: CM to TW, January or February 1949, Folder 2, Box 1, VSC Collection, CSU.

218 "feels constricted": RM to Edwin Peacock, February 20, 1949, Folder 1, Box 1, JZEP Collection.

218 "was able to cut": JM, "Extracts from the 1949 Journals of Jordan Massee," February 17, 1949, Folder 29, Box I, JM/CM Collection.

219 "the best raconteur": Massee, *Accepted Fables,* 13.

219 "'do' for": RM to EP, February 20, 1949, Folder 1, Box 1, JZEP Collection.

219 "Carson requires": JM, Journals, February 24, 1949, "Extracts from the 1949 Journals of Jordan Massee," March 17, 1949, Folder 29, Box I, JM/CM Collection.

220 imperial: JM, Journals, March 23, 1949, "Extracts from the 1949 Journals of Jordan Massee," March 17, 1949, Folder 29, Box I, JM/CM Collection. See also Mariani, *Lost Puritan,* and especially Ben Alexander, "The Lowell Affair," *New England Quarterly* 80 (December 2007): 545–87.

220 devastating: CM to JM and Paul Bigelow, March 29, 1949, Folder 8, Box I, JM/CM Collection.

221 "the long procedure": JM, March 23, 1949, "Extracts from the 1949 Journals of Jordan Massee," March 17, 1949, Folder 29, Box I, JM/CM Collection.

221 "It took a long time": JM, interview 1 by VSC, July 25, 1971, and JM, interview 2 by VSC, July 26, 1971, Folder 21, Box 5, VSC Papers, DU.

221 She was terribly upset: CM to Sidney Isenberg, May 12, 1948, SI Papers.

222 "one large drink": JM, Journals (long version), "Extracts from the 1949 Journals of Jordan Massee," March 17, 1949, Folder 29, Box I, JM/CM Collection.

222 "and the jigger": JM, interview 2 by VSC, July 26, 1971, Folder 21, Box 5, VSC Papers, DU.

222 cheap dry sherry: Ibid.

222 "would get herself": JM, interview 1 by VSC, July 26, 1971, p. 37, Folder 21, Box 5, VSC Papers, DU.

222 "nourishing": Phoebe Pierce Vreeland, in Plimpton, *Truman Capote,* 50. See "Cheers to 200 Years—The Fascinating Story of Guinness in America," Irish Central, October 23, 2017, https://www.irishcentral.com/culture/food-drink /cheers-to-200-years-the-fascinating-story-of-guinness-in-america.

222 hospitalized for malnutrition: Carr, *The Lonely Hunter,* 444. See also JM, "Extracts from the 1949 Journals of Jordan Massee," March 24, 1949, Folder 21, Box I, JM/ CM Collection.

222 "when she gets home": JM, interview by VSC, July 27, 1971, Folder 21, Box 5, VSC Papers, DU.

223   "mathematical genius"; JM, "Extracts from the 1949 Journals of Jordan Massee," March 24, 1949, Folder 21, Box I, JM/CM Collection.

224   "Her idea of a drink": JM, interview by VSC, July 26, 1971, p. 14, Folder 21, Box 5, VSC Papers, DU.

224   Reeves went to an AA meeting: EP, interview by VSC, n.d., Box 6, Series 1, VSC Papers, DU. See also Carr, *The Lonely Hunter*, 328.

224   the chore of fixing: Cheryl Crawford, interview by MSS, c. January 20, 1978, Box 5, Series 3, CD Collection.

224   "the wreck": BB to MEM, December 18, 1970, Folder 2-M, Box 8, Series 2, MEM/CM Collection. Bessie Breuer had nothing good to say about Carson, devoting a whole novel, "Knife My Bride," to a destructive dynamo of a writer, readily identifiable as CM.

224   "sweetest, gentlest": JM, interview 2 by VSC, July 26, 1971, Folder 21, Box 5, VSC Papers, DU.

225   Reeves was committed: CM to MST and Tuck Tucker, c. August 1950, MST Papers.

225   bulwark of support: CM to Hardwick Moseley, c. 1949 [misdated by archivist 1946], HU 46, HM Papers. Carr maintains the matter never went to court, though with the above result. Carr, *The Lonely Hunter*, 311.

225   Whitehead would not have trouble: Carr, *The Lonely Hunter*, 305, somewhat mystifyingly says that the producers knew the play was a high risk for investors. She may have based it on some extensive negative comments that Cheryl Crawford made about the play a year before.

227   "lost her faith": Waters, *His Eye Is on the Sparrow*, 263, 273.

227   "top billing": Bogle, *Heat Wave*, 443.

227   "had been more like training": Clurman, *All People Are Famous*, 246.

228   "It all had to spring": McKay Jenkins, "Dramatizing *The Member of the Wedding*," in R. Barton Palmer, ed., *Twentieth-Century Fiction on Screen* (New York: Cambridge University Press, 2007), 93–94.

228   "everyone was her slave": Julie Harris, interview by MSS, n.d., Cassette 4, Box 1, Series 5, MSS Papers.

228   but Tennessee: It's commonly said that Williams was present at the opening; see Carr, *The Lonely Hunter*, 339. But letters indicate otherwise. John Lahr reports that Merlo returned on January 5, 1950, from his Christmas trip to NYC, the opening night of the Broadway version. See Lahr, 190. A letter dated January 5, 1950, says Merlo got back on January 4; Williams, *Selected Letters*, 2:281.

229   "Neither of us": RM to John and Simone Brown, January 30, 1950, John L. Brown Papers II, Georgetown University.

229   a medical abortion: Carson gives a very different accounting of this pregnancy in *ING*, 46–47, stressing Bébé's role in the affair. Carson portrays her as adamant that Carson be given an abortion for a pregnancy that would otherwise kill her. In this account Bébé calls in Dr. William Mayer for support. The timing of the incident is odd; Carson says that the pregnancy was discovered shortly after the play's opening on January 5, 1950, and that she had a miscarriage at home prior to the scheduled abortion. She indicates that she arrived at the hospital, bloody, in a taxi with Reeves, and that the doctor scolded Reeves for bringing her in so late, as she was now dying. The specificity of the latter detail is convincing, but the rest of the story seems impossibly garbled. It is not clear why it suited Carson to say she had a

miscarriage rather than an abortion. It is unlikely that she hoped to make the story more palatable for public consumption.

231 "loud, honest cheers": All reviews quoted in Savigneau, *Carson McCullers,* 196–97.

232 "waterboy": RM to John and Simone Brown, January 30, 1950, John L. Brown Papers II, Georgetown University.

233 But Tennessee remained: Williams, *Selected Letters,* 2:283n.

12. I AM AN INVALID

234 Though they hadn't: CM to Hardwick Moseley, April 10, 1950, HM Papers. The record does not show when Moseley contacted her.

235 Lasky explicitly stated: Floria Lasky to Hardwick Moseley, March 8, 1950, HM Papers.

236 investors received: Carr, *The Lonely Hunter,* 367.

236 a cerebral hemorrhage: CM to Hardwick Moseley, c. 1950, HM Papers.

236 "her cheeks looked": Williams, *Five O'Clock Angel,* 29.

236 "Deeply mistrustful": Ibid., 45.

237 "cat eyes": Peters, *May Sarton,* 107.

238 "almost pure Irish": Quoted in Carr, *The Lonely Hunter,* 525.

238 "was maintained": Rebecca Pelan, "Real Journeys of the Imagination: Carson McCullers and Ireland," *Irish Journal of American Studies,* no. 3 (2004), http://ijas .iaas.ie/author/rebeccapelan/.

239 "austere": May Sarton, "Elizabeth Bowen," in *A World of Light: Portraits and Celebrations* (New York: W. W. Norton, 1976), 201.

239 marvelous mansion: Carr, *The Lonely Hunter,* 350.

239 an emerald green "demesne": CM to JM, Paul Bigelow, and "Alice," c. May 30, 1950, Folder 23, Box 1, JM/CM Collection.

239 "a bowl of rough grass": Sarton, "Elizabeth Bowen," 199.

239 The older writer: CM to JM, Paul Bigelow, and "Alice," c. May 30, 1950, Folder 23, Box 1, JM/CM Collection.

240 got herself out of: TW to Paul Bigelow, June 7, 1950, in Williams, *Selected Letters,* 2:318–20.

240 Carson had found: CM to Mary Tucker, c. July 1950, MST Papers.

240 she thought she and Jane: CM to TW, c. 1949, VSC Papers, DU.

240 "She's one year": Dillon, *Little Original Sin,* 125.

240 "Certainly [she]": Ibid., 141.

241 "her freaks": Ibid., 209.

241 "streams": CM to MST and "Tuck" Tucker, c. July 1950, MST Papers.

243 "We may go back": RM to MST and "Tuck" Tucker, c. July 1950, MST Papers.

243 "terrible handful": Quoted in Carr, *The Lonely Hunter,* 360.

243 "she remains in my mind": Quoted in Craig, *Elizabeth Bowen,* 158–9.

244 "Get Marty Mann!": TW to Paul Bigelow, June 7, 1950, Williams, *Selected Letters,* 2:318–20.

245 "many times daily": Carr, *The Lonely Hunter,* 361.

247 Marty shouldn't worry: CM to Marty Mann, September 4, 1950, Marty Mann Papers, Syracuse University.

247 "was able to sidestep": Sally Brown and David R. Brown, *Mrs. Marty Mann: The First Lady of Alcoholics Anonymous* (Center City, Minn.: Hazelden, 2001), 222.

13. HARDER THAN MARBLE

249 "Sitwell arrived": JM, "Extracts Pertaining to Carson McCullers from the Journals of JM," October 31, 1950, Folder 29, Box 1, JM/CM Collection.

249 "Sitwell treated": William Sitwell, review of Greene, *Avant-Garde Poet,* in *Sunday Telegram,* March 11, 2011.

251 She was simply: CM to ES, November 26, 1950, Folder 1, Box 98, Sitwell Papers, HRC.

251 "You are a transcendental": ES to CM, November 21, 1950, consulted in JM, Letters from ES to CM, Folder 30, Box 1, JM/CM Collection.

252 "You say what have": ES to CM, February 15, 1951, consulted in JM, Letters from ES to CM, Folder 30, Box 1, JM/CM Collection.

252 She sold the film rights: See James R. and Carson McCullers, NY State Income Tax return, 1950, Folder 4, Box 38, CM Collection, HRC.

252 "a crumpled figure": Garnett, *Great Friends,* 222.

253 "She was in continual": Ibid., 228.

253 "She has several highballs": Quoted in Carr, *The Lonely Hunter,* 373. Emphasis in the original.

253 "Perhaps his part": Quoted in Evans, *Ballad of Carson McCullers,* 159.

253 "glowing": Anne Poor to MEM, October 5, 1967, Folder 1-X, Box 5, Series 1, MEM/CM Collection.

253 "danger signals": Evans, *Ballad of Carson McCullers,* 159.

254 scene on a Rochester bridge: DD, "Diary," n.d., Tape 56b, Box 2, Series 5, MSS Papers.

254 two receipts: Receipts for Carson and J. R. McCullers indicate that they disembarked at Southampton, rather than at the ship's usual destination, Cherbourg, which was possibly why they were issued. See "List of Outward Bound Passengers Traveling First Class on the R.M.S. *Queen Elizabeth,* New York to Southampton, leaving July 28, 1951," nos. 266 and 270, via Ancestry.com.

255 In some fashion: For the outlines of the story, see Carr, *The Lonely Hunter,* 374–75, and Andrew Lyndon, interview by VSC, Folder 19, Box 2, Series 2, CD Collection.

255 "Rita called": JM, "Excerpts from the 1951 Journal of JM," from "Notes on CM by JM," Folder 25, Box 1, JM/CM Collection.

255 Carson wrote to her publisher: CM to Paul [Brooks], August 2, 1951, HM Papers. Something may have been awry even in this letter, for unknown reasons. Someone, presumably Brooks, an editor at Houghton Mifflin, wrote at the top of the page, "I have no idea what this is about." Someone replied below that note, "I don't know."

256 Reeves disgracing himself: Carr, *The Lonely Hunter,* 376.

256 "a very drunk Carson": Hastings, *Rosamond Lehmann,* 244.

256 endearments: CM to RM, August 7, 1951, Folder 9, Box 24, CM Collection, HRC.

258 "a youngish and very seedy": TW to Audrey Wood, August 23, 1951, in Williams, *Selected Letters,* 2:396.

258 "A fish couldn't drink": TW to Frank Merlo, August 29, 1951, in Williams, *Selected Letters,* 2:400.

258 "on whom she had": TW to Audrey Wood, October 27, 1951, in Williams, *Selected Letters,* 2:405.

259 "exhausted from seeing": Lehmann quoted in Carr, *The Lonely Hunter,* 378.

259 in a despair: CM to RM, September 23, 1951, Folder 10, Box 25, CM Collection, HRC.

261 "brooding and mooning": TW to Audrey Wood, October 27, 1951, in Williams, *Selected Letters,* 2:405.

261 "those broad, beautiful shoulders": Kathryn Cohen to CM, c. September 27, 1951, Folder 10, Box 25, CM Collection, HRC.

262 a salubrious: CM to RM, September 29, 1951, Folder 9, Box 24, CM Collection, HRC.

262 "elegant" robe: CM to RM, c. late September 1957, Folder 9, Box 24, CM Collection, HRC. This seems to be a different letter from the one cited above, but the pages of two letters seem to have become confused. She intersperses two confused requests for a blank bank draft for about $2,000 for one of her doctors to buy a car, the currency exchange facilitating the purchase. There is no indication that Reeves or Floria Lasky sent her this sum.

263 Rosamond might not have formed: Carr, *The Lonely Hunter,* 380.

264 "all the gain": Kathryn Cohen to Rosamond Lehmann, November 27, 1951, Rosamond Lehmann Papers, Archive Centre, King's College, Cambridge.

264 "to which the female hypnotist": TW to Audrey Wood, October 27, 1951, in Williams, *Selected Letters,* 2:405.

264 "monster": Andrew Lyndon, interview by VSC, notes, January 8, 1971, Box 4, VSC Papers, DU.

14. GRAPPA RATHER THAN GIN

265 "nest" of talent: Goyen's quotes are from a *Paris Review* interview in Goyen, *Autobiographical Essays,* 87.

266 "not very well": RM to Rosamond Lehmann, November 26, 1951, Rosamond Lehmann Papers, Archive Centre, King's College, Cambridge.

267 she expected him: CM to RM, c. fall 1951, Folder 9, Box 24, CM Collection, HRC.

267 "Ladies and gentlemen": Plimpton, *Truman Capote,* 122. Young misremembers the name of the ship as the *Queen Mary,* and Plimpton (perhaps following Young) misdates the crossing as 1954.

269 "All day Carson groans": Quoted in Carr, *The Lonely Hunter,* 385.

270 "divinely beautiful": Young quoted in Plimpton, *Truman Capote,* 122.

270 "a mad, sympathetic": Quoted in Curtis, *Splendid Intelligence,* 74.

270 "There was this little": Walter, *Milking the Moon,* 164.

271 "hundreds of questions": JM, "Extracts from the 1949 Journals of Jordan Massee," March 18, 1949, Folder 21, Box 1, JM/CM Collection.

272 "I fear it is": TW to Maria St. Just, February 5, 1952, in Williams, *Five O'Clock Angel,* 53.

272 "off and on": RM to Jack Fullilove, April 13, 1952, Folder 9, Box 24, CM Collection, HRC.

272 Carson's white socks: Carr, *The Lonely Hunter,* 389.

272 "people so drunk": John Brown quoted in Savigneau, *Carson McCullers,* 218.

274 "I've got to get me": Walter, *Milking the Moon,* 164.

274 she put him in mind: JM, interview 1 by VSC, July 25, 1971, Folder 21, Box 5, VSC Papers, DU.

275 "a direct lineal": RM to Edwin Peacock and John Zeigler, November 3, 1952, Folder 1, Box 1, JZEP Collection.

275 their estimated income: Warshaw and Clarke to CM and RM, July 31, 1952, Folder 9, Box 29, CM Collection, HRC.

276 "She and Reeves came": TW to Oliver Evans, August 5, 1952, in Williams, *Selected Letters*, 2:445.

276 "one big bundle": TW to Maria St. Just, July 7, 1952, in Williams, *Five O'Clock Angel*, 60.

276 "I am homosexual": TW to VSC, August 18–19, 1970, Box 7, VSC Papers, DU.

279 a cheerful letter: RM to Edwin Peacock and John Zeigler, November 3, 1952, Folder 1, Box 1, JZEP Collection.

279 drinking on the plane: CM to Jack Fullilove, 9, 1952, Folder 3, Box 1, VSC Collection, CSU.

279 "Sister (the famous": Clarke, *Capote*, 233–34.

280 "Well, just a minute": Plimpton, *Truman Capote*, 124–25. Plimpton gives the date as 1954, but it is clearly 1952.

280 "Ahhh": Plimpton, *Truman Capote*, 123.

280 Truman "plundered": Vidal in *Playboy* interview, June 1969, quoted in Lawrence Grobel, ed., *Conversations with Capote* (New York: NAL, 1985), 130.

280 "A leaf, a handful": Capote, *Grass Harp*, 49.

280 was like a baby: JM, interview by MSS, n.d., Cassette 6, Box 1, Series 5, MSS Papers.

280 "a little crook": JM, "Extracts from the 1949 Journals of Jordan Massee," March 18, 1949, Folder 21, Box 1, JM/CM Collection.

281 "some crisp": RM to Edwin Peacock and John Zeigler, November 3, 1952, Folder 1, Box 1, JZEP Collection. A bill from the Salvator Mundi Hospital charges Carson for a room for October 15 through October 20. MSS, Cassette 25, Box 1, Series 5, MSS Papers.

15. A COLOSSAL POWER OF DESTRUCTION

284 "a sensitive and lovable creature": Graver, *Obsession with Anne Frank*, 51; ellipsis in the original.

284 Carson in turn: CM to Mary Tucker, c. spring 1953, Series 1, Box 1, MST Papers. Carson also told Mary Tucker that Otto Frank had visited them in Bachivillers for "several days."

284 "an uncommon understanding": Graver, *Obsession with Anne Frank*, 71.

284 was a departure: CM to Cheryl Crawford, November 17, 1952, Folder 2, Box 24, CM Collection, HRC.

285 "would not be honest": Meyer Levin to CM, c. early November 1952, Folder 5, Box 27, CM Collection, HRC.

286 the "Anne book": Melnick, *Stolen Legacy*, 68.

286 "When I kept reading": Flanner, *Darlinghissima*, 184.

286 "I say to the devil": quoted in Melnick, *Stolen Legacy*, 77.

287 "[She] is so fragile": Ibid., 79.

287 "I don't want to do": Cheryl Crawford to CM, April 15, 1953, p. 2, Box 24, CM Collection, HRC.

287   "funny, hopeful, happy": See Cynthia Ozick, "Who Owns Anne Frank?" *New Yorker,* September 29, 1997.

287   public relations equivalent: Graver, *Obsession with Anne Frank,* 169.

287   "had to feed her": Goyen, *Autobiographical Essays,* 108.

288   "Yes, Reeves": Bébé Smith to MST, May 4, 1950, Box 1, Series 1, MST Papers.

288   "who despite his defects": BB to MEM, December 18, 1970, Folder 2-M, Box 8, Series 2, MEM/CM Collection.

288   "What will happen": Janet Flanner to Natalia Danesi Murray, April 11, 1953, in Flanner, *Darlinghissima,* 194.

288   "Whether we are divorced": RM to CM, September 6, 1953, Folder 2-M, Box 8, Series 2, MEM/CM Collection.

289   "wants to be entirely independent": RM to Floria Lasky, March 24, 1953, Folder 5, Box 41, CM Collection, HRC.

289   "He should have been": Clarke, *Capote,* 251.

289   "disorientation": Janet Flanner to CM, December 5, 1953, Tape 12, Series 5, MSS Papers.

290   "the grace with which": Wineapple, *Genêt,* 183–84.

290   "seductive": Goyen, *Autobiographical Essays,* 108.

290   "Reeves and I": JM, interview 3 by VSC, February 27, 1972, Folder 21, Box 5, CM Collection, DU.

290   "meets the post man": Lamar and Virginia Smith to CM, c. April 1953, Folder 4, Box 29, CM Collection, HRC.

290   "at least once": Virginia Smith to CM, April 27, 1953, Folder 4, Box 29, CM Collection, HRC.

290   saw the "necessity": JM, interview 3 by VSC, February 27, 1972, notes, pp. 12–13, Folder 21, Box 5, VSC Papers, DU.

291   "an AA friend": RM to CM, September 6, 1953, Folder 6-x, Box 19, Series 6–7, MEM/CM Collection.

292   "I am sick of": Janet Flanner to Natalia Danesi Murray, April 11, 1953, in Flanner, *Darlinghissima,* 193–94.

293   "in great distress": TW to Audrey Wood, June 29, 1953, in Williams, *Selected Letters,* 2:490.

293   Reeves was driving: The most complete version of Carson's story is in TW to VSC, August 18–19, 1970, VSC Papers, DU. See also Andrew Lyndon, interview by VSC, January 8, 1971, Folder 19, Box 2, Series 2, CD Collection. Williams gives a shorter version in *Memoirs,* 245. Among the several holes in the story is that Carson said she hitched a ride to the American Hospital; given that she and Reeves were headed there, he would have known just where to find her.

294   flimsy dress: JM, interview by MSS, n.d., Box 1, Series 5, MSS Papers.

294   "dreary, bleary": RM to CM, July 28, 1953, Folder 6-x, Box 19, MEM/CM Collection.

295   "money changer": Carr, *The Lonely Hunter,* 401–2.

295   "so precipitously": Truman Capote to NA, November 20, 1953, in Capote, *Too Brief a Treat,* 232.

295   "my precious children": Jessie McCullers to RM and CM, July 7, 1953. See also the letters dated July 25, July 26, August 31, and September 10, 1953, Folder 3, Box 41, CM Collection, HRC.

296 "Reeves was simply": Quoted in Carr, *The Lonely Hunter,* 402.

297 "might pick up the spark": RM to CM, September 6, 1953, Folder 6-x, Box 19, Series 6–7, MEM/CM Collection.

297 "going West": Wineapple, *Genêt,* 329n49.

297 Reeves's body: American Foreign Service, "Report of the Death of an American Citizen, December 9, 1953," in Ancestry.com, *Reports of Deaths of American Citizens Abroad, 1835–1974.* The cause of death on the form was "natural cause—non-epidemic and non-contagious disease." Strangely, Reeves's occupation was given as "banker." Perhaps the last job his friends or family could remember him holding was his position at Bankers Trust.

298 "tearing him down": MSS, Notes on visit to Lillian Smith, c. late June 1965, Folder 5, Box 2, Series 2, MSS Papers.

16. ENDINGS ARE KNIVES

301 "far more likely": Rita Smith to Floria Lasky, December 18, 1953, Folder 4, Box 44, CM Collection, HRC.

301 "At last Reeves": Bébé Smith, unpublished fragment, n.d., Folder 1, Box 45, CM Collection, HRC.

301 "seems to me to have been decided": Janet Flanner quoted in Wineapple, *Genêt,* 235.

301 "It comes back to me": Dorothy Harvey to CM, November 29, 1953, Folder 1, Box 27, CM Collection, HRC.

301 "In the disappearance of Reeves": Natalia Danesi Murray to CM, c. late 1953, Folder 1, Box 28, CM Collection, HRC.

302 She would banish: CM to NA, c. late 1953, NA Papers.

302 "Reeves died, ultimately": Quoted in Carr, *The Lonely Hunter,* 403.

302 "All of us here feel badly": Bob Myers to CM, n.d., Folder 8, Box 28, CM Collection, HRC.

303 "My youth is gone": Clarke, *Capote,* 251.

304 "A lot of animosity": JM, interview 1 by VSC, July 25, 1971, Folder 21, Box 5, VSC Papers, DU.

304 "The only thing Carson did": Quoted in Carr, *The Lonely Hunter,* 409.

304 an open invitation: Harlan Green, "A Defining Chapter," *Charleston Magazine* (November 2018), https://charlestonmag.com/features/a_defining_chapter.

305 "shrunken and birdlike": Dawn Langley Simmons to MSS, August 30, 1978, Folder 24, Box 3, Series 1, MSS Papers.

305 "purely unintellectual": Hilda Marks and Robert Marks, interview by VSC, May 24, 1971, Box 4, VSC Papers, DU.

305 "The simple life": John Zeigler and Edwin Peacock to Floria Lasky, c. early March, Folder 1, Box 49, CM Collection, HRC.

306 "We certainly do appreciate": Lamar Smith, Jr., and Virginia Smith to Rita Smith, c. spring 1954, Folder 3, Box 43, CM Collection, HRC.

306 Reeves had sent Rita: Rita Smith to CM and RM, July 30, 1952, Folder 6, Box 29, CM Collection, HRC.

306 Rita wrote, perhaps: Rita Smith to CM, c. spring 1954, March 11 and 29, 1954, Folder 6, Box 29, CM Collection, HRC.

308   "very sharp": Carr, *The Lonely Hunter,* 427.

309   "had affected not only her brain": Quoted ibid., 430, based on a 1971 interview.

310   concluding that she would die: Ibid., 438.

310   "drooled": Walter Aschaffenburg quoted ibid., 429.

310   "Carson had a great deal of warmth": Edel quoted ibid., 438, from a 1971 interview.

312   persuaded Tennessee: There are indications that CM and TW made a previous appearance together, perhaps for a radio broadcast. A document at HRC, identified as "Broadcast interview of Carson McCullers and Tennessee Williams" (Folder 11, Box 2, Series 1), is a transcript (words, especially proper names, are misheard and/ or left out) that is much shorter than the transcript of the 92nd Street Y appearance. The same general script is followed, but Williams reads different passages. The event was evidently much shorter, as the transcript is barely six pages to the other event's thirty-one. The questions from the audience are different. In the 92nd Street Y transcript, Williams, before reading an extract from *HLH*, says, "Last time I read the opening paragraph of *The Heart Is a Lonely Hunter.*"

312   "Carson did not read well": Hilda and Robert Marks, interview by VSC, May 24, 1971, notes, Box 4, VSC Papers, DU.

312   A pitcher of clear liquid: "Carson McCullers and Tennessee Williams," transcript of an appearance at the 92nd Street Y, May 8, 1954, MEM/CM Collection.

313   "increased her nervousness": Windham, *Lost Friendships,* 67–68.

313   "monstrous exhibition": Lerman, *Grand Surprise,* 165.

314   "interrupting one another": Spoto, *Kindness of Strangers,* 216.

314   "not such that it can": RM to Floria Lasky, March 24, 1953, Cassette 24, Side A, Box 2, Series 5, MSS Papers.

315   "I don't believe she worked": Quoted in Carr, *The Lonely Hunter,* 430.

315   "is trying to prevail": EA to Rita Smith, c. 1954, Yaddo Papers, NYPL.

316   "disheveled, unloved": Lerman, *Grand Surprise,* 169.

317   in the event: CM to John and Simone Brown, c. summer 1954, John L. Brown Papers II, Georgetown University. See also CM to NA, August 15, 1954, NA Papers.

317   "in the deep": Lerman, *Grand Surprise,* 177.

17. I SEEN THE LITTLE LAMP

318   "a unique friendship": Quoted in Spoto, *Kindness of Strangers,* 190.

318   "blessed" day: Williams, *Selected Letters,* 2:240n.

318   "My fondest dream": Reed, *People Are Crazy Here,* 31.

319   "quite unnecessarily repulsive": Isherwood, *Diaries,* entry dated March 8, 1951, 1:479.

320   "the life of the outcast": Françoise Sagan, *With Fondest Regards,* trans. Christine Donougher (New York: E. P. Dutton, 1985), 46–47, 60. Sagan's memoir mentions a second encounter with Carson in Nyack "two or three" years later, where she met and drank with Carson's dying mother. Bébé died in 1955, less than two months after Sagan met Carson the first time. It does not seem possible that she was writing about an earlier meeting at which Bébé might have been present. It is extremely unlikely that she misremembered Bébé being present, given that she describes her in detail.

320   "swilling my liquor": TW to Maria St. Just, April 27, 1955, in Williams, *Five O'Clock Angel,* 113.

321 "It is much easier": Ibid.

321 Bébé told Ida Reeder: *ING,* 53. Vomiting blood possibly indicates esophageal varices, a common cause of death in alcoholics.

321 Carson heard the news: This account is based largely on Hilda Marks and Robert Marks, interview by VSC, May 24, 1971, notes, Box 4, VSC Papers, DU.

322 Lamar and Rita felt: Carr, *The Lonely Hunter,* 448.

322 a striking example: William Goyen, "*Paris Review* Interview with William Goyen, 1976," in *Autobiographical Essays,* 89.

324 "so excited": Cheryl Crawford, interview by MSS, c. January 20, Folder 7, notes, Box 5, MSS Papers.

324 "whose dream of marriage": BB to Cheryl Crawford and Ruth Norman, c. 1955, Cheryl Crawford Papers, Billy Rose Theatre Division, NYPL.

324 "She really thought she": Quoted in Carr, *The Lonely Hunter,* 441.

325 "No two people": Quoted ibid., 451.

330 "We battled such": Quoted ibid.

331 "In spite of the talk": Quoted ibid., 454.

332 "Rose, precious": TW to Maria St. Just, January 3, 1957, in Williams, *Five O'Clock Angel,* 141.

333 "Laughing at Choppers": TW to Maria St. Just, June 20, 1955, in Williams, *Five O'Clock Angel,* 116.

18. I TRUST YOU

335 Quintero couldn't direct: Matthau, *Among the Porcupines,* 133. See Sydney Stern, *The Brothers Mankiewicz: Hope, Heartbreak, and Hollywood Classics* (Jackson: University Press of Mississippi, 2019), 300, and Kenneth L. Geist, *Pictures Will Talk: The Life and Films of Joseph L. Mankiewicz* (New York: Scribner, 1978), 287–89.

335 Quintero started drinking: JM, interview by VSC, July 26, 1971, Cassette 3, Side A, Folder 22, Box 2, Series 2, CD Collection.

335 "stunning": Leggett quoted in Carr, *The Lonely Hunter,* 460.

336 "sturdy entertainment": Frank Aston quoted ibid., 458.

336 "a trauma in three acts": *New York Daily News,* October 31, 1957.

336 "agonizing exit": Williams, *Memoirs,* 108.

336 "some skulking littérateur": Wolcott Gibbs, *New Yorker,* November 9, 1957.

336 "it was a posthumous argument": Lasky quoted in Savigneau, *Carson McCullers,* 263.

337 "Carson . . . was a hysteric": Baxter quoted in Carr, *The Lonely Hunter,* 452.

338 "really sold": Julie Harris, interview by MSS, c. 1970s, Folder 7, Box 5, Series 1, MSS Papers.

339 "Truman, Carson could have": JM, "In Cold Blood: Recollections of a Conversation with Truman Capote," in "Notes on Carson McCullers in the 1965 Journal," Folder 55, Box 1, JM/CM Collection.

339 "She wouldn't stop drinking": Plagemann, *American Past,* 211.

339 "It saddened me": Plagemann quoted in Carr, *The Lonely Hunter,* 498.

340 They often discussed it: Therapy tape 3, April 21, 1958, Folder 5-A.3 (a), Box 11, Series 5, MEM/CM Collection.

341 "take a prime seat": MEM, interview by MSS, n.d., Folder 15, Box 3, MSS Papers.

341 overcome with fear: Therapy tape 2, April 14, 1958, Folder 5-A.2 (a), Box 11, Series 5, MEM/CM Collection.

342 relating her dreams: CM to MEM, February 3, 1958, Folder 8A-20, Box 27, Series 8, MEM/CM Collection.

343 she was at the outset: Therapy tape 2, April 14, 1958 Folder 5-A.2 (a), Box 11, Series 5, MEM/CM Collection.

343 she believed: CM to MEM, February 6, 1959, Folder 8A-20, Box 27, Series 8, MEM/CM Collection.

344 a constant fear: CM to MEM, February 9, 1959, Folder 8-A21, Box 27, Series 8, MEM/CM Collection.

344 "Honey," "Darling": See John Dalmas, *Rockland County Sunday Journal-News,* August 10, 1975.

345 to which Carson responded: CM to MEM, April 2, 1958, Folder 6, Box 40, CM Collection, HRC.

345 Carson had hopes: CM to MEM, February 6, 1959, Folder 8A-20, Box 27, Series 8, MEM/CM Collection.

345 "Then you had the inspiration": Robbie Lantz to MEM, quoted in Savigneau, *Carson McCullers,* 271.

346 "You are too wise": MEM to Robbie Lantz, March 6, 1970, unsent, Box 27, Series 6, MEM/CM Collection.

346 a lighter, humorous side: Therapy tape 1, April 11, 1958, Folder 5-A.1 (a), Box 11, Series 5, MEM/CM Collection.

346 word got out: MEM, May 1995 interview, quoted in Savigneau, *Carson McCullers,* 272.

346 contacted Carson: Harold Hayes to CM, August 7, 1958, Tape 22, Box 1, Series 5, MSS Papers.

347 celebrity murder: Therapy tape 1, April 11, 1958, Folder 5-A.1 (a), Box 11, Series 5, MEM/CM Collection.

19. THAT GREEN AND GLOWING SPRING

349 She was once again: CM to MEM, April 2, 1958, Folder 8-A, Box 27, Series 8, MEM/CM Collection. The copy of the letter at HRC, Mary Mercer's copy, is initialed "M.E.M." and dated April 4, 1958.

349 ninety longhand pages: RM to Hardwick Moseley, May 19, 1950, HM Papers.

349 this new novel: CM to Hardwick Moseley, c. 1950, HM Papers.

350 "One could walk": Ray Trussell quoted in Carr, *The Lonely Hunter,* 468.

350 she worked on her novel: CM to MEM, February 6, 1959, Folder 8A-20, Box 27, Series 8, MEM/CM Collection.

350 Carson's 1958 therapy sessions: There are nine transcripts, numbered 1 through 10, but transcript 4 never existed. Transcript 9 is severely truncated, and some sessions break off suddenly. Each is dated.

351 long risqué story: Therapy tape 5, April 25, 1958, Folder 5-A.5 (a), Box 11, Series 5, MEM/CM Collection.

352 the harrowing story: Therapy tape 6, April 28, 1958, Folder 5-A.6 (a), Box 11, Series 5, MEM/CM Collection.

352 "There are the threads": Therapy tape 6, April 28, 1958, Folder 5-A.6 (a), Box 11, Series 5, MEM/CM Collection.

352 "You had to act": Therapy tape 8, May 9, 1958, Folder 5-A.8 (a), Box 11, Series 5, MEM/CM Collection.

352 "That is what": Therapy tape 5, April 25, 1958, Folder 5-A.5 (a), Box 11, Series 5, MEM/CM Collection.

353 "And when you really": Therapy tape 10, May 16, 1958, Folder 5-A.10 (a), Box 11, Series 5, MEM/CM Collection. The context is of Carson's last session, so perhaps the excitement is understandable.

353 she was embracing: CM to MEM, June 30, 1958, Folder 8-A.3, Box 27, Series 8, MEM/CM Collection.

353 that "green and glowing" spring: CM to MEM, February 6, 1959, Folder 8A-20, Box 27, Series 8, MEM/CM Collection.

354 "so much more sophisticated": MEM, interview 2 by MSS, c. 1977, Folder 15, Box 3, MSS Papers.

355 to cut down: CM to MEM, July 11, 1958, Folder 8-A.4, Box 27, Series 7, MEM/CM Collection.

355 She got up with the sun: CM to MEM, July 11, 1958, Folder 8-A.13, Box 27, Series 8, MEM/CM Collection.

356 "Mary was a very organized": Quoted in Savigneau, *Carson McCullers,* 282.

357 how difficult the task seemed: Quoted in Carr, *The Lonely Hunter,* 470.

357 "occasional waywardness": Thomas Lask, *New York Times,* May 4, 1958.

357 This compromise: CM to MEM, July 20, 1958, Folder 8-A.10, Box 27, Series 8, MEM/CM Collection.

357 "talking about nothing": Feibleman, *Lilly,* 52.

358 "incensed": MEM to CM, August 1958, Folder 8-A.17, Box 27, Series 8, MEM/CM Collection.

358 "incredible disorder": Unidentified observer quoted in Carr, *The Lonely Hunter,* 462.

359 "looking down": Williams, *Letters to Donald Windham,* 292n1.

359 Carson sprang: CM to MEM, July 24, 1958, Folder 8-A.12, Box 27, Series 8, MEM/CM Collection.

361 "I am an old woman": Quoted in Thurman, *Isak Dinesen,* 267.

361 "she radiates": Quoted ibid., 468.

361 it had all gone: CM to MEM, February 10, 1959, Folder 8-A.22, Box 27, Series 8, MEM/CM Collection.

362 She didn't know what: CM to MEM, February 9, 1959, Folder 8-A.21, Box 27, Series 8, MEM/CM Collection.

20. INSATIABILITY FOR LIVING

363 "Carson McCullers Completes": Nona Balakian, "Carson McCullers Completes New Novel Despite Adversity," *New York Times,* September 3, 1961.

364 "protective angel": Tippins, *February House,* 224.

364 sign of life: CM to MEM, February 13, 1960, Folder 8-A.37, Box 27, Series 6, MEM/CM Collection.

364 "bogged down": MEM to Marielle Bancou, April 3, 1960, Folder 6–6.1, Box 27, Series 6, MEM/CM Collection.

365 she drew two hearts: CM to Paul Brooks, February 28, 1951, HM Papers.

365   "which, no matter": Robert Lantz to Hardwick Moseley, October 12, 1960, HM Papers.

365   old stories to group: MEM to Marielle Bancou, April 5, 1960, Folder 6–6.1, Box 16, MEM/CM Collection.

366   "I think the climate": Lovell Thompson to Hoyt, Fenellosa, and French, November 4, 1960, HM Papers. Philip Roth returned to Houghton Mifflin.

366   "major novel": "DdeS," reader's report, November 3, 1960, HM Papers.

367   "Uncle Jack and": Jordan Massee, Sr., to "My dear Watson," July 20, 1961, JM/CM Collection, CSU. Jordan Jr. said he and his father had "the most violent argument we had ever had" over the book.

367   "any more criticism": JM, interview 2 by VSC, July 26, 1971, Folder 21, Box 5, VSC Papers, DU.

368   from ten-fifteen: JM, "From the 1961 Journals of JM," February 11, JM/CM Collection, CSU.

368   new book about Lizzie Borden: HM, "From the 1961 Journals of JM," February 21, 1961, JM/CM Collection, CSU. Unfortunately, Carson never publicly commented on the Lizzie Borden case.

368   "the first bound copies": Rita Smith to Floria Lasky, n.d., Folder 4, Box 44, CM Collection, HRC.

368   Jordan made clear: JM, "From the 1961 Journals of JM," February 11, February 22, and June 23, 1961, JM/CM Collection, CSU.

369   "She is very lonely": Joyce Hartman to Craig Wylie and Paul Brooks, July 14, 1961, HM Papers.

370   "masterly": Charles Rolo, "A Southern Drama," *Atlantic*, October 1961.

370   "written a perfect": Dorothy Parker, *Esquire*, December 1961.

370   "the novelist mechanically": Irving Howe, *NYTBR*, October 17, 1961.

370   "a novel without direction": *Time*, September 22, 1961, quoted in Savigneau, *Carson McCullers,* 293.

371   "rumpled": Whitney Balliett, *New Yorker,* September 23, 1961.

371   "Fifteen minutes": JM, interview by VSC, July 27, 1971, Folder 21, Box 5, VSC Papers, DU.

371   "Her genius": Gore Vidal, *Times Literary Supplement*, October 20, 1961.

371   "a marvel of a novel": *New York Herald Tribune,* September 27, 1961.

372   "There was never": JM, interview 2 by VSC, July 26, 1971, Folder 21, Box 5, VSC Papers, DU.

373   "delighted": MEM, interview by MSS, n.d., Cassette 10, Box 1, Series 5, MSS Papers. An undated filmed interview of Carson on board ship shows her smoking a cigarette and clearly not inhaling. Of course, it is possible (if unlikely) that she took up inhaling in later years. See "Shipboard Reporter" with Jack Mangan, https://www.youtube.com/watch?v=xkDY_NPbkRs.

373   "with a corps of people": MEM to MST, c. June 1, 1962, MEM Collection of CM/MST Correspondence, 1959–1976, DU.

374   amateurish: Carr, *The Lonely Hunter,* 523–24. See also Mary Rodgers and Jesse Green, *Shy: The Alarming Outspoken Memoirs of Mary Rodgers* (New York: Farrar, Straus & Giroux, 2022). Rodgers is very unkind, describing Carson as "a mess," with "scrambled teeth and short, greasy hair," who received Rodgers in bed, drinking from a glass of Maker's Mark.

374 "a marvelous": CM to MST, February 6, 1966, MEM Collection of CM/MST Correspondence, 1959–1976, DU.

374 "It would be simply awful": Quoted in Russo and Merlin, *Troubles in a Golden Eye,* 133. A copy of this play exists, which was called "A Musical Adaptation of Carson McCullers' *The Member of the Wedding,* book by G. Wood and Theodore Mann, Music and lyrics by G. Wood." A draft of a telegram to G. Wood, signed by Rita Smith, indicates that Rita was involved in the effort, as does the fact that Rita sent the play as part of the archive of Carson's papers that she held. Frankie and John Henry sing a duet called "The We of Me." Folder 1, Box 42, CM Collection, HRC.

374 "for the simple reason": Quoted in Gussow, *Edward Albee,* 195.

375 "I have a feeling": Quoted ibid.

376 "the sun": Quoted ibid.

376 "I wouldn't like": Quoted ibid., 196.

376 sent her a kiss: CM to MST, May 11, 1952, MST Papers.

377 "Carson as unstrung": MEM to MST, c. May 11, 1962, MEM Collection of CM/MST Correspondence, 1959–1976, DU.

377 "I don't like people": MEM, interviews by MSS, February 2, June 30, July 1, 1962, Folder 15, Box 3, MSS Papers.

377 "a bad jolt": MEM to MST, June 1, 1962, MEM Collection of CM/MST Correspondence, 1959–1976, DU.

378 "the looks of Carson": JM, interview by VSC, July 25, 1971, p. 6, Folder 21, Box 5, VSC Papers, DU.

378 "How indescribably frail": JM, Notes, June 13, 1962, Folder 1, Box 1, JM/CM Collection.

378 "my daughter": Carr, *The Lonely Hunter,* 517.

378 "I have more to say": Quoted ibid., 464.

379 "like trojans": MEM to MST, c. June 1962, MEM Collection of CM/MST Correspondence, 1959–1976, DU.

379 "she can use it": MEM, June 16, 1962, MEM Collection of CM/MST Correspondence, 1959–1976, DU.

380 "perennial adolescent": Quoted in Garnett, *Great Friends,* 233.

381 "Queen of England": Marielle Bancou, YouTube interview, January 8, 2008.

381 Carson faded fast: Joanna Gomme to MEM, October 5, 1962, Folder 1-W, pp. 3–6, MEM/CM Collection.

381 "as happy as": Garnett, *Great Friends,* 234.

382 "charming and courteous": Quoted in Zachary Leader, *The Life of Kingsley Amis* (New York: Pantheon, 2007), 485–86.

382 "a great deal": Quoted in Carr, *The Lonely Hunter,* 518.

382 "largely because she was": "Edith Sitwell," Poetry Foundation, https://www.poetry foundation.org/poets/edith-sitwell.

383 "Carson's illnesses": ES to Maurice Bowra, December 17, 1962, in Greene, *Selected Letters of Edith Sitwell,* 451.

21. THE SAD, HAPPY LIFE OF CARSON MCCULLERS

384 "The Dark Brilliance": Quoted in Carr, *The Lonely Hunter,* 502.

384 "Both Child and Sage": Ibid.

384 "to turn all of that": Edward Albee, interview by Digby Diehl, *Transatlantic Review,* no. 13 (Summer 1963): 57–72.

385 "haunting": John McLain, "Albee's 'Ballad' Sings Rugged Drama of Love," *New York Journal American,* October 31, 1963.

385 "the essential atmosphere": Howard Taubman, " 'The Ballad of the Sad Café': Albee's Adaptation of Novella Presented," *New York Times,* October 31, 1963.

385 "our inevitable detachment": Walter Kerr, *New York Herald Tribune,* October 31, 1960.

387 struggling with her AA program: CM to MEM, February 8, 1960, Folder 8-A.33, Box 27, Series 8, MEM/CM Collection. Carson refers to a rehab program that Rita could go to, planning to recommend High Watch.

387 "with letters back": Lamar Smith, Jr., to Rita Smith, June 28, 1961, Folder 3, Box 43, CM Collection, HRC.

388 "It was the first time": Mary McNamara and Booth More, "A Model of Style and Substance," *Orlando Sentinel,* October 17, 2001, https://www.orlandosentinel.com /news/os-xpm-2001-10-17-0110160315-story.html.

388 "Sistah has ruined": Daugherty, *Last Love Song,* 69.

389 More medical trouble: MEM to Rita Smith, July 6, 1990, Folder 6, Box 29, CM Collection, HRC.

389 quantities of Kleenex: JM, interview 2 by VSC, July 26, 1971, Folder 21, Box 5, VSC Papers, DU.

389 Mary's notes about alcohol: MEM, "Notes for Hospitalization," c. 1962, Folder 6-A.3, Box 13, Series 6, MEM/CM Collection.

392 Jordan later said: JM, interview 1 by VSC, July 25, 1971, Folder 21, Box 5, VSC Papers, DU.

392 "Fires burning day": MEM to CM, c. 1962, Folder 6, Box 28, MEM/CM Collection.

392 "Carson was not a religious": MEM, interview by MSS, n.d., Cassette 10, Box 1, Series 5, MSS Papers.

392 "I know you promised": MEM to CM, n.d., Folder 6, Box 28, CM Collection, HRC.

392 kissed Mary's small foot: CM to MEM, August 30, 1966, Folder 8-A.46, Box 27, MEM/CM Collection.

393 "fairly steady": MST to MSS, September 10, 1971, Folder 7, Box 4, Series 1, MSS Papers.

393 handwritten account for 1960: MST to MSS, September 12, 1971, Folder 7, Box 4, Series 1, MSS Papers.

393 letter from Robbie Lantz: Robbie Lantz to CM, August 11, 1967, Folder 6, Box 27, CM Collection, HRC.

393 "may seem slight": Walter Gibson quoted in Carr, *The Lonely Hunter,* 521.

394 "The sky is higher": McCullers, *Sweet as a Pickle and Clean as a Pig,* 10.

396 "Lantz announced": Joyce Hartman, internal Houghton Mifflin memo, March 16, 1967, HM Papers.

396 "I think I'm homosexual": Bob Pace to MSS, April 29, 1977, Folder 20, Box 3, Series 1, MSS Papers.

397 When Tom McCullers was stationed: JM writes about the Diamond/McCullers incident in his entry for March 25, 1949, in his journals, Folder 21, Box 1, JM/CM Collection.

397 like a pig: CM to MST, October 31, 1965, Box 1, MST Papers.

398 "Tenn, honey": JM, interview 1 by VSC, July 24, 1971, Folder 21, Box 5, VSC Papers, DU.

398 "tangible-intangible": MEM, interviews by MSS, June 30 and July 2, 1973, Folder 8-A.46, Box 27, MSS Papers.

399 "a horrible year": JM, "From the 1965 Journal of Jordan Massee," Folder 65, Box 2, JM/CM Collection.

399 "Carson is the same": MEM to MST, September 2, 1965, MST Papers.

399 "I remember her as": Huston, *Open Book,* 330.

399 "very touching": Ibid., 331.

400 "Search your mind": John Huston to CM, n.d., Folder 1, Box 27, CM Collection, HRC.

400 "And what a cast!": Reed, *People Are Crazy Here,* 41.

400 "a hothouse tale": Terrence Rafferty, "*Reflections in a Golden Eye*: A 'Hothouse Tale' of Desire and Simmering Violence," Library of America, February 8, 2017, https:// www.loa.org/news-and-views/1245-_reflections-in-a-golden-eye_-a-hothouse-tale -of-desire-and-simmering-violence.

401 "desire to get out": Marlon Brando to CM, Cassette 11, Box 22, Series 5, MSS Papers.

401 "it looked like": Reed, *People Are Crazy Here,* 41.

401 Mary took Huston: MEM to John Huston and Gladys Hill, January 26, 1967, Folder 17, Box 2, Series 2, CD Collection. These are photocopies of letters in VSC Papers, DU.

401 "giggling like": Reed, *People Are Crazy Here,* 40.

402 "Carson was adorable": Huston, *Open Book,* 334.

403 "I know the trip": Ibid., 335.

403 "more dead than alive": MST to MSS, August 28, 1967, Folder 2, Box 4, MSS Papers.

403 even the thought: Gladys Hill to MEM, April 17, 1967, Folder 1-P, Box 4, MEM/ CM Collection.

403 "perilous journey": Stuart Sherman, "Carson McCullers," *BOMB,* October 1, 1990, https://bombmagazine.org/articles/carson-mccullers/.

405 "stupid but a genius": Ibid.

408 "Every day she wrote": Ibid.

408 "Raggedy Ann grin": Reed, *People Are Crazy Here,* 42.

408 "So we moved her": MEM, interview by MSS, n.d., Cassette 10, Box 2, Series 5, MSS Papers.

EPILOGUE

411 Jordan Massee was left out: The heirs paid him the $1,000 she had originally left for him. Floria Lasky to MEM, October 11, 1967, Folder 6-C, 1.1, Box 14, MEM/CM Collection.

412 "SELL THE PAPERS": Rita Smith to Floria Lasky and Robbie Lantz, November 12, 1972, Folder 4, Box 44, CM Collection, HRC.

413 her 1958 therapy sessions: See Carlos Dews, " 'Impromptu Journal of My Heart': Carson McCullers' Therapeutic Recordings, April–May 1958," in Alison Graham-

Bertolini and Casey Kayser, eds., *Carson McCullers in the Twenty-First Century* (New York: Palgrave Macmillan, 2016).

414   "eclectic band of misfits": "Your Guide to *The Heart Is a Lonely Hunter*," Oprah .com, April 21, 2004, https://www.oprah.com/oprahsbookclub/the-heart-is-a-lonely -hunter-by-carson-mccullers_1/all.

415   "exactly as I saw them": Russo and Merlin, *Troubles in a Golden Eye,* 90.

415   "exactly how right he is": Ibid., 107; Terrence Rafferty, "*Reflections in a Golden Eye*: A 'Hothouse Tale' of Desire and Simmering Violence," Library of America, February 8, 2017, https://loa.org/news-and-views/1245-_reflections-in-a-golden-eye_-a -hothouse-tale-of-desire-and-simmering-violence.

416   "She wrote from within a body": Patricia Lockwood, "Aviators and Movie Stars" (review of the Library of America edition of McCullers), *London Review of Books,* October 19, 2017, 7.

416   "each defines the status quo": Hilton Als, "Unhappy Endings," *New Yorker,* December 3, 2001.

417   "Playing in the Dark": Toni Morrison, *Playing in the Dark: Whiteness and the Literary Imagination* (New York: Vintage, 1993).

417   she would be a transgender man: Sarah Schulman, "White Writer," *New Yorker,* October 21, 2016. Schulman brings up Carson's statement to Capote about being born a boy. She also suggests that if Carson were alive today, she would be in AA and on antidepressants.

419   "a lonely hunter": The title *The Heart Is a Lonely Hunter* is from an 1896 poem by Fiona Macleod, another name for the Scottish poet William Sharp, a pseudonym revealed after his death, an obvious irony in this context.

Bibliography

Abbott, Karen. *American Rose: A Nation Laid Bare: The Life and Times of Gypsy Rose Lee.* New York: Random House, 2010.

Auden, W. H. *"In Solitude, for Company": W. H. Auden After 1940: Unpublished Prose and Recent Criticism.* Edited by Katherine Bucknell and Nicholas Jenkins. New York: Oxford University Press, 1995.

Bain, David Haward, and Mary Smyth Duffy, eds. *Whose Woods These Are: A History of the Breadloaf Writers' Conference, 1926–1992.* Hopewell, N.J.: Ecco, 1993.

Barranger, Milly S. *A Gambler's Instinct: The Story of Broadway Producer Cheryl Crawford.* Carbondale: Southern Illinois University Press, 2010.

Black, Robert W. *The Battalion: The Dramatic Story of the 2nd Ranger Battalion in World War II.* Mechanicsburg, Penn.: Stackpole Books, 2006.

Bloom, Harold, ed. *Carson McCullers: Modern Critical Views.* New York: Chelsea House, 1986.

Bogle, Donald. *Heat Wave: The Life and Career of Ethel Waters.* New York: HarperCollins, 2011.

Britten, Benjamin. *Letters from a Life: Selected Letters and Diaries of Benjamin Britten, 1913–1976,* vol. 2, *1939–1945.* Edited by Donald Mitchell and Philip Reed. Berkeley: University of California Press, 1991.

Calisher, Hortense. *Herself.* New York: Arbor House, 1972.

Capote, Truman. *The Grass Harp.* 1951. Reprint, New York: Vintage, 2012.

———. *Too Brief a Treat: The Letters of Truman Capote.* Edited by Gerald Clarke. New York: Vintage, 2004.

Carpenter, Humphrey. *W. H. Auden: A Biography.* Boston: Houghton Mifflin, 1981.

Carr, Virginia Spencer. *The Lonely Hunter: A Biography of Carson McCullers.* New York: Doubleday, 1975.

———. *Understanding Carson McCullers.* Columbia: University of South Carolina Press, 1990.

Chauncey, George. *Gay New York: Gender, Urban Culture, and the Making of the Gay Male World.* New York: Basic Books, 1994.

Clark, Beverly Lyon, and Melvin J. Friedman. *Critical Essays of Carson McCullers*. New York: G. K. Hall, 1996.

Clarke, Gerald. *Capote: A Biography*. New York: Simon & Schuster, 1988.

Clurman, Harold. *All People Are Famous (Instead of an Autobiography)*. New York: Harcourt Brace Jovanovich, 1974.

———. *Lies Like Truth: Theatre Reviews and Essays*. New York: Grove, 1960.

Cook, Richard M. *Carson McCullers*. New York: Frederick Ungar, 1975.

Craig, Patricia. *Elizabeth Bowen*. Lives of Modern Women Series. New York: Penguin, 1986.

Crawford, Cheryl. *One Naked Individual: My Fifty Years in the Theatre*. Indianapolis: Bobbs-Merrill, 1977.

Curtis, Cathy. *Splendid Intelligence: The Life of Elizabeth Hardwick*. New York: W.W. Norton, 2022.

Daugherty, Tracey. *The Last Love Song: A Biography of Joan Didion*. New York: St. Martin's Press, 2015.

DeLong, Thomas A. *Madame Chiang Kai-Shek and Miss Emma Mills: China's First Lady and Her American Friend*. Jefferson, N.C.: McFarland, 2007.

Dillon, Millicent. *A Little Original Sin: The Life and Works of Jane Bowles*. New York: Holt, Rinehart, and Winston, 1981.

Eller, Jonathan R., ed. *Becoming Ray Bradbury*. Urbana: University of Illinois Press, 2011.

Ellis, Havelock. *My Life*. London: Heinemann, 1940.

Evans, Oliver. *The Ballad of Carson McCullers: A Biography*. New York: Coward-McCann, 1966.

Faderman, Lillian. *Odd Girls and Twilight Lovers: A History of Lesbian Life in Twentieth-Century America*. New York: Columbia University Press, 1991.

———. *Surpassing the Love of Men: Romantic Friendship and Love Between Women from the Renaissance to the Present*. New York: William Morrow, 1981.

Fahy, Thomas. " 'Some Unheard-of Thing': Freaks, Families and Coming of Age in *The Member of the Wedding*." In *Peering Behind the Curtain: Disability, Illness, and the Extraordinary Body in Contemporary Theatre*. Edited by Kimball King and Tom Fahy. New York: Routledge, 2002, 68–83.

Feibleman, Peter. *Lilly: Reminiscences of Lillian Hellman*. New York: William Morrow, 1988.

Flanner, Janet. *Darlinghissima: Letters to a Friend*. Edited by Natalia Danesi Murray. New York: Random House, 1985.

Foley, Martha. *The Story of STORY Magazine: A Memoir by Martha Foley*. Edited by Jay Neugenboren. New York: W. W. Norton, 1980.

Frankel, Noralee. *Stripping Gypsy: The Life of Gypsy Rose Lee*. New York: Oxford University Press, 2009.

Garnett, David. *Great Friends: Portraits of Seventeen Writers*. New York: Atheneum, 1980.

Givner, Joan. *Katherine Anne Porter: A Life*. New York: Simon & Schuster, 1982.

Gladney, Margaret Rose, ed. *How Am I to Be Heard?: Letters of Lillian Smith*. Chapel Hill: University of North Carolina Press, 1993.

Glendinning, Victoria. *Elizabeth Bowen: A Biography*. New York: Alfred A. Knopf, 1977.

Goldstein, Lee Nathalie. "The Art of Fiction: A Study of Carson McCullers." Master's thesis, American University, 1963.

Goyen, William. *Goyen: Autobiographical Essays, Notebooks, Evocations, Interviews*. Edited by Reginald Gibbons. Austin: University of Texas Press, 2007.

Graver, Lawrence. *An Obsession with Anne Frank: Meyer Levin and the Diary*. Berkeley: University of California Press, 1997.

Greene, Richard. *Edith Sitwell: Avant Garde Poet, English Genius*. London: Virago, 2011.

———. *Selected Letters of Edith Sitwell*. London: Virago, 1997.

Grosskurth, Phyllis. *Havelock Ellis: A Biography*. New York: Alfred A. Knopf, 1980.

Gussow, Mel. *Edward Albee: A Singular Journey*. New York: Simon & Schuster, 1999.

Hamilton, Ian. *Robert Lowell: A Biography*. New York: Random House, 1982.

Hastings, Selina. *Rosamond Lehman: A Life*. New York: Random House, 2012.

Hulbert, Ann. *The Interior Castle: The Art and Life of Jean Stafford*. New York: Alfred A. Knopf, 1992.

Huston, John. *An Open Book*. New York: Alfred A. Knopf, 1980.

Isherwood, Christopher. *Christopher and His Kind: 1929–1939*. New York: Farrar, Straus & Giroux, 1976.

———. *Diaries*. Edited by Katherine Bucknell. New York: HarperCollins, 1996.

James, Judith Giblin. *Wunderkind: The Reputation of Carson McCullers, 1940–1990*. Columbus, S.C.: Camden House, 1995.

Kazin, Alfred. *Alfred Kazin's Journals*. Edited by Richard M. Cook. New Haven, Conn.: Yale University Press, 2011.

Kildea, Paul. *Benjamin Britten: A Life in the Twentieth Century*. New York: Penguin, 2013.

Kimberling, Victoria J. *David Diamond: A Bio-Bibliography*. Metuchen, N.J.: Scarecrow Press, 1987.

King, Michael J. *Rangers: Selected Combat Operations in World War II*. Fort Leavenworth, Kans.: Combat Studies Institute, U.S. Army Command and General Staff College, 1985.

Lahr, John. *Tennessee Williams: Mad Pilgrimage of the Flesh*. New York: W. W. Norton, 2014.

Laurence, Patricia. *Elizabeth Bowen: A Literary Life*. London: Palgrave Macmillan, 2019.

Lehman, Beatrix. *Rumour of Heaven*. 1934. Reprint, London: Virago, 1987.

Lerman, Leo. *The Grand Surprise: The Journals of Leo Lerman*. Edited by Stephen Pascal. New York: Alfred A. Knopf, 2007.

MacNeice, Louis. *The Strings Are False: An Unfinished Autobiography*. 1965. Reprint, London: Faber and Faber, 1982.

Madsen, Axel. *The Sewing Circle: Sappho's Leading Ladies*. New York: Kensington Books, 2002.

Mann, Klaus. *The Turning Point: Thirty-Five Years in This Century*. New York: L. B. Fischer, 1942.

Mariani, Paul. *Lost Puritan: A Life of Robert Lowell*. New York: W. W. Norton, 1994.

Marrs, Suzanne. *Eudora Welty: A Biography*. New York: Harcourt, 2005.

Massee, Jordan. *Accepted Fables*. [N.p.]: Indigo Publishing, 2005.

Matthau, Carol. *Among the Porcupines: A Memoir*. New York: Random House, 1992.

Maxwell, Gilbert. *Tennessee Williams and Friends*. Cleveland: World Publishing, 1965.

McDowell, Margaret B. *Carson McCullers*. Boston: G. K. Hall, 1980.

McGee, Micki, ed. *Yaddo: Making American Culture*. New York: Columbia University Press, 2008.

McGill, Ralph. *The South and the Southerner*. 1959. Reprint, New York: Atlantic Monthly Press, 1963.

Meaker, Marijane. *Highsmith: A Romance of the 1950s*. San Francisco: Cleis Press, 2003.

Mellen, Joan. *Kay Boyle, Author of Herself*. New York: Farrar, Straus & Giroux, 1994.

Melnick, Ralph. *The Stolen Legacy of Anne Frank: Meyer Levin, Lillian Hellman, and the Staging of the Diary.* New Haven, Conn.: Yale University Press, 1997.

Oja, Carol J. *Colin McPhee: Composer in Two Worlds.* Washington, D.C.: Smithsonian, 1990.

Peters, Margot. *May Sarton: A Biography.* New York: Alfred A. Knopf, 1997.

Plagemann, Bentz. *An American Past: An Early Autobiography.* New York: William Morrow, 1990.

Plimpton, George, ed. *Truman Capote: In Which Various Friends, Enemies, Acquaintances, and Detractors Recall His Turbulent Career.* New York: Doubleday, 1997.

Powell, Neil. *Benjamin Britten: A Life for Music.* New York: Henry Holt, 2013.

Prater, Donald. *Thomas Mann: A Life.* New York: Oxford University Press, 1995.

Presley, Delma Eugene. "Carson McCullers and the South." *Georgia Review* (Spring 1974).

Rampersad, Arnold. *The Life of Langston Hughes, 1914–1967.* Vol. 2. New York: Oxford University Press, 1988.

Rampersad, Arnold, and David Roessel, eds. *The Selected Letters of Langston Hughes.* New York: Alfred A. Knopf, 2015.

Reed, Rex. *Do You Sleep in the Nude?* New York: Dutton, 1968.

———. *People Are Crazy Here.* New York: Delacorte Press, 1974.

Rowley, Hazel. *Richard Wright: The Life and Times.* New York: Henry Holt, 2001.

Russo, William, and Jan Merlin. *Troubles in a Golden Eye: Starring Taylor and Brando with John Huston.* Xlibris, 2005.

Sarton, May. "Elizabeth Bowen." In *A World of Light: Portraits and Celebrations.* New York: W. W. Norton, 1976.

Savigneau, Josyane. *Carson McCullers: A Life.* Translated by Joan E. Howard. Boston: Houghton Mifflin, 2001.

Schanke, Robert A., and Kim Marra. *Passing Performances: Queer Readings of Leading Players in American Theater History.* Ann Arbor: University of Michigan Press, 1998.

Schenkar, Joan. *The Talented Miss Highsmith: The Secret Life and Serious Art of Patricia Highsmith.* New York: St. Martin's Press, 2009.

Sears, James T. *Edwin and John: A Personal History of the Old South.* New York: Routledge, 2009.

———. *Lonely Hunters: An Oral History of Lesbian and Gay Southern Life, 1948–1968.* New York: Westview Press, 1997.

Simmonds, Roy S. *The Two Worlds of William March.* Tuscaloosa: University of Alabama Press, 2011.

Sitwell, Edith. *Taken Care Of: The Autobiography of Edith Sitwell.* New York: Atheneum, 1965.

Spanier, Sandra, ed. *Kay Boyle: A Twentieth-Century Life in Letters.* Urbana: University of Illinois Press, 2015.

Spoto, Donald. *The Kindness of Strangers: The Life of Tennessee Williams.* 1985. Reprint, New York: Da Capo Press, 1997.

———. *Lenya: A Life.* Boston: Little, Brown, 1989.

Spotts, Frederic. *Cursed Legacy: The Tragic Life of Klaus Mann.* New Haven, Conn.: Yale University Press, 2016.

Stelpflug, Peggy, and Richard Hyatt. *Home of the Infantry: The History of Fort Benning.* Macon, Ga.: Mercer University Press, 2007.

Strandberg, Victor. "*In a Farther Country*: The Goyen-McCullers Freak Show." In *A Goyen*

Companion: Appreciations of a Writer's Writer, edited by Brook Horvath, Irving Malin, and Paul Ruffin. Austin: University of Texas Press, 1997.

Sullivan, Margaret Sue. "Carson McCullers, 1917–1947: The Conversion of Experience." PhD diss., DU, 1966, in Folder 18, Box 1, Series 3, MSS Papers.

Thurman, Judith. *Isak Dinesen: The Legend of a Storyteller.* 1982. Reprint, New York: St. Martin's Press, 1982.

Tippins, Sherill. *February House.* Boston: Houghton Mifflin, 2005.

Unrue, Darlene Harbour. *Katherine Anne Porter: The Life of an Artist.* Jackson: University Press of Mississippi, 2005.

Voss, Ralph F. *A Life of William Inge: The Strains of Triumph.* Lawrence: University Press of Kansas, 1989.

Waldron, Ann. *Eudora: A Writer's Life.* New York: Doubleday, 1998.

Walter, Eugene, as told to Katharine Clark. *Milking the Moon: A Southerner's Guide to Life on This Planet.* New York: Crown, 2001.

Ware, Louise. *George Foster Peabody: Banker, Philanthropist, Publicist.* Athens: University of Georgia Press, 1951.

Waters, Ethel, with Charles Samuels. *His Eye Is on the Sparrow: An Autobiography.* 1950. Reprint, New York: Da Capo Press, 1992.

Webb, Constance. *Richard Wright.* New York: G. P. Putnam's, 1968.

Weiss, Andrea. *In the Shadow of the Magic Mountain: The Erika and Klaus Mann Story.* Chicago: University of Chicago Press, 2008.

Werth, Barry. *The Scarlet Professor: Newton Arvin: A Literary Life Shattered by Scandal.* New York: Doubleday, 2001.

Williams, Tennessee. *Five O'Clock Angel: Letters of Tennessee Williams to Maria St. Just, 1948–1982.* Edited by Maria St. Just. New York: Alfred A. Knopf, 1990.

——. *Memoirs.* Garden City, N.Y.: Doubleday, 1972.

——. *The Selected Letters of Tennessee Williams.* Edited by Albert Devlin and Nancy Tischler. 2 vols. New York: New Directions, 2004.

——. *Tennessee Williams' Letters to Donald Windham, 1940–1965.* Edited by Donald Windham. New York: Holt, Rinehart and Winston, 1977.

Wilson, Andrew. *Beautiful Shadow: A Life of Patricia Highsmith.* New York: Bloomsbury, 2003.

Windham, Donald. *Lost Friendships: A Memoir of Truman Capote, Tennessee Williams, and Others.* 1987. Reprint, New York: Paragon, 1989.

Wineapple, Brenda. *Genêt: A Biography of Janet Flanner.* Lincoln: University of Nebraska Press, 1989.

Index

AA. *See* Alcoholics Anonymous
Adams, John Vincent, 53, *59,* 65–7, 73, 82, 93–4
Adler, Stella, 226
"After great pain a formal feeling comes" (Dickinson), 362
Albee, Edward, 374–6, *375,* 379, 384–6
Alcoholics Anonymous (AA), 59, 205, 222, 224–5, 244–5, 253, 276, 315, 387, 418
alcoholism, 51
  DTs and, 204–5, 391
  enabling of, 222–4, 315–6, 372–3
  of McCullers, Carson, 8, 58–60, 71, 95–6, 155, 184, 198–9, 202–3, 221–2, 239, 245, 253–9, 261, 269, 272–3, 276, 281, 287–93, 298–9, 307, 309, 312–5, 320, 323, 331, 339, 347, 355, 372–3, 382, 389–90, 391, 398, 401
  of McCullers, Reeves, 6, 8, 52, 58–60, 71, 93, 127, 155–6, 164, 198–9, 202–4, 220, 224–5, 241, 244, 253–6, 267, 272–3, 276–7, 279, 287–93, 295, 297, 302, 315
  in McCullers's ancestry, 10, 14, 15, 23–4, 58–9, 222–3
  as theme in literary work, 4, 75, 329–30
Allen, Karen, 415
Allied Military Government for Occupied Territories (AMG), 164, 177–8
Als, Hilton, 416–7

Altman, Dara, 393, 411
Altman, Emily, 393, 411
American Academy of Arts and Letters, 158, 332, 359
American Hospital, Neuilly, France, 201–2, 203, 277, 281, 291, 294
American Legion Cemetery, Neuilly-sur-Seine, France, 299, 303
American Psychiatric Association, 212
Ames, Elizabeth, 122, 129–30, 137–8, 140, 142, 147–8, 153–4, 156–7, 177, 179–80, 194, 199, 270, 309–10, 315, 337
  Communist scare and, 219–20
Amis, Kingsley, 380, 382
Anderson, Maxwell, 98, 140, 308
Anderson, Sherwood, 4
Antabuse, 277, 279, 297
anti-Semitism, 160–1
Antonio, Lou, 385
Arkin, Alan, 415
Army Rangers, 154, 155, 166–7, 351
"Art and Mr. Mahoney" (McCullers), 217
Arvin, Newton, 123, 126, *128,* 128–9, 131–3, 135–7, 139, 146, 152, 154, 158, 161, 172, 177, 178, 194, 211, 272, 302, 311, 316
Askew, Kirk, 120
Aston, Frank, 336
Atkinson, Brooks, 231–2, 411
The Atlantic, 76, 370
Auchincloss, Hugh, 379

Auden, Wystan H., 86, 88–9, 96, 99, *101*, 113, 268, 411
   Seven Middagh residence of, 7, 100–5, 108, 146–7, 156, 351
Austen, Jane, 381

The Bad Seed (March), 308
Balakian, Nona, 370
The Ballad of the Sad Café (McCullers), 372
   anti-Semitism alleged in, 160–1
   book cover of, *159*
   musical adaptation of, 308, 315
   publication of, 159–61, 184, 235–6
   reviews/reception of, 160–1, 197–8
   themes/characters of, 7, 33, 70, 116, 159–61, 385–6, 407, 416
   writing of, 116, 123, 158, 313
The Ballad of the Sad Café (play), 350
   actors in, 385
   director of, 385
   reviews/reception of, 385–7
   themes of, 385–6
   writing of script for, 284, 374–6, 379, 384–5
Bancou, Marielle, 343, 356, 360, 364–5, 380–1, 411
Bates, Sylvia Chatfield, 48, 61–3, 75–6
Baudelaire, Charles, 41, 57, 218, 346
Baxter, Anne, 326, 334–5, 337–8
Bay, André, 198–9
Beaton, Cecil, 279
The Bell Jar (Plath), 388
Bergen-Belsen concentration camp, 283
Bernhardt, Sarah, 363, 405
The Best American Short Stories of 1944, 161
Bigelow, Paul, 182–3, 190, 204, 206, 218, 228, 233, 239–41, 247
Bilderback, Carolyn, 48
Blanch, Lesley, 317
Blick, Alvin, 295
Bloomgarden, Kermit, 287
Bonjour Tristesse (Sagan), 319
Book Week, 186
Borden, Lizzie, 350, 368
Boston Transcript, 82, 114
Botteghe Oscure, 270–1, 349
Boulanger, Nadia, 118
Bowen, Elizabeth, 237–40, *238*, 243–4, 347–8
Bowen's Court (Bowen), 238
Bowles, Jane, 7, 86, *216*, 216–7, 240–1, 247–8

Bowles, Paul, 7, 103, *216*, 216–7, 240–1, 388
Bowra, Maurice, 382
Boyle, Kay, 92, 106–7, 124, 132, *141*, 141–2, 145, 172–3, 176, 180, 195, 197–9, 201, 339, 412
Boy Scouts/Eagle Scouts, 52, 73, 154, 257
Bradbury, Ray, 5, 194, 388
Bragg, Laura, 305
Brando, Marlon, 226, 369, 400–1, 415
Bread Loaf Writers' Conference, 94–6, 114, 123, 129
Breit, Harvey, 228
Breuer, Bessie, 98–9, 119, 132, 135, 139–42, 148, 159, 170–2, 176, 194, 199, 201, 224, 249, 288, 324
Bridges, Ruby, 367
Brin, Irene, 269
Brinnin, John Malcolm, 312
Britten, Benjamin, 7, 103–5, 113, 119, 146, 382
Brooks, Paul, 369
Browne, Roscoe Lee, 385
Brown, John L., 188, 195–6, 197, 232, 234, 240–3, *242*, 272–3, 294, 296–7, 302–3, 316
Brown, Simone-Yvette L'Evesque, 188, 195–6, 232, 240–3, 272–3, 294, 296–7, 316
Brown v. Board of Education (1954), 13
Burnett, Whit, 45–6, 63, 75
Burton, Richard, 415

Caetani, Marguerite, princess of Bassanio, 270–1, 295
Caetani, Roffredo, prince of Bassanio, 270
Caldwell, Erskine, 7, 82–3
Calisher, Hortense, 143, 166
Cameron, Alan, 238
Camino Real (Williams), 275, 287
Camp Wheeler, Macon, Georgia, 177–9
Capote, Truman (née Truman Streckfus Persons), 7, 128, 195, 222, 265, 268, 303, 369, 388
   Carson's relationship with, 5, 180–2, *181*, 188, 278–81, 289, 293, 302, 324, 339, 411, 417
Carroll, Robert E., 379
Carr, Virginia Spencer, 15, 413
Carson, Alphonso, 14
Carson, James, 12
Carson, John Thomas, 11–3

Carson, Joseph Jefferson, 11–2
Carson, Joseph Perryman, 11
Carson, Mabel, 182–3
Carson, Martha Goodwin Raines, 11
Carson McCullers (Schulman), 414
Carson McCullers Center for Writers and Musicians, Columbus, Georgia, 413
Carson, Robert, 13–5, 18, 21
Carson, Susan Sophronia Howe, 11–3
Carson, Thomas, 11
Cartier-Bresson, Henri, 195–6
Cather, Willa, 417
Cat on a Hot Tin Roof (Williams), 318–9
Cerf, Bennett, 190
Chamberlain, Neville, 77
Chapman, John, 336
Chappell, L. H., 20
Charleston, South Carolina, 217–8, 220–1, 304–7, 309, 387, 394
Charlotte, North Carolina, 67–8, 69–77, 307–9, 394
Charlotte Observer, 67
Charm, 99
Chekhov, Anton, 41
Cheltenham Literature Festival, 379–81
Cheney, Brainard, 95
Chiang Kai-Shek, 65
Ciardi, John, 84, 95–6
Civilian Conservation Corps (CCC), 43, 45
civil rights movement, 366–7, 394–6
Civil War, 10–3, 16, 20, 271
Clarac, Achille-Claude, 90
Clarke, Elijah, 11
Clark, Eleanor, 180
Clay, Helena, 170
Cleckley, Hervey, 212, 299
Clift, Montgomery, 226, 279, 324, 369, 415
Clock Without Hands (McCullers)
    advance for, 366
    book cover of, *370*
    publication of, 235, 271, 363–72
    reviews/reception of, 370–2, 373
    themes/characters of, 8, 13, 218, 271, 339, 349, 366–72, 416
    writing of, 218, 235, 284, 294, 314, 339, 341, 349, 363–6, 374, 409
Clurman, Harold, 225–8, 232, 336, 411
Cohen, Dennis, 257–8, 381
Cohen, Kathryn Hamill, *258,* 337
    Carson and, 257–64, 267, 381

Colley, Dudley, 243
Collier's, 374
Columbia-Presbyterian Harkness Pavilion, New York City, 343–4, 353, 368, 378–9, 389, 396
Columbia University, 61, 63, 66, 117, 357
    Carson's studies at, 46–8, 56, 117
    Smith, Rita, as teacher at, 387–8, 411
Columbus Enquirer, 16
Columbus, Georgia, 218–9
    Carson's residence in, 3, 7, 9–11, 13–9, 24–9, *25,* 30–46, 50–61, 64, 106, 109–11, 112–6, 135–8, 155–7, 413
    economy of, 20–1, 44–5
    as theme in McCullers's work, 22–3, 115
Columbus State University, Carson's papers at, 413
Communism, 45, 157, 219–20, 257
    as theme in McCullers's work, 4
Confederacy, 11–3, 16, 20, 371
conversion disorder, 337–9
Copland, Aaron, 105, 216
Cornell, Katharine, 192–3
"Correspondence" (McCullers), 123
Cotlenko, Monique, 198, 303, 343
Cotlenko, Valentin, 198
"Court in the West Eighties" (McCullers), 62, 85
Crane, Cheryl, 347
Crane, Hart, 191
Crawford, Cheryl, *148,* 148–50, 152, 153, 177, 221–2, 224, 226, 237, 272, 283–7, 303, 318, 324, 326, 418
Cunard, Nancy, 89, 381
Cuomo, Ciro, 269
Curtis, Elisabeth, 192

Dahl-Wolfe, Louise, 84, 85, 87
Dangerfield, George, 186
Davidson award, 232
Davis, George, 85–7, 88–9, 97–8, *98,* 132, 140, 159, 169, 180, 194, 196
    Seven Middagh house rental by, 99–102, 104–5, 117, 145–7, 165
"Dear Mr. Brahms" (McCullers), 62
Decision, 89, 117
del Corso, Gaspero, 269
de Santillana, Dorothy, 366
Descartes, 58
De Sica, Vittorio, 278
Dett, R. Nathaniel, 139
Dewhurst, Colleen, 385
de Wilde, Brandon, 227, *229,* 231–2

de Wilde, Fritz, 227
Dews, Carlos, 414
Diamond, David, *118*, 122, 156, 233, 374–5
    Carson's relationship with, 118–21,
        123–8, 129, 133, 136, 138, 148, 151, 158,
        161, 165, 200, 220, 253, 268–9, 281,
        397
    Reeves McCullers's relationship with,
        118–20, 123–7, 129, 158, 165, 200, 220,
        253–4, 268–9, 281
    Tom McCullers's relationship with, 397
The Diary of Anne Frank (Goodrich/
    Hackett), 283–7
The Diary of a Young Girl (Frank), 283–7
Dickinson, Emily, 362, 364
Didion, Joan, 388
Dinesen, Isak (aka Karen von Blixen),
    218, 350, 358–61, *360*, 392, 403
Doctors Hospital, New York City, 254–6,
    331–2
"The Doll's House" (Mansfield), 322–3
Dos Passos, John, 43
Dostoyevsky, Fyodor, 4, 61
Doubleday, 95, 284, 413
Doughty, Howard, 179, 187
DTs, 204–5, 391
"The Dual Angel" (McCullers), 251, 257
    publication of, 270–1
du Gard, Roger Martin, 91
Duncan, Isadora, 35, 66
Dunn, Michael, 385
Dyar, Martyn, 401–2

Early, Jubal, 12
Edel, Leon, 310–1
Edwards, Ben, 385
Ehrlich, Gerald, 168, 179
Ehrlich, Leonard, 147, 148, 168, 179, 187
Einstein, Albert, 113
Elegy in Memory of Maurice Ravel
    (Diamond), 118
Eliot, T. S., 53, 87, 251
Ellis, Edith Lees, 151
Ellis, Havelock, 150–2
Ellison, Ralph, 139
Éluard, Paul, 86
Engels, Friedrich, 43, 53, 58
Erskine, Albert, 129
erysipelas, 114
Esquire, 311, 346, 370
Eustis, Helen "Biddy," 139–40, 147, 168
Evans, Oliver, 249, 253, 276
Evans, Walker, 147

Façade (Sitwell), 250
Fadiman, Clifton, 4–5, 82, 86, 114
Farrar, John C., 94
"The Faucet" (McCullers), 41, 191
Faulkner, William, 4, 7, 10, 53, 82–3, 115,
    357, 378–9, 388
Fayetteville, North Carolina, 72, 76–82
Feibleman, Peter, 357
Fiennes, Audrey, 243
First Baptist Church, Columbia, Georgia,
    14, 18–9, 67
Fisher, Alfred, 139, 147
Flanagan, William, 374
Flanner, Janet (aka Genêt), *200*, 199–201,
    297, 301–3, 340
    Carson's relationship with, 85–6, 97–8,
        139, 253, 286, 288–9, 292–3, 296, 356,
        411, 412
Fleurs du Mal (Baudelaire), 41
Flowering Judas (Porter), 129
"The Flowering Dream" (McCullers),
    311, 345
Foley, Martha, 45–6, 161
Ford Foundation, 298
Forster, E. M., 317, 398
Forster, Robert, 415
Fort Benning, Georgia, 20, 33, 43, 45, 61,
    79, 115, 136, 150, 153, 406
Fort Dix, New Jersey, 165
France, 81, 134
    Carson's residence in, 272–82, *273*,
        283–94, 327–8, 406
    Carson's visits to, 188, 195–6, 197–204,
        206, 240–5
Franckenstein, Bobby, 199
Franckenstein, Faith Carson, 199
Franckenstein, Joseph von, 141, 195
Frank, Anne, 283–7
Franklin, Dr., 224, 316, 340
Frank, Otto, 283–7
Frederickson, Edna, 95
French Resistance, 108–9, 195
Freud, Sigmund, 340, 352
Frost, Robert, 95
Fullilove, Jack, 277, 279, 281–2, 291,
    296–7, 303

Gachet, Ann, 15–6
Gachet, Charles, 15–6
Gachet, James Edward, 16
Gam, Rita, 192
Garnett, David, 252, 380–1
Garrison, Mary, 131

Gary, Romain, 380
Gascoyne, David, 256–7
Gérard, Rolf, 393
Gibbs, Wolcott, 231, 336
G.I. Bill, 178–9, 195
Giehse, Therese, 90, 142
Ginsberg, Allen, 7
Giuliano, Ciro, 198
Givner, Joan, 130
Glasgow, Ellen, 7
The Glass Menagerie (Williams), 190, 191, 206, 227
Goddard, Paulette, 399
Godden, Rumer, 371
Gomme, Jackie, 380
Gomme, Joanna, 380–1
Goodrich, Frances, 287
Goucher College, Maryland, 311
Goyen, William, 239, 265–6, 287, 290, 322–3
The Grass Harp (Capote), 280, 324, 326
the Great Depression, 25, 44–5, 47, 67, 78, 195, 225
Griffith, Dorothy, 38
The G-String Murders (Lee), 102–3
Guggenheim Fellowship, 118, 267
   Carson's award of, 132, 136–7, 146, 158, 188
Guggenheim, Peggy, 102, 141

Hackett, Albert, 287
Haieff, Alexei, 180
Hall, Gordon Langley (later Dawn Langley Simmons), 305
Hamilton, Nancy, 193
Hammerschlag, Ernst, 340–1, 346
Harper's Bazaar, 85, 88, 99, 102, 147, 269, 384
   The Ballad of the Sad Cafe publication by, 159–61, 184
   The Member of the Wedding publication by, 184
   Reflections in a Golden Eye publication by, 86–7, 114–5
Harris, Julie, 227–8, *229–30*, 231, 338, 400–1, 411, 415
Harry Ransom Center, University of Texas, Austin, 412
Hartman, Joyce, 369, 393, 395–6
Harvey, Geoff, 119
Harvey, Helen, 19, 27–8, 40, 43
Havoc, June, 102
Hawthornden Prize, 381

Hawthorne (Arvin), 128
Hayes, Harold, 346
Hayes, Helen, 172, 227
The Heart Is a Lonely Hunter (film), 374, 393, 415
The Heart Is a Lonely Hunter (McCullers), 129
   advance for, 78, 81, 235
   audio excerpts, by Carson, of, 356–7
   book cover of, *80*
   as Oprah Book Club pick, 414
   outline for, 73–5
   publication, European, of, 198
   publication, U.S., of, 3, 80–2, 181, 235, 414
   Reeves McCullers's contributions to, 73–5, 407
   reviews/reception of, 3–5, 82–7, 89, 109, 190, 414, 415
   stage adaptation of, 284
   themes/characters of, 4, 6, 8, 17, 21–2, 28–9, 32–3, 40, 43–4, 73–5, 78–9, 80, 93, 116, 311, 313, 405–6, 415–7, 419
   title, final, 75
   title, working, 78
   translations of, 189, 198
   writing of, 69–79
Hecht, Ben, 86, 171–2
Heller, Joseph, 380, 382
Hellman, Lillian, 357
Hemingway, Ernest, 4, 86–7, 157, 319, 359, 378
Hersey, John, 286
Hicks, Dorothy, 126, 131
Hicks, Granville, 126, 131, 310
Highsmith, Patricia, 7, 259
High Watch rehab facility, 387
Hillyer, Dorothy, 184
Hitler, Adolf, 76–7, 89, 90, 157, 161
Holiday, 298
"Home for Christmas" (McCullers), 217
homosexuality
   McCullers, Carson, and, 6, 32, 37–40, 49, 57–8, 66, 90–4, 106–11, 123–4, 129–30, 148–52, 158, 164–5, 177, 220, 281–2, 324, 345, 351–2, 407, 417–8
   McCullers, Reeves, and, 6, 49, 119–20, 123–7, 129, 150–2, 164–5, 177, 220, 276, 281–2, 396, 407, 418
   societal views on, 150–2, 353
Hopper, Edward, 172, 412
The Horizontal Man (Eustis), 140

Hôtel Château-Frontenac, Paris, 296–7, 302

Houghton Mifflin, 61, 126, 138, 146, 265, 335, 395–6
  The Ballad of the Sad Café publication by, 235–6
  Clock Without Hands publication by, 365–72
  The Heart Is a Lonely Hunter publication by, 3, 75–82, 181, 235, 414
  Literary Fellowship Award of, 75–8, 308
  The Member of the Wedding publication by, 181, 185–7
  The Mortgaged Heart publication by, 412
  Reflections in a Golden Eye publication by, 87, 114
  The Square Root of Wonderful play publication by, 326, *326*, 336
  Sweet as a Pickle and Clean as a Pig publication by, 393

Howard, Jane, 380
Howe, Irving, 370
Hughes, Langston, 139, 157, 304
Hull, Helen, 47
"Hush Little Baby" (McCullers), 395
Huston, John, 393, *402*, 402–4
  Reflections in a Golden Eye film by, 399–401, 415–6

I Have Touched the Earth (Bates), 61–2
Illumination and Night Glare (McCullers), 27
  editing/publication of, 414
  theme/narratives of, 13, 406–7
  writing/dictation of, 405–8
Inge, William, 224, 317, 369
"Instant of the Hour After" (McCullers), 59–60, 62
In the Summer House (Bowles, J.), 217
Irish Times, 402
Isenberg, Sidney, 208–9, 212–3, 221, 299
Isherwood, Christopher, 86, 88–9, 101, 103, 190, 319
Ishigaki Ayako, 180, 188
Ishigaki Eitaro, 179
Italy, 134, 266–72, 278–80
Ives, Marion, 181
"I Want, I Want" (McCullers), 62

Jackson, Stonewall, 11
Jackson, Vannie Copeland, 44
Japan, World War II and, 134–5
Jim Crow laws, 21, 44, 54–6, 226, 371

"The Jockey" (McCullers), 126
the Jofferses, 274–5, 281, 294
Johnson, C. Graham, 14, 15
Johnson, Greer, 208–9, 225, 230, 234–5
Johnson, Martha Elba Smith "Mattie," 15, 24, 41, 67, 317
Johnson, Sidney, 54–6
Jones, Jennifer, 278–9
Jones, Judith, 283
Jordan, Thornton, 413
Joyce, James, 398
Juilliard School, 34, 36, 46, 48

Kallman, Chester, 101, 105, 113, 146
Kanin, Garson, 287
Kantorowicz, Alfred "Kanto," 157, 173
Kantorowicz, Frieda, 157
Kapp, Isa, 186
Kazan, Elia, 226–7, 275, 318
Kazin, Alfred, 143, 158, 161, 219
Keathley, George, 335
Keith, Brian, 400
Keller, Helen, 363, 405
Kerr, Walter, 385
Kierce, Alice, 28
Kinsey, Alfred, 152
Kirchwey, Freda, 96–7
Kirkus Reviews, 61, 185–6
Kirstein, Lincoln, 100, 105, 121
Kiss Me, Kate (musical), 324
Knopf, Blanche, 270
Krafft-Ebing, 152
Kramer, Stanley, 236, 252
Kristin (pet dog), 261, 266, 267, *292*, 303
Ku Klux Klan, 115–6, 271

Lamp unto My Feet (TV show), 357
Lancaster, Ida McCullers, 51, 52, 63
Lancaster, John, 51, 52
L'Ancien Presbytère, Bachivillers, France, *273*, 273–82, 283–97, 302, 307, 327–8, 406
Landowska, Wanda, 148
Landshoff, Ruth, 91
Lang, George, 269
Lang, Tina, 269
Lantz, Robbie, as Carson's agent, 345–6, 365, 369, 392–3, 395–6, 412–3
Lasky, Floria,
  as Carson's estate executor, 412–3
  as Carson's lawyer, 235, 252, 263, 268, 275, 289, 293–6, 301, 311, 314, 336, 369, 380, 392–3

Lawrence, D. H., 41, 80
Ledger-Enquirer (Columbus), 60–1
Lee, Gypsy Rose (née Rose Louise
    Hovick), 7, 102–6, *103*, 107, 347, 352,
    406, 411
Lee, Marguerite McCullers, 396–7
Lee, Robert E., 20
Lee, Stanton, Jr., 396
Leggett, John, 335
Lehmann, Beatrix "Peggy," 257
Lehmann, Rosamond, 243, 256–7, 259,
    263, 266
Lenya, Lotte, 98, 140
Lerman, Leo, 121, 188, 249, 313, 316, 317
Let Me Dance club, Columbus,
    Georgia, 31
Levin, Meyer, 285–7
Library of America, 414
Lieber, Maxim, 85
Life, 207, 208–9
Life and Letters To-Day, 117
"Like That" (McCullers), 62–3
"Lines for an Old Man" (Eliot), 87
Linscott, Robert, 3, 90, 95–7, 114, 117, 126,
    132, 139, 181, 265, 365
Liszt's Second Hungarian Rhapsody,
    28, 34
Littell, Robert, 115
Lobrano, Gus, 147
Locke, Sondra, 415
Lockwood, Patricia, 416
Logan, Joshua, 225
"Loneliness: An American Malady"
    (McCullers), 217
The Lonely Hunter (Carr), 413
"The Lonely Hunter" (Sharp), 75
Longanesi, Leo, 272
"the Lost Generation," 86
Loti, Pierre, 58
Loud-Mouth Dancers, Columbus,
    Georgia, 31
Lover, Beloved (Vega) (album), 414
Lover, Beloved (Vega) (one-woman show),
    414
lover-beloved ideology, 414
    in Carson's life, 94, 143–4, 407
    as narrative theme, 70–1, 385, 407
Lowell, Robert, 157, 219–20, 270
Luce, Clare Boothe, 166–7
Lyndon, Andrew, 53, 205, 255, 264

MacArthur, Charles, 172
Macleod, Fiona. *See* Sharp, William

MacNeice, Louis, 100, 104, 146
"Madame Zilensky and the King of
    Finland" (McCullers), 123
Mademoiselle, 121
    Carson pieces in, 17, 217, 270–1, 329, 349
    Smith, Rita, career at, 169, 180–1, 222,
    278, 329, 387–8
Magnani, Anna, 276, 350
Magny, Claude-Edmonde, 203
Malraux, André, 317
Mangione, Jerry, 179
Mankiewicz, Joseph, 334
Mann, Erika, 88–91, *89,* 93–4, 96–8, 101,
    105, 107, 121, 200
Mann, Golo, 101, 105, 108, 121
Mann, Klaus, 88–91, 98, 101, 105, 117, 121,
    129, 142
Mann, Marty, 244, 254, 315
    Carson's relationship with, 205, 245–8,
    252, 263, 324, 418
Mann, Thomas, 88, 97, 117, 157
Mansfield, Katherine, 322–3
"The Man Upstairs" (McCullers), 395
"The March" (McCullers), 394–5
March, William, 76, 308
Markloff, Edith, 48
Marks, Hilda, 305, 312, 321, 346, 391
Marks, Robert, 305, 312, 321, 391
Marquand, John P., 95
Marre, Albert, 331–2, 334
Marshall, George C., 115
Martin Beck Theatre, New York City, 385
Martineau, Florence, 241, 244–5
Martineau, Stanley, 225, 241, 244–5
Marx, Karl/Marxism, 43, 53, 58, 75
Maschler, Tom, 381
Massee, Jordan, Jr., *183,* 249, 255, 309, 335
    Carson biographies and, 413
    Carson's relationship with, 33, 182–4,
    190, 198, 205, 218–24, 228, 239, 247,
    271, 274, 290, 301, 304, 316, 320–1,
    332, 339, 356, 360, 367–9, 371, 373,
    378, 392, 397, 399, 411, 413
Massee, Jordan, Sr., 182, 219, 367
Massie, Robert K., 412
Matthau, Carol, 335
Mayer, Beata, 105
Mayer, Elizabeth, 105, 113
Mayer, Michael, 105
Mayer, William, 105, 113, 131, 148, 210,
    212, 222, 340, 364
McCarter Theatre, Princeton, New Jersey,
    335

McCarthy, Mary, 405
McClintic, Guthrie, 192
McCormack, Ken, 413
McCullers, Carson (née Lula Carson
    Smith). *See also* narrative themes,
    McCullers; works, McCullers
  alcohol use/abuse by, 8, 58–60, 71,
    95–6, 155, 184, 198–9, 202–3, 221–2,
    239, 245, 253–9, 261, 269, 272–3, 276,
    281, 287–93, 298–9, 307, 309, 312–5,
    320, 323, 331, 339, 347, 355, 372–3, 382,
    389–90, 391, 398, 401
  Ames's relationship with, 122, 129–30,
    137–8, 140, 142, 147–8, 153–4, 156–7,
    177, 179–80, 194, 199, 309–10, 315
  ancestry of, 9–17, 58
  anti-Semitism accusation against,
    160–1
  autobiography of, 13, 27, 405–8, 414
  biographies of, 412–3, 414
  birth of, 16
  Boyle, Kay, relationship with, 92,
    106–7, 124, 132, *141*, 141–2, 145, 172–3,
    176, 180, 195, 197–9, 201, 339, 412
  Bread Loaf fellowship awarded to,
    94–6, 114, 123, 129
  cancer, breast, of, 376–9, 389
  cancer, cervical, of, 388
  Capote's relationship with, 5, 180–2,
    181, 188, 278–81, 289, 293, 302, 324,
    339, 411, 417
  Charlotte, North Carolina, residence
    of, 68, 69–77
  Cheltenham Literature Festival
    appearance by, 379–81
  childhood of, 3, 7, 9, 16–29, *25*
  Cohen, Kathryn, and, 257–64, 267, 381
  at Columbia University, 46–8, 56, 61,
    117
  Columbus, Georgia, residence of, 3, 7,
    9–11, 13–9, 24–9, *25*, 30–46, 50–61,
    64, 106, 109–11, 112–6, 135–8, 155–7,
    413
  conversion disorder and, 337–9
  Crawford's relationship with, *148*,
    148–50, 152, 153, 177, 221–2, 224, 225,
    237, 272, 283–7, 303, 318, 324, 326,
    418
  death/burial of, 408–9, 411
  Diamond's relationship with, *118*,
    118–21, 123–8, 129, 133, 136, 138, 148,
    151, 158, 161, 165, 200, 220, 253,
    268–9, 281, 397

  Dinesen's relationship with, 358–61, *360*
  domestic abuse and, 92–3, 131, 254, 288
  dropping of first name by, 23, 31, 417
  drug/medication regimens of, 373,
    389–91, 398
  early plays written by, 27–9, 40–1
  England visits by, 254–64
  erysipelas suffered by, 114
  family nickname for, 9, 31
  Fayetteville, North Carolina, residence
    of, 72, 76–82
  Flanner's relationship with, 85–6,
    97–8, 139, *200*, 200–1, 253, 286,
    288–9, 292–3, 296, 356, 411, 412
  forgeries committed against, 125–6, 131,
    135, 153–5, 156, 177, 295–6, 302
  France residence of, 272–82, *273*,
    283–94, 327–8, 406
  France visits of, 188, 195–6, 197–204,
    206, 240–5, 272
  Guggenheim fellowships awarded to,
    132, 136–7, 146, 158, 188
  heart failures of, 343, 389
  Huston's relationship with, 399–402,
    402
  hypnosis treatments of, 259–61, 263–4
  Ireland visits, 239, 400–3
  Italy visits, 266–72
  Lamp unto My Feet appearance by, 357
  Lantz as agent of, 345–6, 365, 369,
    392–3, 395–6, 412–3
  Lasky as lawyer of, 235, 252, 263, 268,
    275, 289, 293–6, 301, 311, 314, 336,
    369, 380, 392–3
  lawsuit by Greer against, 209, 225,
    234–5
  literary influences on, 41, 43–4, 58, 80
  Mann, Marty's, relationship with, 205,
    245–8, 252, 263, 324, 418
  Massee's relationship with, 33, 182–4,
    190, 198, 205, 218–24, 228, 239, 247,
    271, 274, 290, 301, 304, 316, 320–1,
    332, 339, 356, 360, 367–9, 371, 373,
    378, 392, 397, 399, 411, 413
  Mercer as therapist of, 340–8, 350–3
  Mercer's romance/relationship with, 37,
    353–6, *354*, 361–2, 364, 367, 372–3,
    375–81, *386*, 387, 389–92, 397–8,
    403–8
  mother's death and, 321–3
  mother's relationship with, 9, 18–9, 23,
    41–3, 92, 110–1, 122, 135–6, 183, 194,
    210–4, 229–30, 290, 305–6

New York City residence of, 46–9,
  62–6, 82–7, 88–111, 112, 116–33, 134,
  136, 146–52, 215–8, 237
at New York University/Washington
  Square College, 61–5, 117
Nyack, New York, residence of, 171–3,
  179, 204–14, 215–8, 236, 309, 317,
  322–5, 332–3, 334–48, 349–62,
  363–80, 384–401, 403–8, 412–3
one-woman show about, 414
papers of, posthumous sale of, 412
paralysis of, 203–11, 215, 236–7, 246,
  251, 277, 287–90, 307–8, 337–9, 344,
  353, 356, 358, 372, 379, 389, 409
photographs of, *10, 31, 59, 65, 84, 98,
  169, 292, 360–1, 373, 375, 386, 402*
physical characteristics of, 5, 31–2, 34,
  35, 83–4, 194, 218–9, 252, 270, 335–6,
  358, 364, 403, 417–8
piano as focus of, 27–9, 30–1,
  32–40, 46
plays written about, 414
pleurisy cases of, 106, 135, 266
pneumonia cases of, 36, 58, 63–4, 112,
  114, 135, 137, 266, 343, 388–9, 399
Porter infatuation of, 129–30, 419
posthumous releases of work by, 411–2,
  414
pregnancy of, 228–9
psychotherapy sessions of, 340–8, 413
Reeves McCullers's courtship of,
  56–63, 65–7, 153–6, 162–6
Reeves McCullers's death and, 298–9,
  314, 326–30
Reeves McCullers's divorce from, 126,
  131–2
Reeves McCullers's marriage to, 3, 5–6,
  66–8, 69–81, 92–4, 97, 109–11, 112,
  116–21, 123–8, 406–7, 418, 419
Reeves McCullers's remarriage to,
  176–9, 184, 194–6, 199–206, 209,
  212–3, 237, 243–5, 252, 259–61,
  262–3, 273, 280, 287–97, 301–2,
  326–30, 338, 343, 351, 406–7, 418, 419
religious observations of, 18–9, 392, 397
rheumatic fever of, 64, 113, 168, 337,
  344
Saint-Subber's relationship with,
  323–32
Schwarzenbach's relationship with, 6,
  88, 90–4, 96–7, 99, 105–10, 112,
  123–4, 127, 135, 142–5, 153, 177, 193,
  345, 351–2, 355, 418

Seven Middagh residency of, 7, 99–111,
  145–52, 156, 347, 351, 381
sexuality of, 6, 32, 37–40, 49, 57–8, 66,
  90–4, 106–11, 123–4, 129–30, 148–52,
  158, 164–5, 177, 220, 281–2, 324, 345,
  351–2, 407, 417–8
Sitwell's relationship with, 249–52, *250,*
  380–3
slavery by ancestors of, 10–3, 16
smoking habit of, 31, 83, 84–5, 95, 258,
  347, 358, 373, 401
strep infections of, 64, 113–4, 135, 344,
  409
strokes suffered by, 8, 64, 112–4, 168–9,
  201–2, 203–14, 229, 309, 337, 344,
  382, 402, 408–9, 416
suicide attempt by, 210–2
tuberculosis suffered by, 63–4, 112,
  114
Tucker, Mary's, relationship with,
  36–40, 70, 124, 185, 240, 241–2, 246,
  284, 286, 288, 327, 350–1, 353, 374,
  376–9, 397, 403–5
"Twenty Years of Writing" lecture by,
  312–4
Watkins as agent for, 180–1, 194,
  208
Williams, Tennessee, relationship with,
  7–8, *189,* 189–94, 198, 205–9, 213–4,
  216–7, 219, 222, 225–8, 233, 236–7,
  240–1, 244, 249, 257–8, 261–2, 264,
  272, 275–6, 279, 304, 312–4, 316,
  318–21, 332–3, 357, 368–9, 404, 407,
  411, 413
Wood as agent for, 208–9, 225, 235,
  261, 264
Yaddo artist residencies by, 119, 120–5,
  129–32, 135, 137–46, 157–9, 168,
  179–80, 187, 306, 308–16, 337, 349
McCullers, James Reeves, Jr. "Reeves"
  (Carson's husband)
alcohol use/abuse by, 6, 8, 52, 58–60,
  71, 93, 127, 155–6, 164, 198–9, 202–4,
  220, 224–5, 241, 244, 253–6, 267,
  272–3, 276–7, 279, 287–93, 295, 297,
  302, 315
birth/childhood of, 50–6, *51*
Carson's courtship by, 56–63, 65–7,
  153–6, 162–6
Carson's divorce from, 126, 131–2
Carson's marriage to, 3, 5–6, 66–8,
  69–81, 92–4, 97, 109–11, 112, 116–21,
  123–8, 406–7, 418, 419

McCullers, James Reeves, Jr. "Reeves"
  (*continued*)
  Carson's remarriage to, 176–9, 184,
    194–6, 199–206, 209, 212–3, 237,
    243–5, 252, 259–61, 262–3, 273, 280,
    287–97, 301–2, 326–30, 338, 343, 351,
    406–7, 418, 419
  characteristics of, 50, 93, 98
  check forgeries by, 125–6, 131, 135, 153–5,
    156, 177, 295–6, 302
  death of, 297–9, 300–4, 312, 314, 321,
    326, 349
  Diamond's relationship with, 118–20,
    123–7, 129, 158, 165, 200, 220, 253–4,
    268–9, 281
  domestic abuse by, 92–3, 131, 254, 288
  drug use by, 156, 202
  England visits, 254–6
  France residence of, 272–82, *273*,
    283–97, 327–8
  France visits, 195–6, 197–204, 206,
    240–5, 272
  funeral of, 302–3
  The Heart Is a Lonely Hunter
    contributions of, 73–5, 407
  Italy visits, 266–72, 278–80
  military service of, 49, 53, 56, 134, 136,
    138–9, 150–1, 153–5, 162–8, 173–5,
    177–9, 194, 351, 406–7
  photographs of, *51, 52, 59, 65, 71*
  seizures experienced by, 204–5
  sexuality of, 6, 49, 119–20, 123–7, 129,
    150–2, 164–5, 177, 220, 276, 281–2,
    396, 407, 418
  suicidal thoughts/suicide of, 126, 254,
    276, 279, 288, 291, 294, 297, 300–1,
    314, 326–30, 396–7
  as WOR accountant, 212–3, 215
McCullers, James Reeves, Sr. "Bud," 51
McCullers, Jessie, 51, 278, 295–6, 303, 397
McCullers, Marguerite, 396–7
McCullers, Tom, 168, 278, 303, 396–7
McCullers, Wiley, 50–1
McCullers, Wiley Mae, 278, 303, 397
McGill, Ralph, 22
McLain, John, 385–6
McMillan, Florence, 48
McNally, Terrence, 356–76
McPhee, Colin, 123
McRae, Emma Rose, 51–2
McRae, Vernon, Jr., 50, 51–2
McRae, Vernon, Sr., 51–2
Mei-ling Soong, 65

Meltzer, Robert, 173
The Member of the Wedding (film), 415
The Member of the Wedding (McCullers)
  advance for, 146
  audio excerpts, by Carson, of, 356–7
  book cover for, 185
  film adaptation of, 252
  musical adaptation of, 374–6, 379
  publication of, 184
  reviews/reception of, 185–7, 190, 191,
    200–1, 230, 232
  themes/characters of, 7, 17, 18, 30, 33,
    40, 80–1, 105–6, 135, 137, 159, 162, 180,
    184–5, 200–1, 284, 394, 406, 416–7
  title, working, 80
  translations of, 189
  writing of, 80–1, 105–6, 116, 132, 135,
    142, 158–9, 172, 179, 313, 349
The Member of the Wedding (play), 208
  actors in, 226–8, *229–30*, 401
  director of, 217, 225–6, 336
  lawsuit by Greer over, 209, 225, 234–5
  off-Broadway productions of, 415
  producers behind, 217, 225
  reviews/reception of, 228–33, 234, 240,
    322, 326, 337, 414–5
  writing of, 191–4, 208–9, 215, 218, 225,
    230, 234–5, 349
Memories of a Catholic Girlhood
    (McCarthy), 405
Memory of Love (Breuer), 98
Mercer, Mary E., *342*
  Carson's death and, 408, 411–3
  as Carson's psychotherapist, 340–8,
    350–3, 413
  Carson's romance/relationship with, 37,
    353–6, *354*, 361–2, 364, 367,
    372–3, 375–81, *386*, 387, 389–92,
    397–8, 403–8
  death of, 413
Meredith, Burgess, 140, 399
Merlo, Frank, 228, 258, 262, 320, 398
MGM Records, 356–7
Miller, Arthur, 359–61
Mills, Emma DeLong, 58, 64–5, 68, 69,
    71–3, 75–8, 82
Minnelli, Vincente, 225–6
"Miriam" (Capote), 180
Mistral, Gabriela, 316
Modern Library, 414
Moe, Henry, 137
Mondadori Publishing, 201
Monroe, Marilyn, 359–61, *360–1*

Monti, Mario, 272
More Fun comics, 47
Morris, Edita, 196, 199, 201
Morris, Ira, 196, 199, 201
Morrison, Ted, 95, 132
Morrison, Toni, 416–7
The Mortgaged Heart (McCullers), 412
Mortimer, Chapman, 399–400
Moseley, Hardwick, 75, 181, 184, 187, 234–5, 349, 365
Murray, Natalia Danesi, 198–9, 200–1, 268, 286, 292–3, 301, 340, 356
Mussolini, 134
My Autobiography of Carson McCullers (Shapland), 414
Myers, Robert, 202, 204, 206–8, 277, 291, 297, 300, 302–4, 307
My Life (Ellis), 151

narrative themes, McCullers
    alcoholism, 4, 75, 329–30
    Columbus, Georgia, 22–3, 115
    hero worship, 26–7
    loneliness/isolation, 22, 70, 160, 370, 419–20
    lover-beloved ideology, 70–1, 385, 407
    outsiders/misfits, 4, 18, 30–1, 82–3, 93, 106, 114–6, 150, 159–60, 184, 240–1, 250, 308, 323, 369, 414, 415–7, 419–20
    race/racism, 4, 8, 13, 43–4, 150, 218, 366–7, 370–1, 394–6, 416–7
    sexuality, 4, 6–7, 32–3, 74–5, 79–80, 86, 114–6, 150, 368–9, 371, 385–6, 415
    suicide, 4, 75, 326–30, 371
National Book Award, 308, 370
National Council on Alcoholism, 244–5
National Institute of Arts and Letters, 271
National Register of Historic Places, 413
The Nation, 96, 170, 226, 336
Nazi Germany, 76–7, 81, 88–9, 101, 134, 157
Neikrug, Sam, 147
Neurological Institute, New York City, 204, 206, 389
Newberry, Edwin, 220, 305, 307–9
New Comics, 47
New Deal programs, 45
Newhouse, Edward, 123
The New Republic, 82, 226
New School for Social Research, New York City, 388, 411–2

New York City, New York, Carson's residence in, 46–9, 62–6, 82–7, 88–111, 112, 116–33, 134, 136, 146–52, 215–8, 237
New York Daily Mirror, 231
New York Daily News, 231, 336, 346–7
New York Drama Critics' Circle Award, 231
The New Yorker, 95, 97, 102, 147, 170, 243, 336, 370–1, 405
New York Herald Tribune, 73, 186, 230, 371, 385
New York Post, 398
The New York Times, 4, 83, 85, 86, 228, 231, 237, 285, 300, 336, 357, 385–6, 393
    Book Review, 186, 370
    Carson feature, 1961, by, 363, 370
New York University, 61–5, 117
"Night Watch over Freedom" (McCullers), 172
Nobel Prize, 316–7
Norman, Ruth, 148–9, 272
North, Sterling, 186
Nyack Hospital, New York, 408
Nyack, New York
    Carson's burial in, 411
    Carson's residence in, 171–3, 179, 204–14, 215–8, 236, 309, 317, 322–5, 332–3, 334–48, 349–62, 363–80, 384–401, 403–8, 412–3

Oak Hill Cemetery, Nyack, New York, 411
O'Connor, Flannery, 83
O'Connor, Frank, 243
O. Henry Prize, 169
Omnibus series, 298
O'Neill, Eugene, 26, 41, 191, 257, 313, 335
"On the Wings of an Angel" (song), 28
The Opening of a Door (Davis), 85–6
Oprah's Book Club, 414
Other Voices, Other Rooms (Capote), 181, 280
Out of Africa (Dinesen), 218, 350, 358

Pale Horse, Pale Rider (Porter), 129
Paris, France, 35, 78, 85–6, 88, 97–9, 118, 168, 216, 218, 234
    Carson's visits to, 188, 195–6, 197–204, 206, 240–5, 272
Paris Review, 265, 357
Parker, Dorothy, 370
Parks, Rosa, 366

the Parnassus Club, New York City, 48
Patterson, Glenn, 401, 404
Patton, Beatrice, 115
Patton, George S., Jr., 115
Payne Whitney Hospital, White Plains,
    New York, 108–9
    Carson's commitment to, 209–12, 213,
        251, 299, 340–1, 348
Peabody, George Foster, 121–2
Peabody, Marjorie Waite, 122
Peacock, Edwin, 36, 43, 45–7, 49, 54, 56,
    59, *59*, 67, 150, 176, 202, 213, 217–9,
    220, 224, 279, 304–7, 309, 358, *386*,
    387
Pearl Harbor attack, 135
Pears, Peter, 7, 103–5, 113, 119, 146, 382
Peck, Priscilla, 244–7, 263
Peffer, Nathaniel, 73
The Pepper Mill cabaret show, 88–9
"The Pestle" (McCullers), 349
Peterson, Virgilia, 186
Philadelphia Bulletin, 228
Philadelphia Daily News, 228
Philadelphia Fine Arts Association, 311,
    317
Pierce, Phoebe, 181
Plagemann, Bentz, 339
Plath, Sylvia, 169, 388
"Playing in the Dark" (Morrison), 417
Poe, Edgar Allan, 346, 417
Poetry Center, New York City, 312–4
"Poldi" (McCullers), 62
Poor, Anne, 99, 140
Poor, Henry Varnum, 98, 119, 132, 140,
    148, 171–2, 176, 253
Poor, Josephine, 140
Poor, Peter, 140
Porter, Cole, 102, 324, 405
Porter, Frederick, 67
Porter, Katherine Anne, 87, 96, 99, 123,
    130, 188, 190
    Carson's infatuation with, 129–30, 419
Porter, Russell, 296, 303
Preston, Stuart, 237
Price, Francis, 284
The Problem We All Live With (painting),
    367
"The Prussian Officer" (Lawrence), 41, 80
Publishers Weekly, 85
Pulitzer Prize, 231, 287
Purple Heart medal, 194

Quintero, José, 335

Rachmaninoff, Sergei, 35, 36, 58, 63, 327
racism/race, 21, 45, 147, 172, 190
    civil rights movement and, 366–7
    as theme in McCullers's work, 4, 8, 13,
        43–4, 150, 218, 366–7, 370–1, 394–6,
        416–7
    Valdosta lynchings and, 54–6
    voting suppression and, 13
The Rainbow (Lawrence), 41
Rainer, Luise, 173
Rainey, Ma, 21
Random House, 181, 265, 365
Ravel, Maurice, 118
Rawlings, John, 84
Rea, Oliver, 225, 230
Redbook, 395
Redman, Ray, 4
"A Reed of Pan" (McCullers), 45, 61
Reed, Carol, 350
Reeder, Ida, 321, 344, 391, 400–3, 405, 411
Reed, Rex, 400–1, 408
Reflections in a Golden Eye (film)
    cast of, 400–1, 415
    director of, 399–401, 415
    payment for rights to, 393
    reviews/reception of, 415–6
    screenwriter of, 399
Reflections in a Golden Eye (McCullers)
    audio excerpts, by Carson, of, 356–7
    dedication of, 145
    publication of, 86–7
    reviews/reception of, 95, 114–6, 123,
        197–8, 416
    themes/characters of, 7, 79–80, 114–6,
        406, 415–6
    and title's origins, 79, 86–7
    translations of, 188–9, 269
    writing of, 79–80, 406–7
Reinhardt, Wolfgang, 279
The Reivers (Faulkner), 378
"Residuum" (McCullers), 62
Retail Credit Company (later Equifax),
    67, 73, 76–7, 79
rheumatic fever, 64, 113, 168, 337, 344
Rimbaud, Arthur, 363, 405
Rockwell, Norman, 367
Rodgers, Mary, 374
Rodriguez, Pancho, 190–3
Rogers, Neal, 277
Rolo, Charles, 370
Roosevelt, Franklin Delano, 45
The Rose Tattoo (McCullers), 228, 233
Ross, Harold, 213, 405

Rothschild, Norman, 30
Rousseau, 58
Royal Festival Hall, UK, 381–3
Rukeyser, Muriel, 117–9, 135–6, 138, 144, 148
Ryan, Thomas, 374

Sagan, Françoise, 319
St. James' Episcopal Church, New York City, 411
St. Just, Maria, 236–7, 272, 276, 320–1, 332–3, 337
Die Sammlung, 88
Sand, George, 58
Sarton, May, 5, 82, 237, 238
The Saturday Review of Literature, 4, 82, 186
Scarborough, Dorothy, 48
Schneider, Alan, 385
Schomburg, Fred, 16–7
Schulman, Sarah, 414, 417
Schwarzenbach, Annemarie, *91*
    career of, 144–5
    Carson's relationship with, 6, 88, 90–4, 96–7, 99, 105–10, 112, 123–4, 127, 135, 142–5, 153, 177, 193, 345, 351–2, 355, 418
    death of, 142–3
Scott, Thomas, 15
Seidlin, Oskar, 129
Selznick, David O., 278–81
Sendak, Maurice, 304
"September 1, 1939" (Auden), 101
Seven Middagh, Brooklyn, 7, 99–106, *100*, 108, 110–1, 116–7, 120–1, 145–52, 156, 180, 182, 188, 200, 202, 216, 347, 351, 381
The Sewanee Review, 95
Sexual Behavior in the Human Male (Kinsey), 152
sexuality, 217
    of McCullers, Carson, 6, 32, 37–40, 49, 57–8, 66, 90–4, 106–11, 123–4, 129–30, 148–52, 158, 164–5, 177, 220, 281–2, 324, 345, 351–2, 407, 417–8
    of McCullers, Reeves, 6, 49, 119–20, 123–7, 129, 150–2, 164–5, 177, 220, 276, 281–2, 396, 407, 418
    as theme in McCullers's work, 4, 6–7, 32–3, 74–5, 79–80, 86, 114–6, 150, 368–9, 371, 385–6, 415
Shadows on the Grass (Dinesen), 359
Shapland, Jenn, 414

Sharp, William (aka Fiona Macleod), 75
Sheriff, Valentina, 262, 266, 291, 296–7, 302
Sherman, Stuart, 403–5, 408
Sherman, William, 12, 20
Silver Star medal, 194
Sims, Marian, 95
Sitwell, Edith, 249–52, *250*, 256–7, 317, 380–3
slavery, in McCullers's ancestry, 10–3, 16
Smedley, Agnes, 157, 168, 219
Smith, Hampton, 54–6
Smith, Lamar "Bill," 219, 278, 290, 387, 411
Smith, Lamar, Jr. (Carson's brother), 17–8, 44, 59, 61, 135, 155, 181, 184, *223*, 229, 278, 290, 306, 350, 352, 387
    Carson's death and, 411–2
    death of, 412
    education of, 222–3
    mother's death and, 321–2
Smith, Lamar, Sr. (Carson's father), 15, 18–22, 24–8, 46, 49, 57, 66, 110–1, 136, 155, 184, 351
    alcohol use by, 23, 59, 156–7, 163, 222
    characteristics of, 16–7
    death of, 169
    marriage of, 16
Smith, Lillian, 9, 15, 42, 44, 298
Smith, Margarita Gachet "Rita" (Carson's sister), 17–8, 24, 110–1, *169*, 203–4, 207, 213, *223*, 230, 234, 254, 290, 296, 298–9, 301, 306, 308–9, 351, 356, 357, 367, 369, 391–2
    alcohol use by, 59, 170, 205, 222–4, 315, 340, 387
    career of, 169, 180–1, 278, 329, 387–8, 395–6, 411–2
    Carson's death and, 411–2
    death of, 412
    education of, 135, 136, 169
    mother's death and, 321–3
    psychotherapy of, 340
Smith, Mary Louise Gachet "Molly" (Carson's grandmother), 16
Smith-McCullers Historic House, Columbus, Georgia, 413
Smith, Oliver, 146, 217
Smith, Simeon, 378
Smith, Vera Marguerite Waters "Bébé" (Carson's mother), 20–2, 24–8, *42*, 49, 57, 62, 66, 112, 151, 155, 203–4, *223*, 249, 280, 299, 301, 316, 351

Smith, Vera Marguerite Waters "Bébé"
  (continued)
  alcohol use by, 58–9, 222, 253
  Carson's relationship with, 9, 18–9, 23,
    41–3, 92, 110–1, 122, 135–6, 183, 194,
    210–4, 229–30, 254, 290, 305–6, 351
  characteristics of, 7, 9, 15, 41–3, 219
  childhood of, 14–5
  death of, 321–3
  health issues of, 277–8, 290, 306, 309
  marriage of, 16–7, 169–70
  Nyack, New York, residence of, 170–2,
    171, 179, 210–4, 222, 236
Smith, Virginia Standard "Jenny," 135,
  181, 184, 219, 290, 306, 387
Smith, William Hooker (Carson's
  grandfather), 16
Snelling, Paula, 298
Snow, Carmel, 99
"The Sojourner" (McCullers), 217, 298
Solano, Solita, 86, 97–8, 200
The Sound and the Fury (Faulkner), 379
Southern Gothic literature, 7, 56, 82–3,
  115, 143, 150
Soviet Union, World War II and, 81, 134
"Spain" (Auden), 101
Spanish Civil War, 77, 101, 117, 157
Spender, Stephen, 100
Spenser, Edmund, 239
Spotto, Donald, 314
The Square Root of Wonderful (McCullers)
  (play)
  autobiographical elements of, 326–30
  cover of stage play, 326
  directors of, 332, 334–5
  producers of, 323, 325, 334
  reviews/reception of, 326, 336–7, 339,
    385
  themes/characters of, 289, 326–8, 330,
    335
  writing of, 323–5, 349
Stafford, Jean, 157
Starkie, Enid, 41
Stark, Ray, 399
Stazione Termini (film), 278–81
Stegner, Wallace, 95–6
Steinbeck, Gwyn, 148
Steinbeck, John, 148
Stein, Gertrude, 4, 86
Stein, Jean, 356–7
Stern, James, 104, 381
Stevenson, Robert Louis, 19
Stewart, Sam, 365

Stirling, Monica, 303
stock market crash of 1929, 45
Stompanato, Johnny, 347
Storey, Virginia, 17–8, 41, 49
Story, 45–6, 76
  "Wunderkind" published by, 62–3
Strange Fruit (Smith), 298
A Streetcar Named Desire (Williams),
  206, 401
strep infections, 64, 113–4, 135, 344, 409
strokes, McCullers's, 8, 64, 112–4, 168–9,
  201–2, 203–14, 229, 309, 337, 344,
  382, 402, 408–9, 416
Studies in the Psychology of Sex (Ellis),
  150–2
Styron, William, 279–80
"Sucker" (McCullers), 26–7, 85
suicide, as narrative theme, 4, 75, 326–30,
  371
Sullivan, Margaret, 15, 38–40, 354, 412–3
Summer and Smoke (Williams), 191–2,
  194, 217, 261, 276
Sunday Telegraph, 380, 382
Svendsen, Clara, 360, 392
Swanner, Dr., 315
Sweet as a Pickle and Clean as a Pig
  (McCullers), 393–4

Talmadge, Eugene, 45
Taylor, Elizabeth, 400–1, 415
Taylor, Laurette, 191
Tchelitchew, Pavel, 250
Terence (poet), 312
Theatre Club, 232
Theatre Guild, 208, 225, 227, 230, 235
This Week, 217
Thompson, Lovell, 366
Thomson, Virgil, 120
Three Arts Club, New York City, 48
The Three Faces of Eve (Cleckley), 212
Thurber, James, 405
Till, Emmett, 366
Time, 52, 115, 123, 166, 186, 370, 414
The Times Literary Supplement, 371
Tolstoy, Leo, 41
Tony awards, 387
transgender identities, 417–8
Trask, Katrina, 121–2, 140
Trask, Spencer, 121
A Tree. A Rock. A Cloud (film), 415
"A Tree. A Rock. A Cloud" (McCullers),
  158, 169, 280, 313, 415
  theme of, 138

Truman, Harry, 366
Trussell, Ray E., 341, 350
tuberculosis (TB), 63–4, 112, 114
Tucker, A. S. "Tuck," 33, 70, 376
Tucker, Buddy, 33
Tucker, Mary Sames, 31, 33–5, 42
    Carson's relationship with, 36–40, 70,
      124, 185, 240, 241–2, 246, 284, 286,
      288, 327, 350–1, 353, 374, 376–9, 397,
      403–5
Tucker, Virginia "Gin," 33–5, 42, 45, 50,
    61, 64, 69–72, 351, 377
Turner, Hayes, 55
Turner, Lana, 347–8
Turner, Mary, 55–6
"Twenty Years of Writing" lecture,
    312–4
Two Serious Ladies (Bowles, J.), 217

United Kingdom (UK), 77, 81, 86, 89,
    103, 134
    Carson's visits to, 254–64
Untermeyer, Louis, 95–6, 132

Vail, Laurence, 141
Valdosta, Georgia, 51–2, 54–6
van Doren, Mark, 359
Vega, Suzanne, 414
Vidal, Gore, 121, 249, 265, 268, 280, 371
Vogue, 84, 172, 244
von Opel, Fritz, 193
von Opel, Margot, 92, 94, 97, 106–8, 193
Vreeland, Diana, 102

Walden, Robert, 43, 220, 305, 307–9, 315
Walker, Margaret, 157
Walnut Theatre, Philadelphia, 228
Walter, Eugene, 270, 274
Walton, William, 250
Washington, George, 19
Washington Square College, New York
    City, 61–5, 117
Waters, Charles Thomas (Carson's
    grandfather), 14, 23, 58, 222
Waters, Elam Bertram, 14
Waters, Ethel, 226–8, *229–30,* 231–2, 411,
    415
Waters, Lula Caroline Carson (Carson's
    grandmother), 12, 13–5, 18–20, 23–4,
    25, 58, 222, 406
Watkins, Ann, 180–1, 194, 208
"We Carried Our Banners—We Were
    Pacifists Too" (McCullers), 172

Weill, Kurt, 98, 140
Wells, Ruth, 391
Welty, Eudora, 83, 95–6, *96,* 123, 129–30,
    190, 243, 272
"When We Are Lost" (McCullers), 300,
    328
"White for the Living" (Smith), 169
Whitehead, Robert, 225–7, 230
White, Katherine, 213
"Who Has Seen the Wind?" (McCullers),
    329–30
Who's Afraid of Virginia Woolf? (Albee),
    375, 385
Williams, Edwina, 189
Williams, Rose, 189–90, 207, 258, 318, 332
Williams, Tennessee (née Thomas Lanier
    Williams III), 116, 182, 195, 253, 271,
    281, 287, 291, 335, 388, 415, 418
    alcohol use/abuse by, 312–4
    Carson biography and, 413
    Carson's relationship with, 7–8, *189,*
      189–94, 198, 205–9, 214, 216–7, 219,
      222, 225–8, 233, 236–7, 240–1, 244,
      249, 257–8, 261–2, 264, 272, 275–6,
      279, 304, 312–4, 316, 318–21, 332–3,
      357, 368–9, 404, 407, 411, 413
    "Twenty Years of Writing" lecture by,
      312–4
Williams, Thomas Lanier, II, 189
Wilson, Bill, 205
Wilson, Edmund, 185, 186–7, 191, 230–1,
    232
Windham, Donald, 198, 214, 313
Winn & Company, 51
With Fondest Regards (Sagan), 320
Wolkenberg, Freddy, 106–8, 109
Women's Christian Temperance Union
    (WCTU), 23–4
Wood, Audrey, 208–9, 225, 235, 261, 264,
    293
Woodruff, Jim, 61
Woodruff, Kathleen, 218
Woolfolk, Harry, 220, 307–8, 337
Woolf, Virginia, 86, 398
works, McCullers. *See also* narrative
    themes, McCullers; *specific works*
    "Art and Mr. Mahoney," 217
    autobiographical characters in, 7, 8, 18,
      28–9, 32–3, 40, 63, 105–6, 162, 184–5,
      326–30
    The Ballad of the Sad Café, 7, 33, 116,
      123, 158, *159,* 159–61, 184, 197–8, 235–6,
      308, 313, 315, 372, 385–6, 407, 416

works, McCullers *(continued)*
   Clock Without Hands, 8, 13, 218, 235,
     271, 284, 294, 314, 339, 341, 349,
     363–74, *370,* 409, 416
   during college years, 62–3
   "Correspondence," 123
   "Court in the West Eighties," 62, 85
   "Dear Mr. Brahms," 62
   "The Dual Angel," 251, 257, 270–1
   "The Faucet" (play), 41, 191
   "A Flowering Dream," 345
   "The Flowering Dream," 311, 345
   The Heart Is a Lonely Hunter, 3–6, 8, 17,
     21–2, 28–9, 32–3, 40, 43–4, 69–79,
     80, 80–7, 89, 93, 109, 116, 129, 181,
     189, 190, 198, 235, 284, 311, 313, 356–7,
     405–6, 407, 414–7, 419
   "Home for Christmas," 217
   "Hush Little Baby," 395
   Illumination and Night Glare, 13, 27,
     405–8, 414
   "Instant of the Hour After," 59–60, 62
   "I Want, I Want," 62
   "The Jockey," 126
   "Like That," 62–3
   "Loneliness: An American Malady," 217
   "Madame Zilensky and the King of
     Finland," 123
   "The Man Upstairs," 395
   "The March," 394–5
   The Member of the Wedding (book), 7,
     17–8, 30, 33, 40, 80–1, 105–6, 116,
     132, 135, 137, 142, 146, 158–9, 162, 172,
     179, 180, 184–7, 189–90, 191, 200–1,
     230, 232, 252, 284, 313, 349, 356–7,
     374–6, 379, 394, 406, 416–7
   The Member of the Wedding (play),
     191–4, 208–9, 215, 217–8, 225–33,
     229–30, 234–6, 240, 322, 326, 336–7,
     349, 365, 401, 414–5
   The Mortgaged Heart, 412
   "Night Watch over Freedom," 172
   "The Pestle," 349
   "Poldi," 62
   posthumous releases of, 411–2, 414
   Reflections in a Golden Eye, 7, 20,
     79–80, 86–7, 95, 114–6, 123, 145,
     188–9, 197–8, 269, 356–7, 406–7,
     415–6
   "Residuum," 62

"The Sojourner," 217, 298
The Square Root of Wonderful, 289,
   323–32, *326,* 334–7, 339, 349, 385
"Sucker," 26–7, 85
Sweet as a Pickle and Clean as a Pig,
   393–4
translations of, 189, 195, 198, 269
"A Tree. A Rock. A Cloud," 138, 158,
   169, 280, 313, 415
"We Carried Our Banners—We Were
   Pacifists Too," 172
"When We Are Lost," 300, 328
"Who Has Seen the Wind?," 329–30
writing/development process behind,
   73–5, 311–3, 395
writing struggles and, 213–4, 326, 330,
   341–4, 349, 356, 363–5, 393–6, 408
"Wunderkind," 9, 26–7, 62–3
World Telegram and Sun, 231, 336
World War I, 64, 257
World War II, 81, 89, 101, 116, 134–5, 283
   D-Day in, 167–8, 174–5
   Reeves's service in, 153–5, 162–8, 173–5,
     194
WOR Radio, 212–3, 215
Worsthorne, Peregrine, 382
Wright, Ellen, 147, 203–4, 303
Wright, Julia, 147
Wright, Richard, 46, 82, 104, 146–7, *202,*
   202–4, 241, 303, 416
"Wunderkind" (McCullers), 9
   Story's publication of, 62–3
   themes of, 26–7
Wylie, Craig, 369

Yaddo artist residence, New York, 270
   Carson at, 119, 120–5, 129–32, 135,
     137–46, 157–9, 168, 179–80, 187, 267,
     306, 308–16, 337, 349
   Communist scare at, 219–20
   racial integration at, 139
The Years with Ross (Thurber), 405
York, R. L., 91
Young, Marguerite, 187, 267–70, 280

Zabel, Morton, 157
Zeigler, John, 213, 218, 220, 279, 304–7,
   309, 358, *386,* 387
Zimmerman, Barbara, 284
Zinnemann, Fred, 415

ILLUSTRATION CREDITS

All photographs are courtesy of Columbus State University Archives and Special Collections, with the exception of those listed below.

Lula Carson Smith © Harry Ransom Center, The University of Texas at Austin

Bébé Smith in armchair courtesy of David M. Rubenstein Rare Book & Manuscript Library, Duke University

Reeves and Carson © Granger/Granger

Reeves McCullers in bathrobe courtesy of David M. Rubenstein Rare Book & Manuscript Library, Duke University

Book covers for *The Heart Is a Lonely Hunter* and *The Member of the Wedding* © General Research Division, New York Public Library

Carson wearing lipstick © Louise Dahl-Wolf

Erika Mann portrait © Library of Congress Prints and Photographs Division, *New York World-Telegram* staff photograph

Annemarie Schwarzenbach © Atelier Binder/ullstein bild via Getty Images

Eudora Welty portrait © MPI/Archive Photos via Getty Images

Carson and George Davis © Henri Cartier-Bresson/Magnum Photos, Henri Cartier-Bresson, Henri Cartier-Bresson Foundation

Seven Middagh Street in Brooklyn courtesy of Municipal Archives, City of New York

Auden portrait © Everett Collection Inc/Alamy Stock Photo

Gypsy Rose Lee © Eliot Elisofon Collection

David Diamond courtesy of Peter Elliott

Newton Arvin courtesy of Smith College

Katherine Anne Porter © Katherine Anne Porter papers, Special Collections and University Archives, University of Maryland Libraries

Kay Boyle portrait © Library of Congress Prints and Photographs Division, *New York World-Telegram and The Sun* Newspaper Photograph Collection

Cheryl Crawford portrait © Billy Rose Theatre Division, New York Public Library for the Performing Arts

Carson and Rita Smith © Henri Cartier-Bresson/Magnum Photos, Henri Cartier-Bresson, Henri Cartier-Bresson Foundation

McCullers Nyack home © Nyack Library, Local History Image Collection

Truman Capote © Graphic House/Archive Photos via Getty Images

Jordan Massee on a slide courtesy of David M. Rubenstein Rare Book & Manuscript Library, Duke University

Carson and Tennessee Williams at table © Harry Ransom Center, The University of Texas at Austin

Janet Flanner portrait © Berenice Abbott, Alamy Stock Photo

Richard Wright portrait © Archivio Cameraphoto Epoche/Hulton Archive via Getty Images

Jane and Paul Bowles with parrot © Pepe Carletón

Rita, Lamar, and Bébé Smith © Harry Ransom Center, The University of Texas at Austin

Production still from *The Member of the Wedding* © Historic Collection/Alamy Stock Photo

Carson at cast party with Ethel Waters and Julie Harris © Ruth Orkin

Elizabeth Bowen © National Portrait Gallery, London

John Brown with book courtesy of Booth Family Center for Special Collections, Georgetown University

Edith Sitwell © *Evening Standard*/Hulton Archive via Getty Images

Kathryn Hamill Cohen portrait, "Death of a Ziegfeld Girl," *Daily Mail,* January 5, 1960 © Patricia Highsmith Papers, Swiss Literary Archives

Arnold Saint-Subber portrait by Friedman-Abeles © New York Public Library for the Performing Arts

Monroe, Dinesen, and Carson © Bettmann via Getty Images

Monroe kissing Carson © Bettmann via Getty Images

Edwin Peacock, Mary Mercer, Carson, and John Ziegler courtesy of David M. Rubenstein Rare Book & Manuscript Library, Duke University

Carson McCullers and John Huston © Jimmy McCormack/*The Irish Times*

A NOTE ON THE TYPE

This book was set in Adobe Garamond. Designed for the Adobe Corporation by Robert Slimbach, the fonts are based on types first cut by Claude Garamond (ca. 1480–1561). Garamond was a pupil of Geoffroy Tory and is believed to have followed the Venetian models, although he introduced a number of important differences, and it is to him that we owe the letter we now know as "old style." He gave to his letters a certain elegance and feeling of movement that won their creator an immediate reputation and the patronage of Francis I of France.

Composed by North Market Street Graphics,
Lancaster, Pennsylvania

Printed and bound by Berryville Graphics,
Berryville, Virginia

Designed by Cassandra J. Pappas